THE REFORMATION

A narrative history related by
contemporary observers
and participants

Hans J. Hillerbrand

THE REFO

BAKER BOOK HOUSE
Grand Rapids, Michigan

RMATION

A narrative history related by
contemporary observers
and participants

Reprinted by Baker Book House
with the permission of the copyright owner

ISBN: 0-8010-4185-6

Sixth printing, February 1987

Printed in the United States of America

Contents

Illustrations

Acknowledgments

GRATEFUL acknowledgment is made to the following publishers for permission to quote copyright material: The American Philosophical Society, Philadelphia, and Dr Charles D. O'Malley in respect of Charles D. O'Malley, *Michael Servetus. A translation of his Geographical, Medical, and Astrological Writings.* . . . (Philadelphia, 1953); Beacon Press, in respect of Roland H. Bainton, *Hunted Heretic* (Boston, 1953); Benziger Brothers, Inc., in respect of Henry VIII, *Assertio Septem Sacramentorum* (New York, 1908); Blackwell & Mott, in respect of *They Saw It Happen. An Anthology of Eye-Witness Accounts of Events in British History 1485–1688* (Oxford, 1957); Cambridge University Press, in respect of G. R. Elton, ed., *The Tudor Constitution* (Cambridge, 1960); Columbia University Press, in respect of Sebastien Chateillon, *Concerning Heretics.* . . . (transl.) by Roland H. Bainton (New York, 1935); Concordia Press, in respect of U. Saarnivaara, *Luther Discovers the Gospel* (St Louis, 1951); Farrar, Straus & Cudahy and Burns & Oates, in respect of James Brodrick, *St Francis Xavier* (New York and London, 1952); M. H. Gill (with Newman Press), in respect of Mary Purcell, *The First Jesuit* (Dublin, 1956; Westminster, 1957); Gütersloher Verlagshaus Gerd Mohn, in respect of *Quellen zur Geschichte der Täufer VII* (Gütersloh, 1959); Harper & Row, Publishers, in respect to Johan Huizinga, *Erasmus and the Age of the Reformation* (New York, 1957) and (with Longmans Green) Albert-Marie Schmidt, *John Calvin and the Calvinistic Tradition* (New York and London 1960); Harvard University Press, in respect of *The Two Treatises of Servetus on the Trinity* (Cambridge, 1932); Herder Book Company, in respect of *Disciplinary Decrees of the General Councils* (St Louis, 1937); Loyola University Press, in respect of *The Letters of St Ignatius of Loyola* (Chicago, 1959); Macmillan & Co. Ltd, in respect of Henry Gee and William J. Hardy, *Documents Illustrative of English Church History* (London, 1896); Mennonite Historical Society, Goshen, Indiana, in respect of *The Mennonite Quarterly Review;* Mennonite Publishing House, in respect of A. L. E. Verheyden, *Anabaptism in Flanders* (Scottdale, 1961), and *The Complete Works of Menno Simons* (Scottdale, 1956); Muhlenberg Press, in respect of *Luther's Works* (St Louis-Philadelphia, 1955 ff.); Thomas Nelson and Sons Ltd, in respect of John Knox's *History of the Reformation in Scotland* (London and New York,

1949–50); Oxford University Press, in respect of B. J. Kidd, *Documents Illustrative of the Continental Reformation* (Oxford, 1911); Henry Regnery Co., in respect of *St Ignatius' Own Story* (Chicago, 1956); Sheed & Ward, in respect of *The Complete Works of Saint Teresa* (London and New York, 1946); Stanford University Press and Barrie and Rockliff, in respect of Edwin Doernberg, *Henry VIII and Luther* (Stanford, 1961); *The Tablet*, London, in respect of *The Dublin Review*; Dr Aiken Taylor, in respect of his translation of the Geneva Ecclesiastical Ordinances; Westminster Press, in respect of *Spiritual and Anabaptist Writers* (London and Philadelphia, 1957); Woodstock Press, in respect of *The Spiritual Journal of St Ignatius* (Woodstock, 1958).

Grateful acknowledgment is also made of the following museums and art galleries for permission to reproduce illustrations for this volume: Museum Boymans-van Beuningen, Rotterdam; British Museum, London; National Portrait Gallery, London; Bibliothèque Publique et Universitaire de Genève, Genève; Öffentliche Bibliothek der Universität Basel; Zentralbibliothek Zürich; Stadt- und Universitätsbibliothek Bern; Kunstverein Winterthur; Herrn Leonard von Matt, Buochs, Switzerland; Herrn Conrad Vetterli, Zürich, Switzerland; Kunsthistorisches Museum, Wien; Österreichische Nationalbibliothek, Wien; Bildarchiv Foto Marburg; Landesmuseum für Kunst und Kulturgeschichte, Münster; Staatliche Graphische Sammlung, München; Germanisches Nationalmuseum, Nürnberg; Staatliche Kunstsammlungen, Weimar; Lutherhalle, Reformationsgeschichtliches Museum, Wittenberg; Szépmüvészeti Muzeum, Budapest; Direction des Musées de France, Paris; Fratelli Alinari, Firenze; Fogg Art Museum, Harvard University; Samuel H. Kress Foundation, New York; The Library of Congress, Washington; Mennonite Historical Library, Goshen, Indiana; Mennonite Historical Library, Harrisonburg, Virginia; Duke University Library, Durham, N.C.

Fratelli Alinari, Firenze, kindly provided the illustration facing p. 49 and the portrait of Henry VIII, facing p. 336; Bildarchiv Foto Marburg provided the illustration facing p. 177; Herr Leonard von Matt in turn provided the two illustrations facing p. 433 and the bottom illustration facing p. 464: they are taken from Leonard von Matt and Hugo Rahner, eds., *St Ignatius of Loyola, A Pictorial Biography* (Chicago, 1956).

Reference must also be made to Max Geisberg, *Der Deutsche Einblatt-Holzschnitt in der ersten Hälfte des XVI. Jahrhunderts* (Munich, 1923 ff.), abbreviated 'Geisberg'.

Preface

THIS volume undertakes to tell the story of the Reformation with the help of contemporary sources. The exciting and dramatic events of the religious upheaval of the sixteenth century are recounted with the autobiographical reflections of the *dramatis personae*, with letters, official documents, polemic pamphlets, and the like. The approach is therefore historical. It is not intended to present an anthology of writings of the important theologians of the time. Such collections are variously available and there is no need to swell the number.

A further delimitation of the volume consists in the concentration on the ecclesiastical developments rather than the history of the entire era with all its manifold expressions. Limitation of space made this mandatory. This will not, it is hoped, detract from the value of this collection.

The structure of the volume is dependent on the course of the religious happenings. It is selective rather than comprehensive and emphasizes the central events and persons. The approach of the individual chapters is determined by the character of their subject matter—the Reformation in England is recounted largely with governmental documents; the story of Calvin with his letters.

The problems of such a volume are many and obvious. The selection of the sources presented certain difficulties. Some of the important events of the Reformation were not recorded by contemporary observers and cause unbridgeable gaps in the sources. Other events in turn are described almost too well, which makes it difficult to select the most appropriate documents. Undoubtedly other sources of equal significance might have been selected. Others might possibly have been omitted.

It was also found to be impossible to include sources illustrative of the less important reformers, such as Melanchthon, Bullinger, Bucer, Lasco, and others. Pertinent biographical materials are rare and the readily available theological documents were excluded by intent. If these reformers appear, therefore, only marginally in this volume, it is not to suggest that their role in the theological course of the Reformation was insignificant.

An anthology of eyewitnesses raises the question of the historical accuracy of judgment on the part of the writers of the materials. The documents, coming as they do from men actively involved in the course of events, are frequently biased. The writers were at times unwilling and often unable to discern happenings objectively. Thus the various descriptions do not in every single instance present a view shared by current historical scholarship. This will need to be remembered in reading the materials. However, obvious errors of fact and judgment have been corrected, either in the text itself or in the notes at the ends of the chapters. Thus it can be said that, taken as a whole, the documents do reflect a reasonably accurate picture of the course of the Reformation. And, whatever the shortcomings, they point out that in order to understand the past, the historian must take contemporary opinion at face value and understand a given event from what might be called subjective perspective. The critical verification of such subjective judgment is, of course, mandatory, and ought to represent a more advanced level of the historian's work. But an awareness of the subjective sentiment present in many historical situations must not be obscured thereby. Tetzel's sale of indulgences serves as a good illustration. The historian today may well reject—on account of a critical verification of the sources—some of the charges made at the time against Tetzel's preaching; the fact remains that a great many people in 1517 and 1518 thought that he had preached the hair-raising claims of which he was accused. The widespread enthusiasm for Luther finds its explanation as much in the content of Luther's message as in the subjective interpretation of this message on the part of the common people.

The introductions to the various chapters are designed to provide a coherent narrative of the course of events.

An attempt has been made to identify important names, dates, and places briefly in the notes at the end of each chapter. These notes also suggest additional literature which will be found helpful in pursuing further studies.

A great number of the documents were freshly translated into English. It is hoped that the translations are both readable and accurate—a result not too easily achieved in light of the difficulties of sixteenth-century German, French and Latin. The translations strive to be accurate without slavishly adhering to the original. Redundant repetitions have been omitted and brief additions were made wherever the text itself was not sufficiently self-explanatory. Likewise personal pronouns have been changed into proper names if clarity of the material made this mandatory. Since virtually none of the texts used in this volume has precise theological relevance, this approach should not be contested. Where existing translations have been used and altered, appropriate acknowledgment is made in the notes.

I gratefully acknowledge the support of the Duke University Research Council. My colleague Dr Arthur B. Ferguson gave me the benefit of his

Preface

competence in Tudor history. My colleague Dr Charles K. Robinson read parts of the manuscript and made many stylistic suggestions. Mr John Yost assisted in compiling the index and Mrs Alfreda Kaplan proved to be a competent and invaluable typist. I stand in all their debt.

H.J.H.

The Divinity School,
Duke University,
Durham, N.C.

ABBREVIATIONS IN THE TEXT

WA   *D. Martin Luthers Werke* (Weimar, 1883 ff.)

WA TR   *D. Martin Luthers Werke, Tischreden*

WA Br   *D. Martin Luthers Werke, Briefe*

WA DB   *D. Martin Luthers Werke, Deutsche Bibel*

CR   *Corpus Reformatorum* (Braunschweig, 1834 ff.)

BRN   *Bibliotheca Reformatoria Neerlandica* ('s-Gravenhage, 1909)

MI   *Monumenta Ignatiana*

Preface to the New Edition

THE objective of this book, originally published in 1965, was not so much to offer a collection of primary sources of the Reformation of the sixteenth century as to attempt a narration of Reformation events through contemporary accounts—in other words, the way men and women in the sixteenth century themselves might have observed or followed the course of events. The book was well received and soon went out of print. I am delighted that it is now made available again. All the same, the reprint of the original 1965 edition prompts a few observations. A great deal of significant research has occurred since 1965 and the reprint needs to be related to new insights and currents of scholarship. Accordingly, a few summary remarks are in order.

1. Most importantly, the bibliography is somewhat outdated. Many outstanding publications have appeared since 1965. To remedy this lacuna, the *Bibliographical Addendum* lists the significant and most accessible of the recent publications. Together with the original bibliography, a comprehensive guide to the important literature on the Reformation is thus available to the reader.

2. As regards scholarly issues of Reformation research, scholars have begun to stress certain aspects of the Reformation which had been somewhat neglected. The common denominator of these scholarly efforts is a more differentiated perspecive of the course of events. Generalized pronouncements are nowadays made with greater reluctance than, say, fifteen years ago. Thus, we have a more differentiated appraisal of the state of society and the church before the Reformation than was the case two or three decades ago. The first chapter of this book reflected, however, the somewhat one-sided view then dominant that pre-Reformation society was eminently characterized by abuse and perversion. Recent research has uncovered evidence of a great deal of spiritual vitality and of ecclesiastical loyalty in the decades before 1517 so that it is no longer possible to see the Reformation all-too-simply as the revival of an utterly decadent and perverted church. The adamant criticism of contempo-

raries and their sorrowful agonizing over ecclesiastical abuses must be seen in the broader setting of a continued presence of spiritual vitality. The religiosity of the people in the early sixteenth century was probably not too different from earlier times. The notion that church and society were like a kind of pressure cooker, inescapably pushing to a crisis, does not express the reality of conditions. Abuse and vitality, worldliness and spirituality, were existing side by side. An equilibrium existed which, no matter how precarious and uneasy, might have persisted for decades—or might have been resolved altogether in a harmonious fashion. The most serious issue of the time immediately preceding the Reformation pertained to the broader relationship of church and society. There can be little doubt that the traditional prerogatives which the church enjoyed were variously attacked—and were crumbling. The church enjoyed legal and fiscal prerogatives which, with the rise of the towns and a literate citizenry, increasingly came under attack. Changing times compelled the redefinition of the place of the church in society. It was taking place at many places, and the Reformation occurred in this context.

The state of theology on the eve of the Reformation calls for an additional comment. The reader will recall that this book does not seek to deal with the unfolding theological history of the Reformation. Still, a great deal of lively research has occurred in this area. In the decades before the Reformation theologians had increasingly come to stress man's involvement, and thus human freedom, as the key to salvation. In contrast to the much richer medieval tradition, this understanding of justification constituted a narrowing of the perspective whose graphic expression was found in Gabriel Biel's statement that man must *"facere quod in se est"* (do what is within him). This notion, while in its proper understanding within the range of authentic Catholicity, was bound to lead to discomforting generalizations. It was against this one-sided emphasis that the reformers reacted. In so doing, they failed to realize the richness of the tradition into which the late fifteenth-century theological discourse was embedded.

3. Significant changes have also occurred in our view of the "radicals" of the Reformation. While research has not continued in as lively a fashion as before, several noteworthy contributions have modified our perspective. Thus, the place of the radicals in the spectrum of the broader Reformation has been defined more modestly. The notion that they were a major force (comparable to, say, Luther) has given way to the view that they were a fringe phenomenon, albeit an interesting and significant one. Moreover,

we have come to embrace a more complex view of the "Left Wing" of the Reformation. The radicals are no longer seen as exclusively influenced by the Reformation. Medieval motifs are accepted as very important factors. In this context, the notion of three clearly structured subgroupings—Anabaptist, Spiritualists, and antitrinitarians—with more or less clearly structured subdivisions has given way to more differentiated distinctions. Scholars tend to see a more heterogeneous Radical Reformation. In particular the Anabaptist movement is taken as having been more diverse than is outlined in this book.

4. Recent Reformation research has paid a great deal of attention to the urban Reformation, which—one might well say—is the focal point of current scholarly interest. So distinguished a scholar as A. G. Dickens has concluded that "the Reformation was an urban event." The publication of Bernd Moeller's *The Imperial Cities and the Reformation* proved to be enormously stimulating for research. Moeller explored the striking proclivity of the Reformation to the free imperial cities in Germany—tellingly expressed in the fact that the overwhelming majority of the cities sooner or later became Protestant. A great deal of research on specific cities and problems has been published in recent years, though it is too early to form generally accepted conclusions about the broad pattern of urban ecclesiastical change. The urban scene at the time of the Reformation manifested several interesting elements—the role of ideas; institutional change; the place of elites; etc.—which make the urban Reformation a fruitful field of endeavor for historians of varying interests.

5. Our perspective as regards the English Reformation has also undergone change. Significant research has focused on the role of Thomas Cromwell, minister to Henry VIII. in the implementation of administrative no less than ecclesiastical change in the 1530s. At the same time, the figure of the king himself has appeared in a bolder relief. Whatever his amorous fancies for Anne Boleyn, Henry is perceived as a more forceful and circumspect ruler, who possessed (guided by others) a clear notion of what kingship was to mean in England. The issue joined in the "great matter," because Henry recognized that in one crucial respect—to have his case decided in England—he was as powerless as the humblest of his subjects. The "great matter" therefore did not merely involve Henry's desire to rid himself of Catherine of Aragon and gain freedom to marry Anne, nor even his desire for a male heir; it involved the very definition of kingship, profound reason enough for Henry to be adamant about the matter.

Such, in brief, is the current state of Reformation studies. If the present book could be written from scratch, a few passages and certain emphases would probably appear differently; some new texts—such as, for example, Johann Kessler's description of his encounter with Luther—would be added. But, even as matters stand, I think it a good and useful book, and once again I commend it to the reader's attention.

H. J. Hillerbrand

City University of New York
9/21/77

Restlessness
Before the Storm

THE Protestant Reformation of the sixteenth century, to be described on the following pages, was no accident—unless all of history is accident. Without going into the intriguing, if insoluble, problem of whether men make history or history makes men, it can be said that the late fifteenth and early sixteenth centuries were a fertile ground for a religious upheaval. The time was a revolutionary one and those who could see beyond their noses could read this in the sky.

Unlike earlier movements for ecclesiastical and religious reform, the Protestant Reformation found in its time many elements of support which had been lacking before. Its eventual success—or at least what the Protestant historian is wont to call success, namely no more and no less than the external consolidation of Protestantism in several European countries —was greatly aided by these elements. To be sure, the Reformation received its primary impetus from one man: Martin Luther, a religious genius of rare stature. The acknowledgment of Luther's centrality leaves, none the less, the phenomenon of his widespread support altogether unanswered. Certainly not all of his followers supported him for the right theological reason. Likewise the ecclesiastical proceedings against Luther could have been swifter, more effective, and more powerful. That they were not was due to the intricate political situation of the time. Whether Martin Luther was significantly stronger than his reforming predecessors can be debated. His enemies, however, most certainly were weaker. If church history can be written in the subjunctive, then one might say that there would have been a religious upheaval in the sixteenth century even if Martin Luther had died in the cradle.

It would be an ambitious undertaking to sketch in sufficient detail the complete picture of Europe at the eve of the Reformation—the widening horizons inaugurating the Age of Discoveries; the new humanism of the Renaissance; the political situation characterized by the large monarchies along the periphery—Spain, France, England, Sweden—and the powerless *Holy Roman Empire of the German Nation* with its innumerable territorial states in the centre. All these aspects of early-sixteenth-century Europe are important. If they are, none the less, here omitted from consideration, this omission is made inevitable by the character of subject-matter and limitation of length of the present volume. We shall try to relate in broad outline some of the more important characteristics of the religious scene at the turn of the sixteenth century.

Germany was, at the eve of the Reformation, an intensely religious country. It differed in this respect from Italy, where the ideals of the Renaissance had made considerable headway. The situation in Germany was characterized by a preoccupation with external religious form, though expressions of deep inner piety were not absent. The formal religiosity can well be illustrated with impressive figures: for example, in Cologne, a town of some 30,000 inhabitants, there were over a hundred churches and chapels, and the same number of monasteries and convents. The Church was the very heart of society and man found himself surrounded by constant reminders that this life was but a prelude for the life to come. There were impressive religious ceremonies and devotional writings in ever-increasing number. The Bible was repeatedly translated into the vernacular; homilies appeared in many editions, and the famous books on *The Art of Dying* depicted, in word and illustration, the Christian teaching concerning the end of life and thereby called attention to the necessity of a right life as appropriate preparation.

The veneration of the saints became more and more popular throughout the fifteenth century. Their number was legion, each with a special relation to a certain region, town, trade, sickness or need, but all with imposing relevance for the Christian believer. Children were given the names of saints and the special observances of memorial days of saints came, at the close of the Middle Ages, almost every week.

It is understandable that such preoccupation with saints had bearing on the role of Mary. She had always occupied a special place in the devotion of the Middle Ages, as is shown by the many churches bearing her name and the numerous works of art depicting her in painting and sculpture. All this was now intensified, largely as a result of the growing emphasis on Mary's immaculate conception. The Virgin personified as 'Our Dear Lady' the warmth and graciousness which were often lacking in Christ, who appeared as the angry judge of the world.

The increasing importance of Mary led to the prominence of her mother, Anne. The glory of the daughter reflected on the mother, particularly since the postulate of Mary's immaculate conception made this almost a theological necessity. Toward the end of the fifteenth century Anne became more and more popular. In Saxony she was the patron saint of the miners—the mining town Annaberg had received its name from hers. Elector Frederick the Wise had one of her thumbs in his collection of relics and Luther called upon her for help when he vowed to become a monk.

The growing popularity of the Rosary as a means of reciting Ave Marias was another outgrowth of Mary's prominence. A great number of Confraternities of the Rosary sprang up whose members agreed to pray three rosaries a week for the salvation of the other members, the mendicant orders, and the universal church. In Cologne there existed eighty and in Hamburg one hundred such Confraternities which were, practically speaking, mutual insurance societies for attaining eternal salvation.

The way was not far from the popularity of the saints to an increased significance of relics, for here the saints became in a way empirically apprehendable. The Church encouraged the prayerful consideration of the remains of holy men and women of old because it knew that the simple Christian would be edified thereby in his devotion. By the fifteenth century the moderate beginnings of such ecclesiastical practice had long given way to a vulgarization which to twentieth-century man, of whatever religious persuasion, is no less than shocking. One blushes to think of the claims of authenticity advanced for relics—from a part of Jesus' diapers to Mary's earwax—and the efforts of the Church to curb such credulity proved to be of little avail. The collection of relics came to be characteristic of late medieval piety. Like stamp collecting in our day, the acquisition of relics was limited only by ingenuity and finances. The extensive collection of Elector Frederick the Wise of Saxony was widely famous. On a trip to the Holy Land he laid the foundation; continuous buying and selling brought about the accumulation of new relics virtually every day. As the beautifully illustrated and concisely annotated catalogue of the collection pointed out, a total of 1,902,202 days of indulgence was available from the collection. There were many other pious collectors of relics. One Nikolaus Muffel, of Nurnberg, vowed publicly to acquire one relic a day for an entire year. On the two hundred and eighth day his pious activities unfortunately came to an abrupt halt when he was hanged for thieving.

Extremes, it is said, often meet. They did in the religious life of the late fifteenth century. For alongside the various expressions of a formal, if at times vulgar, religiosity there is evidence of a noble spirituality which expressed itself in the tradition of late medieval mysticism. Thomas à Kempis's *Imitation of Christ*, the *German Theology*, and the Brethren of the Common Life are illustrative of those segments of the Church which stressed mystic devotion and practical piety. The sacraments of the Church were thought to be less important than the personal appropriation of salvation; the preoccupation with external form, the credulity of the people, and the many abuses in the Church were criticized.

As we turn to formal ecclesiastical life in the century preceding the Reformation we observe two important developments. One was the definite increase in papal power throughout the fifteenth century. Coming as it did at the heels of the Council of Constance (1414–18), it meant that the victory of the conciliar idea proved to lead at once to the renewed rise of papalism. By ending the fateful schism of the Church, where two, and finally three popes had excommunicated one another's followers, the council had consolidated its formidable opponent. Throughout the fifteenth century the popes opposed the conciliar idea which, none the less, continued to live. The unwillingness of the papacy to surrender anew its authority to a council explains in some measure the papal reluctance to convene a general council in the crucial years of the early Reformation.

A second characteristic of pre-Reformation ecclesiastical life was the influence of Renaissance thought upon the Church, especially the papacy. Many of the men who guided the Church in the second half of the fifteenth and early part of the sixteenth centuries were worldly and shrewd. There were ten popes, all in all. One ruled for less than a month; but the nine others left their imprint. They were generally men of good moral character —or at least would have been so considered in their day. They were erudite and added to the aesthetic and cultural splendour of Rome. What they all lacked was what the Church needed most: the ability to understand their pontifical office in terms of a spiritual responsibility.

Thus the papacy became but another worldly Italian court, characterized by all the intrigue and bribery to be found elsewhere. The increased centralization of the administration of the Church in Rome created a bureaucracy where ecclesiastical offices could be bought by the highest bidder, indeed, often by the two highest bidders, with resulting lawsuits before ecclesiastical courts between the two men involved and new income for the papal treasury. In Rome, it was said, everything could be bought from top to bottom. The Church at large followed this example and at the eve of the Reformation corruption was by no means limited to the 'top'.

A reaction was inevitable. A great number of popular pamphlets scorned and denounced Church and clergy—from Sebastian Brant's *The*

Ship of Fools to the *Letters of Obscure Men*. The increasing financial burden placed upon the people, the immorality and ignorance of the clergy, the simony of church offices, the trade with indulgence and relics became increasingly subject to biting attacks. In Germany the critique of the Church was for many a criticism of Rome. It found expression in the various *Gravamina*, or grievances, periodically drawn up and submitted to the Church for alleviation. In 1510 these grievances were ordered to be compiled systematically, and at the Diet of Augsburg in 1518 their alleviation was made a major condition for the fulfilment of the papal request for aid against the Turks.

By the early sixteenth century, then, outward religiosity only scantily covered grave abuse underneath. Anything could happen. But when it did, even those who had expected it were surprised from whence it came.

It came from an Augustinian monk and Professor of biblical literature teaching in what might be called academic 'Siberia', the small University of Wittenberg in Saxony. But this professorial monk Martin Luther almost single-handedly persuaded the German people that the Church had perverted the Christian religion and demanded that a reform of this Church be undertaken. The story of the Reformation is, therefore, in large measure the story of Martin Luther.

The story of his life is dramatic and eventful. He was born on 10th November 1483 at Eisleben, a town on the border between Thuringia and Saxony. His father, Hans Luther, came from peasant stock and combined frugality and hard work, which brought about his rise from a common labourer to a well-to-do mining operator.

Martin attended school at Mansfeld and Magdeburg and, in 1501, enrolled at the University of Erfurt, where he pursued the usual course in the liberal arts. Two years later, after having sworn the customary oath by God and the Holy Gospels that he had regularly attended the lectures and exercises in the prescribed subjects, he received the bachelor's degree. In February 1505 he was awarded the master's degree and in April of that year he commenced the study of law. Up to this point his academic career had been routine enough—all too routine, perhaps, for the son of an ambitious father. Indeed, Martin's studies might very easily have continued in this fashion. But less than three months after beginning to study law Martin Luther had entered the cloister of the Eremites of St Augustine, a strict monastic order, in Erfurt. The immediate cause for this step had been the experience of a thunderstorm, which had prompted his vow to become a monk. At a deeper level, however, his immensely sensitive conscience was perturbed by an uncertainty and restlessness concerning his salvation. The monastery was to resolve his spiritual struggle. He spent the customary novitiate year and, in the autumn of 1506, began to study for the priesthood. In April 1507 he took holy orders.

Martin now began formal theological studies, first at Erfurt and then at the University of Wittenberg. Such studies were in those days a long and tedious affair, where the student had to attain several intermediate academic degrees in order to obtain, after a dozen years or so, the doctorate in theology. Luther received his doctor's degree in October 1512, in an amazingly short time—the university at Wittenberg was young and eager to attract students, and its degree requirements were lenient. The town was small—really a peasants' village with a population of 2,000 and brewing as its chief activity.

Little is known about these years of Martin's life, apart from the fact that he must have faithfully pursued his studies and served, as was customary, as university lecturer both at Erfurt and Wittenberg. In 1511, probably, an event occurred in his life to which he attributed in later years great importance. Together with a monastic brother he was sent to Rome on clerical business. The Augustinian order in Germany was at that time reorganized in order to provide for more centralized administration. Several cloisters, among them Erfurt, opposed this plan (entailing close co-operation between cloisters which strictly observed the Augustinian rule and others which were more lenient) and decided to take their case to Rome. Luther, then still at Erfurt, and his confrère were appointed to argue the case. The mission proved to be a failure, but for Luther the journey meant an acquaintance with the centre of the Church. Its decadence and worldliness made a lasting impression on him.

In 1513 Luther began teaching as professor at Wittenberg. His first lecture on the Psalms was followed by expositions of a number of other biblical books. This academic responsibility led him to an inner clarification of his spiritual problems. Outwardly a man of considerable promise who steadily climbed the hierarchic ladder, he fought inwardly a battle for a 'gracious God'. His spiritual problem arose from his profound conviction of his own sinfulness, which even the monastery and the means of grace offered by the Church had not changed. The Church called upon him to mobilize his own efforts, but he failed to see anything in his life which might be found acceptable in the sight of God. He faced God and his righteousness empty-handedly.

The study of the Scriptures led him gradually to deliverance. He formulated it in terms of a biblical theology to which Paul, Augustine, and German mysticism made important contributions. Luther came to see that he had falsely understood the meaning of the righteousness of God and that its true meaning was that God declares man righteous by grace. God does not count on man's effort, but indeed makes man's inability to do the good the very cornerstone of his pronouncement that man is to be redeemed *sola gratia*, by grace alone. Though the exact time and precise meaning of Luther's 'evangelical experience' have been much discussed in scholarship, it is clear that at least by 1517 Martin Luther had come to an understanding of the Christian religion which was alien to that of the Catholic Church. None the less, he might have lived and died an obscure professor of theology in the early sixteenth century. He might, on the other hand, have died at the stake as a heretic. That he did neither must be attributed to his time, to his Church, but, above all, to his religion.

▶   **A contemporary comments on Martin Luther's birth and early youth.**

On the eve of St Martin's Day, 10th November 1483, Martin Luther was born at Eisleben in the Harz. His parents were Hans Luther, a miner, and Margarethe, his wife. He was baptized on St Martin's Day in the Church of St Peter and received the name Martin.

Our gracious God blessed the mining activities of this child's father and enabled him to acquire two furnaces at Mansfeld. . . . From the proceeds of this property Hans Luther brought up his son honourably in the fear of God. When Martin reached the proper age he was sent to a Latin school, where he industriously and quickly learned the Ten Commandments, the Catechism, the Lord's Prayer, grammar, and Christian hymns. . . . At the age of fourteen his father, with the help of Johann Reineck, sent him to school at Magdeburg, which at that time was unexcelled in its fame. There Martin begged for bread and shouted his *panem propter Deum*.[1]

The following year he went to Eisenach, where there were relatives of his mother. After he had sung for his bread for some time in the streets, a pious lady invited him to her table. His singing and devout prayer had attracted her to Martin.

                                        Johann Mathesius, *Historien*, p. 1.

▶   **Luther himself comments on his background as follows:**

I am the son of a peasant. My great-grandfather, grandfather, and father were peasants. As he [Philipp Melanchthon] said, I should have become a superintendent, a bailiff or the like in the village, a servant with authority over a few. Then my father moved to Mansfeld, where he became a mining operator. This is where I come from.

That I became a baccalaureus and magister, but afterwards took off the brown cap, giving it to others, that I became a monk which brought shame upon me as it bitterly annoyed my father—that I and the Pope came to blows, that I married an apostate nun; who would have read this in the stars? Who would have prophesied it?

                                        WA, TR 5, No. 6250.

▶ The contemporary chronicler recounts Luther's youth and early university studies.

In 1501 the parents sent the young man to Erfurt to the University, supporting him with the profits from their mining property. . . . Here he began to study earnestly and industriously logic as well as the other liberal and rhetoric arts. For a time he studied jurisprudence. Though by nature alert and joyful, he began his studies every morning with prayer and mass. His rule was, 'Eagerly prayed is half studied.' He never overslept or missed a lecture; he consulted and questioned his teachers in honourable fashion. He studied with his fellow students and whenever there were no lectures he spent his time in the library.

On one occasion he came across a Latin Bible such as he had never seen. Greatly astonished, he observed that it contained far more passages, epistles, and gospels than were customarily expounded in the postils and from the pulpits. . . . Since all was so new to him he began to desire earnestly that God would sometime give him a copy of this book.[2]

Early in 1505 after industrious studies in the liberal arts as was the custom in the universities at that time, Martin received the Master's degree at Erfurt. Later that year, after a good friend had been killed and a flash of lightning during a fierce thunderstorm had terribly frightened him, he decided to enter the monastery, in order to serve God there. He meant to propitiate him by saying mass and to earn eternal salvation with monastic holiness.

Johann Mathesius, *Historien*, p. 1.

▶ In the summer of 1505 Luther entered the monastery. Years later he commented on his decision.

On 16th July, St Alexis Day, Luther observed: 'Today is the anniversary of my entrance into the monastery at Erfurt.' Then he began to relate how he had made the vow. Two weeks earlier while travelling near Stotternheim, not far from Erfurt, he was so frightened by a flash of lightning that he exclaimed in terror: 'Help me, St Anne, I will become a monk!' He continued: 'Afterwards I regretted this vow and many counselled me against it. None the less, I remained steadfast. On the day before St Alexis I invited my best friends to a farewell and requested that they should accompany me to the cloister the following day. When they wanted to keep me back, I said: "You will see me today for the last time." They escorted me with tears in their eyes. My father was also very angry about my vow, but I persisted in my decision. I never thought that I would leave the cloister. I had died unto the world.'

WA, TR 4, No. 4707.

▶ Martin Luther's father reacted quite negatively to his son's decision to enter the monastery. Martin recalled later on:

He became a monk altogether against the will of his father. When Martin asked him, at the occasion of his first mass, why he was so angry about his decision, he received the answer: 'Do you not know that it is commanded to honour father and mother?' Martin reasoned that his terror in the thunderstorm had forced him to become a monk, but his father remarked: 'I hope it was not the devil.'

WA, TR 1, No. 623.

▶ Though Luther did not find in monastic life the answer to his spiritual problems, he always insisted that he had earnestly endeavoured to fulfil the monastic ideal.

I was indeed a pious monk and kept the rules of my order so strictly that I can say: If ever a monk gained heaven through monkery, it should have been I. All my monastic brethren who knew me will testify to this. I would have martyred myself to death with fasting, praying, reading, and other good works had I remained a monk much longer.

Martin Luther, *Die kleine Antwort auf Herzog Georg nähestes Buch,* 1533.
WA 38, 143.

▶ The abrupt transfer to Wittenberg is described by Luther in the following letter.

Do not ask why I departed without saying farewell. For my departure was so sudden that it was almost unknown to my fellow monks. I wished to write you, but could not do so, since I had time and leisure for nothing except to regret that I had to break away without saying good-bye. Thus now I am at Wittenberg, by God's command or permission. If you desire to know my situation, I am well, thank God, except that my studies are very severe, especially philosophy, which from the first I would willingly have changed for theology; I mean that theology which searches out the meat of the nut, and the kernel of the grain and the marrow of the bones. But God is God; man often, if not always, is at fault in his pronouncements. He is our God, he will sweetly govern us for ever.

Please accept benevolently this which has been set down in haste and without plan. And if you can get any messengers to me, let me benefit from your letters. I shall try to do the same for you in return. Farewell in the beginning and the end, and believe me such as you wish me. Again farewell.

WA, Br. 1, 16–17.

▶ A trip to Rome, probably in 1511, proved to be important for his attitude toward the Church.[3]

In Rome I was a frantic saint. I ran through all the churches and catacombs and believed everything, their lies and falsehood. I celebrated several masses in Rome, and almost regretted that my father and mother were still living, for I would have liked to redeem them from purgatory with my masses and other good works and prayers. There is a saying in Rome: 'Blessed is the mother whose son celebrates a mass in the Church of St John on Saturday.' I surely would have liked to make my mother blessed! But there was a great commotion and I could not get close. I ate a salted herring instead.

> Martin Luther, *Auslegung des 117. Psalms*, 1530. *WA* 31, 1, 226.

I would not exchange for money my trip to Rome. Otherwise I would not believe what I saw with my own eyes. Godlessness and evil are great and shameless there. Neither God nor man, neither sin nor modesty, are respected. So testify all the pious who were there and all godless who returned worse from Italy.

> *WA, TR* 3, No. 3582A.

I did not stay long in Rome, but found occasion to celebrate and hear many a mass. I still shudder when I think of it now. I heard people laughingly boast in the inn that some celebrated mass saying to the bread and wine: 'Bread art thou and bread wilt thou remain.' Then they elevated it. I was a young and pious monk who was hurt by such words. What should I think? I had to think that in Rome they talked so freely and publicly. If pope, cardinals, and the courtiers celebrated mass that way, I had been deceived, since I had heard many masses by them. I was especially annoyed over the speed with which they said the mass. By the time I reached the gospel the priest next to me had already finished mass and shouted: 'Come on, finish, hurry up.'

> *WA, TR* 3, No. 3428.

▶ The suggestion to undertake advanced theological studies came to Luther from Johann Staupitz, his superior in the Augustinian order. Luther himself recollected:

On one occasion while I was sitting under the pear tree, which still today stands in the middle of my yard, Staupitz, my prior, said to me: 'Master, you should work for a doctorate; that will give you something to do. . . .' When he approached me again under the pear tree concerning the same matter, I showed myself quite reluctant and presented my arguments, most of all the fact that strength would fail me and I would not live long. Thereupon Staupitz responded: 'Do you not know that God must do great things? He needs many wise and intelligent men to assist him. If you should die, you will be his adviser.'

WA, TR 2, 2255A.

▶   With the following letter Luther invited the prior and brothers of the Augustinian convent at Erfurt to his doctoral promotion.

Greetings in the Lord. Reverend, venerable and dear brothers:

The day of St Luke is approaching on which I will celebrate, in obedience toward the Fathers and the Reverend Father, my promotion in theology, as you certainly know from letters of our Reverend Father Prior. I will not accuse myself nor speak of my inadequacy, lest it appear that I wish to obtain pride and praise by such humility. God knows, as does my conscience, how worthy and how grateful I am for such glory and honour.

22nd September, 1512. *WA, Br.* 1, 18.

▶   Luther became professor at the University of Wittenberg in 1512 and subsequently assumed ever more academic and monastic responsibilities.[4] In a letter written in 1516, Luther reflected on his busy life.

In the name of Jesus. Greetings. It almost seems that I need two secretaries or scribes, for I do nothing all day but write letters. Thus I do not know if I am repeating myself. But you will find that out. I am preacher at the convent and reader during the meals. I am also daily in demand as preacher in the parish church, regent of studies, and vicar of our order. This entails the supervision of eleven convents. I also administer the fish pond at Leitzkau and administer the Herzberg affairs at Torgau. I lecture on Paul and collect material for a lecture on the Psalms. In addition there is my correspondence which, as I already mentioned, consumes the greater part of my time. Rarely do I have time for the prayers of the breviary or for saying mass. And besides all that I have to contend against the temptations of the flesh, the world, and the devil. There you see what a lazy-bones I am.

WA, Br. 1, 72.

► Of far-reaching importance was Luther's discovery of a new understanding of the essence of the Christian religion. In various Table Talks and in the Preface to an edition of his Latin writings Luther reflected on the course of his spiritual pilgrimage.[5]

Meanwhile, that same year I had again turned to the exposition of the Psalter, confident that after the academic treatment of the Epistles of St Paul to the Romans and Galatians and the Epistle of the Hebrews I was better trained. Certainly I had been possessed by an unusually ardent desire to understand Paul in his Epistle to the Romans. Nevertheless, in spite of the ardour of my heart I was hindered by the unique word in the first chapter: 'The righteousness of God is revealed in it.' I hated that word 'righteousness of God', because in accordance with the usage and custom of the doctors I had been taught to understand it philosophically as meaning, as they put it, the formal or active righteousness according to which God is righteous and punishes sinners and the unjust.

As a monk I led an irreproachable life. Nevertheless I felt that I was a sinner before God. My conscience was restless, and I could not depend on God being propitiated by my satisfactions. Not only did I not love, but I actually hated the righteous God who punishes sinners. . . . Thus a furious battle raged within my perplexed conscience, but meanwhile I was knocking at the door of this particular Pauline passage, earnestly seeking to know the mind of the great Apostle.

Day and night I tried to meditate upon the significance of these words: 'The righteousness of God is revealed in it, as it is written: The righteous shall live by faith.' Then, finally, God had mercy on me, and I began to understand that the righteousness of God is that gift of God by which a righteous man lives, namely, faith, and that this sentence—The righteousness of God is revealed in the Gospel—is passive, indicating that the merciful God justifies us by faith, as it is written: 'The righteous shall live by faith.' Now I felt as though I had been reborn altogether and had entered Paradise. In the same moment the face of the whole of Scripture became apparent to me. My mind ran through the Scriptures, as far as I was able to recollect them, seeking analogies in other phrases, such as the work of God, by which he makes us strong, the wisdom of God, by which he makes us wise, the strength of God, the salvation of God, the glory of God.

Just as intensely as I had before hated the expression 'the righteousness of God', I now lovingly praised this most pleasant word. This passage from Paul became to me the very gate to Paradise. Afterwards I read Augustine's treatise *On the Spirit and the Letter*, and, contrary to my expectation, I discovered a similar interpretation of the righteousness of God: that with which we are endowed when God justifies us. Although up until now this had been imperfectly explained, and he does not clearly expound everything concerning imputation, he nevertheless seemed to teach the righteousness of God by which we are justified.

Better equipped after these considerations, I began to interpret the Psalms the second time. The result would have been an extensive commentary, but I was again interrupted the following year by the summons of Emperor Charles V to the Diet at Worms.

WA 54, 183f.

These words 'righteous' and 'righteousness of God' struck my conscience as flashes of lightning, frightening me each time I heard them: if God is righteous, he punishes. But by the grace of God, as I once meditated upon these words in this tower and heated room: 'The righteous shall live by faith' and the 'righteousness of God', there suddenly came into my mind the thought that if we as righteous are to live by faith, and if the righteousness of faith is to be for salvation to everyone who believes, then it is not our merit, but the mercy of God. Thus my soul was refreshed, for it is the righteousness of God by which we are justified and saved through Christ. These words became more pleasant to me. Through this word the Holy Spirit enlightened me in the tower.

WA, TR 3, No. 3232.

At first whenever I read or sang the Psalm: 'Deliver me in thy righteousness', I was frightened, and I hated the words 'the righteousness of God' and 'the work of God', for I believed that the righteousness of God meant his severe judgment. Were he to save me accordingly, I should be damned for ever. But the words 'the mercy of God' and 'the help of God' I liked better. Thanks to God, when I understood the matter and learned that the righteousness of God means that righteousness by which he justifies us, the righteousness bestowed as a free gift in Jesus Christ, the grammar became clear and the Psalter more to my taste.

WA, TR 5, No. 5247.

▶   In the autumn of 1516 Luther described, in a letter, an academic disputation which already gave evidence of his new theology.

There is nothing for your followers of Gabriel Biel to marvel at in my propositions, or rather those of Bartholomäus Feldkirchen, although my own colleagues have expressed wonder at them. And the propositions were not composed by me, but by Feldkirchen, moved thereto by the chatter of the detractors of my lectures. He did it so that, by a public discussion held, against custom, under my chairmanship, the mouths of the chatterers might be closed or the opinions of others be heard. I offended everybody greatly by denying that the book on true and false penitence was Augustine's. It is a most bungling and inept book, far removed from Augustine's opinions and learning. I knew, indeed, that Gratian and the Master of the Sentences had taken a good deal from it, which was not medicine, but poison for consciences. But I offended them implacably, especially Dr Carlstadt, because, aware of this, I dared to deny the authenticity of the book.

WA, Br. 1, 65–66.

BIBLIOGRAPHY

By far the best treatment of the sixteenth century in English is the *New Cambridge Modern History*, vol. II, *The Reformation* (Cambridge, 1958). Valuable monographs are Harold J. Grimm, *The Reformation Era* (New York, 1954), and Hajo Holborn, *A History of Modern Germany*, vol. I, *The Reformation* (New York, 1959). The older works by Preserved Smith, *The Age of the Reformation* (New York, 1920) and James Mackinnon, *Luther and the Reformation* (London, 1925ff.) are no longer indicative of current scholarship, but still contain useful details. Myron P. Gilmore, *The World of Humanism* (New York, 1952) describes general conditions at the eve of the Reformation.

Of German language works the monumental *Propyläen-Weltgeschichte* (Berlin, 1930) with its masterly combination of illustrations and essays must be mentioned first. Gerhard Ritter's contribution to the 1940 edition has appeared separately under the title *Die Neugestaltung Europas im 16. Jahrhundert* (Berlin, 1950). It is, in form and content, a masterpiece. See also Erich Hassinger, *Das Werden des neuzeitlichen Europa, 1300–1600* (Braunschweig, 1959). For a detailed introduction, rich with bibliographical information, see Heinrich Hermelinck, *Reformation und Gegenreformation* (Tübingen, 1931).

Describing late medieval piety is Johan Huizinga, *The Waning of the Middle Ages* (London, 1924), Willy Andreas, *Deutschland vor der Reformation* (Stuttgart, 1948), and Gerhard Ritter, 'Why the Reformation Occurred in Germany', *Church History*, 27 (1958), 99–106.

The works of H. Daniel-Rops, *The Protestant Reformation* (London-New York, 1961) and *The Catholic Reformation* (London-New York, 1962), contain factual errors and Catholic bias, but are exceedingly well written.

The best biography of Luther in English comes from the pen of Roland H. Bainton, *Here I Stand: A Life of Martin Luther* (New York, 1950). Narrower in scope, but eminently competent and readable is E. Gordon Rupp, *Luther's Progress to the Diet of Worms* (London, 1951). A detailed and scholarly exposition of the same period is Robert H. Fife, *The Revolt of Martin Luther* (New York, 1957). For a survey of Luther's environment see Ernest G. Schwiebert,

Luther and His Times (St Louis, 1950). There is no comprehensive exposition of Luther's theology, though the following works should be mentioned: Philip S. Watson, *Let God Be God* (Philadelphia, 1949), E. Gordon Rupp, *The Righteousness of God* (London, 1953), and Heinrich Bornkamm, *Luther's World of Thought* (St Louis, 1958). The suggestive essays of the outstanding Luther scholar of this century, Karl Holl, were collected in his *Gesammelte Aufsätze* I, *Luther* (Tübingen, 1923). A brief, but lively study is Gerhard Ritter, *Martin Luther. His Life and Work* (London–New York, 1963); also F. Lau, *Luther* (London–Philadelphia, 1963).

The standard edition of Luther's works is the so-called Weimar edition, *D. Martin Luthers Werke* (Weimar, 1883ff.), here abbreviated *WA*. An extensive English translation—eventually to comprise fifty-five volumes—is at present being published, *Luther's Works, American Edition* (St Louis, Philadelphia, 1957ff.). Other important English translations of Luther's writings are the following: Theodore Tappert, ed., *Martin Luther, Letters of Spiritual Counsel* (Philadelphia, 1955); Preserved Smith and G. M. Jacobs, eds., *Luther's Correspondence*, 2 vols. (Philadelphia, 1913–18). See also *Works of Martin Luther*, 6 vols. (Philadelphia, 1915–32); *Martin Luther. Reformation Writings*, transl. by B. Lee Wolf (London, 1952); *Martin Luther. Selections from his Writings*, edited by John Dillenberger (Chicago, 1961).

Printing contemporary materials about Luther is *Das Buch der Reformation, Geschrieben von Mitlebenden*, Herausgeg. von Karl Kaulfuss-Diesch (Leipzig, 1917); Otto Scheel, *Dokumente zu Luthers Entwicklung (bis 1519)* (Tübingen, 1929); Heinrich Fausel, *D. Martin Luther* (Stuttgart, 1955); Oskar Thulin, *Martin Luther, Sein Leben in Bildern und Zeitdokumenten* (München-Berlin, 1958). Luther's own autobiographical reflections up to the time of his stay on the Wartburg are cited in the *Gesamtregister zu Dr Martin Luthers Werke*, vol. 58, 1 (Weimar, 1948), pp. 1–54.

The first Luther biography came from the pen of Melanchthon and is now available in *CR* 6, 155–70. Famous is Johann Mathesius, *Historien von des ehrwürdigen in Gott seligen teuren Manns Gottes D. Martini Lutheri Anfang, Lehr, Leben und Sterben* (Nürnberg, 1566), now in G. Loesche, ed., *J. Mathesius' ausgewählte Werke*, III. Band (Prag, 1906). A discussion of Luther biographies is given by E. W. Zeeden, *The Legacy of Luther* (London, 1954).

NOTES AND REFERENCES

1. *Panem propter deum* refers to the begging of 'bread for the sake of God'. Luther himself observed, 'I was a crumb-hunter, too, and gathered my bread at people's houses, especially in my dear city Eisenach' (*WA* 30, 2, 576). The woman who took him in was Ursula Cotta. Robert Fife, *op. cit.*, p. 27, is sceptical about Mathesius's authenticity in this regard.

2. Luther himself related similar incidents regarding his first seeing a Bible. See *WA, TR* 1, 44; 3, 598.

3. For other sources for Luther's Roman sojourn, see *WA* 58, 1, 29–33.

4. For a description of Luther's life before the indulgence controversy, see Robert Fife, *op. cit.*, pp. 179–244.

5. The translation used here is that in U. Saarnivaara, *Luther Discovers the Gospel* (St Louis, 1951), pp. 36–37. Saarnivaara provides a good introduction to the difficult problem of time and significance of Luther's apprehension of an 'evangelical' understanding of the Christian faith. See also Wilhelm Link, *Das Ringen Luthers um die Freiheit der Theologie von der Philosophie* (München, 1954); Heinrich Bornkamm, 'Luthers Bericht über seine Entdeckung der justitia dei', *Archiv f. Reformationsgeschichte* 37 (1940); Gerhard Pfeifer, *Das Ringen des jungen Luther um die Gerechtigkeit Gottes* in *Luther-Jahrbuch*, 1959; Ernst Bizer, *Fides ex auditu* (Neukirchen, 1958); Heinrich Bornkamm, 'Zur Frage der Iustitia Dei beim jungen Luther', *Archiv f. Reformationsgeschichte* 52 (1961); 53 (1962).

The
Gathering Storm

A MORE or less routine academic procedure catapulted the Wittenberg professor from the seclusion of his academic and monastic responsibilities into the public limelight and made him, virtually overnight, one of the most widely known figures in Germany. On the day before All Saints', 31st October 1517, Martin Luther posted at the door of the Castle Church in Wittenberg a list of ninety-five theses dealing with the general theme of indulgences. With this he was inviting, as the introduction to the theses emphasized, his academic colleagues to a theological debate on the subject, as was the custom of university life of that time. If we can believe both his own words and the logic of events, then it is obvious that nothing was further from his intention than to instigate widespread dissension or theological controversy. Indeed, it is still one of the mysteries of Reformation history how this proposal for academic disputation, written in Latin, could have kindled such enthusiastic support and thereby have such far-reaching impact. The answer, if there is one, is that Luther had gotten into an ecclesiastical hornets' nest in which there was more than theology involved—prestige and money. In any case, these ninety-five theses were far more conservative in tone than certain propositions which Luther had circulated the year before. Luther's step was prompted by reports of the activities of a Dominican monk named Johann Tetzel, who with skill and eloquence offered indulgences in the vicinity of Wittenberg.

The institution of indulgences was, in Luther's time, a matter complex in theology and perverted in practice, which had come a long way from its beginnings in the eleventh century, with practice usually one step ahead of theory. Indulgence originally arose in connection with the sacrament of penance, which assured the penitent sinner of the forgiveness of sins while making a distinction between the guilt and the punishment of the sin. The former is forgiven by God through the priest. The latter must, however, be met. This is done through certain good works such as fasting, the recitation of certain prayers, pilgrimages, or alms.

Such an understanding, which combined the pedagogical and biblical insight that the penitent sinner must give external evidence of his remorse, had serious drawbacks. It was possible that for a good reason one was prevented from the performance of the assigned good work. The concept of indulgences provided the solution. The Church was willing—on account of her authority over the treasury of merit—to accept substitution. The Crusades first posed the problem—and suggested an answer. Those who went to fight the infidels received the benefits of 'good works' they might have done had they stayed at home to perform them. Financial contributions soon took the place of going on the Crusades and eventually contributions to any good purpose were considered valid. The sinner could cancel his temporal punishment through a payment to the Church. Consequently, an indulgence is defined by the Catholic Church as that remission of temporal punishment which is owed for sins whose guilt has already been removed. It is granted by the Church on the authority of Matt. 16.19 and the treasury of merit—the notion that the Church had at its disposal the merits of those saintly men and women who had done more than their share of good works.

By the early sixteenth century a great many popular misconceptions and vulgarizations clouded the original intent and theological significance of indulgences. Thus the relationship between indulgence and the sacrament of penance was not always properly defined. Similarly the question whether indulgences could also be extended to the dead was anything but settled. The Church failed to correct the false notions spread abroad. One reason for this failure was undoubtedly the financial advantage accruing to the Church on account of such widespread ignorance. Though the disciplinary canons of the Fifth Lateran Council, promulgated in 1517, put on paper sharp proscriptions of the most glaring ecclesiastical abuses, little was altered in practice.

The activities of Johann Tetzel which caught Luther's attention were part of an ambitious ecclesiastical and financial scheme in which the papal desire to provide funds for the construction of St Peter's in Rome and the wish of Albert of Hohenzollern to attain the important archbishopric of Mainz were ingeniously matched. Unfortunately Albert was, when he first became interested in the vacancy at Mainz, only twenty-four years of age and thus greatly below the canonically prescribed age for a bishop. Furthermore, he was already Bishop of Magdeburg and Halberstadt. Thus a special papal dispensation with which a huge financial payment was connected became necessary in order to have this accumulation of ecclesiastical offices approved. Albert hoped, of course, to receive sufficient income from the bishopric to compensate him for his initial financial outlay. Arrangements were also made to offer an indulgence in North Germany; half of the proceeds were to go to Albert and the other half to Rome for the construction of St Peter's. The South German banking house of the Fuggers advanced the dispensation payment to Albert and was entrusted with the administration of the sale of the indulgence.

An efficient organization was established, detailed instructions drawn up, and the actual sale entrusted to a number of 'commissioners' of whom Tetzel had undoubtedly the widest reputation. On Saxon territory the sale was prohibited, but Wittenberg was close enough to the border so that the townspeople only needed to cross the river to avail themselves of Tetzel's offering; since he offered much, they did so in considerable numbers. Luther's attention was directed thereby not only to Tetzel, but also to the problem of indulgences in general. His ninety-five theses were written to clarify the problem. On the day he posted them he sent a copy, together with a covering letter, to the person most acutely involved—Archbishop Albert.

Tetzel quickly responded with theses of his own in which he solemnly insisted that he had preached nothing contrary to the teaching of the Church. Albert in turn asked the University of Mainz for its opinion of the theses and reported the matter post-haste to Rome in order to have Luther's orthodoxy properly examined. Soon a prolific theological controversy ensued. Luther himself published, early in 1518, a lengthy interpretation of his original theses. A meeting of the Augustinian order at Heidelberg in May 1518 gave Luther the opportunity for a disputation. By this time, however, the concern was no longer confined to the indulgences, but dealt with more basic theological issues, such as sin, grace, and man's freedom. Though Luther gained new supporters on this occasion, it became clear that the rift between him and the Church was extensive.

At this point, in all likelihood, Luther would probably have suffered the fate of many heretics before him—to be summarily tried and burned at the stake—had it not been for the protection afforded him by his ruler, Elector Frederick, whose insistence made it possible for Luther to be examined not in Rome, as was ordinarily the case, but in Germany. The examination took place at Augsburg in October 1518. It was conducted by Cardinal Cajetan, one of the most learned Thomist theologians of the time, who was in Germany for the purpose of persuading the German territorial rulers to join in common military action against the Turks. The encounter between Luther and Cajetan proved to be fruitless, for the two men, like two housewives standing on their doorsteps, argued from different premises. Cajetan bombarded Luther with papal and scholastic pronouncements; Luther wanted to be convinced with Scripture. In the end, the differences at two points—the treasury of merit and the confidence of faith—made conciliation impossible. Luther felt that his refusal to submit to Cajetan had endangered his life and he fled overnight from Augsburg, after Staupitz, his monastic superior, had freed him from his monastic vow of obedience.

At this juncture the controversy broadened. The most formidable and erudite spokesman against all theological innovation now was Johann Eck, a Dominican friar and professor at the University of Ingolstadt. Luther himself temporarily deserted the arena, having agreed, after talks with the Papal Chamberlain von Miltitz in January 1519, to submit his case to the German bishops and refrain from writing for the time being. None the less, his place in the controversy was quickly taken by Andreas Bodenstein von Carlstadt, his senior colleague at the University of Wittenberg. Carlstadt was a somewhat erratic character who had a lifelong tendency to push matters to extremes. In July 1518 he had published 379 theses against Eck to which he added twenty-six more for full measure. Eck, always ready for a good theological fight, responded in kind. The controversy between the two men which ensued was to be brought to a public conclusion with a theological debate. Since Eck had kept on needling him, Luther became involved again. The three protagonists met early in July 1519 at Leipzig. First Carlstadt and Eck debated for several days. Then Luther met Eck. Before the debate Luther had drawn up thirteen propositions of which the last denied the supremacy of the Pope. Here Eck centred his attack. In the debate he skilfully succeeded in drawing the admission out of Luther that some of Huss's views, condemned by the Council of Constance, had been good and Christian. Luther had not meant to defend Huss. But he could hardly have made a more disastrous statement, for not only did there exist widespread antipathy against Hussite heresy, but also the Council of Constance was everywhere esteemed as the means which had healed the schism in the Church. Thus Leipzig made it obvious that Luther had broken with the Church. Now it was up to the Church to act against the declared heretic.

But at that time the Church had other worries. Emperor Maximilian had died in January 1519, and the election of an acceptable successor was more important, as far as the Church was concerned, than a monkish squabble. It was to be of utmost importance for Luther that during the

crucial months in which the Church could have acted promptly against
him political considerations were overshadowing everything else. Neither
of the two candidates for the imperial office, Francis of France and Charles
of Spain, was acceptable to the papacy, because in both instances the
combination of political power appeared as a nightmare. Francis already
possessed Milan in northern Italy; Charles owned Naples in the south.
The acquisition of the German Empire in addition to a powerful home-
land meant forebodings of political disaster for the papal states in central
Italy. Pope Leo X supported the candidacy of Henry VIII of England,
but soon settled on Francis who was, compared with Charles, the lesser
of two evils. When it became obvious that Francis could never hope to gain
the necessary majority of the Electors, Leo sought to persuade Elector
Frederick of Saxony to become a candidate. But Frederick, who knew his
political limitations, politely declined. This left in the running only
Charles, a nineteen-year-old youth who could neither speak German
nor understand the German mentality. On 28th June 1519 he was unanimously elected German Emperor. But more than eighteen months passed
before the new Emperor came to Germany.

Once the Emperor's election had been taken care of the Church could
devote its attention anew to Luther. After several months of deliberation
the bull *Exsurge Domine*, published on 15th June 1520, embodied the
official conclusions. Forty-one propositions of Luther were condemned as
heretical. Luther was given sixty days to revoke his views and another
sixty days to report to Rome. Otherwise he was to be placed under the
ban. When Luther first heard of the bull he thought it to be a false
rumour, spread by Eck to discredit him. But in October he was officially
notified of its content—rumour had turned into unquestionable fact. In
November, Luther responded with an aggressive pamphlet *Against the
Accursed Bull of the Anti-Christ*, in which the title itself made it obvious
that he was not going to revoke. One month later—exactly sixty days after
his official notification—Luther, accompanied by a throng of eager
students, marched outside Wittenberg and burned copies of the canon
law and assorted works of medieval theologians, though wisely only of
second-rate men whose books were not too valuable. Perhaps as an after-
thought, a copy of the bull *Exsurge Domine* was thrown into the fire. This
was Luther's answer. On 2nd January 1521 the official bull of excommunication, *Decet Romanum Pontificem*, appeared automatically, even
though its official publication was delayed for some time in order not to
arouse anti-Roman reactions in Germany.

Luther was now an ecclesiastical outlaw. Much depended at this juncture on the attitude of the new Emperor and the territorial rulers. The
question was, of course, whether they would lend their support to the
administration of the ecclesiastical verdict. The papal representative,
Aleander, cognizant of a mounting wave of popular enthusiasm for

Luther, urged an imperial ban against Luther without further delay. On the other hand, the territorial states, as well as the humanist advisers of the Emperor, did not wish to overlook the popular sentiment and favoured a hearing. Finally, after considerable reluctance, Charles agreed, in line with his pledge at his election, not to condemn anybody without a hearing, to have Luther examined at the next diet. After some deliberation, it was decided to give Luther a safe-conduct to appear before the German Diet assembled at Worms.

Luther arrived in the city on 16th April 1521, and appeared before the representatives of the German estates the following day. He was shown his books, asked if he admitted their authorship and was willing to recant. Luther must have anticipated these questions. None the less, to everyone's surprise—and consternation—he requested twenty-four hours to ponder his reply. The following day he admitted the authorship of the books and conceded that he had been vehement in tone at times. He added, however, that unless he were convinced by Scripture and evident reason, he would not recant.

In a speech to the rulers Emperor Charles made it clear the next day that he was unwilling to tolerate a recognized heretic in his realm. Weeks of deliberation followed. On 26th May, after the Diet had officially adjourned and some of the territorial rulers had already left Worms, an edict was published which placed Luther and all his supporters under the ban and ordered all his books to be burned. The secular and the ecclesiastical authorities had thus closed ranks. Theoretically, at least, the case of Martin Luther, heretic, was taken care of and closed. One wonders, though, if Pope and Emperor really thought so.

▶ The sale of the indulgence for the construction of St Peter's in Rome was regulated by a 'Summary Instruction', issued by Albert of Hohenzollern. Here the details of administration were set forth.[1]

Albert, by the grace of God and the Apostolic Chair, Archbishop of Magdeburg and Mainz, Primate and Chancellor of the Holy Roman Empire in Germany, Elector, Administrator of the Churches in Halberstadt, Margrave in Brandenburg, Duke in Stettin, etc.

To all who read this letter: Salvation in the Lord.

We do herewith proclaim that our most holy Lord Leo X, by divine providence present Pontiff, has given and bestowed to all Christian believers of either sex who lend their helpful hand for the reconstruction of the cathedral church of St Peter, the Prince of the Apostles, in Rome, complete indulgence as well as other graces and freedoms, which the

Christian believer may obtain according to the apostolic letter dealing with this matter. . . .[2]

Here follow the four principal graces granted in the apostolic bull. These can be obtained separately. Utmost industriousness should be exercised in order to commend each grace most emphatically to the faithful. . . .

The first grace is the complete remission of all sins. Nothing can be called greater than this grace, since man, living in sin and deprived of divine grace, obtains complete forgiveness by these means and enjoys anew the grace of God. Moreover, through such forgiveness of sins the punishment which one is obliged to undergo in purgatory on account of the offence of the Divine Majesty is all remitted and the pain of purgatory is altogether done away with. And even though nothing satisfactory and worthy could be given in exchange for such a grace—since it is a gift of God and a grace beyond price—yet we decree the following rules in order that Christian believers may obtain it all the more easily:

In the first place: Everyone who is contrite in heart and has confessed with his mouth—or at least has the intention of confessing at a suitable time—shall visit the designated seven churches in which the papal coat of arms is displayed and pray in each church five devout Lord's Prayers and five *Ave Marias* in honour of the five wounds of our Lord Jesus Christ whereby our redemption took place, or one *Miserere* [Ps. 51], which psalm seems particularly appropriate to obtain forgiveness of sins. . . .

Where, however, persons are so weak that they could not easily come to such a church, their confessor or penitentiary should cause to be brought an altar to a suitable place according to his discretion. When such persons visit this place and offer their prayers near the altar or before, they shall receive the indulgence as though they had visited the seven churches.

Those on a sick bed are to be given a holy picture, before or near which they shall offer several prayers according to the decision of the confessor. Thus they shall receive the indulgence in this manner as though they had visited the seven churches. Wherever any person for a certain reason desires to be relieved of the necessity to visit said altars and churches, it may be granted him by the penitentiary. However, a larger amount will become necessary under such circumstances.

Concerning the contribution to the chest, for the building of said church of the chief of the apostles, the penitentiaries and confessors are to ask those making confession, after having explained the full forgiveness and privilege of this indulgence: How much money or other temporal

The sale of indulgences. On a pole, in the form of a cross, hangs the papal authorization for the sale; on the ground lie scales; two sacks of coins show the profit. (*Woodcut by Jorg Breu the Elder, Geisberg,* 353)

goods they would conscientiously give for such full forgiveness? This is to be done in order that afterwards they may be brought all the more easily to make a contribution. Because the conditions of men are many and diverse, it is not possible to establish a general fee. We have therefore fixed the following rates:

Kings, queens, and their sons, archbishops and bishops, and other great rulers should pay, upon presenting themselves to places where the cross is raised, twenty-five Rhenish guilders.

Abbots, prelates of cathedral churches, counts, barons, and others of the higher nobility and their wives shall pay for each letter of indulgence ten such gold guilders. Other lesser prelates and nobles, as also the rectors of famous places, and all others who take in, either from steady income or goods or other means, 500 gold guilders should pay six guilders.

Other citizens and merchants, who ordinarily take in 200 such gold florins, should pay three florins.

Other citizens, merchants, and artisans, who have their families and income of their own, shall pay one such guilder; those of lesser means, pay only one half. . . .

But those who do not have any money should supply their contribution with prayer. For the kingdom of heaven should be open to the poor no less than to the rich.

Even though a wife cannot obtain from the property of her husband without his will, she can still dispose of her dowry or other property elsewhere, which enables her to contribute even against the will of her husband. Where she does not have anything or is hindered by her husband, she is to supply her contribution with prayer. This applies also to sons who are under paternal authority.

Where, however, poor wives and sons yet under paternal authority are able to beg or to receive gifts from rich and devout persons, they are to put those contributions into the chest. If they have no opportunity to obtain the necessary amount, they may obtain said treasure of grace through prayer and intercession both for themselves and also for the dead.

. . . The second principal grace is a letter of indulgence, entailing the greatest, exceedingly quickening and hitherto unheard of powers, which will continue beyond the eight years designated in the present bull. . . . The content of this letter shall be explained by the preachers and confessors to the best of their ability. . . .

The third principal grace is the participation in all the possessions of the Church universal; . . . contributors toward said building, together with their deceased relatives, who have departed this world in a state of grace, shall from now on, and for eternity, be partakers in all petitions, intercessions, alms, fastings, prayers, in each and every pilgrimage, even those to the Holy Land; furthermore, in the stations at Rome, in masses, canonical hours, flagellations, and all other spiritual goods which have been, or shall be, brought forth by the universal, most holy Church militant or by any of its members. Believers who purchase confessional letters may also become participants in all these things. Preachers and confessors must insist with great perseverance upon these advantages, and persuade believers not to neglect to acquire these benefits along with their confessional letter.

We also declare that in order to obtain these two most important graces, it is not necessary to make confession, or to visit the churches and altars, but merely to procure the confessional letter. . . .

The fourth distinctive grace is for those souls which are in purgatory, and is the complete remission of all sins, which remission the Pope brings to pass through his intercession, to the advantage of said souls, in this wise: that the same contribution shall be placed in the chest by a living person as one would make for himself. It is our wish, however, that our subcommissioners should modify the regulations regarding contributions of this kind which are given for the dead, and that they should use their judgment in all other cases, where, in their opinion, modifications are desirable.

It is, furthermore, not necessary that the persons who place their contributions in the chest for the dead should be contrite in heart and have orally confessed, since this grace is based simply on the state of grace in which the dead departed, and on the contribution of the living, as is evident from the text of the bull. Moreover, preachers shall exert themselves to give this grace the widest publicity, since through the same, help will surely come to departed souls, and the construction of the church of St Peter will be abundantly promoted at the same time. . . .

Intructio Summaria (W. Köhler, *Dokumente zum Ablassstreit*, pp. 104–16).

▸ The Dominican monk Johann Tetzel was charged with the sale of the indulgence in parts of Saxony and Brandenburg. Here is one of his sermons.[3]

What are you thinking about? Why do you hesitate to convert yourself? Why don't you have fears about your sins? Why don't you confess now to the vicars of our Most Holy Pope? Don't you have the example of Lawrence, who, compelled by the love of God, gave away his inheritance and suffered his body to be burned? Why do you not take the example of Bartholomew, Stephen, and of other saints who gladly suffered the most gruesome deaths for the sake and salvation of their souls? You, however, do not give up great treasures; indeed you give not even a moderate alms. They gave their bodies to be martyred, but you delight in living well joyfully. You priest, nobleman, merchant, wife, virgin, you married people, young person, old man, enter into your church which is for you, as I have said, St Peter's, and visit the most holy Cross. It has been placed there for you, and it always cries and calls for you. Are you perhaps ashamed to visit the Cross with a candle and yet not ashamed to visit a tavern? Are you ashamed to go to the apostolic confessors, but not ashamed to go to a dance? Behold, you are on the raging sea of this world in storm and danger, not knowing if you will safely reach the harbour of salvation. Do you not know that everything which man has hangs on a thin thread and that all of life is but a struggle on earth? Let us then fight, as did Lawrence and the other saints, for the salvation of the soul, not the body which is today but not tomorrow. Today it is well, but ill tomorrow. Today alive and tomorrow dead.

You should know that all who confess and in penance put alms into the coffer according to the counsel of the confessor, will obtain complete remission of all their sins. If they visit, after confession and after the

Jubilee, the Cross and the altar every day they will receive that indulgence which would be theirs upon visiting in St Peter's the seven altars, where complete indulgence is offered. Why are you then standing there? Run for the salvation of your souls! Be as careful and concerned for the salvation of your souls as you are for your temporal goods, which you seek both day and night. Seek the Lord while he may be found and while he is near. Work, as St John says, while it is yet day, for the night comes when no man can work.

Don't you hear the voices of your wailing dead parents and others who

Caricature of Tetzel's sale of indulgences.
The German verse recounts the famous verse attributed to Tetzel:

As soon as the coin in the coffer rings,
the soul into heaven springs.

(*Lutherhalle, Wittenberg*)

say, 'Have mercy upon me, have mercy upon me, because we are in severe punishment and pain. From this you could redeem us with a small alms and yet you do not want to do so.' Open your ears as the father says to the son and the mother to the daughter . . ., 'We have created you, fed you, cared for you, and left you our temporal goods. Why then are you so cruel and harsh that you do not want to save us, though it only takes a little? You let us lie in flames so that we only slowly come to the promised glory.' You may have letters which let you have, once in life and in the hour of death . . . full remission of the punishment which belongs to sin. Oh, those of you with vows, you usurers, robbers, murderers, and criminals—Now is the time to hear the voice of God. He does not want the death of the sinner, but that he be converted and live. Convert yourself then, Jerusalem, Jerusalem, to the Lord, thy God. Oh, you blasphemers, gossippers, who hinder this work openly or secretly, what about your affairs? You are outside the fellowship of the Church. No masses, no sermons, prayers, sacraments, or intercession help you. No field, vineyard, trees, or cattle bring fruit or wine for you. Even spiritual things vanish, as many an illustration could point out. Convert yourself with all your heart and use the medicine of which the Book of Wisdom says, 'The Most High has made medicine out of the earth and a wise man will not reject it.'

W. Köhler, *Dokumente zum Ablassstreit*, pp. 125–26.

▶ A contemporary chronicler[4] reported on the activities of Johann Tetzel:

At that time a Dominican monk named Johann Tetzel was the great mouthpiece, commissioner, and preacher of indulgences in Germany. His preaching raised enormous amounts of money which were sent to Rome. This was particularly the case in the new mining town St Annaberg, where I, Friedrich Myconius, listened to him for over two years. The claims of this uneducated and shameful monk were unbelievable. Thus he said that even if someone had slept with Christ's dear Mother, the Pope had power in heaven and on earth to forgive as long as money was put into the indulgence coffer. And if the Pope would forgive, God also had to forgive. He furthermore said if they would put money quickly into the coffer to obtain grace and indulgence, all the mountains near St Annaberg would turn into pure silver. He claimed that in the very moment the coin rang in the coffer, the soul rose up to heaven. Such a marvellous thing was his indulgence! In sum and substance: God was no longer God, as he had bestowed all divine power to the Pope: '*Tu es Petrus, tibi dabo claves, quodcunque ligaveritis.*' And then there were the masters of the Inquisition, who banished and burned those saying conflicting words. This indulgence was highly respected. When the commissioner was welcomed to town, the papal bull was carried on velvet or gold cloth. All the priests, monks, councilmen, teachers, pupils, men, women, maids, and children went to meet him singing in solemn procession with flags and candles. The bells tolled and when he entered the church the organ played. A red Cross was put up in the middle of the church to which the Pope's banner was affixed. In short: even God himself could not have been welcomed and received more beautifully.

Friedrich Myconius, *Historia reformationis*, p. 14.

Printed letter of indulgence of 1488. The empty spaces in the middle allow the name of the recipient as well as the date to be entered. The final two paragraphs quote the formula of absolution specified.
(*Staatsarchiv, Berlin*)

▶   Many stories about Tetzel made the rounds, particularly after the indulgences controversy had broken out.

After Tetzel had received a substantial amount of money at Leipzig, a nobleman asked him if it were possible to receive a letter of indulgence for a future sin. Tetzel quickly answered in the affirmative, insisting, however, that the payment had to be made at once. This the nobleman did, receiving thereupon letter and seal from Tetzel. When Tetzel left Leipzig the nobleman attacked him along the way, gave him a thorough

beating, and sent him back empty-handed to Leipzig with the comment
that this was the future sin which he had in mind. Duke George at first
was quite furious about this incident, but when he heard the whole story
he let it go without punishing the nobleman.

Luthers Schriften, herausg. von Walch. XV, 446.

▶   Luther himself, many years after the storm of the controversy
     had calmed down, summarized the course of events as he saw it.

It happened in 1517 that a Dominican monk named Johann Tetzel, a
braggart, caused a great stir. Maximilian once sentenced him to drowning
in the River Inn—presumably because of his great virtue—but Duke
Frederick rescued him in Innsbruck from the punishment of being
drowned. Duke Frederick reminded him of this incident when he began to
denounce us Wittenbergers. Actually, he admitted it quite openly. This
same Tetzel now began to peddle his indulgences. With might and main
he sold grace for money as dearly or as cheaply as he could. At that time
I was preacher here in the cloister and was filled as a new doctor with an
ardent love for the Sacred Scriptures.

When many people from Wittenberg ran after indulgences to Jüterborg and Zerbst, I did not yet know—as surely as my Lord Christ has
redeemed me—what indulgences were, but no one else knew either. I
carefully began to preach that one could do something better and more
certain than to purchase indulgences. On an earlier occasion I had already
preached here in the castle against indulgences, but was not very graciously
received by Duke Frederick, who was fond of his collegiate church. Now,
to speak about the real cause for the 'Lutheran scandal', at first I let
everything continue its course. Then it was reported to me, however, that
Tetzel was preaching some cruel and terrible propositions, such as the
following:

He had grace and power from the Pope to offer forgiveness even if
someone had slept with the Holy Virgin Mary, the Mother of God, as
long as a contribution would be put into the coffer.

Furthermore, the red Cross of indulgences and the papal coat of arms
on the flag in the churches was as powerful as the Cross of Christ.

Moreover, even if St Peter were here now he would have no greater
grace or power than he had.

Furthermore, he would not want to trade places in heaven with St
Peter, for he had redeemed more souls with his indulgences than Peter
with his sermons.

Furthermore, if anyone put money into the coffer for a soul in purgatory, the soul would leave purgatory for heaven in the moment one could hear the penny hit the bottom.

Also, the grace of indulgences is the grace by which man is reconciled with God.

Furthermore, it is not necesssary to show remorse or sorrow or do penance for sins when purchasing indulgences or a letter of indulgence. He even sold indulgences for future sins. Such abominable things he did abundantly. He was merely interested in money.

At that time I did not yet know who was to get the money. Then there appeared a booklet with the illustrious coat of arms of the Bishop of Magdeburg. In it the commissioners of indulgences were ordered to preach some of these propositions. Thus it came to light that Bishop Albert had employed Tetzel, because he was such a braggart.

Martin Luther, *Wider Hans Worst*, 1541. (*WA* 51, 538.)

▶ The outbreak of the indulgences controversy, the publication of the ninety-five theses, and their immediate popularity were described by a chronicler:[5]

In that year several people came to Dr Martin Luther in Wittenberg with letters of indulgence and made confession to him on the basis of the grace offered in those letters. When they were heard to say that they would not desist from adultery, usury, unrightful goods and similar sins and wickedness, Luther would not absolve them, since there was no sign of genuine repentance and improvement. Then the penitents appealed to their papal letters and to Tetzel's grace and indulgence. But Martin did not care about this and called attention to the saying: 'Unless ye improve, ye shall all perish' (Luke 13). When he thus would not absolve them, they went back to Tetzel, complaining that this Augustinian monk would not honour their letters. Tetzel, who was at Jüterborg in Saxony at that time, became furious. He raged in the pulpit and threatened with the Inquisition. In order to instil fear he had fires built in the market square several times a week, pointing out that he had orders from the Pope to burn the heretics who were against the holy Pope and his holy indulgence.

Dr Martin Luther first wrote to the Bishops of Meissen, Frankfurt, Zeitz, and then to Albert, the Bishop of Mainz. He reminded them of their episcopal obligation to prevent the abuse and blasphemy of the name of God as well as the deplorable deception of the poor people. But the Bishop of Mainz scoffed at this and several of the others replied that they could not interfere with papal affairs. When Dr Martin Luther realized that the bishops would not do anything concerning this matter, he composed several propositions concerning indulgences. They begin as follows:[6] '*Dominus et Magister noster Christus dicens: poenitentiam agite, voluit omnem omnium hominum vitam esse poenitentiam.*' Though he had these propositions printed, he merely wanted to enter into a debate with the faculty of the University of Wittenberg concerning the nature, effect, foundation, and significance of indulgences. But hardly fourteen days had passed when these propositions were known throughout Germany and within four weeks almost all of Christendom was familiar with them. It almost appeared as if the angels themselves had been their messengers and brought them before the eyes of all the people. One can hardly believe how much they were talked about. They were quickly translated into German and everyone was highly sympathetic, with the exception, of course, of the Dominicans and the Bishop of Halle, and all those who daily benefited from the Pope.

Friedrich Myconius, *Historia reformationis*, pp. 21–23.

▶ The Castle Church at Wittenberg, where Luther probably posted his ninety-five theses, was famous for its extensive collection of relics, as the following excerpt from what might be called the 'official catalogue'[7] shows.

. . . Three pieces of the city where the Virgin Mary was born. One piece of a yarn which she spun. One piece of the house where she lived at the age of fourteen. Two pieces of the city of Mt Zion where Mary lived. Two pieces of the room where Mary was greeted by the angel. Five particles of the milk of the Virgin Mary. One piece of the tree where Mary nursed the Lord near the Garden of Balsam. Four pieces of the hair of Mary. Three pieces of the shirt of Mary. Three pieces of one robe of Mary. Eight pieces of other robes of Mary. Four pieces of the belt of Mary. Seven pieces of the veil of Mary. Two pieces of the veil of Mary which was sprinkled with the blood of Christ under the Cross. One piece of the city where Mary died. One piece of the wax candle given to Our Lady when she died. Six pieces of the grave of Mary. Two pieces of the earth of the grave of Mary. One piece of the place where Mary ascended into heaven. VI. A silver picture of the little baby Jesus. Four pieces of the city where the Lord Jesus was born. One piece of the diaper in which he was wrapped. Thirteen pieces of the manger of Jesus. One piece of the cradle. Two pieces of the hay. One piece of the straw on which the Lord lay when he was born. One piece of the gold and of the myrrh which the Three Kings offered unto the Lord. One piece of the city where the Lord Jesus was circumcised. VII. Four pieces of the mountain on which the Lord Jesus fasted. Two pieces of the city where Christ preached the

The Castle Church
at Wittenberg. The theses
were posted on the left-
hand door.
(*Cranach, Das Wittemberger
Heiligthumsbuch*)

Lord's Prayer. One piece of the stone on which Jesus stood while weeping over Jerusalem. One piece of the stone from which Christ got on the donkey. Two pieces of the ground where the Lord Christ was arrested. VIII. . . . Five pieces of the table on which the Lord Christ held the Last Supper with his disciples. One piece of the bread of which Christ ate with his disciples during the Last Supper. IX. . . . One piece of the land which was bought for the thirty pieces of silver for which Christ was betrayed. One piece of the Holy Land. Three pieces of the stone where the Lord sweated blood. One piece of the ground where the Lord sweated blood. One piece of the stone sprinkled with the blood of Christ. X. Three pieces of the Mount of Olives and of the rod of Aaron. Two pieces of the rod of Moses. One piece of the burning bush which Moses saw. One piece of an object sprinkled with the blood of Christ. Eleven pieces of Mount Calvary. Two pieces of the Mount of Olives. XI. One piece of the cloth with which the Lord wiped his disciples' feet. One piece of the robe of Christ. One piece of the seamless robe of Christ. One piece of the robe of Christ. One piece of his purple robe. Two pieces of the cloth which St Veronica received from the Lord. Three pieces of the white robe in which the Lord was ridiculed by Herod. Three pieces of the cloth with which our Lord's holy eyes were blindfolded. One piece of the beard of

Martin Luther. (*Painting by Lucas Cranach the Elder*, 1528. *Staatl. Kunstsammlungen, Weimar*)

Pope Leo X (1513–21) who guided the Catholic Church during the first years of the Reformation, with his nephews, Cardinals Medici (subsequently Pope Clement VII) and Rossi. (*Painting by Raphael. Pitti Palace, Florence*)

the Lord Jesus. XII. One piece of the wax of the candles which touched the sudarium of Christ. One piece of the wedge with which the cross of Christ was held. Three pieces of the stone on which the cross stood. Three pieces of the place where the cross of Christ was found. Twelve pieces of the column where the Lord Christ was scourged and flogged.

The Eighth Aisle.

I. One piece of the rope with which Jesus was tied. Three pieces of the rod with which the Lord Jesus was scourged. Three pieces of the whip with which the Lord Jesus was flogged. One piece of the stone upon which the Lord Jesus sat when he was crowned. One piece of the stone which was crushed while the Lord carried the cross. One piece of the sponge with which the Lord was given vinegar and gall. . . . III. Two pieces of the crown of the Lord Jesus. Eight complete thorns of the crown of the Lord Jesus. IV. One large piece of one nail which was driven through the hands or feet of the Lord Jesus. V. A thorn which wounded the holy head of the Lord Jesus. VI. One piece of the holy cross. . . . VII. Three pieces of the holy cross. VIII. Three pieces of the three kinds of wood of the cross of Christ. IX. A particularly large piece from the holy cross. X. Twenty-five pieces of the holy cross. XI. One piece of the stone which lay on the grave of Christ. Twenty-two pieces of the grave of Christ. One piece of the stone from which Christ descended into heaven. XII. A casket lined with silver in which are found sixteen hundred and seventy-eight pieces. Seventy-six pieces of holy remains. Bones from holy places which on account of faded writing can no longer be read and identified.

All in all: five thousand and five pieces. An indulgence of one hundred days for each piece. There are eight halls and each hall has an indulgence of one hundred and one days in addition. Blessed are those who participate therein.

Lucas Cranach, *Wittemberger Heiligthumsbuch*, E iij, E iij b, F ij, F iiij, H iiij b, I iiff.

▶ Luther sent a copy of the ninety-five theses to the person most intimately involved, Archbishop Albert of Hohenzollern, and included the following letter:

In the name of Jesus I bid you the grace and mercy of God, Reverend Father in Christ, Most Illustrious Elector. You must graciously forgive that I, the scum of the earth, am so bold as to dare to address a letter to you. The Lord Jesus is my witness that I am not unaware of my unworthiness and insignificance which has caused me to delay for some time what I am now boldly doing. I am strongly moved by the faithful devotion which I confess to owe to you, Reverend Father in Christ. May you therefore cast a gracious eye upon me, as I am earth and ashes, and with clemency becoming a bishop graciously hear and understand my concern.

There is sold in the country under the protection of your illustrious name the papal indulgence for the building of St Peter's in Rome. In this I do not complain so much about the great clamour of the indulgence preachers whom I have not personally heard. But I am greatly concerned about the false notion existing among the common people which has become a cause of public boast. These unfortunate souls seemingly believe they are assured of their salvation as soon as they purchase letters of indulgence. They also believe that the souls leave purgatory as soon as they put the money into the chest. Furthermore, this grace of indulgence is said to be so powerful that no sin is too large not to be forgiven, even in the impossible case when someone had—to use their words—assaulted the Mother of God. Finally, it is claimed that man can free himself by this indulgence from all punishment and guilt. . . .

How is it possible that the indulgence preachers convey security and fearlessness to the people through false fables and futile promises about indulgences? Indulgences do not contribute to the salvation and sanctification of souls, but only remit temporal punishment which is imposed according to canon law.[8] Therefore works of piety and charity are infinitely more valuable than indulgences and yet they are preached neither with such splendour nor diligence. Indeed, they must silently give way to the more important preaching of indulgences. Yet, it should be the foremost and only care of all bishops to teach the Gospel and the love of Christ to the people. Christ nowhere commanded to preach indulgences, but emphatically insisted on the preaching of the Gospel. What great danger and shame wait for a bishop who allows the Gospel to be silenced, but suffers the pompous proclamation of indulgences and is more concerned about indulgences than the Gospel. Will not Christ say to him, 'Ye strain at a gnat, and swallow a camel'?

But this, Most Reverend Father in the Lord, is not all. The Instructions to the indulgence commissioners issued under your name state—surely without your knowledge and consent—that one of the most precious graces offered consists in the invaluable divine gift of man's reconciliation with God and the remission of all punishment in purgatory. It is also said that those who purchase such letters of indulgences need not be contrite.

What can I do, Most Sublime Bishop and Illustrious Elector, but to beseech you, through our Lord Jesus Christ, to cast your eyes of paternal care on this matter, to do away with these Instructions, and to order the indulgence preachers to preach differently? Otherwise someone may arise to contradict publicly the preachers and the Instructions, thereby bringing you into obliquity. This I deeply dread and yet I fear that something will happen soon unless the matter is taken care of.

I pray that you may accept this humble but faithful admonition graciously as ruler and bishop, even as I submit it with a faithful and devoted heart. For I, too, am one of your sheep. The Lord Jesus guard and guide you for ever. Amen.

Wittenberg, on the eve of All Saints' Day in the year 1517.

If you, Reverend Father, so desire, you might look at the enclosed set of propositions to recognize how indefinite the concept of indulgence is, even though the indulgence preachers consider it altogether certain.

31st October 1517. *WA, Br.* 1, 110-11.

▶   **Excerpts from Luther's ninety-five theses.**

Love for truth and the desire to bring it to light prompt a public discussion[9] of the following propositions at Wittenberg under the chairmanship of the reverend father Martin Luther, Master of Arts and Sacred Theology and duly appointed professor on these subjects at that place. He requests that those who cannot be present to debate orally with us will by letter in their absence.

In the Name of Our Lord Jesus Christ. Amen.

1. When our Lord and Master Jesus Christ said, 'Repent' he wanted the entire life of believers to be one of penitence.

2. This word cannot be understood as referring to penance as a sacrament (that is, confession and satisfaction, as administered by the ministry of priests).

3. This word also does not refer solely to inner penitence; indeed there is no penitence unless it produces various outward mortifications of the flesh.

4. Therefore punishment [of sin] remains as long as the hatred of self (that is, true inward penitence), namely until entering the kingdom of heaven.

5. The Pope neither wishes nor can remit any punishment except that which he imposed by his or by canonical authority.

6. The Pope cannot remit any guilt, except by stating and confirming that it has been remitted by God; or, by remitting [guilt] in cases reserved to his judgment. If his power were disregarded, guilt would certainly remain.

7. God remits guilt to no one without at once submitting him humbly in all things to the priest as his vicar. . . .

20. By full remission of all punishment, the Pope therefore does not actually mean 'all [punishment]' but only that which he imposed.

21. Therefore, those indulgence preachers err who say that man is by papal indulgence absolved from every punishment and saved. . . .

27. They preach human doctrines who assert that as soon as the coin falls into the chest the soul flies upwards [out of purgatory]. . . .

37. Any true Christian, whether living or dead, participates in all the works of Christ and the Church; this is granted him by God, even without [indulgence] letters. . . .

42. Christians are to be taught that it is not the desire of the Pope that the buying [of indulgences] should in any way be compared with works of mercy.

43. Christians are to be taught that giving to the poor or lending to the needy is better than to buy indulgences.

44. Love grows through works of love and man becomes better, but through indulgences he does not become better, as he is only freed from punishment.

45. Christians are to be taught that he who sees a needy man and neglects him, yet gives his money for indulgences, does not buy papal indulgence but God's indignation.

46. Christians are to be taught that, unless they are well taken care of, they should retain enough for their domestic needs and by no means squander it on indulgences.

47. Christians are to be taught that the buying of indulgences is free, not commanded.

48. Christians are to be taught that even as the Pope needs prayer when granting indulgences, he desires devout prayer more than money.
. . .

Disputatio pro declaratione virtutis indulgentiarum, 1517. (*WA* 1, 233ff.)

▶ Albert of Hohenzollern requested the theological faculty at the University of Mainz for an assessment of Luther's theses and received the following reply:[10]

Most Reverend Father in Christ, most illustrious and gracious Prince and Lord! We promise our devoted obedience. We have received with due humility the theses posted at the famous university of Wittenberg by a professor of the order of St Augustine, which were sent us by you. We have read them and among other things we find that they limit and restrict the power of the Pope and the apostolic see and contradict, therefore, the opinions of many blessed and venerable doctors.

17th December 1517. E. Hermann, *Miscellen zur
Reformationsgeschichte*, p. 266.

▶ Early in 1518, after it had become evident what controversy the ninety-five theses had evoked, Luther published his 'Resolutions', a lengthy explanation of his earlier pronouncement. He dedicated this work to Pope Leo X and wrote the following introduction.

Martin Luther, Augustinian monk, wishes eternal salvation to the Most Holy Father, Pope Leo X.

I have heard some bad rumours about me, Most Holy Father. I understand that several 'good' friends have made my name foul with you, claiming that I have tried to do away with the reputation and the power of the keys as well as of the Pontiff. I am accused as heretic, apostate, and false believer, besides being branded with six hundred additional calumnious epithets. My ears are horrified and my eyes amazed, but my innocent and pure conscience still remains the bulwark of my confidence.

Now there is nothing new in such accusations, for here, too, these 'truth-loving' and 'honourable' men have bestowed upon me such glorious titles. In this they betray their bad conscience, since they obviously want to impose upon me their own monstrosities and cover their own disgrace with mine. I pray, Most Holy Father, listen to my own childish and unlearned account of the matter.

Recently the apostolic jubilee indulgence began to be preached in this area. Eventually the preachers surmised that the protection of your name allowed them everything. They dared publicly to teach the most godless heresy, causing grave scandal to and mockery of ecclesiastical authority. . . . They had one means to suppress the uproar of the people, namely the authority of your name, the threat of the stake, and the shame of heresy. One can hardly say how much they like to use these as threats, for they themselves feel the inner contradiction in their loose blabber. This is the way to do away with scandal, indeed, to use blunt tyranny to bring about division and eventually rebellion. One could hear in all the taverns the stories about the greediness of the priests. The people desecrated the keys of Peter, and even the Pope himself, by their talking. Of this our whole land is witness. But I was inflamed with a zeal for Christ or perhaps—as they say—a youthful zeal. I realized that it was not my function to do anything in such an important matter all alone. Therefore I warned in personal letters some of the dignitaries of the Church. I was graciously received by some, by others ridiculed and treated even worse. All in all, the fear of your name and the threats of punishment prevailed. Finally, when I could do nothing else, I felt it right—in all modesty—to contradict them and to debate their teachings. Therefore I published certain theses, inviting only scholars to debate with me, as the preface to my theses expressly states. Even my enemies cannot deny this.

This is the fire which now is burning everywhere, as they say. Perhaps they are annoyed that I all by myself—called by your apostolic authority to be a teacher of theology—claim the right to debate according to custom of all universities and the Church, not only the matter of indulgences, but also immensely higher things, such as the power of the keys, the forgiveness of sins, and especially the relationship of indulgences to divine punishment and forgiveness.[11] I am not worried about the fact that they begrudge my right, which stems from your authority. But I must also suffer that they incorporate Aristotle's dreams into the most sublime teachings of theology and dispense their futile talk concerning God's majesty, for which they have no right.

It is a mystery to me how my theses, more so than my other writings, indeed, those of other professors, were spread to so many places. They were meant exclusively for our academic circle here. This is shown by the fact that they were written in such a language that the common people could hardly understand them. They are propositions for debate, not dogmatic definitions, and they use academic categories. Had I anticipated their widespread popularity, I would certainly have done my share to make them more understandable.

What shall I do now? I cannot recall my theses and yet their popularity makes me to be hated. Unwillingly I must enter the public limelight and subject myself to the dangerously shifting judgment of men. I am no great scholar, I have a stupid mind and little education—this in our flourishing century whose superb literature would even push Cicero, who in his time did not have to fear the educated Roman public, into the corner. But what does it help! Necessity forces me to be a honking goose among singing swans. . . .

Therefore, Most Holy Father, I prostrate myself before your Holiness and dedicate myself to you with whatever I am and have. Raise me up or slay me, approve my work or reject it according to your pleasure: I shall recognize your voice as the voice of Christ, speaking and ruling in you. Should I have deserved death, I will not refuse it. For the earth is the Lord's and the fullness thereof. Blessed be he for ever. Amen. May he always preserve you. Amen.

30th May 1518. *Resolutiones disputationum de indulgentiarum virtute.* (*WA* 1, 527–9.)

▶   Also early in 1518, Luther participated in a theological disputation at Heidelberg which ventured to clarify some of the issues by means of the following theses:

Brother Martin Luther, Master of Sacred Theology, will preside, and Brother Leonhard Beier, Master of Arts and Philosophy, will defend the following theses before the Augustinians of this renowned city of Heidelberg in the customary place. In the month of May 1518.

Distrusting completely our own wisdom, according to that counsel of the Holy Spirit, 'Do not rely on your own insight' [Prov. 3.5], we humbly present to the judgment of all those who wish to be here these theological paradoxes, so that it may become clear whether they have been deduced well or poorly from St Paul, the especially chosen vessel and instrument of Christ, and also from St Augustine, his most trustworthy interpreter.

1. The law of God, the most salutary doctrine of life, cannot advance man on his way to righteousness, but rather hinders him.

2. Much less can human works, which are done over and over again with the aid of natural precepts, so to speak, lead to that end.

3. Although the works of man always seem attractive and good, they are nevertheless likely to be mortal sins.

4. Although the works of God are always unattractive and appear evil, they are nevertheless really eternal merits. . . .

8. By so much more are the works of man mortal sins when they are done without fear and in unadulterated, evil self-security.

9. To say that works without Christ are dead, but not mortal, appears to constitute a perilous surrender of the fear of God. . . .

13. Free will, after the fall, exists in name only, and as long as it does what it is able to do, it commits a mortal sin. . . .

15. Nor could free will remain in a state of innocence, much less do good, in an active capacity, but only in its passive capacity.

16. The person who believes that he can obtain grace by doing what is in him adds sin to sin, so that he becomes doubly guilty.

17. Nor does speaking in this manner give cause for despair, but for arousing the desire to humble oneself and seek the grace of Christ.

18. It is certain that man must utterly despair of his own ability before he is prepared to receive the grace of Christ.

19. That person does not deserve to be called a theologian who looks upon the invisible things of God as though they were clearly perceptible in those things which have actually happened [Rom. 1.20].

20. He deserves to be called a theologian, however, who comprehends the visible and manifest things of God seen through suffering and the cross.

21. A theology of glory calls evil good and good evil. A theology of the cross calls the thing what it actually is. . . .

Disputatio Heidelbergae habita. (*WA* 1, 353-4.)[11a]

▶ In August of 1518, Pope Leo X wrote to Luther's ruler, Elector Frederick of Saxony, in an effort to exert pressure on the Wittenberg professor.

Beloved Son, greeting and the apostolic blessing! . . . It has come to our ears from all quarters that a certain son of iniquity, Friar Martin Luther, of the German Congregation of Augustinian Hermits, forgetting his cloth and profession, which consists in humility and obedience, sinfully vaunts himself in the Church of God, and, as though relying on your protection, fears the authority or rebuke of no one. Although we know this is false, yet we thought good to write to your Lordship, exhorting you in the Lord, that for the name and fame of a good Catholic Prince such as you are, you should retain the splendour of your glory and race unsoiled by these calumnies. Not only that we wish you to avoid doing wrong, as you do, for as yet we judge that you have done none, but we desire you to escape the suspicion of doing wrong, in which Luther's rashness would involve you. . . .

As this affair concerns the purity of the faith of God and the Catholic Church, and as it is the proper office of the Apostolic See, the mistress of faith, to take cognizance of who thinks rightly and who wrongly, we again exhort your Lordship, for the sake of God's honour and ours and your own, please to give help that this Martin Luther may be delivered into the power and judgment of the Holy See, as the said legate will request of you. . . .

23rd August 1518. *Lutheri Opera* (Erlangen, 1865) II, 352. [11b]

▶ The year 1518 also brought the first expressions of enthusiastic support for Martin Luther, coming particularly from the ranks of the humanists. One of them, Wolfgang Capito, later on the reformer of Strassburg, wrote a letter of commendation and warning.

If you will lend an ear to the advice of one who knows, I would warn you to adopt the tactics of Sertorius. Believe me, you can undermine gradually what you can never overthrow by force. Your enemies hold a fortress which is protected on every side. Behind a triple line of defence and beyond the range of cannons they snore peacefully. Their threefold safety lies in the authority of the Pope (that is, of the universal Church), in the powerful protection of the rulers, and in the persistent support of the universities.

Surely you will never succeed in breaking this diabolically stout rope. Another Alexander would be needed to cut this Gordian knot with the sword; the problem is how to do it by mere skill or reason. Simple, pious folk meekly follow the beck and nod of our false Church. The more thoughtful heads have had their spirit quenched by its tyranny. We theologians, who loudly proclaim our special sanctity and knowledge of Christ, constantly compromise his cause by our arrogance. We take advantage of the religious abuses and under the guise of piety we decently guard our own interests.

Therefore I ask you, lest your noble undertaking should fail, to resort to a little dissimulation, so that you may get your hook well fixed in your reader before he suspects your intention. The apostles followed this plan, never pressing anything openly and always maintaining a dignified and kindly attitude. St Paul resorts to similar devices in his Epistle to the Romans. How dexterously he manoeuvres in order to keep their favour! He advances, withdraws, dissimulates, shows the divine treasure from afar, but carefully veils it. In short, he so skilfully balances his presentation that he neither irritates nor wearies his readers. . . .

Thus by indirect means important results may be achieved. I would have you always keep open a safe exit by which you can escape when in danger. . . .

Recently I received Silvester Prierias' foolish pamphlet[12] against your treatment of indulgences. If you are going to reply, I would have you do so in prudent language and so reflect the true spirit of Christ in the Gospel. You should deal with the origin and growth of our religion, the original customs, the nature of hardened error, and the varying decrees of popes and councils, so that your presentation may be visibly confirmed as coming directly from the fountain of truth.

Also remember that certain kinds of abuse are frequently better discredited by ridicule than by laborious effort. Be very careful not to attack the Pope himself. Lay all the blame on Prierias for his impudent flattery and for suggesting motives unworthy of the papal dignity, simply in the interest of his own belly. Oppose yourself to the unblushing sycophant, as if you were endeavouring to cut off the opportunity for evil. Where you seem to see a chance for them to reply, block the way, so that they cannot reach you to strike back. . . .

4th September 1518. *WA, Br.* 1, 197–9.

▶   Also in 1518, young Philipp Melanchthon came to Wittenberg to join the university faculty.[13] Soon an enthusiastic follower of Luther, he played an important role in the course of the

Reformation. Here is one of Luther's early references to Melanchthon and the latter's description of his responsibilities.

. . . The most learned and perfect Grecian Philipp Melanchthon is
teaching Greek here. He is a mere boy in years, but one of us in various
knowledge, including that of almost all books. He is not only master of
Greek and Latin, but of all the learning to which they are the keys, and
he also knows some Hebrew.[14]

16th September 1518. WA, Br. 1, 203.

▶   Melanchthon himself wrote as follows:[15]

. . . I have begun to teach Greek and Hebrew to the Saxons, which
undertaking I hope God will favour. I have also determined to publish
as soon as possible some sacred writings of the Greeks, Hebrews, and
Romans with commentaries. Wherefore I pray you either for the love of
these studies, or for the honour of the Elector Frederick or of our university to order at my expense, from the booksellers of Coburg, a Greek Bible,
for we have the Hebrew Bible extremely well printed here. You will
understand how much this will redound to the credit of the Elector, the
university, and your own name, and I would be the first to declare it, did
you not already have a witness in Luther, that honoured, good and learned
leader of true Christian piety.

24th September 1518. CR 1, 48.

▶   Melanchthon was twenty-one years of age when he joined the
faculty of the University of Wittenberg. His inaugural address on
'The Reform of the Education of Youth' allows us to anticipate
his subsequent co-operation with Luther.

It appears impudent and presumptuous indeed to speak in this illustrious gathering, since both my temperament and the nature of my
studies keep me from such a place and such a laudatory gathering of
orators. The difficulties of the subject-matter, which I am about to consider, could also frighten me, if my respect for true studies and my office
would not exhort me to recommend to you to the best of my ability sound
scholarship and the newly awakening muses. Their cause I have pledged
to guard against the barbarians, who in barbaric fashion, that is, with
might and deception, demand in vulgar fashion the titles and rights of
learned teachers and to this very day with evil cunning frustrate men.
Some stop with sly arguments the German youth which for several years
attempts to enter the arena of scholarly competition. They claim that to
study the newly awakening literary sciences was more difficult than profit-

able; that to learn Greek was a matter of idle minds and nothing but boasting; that Hebrew had little to commend itself. In the meantime the true sciences were allowed to decay, philosophy made into an orphan.

Certain men, be it because of intellectual immoderation or quarrelsomeness, jumped upon Aristotle, a crippled Aristotle who for the Greeks themselves was as mysterious as Apollo's 'Delphic oracle'. . . . Noble studies were more and more neglected, the knowledge of Greek was lost, and the bad was being taught instead of the good. From thence arose Thomas, Scotus, Durandus, the seraphic and cherubinic doctors and their followers in greater number than even the offspring of Kadmos. . . . Such studies were prevalent for about three hundred years in England, France, and Germany—and I will not speak further about what transpired during that time. The inevitably unprofitable results must be obvious from what I have said. To make it very clear, listen carefully:

First of all, the neglect of the old disciplines and the introduction of this bold way of commentating and philosophizing caused both Greek and mathematics to be forgotten and religion to suffer. What worse, more raging evil could one think of? And yet none was ever more widespread. Until that time philosophy had been altogether Greek, and only Cyprian, Hilary, Ambrose, Jerome, and Augustine had excelled in Latin. Greek had been in the West virtually the language of religion. By despising Greek, the inestimable benefit of philosophy for humanistic studies was lost. With this disappeared the participation in religion. This development brought decay for Christian morals and the customs of the Church as well as for literary studies. Alleviation easily might have been possible, if only one thing had not perished. The decay of erudition might have been halted had the ecclesiastical ritual not been touched. With the help of good erudition one could have done away with the corruption in the Church, raised up the fallen spirit of man, strengthened this spirit and called it back to order. Through our guilt or through fate, noble erudition turned into its opposite, and old piety turned into ceremonies, and was put into the hands of human traditions, human decisions, decretals, regulations, moods and the glosses of the scribes. . . .

In theology, too, it is important how education is performed. If any field of studies, then theology requires especially talent, training, and conscientiousness. The aroma of God's salve supersedes all the aromas of human knowledge. Led by the Holy Spirit, but accompanied by humanist studies, one should proceed to theology. . . . But since the Bible is written in part in Hebrew and in part in Greek—as Latinists we drink from the stream of both—we must learn these languages, unless we want to be 'silent persons' as theologians. Once we understand the significance and the weight of the words, the true meaning of Scripture will light up for us as the midday sun. Only if we have clearly understood the language will we clearly understand the content. All the dry glossaries, concordances, disconcordances and the like,· which have been manufactured without number, are only hindrances for the spirit. If we put our minds to the sources, we will begin to understand Christ rightly. Then his commandments will become understandable, and we will have tasted from the blessed nectar of sacred wisdom. And, if we 'harvest the grapes in the vineyards of Engedi', as we read in the Song of Songs, the beloved will encounter us 'jumping over hills and mountains', and sweet odours will lead us into the Garden of Eden . . . in death we will receive the kiss of the beloved: woven into his limbs will we live and die, immersed into Zion's sight. . . . These are the fruits of the heavenly wisdom. Let us adore them purely and untouched by our sophistication—as Paul often admonishes us, especially in his letter to Titus: let the Christian teaching be pure, free from all corruption. Doctrine is to be pure. This means: we are not to dirty the sacred Scripture with unprofitable foreign writings. If we mingle the profane with the sacred, we must know that all the profane desires, hatred, quarrelsomeness and factions, division and anger will appear. Whoever wishes to penetrate into religion, must take off the old Adam and put on a new, incorruptible one. That is, he must shake off and break with human desires and with the yoke of the sly serpent with superior power. . . .

This is what I meant when I said that the Church has decayed by a lack of education and that true and genuine piety was perverted by human additions. Once there was a delight in man's commentaries, one ate instead of the divine manna baal-peor and men ceased to be Christians. This I want to say the way I mean it. I mean nothing but what the order of the Church recognizes as evangelical truth. That will be my 'might and power', as the Hebrews say.

Philipp Melanchthon, *De corrigendis adulescentiae studiis*, CR 11, 15ff.

▶   **Papal efforts to silence Luther are illustrated by the following letter of Pope Leo X to Duke George of Saxony.**[16]

. . . We have heard that Martin Luther, a son of perdition, at the suggestion of that cruel enemy of our salvation, the devil, has not blushed to say evil of us and of the said apostolic see, in preaching, or rather in cursing. Now as this not only savours of heresy, but is worthy of severe punishment, and should not longer be borne by your devotion and obedience to us, desiring to extirpate this tare and coccle from the fertile field of the Lord by your aid, fearing lest, should we wink at it, we would put forth deeper roots among the too credulous people, we have charged Karl von Miltitz, our notary, secret chamberlain and nuncio in the Lord, and a cleric of the church of Meissen, to do so. For the wickedness of the thing demands it, and we hope it can be rightly and swiftly done. We have enjoined the said Karl to expound to you our paternal love, hoping that he can rely on the help of your highness; and we charge you for the sake of all the faithful and of the Catholic Church, and the unity and dignity of our see, that, considering the gravity of the present scandal and the rash and damnable error and boldness of the said Martin, you should favour the said Karl and help him to execute his commission. You will thus please God, whose cause you defend, and you will also win praise from us.

24th October 1518. F. Gess, *Akten und Briefe*, I, 45.

▶   In the autumn of 1518 Luther was examined by Cardinal Cajetan at Augsburg. The Cardinal had received the following instructions from Pope Leo X.[17]

Beloved Son, greeting and the apostolic blessing! After it had come to our ears that a certain Martin Luther, reprobate Augustinian, had asserted some heresies and some things different from those held by the Roman Church, and in addition to this, of his own rashness and obstinacy, forgetting the duty of obedience and not consulting the mistress of the faith, the Roman Church, had dared to publish some slanderous books in divers parts of Germany, we, desirous of paternally correcting his rashness, ordered our venerable brother Jerome, Bishop of Ascoli, General Auditor of the Curia, to cite the said Martin to appear personally before him to be examined under certain penalties and to answer for his faith. The said Auditor Jerome, as we have heard, issued this citation to the said Martin.

But recently it has come to our notice that the said Martin, abusing our clemency and become bolder thereby, adding evil to evil and obstinately persisting in his heresy, has published some other propositions and slanderous books, containing other heresies and errors. This disturbed our mind not a little. Wherefore, agreeably to our pastoral duty, desiring to prevent such a pest from growing strong and infecting the minds of the simple, we, by these presents, direct you (in whose circumspection we confide much in the Lord, on account of your singular learning, your experience and your sincere devotion to this holy see of which you are an honourable member) not to delay on receipt of this letter, but, since the affair has become notorious and inexcusable and has lasted long, to force and compel the said Martin, now declared to be a heretic by the said auditor, to appear personally before you. To accomplish this, call on the assistance of our most beloved son in Christ, Maximilian, Emperor Elect of the Romans, and of the other German princes, cities, corporations and powers, both ecclesiastical and secular; and when you have Martin in your power, keep him under a safe guard until you hear further from us, as shall be determined by us and the apostolic see.

If he shall come to you of his own accord, craving pardon for his rashness, and showing signs of hearty repentance, we give you power of kindly receiving him into the communion of holy Mother Church, who never closes her bosom to him who returns. But if, indeed, persevering in his contumacy, and despising the secular arm, he will not come into your power, then in like manner we give you power of declaring in a public edict like those which were formerly written on the praetor's bill-board, to be posted in all parts of Germany, that he and his adherents and followers are heretics, excommunicated, anathematized and cursed, and are to be avoided by all the faithful as such. And in order that this plague may be the more quickly and easily exterminated, you may admonish and require, by our authority and under pain of excommunication and other penalties mentioned below, all and singular prelates and other ecclesiastical persons, as well secular as regular of all orders, including the mendicants, and all dukes, marquises, counts, barons, cities, corporations and magistrates (except the aforesaid Maximilian Emperor Elect) that, as they desire to be considered Christians, they should seize all his adherents and followers and give them into your charge.

And if (which we deprecate and cannot believe) the said princes, cities, corporations and magistrates, or any of them, should receive Martin or his adherents and followers in any way, or should give the said Martin aid, counsel or favour, openly or secretly, directly or indirectly, for any cause whatever, we subject the cities, towns and domains of these princes, communities, corporations and magistrates to the interdict as well as all the cities, towns and places to which the said Martin may happen to come, as long as he remains there and for three days afterwards. And we also command all and singular princes, cities, corporations and magistrates aforesaid to obey all your requisitions and commands, without exception, contradiction or reply, and that they abstain from giving counsel, aid, favour and comfort to the aforesaid.

Acta Augustana, 1518. (*WA* 2, 23–25.)

▶   **Luther himself described his proceedings with Cajetan as follows:[18]**

I was received by the most reverend lord cardinal legate both graciously
and with almost too much respect, for he is a man who is in all respects
different from those extremely harsh bloodhounds who track down
monks among us. After he had stated that he did not wish to argue with
me, but to settle the matter peacefully and in a fatherly fashion, he proposed that I do three things which, he said, had been demanded by the
Pope: first, that I come to my senses and retract my errors; second, that
I promise to abstain from them in the future; and third, that I abstain
from doing anything which might disturb the Church. Realizing that I
could just as well have done these things at Wittenberg without exposing
myself to danger and going to so much trouble, and that I did not need to
seek this papal admonition in Augsburg, I immediately asked to be instructed in what matters I had been wrong, since I was not conscious of
any errors. Then he referred to the *Extravagante*[19] of Clement VI which
begins with the word *Unigenitus*, because in Thesis 58 I had asserted
contrary to it that the merits of Christ did not constitute the treasure of
merits of indulgences. Then he demanded that I retract and confidently
pursued the matter, sure of victory; for he was certain and secure in
assuming that I had not seen the *Extravagante*, probably relying upon
the fact that not all editions of the canon law contain it.

In the second place he reproached me for having taught in the explanation of Thesis 7 that a person taking the sacrament had to have faith or
he would take it to his own damnation, for he wished to have this judged
a new and erroneous doctrine. According to him, every person going to
the sacrament was uncertain whether or not he would receive grace. By
his boldness he made it appear as though I had been defeated, especially
since the Italians and others of his companions smiled and, according to
their custom, even giggled aloud.

I then answered that I had carefully examined not only this *Extravagante* of Clement, but also the other one of Sixtus IV[20] which emulated
and was similar to it (for I had actually read both and had found them
characterized by the same verbosity, which destroys one's faith in their
trustworthiness, stuffed as they are with ignorance). The *Extravagante*
did not impress me as being truthful or authoritative for many reasons,
but especially because it distorts the Holy Scriptures and audaciously
twists the words (if indeed their customary meaning still should be accepted) into a meaning which they do not have in their context, in fact
into a contrary meaning. The Scriptures, which I follow in my Thesis 7,

are to be preferred to the bull in every case. Nothing is proven in the bull. Only the teaching of St Thomas is trotted out and retold.

Then, in contradiction to what I had said, he began to extol the authority of the Pope, stating that it is above church councils, Scripture, and the entire Church. With the purpose of persuading me to accept this point of view, he called attention to the rejection and dissolution of the Council of Basel and was of the opinion that the Gersonists as well as Gerson[21] should be condemned. Since this was something new to me, I denied that the Pope was superior to the council and Scripture and I praised the appeal made by the University of Paris. Then we exchanged words concerning penance and grace in no prearranged order. The second objection caused me much grief, for I should scarcely have feared anything less than that this doctrine would ever be called into question. Thus in no one point did we even remotely come to any agreement, but as one thing led to another, as is usually the case, so a new contradiction arose. When, however, I saw that nothing was accomplished by such a dispute, except that many points were raised and none solved—indeed we already conjured up nothing but papal bulls—and especially since he was representing the Pope and did not wish to appear to yield, I asked that I be given time for deliberation.

On the next day, when four counsellors of his majesty the Emperor were present, I, with a notary and witnesses who had been brought to the meeting, testified formally and personally by reading in the presence of the most reverend legate the following:

'Above all I, brother Martin Luther, Augustinian, declare publicly that I cherish and follow the holy Roman Church in all my words and actions—present, past and future. If I have said or shall say anything contrary to this, I wish it to be considered as not having been said.

'The most reverend cardinal Cajetan by command of the Pope has asserted, proposed, and urged that with respect to the above disputation which I held on indulgences I do these three things: first, to come to my senses and retract my error, second, to pledge not to repeat it in the future, and third, to promise to abstain from all things which might disturb the Church. I, who debated and sought the truth, could not have done wrong by such inquiry, much less be compelled to retract unheard or unconvicted. Today I declare publicly that I am not conscious of having said anything contrary to Holy Scripture, the church fathers, or papal decretals or their correct meaning. All that I have said today seems to me to have been sensible, true, and catholic.

'Nevertheless, since I am a man who can err, I have submitted and now again submit to the judgment and the lawful conclusion of the holy

Church and of all who are better informed than I. In addition to this, however, I offer myself personally here or elsewhere to give an account also in public of all that I have said. But if this does not please the most reverend lord legate, I am even prepared to answer in writing the objections which he intends to raise against me, and to hear the judgment and opinion concerning these points of the doctors of the famed imperial universities of Basel, Freiburg, and Louvain, or, if this is not satisfactory, also of Paris, the parent of learning and from the beginning the university which was most Christian and most renowned in theology.'

Acta Augustana, 1518. (*WA* 2, 7–9.)

▶ The year 1519 brought the famous debate[22] between Martin Luther and his foremost Catholic opponent, Johann Eck, at Leipzig. Luther proposed to defend the following theses:[23]

Martin Luther will defend the following theses against new and old errors at the University of Leipzig.

1. Every man sins daily, but he also repents daily according to Christ's teaching. . . .

2. To deny that man sins even when doing good; that venial sin is pardonable, not according to its nature, but by the mercy of God; or that sin remains in the child after baptism; that is equivalent to crushing Paul and Christ under foot.

3. He who maintains that a good work and penance begin with the hatred of sins and prior to the love of righteousness and that one no longer sins in doing good work, him we number among the Pelagian heretics; but we also prove that this is a silly interpretation of his holy Aristotle. . . .

7. He who babbles about the free will being the master of good or evil deeds shows he does not know what faith, contrition, or free will are; nor does he know who imagines that he is not justified alone by faith in the Word, or that faith cannot be removed by a heinous sin.

8. It is contrary to truth and reason to state that those who die unwillingly are deficient in love and must therefore suffer the horror of purgatory, but only if truth and reason are the same as the opinions of the would-be theologians.

9. We are familiar with the assertion of would-be theologians that the souls in purgatory are certain of their salvation and that grace is no longer increased in them; but we marvel at these very learned men that they can offer the uneducated no cogent reason for this their faith.

10. It is certain that the merit of Christ is the treasure of the Church and that this treasure is enhanced by the merits of the saints; but no one except a filthy flatterer or one who strays from the truth and embraces

Oldest portrait of Luther, found on the title page of his *Ein Sermon geprediget zu Leypssgk* . . . (Leypssgk, 1519). In the rush the circumscription 'Doctor Martinus Lutter, Augustiner, Wittenb.' was wrongly cut into the block.

certain false practices and usages of the Church pretends that the merits of Christ are the treasure of indulgences.

11. To say that indulgences are a blessing for a Christian is insane, for they are in truth a hindrance to a good work; and a Christian must reject indulgences because of their abuse. . . .

12. Completely unlearned sophists and pestiferous flatterers dream that the Pope can remit every punishment owed for sins in this and the future life and that indulgences are helpful to those who are not guilty. But they cannot prove this with so much as a gesture.

13. The very feeble decrees of the Roman pontiffs which have appeared in the last four hundred years prove that the Roman Church is superior to all others. Against them stand the history of eleven hundred years, the text of divine Scripture, and the decree of the Council of Nicaea, the most sacred of all councils.

Disputatio et excusatio adversus criminationes
D. Iohannes Eccii, 1519. (*WA* 2, 160–1.)

▶ The crucial encounter between Luther and Eck at Leipzig actually came off as follows:

5th July 1519, 2 o'clock in the afternoon.

Luther:

The eminent Doctor has just called my attention to the articles of Wiclif and John Huss. He has also spoken of Boniface, who condemned them. I reply as before that I neither want to nor am in a position to defend the Bohemian schism. I am concerned about the Greek Church with the history of 1,400 years. It is irrelevant as far as I am concerned whether the Bohemians believe as do the Greeks—what is that to me? I know of a certainty that neither the Roman pontiff nor all his flatterers can cast out from heaven so great a number of believers who have never been under papal jurisdiction.

Secondly, it is also certain that many of the articles of John Huss and the Bohemians are plainly most Christian and evangelical. The universal Church cannot condemn these: for example, the statement that there is only one universal Church. This, however, has in hostile fashion been condemned by godless flatterers, even though the universal Church prays, 'I believe in the Holy Ghost, the Holy Catholic Church, the Communion of Saints'. None the less they include this eminent article of faith among the articles of John Huss.

A word also about this proposition: 'It is not necessary for salvation to believe that the Roman Church is superior to others.' As far as I am concerned it makes no difference whether this has been held by Wiclif or Huss. I know that Gregory of Nazianzus, Basil of Caesarea, Epiphanius, Cyprian, and numerous other Greek bishops are among the redeemed, even though they did not believe this article. Neither the Roman pontiff nor the wicked inquisitors have the power to draw up new articles of faith; they must judge according to established ones. No faithful Christian can be forced beyond the Sacred Scripture, which is alone the divine law, unless new and approved revelation is added. Indeed, we are prohibited by divine law to believe unless it is supported by Sacred Scripture or open revelation. This principle was lately asserted by Gerson in many places. St Augustine observed earlier as special rule: 'I have learned to honour thus only those books which are called canonical; the others, however great their doctrine and piety, I read considering them to be true not because [or 'when'] they merely appear so, but only when they can persuade me by means of canonical writings or probable opinion.' Even the jurists themselves established quite unexpectedly in the canon *Significasti de electione* that the view of one individual is more significant than that of the Roman pontiff, council and Church if it can be based on better authority and reasoning. Thus it is irrelevant that the eminent Doctor, wishing to argue against me from divine Law, repudiates such divine Law and argues against me from the collections of the wicked inquisitors.

Therefore, if John Huss's proposition that 'papal authority comes from the emperor' is false, Platina's comment,[24] in his life of Benedict II, must be omitted; for according to him Constantinus IV, the Greek Emperor, asserted that the Roman pontiff is the general vicar of Christ, even though this was not so observed by the Greek bishops.

Thus, as long as the eminent Doctor points to the Bohemians who are not yet one hundred years old, I confront him with the Eastern Church, which is the larger part of the universal Church and 1,400 years old. If they are heretics because they have not acknowledged the Roman pontiff, then I shall charge my opponent with heresy, for he dares to consider many saints damned who are venerated by the universal Church. Concerning Boniface VIII, his stature as pontiff, and the character of his work, I will let history speak.

I conclude and ask the Doctor to admit that the Roman pontiffs have been human beings and are not gods, especially since they have so often judged their own affairs and were at times most unlearned flatterers. At any rate, St Gregory, though himself Roman pontiff, rejected the primacy over the entire world in many letters. He referred to his predecessor Pelagius and stated among other things that the Council of Chalcedon bestowed the honour of primacy on the Roman pontiff although no one dared to accept it. If therefore I am in error, then Gregory and his predecessors were in error first and sinned damnably by not accepting the offered primacy.

With all this I hope to have shown that the more recent decrees, condemnations, and approvals of the Roman Church do not prove anything against me, since they are all suspect and in everything against old truth and custom. None the less, out of reverence and desire to avoid schism I will voluntarily be tolerant and will counsel others to be likeminded. Let us not condemn, however, as it were by divine Law, so many believers of the past. . . .

Eck:

The reverend Father denies, in order to defend himself, that he is a patron of the Bohemians; I should be delighted if the facts would correspond with his words. But the latter do not agree with the former, since he asserts in unchristian fashion, that the most evil errors of the Hussites are Christian. . . .

I have always praised the Greeks and their holy martyrs. But the reverend Father, not well instructed in the art of cooking, mixes the holy Greeks with the schismatics and heretics, in order to protect the faithlessness of the latter with the pretence of the holiness of the former, enfolding 1,400 years. (Dr Martin Luther protests: 'I protest both to you and this gathering that you speak falsely and impudently about me.' Eck insists that he would show with the written and spoken word that the majority of the Greeks have been for a long time heretical and schismatic. There is no agreement between light and Belial, nor between schismatics and holy martyrs and confessors.)

[*Eck continues:*] I should like to speak of the Church which existed for twenty years before the Roman Church, which the reverend Father put before me. I am not concerned that the Greek bishops were not confirmed by the Roman pontiff, for local and ordinary priests are also not confirmed by the Pope. It would none the less be foolish to insist therefore that the Supreme pontiff does not possess the primacy over ordinary priests.

Furthermore, the reverend Father boasts that he interprets Luke 22 [vv. 24ff.] according to divine Law. I respond with an obscure man, Richard Armacanus, who is supported also by the authority of Leo; let him say that I also believe the same Scripture of the Gospel and the divine Law. But the reverend Father, trusting in his intellect, denies that I follow the old interpretation. There is no doubt that Arius (who quoted 'the Father is greater than I') was a heretic and that Athanasius possessed the Scripture. Arius understood the Scripture erroneously, and Athanasius as the Holy Spirit compelled him. . . .

The reverend Father wants to hear my arguments concerning the basic issue. He reproaches me somewhat intemperately for having undertaken to show that according to divine Law the Roman Church is superior to others, and yet remaining with the statements of the Fathers and the Saints. The reverend Father does not get much out of me if he does not or cannot follow my argument or does not want to do so. For this assertion can satisfactorily be shown to be made by divine Law; after all the holy Fathers stated that it is based on divine Law. I furthermore referred to the authority of the holy Fathers. . . .

About the Greeks we have spoken already. I surmise that it must be horrible for all Christian believers that the reverend Father does not hesitate to speak against the sacred and honourable Council of Constance, gathered with the great consent of Christendom, by asserting that some of the articles of Wiclif and Huss were most Christian and evangelical (Luther protests: It is not true that I spoke against the Council of

Constance. Eck on the other hand volunteers to prove it by the written and spoken word), which the universal Church could not condemn. Indeed it sounds bad if it is asserted that Huss's article concerning the necessity to salvation, namely, that the Roman Church is superior to others, was improperly condemned. The Bohemians are therefore delighted, not wrongly. This they prayed for, much to the detriment of the Church. If (as St Augustine at another place concluded) one lie is admitted to the Sacred Scripture, the whole will become suspect. Thus the condemned Hussites, strengthened by the support of the reverend Father, will undoubtedly say (Martin Luther protests: This is a most impudent lie): 'If the council erred in these two most Christian articles, its authority will waver also in other articles.' Thus I will not waste further words in a matter which has already been condemned. . . .

6th July, 7 o'clock in the morning.

Martin Luther:

Yesterday the eminent Doctor assumed not the office of a participant, but a judge. He did so against the arrangement and will of our prince George, our patron. He declared and proclaimed many times that I was a heretic, although it was only his responsibility to deal with the matter at hand. Whether or not I am a heretic, I will leave to the judges. They should also probe whether by his statements the public agreement has not been violated. Now about our dispute, he has first of all objected that I called the pestilential errors of Huss most Christian. Concerning this I protest my innocence. He will never be able to prove this. I challenge him to speak to those articles which, though most pestilential, I have called most Christian or else he should revoke his statement. . . .

Concerning the basic issue he says that he retained the divine Law, because he followed the opinions of the Fathers regarding Matthew 16, 'Thou art Peter.' Especially Ambrose and Augustine said that Peter is the rock. He dared to add that Augustine did not revoke his statement. Consulting Augustine's book on the *Retractions* I find the contrary: he indeed revoked and said that Peter is not the rock, but testified to the rock. He says the same in the homily prayed by all priests on Peter and Paul, 'upon the rock (not "upon thee", but "upon the rock") which thou hast confessed'. The same I find also in Ambrose, though he occasionally speaks differently. . . .

Eck:

The reverend Father's claim that I have assumed the role of a judge is altogether irrelevant. I am a disputant and did not say that he was a heretic, but that his statements support and defend heretics, especially the Bohemians, most of all since he dared to make the horrible statement that several articles of John Huss, condemned by the sacred Council of Constance, were most Christian and evangelical. . . .

I said earlier that Peter was by divine Law the prince of the apostles according to Matthew 16, and cited Jerome, Bernard, Leo, and Cyprian, concerning whom he did not respond. None the less, he himself writes in his booklet that St Cyprian was of the opinion that the Church was founded upon the rock; he dared to add that St Cyprian was here in error. In his response to my comments the reverend Father attempted to refer to Augustine, since Cyprian clearly calls, in the eighth letter to Cornelius, the Roman Church the mother and root of the others. The Doctor insists that I cited a statement which was subsequently retracted by Augustine. The reverend Father will not obscure the judgment of the reader: for Augustine did not regret his earlier opinion enough not to refer as support to St Ambrose. But I mentioned in the beginning that Augustine also identified the rock with Christ. Neither of these sentences did Augustine retract, neither of the two did he prefer: he left it to the reader which of the two opinions are more likely. Augustine, at any rate, did not dare to decide. . . .

Disputatio I. Eccii et M. Lutheri Lipsiae habita, 1519. (*WA* 2, 279ff.)

▶   Luther commented, in a letter, on the debate as follows:

The very hour we arrived in Leipzig, before we had even gotten off our carriage, an order prohibiting the disputation was posted on the church doors on behalf of the Bishop of Merseburg. The new papal pronouncement[25] was referred to and reprinted. Nobody cared, however, for this prohibition and the person who had posted it without the knowledge of the city council was arrested.

When they did not accomplish anything this way, they quickly resorted to something else; they conferred separately with Carlstadt and insisted that the disputation should only take place orally and should not be transcribed by secretaries. This was the desire of Eck, who hoped that he could win with shouting and gestures—which is his customary way of gaining victory. Carlstadt replied that they already had agreed upon this and demanded that the agreement not be broken. Thus the disputation should be recorded by secretaries. In order to gain this concession he had to agree, however, that the recorded disputation should not be published prior to the comment of several judges. Then there arose a new disagreement concerning the judges to be selected.[26] They finally pressed

him into conceding that this matter would be settled after the disputation. Otherwise they would not have agreed to the disputation at
all. . . .

First Dr Eck debated with Dr Carlstadt eight days concerning free
will. Carlstadt, who had brought his books with him, presented his arguments masterly and convincingly with the help of God. When Eck's turn
came he refused to debate unless the books were left at home. But Carlstadt had only brought the books to prove that he quoted the Scriptures
and the Church Fathers correctly and did not treat them as high-handedly
as Dr Eck had done. A new tumult arose. Finally a decision was made in
favour of Eck, stating that the books should be left at home. If the disputation had truly been for the sake of truth, one would have wished that all
books should have been employed. Never did their envy and ambition
show themselves more impudently.

Finally this tricky character agreed with all of Carlstadt's assertions.
Even though he had earlier vehemently denounced them he announced
complete consensus, claiming that he had caused Carlstadt to change his
views. He repudiated Scotus and the Scotists, as well as Capreolus and
the Thomists, and stated that the other scholastic theologians had taught
as Carlstadt did. . . .

The following week Eck debated with me, first of all quite vehemently
concerning papal primacy. His entire argument consisted of the words:
'Thou art Peter' (Matt. 16.18), and 'Feed my sheep', 'Follow me', and
'Strengthen thy brethren' (John 21.17, 22; Luke 22.32). In addition, he
referred to many authoritative passages from the Fathers. . . . Then he
went to the extreme and emphasized exclusively the Council of Constance
where the articles of Huss asserting that the papacy derived from the
emperor had been condemned. There he stood quite courageously, as if
on a battlefield, and reproached me with the Bohemians and called me
publicly a heretic and a supporter of the Hussite heretics. He is an impudent and foolhardy sophist. . . .

I countered his argument with a reference to the Greeks, and their
own tradition of a thousand years, and the early Fathers who were not
under the authority of the Pope. In this I did not repudiate his pre-
eminence. Finally we debated about the authority of councils. Here I
publicly asserted that some articles were condemned at the Council of
Constance in a godless manner, since they were taught openly and clearly
by Augustine, Paul and even Christ himself. Then this serpent bloated
itself and accused me as if I had committed a crime and went to extremes
to please the people of Leipzig. Finally I proved from the words of this
Council itself that not all articles had been condemned as heretical and

erroneous. Therefore he had not achieved anything with his proofs. This is how the matter stands.

The third week we debated concerning repentance, purgatory, indulgences and about the power of a priest to absolve. He did not like to debate with Carlstadt and demanded to debate with me. Indulgence was thrown out the window and he agreed almost completely with me. Indeed, the defence of indulgence became plainly a laughing stock, while I had expected it to be the main point of the disputation. In his sermons Eck conceded all this so that even the common people observed his disregard for indulgences. He is even said to have admitted that he would have agreed with me in all points had I not debated about the authority of the Pope. He said to Carlstadt: 'If I reach the same consensus with Dr Martin Luther as I did with you, I would visit him in his inn.' This is the way he is: erratic and tricky. Although he admitted to Carlstadt that the scholastic theologians teach similarly, he rejected, against me, Gregory of Rimini, who alone of all scholastics agrees with us. For him it is no vice to affirm and to deny the same matter on different occasions. But the people of Leipzig did not even notice this, thereby betraying their stupidity. Even more shocking, however, is the fact that Eck made concessions in the disputation only to preach something different in the pulpit. When Carlstadt approached him regarding this, the impudent man answered: 'One need not tell the common people the same things one would say in a learned debate.' . . .

The people of Leipzig neither welcomed nor visited us, indeed treated us as their mortal enemies. They constantly accompanied my opponent, never left his side, dined with him, and invited him. He received a new gown from them as a gift and went horseback riding with them. In short, everything was done by them to shame us. On top of this they persuaded Caesar Pflug and the prince to give their approval.

For us they did only one thing: they honoured us, as is custom, with a gift of wine. Apparently they didn't feel right about even omitting that. Those who were benevolent to our cause visited us secretly.

20th July 1519. WA, Br. 1, 420f.

▶   Johann Eck, Luther's Catholic opponent, likewise commented in a letter to a friend on the debate.

Recently we held a disputation at Leipzig before an audience of the most learned people who had gathered there from all places. God be honoured and praised that their views have fallen into great disrepute even among the common people, while among the learned they are

virtually discounted. You should have heard the audacity of these men
who are blind and undaunted in their wickedness. Luther denies that Peter
was the prince of the apostles. He denies that ecclesiastical obedience is
derived from divine Law, but holds that it was created only by human
agreement or the concession of the Emperor. He denies that the Church
was built upon Peter, despite the words: 'Upon this rock will I build my
church.' When I quoted Augustine, Jerome, Ambrose, Gregory, Cyprian,
Chrysostom, Leo, Bernard, and even Theophylact, he repudiated them all
without a blush, declaring that he would rather stand alone against a
thousand because Christ and none other is the foundation of the Church,
for other foundation can no man lay. This I disproved with the twenty-
second chapter of Revelation concerning the twelve foundations. Thereupon he defended the schismatic Greeks, insisting that they were saved
even though they are not under obedience to the Pope.

Concerning the tenets of the Bohemians he said that some of the
teachings condemned by the Council of Constance had been most
Christian and evangelical. By such foolish error, he frightened and
alienated many who had been devoted to him.

I asked him, 'If the primacy of the Pope is derived only of human right
and of the consent of the believers, whence do you have the monastic
cloth that you wear? Whence do you have the authority to preach and to
hear the confession of your parishioners?' To this he replied that he
wished there were no mendicant orders. He made also other scandalous
and absurd statements: that a council could err because it consisted of
human beings; that one could not prove from Scripture that there is a
purgatory, etc. . . .

In many matters, however, they hit me unprepared. First of all by
bringing along many books with which they were familiar. These they
even brought to the place of the disputation, perusing them and always
reading from them, though it meant their own derision. Secondly, because they always took the transcript of the debate with them and discussed it at their lodging while I never looked at a single word until the
disputation was over. Thirdly, there were many of them: two doctors,
Lange, the vicar of the Augustinians, two licentiates of theology, a
greatly conceited grandson of Reuchlin, three doctors of law, and a
number of masters who supported them at home and in public, indeed
even during the disputation itself. I, however, stood all alone only in the
company of my good cause. I have asked your monastic brethren to copy
the proceedings of the disputation for you and to send it to you as soon
as possible. I request, for the sake of him whom I serve with all my
power, that you earnestly defend the faith for which you have already

shown concern. Not that I want you to interfere and thus cause hatred upon you and your order. I only desire that you stand by me with your counsel and your learning. The men of Wittenberg took their time with the disputation which they did not wish in the first place. At first Luther did not want to have any university in the world as judge. But the most Christian prince, Duke George of Saxony, would not permit any disputation concerning matters of faith unless competent teachers would judge. Thus Luther was forced into it, urged by his supporters. If he had not debated and agreed to have judges all would have left him. When I left the selection of universities up to him he chose Paris and Erfurt. I do not know the University of Paris, but your order has many good connections with it. I would cordially ask you, Reverend Father, for the sake of the Christian faith, to write to your friends or, if you please, to the entire university so that, upon receiving the disputation from the beloved ruler George with a request for a decision, they do not refuse it, but courageously attack the opponents. We both recognize them as judges. I hope the matter is clear enough that it does not need a long examination. May they at once give their judgment according to the ruler's request and affirm what is in accord with our faith. . . .

The men of Wittenberg left in a fury and virtually without bidding good-bye to their innkeeper. This is already my ninth day here after the debate, which lasted for three weeks. On St Peter's Day, at the place of the disputation, Luther preached, in the absence of the prince, a Hussite sermon full of error. Thereupon I preached both on the day of the Visitation of Mary and on the following day before as large a congregation as I ever have against his errors so that the people became fearful of them. Tomorrow I will do it again and then bid good-bye to Leipzig.

Luthers Sämmtliche Schriften, herausg. Walch. XV, 1451.

▶ Duke George of Saxony approached the universities of Paris and Erfurt for their opinion of the debate. Here is his letter to Paris and the evasive answer from Erfurt.[27]

Greeting. The Rector and Professors of our University of Leipzig are sending you the recent debate of Johann Eck of Ingolstadt and Martin Luther of Wittenberg, professors of theology, which was held on some matters of theology and the Bible a few days ago with our permission at the University of Leipzig, and which was taken down from the mouths of the debaters by notaries public. Both sides agreed to refer judgment to the canonists and theologians of your ancient university, excluding the

Augustinians and Dominicans, and we also desire this for the sake of the public peace and the pure doctrine.

4th October 1519. F. Gess, *Akten und Briefe*, I, 100.

We have received your letter recently sent us, concerning certain articles and points which Dr Eck, Dr Luther and Dr Carlstadt publicly debated at your University of Leipzig, and stating your desire and the said university's friendly request that we should diligently examine the said disputation and give you our opinion and judgment on the same. In this as in all other matters we desire to serve you with all our power, but, after repeated consultation, we find that in this case it is not fitting for us to decide and judge the contentions which were brought forward between the aforesaid doctors in this debate, inasmuch as the disputants did not agree to ask our opinion, either in letters or otherwise. Moreover we are credibly informed that they are not of one mind and accord on this matter. Furthermore it is not agreeable to us to exclude from the decision the learned doctors of the two orders, Dominicans and Augustinians in our university, as your Grace requests. Wherefore, we humbly pray your Grace to excuse us. . . .[28]

29th December 1519. F. Gess, *Akten und Briefe*, I, 113.

▶ By 1519, Luther's writings were printed—and read—quite widely, as is shown by the following letter of the Basel publisher Johann Fröben to Luther:

Blasius Salmonius, a printer of Leipzig, gave me some of your books, which he had bought at the last Frankfurt Fair, which, as they were approved by all the learned, I immediately reprinted. We have sent six hundred copies to France and Spain; they are sold at Paris, and are even read and approved by the doctors of the Sorbonne, as certain of our friends have assured us; for some of the most learned say that they have hitherto missed among those who treat Scripture the same freedom that you show.

Francis Calvus, also a bookseller of Pavia, a most learned man, one devoted to the Muses, has taken a good part of your books to Italy to distribute them among all the cities. Nor does he do it so much for gain as to aid piety. He has promised to send epigrams written in your honour by all the learned in Italy, so much does he like your constancy and skill. . . .

We have sold out all your books except ten copies, and never remember to have sold any more quickly.

14th February 1519. *WA, Br.* I, 332–3.

Ulrich von Hutten.
(*Woodcut by Erhard Schoen.*
Geisberg, 1297)

▶ It was to be of great importance for Luther's cause that it could be identified, at least temporarily, with the anti-Roman sentiments of the German nationalists. Of these, Ulrich von Hutten was waging a vehement battle against the Roman Church. His dialogue 'Vadiscus, or the Roman Trinity', published early in 1520, provides a good illustration.[29]

Hutten: Five books of the writings of the historian Tacitus were recently printed at Rome. When I took them to one of our publishers he declared that he dare not reprint them on account of a bull of Leo X which forbade, in the interests of the Roman printer, anyone to publish the work again within ten years.

Ernhold: Then we Germans cannot read the book for ten years? After all, works printed in Rome rarely reach Germany.

Hutten: This irritates me especially. I am increasingly vexed every day to see how our people refuse to leave their superstitions and think that such a bull should be observed which prevents us from advancing our studies and sharpening our wits. The printer said that if he did as I wished and pleased the scholars he would be immediately excommunicated. I asked him if, should the Pope forbid us Germans, under pain of his curse, to have vineyards or make money, we should drink water and throw away our gold. He replied that we should not. . . . I would have persuaded him had not a papal legate, who is here now, roused his apprehensions, telling him that it would be a terrible sin to print the book and that Leo would be very angry if he did so. I was quite furious about the outcome of the affair.

Ernhold: This I can understand; I think there are plenty of other things we must suffer: settling for archbishops' palliums, and paying annates, pensions, and six hundred other exactions. When will the Romans moderate their demands? I fear that we Germans will not stand them much longer, for things are getting worse, and there is no end to their robbery and extortions.

Hutten: As you well say, unless they are more reasonable and show some restraint in their mode of life, this nation of ours will finally have its eyes opened. It will see how miserably it has been misled and swindled. It will recognize the deceptions which have been employed to delude a free people and bring into contempt a brave and strong nation with its noble princes. I already notice that many are beginning to talk freely and act as if we were about to cast off this yoke.

Ernhold: God grant that we may soon cease to be the victims of foreigners!

Vadiscus. (Ulrich von Hutten's Schriften, IV, 153-4.)

▶   A letter of Ulrich von Hutten,[30] addressed to the Elector of Saxony in September 1520, conveys the same anti-Roman sentiment.[31]

We see that there is no gold and almost no silver in our German land. What little is left is drawn away daily by the new schemes invented by the council of the most holy members of the Roman curia. What is thus squeezed out of us is put to the most shameful uses. . . .

Leo gives some to his nephews and relatives (who are so numerous that a proverb in Rome says, 'As thick as Leo's relations'). A portion is consumed by a host of most reverend cardinals (of which the holy father created no less than thirty-one in a single day), as well as in supporting innumerable referendaries, auditors, protonotaries, abbreviators, apostolic secretaries, chamberlains, and a variety of officials forming the *élite* of the great head Church.

These in turn draw after them, at untold expense, copyists, beadles, messengers, servants, scullions, mule drivers, grooms, and an innumerable army of prostitutes and of the most degraded followers. They maintain dogs, horses, monkeys, long-tailed apes, and many more such creatures for their pleasure. They construct houses all of marble. They have precious stones, are clothed in purple and fine linen, and dine sumptuously, frivolously indulging themselves in every species of luxury. In short, a vast number of the worst of men are supported in Rome in idle indulgence by means of our money. . . .

Do you not clearly see how many bold robbers and cunning hypocrites are engaged constantly in committing the greatest crimes under the cover of the monk's cowl? How many crafty hawks feign the simplicity of doves, and how many ravening wolves simulate the innocence of lambs? And although there be a few truly pious among them, even they cling to superstition and pervert the law of life which Christ gave us.

This money, in such quantities as might be available, might be put to better uses, as, for example: to put on foot great armaments and extend the boundaries of the empire; to conquer the Turks, if this seems desirable; to enable many who, because of poverty, now steal and rob, to earn honestly their living once again; to give to those who otherwise must starve contributions to mitigate their need; to help scholars, and to advance the study of the arts and sciences and of good literature; above all, to make it possible that every virtue receive its reward, that want is relieved at home, indolence banished, and deceit killed. . . .

The Russians would also become Christians and join us—when they recently proposed to embrace Christianity, they were repelled by the papal demand for a yearly tribute of four hundred thousand ducats to be levied upon them. Even the Turks would hate us less; no heathen would have occasion to molest us as before. For until now the shameful lives of the heads of the Church have made the Christian name hateful to all strangers.

Ulrich von Hutten's Schriften, I, 393–4.

▶   As late as 1520 Luther addressed the Pope quite respectfully.

I will freely and publicly confess that I am not conscious of anything but that I, whenever I thought of your person, always said the most honourable and best of you. Had I failed to do so once I could not praise this, but would have to confirm in all recognition the judgment of my accusers. I would gladly sing a counter-song to such wickedness on my part and revoke my punishable statement. I called you a Daniel in Babylon. . . .

So I come, Holy Father Leo, and lie prostrate at your feet. I ask that you would, if possible, lend your arm to restrain those flatterers who are the enemies of peace though they talk peace. But to revoke my teaching

. . . I cannot do it. No one should anticipate it, unless he would want to force the matter into even greater confusion. I cannot suffer human rules or criteria for the understanding of the Scriptures. For the Word of God which teaches freedom shall not and may not be imprisoned. If these two are mine nothing is to be loaded upon me which I would not gladly and voluntarily accept.

Sendbrief an den Papst Leo X, 1520. (*WA* 7, 3ff.)

▶   **After much delay, the papal bull 'Exsurge Domine' was published in June 1520. It condemned some forty-one errors of Martin Luther and threatened him with excommunication if he would not recant.**

Leo, Bishop, servant of the servants of God, to eternal memory.

Arise, O Lord, and judge thy cause. Be mindful of the daily slander against thee by the foolish, incline thine ear to our supplication. Foxes have arisen which want to devastate thy vineyard, where thou hast worked the wine-press. At thy ascension into heaven thou hast commanded the care, rule and administration of this vineyard to Peter as head and to thy representatives, his successors, as the Church triumphant. A roaring sow of the woods has undertaken to destroy this vineyard, a wild beast wants to devour it.

Arise, O Peter, according to thy responsibility and care, bestowed upon thee by God. Be eagerly mindful of the cause of the holy Roman Church, mother of all churches and mistress of the faith, which thou hast sanctified according to God's commandment with thy blood and against which, as thou hast said, deceitful teachers have arisen, establishing sects and divisions. . . .

Arise, O Paul, we pray, for thou hast enlightened the Church with thy teaching and the same martyrdom. A new Porphyry has arisen who, like the one of old, attacks the holy twelve apostles, strives against the holy popes, our predecessors, and against thy teaching. He does so not with prayer, but with chiding, biting, and ravening. Since he despairs of his cause, he is not ashamed to employ abusive language as is custom of the heretics whose last help and aid is, as St Jerome observed, to pour out their vile poison with their tongue, when they see that their teaching is about to be condemned. Seeing themselves convicted, they use invectives. And even though thou hast said that heresy must be for the strengthening of Christian believers, yet it must be extinguished in the beginning through thy intercession and work lest it increase. . . .

Finally, arise and lift yourself up, thou entire communion of the saints

Luther's *Ninety-five Theses* in one of the earliest prints extant. The non-consecutive numbering of the theses is noteworthy. (*Staatsbibliothek, Berlin*)

Anti-catholic cartoon depicting five of Luther's opponents—Murner, Emser, Pope Leo X, Eck, Lemp. Each of the five is the animal suggested by a pun on the name: Murner a cat, Emster a goat, Leo a lion, Eck a pig and Lemp a dog. (*Germanischer National Museum, Nürnberg*)

and thou entire Christian Church, whose truthful interpretation of the Sacred Scriptures is perturbed, some of whom the Father of Lies has blinded the senses so that they, according to the ancient custom of heretics, in their own wisdom, force, bend, and forge the Scriptures to have a meaning different than that dictated by the Holy Spirit. Thus, as St Jerome observed, the Gospel is no longer of Christ, but of men, indeed of the devil. Arise, I say, thou entire holy Church of God, and intercede together with the blessed apostles before Almighty God that he might be pleased to bring about, after the cleansing of the errors of his sheep and after the expulsion of all heresies from the habitation of the faithful, peace and unity in his Church.

Reputable men have reported to us what we can hardly express without fearfulness and pain. We have unfortunately seen and read with our own eyes many and various errors, some of which have already been condemned by the councils and definitions of our predecessors, since they incorporate the heresies of the Greeks and the Bohemians. . . .

This we find all the more painful because our predecessors and we ourselves have always had particular fondness for the German people. . . . The German people have truly been the friends of Christian truth and always the most serious opponents of heresy. This is shown by the commendable laws of the German emperors for the freedom of the Church and their laws always to suppress heretics from German territory. If these laws were kept today we would not find ourselves in this difficult situation. This is furthermore shown by the condemned and punished faithlessness of the Hussites, of Wiclif and Jerome of Prague at the Council of Constance. This is indeed shown by the German blood shed so often against the Bohemians. This is shown by the erudite as well as truthful repudiation, rejection and condemnation of these famous errors, or at least many of them, by the universities of Cologne and Louvain. . . . Thus, prompted by the responsibility of our episcopal office, which is entrusted to us, we can no longer suffer the deadly poison of the described errors to lead to the diminishing of the Christian faith. Therefore we have enumerated some of these errors in this bull. . . .[32]

1. It is an heretical opinion, but a common one, that the sacraments of the new law give pardoning grace to those who do not set up an obstacle.

2. To deny that in a child after baptism sin remains is to treat with contempt both Paul and Christ.

3. The inflammable sources of sin, even if there be no actual sin, delays a soul departing from the body from entrance into heaven. . . .

5. That there are three parts to penance: contrition, confession, and

satisfaction, has no foundation in Sacred Scripture nor in the ancient sacred Christian doctors. . . .

13. In the sacrament of penance and the remission of guilt the Pope or the Bishop does no more than the lowest priest; indeed, where there is no priest, any Christian, even if a woman or child, may equally do as much. . . .

16. It seems to have been decided that the Church in general council established that the laity should communicate under both kinds; the Bohemians who communicate under both kinds are not heretics, but schismatics.

17. The treasures of the Church, from which the Pope grants indulgences, are not the merits of Christ and of the saints.

18. Indulgences are pious frauds of the faithful, and remissions of good works; and they are among those things which are allowed, and not those which are advantageous. . . .

20. They are led astray who believe that indulgences are salutary and useful for the fruit of the spirit.

22. For six kinds of men indulgences are neither necessary nor useful; namely, for the dead and those about to die, the infirm, those legitimately hindered, those who have not committed crimes, those who have committed crimes, but not public ones, and those who devote themselves to better things.

23. Excommunication is only an external penalty and does not deprive man of the common spiritual prayers of the Church.

24. Christians must be taught to cherish excommunications rather than to fear them.

25. The Roman Pontiff, the successor of Peter, is not the vicar of Christ over all the churches of the entire world, instituted by Christ himself in blessed Peter. . . .

27. It is certain that it is not in the power of the Church or the Pope to establish articles of faith, much less laws concerning morals or good works.

28. If the Pope with a great part of the Church thought so and so, and did not err; still it is not a sin or heresy to think the contrary, especially in a matter not necessary for salvation, until one alternative is condemned and another approved by a general council. . . .

30. Some articles of John Huss condemned in the Council of Constance are most Christian, altogether true and evangelical; these the universal Church could not condemn.

31. In every good work the righteous man sins.

32. A good work done very well is a venial sin.

33. To burn heretics is against the will of the Spirit.

34. To go to war against the Turks is to resist God, who punishes our iniquities through them.

35. No one is certain that he is not always sinning mortally; because of the truly hidden vice of pride.

36. Free will after sin is a matter of name only; and as long as one does what is in him, one sins mortally.

37. Purgatory cannot be proved from canonical Sacred Scripture. . . .

41. Ecclesiastical prelates and secular rulers would not act badly if they would destroy all of the money-bags of beggary.

Since these errors, as well as many others, are found in the writings or pamphlets of a certain Martin Luther, we condemn, reject and denounce these pamphlets and all writings and sermons of this Martin, be they in Latin or in other languages, in which one or more of these errors are found. For all times do we want them condemned, rejected and denounced. We order in the name of the holy obedience and the danger of all punishment each and every Christian believer of either sex, under no circumstances to read, speak, preach, laud, consider, publish or defend such writings, sermons, or broadsides or anything contained therein. . . .

Indeed, they are, upon learning of this bull, wherever they may be, to burn his writings, publicly and in the presence of clerics and laity in order to avoid the punishment stated above.

As regards Martin: dear God, what have we failed to do, what have we avoided, what paternal love did we not exercise, to call him back from his errors? After we had cited him in order to proceed and deal graciously with him, we summoned and admonished him variously through our legates. We reminded him through our writings that he should desist from his error or else, with safe conduct and the necessary provisions, without fear or trembling (which perfect love casts out), to come to us and talk with us, not secretly, but publicly as our Saviour and the holy Apostle Paul did. Had he done so, we believe, he would have come to himself and recognized his errors. He would not have found at the Roman curia as much error as he charges, listening unduly to the false rumours of evil men. We would have clearly instructed and taught him that the holy popes, our predecessors, whom he chides without all reason, never erred in their statutes and regulations which he boldly destroys. . . .

But he remained disobedient and disregarded our citation and invitation, indeed everything we have just mentioned. He refused to come and has remained, to this very day, disobedient and with a hardened heart for more than a year. Knowing of this citation and invitation he none the less appealed in wicked manner to a future council acting in it against the regulation of our predecessors Pius II and Julius II. . . .

We prohibit this Martin from now on and henceforth to contrive any preaching or the office of preaching. And even though the love of righteousness and virtue did not take him away from sin and the hope of forgiveness did not lead him to penance, perhaps the terror of the pain of punishment may move him. Thus we beseech and remind this Martin, his supporters and accomplices of his holy orders and the described punishment. We ask him earnestly that he and his supporters, adherents and accomplices desist within sixty days (which we wish to have divided into three times twenty days, counting from the publication of this bull at the places mentioned below) from preaching, both expounding their views and denouncing others, from publishing books and pamphlets concerning some or all of their errors. Furthermore, all writings which contain some or all of his errors are to be burned. Furthermore, this Martin is to recant perpetually such errors and views. He is to inform us of such recantation through an open document, sealed by two prelates, which we should receive within another sixty days. Or he should personally, with safe conduct, inform us of his recantation by coming to Rome. We would prefer this latter way in order that no doubt remain of his sincere obedience.

If, however, this Martin, his supporters, adherents and accomplices, much to our regret, should stubbornly not comply with the mentioned stipulations within the mentioned period, we shall, following the teaching of the holy Apostle Paul, who teaches us to avoid a heretic after having admonished him for a first and a second time, condemn this Martin, his supporters, adherents and accomplices as barren vines which are not in Christ, preaching an offensive doctrine contrary to the Christian faith and offend the divine majesty, to the damage and shame of the entire Christian Church, and diminish the keys of the Church as stubborn and public heretics. . . .

Bullarum, diplomatum et privilegiorum, V, 748–57.

▶ The sixty days granted Martin Luther to recant expired on 10th December 1520. That morning the students at the University of Wittenberg found the following note on the bulletin board.

All who adhere to evangelical truth are asked to come to the Chapel of the Holy Cross, outside the gates of the city, and meet there at nine o'clock this morning. At that time the godless papal constitutions and writings of the scholastics will be burned according to an ancient, indeed apostolic custom. This is done because the enemies of the Gospel have stated their

intention to burn Luther's pious and evangelical books. Hurry, pious
students, and witness this holy and God-pleasing spectacle! Perhaps this
is the time when the Antichrist will be revealed.

WA 7, 184.

▶   **The subsequent happenings at Wittenberg on that day are re-
    corded in a contemporary broadside.**

In the year of our Lord and Saviour 1520, on the tenth day of the Christ
month, the students at Wittenberg were informed by a notice on the
bulletin board in front of the lecture building that the anti-Christian
decretals were to be burned at nine o'clock in the morning. At that hour
a large throng of students gathered at a place outside the Elster Gate
behind the hospital. There a master made preparations for a bonfire, put
wood together and kindled it. Then Dr Martin Luther threw the anti-
Christian decretals, together with the recent bull of Leo X, into the fire.
He said: 'Because you have grieved the saints of the Lord, may eternal
fire grieve you.' Thereupon the honourable man returned to the city and
many doctors, masters, and students went with him. About one hundred
students stayed on, however, and stood around the fire. Some sang with
solemn voice *Te Deum Laudamus*, others celebrated a requiem for the
decretals. There were also other pranks which cannot be enumerated.
Then they went to dinner.

After dinner they got hold of a farmer's wagon. . . . In front sat four
students reciting Hebrew sentences. Beside them a flag bearer held a long
pole with a 'papal bull' four feet long which supposedly had been purchased in Rome for twenty ducats. It was held up high so that it floated
like a flag in the wind. There was also a trumpet player on the wagon who
made a terrible noise with his trumpet and who was in the eye of everyone.
He held the trumpet in his right hand, and in his left he grasped a sword
which had twice pierced a bull of indulgences with the seal hanging
down. . . . Also on the wagon there were twigs to kindle a fire. Neither
Dr Luther nor Melanchthon or Carlstadt was present for this afternoon
spectacle. In the backyard of the Master of Philosophy, Vach, the wagon
was further supplied and then taken to the yard of the school, where a
huge crowd had been called together by the sound of the trumpet. Books
of the papists, of Eck, and of the sophists were brought from all sides,
thrown on to the wagon and put into a large basket. Then the journey
continued. Everywhere people looked out of the windows or stood in the
doorways, amazed at the sound of the trumpet, the Hebrew chanting, and
the confusion of the great crowd. Many were delighted about this new

and unusual procession, and applauded and accompanied it to the fire. The fire of the forenoon had not yet died down, since some had stayed around, plundering nearby houses or sheds and feeding the shingles into the fire. The trumpeter gave a signal and all who had followed the procession assembled at one place. They were joined by those who had been on the wagon and everyone marched with little flags around the fire. Some sang *Te Deum Laudamus*, others, *Oh, Thou Poor Judas*, and again others, *Requiem Aeternam*, as if they were saying and singing a requiem for the decretals. Everyone sang whatever came to his mind. In the meantime, the man who had guided the wagon ascended a lectern, which had been prepared at the place, and recited the bull, together with annotations, to the laughing crowd. After the bull, he read from a book by Ochsenfurt, to the laughter of the onlookers; then from one by Eck and also others which stuck out of the basket. Finally he came down from the lectern in order to collect money for a mass for those evildoers about to be burned. At this point he threw the bulls, the books, together with the basket and the flags, into the fire. Some took sticks and pulled pages of the books out of the fire, holding them up in the air and shouting that they would send them to the Pope and the papists. Others began to sing various songs and did silly things with the ashes. Finally everyone left to go home.

The next day after his lecture on the Psalms, Dr Martin Luther admonished those present that they should beware of papal laws and statutes. It had been but a child's play to burn the decretals. It were needful indeed now to burn the Pope, that is, the Roman papacy, together with his teaching and cruelty. Furthermore, he said earnestly: Unless you contradict with your whole heart the ridiculous rule of the Pope, you shall not be saved. For the kingdom of the Pope is so contrary to the kingdom of Christ and to Christian life that it would be better and safer to live all alone in a desert than to live in the kingdom of the Antichrist.

Exustionis Antichristianorum decretalium acta. (*WA* 7, 184-6.)

▶   From Luther's own pen came the following brief report of what had taken place.

Greetings. On 10th December 1520, at nine o'clock in the morning, all the books of the Pope were burned at Wittenberg at the East Gate near the Holy Cross Chapel. The *Decretum*, the *Decretals*, the *Sextus*, the *Clementines*, the *Extravagantes*, the latest bull of Leo X, also the *Summa Angelica*, the *Chrysopassus* by Eck as well as other writings by him and Emser.[33] Other books were also thrown into the fire. Perhaps the papal incendiaries will become aware that it is no outstanding achievement to burn books which cannot be repudiated by argument.

10th December 1520. *WA, Br.* 2, 234.

▶ The most important development of the year 1521 was Luther's appearance before the Diet of the German Empire held at Worms.[34] Here Luther was given another opportunity to recant. This was in line with the Election Agreement of Charles.[34a]

We will also see to it and in no way allow that henceforth anybody, of high or low estate, elector, ruler or otherwise, is without cause and without having been heard declared an outlaw. In all such cases a regular proceeding according to the statutes of the Holy Roman Empire is to be held and administered.

Die Wahlkapitulation Karls V., pp. 30–31.

▶ Charles's election to the German imperial crown was, incidentally, due in some measure to the financial support of the banking house of the Fuggers. The following letter, written early in 1523 to Charles by Jacob Fugger,[35] illustrates this point rather vividly.

Undoubtedly your Majesty is well aware of the desire, on the part of myself and my cousins, to serve loyally the house of Austria for its wellbeing. Thus we agreed with the late Emperor Maximilian to help you to obtain the Roman crown, advising accordingly several rulers who would put their trust and faith only in me and no one else. I furthermore advanced to your proper representatives a considerable amount of money in order to further this cause. This money came not only from me and my cousins, but was obtained, with great difficulty, from other lords and friends, so that this laudable undertaking should be to the honour and welfare of your Majesty. It is known and thus need not be emphasized that your Majesty could not have obtained the Roman crown without my help. This can be supported by documents from your representatives. In all this I did not look at my own advantage. . . .

Your Majesty owed me of the amount which we agreed upon at the recent Diet held at Worms . . . at the end of August 1521, according to two contracts, 152,000 ducats, together with interest accrued since. I myself must pay interest on the money which I raised. . . .

In light of this, it is my respectful request and petition that your Majesty will be mindful of my faithful and obedient service rendered for the good and will instruct and order Lord Vargas or somebody else so that this outstanding amount together with interest will be paid back without further delay.

Max Jansen, Jakob Fugger der Reiche, III, 249f.

▶   A 'newspaper'[36] reported on Luther's appearance at Worms as follows:[37]

In the year AD 1521 on Tuesday after *Misericordia Domini*, shortly before ten in the morning, the Augustinian monk Dr Martin Luther arrived in Worms under imperial safe-conduct and stayed for eleven days, until Friday after *Jubilate* or St George. . . .

Many a pious Christian soul found comfort and admonition in Dr Martin's courageous appearance despite the fact that a mandate had been issued against him in the name of the Emperor together with the imperial safe-conduct. The enemies hoped that this mandate would keep him away, which then would have justified them to charge him with disobedience and proceed against him. But the good pater came and carried himself in a Christian manner, thereby indicating that he feared nothing on earth, but would rather give a hundred necks, bodies, and lives before revoking a single letter without being compelled by the Word of God.

On Wednesday after *Misericordia Domini*, the Emperor called Dr Martin to appear before him and the electors, rulers, and estates of the Empire. This was to be at four o'clock in the afternoon in the Bishop's palace, where the Emperor and his brother, Archduke Ferdinand, had taken residence. When Dr Martin appeared, the councillor of Trier demanded to know, on behalf of the Emperor, if Dr Martin would confess the authorship of the books which had been published under his name and whether he would revoke them. Dr Martin admitted to be the author. Regarding the second question, whether he would revoke, he asked for time to consider. Since the matter concerned the Word of God, the highest thing in heaven and on earth, he wished to be sure. . . . Thereupon the Emperor granted him time to consider the matter until Thursday at four o'clock in the afternoon.

Shortly after four o'clock Dr Martin arrived at the palace, but had to wait until past six o'clock. He delivered a Christian speech, answer and defence both in Latin and German. After he had stated causes for his writing and action he concluded that he could not see how he could revoke anything unless he were better instructed by Sacred Scripture. Even though the Emperor threatened to try him as would be proper in such cases, he would remain true to his conviction, asking, for God's sake, not to force him against his conscience and the Word of God. But where the divine Word could point to an error in his writings, he would gladly revoke and as the first one burn his writings and crush them with his feet.

Here follows the German speech of Dr Martin before the Emperor delivered on said Thursday: 'Most serene and powerful Emperor, most illustrious rulers, most gracious and gracious lords. I obediently appear at the time appointed yesterday evening. I pray, through the mercy of God, that your most serene Imperial Majesty and Lords may graciously listen to this matter of justice and truth. If, due to my lack of experience, I should fail to give anyone the titles due to him or should act with some gestures or manner against courtly etiquette I ask for gracious forgiveness. I was not educated at a noble court, but grew up in a cloister. I can say nothing for myself than that I have hitherto sought on earth through the simple-mindedness of my writings and teachings nothing but God's honour and the edification of the believers.

'Most serene Emperor, gracious electors, nobles and lords. Yesterday I was asked two questions: whether I would confess those pamphlets which were published under my name to be mine and whether I would persist in them or revoke them. To this I answered readily and clearly that I would now and for all eternity admit that these books were mine and were published under my name unless my opponents had changed them with deception or meddlesome wisdom or given false quotations. For I confess nothing but what I myself have written and certainly not the painstaking interpretations and comments of others.

'Now I am called upon to answer the second question. I humbly pray your Imperial Majesty and lords, to consider carefully that my books are not all of the same kind. There are some in which I dealt with faith and life in such an evangelical and simple manner that even my opponents must admit that they are useful, innocent and worthy to be read by Christian people. Even the bull, which is otherwise quite fierce and cruel, considers some of my books to be harmless, though it condemns them on the basis of an unnatural judgment. Would I now revoke these books I would do nothing but condemn the truth which is confessed by all, friend and foe alike. I of all men would be against a common and general confession.

'The second group of my books is written against the papacy and papal scheming and action, that is against those who through evil teaching and example have ruined Christendom laying it waste with the evils of the spirit and the soul. No one can deny or obscure this fact, since experience and complaint of all men testify that the conscience of Christian believers is sneered at, harassed and tormented by the laws of the

Pope and the doctrines of men. Likewise the goods and wealth of this most famous German nation were and are devoured through unbelievable tyranny in unreasonable manner, through decretals and laws, regulations and orders. Yet Canon Law states (Distinctions 9 and 25, Questions 1 and 2) that the law and teaching of the Pope, whenever contrary to the Gospel and the opinions of the holy Fathers, are to be considered in error and be rejected. Were I, therefore, to revoke these books I would only strengthen this tyranny and open not only windows, but also doors for such unchristian ways, which would then flourish and rage more freely than ever before. The testimony of my opposition will make the rule of their bold and ignominious malice most intolerable for the poor suffering people. . . .

'The third group of my books consists of those I have written against certain private individuals who attempted to defend such Roman tyranny and denounce my pious doctrine. I confess that I have been more bitter and vehement against them than is in keeping with my Christian estate and calling. I do not claim to be a saint, nor do I proclaim my life, but rather the doctrine of Christ. Thus I cannot revoke these books, since my revocation would mean the continuance of their tyrannical, violent and raging rule due to my compliance and hesitancy. The people of God would be treated more violently and unmercifully than ever.

'What more shall I say? Since I am a man and not God, I cannot support my pamphlets through any other means than that which the Lord Jesus employed when he was questioned before Ananias and asked concerning his teaching and smitten on his cheek by a servant. He said then: "If I have spoken evil bear witness of the evil." If the Lord, who knew that he could not err, did not refuse to hear testimony against his doctrine even from the most miserable servant, how much more should I, the scum of the earth and prone to error, hope and expect that someone should testify against my doctrine. Therefore I pray by the grace of God that your Imperial Majesty and Lordships, and everyone, high or low, should give such testimony, convict me of error and convince me with evangelical and prophetic writings. Should I thus be persuaded, I am most ready and willing to revoke all errors and be the first to throw my books into the fire.

'From this it should be evident that I have carefully considered and weighed such discord, peril, uproar and rebellion which is rampant in the world today on account of my teaching, as I was gravely and urgently made aware yesterday. It is quite revealing as far as I am concerned that the divine Word causes factions, misunderstanding, and discord to arise. Such, of course, must be the fate and the consequence of the divine

Word, even as the Lord himself said: "I am come not to send peace but a sword, to set a man against his father, etc." Therefore we must ponder how wonderful and terrible God is in his counsels, plans and intentions. Perhaps we condemn the Word of God if we do away with our factions and dissensions. It would be a deluge of inestimable evils, indeed a cause of concern lest the imperial rule of our most pious and youthful Emperor (in whom, next to God, great hope is to be placed) should have an unfortunate beginning. . . .

'Finally I commend myself to your Majesty and to your Lordships, humbly praying that you will not suffer me, against your will, to be subjected to disgrace and defamation by my enemies.'

After this statement the spokesman for the Empire claimed angrily that I [Luther] had not given a clear answer. Furthermore there was no need to discuss what has already been condemned and decided by councils. Therefore I was asked to answer in a simple and unsophisticated manner whether I would revoke. Thereupon I said: 'Since your Imperial Majesty and Lordships demand a simple answer I will do so without horns or teeth as follows: Unless I am convicted by the testimony of Scripture or by evident reason (for I trust neither in popes nor in councils alone, since it is obvious that they have often erred and contradicted themselves) I am convicted by the Scripture which I have mentioned and my conscience is captive to the Word of God. Therefore I cannot and will not recant, since it is difficult, unprofitable and dangerous indeed to do anything against one's conscience. God help me. Amen.'

Afterwards they allowed Dr Martin to stay until Wednesday after St George and dealt no further with him. In the meantime the Emperor threatened to place him and all his followers under the most severe ban. The imperial estates deliberated about this matter.

Die gantz Handlung (Deutsche Reichstagsakten II, 573–83).

▶   **Luther himself reflected, many years later, on his appearance before the Emperor.**

At first Emperor Charles asked me to appear before the Diet granting me safe-conduct and a herald, who accompanied me to Worms. When the two of us came to Weimar, where I received money for our expenses from Duke John, it was rumoured that Dr Martin and his books had already been condemned at Worms. This was actually the case. Moreover I saw imperial messengers who were to publish in all towns imperial mandates, according to which Dr Martin Luther had been condemned by the

Elector Frederick the Wise of Saxony, Luther's ruler whose concern for a just treatment of Luther enabled his appearance at Worms. (*Woodcut by Lucas Cranach the Elder. Geisberg,* 634)

Emperor. Thus the herald asked me, 'My doctor, do you want to continue?' I answered, 'Yes, even though I have been placed under the ban which has been published in all towns, I want to keep myself to the imperial safe-conduct.' This was the first plot undertaken by the Bishop of Mainz. He was of the opinion that he could thus prevent my appearance before the Diet, hoping to be able to proceed against me, since I had supposedly rejected the imperial safe-conduct and had become contumacious. Arriving at Oppenheim with only three days of safe-conduct remaining, the Bishop of Mainz was at work again. He sent Bucer to persuade me to go to Franz Sickingen at Ebernburg, for Lavius, the confessor of the Emperor, would talk with me about certain matters. But I observed that the Bishop of Mainz was not interested in this matter, but wanted me to loiter around so that my safe-conduct would have expired by the time I arrived at Worms. I said to Bucer, 'I want to be on my way. If the confessor of the Emperor has something to tell me, he can do so at Worms.'

Thus I continued on my journey. This was the second plot of the Bishop of Mainz which failed. Since then I have learned that it was he who had pursued all this.

When I was not far from Worms, Spalatin, who was there with Duke Frederick, sent a messenger to warn me privately not to go there to face such danger. But I let him know that even if there were as many devils in Worms as tiles on the roofs I would still come. For I was unperturbed and unafraid. God can make us courageous. I do not know if I would still be so courageous.

I entered Worms in an open carriage, wearing my monkish gown. All the people came out to the street, wanting to see the monk Martin Luther. Thus I proceeded to Duke Frederick's lodging. Even Duke Frederick had been somewhat frightened over my coming to Worms. . . .

The Bishop of Mainz had not expected me to come to Worms. Had I been as fearful as he, I would not have come. After several days I was ordered to appear before all the rulers in the Diet at six o'clock in the evening. There Dr Eck, the chancellor of the Bishop of Trier, spoke on behalf of the Empire and said: 'Martin, do you confess that these books are yours?' All my books lay on a bench. From where they got them I do not know. I almost said 'Yes', but Dr Hieronymus Schurff shouted loudly, 'Let the titles of the books be read!' Then they read the titles of the books. They were all mine. Then I said, 'Most gracious Emperor and gracious lords and rulers, this matter is important and significant. I cannot give, at this time, an answer concerning the books. I pray to be given time to consider it.' This was granted and the Diet adjourned. . . .

When I was asked to appear again before the Diet a great number of people was in the hall, for everyone wanted to hear my answer. High on the walls were many torches, since it was dark. I was not accustomed to such turmoil and activity. When they asked me to speak, I said, 'Most gracious Emperor, gracious electors and rulers! The books which I was recently shown are mine. Several of them are textbooks interpreting the Sacred Scriptures. I willingly confess that they are mine. There is nothing bad in them. The others are polemical writings in which I quarrelled with the Pope and my opponents. Should anything bad be in them, it could be changed. Thirdly there are books in which I deal with Christian teachings. They are only proposition for debate. I will cling to them, whatever may happen according to God's will.' After I had spoken these words I was asked to repeat them once more in Latin, but I sweated considerably and felt warm on account of this turmoil, since I stood in the midst of the rulers. Then Friedrich von Thun said to me that if I could not repeat, it would be sufficient. But I repeated all my words in Latin.

This pleased the Elector Frederick considerably. After I had spoken, I was granted leave.

WA, TR 5, No. 5342b.

▶   **The morning after Luther's second appearance Emperor Charles V[38] assembled the rulers and stated his own position.**

You know that my ancestors were the most Christian Emperors of the illustrious German nation, the Catholic kings of Spain, the archdukes of Austria, and the dukes of Burgundy, who all were, until death, faithful sons of the Roman Church. Always they defended the Catholic faith, the sacred ceremonies, decretals, ordinances and holy rites to the honour of God, the propagation of the faith and the salvation of souls. After their deaths they left, by natural law and heritage, these holy Catholic rites, for us to live and to die following their example.

I am therefore resolved to maintain everything which these my fore-bears have established to the present, especially that which my prede-cessors ordered at the Council of Constance and at other councils. It is certain that a single monk errs in his opinion which is against what all of Christendom has held for over a thousand years to the present. According to his opinion all of Christendom has always been in error. To settle this matter I am therefore determined to use all my dominions and posses-sions, my friends, my body, my blood, my life and my soul. It would be a great disgrace for you and me, the illustrious and renowned German nation, appointed by privilege and singular pre-eminence to be the defenders and protectors of the Catholic faith, as well as a perpetual dis-honour for both us and our posterity, if in our time not only heresy, but the suspicion of heresy and the degradation of the Christian religion were due to our negligence.

After the impertinent reply which Luther gave yesterday in our presence, I declare that I now regret having delayed so long the pro-ceedings against him and his false doctrines. I am resolved that I will never again hear him talk. He is to be taken back immediately according to the arrangements of the mandate with due regard for the stipulations of his safe-conduct. He is not to preach or seduce the people with his evil doctrine and is not to incite rebellion. As said above, I am resolved to act and proceed against him as against a notorious heretic, asking you to state your opinion as good Christians and to keep the vow given me.

Deutsche Reichstagsakten, II, 595–6.

▶ In May 1521, Emperor Charles V issued, in the name of the Diet, the following edict against Luther and his followers:

As it pertains to our office of Roman emperor, not only to enlarge the bounds of the Holy Roman Empire, which our fathers of the German nation founded for the defence of the Holy Roman and Catholic Church, subduing unbelievers by the sword, through the divine grace, with much shedding of blood, but also, adhering to the rule hitherto observed by the Holy Roman Church, to take care that no stain or suspicion of heresy should contaminate our holy faith within the Roman Empire, or, if heresy had already begun, to extirpate it with all necessary diligence, prudence, and discretion, as the case might demand;

Therefore we hold that if it was the duty of any of our ancestors to defend the Christian name, much greater is the obligation on us. . . .

Certain heresies have sprung up in the German nation within the last three years, which were formerly condemned by the holy councils and papal decrees, with the consent of the whole Church, and are now drawn anew from hell; should we permit them to become more deeply rooted, or, by our negligence, tolerate and bear with them, our conscience would be greatly burdened, and the future glory of our name would be covered by a dark cloud in the auspicious beginnings of our reign.

Since now without doubt it is plain to you all how far these errors and heresies depart from the Christian way, which a certain Martin Luther, of the Augustinian order, has sought violently and virulently to introduce and disseminate within the Christian religion and its established order, especially in the German nation, which is renowned as a perpetual destroyer of all unbelief and heresy; so that, unless it is speedily prevented, the whole German nation, and later all other nations, will be infected by this same disorder, and mighty dissolution and pitiable downfall of good morals, and of the peace and the Christian faith, will result. . . .

And although, after the delivery of the papal bull and final condemnation of Luther, we proclaimed the bull in many places in the German nation, as well as in our Burgundian lands, and especially its execution at Cologne, Trier, Mainz and Liège, nevertheless Martin Luther has taken no account of it, nor lessened nor revoked his errors, nor sought absolution from his Papal Holiness or grace from the holy Christian Church; but like a madman plotting the manifest destruction of the holy Church, he daily scatters abroad much worse fruit and effect of his depraved heart and mind through very numerous books. . . .

Therein he destroys, overturns and abuses the number, arrangement

Paſſional Chriſti und

Christ is given a crown of thorns . . .
(*John* 19)

Antichriſt.

The Pope claims to have received an
emperor's crown from Emperor
Constantine

Paſſional Chriſti und

Christ washes his disciples' feet . . .
(*John* 13)

Antichriſti.

The Pope demands that his feet be
kissed

Pages from the widely read

Passional Christi und

Christ drives the money-changers
out of the temple . . . (*John* 2)

Antichristi.

The Pope sells special favours

Passional Christi und

Christ ascends to heaven . . .
(*John* 12)

Antichristi.

The Pope will descend into hell

Passional of Christ and Antichrist of 1521

and use of the seven sacraments, received and held for so many centuries by the holy Church, and in astonishing ways shamefully pollutes the indissoluble bonds of holy matrimony; and says also that holy unction is a mere invention. He desires also to adapt our customs and practice in the administration of the most holy sacrament of the holy Eucharist to the habit and custom of the condemned Bohemians. And he begins to attack confession—most wholesome for the hearts that are polluted or laden with sins—declaring that no profit or consolation can be expected from it. . . .

He not only holds the priestly office and order in contempt, but also urges secular and lay persons to bathe their hands in the blood of priests; and he uses scurrilous and shameful words against the chief priest of our Christian faith, the successor of St Peter and true vicar of Christ on earth, and pursues him with manifold and unprecedented attacks and invectives. He demonstrates also from the heathen poets that there is no free will, because all things are determined by an immutable decree.

And he writes that the mass confers no benefit on him for whom it is celebrated. Moreover he overthrows the custom of fasting and prayer, established by the holy Church and hitherto maintained. Especially does he impugn the authority of the holy fathers, as they are received by the Church, and would destroy obedience and authority of every kind. Indeed, he writes nothing which does not arouse and promote sedition, discord, war, murder, robbery and arson, and tend toward the complete downfall of the Christian faith. For he teaches a loose, self-willed life, severed from all laws and wholly brutish; and he is a loose, self-willed man, who condemns and rejects all laws; for he has shown no fear or shame in burning publicly the decretals and canon law. . . .

He does not blush to speak publicly against holy councils, and to abuse and insult them at will. Especially has he everywhere bitterly attacked the Council of Constance with his foul mouth, and calls it a synagogue of Satan, to the shame and disgrace of the whole Church and of the German nation. . . . And he has fallen into such madness of spirit as to boast that if Huss were a heretic, then he is ten times a heretic.

But all the other innumerable wickednesses of Luther must, for brevity's sake, remain unreckoned. This fellow appears to be not so much a man as the wicked demon in the form of a man and under a monk's cowl. He has collected many heresies of the worst heretics, long since condemned and forgotten, together with some newly invented ones, in one stinking pool, under pretext of preaching *faith*, which he extols with so great industry in order that he may ruin the true and genuine faith. . . .

And now, particularly on account of these things, we have summoned here to Worms the electors, princes and estates of this our Holy Empire, and carefully examined the aforesaid matters with great diligence, as evident necessity demands, and with unanimous advice and consent of all, we decree what follows.

Although one so condemned and persisting in his obstinate perversity, separated from the rites of the Christian Church and a manifest heretic, is denied a hearing under all laws; nevertheless, to prevent all unprofitable dispute . . . we, through our herald, gave him a safe-conduct to come hither, in order that he might be questioned in our own presence and in that of the electors, princes, and estates of the empire; whether he had composed the books which were then laid before his eyes. . . .

And as soon as these books were enumerated, he acknowledged them as his own, and moreover declared that he would never deny them. And he also says that he has made many other books, which we have not mentioned herein because we have no knowledge of them. . . .

Accordingly, in view of all these considerations and the fact that Martin Luther still persists obstinately and perversely in maintaining his heretical opinions, and consequently all pious and God-fearing persons abominate and abhor him as one mad or possessed by a demon . . . we have declared and made known that the said Martin Luther shall hereafter be held and esteemed by each and all of us as a limb cut off from the Church of God, an obstinate schismatic and manifest heretic. . . .

We strictly order that immediately after the expiration of the appointed twenty days, terminating on the fourteenth day of May, you shall refuse to give the aforesaid Martin Luther hospitality, lodging, food, or drink; neither shall anyone, by word or deed, secretly or openly, succour or assist him by counsel or help; but in whatever place you meet him, you shall proceed against him; if you have sufficient force, you shall take him prisoner and keep him in close custody; you shall deliver him, or cause him to be delivered, to us or at least let us know where he may be captured. In the meanwhile you shall keep him closely imprisoned until you receive notice from us what further to do, according to the direction of the laws. And for such holy and pious work we will indemnify you for your trouble and expense.

In like manner you shall proceed against his friends, adherents, patrons, maintainers, abettors, sympathizers, emulators and followers. And the property of these, whether personal or real, you shall, in virtue of the sacred ordinances and of our imperial ban and over-ban, treat in this way; namely, you shall attack and overthrow its possessors and wrest their property from them and transfer it to your own custody and uses; and no one shall hinder or impede these measures, unless the owner shall abandon his unrighteous way and secure papal absolution.

Consequently we command you, each and all, under the penalties already prescribed, that henceforth no one shall dare to buy, sell, read, preserve, copy, print, or cause to be copied or printed, any books of the aforesaid Martin Luther, condemned by our holy father the Pope as aforesaid, or any other writings in German or Latin hitherto composed by him, since they are foul, harmful, suspected, and published by a notorious and stiffnecked heretic. Neither shall any dare to approve his opinions, nor to proclaim, defend, or assert them, in any other way that human ingenuity can invent, notwithstanding he may have put some good in them to deceive the simple man.

Der Römischen Kaiserlichen Maiestät Edict
(*Deutsche Reichstagsakten*, II, 643–59).

BIBLIOGRAPHY

All the standard biographies of Luther and histories of the Reformation discuss, in varying lengths, the happenings between 1517 and 1525. The reader is therefore referred to the bibliography of Chapter I. See also Paul Kalkoff, *Luther und die Entscheidungsjahre der Reformation* (München, 1917).

A collection of important sources, both about the history of indulgences in general and the controversy of 1517 in particular, is found in Walther Köhler, *Dokumente zum Ablassstreit von 1517* (Tübingen, 1934). Pertinent materials from Luther's pen are in *Luther's Works, American Edition*, vol. 31, *Career of the Reformer I*, edited by Harold J. Grimm (Philadelphia, 1957).

NOTES AND REFERENCES

1. There is an English translation of the *Instructio* which was consulted for our rendering in James H. Robinson, *Readings in European History* (Boston, 1906), II, 55–57.

2. For the details of the transaction between the papal curia and Albert see Ernst Schwiebert, *op. cit.*, pp. 306–14.

3. See also J. E. Kapp, *Schauplatz des Tetzelischen Ablass-Krams* (Erfurt, 1717), pp. 46ff. A free German translation is found in *Dr Martin Luthers Sämmtliche Schriften*, herausgeg. von Joh. Gg. Walch, vol. 15 (St Louis, 1899), pp. 340–1. An English translation of another Tetzel sermon is found in *Translations and Reprints from the Original Sources of European History* (Philadelphia, 1894ff.), vol. II, No. 6, pp. 9–10.

4. Friedrich Myconius (1490–1546), the Reformer of Thuringia, was origin-

ally a Franciscan monk, from 1524 Protestant minister at Gotha. The Latin quotation reads, translated: You are Peter, I will give you the keys; whatever you will have bound. . . .

5. A detailed study of the development leading to the posting of the Theses, together with the suggestion of 1st November 1517, as the actual date, is given by Hans Volz, *Martin Luthers Thesenanschlag und dessen Vorgeschichte* (Weimar, 1959). Most scholars have rejected the new date, while asserting at once the insignificance of the question. See Heinrich Bornkamm, 'Der 31. Oktober als Tag des Thesenanschlags', *Deutsches Pfarrerblatt* 61 (1961), 508f.

More recently Erwin Iserloh, *Luthers Thesenanschlag, Tatsache oder Legende?* (Wiesbaden, 1962), has even suggested that the Theses were never posted at all. Here, too, the scholarly reaction has been sceptical. See Kurt Aland, 'Luthers Thesenanschlag, Tatsache oder Legende?' *Deutsches Pfarrerblatt* 62 (1962), 241ff.

6. The Latin quotes the first of Luther's ninety-five theses: When our Lord and Master Christ said 'Repent' he wanted that the entire life of man be one of penitence.

7. *Wittemberger Heiligthumsbuch, illustrirt von Lucas Cranach d. Ält* (Wittemberg, 1509). The edition used is the facsimile edition of Munich 1884.

8. The term *canon* refers to ecclesiastical decrees pertaining to discipline and is distinguished from *decretum* which pertains to doctrinal matters.

9. The formal scholarly disputation which Luther's ninety-five theses were to evoke, never took place.

10. The translation used here is from Preserved Smith, *op. cit.*, pp. 65–66. E. Herrmann's *Miscellen* are in *Zeitschrift für Kirchengeschichte* 23 (1902), 266.

11. Luther's Latin Sermon on Penitence (*WA* 1, 317–24) was published in 1518. His German Sermon on Indulgence and Grace (*WA* 1, 239–46) was published in the same year.

11a. The translation used here is from *Luther's Works*, vol. 31, pp. 39f.

11b. The translation used here is from Preserved Smith, *op. cit.*, p. 105.

12. Silvester Prierias (Mazzolini) (1460–1523), Master of the Sacred Palace at Rome, was the first to attack Luther; perhaps this is attributable to his position as official censor of books at the curia.

13. Melanchthon, who stood both as person and as theologian in Luther's shadow, has not had extensive scholarly treatment. Recent biographies are by Clyde Manschreck, *Melanchthon, The Quiet Reformer* (New York, 1958), and Robert Stupperich, *Melanchthon* (Berlin, 1960). See also Franz Hildebrandt, *Melanchthon—Alien or Ally* (New York, 1946). The first biography of Melanchthon came from the pen of his close friend Joachim Camerarius, *De vita Ph. Melanchthonis narratio*, 1556, available in an edition of G.Th.Strobel (Halle, 1777).

14. Melanchthon's works are found in the *Corpus Reformatorum*, vols. 1–28 (Halle, 1834–60), and the *Supplementa Melanchthonia*, 4 vols. (Leipzig, 1910–29). More recent, and more definitive is Robert Stupperich *et al.*, ed., *Melanchthon's Werke in Auswahl* (Gütersloh, 1951). An English translation of Melanchthon's *Loci* was published by Charles Leander Hill, *The Loci Communes of Philip Melanchthon* (Boston, 1944); there is also *Melanchthon: Selected Writings*, transl. from the Latin by Charles Leander Hill, ed. by

Elmer E. Flack and Lowell Sabre (Minneapolis, 1962).

15. The translation used here is from Preserved Smith, *op. cit.*, p. 113.

16. The translation used here is from Preserved Smith, *op. cit.*, p. 113.

17. The translation used here is from Preserved Smith, *op. cit.*, pp. 102–4.

18. The translation used here is from *Luther's Works*, vol. 31, pp. 261–4.

19. Extravagants are the portions of the canon law which 'wander over' various matters not covered by the Decretals. The reference is to the *Extravagantes Decretales quae a diversis Romanis Pontificibus post sextum emanaverunt, Liber V, Titulus IX, De Poenitentiis et Remissionibus, Cap. II, Clemens VI. Archiepiscopo Tarraconensi eiusque Suffraganeis:—Corpus Iuris Canonici*, ed. Aemilius Friedberg (Leipzig, 1881), II, 1304–6.

20. Sixtus IV was one of the Renaissance popes from 1471–84.

21. Jean Gerson (1363–1429) was a leading conciliarist of the University of Paris. The University of Paris had in 1518 issued an appeal to a general council.

22. The proceeding of the Leipzig Debate is entitled *Disputatio Johannis Eccii et Martini Lutheri Lipsiae disputatis* (*WA* 2, 250ff.)

23. The translation used here is from *Luther's Works*, vol. 31, pp. 317–18.

24. Bartolomeo Platina (1421–81), humanist and author of the first history of the Roman pontiffs, *Opus de vitis ac gestis Summorum Pontiff. ad Sixtum IV* (Venice, 1479). An English translation appeared as late as 1888.

25. The 'papal pronouncement' refers to the papal definition of indulgence *Cum Postquam* of November 1518, which, upon Cardinal Cajetan's recommendation, declared the teaching opposed by Luther as correct. All conflicting teaching was prohibited at *poena excommunicationis latae sententiae*.

26. The references concerning the Pope indicate Luther's and Carlstadt's unwillingness to have the pontiff act as judge of the debate.

27. The translation used here is from Preserved Smith, *op. cit.*, p. 222.

28. The translation used here is from Preserved Smith, *op. cit.*, p. 268.

29. The translation used here is from James H. Robinson, *op. cit.*, pp. 70–71.

30. On Ulrich von Hutten see Hajo Holborn, *Ulrich von Hutten and the German Reformation* (New Haven, 1937). Hutten's writings were edited by Eduard Boecking in five volumes, 1859–61.

31. The translation used here is from James H. Robinson, *op. cit.*, pp. 72–73.

32. The English translation of Luther's forty-one errors is from Denzinger, *The Sources of Catholic Dogma*, translated by Roy J. Deferrari (St Louis, 1957), pp. 240–3.

33. Of the books mentioned in the text, the first five refer to medieval ecclesiastical law. The bull of Leo X is, of course, the *Exsurge Domine*. The *summa angelica* comes from the pen of Angelius de Clavassio (d. 1495) and deals with matters of confession. *Chrysopassus* was a work of Johann Eck dealing with predestination. Hieronymus Emser (1477–1527) was secretary of Duke George of Saxony and a bitter literary opponent of Luther.

34. The sources pertaining to the Diet of Worms, 1521, are found in *Deutsche Reichstagsakten*, Jüngere Reihe, II. Band (Gotha, 1896). The documents relating to Luther's appearance are on pp. 489–660. The sources on the deliberations with Luther after his appearance before the Diet are found in the *Reichstagsakten* 2, 559ff. and 599ff.

34a. *Kaiser, Reich und Reformation, 1517–1525* (Bern, 1952), pp. 30–31. See also *Deutsche Reichstagsakten*, Jüngere Reihe, I. Band (Gotha, 1893), pp. 865f.

35. Max Jansen, *Jakob Fugger der Reiche, Studien und Quellen* (Leipzig, 1910). See also the definitive biography by G. Frhr. von Pölnitz, *Jakob Fugger*, 2 Bde (Tübingen, 1949–51).

36. *Die gantz Handlung, so mit dem hochgelehrten Doctor Martin Luther* ... (n.p., n.d.). This friendly source incorporates Luther's address and parenthetical comment, and goes back, therefore, to another document.

37. English translations of Luther's address are found in Preserved Smith, *The Life and Letters of Martin Luther* (London, 1911), pp. 115–18, and, based on a different report (*WA* 7, 814ff.), in *Luther's Works*, vol. 32, pp. 101–32.

38. The basic work on Charles V is the two volumes by Karl Brandi, of which the first volume has been translated into English under the title *The Emperor Charles V* (London, 1949).

Zwingli and the Reformation in Zürich

ULDREICH ZWINGLI, the Swiss reformer, was born on 1st January 1484. Thus he was about Luther's age—but there, so the historian is almost prompted to observe, the similarity ends. He studied at the University of Vienna and then at Basel, where he received the Master's degree in 1506. Instead of commencing the study of theology, Zwingli chose to enter the parish ministry. Not yet twenty-three years of age, he became a priest at Glarus, where he remained for a full decade. In contrast to Luther, Zwingli had received no formal theological education. He became a self-made theologian—quite an amazing fact considering his ministerial responsibilities at Glarus. But he was too profoundly affected by the humanist quest for learning to desist from his self-educational endeavour. He bought books on mathematics, geography, philosophy, and the classical authors. Whereas Luther was absorbed by the intricate problems of late medieval theology, Zwingli had little understanding, background or interest for such studies. His first literary products were patriotic exhortations. From the beginning there was a distinct political tone in Zwingli which was for the most part lacking in Luther. Twice he accompanied Swiss soldiers to Italy as a chaplain. He vigorously opposed French domination of the Swiss confederation, a fact which subsequently was to aid his call to Zürich.

In 1516, Zwingli moved from Glarus to Einsiedeln, a pilgrimage centre. Here he had a first-hand opportunity to observe a different kind of religiosity. He witnessed the superstition and worship of relics and saints which were rampant among the common people. Zwingli soon preached vigorously against the grosser forms of abuse. But, like all medieval criticism, Zwingli's preaching was directed not against the system from which the abuses flowed, but only against the abuses themselves. Indicative of the limited scope of Zwingli's early criticisms is the fact that he himself undertook a pilgrimage in 1517, the very year in which Luther published his ninety-five theses.

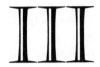

Late in 1518 he became actively interested in an appointment as people's priest in Zürich, one of the leading towns of the Swiss confederation. Zwingli wished not only for the reputation accompanying this distinguished position, but also hoped for greater opportunities to pursue his scholarly studies. His popularity as a preacher made him a likely candidate. None the less, there was considerable reluctance on the part of the election committee to appoint him on account of rumours about his personality and morals. Zwingli cleared the air with a famous letter in which he frankly confessed his previous shortcomings.

In December 1518, Zwingli was elected to the position. In January of the following year he began an ambitious programme of preaching on biblical books, starting with the Gospel according to Matthew on the assumption that a portrayal of the life of Jesus should come first. Then followed a consideration of the Book of Acts in order to depict the life of the early Church. Afterwards came several of the Pauline epistles. In six years Zwingli had covered the entire New Testament. Unfortunately, it is difficult to reconstruct the content of his proclamation. It appears that a positive delineation of the teachings of Jesus was coupled with characteristic denunciation of the 'pensioners': the wasteful and lazy, who received financial subsidies from foreign rulers and themselves oppressed the poor. The fresh and vigorous manner of Zwingli's presentation, the use of homely illustrations, his critique of the obvious ecclesiastical abuses—all this made him a widely known man.

Not long after Zwingli's coming to Zürich, Luther's name appeared for the first time in his correspondence. Soon there were many additional references to the Wittenberg professor. Eagerly Zwingli sought to learn of the developments in Germany and to obtain copies of Luther's writings. He read and propagated them and was exuberant in praise of their author. In later years, however, Zwingli denied vigorously any direct influence of the Wittenberg reformer upon him and insisted that he had preached the

Gospel before anybody in Switzerland had ever heard of Luther. Though this was a surprising statement, Zwingli in a certain sense was right. But the 'Gospel' he had preached had been that of Erasmus and not that of Paul: the proclamation of an ethic of love, a 'philosophy of Christ', a rule of life. This was indeed a deep understanding of the Gospel. None the less, it was not Luther's. For the German reformer the Gospel was God's gracious gift of redemption in Jesus Christ, and without doubt Zwingli received *this* understanding from Luther. When in 1519 he fell sick with the plague which brought him face to face with death, his theological understanding became an intensely personal one. Zwingli's autobiographical reflection on his sickness marks one of the most profound testimonies from his pen. The widespread versatility of Zwingli's early experiences makes it understandable that he could later be under the impression that no single outside influence had been decisive in his early thought and work.

The Reformation in Zürich began simply and quite undramatically. As in Martin Luther's case, Zwingli's inner conviction found, in due time, a forceful external expression. On Ash Wednesday 1522 a group of distinguished Zürich citizens met in a private house to eat two pork sausages. Zwingli, who was present, carefully avoided touching the 'forbidden fruit'. Though Froschauer, the printer, who had been the host for this occasion subsequently insisted that he had to eat meat in order to have sufficient strength to bring out the Pauline Epistles by Easter, it was obvious that at stake was the legality of ecclesiastical forms prescribed by the Church. In the ensuing controversy Zwingli actively supported those who had broken the fast and published his first reformatory treatise *Concerning Freedom and Choice of Food*, in which he discussed the problem from a scriptural point of view. Continuing restlessness and controversy in the city caused the Zürich City Council to call a theological disputation for January 1523, which was to arrive at a definite conclusion concerning the religious orientation of the city.

Though there is evidence to suggest that the disputation was rigged and its outcome clear from the very beginning—a fact quickly recognized by the proponents of the old faith—it was none the less an occasion of great significance. After all, a community went on record asserting its right to repudiate ecclesiastical authority at large and determine its faith on its own. Accordingly the Catholic bishop bluntly denied the gathering any authority in matters of faith and morals. The disputation was held on 29th January 1523. Zwingli (who had written the '67 conclusions', the programme for the occasion) sat at a table with Bibles in Latin, Greek and Hebrew before him and made an eloquent plea for the preaching of the pure Gospel. Since there was nobody present to defend the position of the Roman Church, the disputation dragged on somewhat haphazardly, until finally in the afternoon the spokesman for the City Council declared that inasmuch as no one had repudiated Zwingli, he should henceforth continue to preach the Gospel.

A second disputation was held in October of the same year and specifically addressed itself to the question of the mass and images. As a result of this October disputation, reforms were undertaken in Zürich which were, in the end, farther-reaching than those in Wittenberg. Not only were relics and images done away with in the churches, but also church organs and singing—a surprising fact in light of Zwingli's accomplished musicianship. Worship in Zürich consisted until the end of the century of a rather unexciting sequence of Scripture reading, prayer, and the sermon. Since worship was held daily and obviously exposed the congregation to greater demands than the mass, church attendance soon declined and had to be reinforced throughout the century by numerous city ordinances which made proper attendance at worship virtually a civic responsibility. On Easter 1525 the first Protestant communion service was held: Zürich was now in practice, as well as in theory, a Protestant town.

There were, however, complications. The conservative elements in Zürich were strong and exerted considerable pressure which at times endangered Zwingli's life. Radical disciples ventured to push the course of reform to consequences which Zwingli himself did not approve. But above all, the Reformation in Zürich took place within the political context of the Swiss confederation. The acceptance of new faith by Zürich went hand in hand with a quest for political pre-eminence in the Swiss confederation. Some of the other cantons in turn were unwilling to give up not only the old faith but also their traditional political leadership in the confederation. By the mid-'twenties they had already banded together in an alliance, which in 1529 was enlarged to include Austria, the traditional arch-enemy of the Swiss.

Zwingli, for whom the welfare of Switzerland under Zürich leadership was as important as the reform of the Church, sought to consolidate the political position of Zürich by an alliance. The Catholic cantons had linked themselves with Catholic Austria. Zürich consequently turned to the German Lutheran territories. Moreover, Zwingli conceived the idea of an alliance with grandiose and venturesome dimensions: including Denmark as well as Venice, Saxony as well as France, it was to be a manifestation of power, not necessarily Protestant, but certainly anti-Austrian.

Zwingli formulated such plans at a strategic time. In 1529, the situation in the German Empire had become crucial for the Protestant territories. The majority of the German states rescinded that year at the Diet of Speyer the resolution passed three years earlier which had granted temporary freedom of religion. The Emperor had just concluded peace with France and the papacy. It was possible that he might use his new strength to settle the religious question in Germany politically. It was

Landgrave Philipp of Hesse who actively pursued the plan of a Protestant alliance to provide the necessary counterbalance against Emperor Charles. Zwingli, we have seen, had similar concerns. None the less, the plan failed. For one, Luther was strongly determined to keep religion and politics separate. A Protestant political alliance was for him dangerously akin to the programme of the peasants—a mixture of religious and political considerations. Also, the very prerequisite for an alliance, a common faith, was in fact absent. For Luther, Zwingli's teaching was as bad as that of the radicals. The main point of difference—though there were others— concerned communion. Here Luther and Zwingli and their followers had been engaged since 1525 in a bitter theological controversy, centring in the question of Christ's bodily presence in the communion elements. This Luther emphatically affirmed and Zwingli emphatically denied.

The sacrament of the altar had not been a controversial point in the early years of the Reformation, but Luther's repudiation of the Catholic system of sacramentalism had made the eventual redefinition of communion a necessity. The problem had been thrown into the theological debate by a Dutch physician, Cornelis Hoen, who proposed a symbolic interpretation of the words of institution. Soon afterwards Andreas Carlstadt followed suit with almost a dozen tracts on the question, and by the mid-'twenties the controversy had involved both Zwingli and Luther.

Landgrave Philipp knew that the conciliation of theological differences between the Lutheran and the Zwinglian Reformation was the prerequisite for political agreement. He succeeded in getting the two parties together for a colloquy at Marburg in October 1529. For three days the meaning and Scriptural basis of communion were discussed, though without avail. The theological differences were simply too great. Luther's attitude made it clear from the very beginning that any 'agreement' must consist in the surrender of his opponents. So that there would be no doubt about this, he wrote squarely on the table with chalk, 'This is my body', making it evident to everyone that he was not going to change his literal interpretation of the words of institution. In the end he refused the fraternal embrace.

After the colloquy the participants signed a communiqué, which mentioned the points of agreement. The paragraph dealing with communion spoke first of the common points and only then proceeded to state that none the less an agreement concerning the mode of Christ's presence in the sacrament had not been reached.

The failure to reach theological agreement was for Zürich and Zwingli politically disastrous. When at the Diet of Augsburg the following year Zwingli ventured, like the Lutherans, to present a confession of faith, it was not accepted. The Emperor made it clear that he would not even talk with the Swiss.

This development weakened Zwingli's position in Zürich. The strict ecclesiastical supervision of private lives became repulsive to many Zürich citizens, as did the one-sided ecclesiastical orientation of foreign policy, which led to a steadily increasing deterioration of relations between the five Catholic cantons and Zürich. Zwingli, convinced that a military showdown would be the only answer, submitted his resignation, but was prevailed upon to stay.

Instead of open hostilities, an embargo of wheat, salt, iron and wine was inaugurated against the five cantons. After several months of tense uncertainty the Catholics furiously went to war against Zürich. The day was 9th October 1531. Zürich was unprepared, her soldiers had become weary of the frequent mobilizations during the past several years. Confusion and treason reigned. When battle came, near Cappel, two days later, the Zürich forces were no match for their opponents. It was a tragic day. Zürich was defeated. Zwingli, who had joined the Zürich forces in helmet and armour as a fighting soldier, lay dead on the field with a dozen other preachers, and many soldiers.

But more had died at Cappel than Zwingli and the soldiers. Militarily the battle was an insignificant affair, but politically it was of the utmost importance. For the first time the unsettled questions of religion were to be solved on the battlefield—a sad event repeated again and again during the next century. At Cappel, Protestants had been defeated at the hands of Catholics. And all of Europe had watched as spectators. When peace was concluded, the advance of the new Protestant faith in Switzerland came to a halt. Protestantism did not have to retreat, but it was kept from advancing further, and thus lost its chance of spreading the Reformation throughout the Swiss confederation. Switzerland was divided into two religious camps. This foreshadowed the future, for such a division was to be the fate of Germany, and indeed of Europe.

▶   **A chronicler describes Zwingli's youth and academic studies:**[1]

Huldreich Zwingli of Wildhaus in the county of Doggenburg, a legitimate son of Ulrich Zwingli, the warden there, of honest, pious parents, was born on the first day in January 1484. He was brought up in Wesen by his father's brother, who sent him to school at Bern. There the mendicant monks persuaded him, while he was still very young and immature, to enter the monastery *ad annum probationis*. But his cousin, Bartlime Zwingli, dean and priest at Wesen, would not let him enter the monastery, and took him out before he received orders. He sent him to Vienna, in Austria, where he was to study the liberal arts. He received, in particular, musical instruction in such instruments as the harp, the lute, violin, flute, cornet . . . and became well accomplished and a good composer.

Johann Stumpf, *Chronica vom Leben und Wirken des Ulrich Zwingli*, p. 17.

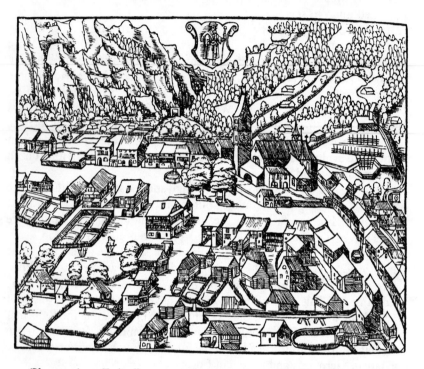

Glarus, where Zwingli spent ten important years. The illustration shows the rural character of the town. (*Woodcut in Johannes Stumpf*, Chronik der Eydgenossen)

▶ **Then came Zwingli's appointment to Glarus and his quest for further knowledge.**

At that time the people of Glarus lost their priest through death. They prevailed upon Master Ulrich Zwingli to become their priest. He responded favourably and took holy orders from the Bishop of Constance, as was customary at that time. Before he said mass, he preached his first sermon at Rapperschwyl in 1506. Afterwards he said his first mass at Wildenhaus on Michael's Day and then began to administer the parish of Glarus. Throughout his stay at Glarus, which lasted until 1516, he devoted himself eagerly to reading. He learned Valerius Maximus by heart, read many historical books, but especially the sacred Scriptures. After having attained some proficiency in Greek, he continued to study it industriously by reading Lucian and other easy Greek authors. He also praised the work of Johannis Pici Mirandulani,[2] especially his *Resolutions on the Propositions*, which Mirandulani had discussed in Rome. Several priests were vexed and began to berate him on account of this. He disregarded them, however, and continued both his reading, studying, and debating with priests, as well as his preaching. He pointed aggressively to abuses and denounced them.

Among other studies, he copied Paul's Epistles in Greek and learned them by heart. When the first *Annotations* of Erasmus of Rotterdam were published, he copied several important passages and added them to his own.[3] He also took notes from Origen, Chrysostom, Ambrose, Jérôme. . . . In sum: he became well acquainted with the sacred Scriptures, and especially the New Testament.

He greatly valued books by good authors,[4] which were in those days quite expensive, though he was not very rich. When he received a stipend from the papal legate in Switzerland, he used it to buy books. But, according to a comment he made to his brothers, he soon lost this pension or stipend and did not receive it any more.

When Zwingli was priest at Glarus several military campaigns to Milan were undertaken on account of the Popes Julius II and Leo X. Since he was a preacher and it was customary in Switzerland for priests and preachers to go along to war, Zwingli accompanied the forces of Glarus on two occasions to Milan, the first time against Novara, the second time for the battle of Marignano outside Milan. He preached frequently in the army camp; on the battlefield he was honest and courageous with counsel, word and deed.

Heinrich Bullinger, *Reformationsgeschichte* I, 7.

▶ **A letter from Zwingli's pen, written in 1513, illustrates his eagerness to pursue classical studies.**

Though I know Latin only poorly, I have now taken up Greek. Therefore give me good advice lest my toil be in vain. What should I study after Chrysoloras' *Grammar*? I have so firmly resolved to study Greek that aside from God no one indeed can divert me from it. I do not care for the fame—which to seek is not always honourable—but am concerned about the sacred writings.

23rd February 1513. *Zwinglis Sämtliche Werke* VII, 22.

▶   Zwingli's humanistic inclinations toward praise and verbosity
        are well illustrated by a letter he wrote to Erasmus in 1516.

The splendour of your learning frightens me from writing to you,
noble Erasmus, since it longs for a more mature world than is visible.
Yet I am beckoned by your most gracious friendliness which you showed
me when in the early spring I came to Basel to see you. It was an extraordinary proof of kindness that you did not despise an insignificant man,
an unknown ignoramus. Undoubtedly you did it as a favour for that
Swiss, our friend Heinrich Glarean with whom you are, as I saw, connected in intimate friendship. You may have asked yourself why I did not
remain at home, since I did not seek from you the solution of a difficult
question, as the pseudo-theologians are accustomed to doing. But when
you consider that I only sought one thing, namely to discern your intellectual prowess, you will no longer be astonished. . . .

But why do I bother your erudite ears? I am well aware that jackdaws
should eat from the ground. I want you to know that in no wise do I
regret my visit to see you. In former times Spaniards and Frenchmen came
to Rome to see Livy, as St Jerome tells us. I have attained great distinction, since I can glory in nothing less than having seen Erasmus, the man
so distinguished in letters and the secrets of the sacred Scriptures.

                            29th April 1516. *Zwinglis Sämtliche Werke* VII, 35-36.

▶   In 1516, Zwingli accepted a position at Einsiedeln, where he
        gained a reputation for his preaching.

After this time, Zwingli left his parish at Glarus to accept a pastoral
position at Einsiedeln. Two reasons prompted him to do so. For one,
many people from Germany made pilgrimages to Einsiedeln. Zwingli
hoped to be of great service through his preaching, thus bringing the
knowledge of Christ to many people. . . . The second reason bringing him
to Einsiedeln was that the Abbot of the church, Conrad of Rechperg, a
very old man, did not think much of monks and 'superstition'. He frequently expressed his sentiments in this regard. When this Abbot became
old he turned over the administration of the cloister to a member of the
convent, Diebold of Geroltzegg, who held the Word of God and erudite
people, especially Zwingli, in high esteem. Zwingli was brought to
Einsiedeln by him.

During Zwingli's preaching at Einsiedeln he requested in a friendly
and serious way of Hugen, the Bishop of Constance, to let the clear and
pure Word of God be preached freely in his diocese. He also asked him
to consider ways to help the Church so that the many abuses and super-

stitions would disappear. Such a care was, after all, the responsibility of his episcopal office. If nothing was done, there was danger that mischief would arise.

Heinrich Bullinger, *Reformationsgeschichte* I, 8–10.

▶   A letter of the papal legate Pucci, of 1518, comments on Zwingli as follows:[5]

The preacher of the town is Master Zwingli. He receives a stipend of fifty florins. I believe it is well spent. Even though he is presently living in Einsiedeln, he is still retaining the parish and is able, if need should arise, to go to Glarus and produce whatever good effects he can.

Wirz, *Quellen zur Schweizer Geschichte* XVI, 135.

▶   A vacancy at the Great Minster in Zürich in 1518 ushered in a new phase of Zwingli's life. In October of that year a friend informed Zwingli of the opening.

Recently I was asked to write you concerning the vacancy in the parish in Zürich, if I may call it such. You will, of course, decide yourself as to what to do. No doubt you are aware of the responsibilities of this position. Therefore I advise you neither for nor against it. If it should be in your interest, I would certainly be delighted to see you as preacher in Zürich. Indeed, I wish nothing more for you than that you attain a worthy place.

29th October 1518. *Zwinglis Sämtliche Werke* VII, 102.

▶   Zwingli's response made it obvious that he was interested in the position.

Next Wednesday I shall be in Zürich around noon. We can then talk about necessary matters. In the meantime inquire about the position: Does the preacher have to hear confession and visit the sick? Who are his superiors and what is his income? If you could learn these and additional details I would not make a decision in this matter without your advice.

29–30th October 1518. *Zwinglis Sämtliche Werke* VII, 103.

▶   Shortly thereafter came a second letter from Zwingli's pen.

The rumour is spreading here that Laurentius Mär, the Swabian who preached popular sermons at Chur, was chosen for the Zürich parish. Then a letter of Master Michael, the Cardinal's secretary, killed this rumour. I was indeed compelled to think that a prophet has no honour in his country if in place of a Swiss a Swabian is preferred, a man to whom I would not yield even in his native land. . . . Please represent my case! Frankly, I have come to desire this position ardently after I found out about that fellow's interest. Under other circumstances I would have accepted his appointment gracefully. Now I consider it as an insult, which is, of course, against the rule of Paul, who includes the quarrelsome among the carnal-minded. I had intended, first of all, to preach on the entire Gospel according to Matthew—something unheard-of for Germans. If they take this foreigner, they can see what he will produce from his pig-pen. Take good care of this matter, and be active in my behalf. I trust you.

2nd December 1518. *Zwinglis Sämtliche Werke* VII, 105–6.

▶   The friend's reply described the situation in Zürich, pointing out the rumour spread about Zwingli's moral character.

Your letter was welcome, particularly because it revealed you as a friend. Let me answer briefly: To my knowledge, Mär will remain rumour. My Lords found out that he is father of six children and encumbered with benefices. I for one do everything within my power to support your candidacy. I am almost a nuisance. You have friends here, but there are also some critical fault-finders. The latter are few in number, whereas the former are numerous and enthusiastic. Everyone, none the less, praises your erudition to the skies. Frankly, your musical inclinations prejudice some against you. They call you pleasure-seeking and a worldling. Others find fault with your past, since you supposedly associated yourself too intimately with easy-going characters.

I have been refuting this charge to the best of my ability. First of all, I saw to it that Mayor Röist was made aware of your learning. He likes you. Master Conrad, who as people's priest was in his days a severe and harsh preacher, as you perhaps know, inquired not about your learning— he said nothing is lacking here—but about your life. I commended you in a friendly and sincere manner and sought to interest him in you. He is a member of the committee preparing the election, which is important. . . . After I had praised the integrity, reputation, and purity of your life to Conrad, he left very gladly. Three days later he came back and said, 'The other day you commended Zwingli especially on account of the purity of his life. I was greatly pleased about this. Just now I had a visitor, however, who mentioned Zwingli's agreement with an official whose daughter he had seduced. Please tell me if this is true.' I replied that this was altogether unbelievable and novel and appeared to be a lie spread by the jealous. Thereupon he said that he hoped this were the case. But he wanted me to find out the truth. Afterwards I called on Luchsinger and let my anger have its say. I also went to see Jacob Ammann, who had visited with you the day before. Nobody knew anything about the matter. This I reported to Conrad. He was very happy and is on your side, at least I could not observe any evidence to the contrary. You know what to think of the Prior or of Utinger.

I am writing you to take heart and not get discouraged. Do you not think that the people of Zürich will praise you highly after all these fables have been refuted? I especially would request that you would please write a word concerning the 'seduced' girl. I know that the charges are not true, but I would like to refute boldly those who wish you ill.

3rd December 1518. *Zwinglis Sämtliche Werke* VII, 107ff.

▶ **Zwingli's famous response to the rumour is addressed to a member of the election committee responsible for filling the vacancy.**

A very learned and intimate friend of mine has written that according to a rumour in Zürich I seduced the daughter of an influential citizen here. Understandably enough, many of my friends are offended. I feel constrained to answer this slander, for otherwise this false rumour could cause you and others to find my character detestable. I will let my pen run its course and will talk openly and confidently with you. First of all, you must know that some three years ago I firmly resolved not to touch any woman, since Paul stated that it is not good to do so. I succeeded poorly in this, however. In Glarus I kept my resolution about six months, in Einsiedeln about a year, not longer, for no one would participate in such a resolution with me. There were many seducers. Alas, I fell and became like the dog who, according to the Apostle Peter, turned back to his own vomit. With deep shame—God knows—I empty the depth of my heart. . . .

Regarding the seduction I need not ponder long for an excuse. The girl is said to be the daughter of a powerful man. This I do not deny. For some men are powerful since they can touch even the emperor's beard without punishment: I am speaking of barbers. The girl is the daughter of a barber. Nobody denies this fact apart from the father, perhaps, who frequently accuses his wife, the daughter's mother, a faithful and modest woman, of adultery: a shameless, but false charge. About two years ago he also expelled this daughter from his home, providing her with neither food nor clothing. She is the daughter of this kind of man. She is called a virgin—which is a more serious charge, as regards me. It is easily answered none the less. I only need to state briefly my principles. I resolved not to destroy a marriage, since the blanket, as Isaiah says, is too short to cover two men. I also did not want to seduce a virgin, whom I piously shunned in light of Paul's teaching, nor did I mean to defile a nun, which would indeed be sacrilege. I call as witnesses all with whom I have lived. . . . I do not now act so abominably. Day and night I study with unceasing industriousness the Greek and Latin philosophers and theologians. Such vigorous work tames and perhaps extinguishes unchaste desires. Furthermore, modesty always constrained me in this matter, so that whenever I became guilty at Glarus, it happened secretly so that even my friends were hardly aware. . . .

That girl was a 'virgin' during the day and a 'woman' at night. She was such a 'day' virgin, however, that everyone in Einsiedeln knew exactly her role. . . . She had had affairs with many men, finally with me. Or let me say it better: She seduced me with more than flattering words. As far as I am concerned, I knew that she was not a virgin any more. . . . When I frequently came to the barber shop she flirted with me. Thus it happened that she became pregnant on my account, if she can know this definitely. This is, as I said, well known here, but no one in Einsiedeln accuses me of having deprived her of virginity. Indeed all her relatives know that she was no longer a virgin when I came to Einsiedeln. I am not at all concerned in this regard. She furthermore had relations with several clerical assistants in Einsiedeln, which is also widely known. She herself does not deny it.

Now these fine moralizers come along and restore her virginity in order to accuse me of a crime which is far from me. . . . If girls in Zürich are called virgins, though they have had affairs with men, who then is a common woman or prostitute? If this disgraced and virtually disgraceful girl is considered a virgin in Zürich, not merely by her friends, she should be grateful to have found judges who so easily forgive her faults and mistakes. At present she is in Zürich awaiting the delivery, but I do not know exactly where she may be found. This is, briefly, the situation. No virgin has ever been defiled by me. If she claims that I caused her pregnancy, I will not deny it. I have long ago confessed my guilt to my Highest God. Those who wish me evil should realize this and recall that a just man stumbles daily seven times and that Peter was asked to forgive seventy times seven. If they come and argue that I will continue in evil habits in the future, you may answer that there is no danger, even though I am not making a vow, being surrounded with weakness. . . .

Some have laid my musical inclinations against me. What shameless and foolish jackasses they are! I have played my instruments at home for my edification. Whenever they hear of an artist or musician they think at once that they must make a contribution. I play for myself and delight in the beautiful harmony of melodies and do not desire any recognition. I must close. In my chatter some things came out rather facetiously, but this is the way we human beings work. Talk with anybody with whom a conversation might be profitable.

5th December 1518. *Zwinglis Sämtliche Werke* VII, 110ff.

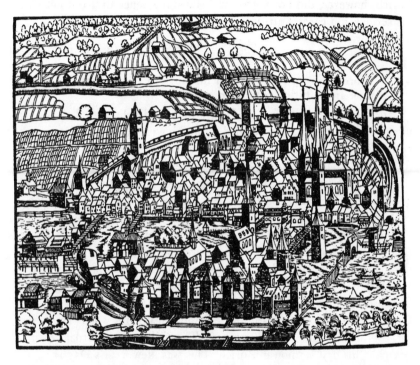

Zürich in Zwingli's time. The Great Minster is on the right, the river Limat flows through the town with its 5,000 inhabitants. (*Woodcut in Johannes Stumpf*, Chronik der Eydgenossen)

▶   **In a letter Zwingli was informed of the state of affairs.**

It seems that those who favour you for the Zürich parish outweigh the others both in influence and number. Be of good courage. The opponents are spreading rumours. They may have caused some disinclination, but have not alienated the goodwill of the well-disposed. I hope that with God's help everything will go as desired. The decision in the matter will be made on the eleventh of this month. At that time the canons will cast their ballots.

7th December 1518. *Zwinglis Sämtliche Werke* VII, 118.

▶   In his 'History of the Reformation', Bullinger reported Zwingli's
      election.

Master Ulrich Zwingli was elected people's priest on Saturday, the
eleventh of December, 1518. At once a letter of invitation was written to
him. Thus Zwingli left Einsiedeln. He came to Zürich on the day of John
the Evangelist and was honourably and well received. Many people in
Zürich, however, did not delight in his coming, since they did not share
his serious and earnest attitude.

Heinrich Bullinger, *Reformationsgeschichte* I, 11.

▶   From the very beginning of his work in Zürich, Zwingli under-
      took an ambitious programme.

After he had duly expressed his gratitude and volunteered all his services he stated that he had decided to preach with the help of God on the
entire Gospel according to Matthew, one chapter after the other, and not
follow the *Evangelia dominicalia* in piecemeal fashion. He wanted to
interpret the Scripture, and not the opinions of men, to the honour of God
and his only Son, our Lord Jesus Christ, as well as to the true salvation of
souls and the edification of pious and honourable men. Some of the
chapter were greatly pleased and delighted by this proposal. Others
thought poorly of such change and innovation. To them Zwingli said that
this had been ancient order; it was therefore no innovation to preach in
this fashion. After all, the Homilies of Chrysostom and Augustine's
Treatises on John were well known. He would strive to proceed in such a
Christian manner that no admirer of evangelical truth would have cause
for complaint. And so it happened. The following Saturday Zwingli
preached his first sermon in Zürich. This was New Year's Day 1519, the
day on which he had been born thirty-four years ago. He announced that
he would that Sunday begin to interpret the entire Gospel according to
Matthew according to divine truth and not human vanity. This he did.
Soon many people, especially from among the common folk, came to hear
Zwingli's evangelical proclamation. He praised God the Father, and
taught men to trust only in the Son of God, Jesus Christ, as saviour. He
vehemently denounced all unbelief, superstition and hypocrisy. Eagerly he
strove after repentance, improvement of life, and Christian love and faith.
He rebuked vice, such as idleness, excesses in eating, drinking and apparel, gluttony, suppression of the poor, pensions, and wars. He insisted
that the government should maintain law and justice, and protect widows
and orphans. The people should always seek to retain Swiss freedom. The
mistresses of the rulers and lords should be banned. This proclamation

soon caused a division among the people. Some in the congregation, including men of temporal and spiritual authority, were eager to hear it and praised God. Others were dissatisfied and gave bad names to Zwingli as one who would lead Zürich to great suffering.

Heinrich Bullinger, *Reformationsgeschichte* I, 12.

▶ Zwingli himself later commented, in 1522, on his work in Zürich:

I will give you an account of my Zürich preaching. . . . After the Gospel according to Matthew I continued with the Acts of the Apostles to show to the Church in Zürich how and through whom the Gospel had been planted and propagated. Then came Paul's First Letter to Timothy. It seemed especially profitable for the sheep of my flock, as it contains guiding principles for the Christian life. Since some possessed only a superficial knowledge of the faith, I omitted the Second Letter to Timothy until I had expounded the Letter to the Galatians. The men with superficial knowledge blasphemed Paul's name in godless madness by asking 'piously', 'Who is Paul anyhow? Is he not human? Admittedly he is an apostle, but not an authentic one, for he did not belong to the Twelve, did not commune with Christ, nor compose articles of faith. I believe Thomas or Scotus as much as Paul.' Accordingly I also interpreted the two letters of Peter, the Prince of the apostles, to show them that the two apostles proclaimed the same message, moved by the same Spirit. Afterwards I dealt with the Letter to the Hebrews so that the work and honour of Christ could be more clearly recognized. . . . Thus I planted. Matthew, Luke, Paul, and Peter watered, but God in a wonderful manner gave the increase.

Zwinglis Sämtliche Werke I, 285f.

▶ Contemporary observers have given us brief sketches of Zwingli's life, such as the following:

In the morning he devoted himself until ten o'clock to reading, the exposition of Scripture, studies, and correspondence, according to time and opportunity. After dinner he received reports, listened to supplicants, conversed, or walked with friends until two o'clock. Then he returned to work. After supper he took a short walk and then wrote letters, at times until midnight. . . .

He industriously read the old teachers and other books, especially commentaries on the Bible. When I briefly visited him in 1524, I saw him with a large book, in which he had industriously recorded the opinions and thoughts of the Fathers, all properly arranged. He also studied Greek, read Aristotle, Plato, Thucydides, and especially Homer. Latin authors he read no less: Horace, Sallust, and Seneca and his *Animorum Agricolam*. At that time Andreas Böschenstein, who was well versed in Hebrew, came to Zürich. He had written one of the first grammars of that language and had taught it. Zwingli took him as teacher and studied Hebrew, together with other Zürich citizens, especially Felix Mantz. Soon thereafter Zwingli's competence increased to the point where he could read the Bible in Hebrew. This aided his acquaintance with the Old Testament.

Ulrich Zwingli, p. 7
Heinrich Bullinger, *Reformationsgeschichte* I, 30.

▶   The year 1519 brought for Zürich—and Zwingli—the plague. Thus Bullinger reports:

In the year 1519 death reigned in the Swiss confederation. The plague caused the death of many people both in towns and in the country. In Zürich it began in August, around St Laurentius, increased in vehemence around 12th September, and continued after Christmas until Candlemas. In the three parishes of Zürich more than 1,500 people died. Andreas Zwingli, a young man of great promise, died also, to the great sorrow of Master Ulrich Zwingli. In August, Zwingli himself fell sick with the plague.

Heinrich Bullinger, *Reformationsgeschichte* I, 28.

▶   The statutes of the Great Minster, where Zwingli was serving, included a provision for such times of catastrophe:

In case of widespread death or the plague the people's priest is not to leave his colleagues, his congregation, or the city of Zürich.

Zwinglis Sämtliche Werke VII, 200.

▶   Andreas Zwingli, who was soon to die of the plague, wrote a letter to his brother in Zürich:

I am eager to learn how you are doing. Since you have not written, we do not know how it is going with you. When I departed you said that the Abbot would soon receive a letter from you, but I see this has not been the case. I do not know the reason. The Abbot seems to be disappointed that you do not favour him more frequently with letters. The plague is rampant here among us. Seven or eight persons have already died. I am still well, according to God's will. A servant of our brother Klaus has died, though not in his house. The Abbot and our brothers greet you heartily. The Abbot wants you to write him as soon as your work allows it. Please love me always.

13th October 1519. *Zwinglis Sämtliche Werke* VII, 211.

▶ Zwingli, who had been seriously sick, could write in November to his friend Myconius:

I am doing fine. Yesterday I finally removed the last patch from my pestilential boil.

Zwinglis Sämtliche Werke VII, 372.

▶ From Zwingli's sickness came a moving testimony—the Song of Pestilence.

I. *At the Beginning of the Illness*

Help, Lord God, help
In this trouble!
I think Death is at the door.
Stand before me, Christ;
For thou hast overcome him!
To thee I cry:
Is it thy will,
Take out the dart,
Which wounds me!
Let me not have an hour's
Rest or repose!
Yet should thou will
That Death take me
In the midst of my days.
So let it be!
Do what thou wilt;
I am completely thine
Thy vessel am I;
Make whole or break,
For, if thou takest away
My spirit
From this earth,
Thou doest it,
That it may not grow worse,
Nor spot
The pious lives and ways of others.

II. *In the Midst of the Illness*

Console, Lord God, console!
The illness grows.
Pain and fear seize
My soul and body.
Come to me then!
My tongue is dumb;
It cannot speak a word.
My senses are all blighted.
Thus is it time
That thou shouldst carry
My fight hereafter
With thy grace, my only consolation!
Which surely saves
Everyone, who sets
His heart's desire
And hope on thee,
And who besides
Despises all gain and loss.
Now all is over,
Since I am not so strong
That I could bravely
Resist
The temptations of the Devil and his treacherous hand.
Yet my spirit will
Constantly abide by thee, however much he rages.

III. *During Convalescence*

Recovered, Lord God, recovered!
I think, I am
Already being restored.
Yes, if it be thy will
That no spark of sin
Should rule me still,
Then my lips must bespeak
Thy praise and teaching
More than ever before—
However it may go—
In simplicity and without danger,
Although I must endure

> The punishment of death
> Sometime,
> Perhaps with greater anguish
> Than would have been the case,
> Lord, at this time
> Since now I came so near.
> Yet I will still
> Bear joyfully the spite and boasting
> Of this world
> For the sake of a reward
> By thy help,
> Without which nothing can be perfect.
>
> Heinrich Bullinger, *Reformationsgeschichte* I, 29.

▶ **Late in 1518 Zwingli had heard first about Luther. He was eager
to obtain detailed information about the Wittenberg professor,
then expressed enthusiastic approval—only to deny later on that
he had ever been directly influenced by Luther. Here Zwingli's
humanist friend, Beatus Rhenanus, wrote:**

The day before yesterday a bookseller arrived here from Bern, who
bought many books by Luther and took them back with him. I rejoice
greatly, dear Zwingli, whenever I see that the world becomes wise,
repudiating the fantasies of thoughtless blabbermouths and following
genuine teaching. My countrymen have already shown interest. I am all
the more surprised over the negligence of the people of Zürich, who
despite your admonishing words fail to do what others do of their own
accord. But this is how human beings are. What is commanded or admonished, we do slowly. What is done by our own impulse, we do
speedily. At any rate, I cannot believe that you have not admonished the
people of Zürich.

Zwinglis Sämtliche Werke VII, 123.

▶ **A reply from the pen of Zwingli, written in February 1519, suggests his enthusiasm for Luther:**

Thank you for writing so conscientiously about Martin Luther. Recently the Abbot of St John showed me most opportunely a letter from a
teacher in Wittenberg, in which he is congratulated for reading Luther's
tracts, since he is a man who truly reflects the image of Christ. He adds
that Luther returned straight to Wittenberg after he had left Cardinal

Cajetan in Augsburg. Highly admired by all, he now firmly proclaims Christ and is willing even to be crucified for him.

22nd February 1519. *Zwinglis Sämtliche Werke* VII, 138.

▶   Another letter from Rhenanus shows that Zwingli was kept informed about developments in Germany:

You will soon receive Martin Luther's Theses which he is to defend at Leipzig against new and old errors, together with a letter in which he portrays Eck better than any artist ever could.

7th May 1519. *Zwinglis Sämtliche Werke* VII, 167.

▶   Hardly two weeks later another letter from Rhenanus provides further information:

The printer Adam Petri, whom I think you know, is about to print several new tracts of Luther in German: a beautiful commentary on the *Lord's Prayer*, which is characteristic of Luther; also a *German Theology*,[6] which will make that clever theology of Scotus appear awkward and dull; and other similar books. If you commend these writings from the pulpit to the people, that is, give the advice to buy them, your own work will succeed according to your desires. . . . I send you as a gift Luther's theses against Eck and the German commentary on the *Lord's Prayer*. . . . You should admonish the other preachers that they promptly recommend these works by Luther to the people.

24th May 1519. *Zwinglis Sämtliche Werke* VII, 175.

▶   In June, Zwingli expressed further interest in a letter:

I do not think that Luther's commentary on the *Lord's Prayer* or his *German Theology* will disappoint me. I take it from your letter that the latter will be completed and published any day. We will buy immediately a great number of copies, especially if Luther should deal, in the *Lord's Prayer*, to some extent with the adoration of saints. I have forbidden such adoration. Since I have not been here very long the people would be more thoroughly persuaded if someone else should say the same thing. I still allow the imploring of the saints, for I did not want to destroy it root and branch.

7th June 1519. *Zwinglis Sämtliche Werke* VII, 181.

▶   In July, Zwingli received this letter from Beatus Rhenanus:

If you feel that Lucius, who brings this letter, has discretion and integrity, I should like him to sell Luther's writings, especially the commentary on the *Lord's Prayer*, for the laity. He would go from town to town, and village to village, indeed from house to house. This will greatly profit our plans and help him at the same time. Surely he will be grateful to you that he has been changed, with your help, from a tramp to a book-agent. Think of this! Since he is so widely known, he will easily find buyers. Who will hesitate to give him a silver coin for an excellent book after having given him a few pennies for his begging? He should not offer any other books for sale, especially not at the present time. For he will sell more of Luther's tracts if he has no others to offer. This will virtually force people to buy them, which would not be the case if there were a wide selection. If you do not consider him sufficiently qualified for this responsibility, look for somebody else and recommend him, by letter, to your friends.

2nd July 1519. *Zwinglis Sämtliche Werke* VII, 193.

▶   **In 1523, Zwingli was far more restrained in his enthusiasm for Martin Luther than he had been three or four years earlier.**

The high and mighty of this world have begun to persecute and hate Christ's teaching under the presence of the name of Luther. They call all of Christ's teaching 'Lutheran', no matter who on earth proclaims it. Even if one never read about Luther and is faithful solely to the Word of God, he would yet be scolded to be a 'Lutheran'. This is now my fate. I began to preach the Gospel of Christ in 1516, long before anyone in our region had ever heard of Luther. I never went into the pulpit without taking the words read the same morning in the mass as the Gospel and interpreting them according to biblical Scripture. . . . When I began to preach in Zürich in 1519 I announced that, God willing, I would proclaim the Gospel according to Matthew, without human speculation. From this I would neither move nor change. Early that year no one here among us knew anything about Luther, except that he had published something concerning indulgence. This taught me little, since I knew all along that indulgences were a deception and farce. . . . Therefore Luther's writings helped me little at that time in my preaching on Matthew. Those who were eager for the Word of God flocked together so unceasingly that I was amazed. I ask the enemies of Christ's teachings, 'Who called me then a Lutheran?' When Luther's booklet on the *Lord's Prayer* was published, after I had already interpreted it in my exposition of Matthew, I knew well that many pious people would suspect that I had written the booklet and published it in Luther's name. Who could accuse me of being a Lutheran? Why did not the Roman cardinals and delegates living in Zürich at that time, who hated me and tried to bribe me with money, call me a Lutheran until they had declared Luther to be a heretic? This is my testimony and all here can testify to it. . . .

Who called me to proclaim the Gospel and to interpret an entire Gospel? Was it Luther? Why, I began to preach in this fashion long before I ever heard of Luther. For this reason I began some ten years ago to study Greek in order to learn Christ's teaching in the original language. I leave it to others to judge how well I comprehended it. At any rate, Luther did not teach me anything. Two years after I concerned myself solely with biblical writings, his name was still unknown to me. The papists none the less burden me and others maliciously with such names and say, 'You must be a Lutheran, for you preach the way Luther writes.' I answer them, 'I preach the way Paul writes. Why do you not also call me a follower of Paul? Indeed, I proclaim the word of Christ. Why do you not call me a Christian?' They are full of malice. Luther is, as I gather, an admirable warrior for God, who earnestly searches the Scriptures, as has not been the case on earth for a thousand years. (I do not mind if the papists consider me a heretic with him.) Not since the papacy has been in existence has his manly, courageous mind, with which he attacked the Roman Pope, had an equal. Who did such deed? God or Luther? Ask Luther himself. I know that he will say, God. Why then do you ascribe the teachings of other men to Luther when he himself ascribes everything to God? . . .

I do not wish to bear Luther's name, for I have read little of his teaching and have often purposely desisted from reading his books in order to conciliate the papists. What I have read of his writings (concerning the doctrines, teachings, views, and meaning of the Scripture—his later writings I have not read) is altogether so well discussed and based on the Word of God that nobody can repudiate it. I also know that in some respects he yields to the weak, but would on principle act differently. Here I do not agree with him. Not that he says too much; rather he does not say enough. . . .

Therefore, let us not change the honourable name of Christ into the name of Luther. For Luther did not die for us, but teaches us to recognize him from whom alone we have all salvation. . . . Yet, I will bear no name than that of my Captain Christ. I am his soldier. He will give me titles and reward according to his good pleasure. I hope that everyone understands why I do not want to be called Lutheran even though I esteem Luther as much as any other living person. I testify before God and all men that I never wrote a single letter to him nor he to me. . . . I did not refrain from this because I was fearful, but because I wanted to show how uniform is the Spirit of God. Though far distant from each other, we still unanimously proclaim the teaching of Christ without any explicit agreement.

Auslegen und Gründe der Schlussreden, 1523:
Zwinglis Sämtliche Werke II, 144–8.

▶ **The actual Reformation in Zürich began in the spring of 1522, when several citizens broke the fast on Ash Wednesday. Bullinger reported on the happening as follows:[7]**

In the Roman Church it was forbidden, at certain times and days, to eat a number of foods, though the Pope made exceptions for money. . . . Yet the Word of God allows clearly the eating of all food at all times and calls it a teaching of Satan to prohibit food which was created by God and is to be used with gratitude. Master Zwingli taught this in Zürich from the pulpit. Because of this Christian teaching, several citizens began, during Lent and on Fridays, to eat meat and other foods prohibited by the Pope. When the City Council learned of this, it punished several with the tower and with other fines. Zwingli thereupon began to preach vehemently concerning this matter and also wrote a booklet *Concerning Freedom and Choice of Food* which he published in April. It was his first book.

Heinrich Bullinger, *Reformationsgeschichte* I, 69.

▶ **In the official investigation of the incident, the following statements were made:**

Inquiry as to who had been eating meat and eggs in Lent.

Elsi Flammer, maid of the printer in the Niederdorf, said she had by her master's orders cooked some sausages on Ash Wednesday, and that the people's priest [Leo Jud] of Einsiedeln, Bartholime Pur, and Michael Hirt, had eaten them. Afterwards several vine-dressers of her master's had eaten of this meat.

Hans Berker saw how eggs and sausage were prepared at the printer's house.

Bartholime Pur, the baker, said: On Ash Wednesday he and Master Huldreich Zwingli, people's priest at the Great Minster, Master Leo Jud, people's priest at Einsiedeln, Master Lorenze Keller, parson of Egg, Heini Aberli, Michael Hirt the baker, Conrad Luchsinger, and Conrad Escher, were in the kitchen of the printer Froschauer's house: and the printer produced two fried sausages. They cut them up and each had a little bit. All ate of them, except Master Huldreich Zwingli, people's priest at the Great Minster. . . .

Emil Egli, *Aktensammlung*, No. 233.

▶   The most prominent person involved in the breaking of the fast
    was the printer, Christoph Froschauer.[8] In justification of his
    participation he wrote a lengthy letter to the Zürich City Council.

It has been reported to you that I have eaten meat in my house. This
I admit and give the following reasons: I am greatly loaded with responsibilities which demand much of my strength, property, and work.
I have to work day and night, weekdays and holidays, in order to complete
the work by the time of the Frankfurt Fair. I am referring to the Letters
of St Paul. My workers and I can hardly sustain ourselves simply with
cereal and I am not able to buy fish all the time.

Furthermore, upon some reflection, I became convinced that the
almighty and gracious God has visited and enlightened us with the light
of truth, the Word of God. This we must truly believe if we want to be
saved. God has left us nothing on earth in which to trust, except the holy
Gospel, his divine Word, which we must believe and accept and keep.
Indeed, unless we direct our lives and deeds by the rule of the Gospel, we
are not Christians. I also became convinced that God has provided the
city of Zürich with a preacher who is without equal in all of Germany,
and who brings honour and praise to our city and is the object of the conversation of fair-minded and learned people everywhere. There are also
in Zürich many educated young people from whom one may expect much
good. My gracious Lords, I do not want to blame or accuse anyone in this
matter. Whatever I did was neither to please nor to hurt. Indeed, I did
not want to do any wrong. Therefore, I am ready to give an account,
since I do not desire to be against the law or the sacred Scriptures. For I
believe the sacred scriptures which assert that a Christian life does not
consist in eating or drinking, indeed not in external works, but solely in
true faith, trust and love. We are called to live one with another in true,
just, friendly and simple manner. I believe the Scriptures and no one
can take them away from me. I would follow them as God gives me grace
and help.

                                Emil Egli, *Aktensammlung*, No. 234.

▶   Zwingli had carefully abstained from breaking the fast in Fro-
    schauer's house. But in a sermon 'Concerning Freedom and
    Choice of Food' preached less than three weeks later he made it
    obvious that he concurred with those who had actually broken
    the prescribed fast.[9]

Dearly Beloved in God, after you have heard so eagerly the Gospel and
the teachings of the holy Apostles now for the fourth year, teachings
which Almighty God has been merciful enough to publish to you through

my weak efforts, the majority of you, thank God, have been greatly fired with the love of God and of your neighbour. You have also begun faithfully to embrace and to take unto yourselves the teachings of the Gospel and the liberty which they give, so that after you have tried and tasted the sweetness of the heavenly bread by which man lives, no other food has since been able to please you. And, as when the children of Israel were led out of Egypt, at first impatient and unaccustomed to the hard journey, they sometimes in vexation wished themselves back in Egypt, with the food left there, such as garlic, onions, leeks and flesh-pots, they still entirely forgot such complaints when they had come into the promised land and had tasted its luscious fruits: thus also some among us leapt and jumped unseemly at the first spurring—as still some do now, who like a horse neither are able nor ought to rid themselves of the spur of the Gospel; still, in time they have become so tractable and so accustomed to the salt and good fruit of the Gospel, which they find abundantly in it, that they not only avoid the former darkness, labour, food and yoke of Egypt, but also are vexed with all brothers, that is, Christians, wherever they do not venture to make free use of Christian liberty. And in order to show this, some have issued German poems, some have entered into friendly talks and discussions in public rooms and at gatherings; some now at last during this fast—and it was their opinion that no one else could be offended by it—at home, and when they were together, have eaten meat, eggs, cheese, and other food hitherto unused in fasts. But this opinion of theirs was wrong; for some were offended, and that, too, from simple good intentions; and others, not from love of God or of his commands (as far as I can judge), but that they might reject that which teaches and warns common men, and they that might not agree with their opinions, acted as though they were injured and offended, in order that they might increase the discord. A third kind of false hypocrite did the same, and secretly excited the civil authorities, saying that such things neither should nor would be allowed, that it would destroy the fasts, just as though they never could fast, if the poor labourer, at this time of spring, having to bear most heavily the burden and heat of the day, ate such food for the support of his body and on account of his work. Indeed, all these have so troubled the matter and made it worse, that the Council of our city was obliged to attend to the matter. . . . What should I do, as one to whom the care of souls and the Gospel have been entrusted, except search the Scriptures again, and bring them as a light into this darkness of error, so that no one, from ignorance or lack of recognition, injuring or attacking another come into great regret, especially since those who eat are not triflers or clowns, but honest folk and of good conscience? Wherefore, it would stand very evil with me, that I, as a careless shepherd and one only for the sake of selfish gain, should treat the sheep entrusted to my care, so that I did not strengthen the weak and protect the strong. I have therefore written a sermon about the choice or difference of food, in which nothing but the Gospels and the teachings of the Apostles have been used, which greatly delighted the majority and emancipated them. But those, whose mind and conscience are defiled, as Paul says [Titus 1.15], it only made mad. . . .

Whether Anyone Has Power to Forbid Foods

I. The general gathering of Christians may accept for themselves fasts and abstinence from foods, but not set these up as a common and everlasting law. . . .

III. If one could not and should not add to the Old Testament, then much less to the New.

IV. For the Old Testament has passed away and was not otherwise given except that it should pass away in its time; but the New is everlasting, and can never be done away with. . . .

VII. How dare a man add to the testament, to the covenant of God, as though he would better it?

VIII. Gal. 1.9, Paul curses what is preached otherwise concerning the Gospel thus: 'If any other gospel is preached to you than ye have heard, let him that preached it be accursed.' . . .

X. Again, Gal. 5.1: 'Stand fast therefore in the freedom wherewith Christ has made us free, and be not entangled again with the yoke of bondage.'

XI. If he is to be cursed who preaches beyond what Paul preached, and if Paul nowhere preached the choice of food, then he who dares command this must be worthy of a curse.

XII. If we are not bound by any law but the law of love, and if freedom as to food insures not the love of one's neighbour, in case this freedom is rightly taught and understood, then we are not subject to this commandment or law.

XIII. If Paul commands us to remain in the liberty of Christ, why do you command me to depart from it? Indeed, you would force me from it.

XIV. When Christ said to his disciples, 'I have yet much to say to you', he did not say, 'I have much yet to teach you how ye shall lay commands on men', but he spake of things which he held up before them and which they, however, scarcely understood. But when the Spirit of Truth shall come, it will teach you all the truth, that they will understand all things according to the light of the Holy Ghost—that is, providing they do not at that time understand, either from ignorance or trouble and fear.

XV. For if such commands are to be understood in this matter, then the disciples have sinned, in not having forbidden labour and the eating of meat, running to the saints, putting on cowls. . . . These points have forced me to think that the church officers have not only no power to command such things, but if they command them, they sin greatly; for whoever is in office and does more than he is commanded is liable to punishment. How much more then when they transgress that which is forbidden them; and Christ forbade the bishops to beat their fellow servants. Is it not beating, when a command is placed upon a whole people, to which command the general assembly has not consented? Therefore, in these articles I leave to each free judgment, and still hope I have to those thirsting for Christian freedom made this clear, in spite of the enmity to me that will grow out of it. It is those who fear the spit [on which their meat roasts] will burn off. God be with us all! Amen. I have written all this hastily; therefore may each understand it as best he can.

Zwinglis Sämtliche Werke I, 88–92, 133–6.

▶   In April 1522 the Zürich City Council issued a mandate which upheld the position of the Church, but demanded that reform be undertaken:

Inasmuch as some persons at the beginning of Lent have unnecessarily eaten meat, thereby causing much contention, restlessness and strife, our Lord Mayor, Councillors and Great Council of the city of Zürich proclaim and admonish everybody in town and country that they should not eat meat during Lent without good reason and permission until further instruction is given following a consultation with our Lord of Constance. It is also the will and opinion of our Lords that no one should become involved in quarrel and strife or employ offensive and inept words against one another concerning the eating of meat, preaching or similar matters. Everyone is to be peaceful and calm.

Emil Egli, *Aktensammlung*, No. 237.

▶   A religious disputation called for January 1523 was to settle the controversy. Here is the invitation to the disputation issued by the City Council:

We, the Mayor, Council and the Great Council, called the Two Hundred of the city of Zürich, send to every people's priest, preacher, minister, and clergyman living in our town and country, our greetings, favourable and affectionate disposition, and would have you know that for some time much dissension and disagreement have existed among those who preach the Gospel to the common people. Some believe that they have truly and completely proclaimed the Gospel, while others reprove them for not having done it skilfully and properly. Consequently the latter call the former errorists, traitors, and even heretics, who, none the less, want to do whatever they can for the honour of God, for peace and Christian unity, and are willing to give an account and proof of their doctrines out of Holy Scriptures. Therefore, we order, wish and desire: Priests, curates, preachers, collectively and individually, or any priest with benefices in the city or territory of Zürich, wishing to speak about this matter in order to reprove or instruct the other side, should appear before us on the day after the Emperor Charles's Day, January 29th, at early Council time, at the town hall here in Zürich. The participants should use the divine Word and the German tongue. With the help of several scholars, if it seems good to us, we will give our careful attention, and will dismiss the meeting with appropriate instructions as to further preaching in light of what shall prove itself as consonant with the Holy Scriptures and truth; thereupon no one may preach from the pulpit what seemed good to him without foundation in the Holy Scriptures. We will also inform our gracious Lord of Constance of our intention, so that he or his representative, if he so desire, may also be present. If anyone disregards óur regulation and does not cite the Holy Scriptures we will proceed against him according to our knowledge, in a way from which we would gladly be relieved.

3rd January 1523. *Zwinglis Sämtliche Werke* I, 466f.

▶   As topics for the disputation, Zwingli drew up '67 Conclusions' which, in a nutshell, summarized the nature and character of his work:[10]

The articles and opinions below, I, Huldreich Zwingli, confess to have preached in the city of Zürich as based upon the Scriptures, which are called inspired by God. I offer to defend and discuss these. Where I have not now correctly understood the Scriptures I shall allow myself to be taught better, but only from the Scriptures.

I. All who say that the Gospel is invald without the confirmation of the Church err and slander God.

II. The sum and substance of the Gospel is that our Lord Jesus Christ, the true Son of God, has made known to us the will of his heavenly Father, and has with his innocence released us from death and reconciled God.

III. Hence Christ is the only way to salvation for all who ever were, are and shall be.

IV. Who seeks or points out another door errs; yes, he is a murderer of souls and a thief.

V. Hence all who consider other teachings equal to or higher than the Gospel err, and do not know what the Gospel is.

VI. For Jesus Christ is the guide and leader, promised by God to all human beings, which promise was fulfilled. . . .

X. Even as a man is mad whose limbs do something without his head, such as tearing, wounding, injuring himself, so likewise the members of Christ who undertake something without their head, Christ, are mad and injure and burden themselves with unwise ordinance.

XI. Hence we see in the so-called clerical ordinances and their splendour, riches, classes, titles, laws, a cause of foolishness, for they do not also agree with the head. . . .

XIV. Therefore all Christian people shall use their best diligence that the Gospel of Christ be preached alike everywhere.

XV. For in faith rests our salvation, and in unbelief our damnation; for all truth is clear in him.

XVI. In the Gospel one learns that human doctrines and decrees do not aid in salvation.

XVII. Christ is the only eternal high priest. Therefore those who have called themselves high priests have opposed the honour and power of Christ, yea, cast it out.

XVIII. Christ, having sacrificed himself once, is to eternity a certain and valid sacrifice for the sins of all faithful. Therefore the mass is not a sacrifice, but is a remembrance of the sacrifice and assurance of the salvation which Christ has given us.

XIX. Christ is the only mediator between God and man. . . .

XXI. When we pray for each other on earth we do so believing that all things are given to us through Christ alone.

XXII. Christ is our righteousness. Therefore our works in so far as they are good are of Christ, but in so far as they are ours, are neither right nor good.

XXIII. Christ scorns the property and pomp of this world. Therefore those who attract wealth to themselves in his name slander him terribly when they make him a pretext for their avarice and ambition.

XXIV. No Christian is bound to do those things which God has not decreed. Therefore one may eat at all times all food, wherefrom one learns that the decree about cheese and butter is deception. . . .

Zwinglis Sämtliche Werke I, 458–61.

▶   **Shortly thereafter, still before the disputation, Zwingli received
the following letter from Pope Adrian VI:**

We are sending the Venerable Brother Ennius, Bishop of Veroli, our
domestic prelate and apostolic nuncio, a man distinguished in prudence
and faith, to that invincible nation so closely linked unto us and the Holy
See in order to discuss important matters concerning the Holy See and all
Christendom. Although we asked him to conduct such deliberations
publicly and in consultation with everyone, we are informed of your
distinguished activities and esteem and prize your loyalty to us, which
prompts us to place our special trust in you. Therefore we have commissioned said Bishop, our nuncio, to transmit a special letter to you and
to assure you of our good will. We exhort you to receive him faithfully
and to continue on the way of the Apostolic See. This will earn no small
thanks from us. Your honour and welfare are concerns of our heart.

Zwinglis Sämtliche Werke VIII, 13f.

▶   **Bullinger commented on the disputation as follows:**

On the day appointed for the disputation a great crowd of some 600
learned and noble persons appeared in the Zürich town hall. . . . There
were also present, in order to listen to this disputation, all the preachers,
ministers and clergy of town and territory of Zürich, as well as other
temporal and ecclesiastical lords from other places, likewise doctors,
masters and learned men from several universities and distant places.
Many people were wondering about the outcome of the matter. No one
was present from the towns of the Swiss confederation, since attendance
had been prohibited by the respective authorities.

Heinrich Bullinger, *Reformationsgeschichte* I, 97.

▶   **Here are the opening remarks of the Mayor of Zürich:**

For some time discord and strife have prevailed in city and country
of Zürich because of certain sermons and doctrines presented to the
people from the pulpit by Master Huldreich Zwingli, our preacher here
in Zürich. He has been reproached and called a deceiver by some and a
heretic by others. This has caused, not only in our city of Zürich but also
in the country under our authority, the increase of discord among priests
and laity alike. Complaints are daily coming before my Lords in this
regard and there seemingly is no end to angry words and strife. Master
Huldreich Zwingli has frequently offered from the pulpit to explain and
defend his proclamation and doctrine which he preached here in Zürich
in open disputation before both clergy and laity. The City Council has

granted Master Huldreich's request in order to end the great unrest and discussion. A public disputation in the German language is to be held before the Great Council of Zürich, called the Two Hundred, to which all the people's priests and curates from our territory have been invited. Also invited was the Bishop of Constance, who has kindly sent the deputation here present, for which the Council of Zürich expresses its special gratitude. Therefore, if anyone is here present who is displeased or doubtful about Master Huldreich's preaching and doctrine as proclaimed from the pulpit, or who is persuaded to hold that such preaching and doctrine are not true, but seditious or heretical, let him freely, boldly, and without fear of punishment convict Master Huldreich of error with the help of the sacred Scriptures.

Zwinglis Sämtliche Werke I, 483–4.

▶ Zwingli, in turn, made the following opening remarks:[11]

'In our own time as in the past, the clear and pure light, the Word of God, has been dimmed, confused and diluted with human principles and teachings so that all those who call themselves Christian do not know the divine will. They only have their self-invented worship, holiness and external spiritual knowledge which is man-made. Those who are learned and leaders persuaded them that such external and false spiritual appearance and self-invented worship were necessary for salvation. Yet our salvation, consolation and redemption do not rest in our own merit, nor even in external works, but only in Christ Jesus, our saviour, concerning whom the heavenly Father himself gave witness that we should hear him as his beloved Son. His will and true service we can discover alone in his true Word, as it is found in the holy Gospels and the trustworthy writings of his apostles, but not in human laws and statutes. Inspired by God's Holy Spirit, some pious souls are preaching this message now. None the less, they are not called Christians, but persecutors of the Christian Church, and even heretics. I am considered one of them by many of both the clergy and the laity in Switzerland. I know that I have preached nothing in Zürich for the past five years but the true, pure and clear Word of God, the holy Gospel, the glad tidings of Christ, the sacred Scripture, which were spoken and proclaimed not by men, but by the Holy Spirit. Yet I am accused by some as heretic, liar, deceiver, disobedient servant of the Christian Church, as my Lords of Zürich well know. . . .

'I have also brought together in outline the contents and import of all my speeches and sermons delivered at Zürich, and have published it in

German. Thus everyone can see and know what my doctrine and sermons at Zürich have been, and will be, unless I am convinced otherwise. I hope and am confident, indeed I know, that my sermons and doctrine are nothing else than the holy, true and pure Gospel, which God wanted me to speak by the intuition and inspiration of his Spirit. . . . I offer to anyone who thinks that my sermons or teachings are unchristian or heretical to give the reasons and to answer kindly and without anger. Now let them speak in the name of God. Here I am.'

At such remarks of Master Huldreich the Vicar from Constance arose, and answered as follows:

'. . . My good fellow brother and lord, Master Huldreich, asserts that he has preached the Gospel publicly in Zürich. Of this I have no doubt, for who would not truly and faithfully preach the Gospel and St Paul, if God had ordained him as a preacher? I am also a preacher, or priest, though perhaps unworthy, but I have taught those entrusted to me for instruction in the Word of God in nothing but the true Gospel, which I can prove. I will not, even in the future cease this proclamation, unless God requires me for other labours in the service of my Lord of Constance. For the holy Gospel is a power of God, as St Paul writes to the Romans (1.16), to each one who believes therein.

'Now Master Huldreich complains that certain people blame him as not having spoken and preached the truth. He stands ready to give an account regarding his speeches and sermons to anyone, even in Constance. If Master Huldreich, my good friend, should come to Constance I would extend him my friendship and honour as far as lay in my power. I would entertain him in my house, not only as a good friend, but also as a brother. Of this he is assured. Furthermore, I did not come here to oppose evangelical and apostolic doctrines, but to hear those who are said to speak or to have spoken against the doctrine of the Gospel.' . . .

Since thus everyone was silent, and no one was anxious to speak against Master Huldreich, who had been called a heretic, Master Huldreich himself arose and said, 'For the sake of Christian love and truth I ask and request all who have spoken to me about my preaching to step forward and to instruct me, for the sake of God, in the truth. If they do not do this I will name them publicly, since many of them are present. On account of brotherly love I want to inform them beforehand, so that they would speak and prove me a heretic without my urging.' But no one desired to come forward or say anything against him.

Meantime Gutschenkel, standing in front by the door, cut a ridiculous caper, and shouted, 'Where are now the "big moguls" that boast so loudly and bravely on the streets? Now step forward! Here is the man.

You can all boast over your wine, but here no one stirs.' All laughed at that.

Then Master Huldreich arose again, asked and requested a second time all who had accused and attacked him about his proclamation to step forth and prove him a heretic. If they did not do that, and did not speak without his urging, he would for a third time publicly name them, etc., as above. When everyone remained silent despite the invitation and challenge of Master Huldreich a priest by the name of Jacob Wagner arose, a clergyman at Neftenbach, and spoke as follows: 'Since there is no one who wishes to speak of these matters after the repeated requests of Master Huldreich, I must, though unskilled, say something. It is well known to you all, gentlemen, that our gracious Lord of Constance this year issued a mandate ordering people to retain and keep the *traditiones humanas* until they were rescinded and changed by a general council. Now since no one will say anything against Master Huldreich's articles, which oppose the *constitutiones humanas*, I say for my part that we ought not to be bound to keep that mandate, but should preach the Word of God, pure and unadulterated by human additions. You know also, dear Lords, how the clergyman of Fislisbach was arrested according to the mandate, taken to Baden before the Diet, which afterwards gave him into the keeping of the Bishop of Constance, who finally put him in prison. If we are to teach and preach according to the contents of the mandate, then Master Huldreich's words have no force. But since there is no one here present who dares to show them untrue, it is plain that proceedings with the gentleman from Fislisbach were too short. . . .'

At such complaint the Vicar from Constance again arose, and spoke as follows: 'These remarks are meant to refer partly to my gracious Lord of Constance and partly to me as his Vicar; therefore it is proper that I answer them. The good gentleman—I really do not know who he is— said first that this year our gracious Lord of Constance issued a mandate ordering people to keep the *constitutiones humanas*, the human ordinances and praiseworthy customs. To this I say, dear lords and gentlemen, there are truly many unfair, ungodly, unchristian opinions and errors at hand, which very often are preached and put before the people, not only here in Switzerland but also elsewhere in my gracious Lord's bishopric by unskilful preachers, which opinions and errors, my dear lords and gentlemen, serve more to disobedience, disturbance and discord than the furthering of Christian unity. For they desire to estrange us from the good old inherited customs and usages descended upon us from our old pious Christian fathers many hundred years ago. Perhaps it was with this in mind that my gracious Lord issued the mandate for the sake of peace and unity in his bishopric. What the real contents of the mandate were I have no accurate knowledge, for at that time, as is known to many, I was absent from home. Therefore, as far as concerns this mandate I do not desire to speak further. But since the good, pious gentleman (I do not know where he sits, because I cannot see him) referred to the priest imprisoned at Constance, my office requires me to make answer. You all know, dear sirs, how this priest was turned over to my gracious Lord of Constance by Swiss citizens at the Diet of Baden as a guilty man. Accordingly my gracious Lord had the prisoner examined and questioned and he was found to be an ignorant and erring man in the sacred Scriptures. I myself have often pitied his unskilful remarks. For by my faith I can say that I questioned him myself, went to him in Christian love, set forth to him some of the Scriptures from St Paul, and he made—what shall I say?—very inaccurate answers. Ah, my dear sirs, what shall I say about this good, simple fellow? He is really untutored, and does not even know Latin. For in Christian brotherly love, kindly and without any anger, I mentioned to him some Scriptures, as for instance, that Paul exhorted Timothy, saying, *Pietas ad omnia utilis* (kindness and greatness are good in all things), and his answer was so childish and unchristian as to be improper to mention and report in Switzerland. But that you may really know, my dear sirs, I spoke with him about praying to the saints and to the mother of God, also about their intercession, and I found him so ignorant and unchristian on these points that I pity his error. He insists on "making a living out of the dead", although the Scriptures show that also before the birth of Christ the saints were prayed to and called upon for others, as I finally convinced and persuaded him by means of Scriptures, that is, by Genesis, Exodus, Ezekiel and Baruch. I also brought him to recant this error, as well as his errors about the mother of God and the saints. I also hope that he will be grateful to me and soon be released. . . .'

Vicar

'When for the first time today I looked and glanced through the Articles of Master Huldreich (I did not read them before), it seemed to me indeed that these altogether disagree with the ritual (i.e. are opposed to the praiseworthy institutions of the churches established for the praise and honour of God), to the loss of the divine teaching of Christ. This I shall prove.'

Zwingli

'Do so. We would like to hear that very much.'

Vicar

'It is written, Luke 9.50: *Qui non est adversum vos*, etc.—"He that is not against us is for us."' Now these praiseworthy institutions of the churches (like fasting, confession, having festival days, singing, reading, consecrating, reading mass and other similar things) have always been decreed and ordered by the holy fathers, not against God, but only for the praise and honour of God Almighty, and it seems very strange and unjust to me to consider and refute them as wrong.'

Title page of the proceedings of the January disputation in Zürich. (*Zentralbibliothek, Zürich*)

Zwingli

'When the vicar quotes from the Gospel, "He that is not against us is for us", I say that is true. "Now the customs and ordinances of the church are ordered and decreed by men, not against God," etc. Vicar, prove that. For Christ always despises human ordinance and decree, as we have in Matt. 15.1–9. When the Jews and Pharisees attacked the Lord because his disciples did not obey the doctrine and ordinance of the

ancients, Christ said to them, "Why do ye also transgress the commandment of God by your tradition?", etc. . . . One sees here that God does
not desire our decree and doctrine when they do not originate with him,
that he despises them, and says we serve him in vain. This also St Paul
shows when he writes, Dear brethren, let no man beguile you by human
wisdom and deceit, in accordance with the doctrine or decree of men, in
accordance with the doctrines of this world, and not those of Christ. . . .
God cares more for obedience to his word than for all our sacrifices and
self-created church customs, as we have it in all the divine writings of the
prophets, twelve apostles and saints. The greatest and most appropriate
honour to show to God is to obey his word, to live according to his will,
not according to our ordinances and best opinion.'

Vicar

'Christ said, according to John 16.12: "I have yet many things to say
unto you, but ye cannot bear them now. Howbeit when he, the Spirit of
truth, is come, he will guide you into all truth." Much has been inaugurated by the holy fathers inspired by the Holy Spirit, especially the
fasts and Saturday, by the twelve apostles, which also is not described in
the Gospel. Here without doubt the Holy Spirit taught and instructed
them.'

Zwingli

'Vicar, prove from the Scriptures that the twelve apostles have inaugurated Saturday and fasts. Christ said in the aforesaid place the Spirit
of God will teach them all truth, without doubt not human weaknesses.
. . . As if he said undoubtedly, not what you think fit, but what the Holy
Spirit teaches you in my name in accordance with the truth, not with
human thoughts. Now then the holy apostles have never taught, inaugurated, ordered and decreed otherwise than as Christ had told them in
the Gospel. For Christ said to them, ye are my friends if ye do that
which I have decreed and commanded. This the dear disciples diligently
did, and did not teach otherwise than as the right Master had sent them
to teach and instruct, which is proven by the epistles of St Paul and St
Peter. Hence your arguments cannot avail anything. For that I can say
truly that I could name more than sixty in this room from among my
lords, laymen not learned in the Scriptures, who all could refute your
argument as presented until now, and by means of the Gospel overcome
and refute.'

Vicar

'Very well, Master Huldreich, do you admit this, that one should only
keep what is writ in the Gospel, and nothing besides? Do you admit that?'

Zwingli

'Vicar, I pity you that you present such sophistical, hair-splitting and useless arguments. Perhaps I could also indulge in such devices, as I have also formerly read the sophists, hence I do not wish to be entrapped by such subterfuges and tricks. I shall answer and argue with the pure Scriptures, saying there it is written. It is befitting a scholar, to defend his cause by the Scriptures.'

Vicar

'You have read in St Paul that he accepted and taught traditions which formerly were not written in the Gospel. [Zwingli interrupts: That we wish to hear.] For when he inaugurated among the Corinthians the custom of the sacrament as he had received it from the Lord he said among other things: *Cetera, cum venero, disponam*, I Cor. 11.34: "And the rest I will set in order when I come." There St Paul announces that he will further teach them to honour and to use the sacrament. But that such was true, and that the twelve apostles gave instructions, presenting them as traditions which were not decreed by the Gospel, I shall prove from St Paul to the Thessalonians.' Master Huldreich interrupts, asking, 'Where is it written?' The Vicar answers, 'You will find it in the second chapter.' Zwingli says: 'We will look at it. But it is not there; we will look for it in the last epistle. But very well, continue.' The Vicar answers: 'Thus says St Paul, ". . . Therefore, brethren, stand fast and hold the traditions (i.e. teachings) which ye have been taught, whether by our word or our epistle." [Here Master Huldreich said, 'He is misusing the Scriptures; I shall prove it.'] St Paul says here that one should stand fast and hold the traditions, whether emanating from his words or his epistle. This is proof that he taught and instructed that which formerly had not been written, but clearly and openly invented.'

Zwingli

'In the first place, when he says St Paul gave traditions to the people of Corinth which before had not been decreed, I say no, for he says in the same place: "For I have received of the Lord that which also I delivered unto you." But when he says, "And the rest will I set in order when I come", it does not mean what the Vicar says; on the contrary he is punishing the Corinthians on account of misuse and mistake in the taking and use of the divine sacrament. For of the wealthy, who assembled in the churches for the sacrament, some overate themselves and became satiated, while the other poor people, at times hungry, had nothing to eat. . . . Therefore St Paul concludes: "And the rest will I set in order when I come." Not that he wishes to teach otherwise than as Christ has ordered him, but in order to stop and better their misuse does he say this. . . .

Secondly, the Vicar pretends that human ordinance and teaching are to be held; this also is not written in the Gospel. He refers to St Paul to the Thessalonians, where he writes: "Therefore, brethren, stand fast and hold the traditions which ye have been taught, whether by word or our epistle." I say Paul did not speak, teach, write or instruct in anything except what the Lord had ordered him. For he testifies everywhere, and also proves it to be true, to have written or preached naught except the Gospel of Christ, which God had promised before in the Scriptures of his Son through the prophets.'

Zwinglis Sämtliche Werke I, 489–90, 500–1, 502–4, 548–55.

▶ At the end of the debate the following edict was issued by the City Council:

Whereas a year has elapsed since a delegation of our Bishop of Constance appeared here in Zürich before Mayor, Council and Great Council, to consider such matters as were before you today, whereupon, after discussion, it was asserted that our Bishop of Constance would call together the learned in his diocese along with the preachers of adjoining dioceses to advise and confer with them in order to reach a unanimous decision which would instruct everyone how to conduct himself; but since then, perhaps for good reasons, nothing significant has been done in this matter by our Bishop of Constance, yet discord increases continuously among clergy and laity alike. Thus Mayor, Council and Great Council of Zürich have designated this day, in the name of God, for the sake of peace and Christian unity, and, supported by the delegation of our Bishop of Constance (for which they give their gracious and eager thanks), have also to this end invited by letter all the people's priests, preachers, curates, both collectively and individually to come to Zürich, in order that in a disputation those might be confronted who mutually accuse one another of being a heretic.

Master Huldreich Zwingli, canon and preacher at the Great Minster in Zürich, has in the past been much attacked and accused. Yet no one opposed him after he had stated and explained his articles nor did anyone disprove them on the basis of sacred Scripture. Several times he challenged those who have accused him of heresy to step forward, but no man proved any heresy in his doctrine. Therefore Mayor, Council and Great Council of Zürich, in order to do away with disturbance and discord, have upon due deliberation and consultation decided and resolved that

Master Zwingli should continue as heretofore to proclaim the Gospel and the pure sacred Scriptures, until he is instructed better.

Furthermore, all people's priests, curates and preachers in their towns, territories and dependencies, are to preach nothing but what can be proved by the Gospel and the pure sacred Scriptures: Likewise they are not in the future to use such terms as 'despicable', 'heretical', or other insulting words when referring to each other.

Whoever are disobedient and do not satisfactorily comply with this statute will be put under restraint so that they will discover the wrong they have committed.

29th January 1523. *Zwinglis Sämtliche Werke* I, 469–71.

▶ As a concrete result of the Reformation in Zürich, an ordinance of September 1523 provided for certain changes of the statutes of the Great Minster:[12]

First, inasmuch as divers troubles have arisen by reason of the clergy making overcharge in the matter of tithes, fees and burdens, whereof the common man complains, the Provost and Chapter hereby agree to surrender all their church-dues at the Great Minster, viz. the burdens which the common man has hitherto had to pay. Further, they agree that at the Great Minster no one shall be required to pay for baptism, for the administration of the sacraments, for spiritual advice, or for a grave-space, without a gravestone; though if anyone wishes to have a gravestone, he must pay for it. No one is to be required to set up candles at a funeral; though if anyone wishes to stick them up, he must be charged for them. And if anyone wishes to have the bells tolled for the departed in the Minster only, then he need not pay; but if in the Minster and in other churches as well, then he must pay the fee as hitherto. . . .

Further, it is thought good that the number of priests and clergy be reduced, so far as can be done with a good conscience, until no more persons remain than suffice for the preaching of God's Word and other Christian purposes. Those who are now occupied as canons and prebendaries may remain, and die in peace. But no one is to be appointed in their place, till a number is reached to be determined by both sides; and their prebends are to be devoted to Christian and useful purposes hereafter to be determined.

Further . . . it is resolved that well-learned, able and honest men be appointed to give public lectures day by day in Holy Scripture, for an hour in the Hebrew, an hour in the Greek, and an hour in the Latin tongue, as is necessary for the right understanding of divine Scripture. . . .

Further, provision should be made for an honourable, learned and discreet priesthood, to the honour of God and of our city and country, and for the salvation of souls.

Emil Egli, Aktensammlung, No. 426.

▶ **A second disputation, in October 1523, was to provide further guidance for the reform of the Church in Zürich. Here are Zwingli's opening comments at that time:**

In the Name of God, Amen. Dear brethren in Christ Jesus, our Lord, the true Word of God, which does not deceive, assures us that where two or three are gathered in the name of Jesus Christ, he is in the midst of them, giving to them all they demand or desire from God. Our Christian people have during the past several days earnestly called upon the help of God in the churches. Since it is impossible, on account of this great crowd, to kneel down, let us call upon God in our hearts. He will certainly be with us and not forsake us, drawing unto him all who are against the Word of God, enlightening those who do not understand it, and correcting those who use it wrongly. Amen.

Zwinglis Sämtliche Werke II, 680.

▶ **Following the disputation the Zürich City Council issued an ordinance regarding the use of images.**

Concerning images, we order that no one, ecclesiastic or otherwise, is to carry images into churches or take them from there until further notice, which, God willing, will be announced shortly according to the Word of God.

This does not apply to those who have placed private images in the churches. These may be removed in a way that no tumult emerges therefrom.

Emil Egli, Aktensammlung, No. 436.

▶ **By early 1525 the Reformation in Zürich was virtually completed. On 16th April 1525 communion was observed according to a new form.**

To the great surprise of many people and the even greater joy of the believers, the Lord's Supper was celebrated in the churches of Zürich on Maundy Thursday, Good Friday, and Easter Day. It was also celebrated on two days at Pentecost and two days at Christmas. . . . The entire territory accepted it as it is used in Zürich, with the exception that at many places the sacrament is not carried around, because of a lack of ministers. The people there go to the table of the Lord. Otherwise, the order is the same. Several Zürich citizens clung to the mass and the papacy and de-

Ulrich Zwingli.
(*Painting by
Hans Asper.
Kunstverein,
Winterthur*)

Title page of Zwingli's
first reformatory treatise,
*Concerning Freedom
and Choice of Food*,
of 1522.
(*Zentralbibliothek,
Zürich*)

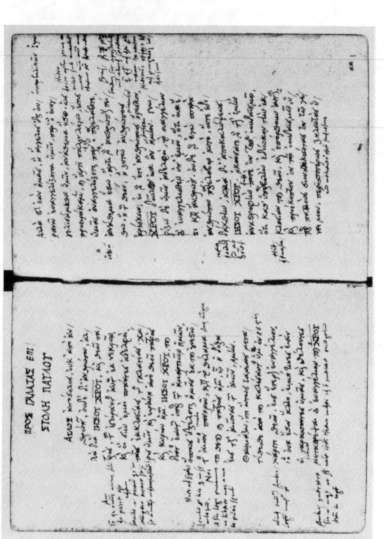

Zwingli's handwritten copy of the Pauline Epistles in Greek—the beginning of Galatians with his annotations. The marginal annotations in Latin contain Zwingli's references to Church Fathers, such as Jerome and Ambrose. (*Zentralbibliothek, Zürich*)

clared that since no one is to be coerced in matters of faith, they should be given a church in which mass could be read and heard. For many reasons this was turned down, however. But for the sake of peace, they were allowed to go to places where the mass and sacrament were still to be found. Thus, they ran to Schlieren, Dieticken, Baden and Einsiedeln. After the disputation of Bern, everybody was forbidden to attend mass.

Heinrich Bullinger, *Reformationsgeschichte* I, 264f.

▶ The Reformation in Zürich was largely effected with the aid of the City Council. Here Zwingli discusses the theological framework within which the Council worked:

I will here briefly comment on the function of the Council of Two Hundred. For we are put into ill repute by certain people who charge that the Two Hundred exercise what should be the responsibility of the entire congregation, which numbers, in town and country, almost seven thousand souls. I reply to those slanderers as follows: We, the ministers of the divine Word in Zürich, have often reminded the Two Hundred that we submit to them those matters which ought to be decided by the entire congregation only under the condition that they counsel and decide under guidance of the divine Word. Furthermore, we have reminded them that they are repesentatives of the Church only as long as the people willingly accept the pronouncements and mandates of the Council. This position has been stated to the entire congregation. In these days, in which some people are torn by stupid passions, eagerly responding to visions of the Spirit, certain matters cannot be entrusted to the mass of people. The Highest God, we are certain, will not forsake the guidance of his Church.

Zwinglis Sämtliche Werke IV, 479.

▶ Like Luther, Zwingli felt that the Catholic injunction against a married priesthood was invalid and accordingly got married. A letter from a friend congratulated him on this step.

When I read in your letter to Capito[13] that you had publicly announced your marriage I was almost beside myself in my great satisfaction. For this was the one thing I desired for you. Not that I attributed to you so great a lack of faith as to think you feared that Christ would not use you as a married man fruitfully in the business of his Word, and that he has employed you to evil results as a celibate. After all, you daily proclaimed things which Antichrist could endure more easily than the announcement of your marriage. I did not think that you were unmarried after you indicated to the Bishop of Constance in a tract that you desired the gift of marriage. When I realized that you were considered a fornicator by some, and a man of little faith in Christ by others, I could not understand why you concealed your marriage so long and did not announce it openly with candour and diligence. I had no doubt that you were led by considerations not easily set aside by a conscientious man. However that may be, I glory in the fact that now you have realized in all things the apostolic definition.

4th April 1524. *Zwinglis Sämtliche Werke* VIII, 170–1.

▶   Unfortunately only one letter of Zwingli to his wife is extant. It was written on what we would take to be a joyful occasion—the birth of a child—but is somewhat unexciting.

Grace and peace from God. My dearest wife, I thank God that he has granted you so joyful a delivery. He will let us bring up the child according to his will. Please send my cousin one or two coifs of the same quality and style as those you wear yourself. She dresses as becomes a woman of her station, but not like a Beguine. She is a married woman of forty, in all respects as Master Jörgen's wife described her. She has been kind to me and to us all beyond measure.

May God take care of you! Remember me to the godmother and wife of the administrator; to Ulmann Trinckler and the wife of magistrate Effinger; and to all whom you love. Pray God for me and us all. Written at Bern, January 11. Remember me to all your children; especially Margreten and comfort her in my name.

Your husband Huldreich Zwingli.

P.S. Send me, as soon as you can, my work clothes.

11th January 1528. *Zwinglis Sämtliche Werke* IX, 346–7.

▶   Zwingli's victory in Zürich did not mean that he had no opponents and enemies. As a chronicler describes, there were many:

After the priests and monks had abdicated and a mandate had been published against the so-called pensioners, it was attempted to get rid of 'that man' through sly cunning. . . . On one occasion, someone came to Zwingli's house after midnight requesting that Zwingli should visit a desperately sick person. The servant who answered for his master offered to go himself, since Zwingli should not be awakened on account of the burden of work he has during the daytime. The caller persistently refused to accept the servant's offer. This made him suspicious. The servant left the caller as if to report to his master and locked the door behind him. The caller stood outside, outwitted in his scheming. In the morning it was learned that Zwingli was to have been kidnapped on a boat, with a gag in his mouth keeping him from shouting. Then he was to be taken away secretly. Not long thereafter a horse was to be used for the same purpose. Also, a bailiff was seen in Zürich, presumably from another town, without a top coat, walking about with a long sword, hoping to meet Zwingli at an opportune occasion and kill him. He was reported to the authorities, arrested, but he escaped hurriedly. Two Zürich citizens, whose names I intentionally do not mention, threw stones against Zwingli's house at night under the influence of wine, broke windows, shouted, scolded and raged in such terrible, disgraceful and indecent manner that the neighbours did not dare to move behind their windows. Only when their stones, words and energy were exhausted, did they stop. Such tumult was reported to the Mayor. Early in the morning the city gates were closed and armed men searched all corners of the city without success. Finally female confidants unwillingly betrayed one of the culprits. The other one had already escaped. He was pulled out of the wine barrel belonging to a priest and taken to the prison by indignant citizens. After several trials he was sentenced to life imprisonment. He was kept several weeks, but then released upon request of Bern.

Ulrich Zwingli, p. 12.

▶ The Catholic opposition against Zwingli and Zürich dominated the disputation at Baden in May 1526.[14] Here is an account of the initial proceedings:

On Saturday afternoon before Pentecost [19th May] the two factions, all the scholars and the representatives of the Swiss confederation assembled in the church at Baden. There Lord Barnabas, Abbot of the church of Engelberg, welcomed the learned men from the various places and all others with friendly words and greetings on behalf of the Swiss confederation. He called attention to the reason for the gathering. Since many words had been spoken on both sides, it seemed unnecessary to repeat them at this time. Afterwards four secretaries, two from each side, were elected, who swore the customary oath concerning the transcription of the disputation. The representatives of the various towns then elected four chairmen and agreed upon an agenda, which was posted at the church door and read as follows:

In the Name of the Holy Trinity.

To the honour and praise of Almighty God, and the furtherance of this disputation and Christian colloquy the Lords of the Twelve Towns and the assembled representatives have agreed on this agenda. They desire that everyone should adhere to it.

First of all, the office of holy mass should be observed every day at five o'clock in the morning to the honour and praise of Almighty God. Afterwards a sermon of about half an hour should be preached asking Almighty God to aid us, through his grace and the Holy Spirit, in a good beginning, a better continuation and best conclusion of this disputation, through which we hope to attain true knowledge and a common Christian faith and come to concord and peace. . . .

Thirdly, each party should name two capable and pious secretaries to transcribe all proceedings. Two additional men from each party should be instructed to sit near these secretaries to see to it that the proceedings are recorded correctly. The four secretaries and the four assistants should daily get together in the evening to check the transcriptions. Possible discrepancies should be reported to the chairman for a decision. Likewise the transcription of the proceedings should always be deposited with the chairman.

Fourthly, my Lords earnestly desire and command that those who do not participate in the debate should not record anything. Any notes taken down by anyone contrary to this provision in his lodging or elsewhere and published afterwards will be considered by my Lords even now false, unprofitable and untrue. All such efforts are also to be punished by the proper authorities.

In the fifth place, the propositions which are to be debated shall be publicly posted at the church door.

In the sixth place, anyone wishing to participate in the debate, briefly or at some length, should give his name to the chairman. After his participation he should await the conclusion and decision of the disputation. Without knowledge and permission of the four chairmen, no participant is to leave Baden.

On the afternoon of the day before Whitsunday, Dr Eck posted the following propositions on the churches and the town hall of Baden:[15]

Propositions concerning the true, old faith presented against Zwingli by Johann Eck.

1. The true body of Christ and his blood are present in the sacrament of the altar.

2. The true body of Christ and his blood are also truly offered in the mass for the quick and the dead.

3. Mary and the saints are to be invoked as intercessors.

4. Images of our Lord Jesus and of the saints are not to be done away.

5. After this life there is a purgatory.

6. Children of Christians are born in original sin.

7. The baptism of Christ, and not of John, removes original sin.

In addition I will defend our true and undoubted faith against all contentions which Zwingli might raise against it. *Soli deo gloria.*

Eidgenössische Abschiede IV, 1a, 926f.

▶ **At the end of the disputation Zwingli was officially condemned.**

Zwingli, the main exponent and originator of the false and seductive teaching in Switzerland, chose not to appear in order to give an account of his faith despite all our offers and concessions of safe-conduct, indeed despite his own earlier statement. Those Swiss preachers who agree with Zwingli's seductive teaching and who were ordered by their authorities to be present at this disputation were not willing to be instructed or to desist from their error, even though they were admonished in open and friendly fashion and were dissuaded. Those present can testify sufficiently to this fact as indeed any faithful and humble Christian can learn from the proceedings. Since the Church ruled and agreed many hundred years ago to condemn anyone who dares to revive or to support old and condemned errors (Zwingli and his followers quote and defend not only Wiclif and Huss, but the doctrines of all the old heretics as well), it is hereby resolved that Zwingli and his followers are to be placed, without further explanation, under the ban and cut off from the Church. They are to be expelled and considered condemned by the entire Christian Church.

Eidgenössische Abschiede IV, 1a, 935f.

▶ Overshadowing other events in the last few years of Zwingli's life was the controversy with Luther concerning communion.[16] A letter of the Dutch physician, Cornelis Hoen, brought the problem of the proper interpretation of communion out into the open.

Our Lord Jesus Christ, who repeatedly promised forgiveness of sins to his own and who wanted to strengthen their hearts at his Last Supper, included a pledge of his promise to remove their uncertainty. In similar fashion the bridegroom, who wants to assure his bride of his love lest she doubt, gives her a ring with the words, 'Take this ring; I give myself to you with it.' She takes the ring and believes that the bridegroom is hers. She turns away from all other suitors and strives to please her groom.

Thus anyone receiving communion, the pledge of his groom, who sacrifices himself according to his testimony, must firmly believe that Christ is his, given for him and his blood shed for him. He will then turn his heart from everything which he hitherto loved and will trust only in Christ. . . . This is what it means to eat Christ and to drink his blood, as the Saviour says in John 6: 'He who eats my flesh and drinks my blood stays in me and I in him.' He who receives communion without such faith eats Jewish bread rather than Christ. But some insist that the Word of God says, 'This is my body.' Yes, you have the Word of God. The apostles, however, did not talk in such a fashion about this sacrament. They broke 'bread', spoke about 'bread', and said nothing about the Roman interpretation. Paul does not contradict my argument in First Corinthians 10. To be sure, he asks, 'The bread which we break, is it not the communion of the body of Christ?' But he does not say 'the bread is the body of Christ'. It is almost obvious therefore that the *is* must be explained by *signifies*. . . . We must distinguish between the bread which is received by the mouth and Christ who is received by faith. Whoever does not so distinguish the body of the Lord and thinks he receives nothing but what he receives with the mouth, is guilty of the body and blood of the Lord and eats and drinks to his judgment. By his eating and drinking, he shows that Christ is near unto him, while he, by his unbelief, is far from Christ.

Cornelis Hoen: *Zwinglis Sämtliche Werke* IV, 512f.

▶   In a letter of November 1524, Zwingli commented on the central problem concerning communion, as he saw it.

Now comes the most difficult aspect of this matter, namely, how we must interpret the words of Christ which are called the words of consecration. Since Christ said, 'This is my body, given for you', these words must mean that the bread, which Christ offered, is his body, not the spiritual, but the true body of Christ, given for us on the Cross. The words are plain and clear. Heaven and earth will disappear more easily than they. . . .

We maintain that everything depends on one syllable, namely on this word 'is', which does not always, we know, have the meaning 'to be', but sometimes 'to signify'. . . . The meaning is then as follows: 'Take and eat; what I now ask you to do will signify to you, or remind you of my body which is given for you.' . . . The meaning of the words of Christ will then be clearly revealed: This supper signifies or is a sign, through which you are reminded that the body of the Son of God, your Lord and Master, was given for you.

Zwinglis Sämtliche Werke III, 342, 345.

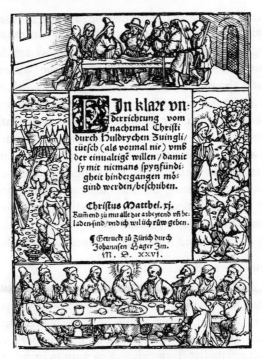

In klare vn=
derrichtung vom
nachtmal Chriſti
durch Huldrychen Zuingli/
tütſch (als vormal nie) vmb
der einualtigē willen /damit
ſy mit niemans ſpyßfündi=
gheit hindergangen mö=
gind werden/beſchriben.

Chriſtus Matthei. rj.
Kumēend zū mir alle die arbeytend vſi be=
laden ſind/vnd ich wil üch rūw geben.

Getruckt zū Zürich durch
Johannſen Hager Zm.
M. D. xxvi.

Title page of Zwingli's first pamphlet dealing with communion, *A Clear Instruction Concerning the Lord's Supper*. The bottom shows the original institution, the top current practice. (*Zentralbibliothek, Zürich*)

▶ **Zwingli described his own position as follows:**

I realized that the words 'this is my body' were meant symbolically, but did not know in which word was the symbol. Then two pious and learned men, whose names I will keep secret[17] [Johannes Rhode, Georg Saganus] visited Leo [Jud] and myself to confer about this matter. When they heard our views, they praised God. They did not divulge their own views; in those days one could not express his ideas without danger. But they informed me of the letter of a learned and pious man from Holland which since then has been anonymously published. There I found the precious pearl: that the 'is' of the words of institution must be understood as 'means'.

Zwinglis Sämtliche Werke IV, 560.

▶ Early in 1529 came an invitation from Philipp of Hesse to Zwingli
to participate in a theological colloquy on communion.

We are presently attempting to call together Luther and Melanchthon,
as well as those who share your views concerning the sacrament. Perhaps
the gracious and almighty God will bestow his grace so that on the basis
of the sacred Scriptures concord can be achieved concerning this article
which would enable us to live in common Christian understanding. At this
diet the papists attempt to support their false life and morals by insisting
that we, who adhere to the pure and clear Word of God, are not of one
accord concerning our faith. Thus I graciously request that you will
eagerly do your part to bring together at an appointed time and place
both you and the Lutherans so that, as I said before, the matter can
rightly be brought to a Christian consensus.

22nd April 1529. *Zwinglis Sämtliche Werke* X, 108–9.

▶ Zwingli responded promptly:

I received your letter with great joy. It seems to me that our present
confusion stems largely from our lack of rulers who are your equal. If
others would act like you, no one would be publicly denounced without a
hearing. In this great controversy concerning an important matter you
alone are concerned to dispel ignorance. You want to bring the antagonists
of this controversy together so that jointly they can learn what they do
not know singly and what is feared by stubborn ignorance. I praise God
for this. Though he is in heaven, he guides and directs everything on
earth. He wisely enlightens your mind so that you learn how to prevent
insecurity. He strongly fortifies your heart so that concord is restored to
the pious. I beg you to continue on this path and let not any obstacles
thwart your pious desire for peace.

I myself will gladly attend such a colloquy if it is pleasing to divine
providence, of which we can be assured unless we provoke God's wrath.
Inform me of place and time. Both should be appropriately chosen.
Those whom you wish to be present should know of the arrangements
before our opponents. Thus we will be together before the enemies of
truth know about our travel. But can I, a blind man, show the way to
someone who is far-sighted? After the details have been arranged, send a
letter to our City Council in which you officially invite me to the colloquy.
Have this invitation delivered to me so that I can pass it on at the proper
time. Should the Council refuse to give me permission to leave, I will, with
the help of God, come anyhow. Farewell, glorious Ruler. I am writing in
Latin because the Swiss German dialect is foreign to you.

7th May 1529. *Zwinglis Sämtliche Werke* X, 117–18.

▶ Early in September 1529, Zwingli addressed himself to the Mayor and City Council of Zürich, informing them of his decision to depart for the Colloquy.

You are aware, my Lords, that considerable controversy has arisen concerning the Lord's Supper between various factions in Germany, even among Christian preachers. Such discord, I am told, has caused evident offence at the recent diet of Speyer and enabled the papists to despise and condemn the Gospel. Therefore, Almighty God moved the pious Christian ruler, the Landgrave of Hesse, to call for a friendly and conciliatory colloquy in order to discuss this matter. Dr Martin Luther and others sharing his opinion and conviction, as well as Oecolampadius of Basel, Bucer of Strassburg, and I are to meet in his territory to compare and assess sacred Scripture in friendly fashion. We hope God Almighty will bestow grace for a unanimous concord resulting in peace, unity, and brotherly faithfulness. . . .

The distance is sixty miles and the proposed place indeed unfavourable to us regarding doctrine. Since it is situated in the territory of the Landgrave there is no personal danger, but the scholars are all opposed to us and we are only three in number. There are few friends who could comfort us between Zürich and there. None the less, it did not seem right to me not to go, for then all endeavour would be in vain and many of our esteemed opponents would travel in vain. They might even say that we had shied away from a friendly colloquy. Therefore, I humbly ask that you do not consider my departure as contempt, which displeases me even in others. Please consider that my failure to go would be to the disadvantage of truth and mean a decrease of your reputation. . . . I am taking Rudolf Collin, the Greek teacher, with me and ask you not to put this to his disadvantage since I have great confidence in him.

4th September 1529. *Zwinglis Sämtliche Werke* X, 292f.

▶ A few days later another letter informed Mayor and City Council of more recent developments:

On Sunday [5th September] I arrived at Basel and was informed that the Lords of the Secret Council appointed Rudolf Frei to accompany Oecolampadius. Tomorrow this will be confirmed. I agreed with him that he would not leave until I received word from you whether or not you will send a messenger. Tomorrow we plan, with the help of God, to proceed to Strassburg. Our Christian fellow citizens of Basel have asked several trustworthy merchants to accompany us on the boat. We hope to be on schedule and plan to leave Strassburg by the eighteenth of this month. I also ask you, my gracious Lords, to forward twenty crowns temporarily, which I will repay you. It was expensive to borrow horses to travel to Basel. We were also advised to purchase horses at Strassburg, which will mean additional expense. I took thirty-five crowns along. Should I buy a horse, little will remain for food. If I borrow money here, I would be a cause of derision. Please do what you can and forgive me my departure without proper permission. I am confident that the matter will turn out to the good.

Master Stoll should tell my wife as much as a woman needs to know. I left her under the pretence of going to Basel to attend to business.

5th September 1529. *Zwinglis Sämtliche Werke* X, 298f.

▶　　Bullinger reported on the events leading up to the Marburg colloquy as follows:

Accompanied only by Rudolf Collin, who was professor of Greek in Zürich, Zwingli left on 3rd September and proceeded quietly to Basel. Thus initially no one but the Secret Council in Zürich knew about it. When his departure and the reason for his travel were made public the following day a council official and Master Ulrich Funk were sent after him, together with a servant and guards. During Zwingli's absence Master Conrad Schmidt, commander of Küssnacht on Lake Zürich, a capable, courageous and learned man, preached for him.

Many rumours concerning Zwingli began to spread in Switzerland. Some said that he had run away with rogues. Others claimed the devil had visited him visibly and had taken him away. Countless other arrogant, worthless and faked comments were made. In Basel, Zwingli was joined by Johann Oecolampadius[18] and a council official. He travelled to Strassburg, where he was cordially welcomed. Here he preached a sermon, which brought him great praise. He was joined by Martin Bucer and Dr Caspar Hedio, and several council officials. The group was also accompanied by Jacob Sturm, counsel of Strassburg, and Jacob Dubenheim, a lord or nobleman from Meissen, whom Landgrave Philipp had delegated for this purpose.

Later Dr Martin Luther came to Marburg. He had tarried for some time in Saxon territory, until the arrival of the escort from the Landgrave which accompanied him from there, for he did not want to leave Saxony without this protection. Landgrave Philipp was prompted to observe therefore: 'Zwingli and his company came from Switzerland without escort. Dr Luther, however, asked for it as if he trusted us less.' Luther was accompanied by Philipp Melanchthon and Justus Jonas from Saxony,

Stephan Agricola from Augsburg, Andreas Osiander from Nürnberg, and Johann Brenz from Schwäbisch Hall.

Other scholars came from many places to hear the disputation between these eminent and famous men, but only a few of them were admitted. First Landgrave Philipp suggested that several of those whom he had invited should talk separately with each other, namely Luther and Oecolampadius, Zwingli and Melanchthon. It was felt unprofitable if Luther and Zwingli, both quite vehement and fiery, would meet at the very outset. Since Oecolampadius and Melanchthon were more gracious and gentle, they were asked to confer with the more vehement ones.

Zwingli and Melanchthon talked especially about Christ's deity, original sin, the Word of God, and communion. The same topics were also discussed by Luther and Oecolampadius.

Heinrich Bullinger, Reformationsgeschichte II, 223f.

▶ Here are excerpts from a reconstruction of the proceedings of the Marburg colloquy.[19]

Hessian Chancellor Feige:

My gracious Prince and Lord has called for you, prompted by the situation of the time, in order to compose the quarrel concerning the Lord's Supper. Much depends on this matter. My gracious Prince and Lord wishes that no one should seek his own advantage, but rather God's honour, the profit of Christendom and brotherly concord. Both parties are to present their arguments in modesty as becomes this matter.

Luther:

Illustrious Prince, gracious Lord! I do not doubt that this colloquy has been arranged and planned with good intentions. Two years ago I turned it down, since I knew that enough had been written on either side and no new argument was left. My own conviction was firm and I was going to adhere to it until the end of my days. When, however, my gracious Prince and Lord, Landgrave Philipp began at the Diet of Speyer to make preparations for such a colloquy, I agreed. I felt that I had to obey the desires of this most excellent ruler. Not that I want to change my view, which is as firm as a rock. I want to point out the basis of my faith and point out to the others where they err. I am indeed interested in talking about the Lord's Supper. However, before discussing the Lord's Supper I must mention certain points concerning which the churches of Zürich, Basel, and Strassburg are in error, if their writings give a correct interpretation of their teaching. I am informed by letter that at Strassburg several men asserted that Arius—as his writings, were they extant, would indicate— had taught more correctly concerning the Trinity than St Augustine and other orthodox Fathers. If his writings were still extant, this could be settled. The two natures of Christ are distinguished in such a way that one person is virtually made into two. . . . Some deny that original sin damns. Some teach that baptism is not the seal of faith, but only a sign of external affiliation. Justification is likewise not attributed solely to our faith in Christ, but in part also to our own powers. My enemies accuse me of teaching falsely concerning the spoken Word and the ministry of the Word, purgatory and perhaps even several other points of Christian faith and doctrine. Unless we are agreed in these matters, our consideration of the Lord's Supper will be of no avail.

Oecolampadius:

I am not aware that in said articles I ever taught anything contrary to Dr Luther's doctrine. This present colloquy was called for the purpose of discussing our respective views concerning the Lord's Supper. Thus I consider it appropriate to discuss it first of all. Should it become evident that some people have not taught correctly in other points, I hold that each person should himself give an account.

Zwingli:

I agree. After all, I discussed these points with Master Philipp. My views on justification are expressed in my pamphlet, *On the Clarity and Certainty of the Word of God*. Let us first of all deal with the Lord's Supper. Afterwards we can consider other points.

Luther:

Be it as you desire. But I testify publicly that I do not agree with said writings. I want to state this lest it is said at home that I was not allowed to open my mouth.

In regard to the Lord's Supper you have these basic arguments: You want to prove conclusively that a body cannot be in two places and you argue that a body cannot be without limitation. You appeal to natural reasons.

I do not ask how Christ is God and man and how these natures can be united. God can do more than our imagination presumes. One must accept the Word of God. It is up to you to prove that the body of Christ is not here, when the Word says, 'This is my body!' I do not want to hear reason. Carnal and geometrical arguments I repudiate altogether. . . . God is above all mathematics. The words of God are to be adored and

observed with awe. God commands: 'Take, eat; this is my body.' I desire
a persuasive proof from sacred Scripture.

(Luther writes the words 'This is my body' with chalk on the table
and covers the table with the cloth.)

Oecolampadius:

The sixth chapter of John explains the other passages of Scripture.
Christ does not speak there of a local presence. He says, 'The flesh profiteth nothing.' I do not want to appeal to reason or geometry—I do not
deny the power of God—but because I possess the sum total of faith I
speak out of it. Christ is risen and is sitting at the right hand of the
Father; consequently he is not in the bread. Our point of view is neither
new nor against God; it rests upon faith and Scripture. One must proceed
from a carnal eating to spiritual eating. The holy Scriptures use figures of
speech, metaphors, metonymies, and the like, where the words mean
something else than they say. Thus it is possible that the words 'This is
my body' are figurative speech, as we find it in some other passages:
'John is Elias' (Matt. 11.14); 'I am the vine' (John 15.1); 'The rock is
Christ' (I Cor. 10.4); 'The seed is the Word of God' (Luke 8.11).

Luther:

Oecolampadius referred to the various modes of speech in the holy
Scriptures, as, for example, 'I am the vine'. He admonishes us to a spiritual eating and says: The Fathers are on our side. To this I reply without
using many words: I do not deny that there are many metaphors in the
holy Scriptures. But you must prove that here 'This is my body' is a
metaphor. Do not talk about things we all know. If Christ would say
demonstratively 'I am the vine' I would also believe it. Common speech
permits a metaphor. Here is a *demonstratio*, a descriptive assertion. Therefore you must prove that it is a metaphor. This has never been done. At
any rate, how does spiritual eating exclude bodily eating so that bodily
eating is altogether worthless? I admit that the Fathers are, in part, on
your side, if we accept your interpretation. But what do we need of them
anyhow, as long as they do not prove that 'body'—'This is my body'—
stands for 'figure of body'? Please, speak to the point without delay!

Oecolampadius:

'I am the vine' is also a *demonstratio*. At least it could be one.

Luther:

I do not deny that there is figurative speech, but you must prove that we have a case here. It is not enough that the words 'This is my body' can be understood in this way. You must prove that they must be understood figuratively. Your argument is based upon a preconceived opinion, a *petitio principii*! Since Christ speaks in John 6 of spiritual eating, you insist that there is no other. You want me to base my belief on this foundation. But by your failure to prove your case my faith is strengthened. I have a precious and powerful text. Interpret it. I have always felt that you do not prove what you ought to prove.

Oecolampadius :

All right, I will show that the words 'This is my body' must be understood figuratively. Listen to John 6. Christ speaks here to the Jews and also to his disciples of the eating of his body and the drinking of his blood. When they, understanding it as bodily eating, shuddered, he answered, 'It is the spirit that giveth life, the flesh profiteth nothing.' Thus it is clear that he dismissed once and for all the carnal eating of his body. It should follow that we neither should nor could introduce again what he had once repudiated.

Luther :

Let me repeat the words from John. You assume that Christ by spiritual eating leads away from physical eating. I reply: He wanted to teach the Jews, the Capernaites, that he is not eaten like bread and meat in a dish and like roast pork. If I eat Christ bodily in the bread it is not an ordinary understanding, but a gift of the Holy Spirit. Thus it is not base or rejectable, but a superior eating. Man can believe the words that here is the body of Christ.

Oecolampadius :

I take you at your word: There is a twofold understanding and meaning of the Word of God. One is lowly and carnal; the other is superior and spiritual. It is a low understanding to speak of the eating of the body of Christ the way you do, Dr Luther. Christ emphatically repudiated it. Instead he commanded the superior understanding and spiritual meaning which we teach.

Luther :

I hear a great deal of the distinction of a twofold understanding of Scripture. But I can and will not tolerate that you understand the words of the Supper as something carnal without the testimony and authority of the holy Scriptures. These words may seem carnal to you. They are, none the less, as no one can deny, the words and deeds of the highest Majesty and are therefore in no wise carnal and base. Through the power of the Word of God forgiveness of sins, eternal life and the kingdom of heaven are attached to such carnal and low things. Therefore one must not void and reject them, but rather they must be esteemed sublime and spiritual.

Oecolampadius:

You consider it faith that Christ is in the bread. It is an opinion and not faith. It is wrong to attribute too much to the element. Listen to Augustine's *De Doctrina Christiana.* ('When a word that is meant figuratively is accepted literally, it is understood in a carnal way.')

Luther:

Let me return once more to the words of the Lord's Supper. If I speak of the 'body which is given for us', then this is not a base understanding of Scripture. Even if we had to deal with bread only it would not be a base understanding of Scripture. Indeed, to lift up a straw, by the command of the Lord, is a spiritual act. We baptize with simple water. One must not be concerned with what is said, but rather who says it. Since God says it, his words should be revered. Take the example of a prince who orders a horse to be shod: a horseshoe is a lowly thing; lowly things are involved. To suffer hunger is also a lowly matter—and yet those who hunger are called blessed. The same can be said of the words 'Baptize in water'. We do not ascribe the cleansing to the water, but to the Holy Spirit. We are all agreed as to the element. We do not ascribe dignity to the bread, but to the Word, and him who does it, namely, Jesus Christ. Just like the prince who sends his servant to shoe the horse dignifies the iron by putting it to the horse's hoof. Dignify the Cross! God often miraculously uses lowly matters. Thus he acted with Abraham, who was to sacrifice his son; thus he forbade Adam to eat of the tree. As often as we speak of the body of Christ, we speak of the body who is at the right hand of the Father. We should like to accept your views, but cannot, for you have a vague understanding. Please forgive, gracious Prince and Lord! The words 'This is my body' have captivated me! Even if Augustine and other Fathers want to interpret the words, they should stand behind Christ and let him give the interpretation. If they do this, we can depend on them and trust them. If not, let us discard the Doctors and trust Christ. At any rate, we must not agree with them just on account of the Doctors. Now it is up to you to speak!

Oecolampadius:

I accept your illustration. You suggest that the Word brings the body of Christ into the bread.

Luther:

That is correct. For example: A prince orders an iron horseshoe, someone else one made of gold. Thereby the lowly is made sublime. We have already learned the meaning of Christ.

Oecolampadius:

Since we have the spiritual eating, why do we need a bodily eating?

Luther:

What you are actually saying is that since we have the spiritual eating we do not need any bodily eating. I reply: We do not at all deny the spiritual eating, but teach and believe it to be necessary. But from this does not follow that bodily eating is useless or unnecessary. I do not inquire whether it is necessary or not. This is not my business. It is written: 'Take, eat; this is my body.' Thus one must above all things do it and believe. One must do it. . . . Christ gives himself to us in many ways: in preaching, in baptism, in brotherly consolation, in the sacrament. Again and again the body of Christ is eaten, for he himself commands us so. If he ordered me to eat manure, I would do it, since I would altogether know that it would be to my salvation. Let not the servant brood over the will of his Master. We have to close our eyes.

Oecolampadius:

But where is it written that we must walk with closed eyes through Scripture, Dr Luther?

Luther:

Even if we debate for a hundred years, we are not going to prove anything. Explain the text and I am satisfied. He who spoke the words of John 6 also spoke the words 'This is my body.'

Oecolampadius:

In John 6 we read: 'The flesh profiteth nothing.' If the eating of the flesh profiteth nothing, but the Spirit, then we must look for that which does profit and obey God's will. Let us read Scripture intelligently, comparing passage with passage. This is what Augustine does. I maintain what I said.

Luther:

And I stay with my text. . . .

Jacob Sturm :

Illustrious Prince, gracious Lord! I left home under the impression that there was only one point of disagreement between us. But Dr Luther made some statements at the beginning of the colloquy which could be interpreted to the disadvantage of the City of Strassburg, namely, that we do not rightly preach the Trinity and other doctrines. If I would remain quiet and this matter would not be taken care of, I would not fulfil my obligation. Having been sent here by decision of the City Council, I would bring home two disagreements instead of one. I request that Martin Bucer be permitted to dispel such suspicion and speak concerning the matter.

(After a short deliberation, Bucer is permitted to speak.)

Bucer :

Let me state very briefly our views concerning the Trinity, Christ, justification, baptism, etc. . . . I ask you, Dr Luther, to confirm that we teach correctly.

Luther :

No, I cannot do that. I am not your Lord or judge. It makes no difference to me how you teach in Strassburg. Since you do not want my teaching, I cannot have you as my disciples. We have learned earlier that you wanted to spread your teaching under my name. I have now heard you, but I do not know whether you teach at home the same way as here. Therefore I cannot confirm anything. You do not need it anyhow. After all, you boast everywhere that you did not learn from us. One can well see that you have not learned anything from us; I should rather not have such disciples. I do not want to be your teacher. You have my writings and my confession.

Bucer :

I ask: Will you recognize me as brother or do you think that I err so that I can overcome them? Please tell us what displeases you in our teaching!

Luther :

I am neither your master nor your judge nor even your teacher. Your spirit and our spirit do not go together. It is evident that we do not have the same spirit. For there cannot be the same spirit if one side simply believes the words of Christ and the other side reprimands, attacks, denies and blasphemes this faith. Thus, as said before, we commend you to the judgment of God. Teach as you will be able to defend before God.

Chancellor Feige:

My gracious Prince and Lord wishes to express his gratitude to all who have accepted his invitation and participated in this colloquy. If the Landgrave should ask you to meet again, either individually or as a group, you are to accept his bidding. The Landgrave wants to take counsel and you are requested not to leave.

Walther Köhler, Das Marburger Religionsgespräch, pp. 6–13, 37–38.

▶   **After the colloquy, Zwingli reported to his friend Vadian:**

Grace and peace from the Lord! Let me write briefly about what you so eagerly want to know. After we had reached Marburg under safe conduct and Luther with his party had likewise arrived, the Landgrave suggested that Oecolampadius and Luther, Melanchthon and Zwingli, should talk privately to explore the possibility of agreement. Luther treated Oecolampadius in such a way that the latter complained to me privately that he had met another Eck. I write this confidentially.

Melanchthon was slippery and changed into everything after the manner of Proteus that he forced me to seize a reed, arm my hand and dry it as with salt and so hold him firmly as he glided around in all sorts of escapes and subterfuges. . . . There were four sessions in all in which we contended successfully. We challenged Luther that he had made the following utterly foolish statements which needed explanation: that Christ suffered in his divine nature; that the body of Christ is everywhere; and that the flesh would only profit as he, Luther, asserted. But the fine fellow did not respond except that he said as regards the flesh being of no profit, 'You know, Zwingli, that with passing time and growing judgment all the Fathers treated the passages of Scripture differently than the earlier expositors.' Then he said, 'The body of Christ is eaten corporeally in our body, but in the meantime I will withhold comment whether the body is eaten by the soul.' And yet a little before he had said, 'The body of Christ is eaten with the mouth corporeally, but the soul does not eat him corporeally.' He also said, 'The body of Christ is produced by these words, "This is my body", no matter how wicked the man is who pronounces these words.' He conceded that the body of Christ is finite. He admitted that the Eucharist can be called the sign of the body of Christ.

20th October 1529. Zwinglis Sämtliche Werke X, 316ff.

►   Luther, in turn, commented on the colloquy in a letter to his wife:[20]

Grace and peace in Christ. Dear Lord Kathie, I do want you to know that our friendly colloquy at Marburg has come to an end. We have reached agreement virtually on every point, except that our opponents wanted to have mere bread in the Lord's Supper and acknowledge Christ spiritually in the bread. Today the Landgrave wants us to attempt to reach an agreement after all. If we reach none, we are to acknowledge one another as brethren and members of Christ. He is so greatly concerned to reach this goal. We, however, do not want to hear about brethren and members, though we do want peace and goodwill. Probably tomorrow or the following day we will leave here. . . .

Tell Pommer [Bugenhagen] that Zwingli's best argument was that *corpus non potest esse sine loco, ergo Christi corpus non est in pane*. Of Oecolampadius: This *sacramentum est signum corporis Christi*. I think God has blinded their eyes so that they could not present any arguments.

4th October 1529. *WA, Br.* 5, 154.

►   The victory of the Reformation in Zürich did not mean that all religious problems were dispelled. In 1530 the City Council had to enforce church attendance by a government mandate.

The Kingdom of God is to be sought above all other things. The Word of God is the proper guide for this Kingdom and constitutes the true certainty of our salvation. None the less, we are informed that some come only occasionally, others virtually not at all, and still others arrive too late to hear the Word of God, thereby offending the Church not a little. This is especially the case where there are Anabaptist supporters and adherents. They stand outside under the doors and in the church-yard, or spend the time of the sermon voluptuously in inns. Some of them even ridicule and abusively insult the Word of God and its proclaimers. Despite these facts there prevails on the part of the authorities, officials and wardens, no attention to God, nor fear of him. Therefore we earnestly order everybody, be he of high or low estate, woman or man, child or servant who resides and lives in our town, country, authority, and rule— unless excused by sickness or other true, sincere cause which is generally acceptable—to attend at least each Sunday, at the stated time, service and sermon. Everybody is to be obediently présent at the third ringing of the bells. Nobody is to evade this.

We also do not wish that anybody, young or old, stands in the church-yard or under the door, or spends the time prior to or during the sermon in his room, in wine or food taverns nor at other places (as is custom at present). We desire everybody to go to church, to hear the Word of God with proper seriousness and discipline as becomes true Christians, and remain until the end. . . .

Emil Egli, *Aktensammlung*, No. 1656.

▸   One year later another mandate for churchgoing became necessary.[21]

Whereas the mandate for churchgoing put out last year, 1530, has been badly observed; and young and old, men and women, idly wander about hither and thither during sermon time, on the bridges, down the alleys, by the gates and alongside the moats; therefore my Lords order all persons who have concern and oversight as regards church attendance and particularly, since need requires it, such as ought always to go from time to time, and hereby earnestly command that every man shall strictly observe the mandate to go to church on Sundays and holy days. And that no one may be able to say that he went to another church, henceforth the preachers in all the three churches shall begin to preach at the same time, which is convenient to all.

Emil Egli, *Aktensammlung*, No. 1780.

▸   Overshadowing the Reformation in Zürich was the steadily increasing political opposition of the Catholic cantons. Early in 1531, Zürich undertook sterner measures against the cantons to alleviate the pressing situation. Bullinger reported on the blockade:

On Sunday, 14th May, representatives of the Christian territories came to Zürich. On the following Monday they emphatically admonished Zürich to cease from its proposed expedition against the five cantons. Instead a blockade of supplies should be inaugurated. Zürich was considerably concerned about this proposal. For the present advantage would be lost and the allies would be kept waiting until the five cantons were armed well enough to attack and harm them. . . . It seemed unchristian to take the bread away from the guilty and the innocent, the sick and the aged, from the pregnant women, children and other needy people and break their will by famine. . . . The common folk would be displeased about this and many friends would become enemies. Thus the matter would eventually take a bad ending. Against this point of view it was argued, particularly by Bern, that this would still be preferable to an armed conflict. . . .

Thus all foodstuff and supplies were taken away from the five cantons. . . . Accordingly they soon experienced great lack of bread, wine, salt, steel, iron . . . and the other provisions necessary for life. Thus there was great need and complaint among them. . . . Many people in Switzerland as well as abroad considered this blockade of supplies neither successful nor Christian, especially since Paul had written to the Romans, as Solomon had asserted earlier: 'If your enemy hungers, feed him. If he thirsts, give him to drink. By so doing you will gather fiery coals on his head.' The five cantons complained bitterly that famine was to force them from their true faith, their freedom and justice; that both the peace of the land and other treaties had been violated.

Heinrich Bullinger, *Reformationsgeschichte* II, 283f.

▶   In October 1531 open conflict broke out between Zürich and the Catholic cantons. Near Cappel the opposing forces met.

On the eleventh of October a vagabond who had previously been expelled from Zürich territory came to the city. He asked for mercy and reported that the five cantons were proceeding towards Zürich and had already occupied Cappel. The people believed the traitor and sent out an artillery detachment under the leadership of George Göldli. This detachment was followed by the unprepared soldiers. Zwingli accompanied them fully armed on horseback. Outside the city the vagabond who had been given arms was dispatched to explore where and how the enemy was advancing. But he hardly disappeared from our sight when he threw away the arms and returned straightway to the enemy. He revealed everything about us. . . . The soldiers of the five cantons used convenient opportunity to break forth from the woods where they had been hiding, and enticed us thereby to battle. We courageously attacked in battle formation, first with cannons, which also fulfilled their task well at the second attack. In close fight our soldiers were courageous indeed and forced the enemy to give up his favourable position. The decision was already near when the soldiers of the five cantons saw perchance that the farmers who had been asked to protect our cannons were fleeing. Thus encouraged they attacked a third time in superior numbers. On both sides there was fierce and obstinate fighting, finally, with table knives, biting and scratching.

When Zwingli saw his own in danger, he joined the second row and there died courageously. Sixteen cannons, two flags, and all equipment were lost. After the great flag had changed hands three times, an eighteen-year-old youth rolled it up and brought it to Zürich. The enemies took their dead with them so that we do not know their number. Zwingli's corpse was shamelessly dealt with, as a prisoner reported to Zürich. There is great mourning in Zürich. Fifteen members of the Council were killed. . . . More than four hundred are said to be missing, a great many of them Zürich citizens, indeed the best ones. What sadness!

> 23rd October 1531. Martin Bucer to Ambrosius
> Blaurer: Th. Schiess, *Der Briefwechsel der*
> *Gebrüder Blaurer* I, 281.

▶   **Zwingli, who had accompanied the Zürich forces to battle, was**
    the most prominent of many casualties:[22]

Three times Zwingli was thrown down by the onstorming masses, but each time he regained his feet. The fourth time a lancet hit him below the chin. Sinking to his knees, he exclaimed, 'What does it matter? The body they can kill, but not the soul.' Soon afterwards he departed in the Lord. After the battle the enemies had time to look for Zwingli's corpse— we had withdrawn to a secure position. Who told them so quickly about his presence or his death? The corpse was found and the sentence pronounced over it. It was cut into four pieces, thrown into the fire, and burned down to ashes. Three days later, after the departure of the enemies, Zwingli's friends arrived to find some remains of him. Miraculously his heart, altogether whole and intact, was found in the ashes. The people were amazed and sensed a miracle, but did not understand it. They ascribed this to God and rejoiced. They were assured, by supernatural means, of the purity of Zwingli's heart. Shortly thereafter a man whom I know well came to me to ask if I wished to see a part of Zwingli's heart which he had with him in a capsule. I declined, since awe struck me upon hearing such unexpected words. Thus I have not seen it with my own eyes.

> Oswald Myconius, *Ulrich Zwingli*, pp. 15f.

▶   **The Peace of Cappel concluded the first phase of the Zürich**
    Reformation.

First, we of Zürich shall and will let our trusty and well-beloved confederates of the five cantons, as well as their dear fellow citizens and countrymen of Wallis and all their allies, spiritual and temporal, abide without any contradiction or dispute, in their true undoubted Christian faith, now and hereafter, throughout their cities, lands, territories and lordships. We will dismiss and put away all evil devices, evasions, deceit, and fraud. In our turn we of the five cantons will also let our confederates of Zürich and their allies abide by their faith. . . .

Secondly, we of both sides shall allow each party to continue all liberties, lordships and jurisdictions which we have in the common lordships and bailiwicks, altogether without hindrance. It is also further resolved and concluded between both parties, that if, in these common lordships, any parish, community or lordship has accepted the new faith and wishes to abide thereby, it may be suffered to do so. If any of those, who have received the new faith desire once more to turn therefrom and receive again the old true Christian faith, they shall, without let or hindrance, have free permission, full right, power and authority so to do. Similarly, if anyone in the aforesaid lordships has not yet secretly or openly renounced the old faith, he shall be allowed to abide by his old faith without opposition or hatred. If, moreover, in one or more places it should be desired to set up again and maintain the seven sacraments, the celebration of the holy mass and other ordinances and ceremonies of the Christian Church, then they shall and may do so and maintain them, no less than the other side its preachers. The church goods also and the property of the benefice shall be assigned at a fixed rate to the priest, and the balance handed over to the preachers. Neither party shall revile or abuse the other because of its faith: and whosoever shall do otherwise shall be punished by the magistrate, according to the nature of the offence.

Zweiter Kappeler Landfrieden : in *Religionsvergleiche des 16.*
Jahrhunderts, Bern, 1945, pp. 7–9.

BIBLIOGRAPHY

The scholarly edition of Zwingli's works is that of the *Corpus Reformatorum,* vol. 88ff.: *Huldreich Zwinglis Sämtliche Werke* (Leipzig, 1905ff.). A good selection which translates the Latin works into German is Huldreich Zwingli, *Hauptschriften* (Zürich, 1940ff.). A collection of biographical sources, on which the present selections rely heavily, is Walther Köhler, *Das Buch der Reformation Huldreich Zwinglis* (Munich, 1926). The following English translations of Zwingli's writings are to be noted: Samuel M. Jackson, ed., *Selected Works of Huldreich Zwingli* (Philadelphia, 1901). Samuel M. Jackson, ed., *The Latin Works and Correspondence of Huldreich Zwingli,* 3 vols. (New York, 1912; Philadelphia, 1922, 1929); G. W. Bromiley, *Zwingli and Bullinger* (London and Philadelphia, 1953). A historiographical survey of recent Zwingli scholarship is given by Bard Thompson, 'Zwingli Study Since 1918', *Church History* 19 (1950). Among the biographies are to be noted the probably definitive one by Oskar Farner, *Huldrych Zwingli,* 4 vols. (Zürich, 1943–59), and the older one by Samuel M. Jackson, *Huldreich Zwingli* (New York, 1901). A concise assessment of Zwingli's thought is given by Jacques Courvoisier, *Zwingli, A*

Reformed Theologian (Richmond, 1963). See also *Ulrich Zwingli, Eine Auswahl aus seinen Schriften* (Zürich, 1918), and Gottfried W. Locher, 'Die Wandlung des Zwingli-Bildes in der neueren Forschung', *Zwingliana* 11 (1963).

NOTES AND REFERENCES

1. For a discussion of sixteenth-century biographies of Zwingli, see the introduction to Johann Stumpf, *Chronica vom Leben und Wirken des Ulrich Zwingli* (Zürich, 1932), pp. 5ff.

2. Giovanni Pico della Mirandola (1463–94), an Italian philosopher and mystic, combined neoplatonic and Kabbalistic ideas.

3. The work mentioned in the text is Erasmus's *Novum Instrumentum Omne*, published in 1516 by Fröben at Basel, which includes, together with the Greek original and Latin translation, short annotations on difficult passages of the text.

4. Oskar Farner, *op. cit.*, II, 122, lists both Pico's *Opera* (Venice, 1513) and the tract *de providentia dei* (Strassburg, 1509) as part of Zwingli's library. In 1529 Zwingli preached a sermon at Marburg with identical title and similar content.

5. Caspar Wirz, *Akten über die diplomatischen Beziehungen der römischen Kurie zu der Schweiz, 1512–1552* (Basel, 1895).

6. The *German Theology* is a late-fourteenth-century anonymous work which stresses the union of man's soul with God, disregarding the external forms of ecclesiastical life. Luther was for a time influenced by this writing and published it in 1516 (*WA* 1, 152–3) and 1518 (*WA* 1, 375–9).

7. The translation used here is from B. J. Kidd, *Documents*, pp. 390–1.

8. Christoph Froschauer (*c.* 1490–1564), contributed, as printer of Protestant tracts, much to the spread of the Reformation. P. Leeman-van Elck, *Die Offizin Froschauers* (Zürich, 1939). The document is taken from Emil Egli, *Aktensammlung zur Geschichte der Züricher Reformation in den Jahren 1519–1533* (Zürich, 1879).

9. The translation used here is from S. M. Jackson, *Huldreich Zwingli*, pp. 404–7, 448–50.

10. The translation used here is from S. M. Jackson, *Selected Works*, pp. 111–13.

11. The translation used here is from S. M. Jackson, *Selected Works*, pp. 49–50, 58–59, 61–62, 95–100.

12. The translation used here is from B. J. Kidd, *Documents*, p. 426.

13. Wolfgang Capito (*c.* 1478–1541), humanist, since 1523 in Strassburg, where he introduced the Reformation. See Otto Erich Strasser, *La penseé théologique de Wolfgang Capito* (Neuchâtel, 1938).

14. On the Baden Disputation, see Leonhard von Muralt, *Die Badener Disputation* (Leipzig, 1926).

15. *Amtliche Sammlung der älteren Eidgenössischen Abschiede*, vol. IV, 1, *1521–1528* (Bern, 1873).

16. The Communion Controversy of the sixteenth century is ably discussed

by Walther Köhler, *Zwingli und Luther, Ihr Streit über das Abendmahl,* 2 vols. (Leipzig-Gütersloh, 1924–53).

17. Later Zwingli mentioned the two names; see *Sämtliche Werke* 8, 568–668. For studies of the Marburg Colloquy, see Walther Köhler, *Zwingli und Luther. Ihr Streit über das Abendmahl,* 2 vols. (Leipzig-Gütersloh, 1924–53), as well as Hermann Sasse, *This Is My Body* (Minneapolis, 1959). The Diet referred to in the document is that of Speyer in 1529. See Johannes Kühn, *Die Geschichte des Speyrer Reichstages 1529* (Leipzig, 1929). For Philipp of Hesse (1504–67) there is no recent biography. See *Religion in Geschichte und Gegenwart,* 3. Aufl. V, 332–3.

18. Johann Oecolampadius (1482–1531), was the Reformer of Basel. For Martin Bucer (1491–1551), the Reformer of Strassburg, see H. Eells, *Martin Bucer* (New Haven, 1931), and Wilhelm Pauck, *The Heritage of the Reformation* (Glencoe, Ill., 1961).

19. Walther Köhler, *Das Marburger Religionsgespräch 1529* (Leipzig, 1929), reconstructs the colloquy, cites the various sources and mentions other attempts at reconstructing the proceedings. Hermann Sasse, *op. cit.,* pp. 223–68, prints an English translation based on his source preference. For another sixteenth-century source see Johannes Stumpf, *Beschreibung des Abendmahlstreites auf Grund einer unbekannt gebliebenen Handschrift* (Zürich, 1960).

20. The Latin reads in translation: 'A body cannot be without a place; therefore the body of Christ is not in the bread', and 'this sacrament is a sign of the body of Christ'. That Kathie knew Latin well enough to participate in theological conversation is also attested otherwise. See *WA, TR* 4, No. 4860, and 5, No. 5567.

21. The translation used here is from B. J. Kidd, *Documents,* p. 450.

22. For the contemporary response to Zwingli's death, see A. Erichson, *Zwingli's Tod und Dessen Beurtheilung durch Zeitgenossen* (Strassburg, 1883); the story concerning Zwingli's heart is discussed by Gottfried W. Locher, 'Die Legende vom Herzen Zwinglis neu untersucht,' *Zwingliana* 9 (1949/53), 563ff.

Calvin and the
Reformation in Geneva

MARTIN LUTHER was well on his way in his theological studies when Jean Cauvin, or John Calvin, was born at Noyon, in northern France, in 1509. John's father had worked himself up from moderate beginnings to the respected position of a financial secretary to the resident bishop. Young John enrolled at the University of Paris at the age of fourteen, took a course in the liberal arts, and received the master's degree in 1528. His father wanted him to study law, but John pursued studies also in Greek, Hebrew and classical antiquity. He had contacts with Christian humanism and published, in 1532, a commentary on Seneca's treatise *On Clemency*. He hoped that this learned and thoughtful book would bring him fame—it even dared disagree with Erasmus—but no one took any notice.

About that time Calvin must have also had his first contact with Protestantism. He himself spoke later on of his 'sudden conversion', but the few clues hardly allow a definitive date. When in 1533 the Rector of the University of Paris, Nicolas Cop, gave an inaugural address replete with Protestant ideas, Calvin was probably involved as the writer of the address. Protestantism, at that time, was actively suppressed in France, but more perhaps on account of the King's insistence on autocratic sovereignty than on account of religious considerations. Such suppression did not, however, thwart Protestant aggressiveness. In the autumn of 1534 a Protestant poster was affixed to the door of the King's bedroom. The consequences for the Protestants were disastrous. Persecution was intensified and Calvin, together with many others, found it necessary to leave France.

He settled temporarily at Basel, vigorously pursuing theological studies. Not yet twenty-seven years of age, he published early in 1536 a brief but systematic exposition of the Protestant faith, the *Institutes of the Christian Religion*, which became, variously revised and enlarged, the most significant single exposition of Protestant theology in the sixteenth cen-

tury. What the commentary on Seneca had not accomplished was now achieved: Calvin became a famous man. But he was yet without a definite vocational goal. He decided to devote himself to further studies. He travelled to Italy, then returned secretly to France in order to settle his personal affairs. From there he planned to proceed to Strassburg to lead the quiet life of a scholar.

However, war between Charles V and Francis forced him to make an unanticipated detour via Geneva. In this important city in the south-west corner of the Swiss confederation, the Protestant faith had been introduced in 1532, though not without some difficulty and opposition. When Guillaume Farel, the leading minister of Geneva, learned, quite by accident, of Calvin's temporary presence in the city, he pleaded with him to stay. Calvin—only twenty-seven years of age, shy, and hesitant to step into the public limelight—at first refused, then agreed. His responsibilities at first were few and his work simple: he was to hold daily Bible studies on the Pauline Epistles. In 1537 he drew up a church order which provided for ecclesiastical discipline and required the citizens to subscribe to a confession of faith. Many refused to swear, and serious dissension entered the city. The following year brought the election of a new city council, whose members were hostile to Calvin and Farel. This 'devil's council', as Calvin called it, ordered the adoption of the church order of Bern rather than the one drawn up locally. Outwardly, there were only minor differences between the Bernese order and the one proposed by Calvin and Farel. But for the two ministers the issue was more fundamental: Should the city council or the ministers direct religious affairs in the city? Calvin and Farel were unwilling to compromise their conviction that governmental authority had no right to dictate ecclesiastical practice. As a result the two ministers were expelled from Geneva in April 1538.

Calvin proceeded northward to Strassburg—completing, as it were, after a two-year delay, his original journey. The apparent failure of his public ministry made him all the more determined to lead henceforth the withdrawn life of a scholar. Hesitantly he became minister of a congregation of French refugees and participated in religious discussions. In addition, he studied, wrote and gathered new experiences in some of the religious colloquies which were held at that time in Germany in a last effort to bridge the gap between the old and the new faith.

Geneva, in the meantime, was experiencing religious and political difficulties. Bern increasingly attempted to subject Geneva to her control. The religious atmosphere in Geneva was made tense by the absence of any positive programme of reform, after all sorts of elements had earlier united in their negative repudiation of the Roman Catholic Church. Calvin's return to Geneva seemed to many the solution for political and religious order. After several pleas from the Genevan city council, Calvin agreed in September 1541 to return. In November a new church order, the *Ordonnances Ecclésiastiques*, was adopted by the city council. This had been the price for Calvin's return. The Church of Geneva was to be ordered in accord with this set of regulations. Since Church and State were but two sides of the same commonwealth, these *Ordonnances* also ordered civic life in the town. Judging from the document as well as from subsequent practice, it appears that in Geneva, if anywhere, the path to Christian perfection was narrow and straight. Rigorous control and supervision of all of life prevailed in the city. Not only was absence from worship punishable, but singing worldly songs, dancing and card playing were objectionable behaviour. The consistory, composed of the ministers of Geneva and twelve elders (to each of whom was assigned a particular section of the city) was entrusted with the maintenance of pure faith and morals. Since this body acted both as prosecutor and judge, it became infamous indeed—any citation meant conviction.

It took Calvin fifteen struggling years to get the principles for which he stood—and which had been incorporated into the *Ordonnances*— accepted in Geneva. The struggle with the opponents seemed endless.

One opponent was Pierre Ameaux, a manufacturer of playing cards, whose business was drifting toward bankruptcy on account of the austere morality in the city. Enranged, he called Calvin a false preacher. Though this had been said confidentially among good friends, soon the whole city knew it. Ameaux was cited before the authorities and punished. In January 1546 he had to walk through the streets of Geneva in a penitent's garb. Calvin himself had insisted on this as punishment, asserting that God's honour, not his, was at stake. Then there was the case of Sebastian Castellio, a young schoolteacher whom Calvin had brought back with him from Strassburg. Castellio wanted to be ordained to the ministry, but the routine examination revealed that his views on certain theological matters were not altogether in harmony with church tradition. Thus he held the Song of Solomon to be a simple love poem. A translation of the

Holy Scriptures on which he had been working was promptly denounced by Calvin for various doctrinal and stylistic flaws. The atmosphere became tense, and in 1545 Castellio felt it advisable to leave Geneva. He settled in Basel and became one of Calvin's most vigorous literary opponents, using a brilliant mind and a gifted pen to denounce the Genevan Reformer.

In 1541 Jerome Bolsec, a former Catholic monk, attacked Calvin's doctrine of predestination and charged that in it God was made the origin of evil. This charge, of course, hit the core of Calvin's theological system. Bolsec had to leave Geneva, but this was another case of evicted but not convicted: he became a lifelong enemy of Calvin. In later years he returned to Catholicism and wrote a bitter and hostile biography of Calvin, indeed a veritable arsenal of uncomplimentary epithets.

The most serious controversy, recounted in the next chapter, centred in Michael Servetus. Calvin weathered the storm of the trial, as well as the violent denunciation from Castellio's pen after Servetus's execution. With surprising unanimity Protestant theologians all over Europe came to Calvin's literary and theological rescue.

The Genevan Reformer emerged from this episode more strongly than he had entered it. His position in the city became unchallenged. The elections to the City Council in 1555 brought a majority for Calvin's supporters. Geneva was now the city of Calvin; indeed, it was the very heart of Protestantism. The Geneva Academy, founded in 1559, trained future ministers, who came from many European countries and returned entrusted and enthused with Calvin's evangel.

Frail, timid, but determined, John Calvin, the man who had wrought 'this most perfect school of Christ since the days of the Apostles' (as John Knox was persuaded to call it), died in 1564. His funeral was simple, even as his life and his piety had been simple. Few words were spoken, no hymns sung. His epitaph was his life: *Soli deo gloria*, To God alone the glory. His work lived on—not only in Geneva, but in France, Scotland, Holland and Hungary. Calvin had taught Christians to be warriors for God; from the middle of the century for many decades to come Calvinism proved to be the most vital and powerful expression of the Protestant Reformation.

▶   In a brief biography[1] written in the year of Calvin's death, Theodore Beza,[2] his close associate, described the background and youth of the great Reformer.

John Calvin was born at Noyons, a celebrated town in Picardy, or at least on the confines of Picardy, on the 27th July, in the year of our Lord

1509. His father's name was Gerard Calvin, his mother's Joan Franc, both of them persons of good repute, and in easy circumstances. Gerard being a person of no small judgment and prudence, was highly esteemed by most of the nobility of the district, and this was the reason why young Calvin was from a boy very liberally educated, though at his father's expense. . . . Calvin, who was a most diligent student, made such progress that he left his fellow students behind in the Grammar course, and was promoted to the study of Dialectics, and what is termed Arts.

His father had at first intended him for the study of Theology, to which he inferred that he was naturally inclined; because, even at that youthful age, he was remarkably religious, and was also a strict censor of everything vicious in his companions. This I remember to have heard from some Catholics, unexceptionable witnesses, many years after he had risen to celebrity.

Being thus, as it were, destined to the sacred office, his father procured a benefice for him from the Bishop of Noyons, in what is called the Cathedral church. . . . The design of making him a priest was interrupted by a change in the views both of father and son—in the former, because he saw that the Law was a surer road to wealth and honour, and in the latter because he became acquainted with the true Church. . . .

Having set out for Orleans, to study law . . . Calvin, in a short time, made such astonishing progress, that he very often officiated for the professors, and was considered rather a teacher than a pupil. On his departure, he was presented with a Doctor's degree, free of expense, and with the unanimous consent of all the professors, as a return for the services which he had rendered to the Academy. Meanwhile, however, he diligently cultivated the study of sacred literature, and made such progress that all in that city who had any desire to become acquainted with a purer religion often called to consult him, and were greatly struck both with his learning and his zeal. Some persons, still alive, who were then on familiar terms with him, say that, at that period, his custom was, after supping very frugally, to continue his studies until midnight, and on getting up in the morning, to spend some time meditating, and, as it were, digesting what he had read in bed, and that while so engaged he was very unwilling to be interrupted. By these prolonged vigils he no doubt acquired solid learning, and an excellent memory; but it is probable he also contracted that weakness of stomach which afterwards brought on various diseases, and ultimately led to his untimely death.

Theodore Beza, *Life of Calvin*, pp. lix-lxi (CR 49, 121-2).

▶ Earliest expression of Calvin's studies was the publication of a commentary on the Roman philosopher Seneca's work, 'De Clementia'.[3] Beza reports on this as follows:

A sudden intimation of the death of his father called him back to his native town. Shortly after, in his twenty-fourth year, he went to Paris, and there wrote his excellent Commentary on Seneca's Treatise, *De Clementia*. This very grave writer, being obviously in accordance with Calvin's disposition, was a great favourite with him. A few months' residence here made him known to all who desired a reform in religion.

Theodore Beza, *Life of Calvin*, p. lxii (*CR* 49, 122).

▶ Calvin himself wrote to a friend:

. . . Well, at length the die is cast. My Commentaries on the Books of Seneca, *De Clementia*, have been printed, but at my own expense, and have drawn from me more money than you can well suppose. At present, I am using every endeavour to collect some of it back. I have stirred up some of the professors of this city to make use of them in lecturing. In the University of Bourges I have induced a friend to do this from the pulpit by a public lecture. You can also help me not a little, if you will not take it amiss; you will do so on the score of our old friendship; especially as, without any damage to your reputation, you may do me this service, which will also tend perhaps to the public good. Should you determine to oblige me by this benefit, I will send you a hundred copies or as many as you please. Meanwhile, accept this copy for yourself, while you are not to suppose that by your acceptance of it, I hold you engaged to do what I ask.

23rd May 1532, *Letters* I, pp. 31–32 (*CR* 38, No. 13).

▶ The most momentous experience of his life as a student was his conversion,[4] described here by himself.

When I was as yet a very little boy, my father had destined me for the study of theology. But afterwards, when he considered that the legal profession commonly raised those who followed it to wealth, this prospect induced him suddenly to change his purpose. Thus it came to pass that I was withdrawn from the study of philosophy, and was put to the study of law. To this pursuit I endeavoured faithfully to apply myself, in obedience to the will of my father; but God, by the secret guidance of his providence, at length gave a different direction to my course. And first, since I was too obstinately devoted to the superstitions of Popery to be easily extricated from so profound an abyss of mire, God by a sudden conversion subdued and brought my mind to a teachable frame, which was more hardened in such matters than might have been expected from one at my early period of life. Having thus received some taste and knowledge of true godliness, I was immediately inflamed with so intense a desire to make progress therein that although I did not altogether leave off other studies, I yet pursued them with less ardour.

I was quite surprised to find that before a year had elapsed, all who had any desire after purer doctrine were continually coming to me to learn, although I myself was as yet but a mere novice and tyro. Being of a disposition somewhat unpolished and bashful, which led me always to love the shade and retirement, I then began to seek some secluded corner where I might be withdrawn from the public view; but so far from being able to accomplish the object of my desire, all my retreats were like public classes. In short, whilst my one great object was to live in seclusion without being known, God so led me about through different turnings and changes that he never permitted me to rest in any place, until, in spite of my natural disposition, he brought me forth to public notice.

Commentaries, Psalms, pp. xl–xli (*CR* 59, 21–23).

▶   In November 1533 the rector of the University of Paris, Nicolas Cop, gave an address which had a Protestant tenor. Calvin, most probably, had a hand in this lecture, of which an excerpt follows below.[5]

'Blessed are the poor in spirit' (Matt. 5). . . . And first of all, what we must find out most carefully is the aim of this Gospel, and how everything is related to it. It is easy to do so if we first of all define the Gospel and define the Law and then compare them with each other. Consequently the Gospel is the good news and the saving preaching of Christ proclaiming to us that he has been sent by God the Father to bring his help to all and to assure us of eternal life. The Law is contained within the commandments; it threatens us, it compels us, it contains no gracious promise. The Gospel makes no threats, does not bind anybody with precepts, teaches the sovereign goodwill of God towards us. Whoever consequently wants to give an untarnished and exact interpretation of the Gospel must not go beyond these definitions. Those who do not follow this way of understanding these things will never succeed in becoming conversant with the philosophy of Christ.

A. L. Herminjard, *Correspondance des Réformateurs*
(Geneva, 1866–97) III, 418ff.

The proclamation of mayor and city council of Zürich, calling for the January 1523 disputation. See p. 131. (*Staatsarchiv, Zurich*)

Zwingli's only extant letter to his wife Zwingli's signature is here in the German form. See p. 146. (*Graphische Sammlung, Zentrabibliothek, Zürich*)

Signatures of the Marburg Colloquy 1529. Martin Luther, Justus Jonas, Philipp Melanchthon of Wittenberg, Andreas Osiander of Nürnberg, Stephen Agricola of Augsburg, Johann Brenz of Schwäbisch Hall, Johann Oecolampadius of Basel, Huldrych Zwingli of Zürich, Martin Bucer, and Caspar Hedio of Strasburg. (*Staatsarchiv, Marburg*)

▶   Beza described the developments ensuing from Cop's address.

About this time, Calvin renouncing all other studies, devoted himself to God, to the great delight of all the pious who were then holding secret meetings in Paris. It was not long before an occasion occurred for strenuous exertion. The person who at this time held the office of Rector in the University of Paris was Nicolas Cop, son of Guillaume Cop of Basel, physician to the King. He having, according to custom, to deliver an oration on the 1st of November, the day on which the festival of All Saints is celebrated by the Papists, Calvin furnished him [in part] with one in which religion was treated more purely and clearly than it was previously wont to be. This could not be tolerated by the Sorbonne, and being also disapproved by the Senate, or Parliament, which cited the Rector to appear before them. He accordingly set out with his officers, but being warned on the way to beware of his enemies, turned back, and afterwards quitting the country, retired to Basel. Search was made at the College of Fortet, where Calvin was then residing. He happened not to be at home, but his papers were seized, and among them numerous letters from his friends. However, the worst which happened was that the lives of many of them were brought into the greatest jeopardy. . . . This tempest the Lord dispersed by the instrumentality of the Queen of Navarre (only sister of Francis, the reigning monarch), a woman of distinguished genius, and at this time a great patroness of the Reformers. Inviting Calvin to her Court, she received him, and listened to him with the greatest respect.

Calvin after this left Paris, and removing to the province of Saintonge, became assistant to a friend, at whose request he wrote certain brief Christian exhortations, which in some parishes were read during divine service, in order that the people might be gradually trained to the investigation of the truth.

Theodore Beza, *Life of Calvin*, pp. lxii–lxiii (*CR* 49, 126).

▶   Calvin's new Protestant conviction made a continued stay in France impossible. Beza described his experiences:

He set out to Basel, by way of Lorraine; but when not far from the town of Metz, was brought into the greatest difficulty by the perfidy of one of his servants, who ran off with all the money belonging to both, and being mounted on the stronger horse, suddenly fled with such speed that it was impossible to overtake him. His masters were thus left so unprovided with the means of travelling that they were obliged to borrow ten crowns from the other servant, and in that way arrived with difficulty, first at Strassburg, and afterwards at Basel. There he lived on intimate terms with those two distinguished men, Simon Grynaeus[6] and Wolfgang Capito, and devoted himself to the study of Hebrew. Though most desirous to remain in retirement, as appears from a letter which Bucer addressed to him in the following year, he was compelled to publish his *Institutes of the Christian Religion*, a rude sketch of that most celebrated work.

Theodore Beza, *Life of Calvin*, p. lxv (*CR* 49, 124).

▶   Calvin himself wrote as follows:

Leaving my native country, France, I in fact retired into Germany, expressly for the purpose of being able there to enjoy in some obscure corner the repose which I had always desired, and which had been so long denied me. But lo! whilst I lay hidden at Basel, and known only to a few people, many faithful and holy persons were burnt alive in France; and the report of these burnings having reached foreign nations, they excited the strongest disapprobation among a great part of the Germans, whose indignation was kindled against the authors of such tyranny. In order to allay this indignation, certain wicked and lying pamphlets were circulated, stating that none were treated with such cruelty but Anabaptists and seditious persons, who, by their perverse ravings and false opinions, were overthrowing not only religion but also all civil order. Observing that the object which these instruments of the court aimed at by their disguises was not only that the disgrace of shedding so much innocent blood might remain buried under the false charges and calumnies which they brought against the holy martyrs after their death, but also, that afterwards they might be able to proceed to the utmost extremity in murdering the poor saints without exciting compassion towards them in the breasts of any, it appeared to me, that unless I opposed them to the utmost of my ability, my silence could not be vindicated from the charge of cowardice and treachery. This was the consideration which induced me to publish my *Institutes of the Christian Religion*.[7] My objects were first, to prove that these reports were false and calumnious, and thus to vindicate my brethren, whose death was precious in the sight of the Lord; and next, that as the same cruelties might very soon after be exercised against many unhappy individuals, foreign nations might be touched with at least some compassion towards them and solicitude about them. When it was then published, it was not that copious and laboured work which it now is, but only a small treatise containing a summary of the principal truths of the Christian religion; and it was published with no other design than that men might know what was the faith held by those whom I saw basely and wickedly defamed by those flagitious and perfidious flatterers. That my object was not to acquire fame, appeared from this, that immediately after I left Basel and particularly from the fact that nobody there knew that I was the author.

Commentaries, Psalms, pp. xli–xlii (*CR* 59, 23).

▸ **After a short return to his native France, Calvin found himself, almost accidentally, in Geneva. Here is Beza's description:**

After settling his affairs, and taking with him Antoine Calvin, his only surviving brother, his purpose was to return to Basel or Strassburg. Owing to the war, the other roads were shut up, and he was obliged to proceed through Switzerland. In this way he came to Geneva, having himself no thought of this city, but brought thither by Providence, as afterwards appeared. A short time before, the Gospel of Christ had been introduced in a wonderful manner into that city by the exertions of two most illustrious men, viz. Guillaume Farel from Dauphine . . . and Pierre Viret of Orbe, in the territory of Bern and Fribourg, whose labours the Lord afterwards most abundantly blessed. Calvin having, in passing through Geneva, paid them a visit, as good men are wont to do to each other, Farel, a person obviously inspired with a kind of heroic spirit, strongly urged him, instead of proceeding farther, to stay and labour with him at Geneva. When Calvin could not be induced to consent, Farel thus addressed him: 'You are following only your own wishes, and I declare, in the name of God Almighty, that if you do not assist us in this work of the Lord, the Lord will punish you for seeking your own interest rather than his.' Calvin, struck with this fearful denunciation, submitted to the wishes of the presbytery and the magistrates, by whose suffrage, the people consenting, he was not only chosen preacher (this he had at first refused), but was also appointed Professor of Sacred Literature—the only office he was willing to accept. This took place in August 1536.

Theodore Beza, *Life of Calvin*, pp. lxvi–lxvii (*CR* 49, 125–6).

▸ **Calvin himself wrote, more modestly, these words:**

Wherever else I have gone, I have taken care to conceal that I was the author of that performance; and I had resolved to continue in the same privacy and obscurity, until at length Guillaume Farel detained me at Geneva, not so much by counsel and exhortation, as by a dreadful imprecation, which I felt to be as if God had from heaven laid his mighty hand upon me to arrest me. As the most direct road to Strassburg, to which I then intended to retire, was shut up by the wars, I had resolved to pass quietly by Geneva, without staying longer than a single night in that city. A little before this, Popery had been driven from it by the exertions of the excellent person whom I have named, and Pierre Viret; but matters were not yet brought to a settled state and the city was divided into unholy and dangerous factions. Then an individual who now basely apostatized and returned to the Papists, discovered me and made me known to others. Upon this, Farel, who burned with an extraordinary zeal to advance the Gospel, immediately strained every nerve to detain me. And after having learned that my heart was set upon devoting myself to private studies, for which I wished to keep myself from other pursuits, and finding that he gained nothing by entreaties, he proceeded to utter an imprecation that God would curse my retirement, and the tranquillity of the studies which I sought, if I should withdraw and refuse to give assistance, when the necessity was so urgent. By this imprecation I was so stricken with terror that I desisted from the journey which I had undertaken.

Commentaries, Psalms, pp. xlii–xliii (*CR* 59, 23–25).

▶   **On 5th September 1536 the minutes of the Genevan City Council made the first mention of Calvin.**

Master Guil. Farel points out how necessary the lecture is which that Frenchman began in St Peter's. He also petitioned that he be retained and supported. Concerning this he was advised that his support would be considered.

CR 49, 204.

▶   **So Calvin began his work in Geneva.**

Endeavouring afterwards, with Farel and Coral, to settle the affairs of the Church—most of his colleagues, from timidity, keeping aloof from the contest, and some of them (this gave Calvin the greatest uneasiness) even secretly impeding the work of the Lord—his first object was to obtain from the citizens, at a meeting attended by the whole body of the people, an open abjuration of the Papacy, and an oath of adherence to the Christian religion and its discipline, as comprehended under a few heads. Although not a few refused, as might have been expected in a city which had just been delivered from the snares of the Duke of Savoy, and the yoke of Antichrist, and in which factions still greatly prevailed, yet by the good hand of the Lord, on the 20th of July 1537 (the clerk of the city taking the lead), the senate and people of Geneva solemnly declared their adherence to the leading doctrines and discipline of the Christian religion.

Theodore Beza, *Life of Calvin*, pp. lxvii–lxviii (*CR* 49, 126).

▶ In January 1537 Calvin and Farel submitted a proposal for the administration[8] of church affairs to the Geneva City Council.[9]

Our Lord established excommunication as a means of correction and discipline, by which those who lead a disorderly life unworthy of a Christian, and who despise to mend their ways and return to the strait way after they have been admonished, are expelled from the body of the Church and cut off as rotten members until they come to themselves and acknowledge their fault. . . . We have an example given by St Paul (I Timothy 1 and I Cor. 5), in a solemn warning that we should not keep company with one who is called a Christian, but who is, none the less, a fornicator, covetous, an idolator, a railer, a drunkard, or an extortioner. So if there be in us any fear of God, this ordinance should be enforced in our Church.

To accomplish this we have determined to petition you to establish and choose, according to your good pleasure, certain persons of upright life and good repute among all the faithful, likewise constant and not easy to corrupt, who shall be assigned and distributed in all parts of the town and have an eye on the life and conduct of every individual. If one of these sees any obvious vice which should be reprehended, it shall be brought to the attention of one of the ministers, who will admonish the one at fault and exhort him in a brotherly way to correct his ways. If it is apparent that such remonstrances do no good, he shall be warned that his obstinacy will be reported to the Church. . . . If he will not listen to warnings, it shall be time for the minister to declare publicly to the congregation the efforts which have been made to bring the sinner to amend, and how all has been in vain.

Should it appear that he proposes to persevere in his hardness of heart, it shall be time to excommunicate him. The offender shall be regarded as cast out from the companionship of Christians and left in the power of the devil for his temporal confusion, until he shall give good proofs of penitence and amendment. In sign of his casting out he shall be excluded from communion, and the faithful shall be forbidden to converse with him. Nevertheless he shall not omit to attend the sermons in order to receive instruction, so that it may be seen whether it shall please the Lord to turn his heart to the right way.

The offences to be corrected in this manner are those named by St Paul above, and others like them. When others than the said elders—for example, neighbours or relatives—have first knowledge of such offences, they may make the necessary remonstrances themselves. If they accomplish nothing, they shall notify the elders to do their duty.

This, then, is the manner in which it would seem expedient to us to introduce excommunication into our Church and maintain it in its full force; for beyond this form of correction the Church does not go. But should there be insolent persons, abandoned to all perversity, who only laugh when they are excommunicated and do not mind living and dying in that condition of rejection, it shall be your affair to determine whether you should long suffer such contempt and mocking of God to pass unpunished. . . .

If those who agree with us in faith are punished by excommunication for their offences, how much more should the Church refuse to tolerate those who oppose us? We wish to petition you to require all the inhabitants of your city to make a confession and give an account of their faith, so that you may know who agree with the Gospel and who, on the contrary, prefer the kingdom of the Pope to the kingdom of Jesus Christ.

CR 10, 1, 9f.

▶   **The temporary conclusion of the matter, two years later, is described with characteristic restraint by Calvin himself.**

Being, as I acknowledge, naturally of a timid, soft and pusillanimous disposition, I was compelled to encounter these violent tempests as part of my early training; and although I did not sink under them, yet I was not sustained by such greatness of mind, as not to rejoice more than it became me, when, in consequence of certain commotions, I was banished from Geneva.

Commentaries, Psalms, p. xliii (*CR* 59, 25).

▶   **The cause of conflict was the claim of the City Council to order ecclesiastical affairs in the city. The minutes of the council report the following:**

A letter was received from Bern concerning the observance of Communion at Lausanne with the inquiry if we want to observe the ceremony as contained therein. This has been decided to be so observed by the Great Council. If there are no objections, it is proposed that said letter is shown to the ministers Farel and Calvin and read to them with the question if they want to observe said ceremonies or not, giving them time to respond. It was resolved that the form of said letter, particularly as it pertains to Communion, should be followed. The ministers have asked that under no circumstances innovations should take place before Whitsuntide and that between now and then it should be observed as at Zürich and Strassburg. . . .

It was resolved that Communion [on 21st April, Easter] should be observed, if possible, according to the form of said letter [from Bern]. The ministers Calvin and Farel are to be asked if they will preach according to the form proposed to them today in the letter of Bern. If not, to send for the two ministers whom the Bailiff of Ternier has suggested to us. . . . Le Soultier returns from Farel and Calvin and reports that they do not want to preach or celebrate Communion according to said letter.

CR 49, 223-4.

▶ The stay at Strassburg[10] was to afford Calvin solitude and time for studies. It was to come differently. Here are Calvin's words:

By this means set at liberty and loosed from the tie of my vocation, I resolved to live in a private station, free from the burden and cares of any public charge, when that most excellent servant of Christ, Martin Bucer, employing a similar kind of remonstrance and protestation as that to which Farel had recourse before, drew me back to a new station. Alarmed by the example of Jonah which he set before me, I still continued in the work of teaching. And although I always continued like myself, studiously avoiding celebrity, yet I was carried, I know not how, as it were by force to the Imperial assemblies, where, willing or unwilling, I was under the necessity of appearing before the eyes of many.

Commentaries, Psalms, p. lxiii (*CR* 59, 25-27).

▶ Among others, Calvin met and conversed with Melanchthon.

I had much conversation with Philipp [Melanchthon] about many things, having written to him beforehand on the subject of agreement, that I might with certainty declare their opinion to several worthy men. Therefore, I had submitted a few articles, in which the whole matter was summed up. To these, without any controversy, he himself at once assented, but confessed that there were in that party some persons who required something more gross and palpable, and that with so great obstinacy, not to say despotism, that for long he seemed to be in actual jeopardy, because they saw that he differed from them in opinion. But although he does not think that a solid agreement can be come to, he, nevertheless, wishes that the present concord, such as it is, may be cherished, until at length the Lord shall lead both sides into the unity of his own truth. As for himself, you need not doubt about him, but consider that he is entirely of the same opinion as ourselves. It would be tiresome to relate what conversation we had about other matters; but this will form the subject of pleasant discourse some time or other between ourselves. As for discipline, like other people, he heartily deplores the want of it. Indeed, one is more at liberty to lament the wretched state of the Church in this respect than to correct the evil; do not, therefore, suppose that you suffer alone in this matter. Instances occur daily everywhere which ought to make everyone bestir himself in the endeavour to find out the desired remedy. Not very long since, a learned and worthy man was driven away from Ulm with great disgrace, because he would not consent to wink at the vices of the inhabitants any more. He was sent away by all his colleagues with honourable recommendation, especially that of Frecht.

March 1539. *Letters* I, pp. 129–30 (*CR* 38, No. 164).

Of late, I have plainly told Philipp to his face how much I disliked that overabounding of ceremonies; indeed, that it seemed to me the form which they observe was not far removed from Judaism. When I pressed him with argument, he was unwilling to dispute with me about the matter, but admitted that there was an overdoing in these either trifling or superfluous rites and ceremonies. He said, however, that it had been found necessary to yield in that matter to the Canonists, who are here the stumbling-block in the way; that, however, there was no part of Saxony which is not more burdened with them than Wittenberg, and even there much would be retrenched by degrees from such a medley. But he made a small reservation, to the effect that the ceremonies which they had been compelled to retain were not more approved of by Luther than was our sparing use of them.

April 1539. *Letters* I, pp. 136–7 (*CR* 38, No. 169).

▶   **But there was also time for more mundane matters.**

Concerning the marriage[11] I shall now speak more plainly. Previous to the departure of Michael, I do not know whether anyone made mention of that person concerning whom I wrote. But always keep in mind what I seek to find in her; for I am none of those insane lovers who embrace also the vices of those they are in love with, where they are smitten at first sight with a fine figure. This only is the beauty which allures me, if she is chaste, if not too nice or fastidious, if economical, if patient, if there is hope that she will be interested in my health; therefore, if you think well of it, set out immediately, in case someone else get beforehand with you. But if you think otherwise, we may let that pass. After this, I shall not write again until you come.

19th May 1539. *Letters* I, p. 141 (*CR* 39, No. 172).

Nevertheless, in the midst of such commotions as these, I was so much at my ease as to have the audacity to think of taking a wife. A certain damsel of noble rank has been proposed to me, and with a fortune above my condition. Two considerations deterred me from that connection— because she did not understand our language, and because I feared she might be too mindful of her family and education. Her brother, a very devout person, urged the connection, and on no other account than that, blinded by his affection to me, he neglected his own interests. His wife also, with a like partiality, contended, as he did, so that I would have been prevailed upon to submit with a good grace, unless the Lord had otherwise appointed. When, thereupon, I replied that I could not engage myself unless the maiden would undertake that she would apply her mind to the learning of our language, she requested time for deliberation. Thereupon, without further parley, I sent my brother, with a certain respectable man, to escort hither another, who, if she answers her repute, will bring a dowry large enough, without any money at all. Indeed, she is mightily commended by those who are acquainted with her. If it come to pass, as we may certainly hope will be the case, the marriage ceremony will not be delayed beyond the tenth of March. I wish you might then be present, that you may bless our wedlock.

6th February 1540. *Letters* I, pp. 173–4 (*CR* 39, No. 206).

▶   **In the spring of 1540 Calvin was asked to return to Geneva. The official invitation read as follows:**

Our good brother and special friend:

We commend ourselves most affectionately to you. Because we know that you desire nothing but the increase and advancement of the glory and honour of God and his Holy Word, we ask you, on behalf of the Little, Grand and General Council, that you will move to us and return to your former place and ministry. With the help of God this will be, we hope, a great good and advantage to the furtherance of the holy Gospel. Be assured that our people greatly desire you. We will treat you in such a way that you will have occasion to be pleased.

Herminjard, *Correspondance des Réformateurs*, VI, No. 900.

▶   **Calvin was reluctant and fearful.**

Michael, also, the printer, has communicated to me at Blecheret, that my return thitherward might be brought about; but rather would I submit to death a hundred times than to that cross, on which one had to perish daily a thousand times over. This piece of information I have wished incidentally to communicate to you, that to the utmost of your power you may set yourself to oppose the measures of those who shall endeavour to draw me back thither.

> 29th March 1540. *Letters* I, p. 175 (*CR* 39, No. 214).

I read that passage of your letter, certainly not without a smile, where you show so much concern about my health, and recommend Geneva on that ground. Why could you not have said at the cross? for it would have been far preferable to perish once for all than to be tormented again in that place of torture. Therefore, my dear Viret, if you wish well to me, make no mention of such a proposal.

> 19th May 1540. *Letters* I, p. 187 (*CR* 39, No. 217).

▶   **In an initial reply to Geneva, Calvin pointed to his responsibilities at Strassburg.**

I reply, I can testify before God that I hold your Church in such consideration that I would never be wanting in her time of need to do whatsoever I could for her help. Furthermore, I have no doubt whatever but that she must be very desolate, and also in danger of being broken up and scattered besides, if that has not happened already. And on this account I am in singular perplexity, having the desire to meet your wish, and to wrestle with all the grace that God has given me, to get her brought back into a better condition, while, on the other hand, I cannot slightingly quit the charge or lay it down lightly, to which the Lord has called me, without being relieved of it by regular and lawful means; for so I have always believed and taught, and to the present moment cannot persuade myself to the contrary, that when our Lord appoints a man as pastor in a church to teach in his word, he ought to consider himself as engaged to take upon himself the government of it, so that he may not lightly withdraw from it without the settled assurance in his own heart, and the testimony of the faithful, that the Lord has discharged him.

> 23rd October 1540. *Letters* I, 209 (*CR* 39, No. 246).

▶   **After several refusals, Calvin finally agreed to come back.**

The city began to long for its Farel and its Calvin. As there seemed very little hope of getting back Farel from Neuchâtel, the State turns its whole attention to Calvin, and employing the mediation of Zürich, sends an embassy to Strassburg to obtain the consent of the inhabitants to his return. These expressed great reluctance to part with him. Calvin himself, although the injuries which he had received at the instigation of certain wicked men had made no change upon his affection for the Genevese, yet having an aversion to disturbances, and seeing that the Lord had blessed his ministry in the Church of Strassburg, stated plainly that he would not return. Bucer, also, and others, declared that they would have the greatest objection to part with him. The Genevese, however, persisting, Bucer came to be of opinion that their prayers should be complied with; but he never would have obtained Calvin's consent, had he not given warning of divine judgment, and appealed to the example of Jonah.

Theodore Beza, Life of Calvin, p. lxxv (CR 49, 130–1).

▶ **Afterwards, Calvin reflected on his decision.**

Afterwards, when the Lord having compassion on this city, had allayed the hurtful agitations and broils which prevailed in it, and by his wonderful power had defeated both the wicked counsels and the sanguinary attempts of the disturbers of the Republic, necessity was imposed upon me of returning to my former charge, contrary to my desire and inclination. The welfare of this Church, it is true, lay so near my heart, that for its sake I would not have hesitated to lay down my life; but my timidity nevertheless suggested to me many reasons for excusing myself from again willingly taking upon my shoulders so heavy a burden. At length, however, a solemn and conscientious regard to my duty prevailed with me to consent to return to the flock from which I had been torn; but with what grief, tears, great anxiety and distress I did this, the Lord is my best witness, and many godly persons who would have wished to see me delivered from this painful state, had it not been that that which I feared, and which made me give my consent, prevented them and shut their mouths.

Commentaries, Psalms, pp. xliii–xliv (CR 59, 25–27).

▶ **On 13th September 1541 Calvin arrived in Geneva. The council minutes record the following:**

Calvin, having arrived from Strassburg, presented himself to the Council, to whom he brought letters from the Magistrates and Ministers of Strassburg. He excused himself on account of his journey having been delayed. He represented that it would be necessary to set about the work of ecclesiastical ordinances. Resolved, that they would apply themselves to it immediately, and for that purpose appointed, along with Calvin, Claude Pertemps, Amy Perrin, Claude Roset, Jean Lambert, Poralis, and Jean Balard. Resolved also to retain for Calvin twelve measures of corn, and two tuns of wine.

CR 49, 282.

▶   **Three days later Calvin wrote to Farel.**

Immediately after I had offered my services to the Senate, I declared that a Church could not hold together unless a settled government should be agreed on, such as is prescribed to us in the word of God, and such as was in use in the ancient Church. Then I touched gently on certain points from which they might understand what my wish was. But because the whole question of discipline was too large to be discussed in that form, I requested that they would appoint certain of their number, who might confer with us on the subject. Six were thereupon appointed. Articles concerning the whole ecclesiastical polity will be drawn up, which we shall thereafter present to the Senate.

16th September 1541. *Letters* I, 284–5 (*CR* 39, No. 355).

▶   **One of the conditions for Calvin's return to Geneva had been the drawing up of a church order for the city.**

Calvin being thus restored at the urgent entreaty of his Church, proceeded to set it in order. Seeing that the city stood greatly in need of a curb, he declared, in the first place, that he could not properly fulfil his ministry, unless, along with Christian doctrine, a regular presbytery with full ecclesiastical authority were established. At that time, therefore . . . laws for the election of a presbytery, and for the due maintenance of that order, were passed, agreeably to the Word of God, and with the consent of the citizens themselves. These laws Satan afterwards made many extraordinary attempts to abolish, but without success. Calvin also wrote a Catechism in French and Latin, not at all differing in substance from the former one, but much enlarged, and in the form of question and answer.

Theodore Beza, *Life of Calvin*, p. lxxvi (*CR* 49, 131–2).

▶   **The 'Ecclesiastical Ordinances' ordered the affairs of the Genevan Church and, what is more, the life of the city.**[12]

In the name of God Almighty, we Syndics, Little and Grand Council, together with our people assembled at the sound of the trumpet and great bell, according to our ancient custom, having determined that the matter is worthy of recommendation above all others, that the doctrine of the holy Gospel of our Lord may be well preserved in its purity, and the Christian Church duly maintained, that the young may be faithfully instructed for the future, the hospital well run in good order for the sustentation of the poor, which cannot be done except there be a strict rule and regulations by which each one shall understand the duties of his office; for these reasons it has seemed good to us that the spiritual government which our Lord taught and instituted by his Word, be observed among us. And thus we have ordered and decreed that in our city and territories the regulations which follow shall be observed and kept, inasmuch as it seems to us that they are taken from the Gospel of Jesus Christ.

To begin with there are four sorts of offices that our Lord instituted for the government of his Church.

That is to say, first pastors, then teachers, after which elders and, in the fourth place, deacons. . . .

With respect to the pastors, whom the Scriptures variously designate supervisors, elders and ministers, it is their duty to proclaim the Word of God so as to indoctrinate, admonish, exhort and reprimand both publicly and privately; to administer the sacraments and exercise fraternal discipline with the elders and commissioners. . . .

The examination (of the ministerial candidate) should consist of two parts, the first of these dealing with doctrine, to see if the candidate possesses a good and sound knowledge of the Scriptures. And then, whether he can fittingly and properly communicate the same to the people unto edification.

Moreover, to make certain that the candidate does not hold to any harmful opinions, it will be well to have him swear that he accepts and follows the doctrines approved by the Church. . . .

The second part touches his life, whether he possesses good manners and always conducts himself so as to remain above reproach in conduct. The rule to follow is that one which was so well outlined by St Paul. By this rule we must abide. . . .

In order to maintain purity and harmony of doctrine among themselves, it will be expedient for all the ministers to gather on a convenient day each week to study together the Scriptures. From this meeting none shall be excused without a good reason. If any shall be negligent in this matter, let him be admonished. . . .

If any differences in doctrine shall appear, the ministers shall assemble to discuss the matter. If it should seem expedient, it shall be their duty to call in elders commissioned by the authorities to assist in settling the dispute. Finally, if they cannot reach an agreement, due to the obstinacy of one of the parties concerned, the matter shall be placed before the magistrates for final decision.

To avoid scandalous deportment, it will be well to have regulations drawn governing the ministry, similar to those set forth below, which shall be equally the means by which the ministry shall be kept in reverence

and the Word of God be not dishonoured by the evil reputation or mis-
conduct of ministers. . . .

But first it should be noted that some crimes are always intolerable in
a minister; and that, on the other hand, there are vices which may be
forgiven if the person involved submits to fraternal admonitions. The
first are:

Heresy.
Schism.
Rebellion against ecclesiastical authority.
Blasphemy of a nature sufficiently serious to merit civil punishment.
Simony and any corruption in benefices.
Intrigue against a brother minister.
Deserting a church without proper permission or sufficient excuse.
Insincerity.
Perjury.
Lewdness.
Larceny.
Drunkenness.
Assault of a nature sufficiently serious to warrant punishment by law.
Usury.
Forbidden or scandalous amusements.
Dancing and like dissolute behaviour.
Crimes against civil law.
Any wrong that in another would merit excommunication.

The second are:

Perverting the content of Scripture, so that it scandalizes.
Fruitless preoccupation with vain questions.
Introducing unapproved doctrines or ceremonies into the Church.
Negligence in the study and especially in the reading of the holy
Scriptures.
Negligence in reproving evil; susceptibility to flattery.
Negligence in any of the obligations pertaining to his office.
Vulgarity.
Lying.
Slander.
Careless speech.
Injurious speech.
Indiscretion or chicanery.
Avarice and penuriousness.

Unreasoning anger.

Quarrelsomeness and fomenting disharmony.

Indecent dissoluteness in a minister, as much in dress as in actions and manners.

When someone is accused of a crime that cannot be ignored, if these are civil offences, that is to say, those which should be punished by law, and a minister shall fall therein, let the authorities lay hand on him and besides the common punishment meted out to others, let them punish him by deposing him from his office.

As for other offences concerning which the first investigation belongs to the ecclesiastical assembly, let the commissioners or elders together with the ministers attend to it. . . .

Of the Frequency, Place and Time of Preaching

Each Sunday, at daybreak, let there be a sermon in St Peter's and St Gervaise's, and at the usual hour at the aforesaid St Peter, Magdalene, and St Gervaise. At three o'clock, as well, in all three parishes, the second sermon.

For purposes of catechetical instruction and the administration of the sacraments, as much as possible let the bounds of the parishes be observed. That is, let St Gervaise be used by those who have used it in the past; likewise with Magdalene. . . .

On work days, besides the two sermons mentioned, let there be preaching three times each week, viz. on Monday, Wednesday and Friday, and that these sermons be announced for an hour early enough so that they may be finished before the day's work begins. If a special day of prayer be appointed, the Sunday order is to be observed. . . .

Next, of the Second Order, which We have Called Teachers

The proper duty of teachers is to instruct the faithful in sound doctrine, in order that the purity of the Gospel may not be corrupted, either by ignorance or evil opinions. Nevertheless, as matters now stand, we include in this title the aids and instructions necessary to preserve divine doctrine and keep the Church from becoming desolate for lack of pastors and ministers. So, to use a more familiar expression, we shall call this section regulations for the schools.

The order nearest to the ministry and most closely associated with the government of the Church is that of lecturer in theology, in which office it shall be well to include the teaching of the Old and New Testaments.

But since it is impossible to profit by such instruction without first being instructed in languages and in the humanities, and also since there is need to raise up seed against the future in order that the Church may not be deserted by our children, it will be necessary to establish a school to instruct them, to prepare them not only for the ministry but for civil government.

To begin with, it will be necessary to designate a proper place for teaching purposes, fit to accommodate children and others as well who wish to profit by instruction; to secure someone who is both learned in subject matter and capable of looking after the building (who can also read), employ him and place him under contract on condition that he provide lecturers both in languages and in dialectics, if possible. . . .

NEXT, THE THIRD ORDER, WHICH IS THAT OF ELDERS, that is, those commissioned or appointed to the Consistory by the authorities.

Their office is to keep watch over the lives of everyone, to admonish in love those whom they see erring and leading disorderly lives and, whenever necessary, to report them to the body which will be designated to make fraternal corrections—joining with the others in making such corrections.

If the Church deems it wise, elections may be made on the following basis: two from the Little Council, four from the Council of Sixty, and six from the Council of Two Hundred, honest men of exemplary life, without reproach and free from all suspicion, above all fearing God and possessed of good, spiritual judgment. And it will be well to elect them from every part of the city so as to maintain supervision over all. . . .

THE FOURTH ORDER OF ECCLESIASTICAL GOVERNMENT, OR THE DEACONS

There were always two orders of deacons in the ancient Church, the one being charged with receiving, distributing and guarding the goods of the poor, their possessions, income and pensions as well as the daily offerings; the other, to take watch and ward of the sick and administer the pittance for the poor. And this custom we have preserved to the present. And, in order to avoid confusion, for we have both stewards and managers, let one of the four stewards of the aforesaid hospital act as receiver of all its goods and let him receive adequate remuneration in order that he may better exercise his office. . . .

THE VISITATION OF THE SICK

Because some neglect to find consolation in the Word of God in times of sickness and, as a consequence, have died without admonition or instruction in doctrine (which is for man more salutary at such times than at others), it will be well and for this cause we advise and order that no one shall remain sick abed longer than three days before notifying the ministers. Anyone shall be free to call the ministers whenever he desires; provided it be at an opportune time, in order that they may not be unreasonably interrupted in their duties on behalf of the common welfare of the Church; and to foil every excuse we have resolved that it be so. And, above all, parents, friends and guardians must not wait until the person is at the point of death, for in such extremity solace avails but little. . . .

GENERAL ORDINANCES REGARDING PROPER ORDER IN THE CHURCH

The aforesaid commissioners shall assemble together with the ministers once each week, viz. on Thursday morning, to ascertain if there be any disorder in the Church and to deal in assembly with whatever remedies may be needed. . . .

NEXT, OF THE PERSONS WHOM THE ELDERS SHOULD ADMONISH AND HOW THEY SHOULD PROCEED

If anyone shall lay down opinions contrary to received doctrine, he shall be summoned to appear. If he recant, he shall be dismissed without prejudice. If he is stubborn, he shall be admonished from time to time until it shall be evident that he deserves greater severity. Then, he shall be excommunicated and let this action be reported to the magistrate.

If anyone is negligent in attending worship to such an extent that a noticeable contempt is evident for the communion of the faithful, or if anyone shows himself contemptuous of ecclesiastical discipline, he shall be admonished and, if he becomes obedient, he shall be dismissed in love. If he persists, passing from bad to worse, after having been admonished three times, he shall be excommunicated and the matter shall be reported to the authorities.

For the correction of faults within the life of anyone, it is necessary to proceed after the ordinance of our Lord. That is, secret vices shall be dealt with secretly and no one shall be brought before the Church for accusation if the fault is neither public nor scandalous, unless he has been found rebellious in the matter.

For the rest, those who scorn private admonitions shall be admonished again this time by the Church and, if they will not come to reason nor recognize their error, when they are convicted they shall be ordered to abstain from Communion until they improve their attitude.

As for obvious and public evil, which the Church cannot overlook: if the faults merit no more than admonition, the duty of the commission of elders shall be to summon those concerned, remonstrate with them in love in order that they may be reformed and, if they correct the fault, to dismiss the matter. If they persevere in evil doing, they shall be admonished again. And if, in the end, such action proves unprofitable, they shall be denounced as contemptuous of God and ordered to abstain from Communion until it is evident that they have changed their way of life.

As for crimes that merit not only admonition but punitive correction: Anyone who falls into such error, according to the requirements of the case, shall be commanded to abstain from Communion in order that he may humble himself before God and better repent of his error. . . .

Nevertheless, all these measures shall be applied in moderation. There shall not be such a degree of rigour that anyone will be cast down—for all corrections are but medicinal, to bring back sinners to our Lord. . . .

These ordinances shall be binding, not only within the city, but also upon those villages under the jurisdiction of the authorities.

Ordonnances Ecclésiastiques: CR 38, 5ff.

▶   **The villages under the jurisdiction of Geneva received likewise a new order for ecclesiastical affairs.[13]**

The whole household shall attend the sermons on Sunday, except those left at home to tend the children or cattle.

If there is preaching on weekdays, all who can must come—unless there be some good excuse—so that at least one from each household is present. Those who have men-servants or maid-servants shall bring them whenever possible, so that they shall not live like animals without instruction. . . . Anyone coming after the sermon has begun is to be warned. If he does not amend, he is to pay a fine of three sous. The churches should be locked except for service, so that no one may enter at other hours from superstitious motives. Anyone who is discovered engaging in some superstition within or near the church is to be admonished. If he will not give up his superstition, he is to be punished.

Those who are found to have rosaries or idols to adore are to be sent before the Consistory. In addition to being reproved they are to be sent before the council. The same applies for those who go on a pilgrimage. Those who observe feasts or papal fasts shall only be admonished. Those who go to mass shall, besides being admonished, be sent before the council, which will consider the punishment of the offenders by imprisonment or special fines, as it judges best.

Those contradicting the Word of God shall be sent before the consistory for reproof, or before the council for punishment, as the case may require.

No one shall invite another to drink under penalty of three sous.

Taverns shall be closed during the sermon, under penalty that the tavern-keeper shall pay three sous, and whoever may be found therein shall pay the same amount.

If anyone be found intoxicated he shall pay for the first offence three sous and shall be remanded to the Consistory; for the second offence he shall be held to pay the sum of six sous, and for the third ten sous and be put in prison. . . .

Anyone singing indecent, licentious songs, or dancing *en virollet* or otherwise, shall be kept in prison three days and then sent to the council.

Ordonnances sur la police des églises de la campagne: CR 38, 51ff.

▶   The official records indicate the nature of the work of the Consistory. Here are some excerpts:[14]

Jean Ballard was interrogated why he refused to hear the word of God. He replied that he believed in God, who taught him by his spirit. He could not believe our preachers. He said that we could not compel the sermon against his conscience. . . . We admonished him that he should within three days obey the proclamation or show just cause why he should not. He replied, 'I wish to live according to the gospel of God, but I do not wish to adopt the interpretation of certain individuals, but to follow that of the Holy Spirit through the holy mother Church universal in which I believe.' Asked to say wether he would go to the sermon, he replied that his conscience would not permit him to go, and that he would not act against his dictates; for it was directed by a higher authority than that of preachers. Having heard these things, the council ordered that if he did not obey and go to the sermon as established, he and his family should leave the city within ten days.

24th July 1536. *CR* 49, 203.

Antoine Simon, artisan of Vienne, lives near the bridge of the Rhone. Is asked if he is married and has children. He answers that he is married and has one child. Is asked if he hears the sermons. He answers that he hears them whenever he can. His son is not yet three years of age and cannot understand too well. Is questioned about his faith and belief. He answers that he does not understand very well. Was able to recite the Lord's Prayer, but not the Confession. . . . Is given proper admonition to attend sermons more frequently and to take steps to be instructed in the Confession. . . .

16th March 1542. *CR* 49, 292.

Donna Jane Peterman is questioned concerning her faith and why she does not receive communion and attend worship. She confesses her faith and believes in one God and wants to come to God and the holy Church and has no other faith. She recited the Lord's Prayer in the vernacular. She said that she believes what the Church believes. Is questioned why she never participates in communion when it is celebrated in this town, but goes to other places. She answers that she goes where it seems good to her. Is placed outside the faith. . . .

4th April 1542. CR 49, 293–4.

The sister of Sr Curtet, Lucresse, to whom remonstrances have been made on account of her going with certain monies to have masses said at Nessy by the monks of St Claire. Questioned whether she has no scruples as to what she says. Replied that her father and mother have brought her up to obey a different law from the one now in force here. However, she does not despise the present law. Asked as to when was the festival of St Felix, she replied that it was yesterday. Asked if she had not fasted, she replied that she fasted when it pleased her. Asked if she did not desire to pray to a single God; said that she did. Asked if she did not pray to St Felix; said that she prayed to St Felix and other saints who interceded for her. She is very obstinate. Decision that she be sent to some minister of her choice every sermon day and that the Lord's Supper be withheld from her. Calvin present.

31st August 1546. CR 49, 387.

▶   For more than a decade Calvin experienced trying difficulties in his attempt to mould the Church in Geneva. In retrospect he wrote as follows:

Were I to narrate the various conflicts by which the Lord has exercised me since that time, and by what trials he has proved me, it would make a long history. But that I may not become tedious to my readers by a waste of words, I shall content myself . . . that I have been assailed on all sides, and have scarcely been able to enjoy repose for a single moment, but have always had to sustain some conflict either from enemies without or within the Church. Satan has made many attempts to overthrow the fabric of this Church; and once it came to this, that I, altogether feeble and timorous as I am, was compelled to break and put a stop to his deadly assaults by putting my life in danger, and opposing my person to his blows. Afterwards, for the space of five years, when some wicked libertines were furnished with undue influence, and also some of the common people, corrupted by the allurements and perverse discourse of such persons, desired to obtain the liberty of doing whatever they pleased, without control, I was under the necessity of fighting without ceasing to defend and maintain the discipline of the Church. To these irreligious characters and despisers of the heavenly doctrine, it was a matter of entire indifference, although the Church should sink into ruin, provided they obtained what they sought—the power of acting just as they pleased. Many, too, harassed by poverty and hunger, and others impelled by insatiable ambition or avarice and a desire of dishonest gain, were become so frantic that they chose rather, by throwing all things into confusion, to involve themselves and us in one common ruin, than to remain quiet by living peaceably and honestly. During the whole of this lengthened period I think that there is scarcely any of the weapons which are forged in the workshop of Satan which has not been employed by them in order to obtain their object. And at length matters had come to such a state that an end could be put to their machinations in no other way than cutting them off by an ignominious death; which was indeed a painful and pitiable spectacle to me. They no doubt deserved the severest punishment, but I always rather desired that they might live in prosperity, and continue safe and untouched; which would have been the case had they not been altogether incorrigible, and obstinately refused to listen to wholesome admonition.

The trial of these five years was grievous and hard to bear; but I experienced not less excruciating pain from the malignity of those who ceased not to assail myself and my ministry with their envenomed calumnies. A great proportion of them, it is true, are so blinded by a passion for slander and detraction that, to their great disgrace, they betray at once their imprudence, while others, however crafty and cunning, cannot so cover or disguise themselves as to escape being shamefully convicted and disgraced.

But sensible of my natural bashfulness and timidity, I would not bring myself under obligation to discharge any particular office. After that, four months had scarcely elapsed, when, on the one hand, the Anabaptists began to assail us, and, on the other, a certain wicked apostate, who being secretly supported by the influence of some of the magistrates of the city, was thus enabled to give us a great deal of trouble. At the same time, a succession of dissensions fell out in the city which strangely afflicted us.

Commentaries, Psalms, p. xliv (*CR* 59, 27–29).

▶   **The following poster was found appended in July 1555 to the corpses of previously executed people near Geneva. It shows well the anti-Calvin sentiment:**

1555—The Works of Calvin

Wanderer, reflect on the evil accomplished by Calvin

Who, deprived of L and V, presents himself as a second CAIN.
Take out one L, which so imprudently flies
Take out one open V: by all the evil of *Calvin*,
You know his violent rage.
Knowing him, you judge him *Cain*.

Hierosme Hermes Bolsec, *Histoire de la Vie . . . Jean Calvin*, p. 243.

▶   One of the major controversies in which Calvin found himself in-
     volved in 1542 was with Sebastian Castellio.[15] It began altogether
     insignificantly as Calvin pointed out in a letter.

Now listen to the freaks of our friend Sebastian, which may both raise
your bile and your laughter at the same time. The day before yesterday
he came to me, asked whether I could agree that his edition of the New
Testament should be published. I replied that there would be need of
many corrections. He inquired the reason why. I pointed them out to
him from those few chapters which he had already given me as a speci-
men. Thereupon he answered that he had been more careful in what
remained. Then he asked me over again what I thought as to the publication. I answered, that it was not my wish to hinder the publication; but
that I was ready, nevertheless, to perform the promise which I had made to
Jean Girard, that I would look it over and would correct, should there
appear to be anything that required to be corrected. This arrangement
he refused. He offered, however, to come and read it to me if I would fix
a time. This I refused to do, even were he to offer me a hundred crowns,
to bind myself to certain hours; moreover, that I would be obliged sometimes to dispute for a couple of hours, perhaps, over some little insignificant word. And so he left me, dissatisfied as appeared. That you may
understand how faithful an interpreter he is; while in many ways he wishes
to·change and innovate, in most things he corrupts the meaning. One
passage I may mention as an instance: where there occurs, 'The Spirit
of God which dwells in us', he has changed to 'haunts in us', when to
'haunt', in French, does not mean to 'dwell', but is used to signify to
'frequent'. One such boyish mistake may stamp a bad character upon the
book. Such unseasonable trifling as this I swallow, nevertheless, in
silence.

11th September 1542. *Letters* I, 350–1 (*CR* 39, No. 421).

▶   Two years later tensions between the two men broke out more
     openly. Again, Calvin reported in a letter.

On the other hand, our friend Sebastian has been raging against us
with the utmost violence. There were about sixty persons present yesterday

when the Scripture was being expounded. The passage under consideration was: 'Approving themselves as the ministers of God in all long-suffering', etc. He shrouded his attack under cover of a perpetual antithesis, in such a way as to show that we were in all respects the very opposite of what the ministers of Christ ought to be. It was much after this fashion that he played with the subject: That Paul had been the servant of God, we served ourselves; that he had been one of the most patient of men, we the most impatient; that he had been a night-watcher in order to lay himself out for the edification of the Church, but that we kept watch by playing ourselves; that Paul was sober, we were drunken; that he and the Christians of his time had been harassed and vested on account of seditions, while we made it our business to set them astir; that he was chaste, while we had been whoremongers; that the apostle had himself been shut up in prison, but we got people cooped up even for an offensive word; that he used only the power of God, while we had recourse to that of the magistrate; that he had suffered from the attack of others, while we made it our study to persecute the innocent. What more need I say? It was certainly altogether a bloody oration. At the time, I was quite mute, lest some greater strife might be kindled in the presence of so many strangers, but I laid a complaint before the Syndics. These were the ominous intimation of the commencement of all sorts of schism. It was not so much the perverse manner of his setting about the attack, and the wrong-headed obstinacy of his ill-minded malediction, that has moved me to undertake the repression of the man's restless and froward temper, as because he had slandered us by the falsest calumnies. You must now perceive the kind of straits and difficulties which so weigh me down.

31st May 1544. *Letters* I, 418–19 (*CR* 39, No. 554).

▶   Another manifestation of hostility against Calvin was the following handbill posted in Geneva by one Jacques Gruet on 27th June 1547. Gruet was arrested, tried and executed.

You puffed-up hypocrite! You and your colleague would do well to be quiet. Once you made us furious, nothing will keep you from being silenced. It seems to me that you will soon curse the hour in which you threw off your cowl. Long enough I reprimanded that the devil and all his cursed godless priests have come to damn us. Patience is now over; vengeance is near. Watch out that you won't share the fate of Master Werly of Fribourg. We do not want so many masters. Let this be said to you.

CR 40, 546.

▶   Calvin described the subsequent development in a letter.

A note was found in a pulpit. It threatened us with death if we would
not keep silent. I am sending you a copy. The council was perturbed by
such audacity and ordered a strict investigation of the conspiracy. The
task was turned over to a small committee. Since the suspicion of many fell
on Gruet, he was at once arrested. But it was not his handwriting. But
when his papers were examined, much was found of no less importance:
for example, a supplication, which he had intended to put before the
people at election time, that nothing should be punished by law unless it
actually endangered the commonwealth. Thus was the custom in Venice,
which was greatly experienced in the art of governing. There was indeed
danger that this city, submitting to the brainstorms of one melancholic
man, would lose in an insurrection a thousand citizens. There were also
found letters addressed partly to André Philipp, partly to others. In some
I was personally mentioned. In others images are used which, however,
indicate such a rude artificiality that one can easily know what he had
in mind. There was also found a two-page essay in Latin which ridicules
the entire Scripture, denounces Christ, calls the immortality of the soul
a dream and fable, in short which destroys our entire religion. I do not
believe that he is the author, but since it is in his handwriting he will have
to be responsible. It is, of course, possible that he put together what he
heard from others as he understood it for his diary. They are half-sentences
full of false expressions and idioms.

CR 40, 546–7.

▶   On 26th July 1547 sentence was passed against Gruet:

We Syndics and Judges of criminal matters of this city of Geneva,
having heard the case against you, Jacques Gruet, son of Humbert Gruet
of Geneva . . . find and hold that you have greatly offended and blasphemed God, transgressed against the Sacred Scriptures and also undertaken matters against the authorities, insulted, threatened and slandered
the servants of God and committed the crime of *lèse-majesté* requiring
bodily punishment. For this reason we have held court in the place of our
superiors. With God and his Sacred Scriptures before our eyes we say, in
the name of the Father, the Son and the Holy Spirit, Amen: . . . We condemn you, Jacques Gruet, to be taken to Champel and there have your
body attached to a stake and burned to ashes and so you shall finish your
days to give an example to others who would commit the like.

CR 40, 567f.

► The official minutes of the 'Venerable Company' also tell the intriguing story of Jerome Bolsec,[16] later to become—understandably enough—Calvin's bitter opponent.

15th May 1551:

On this day was called before the Company of the Brethren Mr Jerome Bolsec, M.D. He holds various wild notions concerning free will and predestination. He was emphatically corrected by Scripture passages. Said Jerome showed himself very obstinate until the passage from Ezekiel (18.23; 33.11) was read to him.

CR 49, 481.

16th October 1551:

Mr Jerome Bolsec began again, as before, to present his false propositions concerning election and reprobation, denying that these were *ab aeterno* and saying, with great protestation and exhortation, that one should know no other election or reprobation than that evidenced in faith or unbelief. And that those who know of an eternal will of God by which he has ordained some to life and others to death, make him a tyrant or an idol as the pagans made Jupiter: 'Thus I wish it, thus I order, may it happen according to the rationale of the will.' He says that this is heresy and that such doctrine brings great scandal, since one is made to believe that St Augustine was of this opinion, which was erroneous, as he would show. Moreover, several passages of Scripture had been perverted to support this false and perverse doctrine. . . . He added several other calumnies and blasphemings by which he showed well the poison he had hid in his heart, waiting for the hour of opportunity to vomit it into public.

CR 36, 144.

► On 23rd December came the sentence:

In accord with the deliberations held presently before us, aided by our lieutenant . . . against you Jerome Bolsec, of Paris, according to which and to your voluntary response . . . we find that you, Jerome Bolsec, have audaciously risen against the venerable company of our ministers and have proposed false opinion both against the Sacred Scriptures and the pure evangelical religion . . . by this definite sentence—we condemn you, Jerome Bolsec, that you are to be perpetually banned and we ban you for ever from this our city and territory.

CR 36, 247.

▶ **The end, at least temporarily, was this sentence in the minutes of the 'Venerable Company':**

On the 23rd day of this month [December] Mr Jerome was banned from the territory of Geneva.

CR 49, 498.

▶ **In the mid-forties Calvin engaged, for a short time, in a correspondence with Michael Servetus, who was then residing at Lyons. Both used pseudonyms, but neither was deceived as to the identity of the other. Calvin terminated the exchange of letters rather abruptly.**

By cause that your last letter was brought to me at my going away, I had not leisure to reply to what was inclosed therein. Since my return, at the first leisure that I have had, I have been quite willing to satisfy your desire; not that I have had great hope of late of being profitable to a certain person, judging from the disposition in which I see him to be; but in order to try once more if there shall be any means of bringing him back, which will be, when God shall have wrought in him so effectually, that he has become entirely another man. Since he has written to me in so proud a spirit, I would fain have beaten down his pride a little, speaking more harshly to him than is my wont; but I could scarcely do otherwise. For I do assure you that there is no lesson which is more necessary for him than to learn humility, which must come to him from the Spirit of God, not otherwise. But we must observe a measure here also. If God grants that favour to him and to us, that the present answer turns to his profit, I shall have whereof to rejoice. If he persists in the same style as he has now done, you will lose time in asking me to bestow labour upon him, for I have other affairs which press upon me more closely; and I would make a matter of conscience of it, not to busy myself further, having no doubt that it was a temptation of Satan to distract and withdraw me from other more useful reading. And therefore I beg you to content yourself with what I have done in the matter, unless you see some better order to be taken therein.

Wherefore, after my commendation to you, I beseech our good Lord to have you in his keeping.

Your servant and hearty friend,
CHARLES d'ESPEVILLE

13th February 1546. *Letters* II, 30–31 (*CR* 40, No. 766).

▶   To Farel, Calvin wrote at the same time these harsh words:

Servetus lately wrote to me, and coupled with his letter a long volume
of his delirious fancies, with the Thrasonic boast, that I should see something astonishing and unheard of. He takes it upon him to come hither,
if it be agreeable to me. But I am unwilling to pledge my word for his
safety, for if he shall come, I shall never permit him to depart alive, provided my authority be of any avail.

13th February 1546. *Letters* II, 33 (*CR* 40, No. 767).

▶   Calvin's concerns reached beyond Geneva—here he comforted
five young Protestants who were imprisoned by the Inquisition
in Lyons.

MY VERY DEAR BRETHREN,—Hitherto I have put off writing to
you, fearing that if the letter fell into bad hands, it might give fresh
occasion to the enemy to afflict you. And besides, I had been informed
how that God wrought so powerfully in you by his grace, that you stood
in no great need of my letters. However, we have not forgotten you,
neither I nor all the brethren hereabouts, as to whatever we have been
able to do for you. As soon as you were taken, we heard of it, and knew
how it had come to pass. We took care that help might be sent you with
all speed, and are now waiting the result. Those who have influence with
the prince in whose power God has put your lives are faithfully exerting
themselves on your behalf, but we do not yet know how far they have
succeeded in their suit. Meanwhile, all the children of God pray for you
as they are bound to do, not only on account of the mutual compassion
which ought to exist between members of the same body, but because
they know well that you labour for them, in maintaining the cause of their
salvation. We hope, come what may, that God of his goodness will give
a happy issue to your captivity, so that we shall have reason to rejoice.
You see to what he has called you; doubt not, therefore, that according
as he employs you, he will give you strength to fulfil his work, for he has
promised this, and we know by experience that he has never failed those
who allow themselves to be governed by him. Even now you have proof
of this in yourselves, for he has shown his power, by giving you so much
constancy in withstanding the first assaults. Be confident, therefore, that
he will not leave the work of his hand imperfect. You know what Scripture
sets before us, to encourage us to fight for the cause of the Son of God;
meditate upon what you have both heard and seen formerly on this head,
so as to put it into practice. For all that I could say would be of little service
to you, were it not drawn from this fountain. And truly we have need of

a much more firm support than that of men, to make us victorious over such strong enemies as the devil, death and the world; but the firmness which is in Christ Jesus is sufficient for this, and all else that might shake us were we not established in him. Knowing, then, in whom ye have believed, manifest what authority he deserves to have over you.

10th June 1552. *Letters* II, 350–1 (*CR* 42, No. 1631).

▶   In 1549 Idelette de Bure, Calvin's wife, died. In a letter the Genevan Reformer expressed his grief.

Although the death of my wife has been exceedingly painful to me, yet I subdue my grief as well as I can. Friends, also, are earnest in their duty to me. It might be wished, indeed, that they could profit me and themselves more; yet one can scarcely say how much I am supported by their attentions. But you know well enough how tender, or rather soft, my mind is. Had not a powerful self-control, therefore, been vouchsafed to me, I could not have borne up so long. And truly mine is no common source of grief. I have been bereaved of the best companion of my life, of one who, had it been so ordered, would not only have been the willing sharer of my indigence, but even of my death. During her life she was the faithful helper of my ministry. From her I never experienced the slightest hindrance. She was never troublesome to me throughout the entire course of her illness; she was more anxious about her children than about herself. As I feared these private cares might annoy her to no purpose, I took occasion, on the third day before her death, to mention that I would not fail in discharging my duty to her children. Taking up the matter immediately, she said, 'I have already committed them to God.' When I said that that was not to prevent me from caring for them, she replied, 'I know you will not neglect what you know has been committed to God.' Lately, also, when a certain woman insisted that she should talk with me regarding these matters, I, for the first time, heard her give the following brief answer: 'Assuredly the principal thing is that they live a pious and holy life. My husband is not to be urged to instruct them in religious knowledge and in the fear of God. If they be pious, I am sure he will gladly be a father to them; but if not, they do not deserve that I should ask for aught in their behalf.' This nobleness of mind will weigh more with me than a hundred recommendations. Many thanks for your friendly consolation. Adieu, most excellent and honest brother. May the Lord Jesus watch over and direct yourself and your wife. Present my best wishes to her and to the brethren.

7th April 1549. *Letters* II, 216–17 (*CR* 41, No. 1173).

▶ Calvin's message spread throughout Europe. The extent of its expansion into France can be seen from the following report of a Venetian ambassador in 1561.

Unless it otherwise pleases the Almighty, religious affairs will soon be in an evil case in France, because there is not one single province uncontaminated. Indeed in some provinces, such as Normandy, almost the whole of Britany, Touraine, Poitou, Gascony, and a great part of Languedoc, of Dauphiny, and of Provence, comprising three-fourths of the kingdom, congregations and meetings, which they call assemblies, are held; and in these assemblies they read and preach, according to the rites and uses of Geneva, without any respect either for the ministers of the King or the commandments of the King himself. This contagion has penetrated so deeply that it affects every class of persons, and, what appears more strange, even the ecclesiastical body itself. I do not mean only priests, friars and nuns, for there are but few monasteries that are not corrupted, but even bishops and many of the principal prelates, who hitherto had not shown any such disposition; and it is only on account of the rigorous execution of the law that other persons besides the populace have not disclosed themselves, because they have restrained themselves for the time being from fear of the loss of their property and lives. But your Serenity must learn that while the people and the populace show fervent devotion by frequenting the churches and observing the Catholic rites, all other classes are supposed to be disaffected, and the nobility perhaps more than any other class, and, particularly, persons of forty years of age and under. If these disaffected individuals continue to attend mass and the Divine offices, and externally to practise Catholic rites, they do so for show and from fear; because when they either are, or believe themselves to be, unobserved, they avoid and even fly from the mass above all things, and also from the churches as far as they are able, and more so since it became known that by imprisonment, chastisement and burnings, no remedy was found. It has now been determined not to proceed against any disaffected persons unless they venture to preach, persuade and to take part publicly in congregations and assemblies. All other such persons are allowed to live, and some have been set at liberty, and released from the prisons of Paris and of other parts of the kingdom. A great number of these last have still remained in the kingdom, preaching and speaking publicly, and boasting that they have gained their cause against the Papists, as they delight to style their adversaries; . . . Your Serenity will hardly believe the influence and the great power which the principal minister of Geneva, by name Calvin, a Frenchman, and a native of Picardy, possesses in this kingdom; he is a man of extraordinary authority, who by his mode of life, his doctrines and his writings rises superior to all the rest; and it is almost impossible to believe the enormous sums of money which are secretly sent to him from France to maintain his power. It is sufficient to add that if God does not interfere, there is great and imminent danger that one of two things will happen in this kingdom: either that the truce, which is desired and sought publicly, will end by the heretics having churches wherein they can preach, read and perform their rites, according to their doctrine, without hindrance, and in like manner as they obtained churches by command of the late King, given at Fontainebleau, at the end of August, in compliance with a petition presented to him . . . or, else, that we shall see an obedience to the Pope and to the Catholic rites enforced, and shall have resort to violence and imbrue our hands in noble blood. For these reasons I foresee a manifest and certain division in the kingdom, and civil war as a consequence; and this will be the cause of the ruin both of the kingdom and of religion, because upon a change in religion a change in the State necessarily follows.

Calendar of State Papers: Venetian VII, 322-3.

▶   **Calvin's first biographer, Beza, related the Reformer's final weeks as follows:**

The year 1564 was to him the commencement of perpetual felicity, and to us of the greatest and best-founded grief. On the 6th of February, the asthma impeding his utterance, he delivered his last sermon; and from that time, with the exception of his being sometimes carried to the meeting of the congregation, where he delivered a few sentences (the last occasion was on the last day of March), he entirely desisted from his office of preaching. His diseases, the effect of incredible exertions of body and mind, were various and complicated. . . . Besides being naturally of a feeble and spare body, inclining to consumption, he slept almost waking, and spent a great part of the year in preaching, lecturing and dictating. For at least ten years he never dined, taking no food at all till supper; so that it is wonderful he could have so long escaped consumption. . . . Partly also from overstraining his voice, and partly from the immoderate use of aloes, a circumstance not attended to till it was too late, he became afflicted with ulcerated haemorrhoids, and occasionally, for about five years before his death, discharged considerable quantities of blood. . . . While oppressed with so many diseases, no man ever heard him utter a word unbecoming a man of firmness, far less unbecoming a Christian.

Only raising his eyes towards heaven, he would say, 'O Lord, how long.'

Theodore Beza, *Life of Calvin*, pp. cxx–cxxi (*CR* 49, 160–1).

▶   **On 25th April 1564 Calvin dictated his Last Will and Testament.**

In the name of the Lord, Amen. I, John Calvin, minister of the Word of God in this Church of Geneva, being afflicted and oppressed with various diseases, which easily induce me to believe that the Lord God has determined shortly to call me away out of this world, have resolved to make my testament, and commit my last will to writing in the manner following: First of all, I give thanks to God, that taking mercy on me, whom he had created and placed in this world, he not only delivered me out of the deep darkness of idolatry in which I was plunged, that he might bring me into the light of his Gospel, and make me a partaker in the doctrine of salvation, of which I was most unworthy; and not only, with the same mercy and benignity, kindly and graciously bore with my faults and my sins, for which, however, I deserved to be rejected by him and exterminated, but also vouchsafed me such clemency and kindness that he has deigned to use my assistance in preaching and promulgating the truth of his Gospel. And I testify and declare that it is my intention to spend what yet remains of my life in the same faith and religion which he has delivered to me by his Gospel; and that I have no other defence or refuge for salvation than his gratuitous adoption, on which alone my salvation depends. With my whole soul I embrace the mercy which he has exercised towards me through Jesus Christ, atoning for my sins with the merits of his death and passion, that in this way he might satisfy for all my crimes and faults, and blot them from his remembrance. I testify also and declare, that I suppliantly beg of him that he may be pleased so to wash and purify me in the blood which my Sovereign Redeemer has shed for the sins of the human race, that under his shadow I may be able to stand at the judgment-seat. I likewise declare that, according to the measure of grace and goodness which the Lord hath employed towards me, I have endeavoured, both in my sermons and also in my writings and commentaries, to preach his Word purely and chastely, and faithfully to interpret his sacred Scriptures. I also testify and declare that, in all the contentions and disputations in which I have been engaged with the enemies of the Gospel, I have used no impostures, no wicked and sophistical devices, but have acted candidly and sincerely in defending the truth. But, woe is me! my ardour and zeal (if indeed worthy of the name) have been so careless and languid that I confess I have failed innumerable times to execute my office properly, and had not he, of his boundless

goodness, assisted me, all that zeal had been fleeting and vain. Nay, I
even acknowledge, that if the same goodness had not assisted me, those
mental endowments which the Lord bestowed upon me would, at his
judgment-seat, prove me more and more guilty of sin and sloth. For all
these reasons, I testify and declare that I trust to no other security for
my salvation than this, and this only, viz. that as God is the Father of
mercy, he will show himself such a Father to me, who acknowledge myself to be a miserable sinner. As to what remains, I wish that, after my
departure out of this life, my body be committed to the earth (after the
form and manner which is used in this Church and city), till the day of
happy resurrection arrive.

> Theodore Beza, *Life of Calvin*, pp. cxxi–cxxv (*CR* 49, 162–3).

▶ **Three days later, on 28th April 1564, Calvin asked the Genevan
ministers to come to him. At this occasion he addressed them as
follows:**

When I first came to this city the Gospel was, indeed, preached, but
matters were in the greatest confusion, as if Christianity had consisted in
nothing else than the throwing down of images; and there were not a
few wicked men from whom I suffered the greatest indignities; but the
Lord our God so confirmed me, who am by no means naturally bold (I
say what is true), that I succumbed to none of their attempts. I afterwards
returned thither from Strassburg in obedience to my calling, but with an
unwilling mind, because I thought I should prove unfruitful. For not
knowing what the Lord had determined, I saw nothing before me but
numbers of the greatest difficulties. But proceeding in this work, I at
length perceived that the Lord had truly blessed my labours. Do you also
persist in this vocation, and maintain the established order.

> Theodore Beza, *Life of Calvin*, pp. cxxxi–cxxxii (*CR* 49, 167).

▶ **A month later, 27th May 1564, Calvin died.**

On the day of his departure, viz. the 27th of May, he seemed to be
stronger, and to speak with less difficulty. But it was nature's last effort,
for in the evening, about eight o'clock, symptoms of approaching death
suddenly appeared. I had just left him a little before, and on receiving
intimation from the servants, immediately hastened to him with one of
the brethren. We found he had already died, and so very calmly, without
any convulsion of his feet or hands, that he did not even fetch a deeper
sigh. He had remained perfectly sensible, and was not entirely deprived
of utterance to his very last breath. Indeed, he looked much more like one

John Calvin. (*Unknown master about* 1550. *Museum Boymans—van Beuningen, Rotterdam*)

John Calvin, as a student's doodle sketched him. (*Bibliothèque Publique et Universitaire, Geneva*)

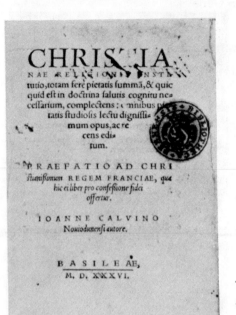

Title page of John Calvin's *Institutes of the Christian Religion.* (*Stadt- und Universitätsbibliothek, Bern*)

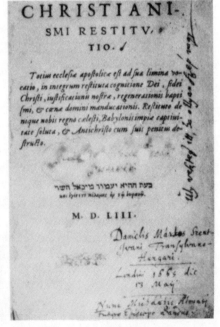

Title page of Michael Servetus' *Restitution of Christianity.* For translation see p. 297. (*Österreichische Nationalbibliothek, Wien*)

sleeping than dead. On that day, then, at the same time with the setting sun, this splendid luminary was withdrawn from us.

Theodore Beza, *Life of Calvin*, p. cxxxiv (*CR* 49, 168).

▶   **In his grief, Beza wrote these words:**

He lived 54 years, 10 months, 17 days, the half of which he spent in the ministry. He was of moderate stature, of a pale and dark complexion, with eyes that sparkled to the moment of his death, and bespoke of his great intellect. In dress he was neither overcareful nor mean, but such as became his singular modesty. In diet he was temperate, being equally averse to sordidness and luxury. He was most sparing in the quantities of his food, and for many years took only one meal a day, on account of the weakness of his stomach. He took little sleep, and had such an astonishing memory that any person whom he had once seen he instantly recognized at the distance of years, and when, in the course of dictating, he happened to be interrupted for several hours, as often happened, as soon as he returned he commenced at once to dictate where he had left off. Whatever he required to know for the performance of his duty, though involved in a multiplicity of other affairs, he never forgot. On whatever subject he was consulted his judgment was so clear and correct that he often seemed almost to prophesy; nor do I recollect of any person having been led into error in consequence of following his advice. He despised mere eloquence, and was sparing in the use of words; but he was by no means a careless writer. No theologian of this period (I do not speak invidiously) wrote more purely, weightily and judiciously, though he wrote more than any individual either in our recollection or that of our fathers. For, by the hard studies of his youth, and a certain acuteness of judgment, confirmed by practice in dictating, he was never at a loss for an appropriate and weighty expression, and wrote very much as he spoke. In the doctrine which he delivered at the first, he persisted steadily to the last, scarcely making any change. Of few theologians within our recollection can the same thing be affirmed. With regard to his manners, although nature had formed him for gravity, yet, in the common intercourse of life, there was no man who was more pleasant. In bearing with infirmities he was remarkably prudent; never either putting weak brethren to the blush, or terrifying them by unseasonable rebuke, yet never conniving at or flattering their faults. Of adulation, dissimulation, and dishonesty, especially where religion was concerned, he was as determined and severe an enemy as he was a lover of truth, simplicity and candour. He was naturally of a keen temper, and this had been increased by the very laborious life which he had led. But the Spirit of the Lord had so taught him to command his anger, that no word was heard to proceed from him unbecoming a good man.

Theodore Beza, *Life of Calvin*, pp. cxxxv–cxxxvi (*CR* 49, 169-70).

▶   The opponents, however, saw the Genevan Reformer in an altogether different light. From the pen of Jerome Bolsec, a Catholic who had turned Protestant, quarrelled with Calvin, and then returned to Catholicism, came in 1577 a vitriolic account of Calvin's life. Here are some excerpts:

Among all the evil introduced into this world by the father of lies and author of sin after the fall of the first parents, heresy has caused more troubles, sedition and division in all times and ages. This terrible and most pernicious monster has given rise to pride and ignorance. And the heretic participates in these as much as did his immediate parents and ancestors. For all heretics are arrogant, proud and presumptuous . . . until they despise all others who are not of their sect and bear hatred against them together with a great number of other fantastic brains who uphold many questions and opinions in favour of the working of the Holy Spirit, of the invocation of the saints, of the prayer for the transgressions and several similar controversies.

But it seems that in our day this enemy of God and Christian unity has gathered most of the described heresies and false doctrines already long refuted and condemned and stowed them away in the city of Geneva through Jean Calvin of Noyon, a man, among others of the world, ambitious, presumptuous, arrogant, cruel, malicious, vindictive and, above all, ignorant.

Hierosme Hermes Bolsec, *Histoire de la Vie . . . Jean Calvin*, pp. 9-12.

▶   Bolsec left no stone unturned to discredit Calvin—including his personal morals.

At that time a lady of Mougis left her husband at Lausanne, without saying good-bye to him, to take up residence at Geneva, where her husband would not dare to go. Even before this time, I know well, that it was rumoured concerning several ladies and girls who rather tamely went to find him at home without any company aside from a small child . . . with a Bible under the arm. When, on the way, they were met by some of their relatives or friends and were asked where they were going, they answered, in jolly fashion, that they were going to that saintly man to have a doubt resolved: and they stayed a long time.

There was also a great clamour and rumour concerning the wife of a lord from abroad who had come, for religious reasons, to these parts. . . . But his residence was very near Geneva and also near Saconnoy and Gez. That lady was young, beautiful and gay. Calvin came to supper and stayed overnight even when the husband was absent from home and region. And I, among others, know well that the maid who was there with that lady revealed under oath that she found indication of two people in the bed of her mistress, although her husband was absent from home. But Calvin had dined and stayed that night. On account of such words the maid was threatened and driven from the house. This may be true or not: but I say, along with worthy men and men of good judgment, that at least Calvin ought to remember and practise Paul's statement in the fifth chapter of Thessalonians: 'Abstain from all evil.'

I cannot let a certain point, quite known to several people concerning Madame Iolland de Brederode, who was the wife of Lord Iaques de Bourgougne, Lord of Fallais. . . . That gentleman, since his arrival at Geneva, was sick and continually under the treatment of physicians. Calvin came several times to visit and several times said to that Lady Iolland, wife of the Lord of Fallais: 'What are you going to do? This man is very ill and will never be able to serve you. Believe me, let him die, as he is almost dead. And when he is dead, let us get married.' After this proposal the Lady was indignant and was scandalized and persuaded her husband to leave Geneva and proceed to Bernese territory, which he did. And that Lady could not hide this incident and spoke of it to several good and honourable persons. And I heard it myself from her mouth in the presence of the Lord, her husband.

And it is necessary to note that no people living in Geneva and under its jurisdiction murmur and speak against Calvin by punishment of excommunication and expulsion by the consistory or even the penalty of death.

Hierosme Hermes Bolsec, *Histoire de la Vie . . . Jean Calvin*, pp. 67–69.

BIBLIOGRAPHY

Calvin's works are edited in the *Corpus Reformatorum*, vols. 29–87 (Braunschweig, 1863–1900); vols. 86 and 87 contain a Calvin bibliography up to 1900. Unfortunately, some of the volumes are not indicative of recent scholarship. A competent selection of works is *J. Calvini Opera Selecta*, 5 vols. (Munich, 1926–52). An excellent English translation of the *Institutes* was edited by John T. McNeill (London and Philadelphia, 1960). There is a two-volume edition of

Calvin's letters, *Letters of John Calvin* (Philadelphia, n.d.). A bibliographical survey of Calvin studies for the time 1901–59 was compiled by Wilhelm Niesel, *Calvin Bibliographie 1901–1959* (Munich, 1961). Recent surveys in English are John T. McNeill, 'Thirty Years of Calvin Study', *Church History* 17 (1948), and Edward A. Dowey, Jr., 'Studies on Calvin and Calvinism', *Church History* 24 (1955); 29 (1960).

There are three biographies of Calvin from the pen of his co-worker Theodore Beza, the one published in 1564 as preface to Calvin's posthumous Joshua Commentary, the second in 1564 (with the help of his associate Nicholas Colladon), the third in 1575. All three are now available in *CR* 49. A hostile biography was published in 1577 by Jerome Bolsec under the title *Histoire de la vie, moeurs, actes, doctrines, constance et mort de Jean Calvin*. Bolsec had, as Protestant, bitterly quarrelled with Calvin concerning predestination, and subsequently returned to Catholicism.

The most elaborate biography of the Genevan reformer is that of Calvinus redivus Émile Doumergue, *Jean Calvin, les hommes et les choses de son temps* (Lausanne, 1899–1927). The iconography of Calvin is discussed by É. Doumerque, *Iconographie Calvinienne* (Lausanne, 1909).

From the pen of Emmanuel Stickelberger comes a readable but knowledgeable portrait, *Calvin: A Life* (Richmond, 1954).

Recent biographies come from Jean Cadier, *The Man God Mastered, A New Biography of John Calvin* (Grand Rapids, Mich., 1960), and Albert-Marie Schmidt, *John Calvin and the Calvinistic Tradition* (New York and London, 1960).

For Calvin's early development, see Quirinus Breen, *John Calvin: A Study of French Humanism* (Grand Rapids, 1932). Calvin's thought is briefly but well presented by Wilhelm Niesel, *The Theology of John Calvin* (Philadelphia, 1956). Competent is John T. McNeill, *The History and Character of Calvinism* (New York, 1954). See also Georgia Harkness, *John Calvin, the Man and His Ethics* (New York, 1958). See also François Wendel, *Calvin. Sources et évolution de sa pensée religieuse* (Paris, 1950), translated under the title *Calvin. Origin and Development of His Religious Thought* (London–New York, 1963).

NOTES AND REFERENCES

John Calvin, *Commentary on the Book of Psalms* (Grand Rapids, 1949)—referred to as *Commentaries, Psalms*.

Letters of John Calvin (Philadelphia, n.d.)—referred to as *Letters*.

1. Theodore Beza, *Life of Calvin*, in *John Calvin, Tracts and Treatises on the Reformation of the Church*, vol. I (Grand Rapids, 1958).

2. For a biography of Theodore Beza one must go back to H. M. Baird, *Theodore Beza, the Counsellor of the French Reformation* (New York, 1899).

3. On French Humanism, and particularly Jacques LeFèvre d'Etaples (*c.* 1455–1536), see M. Mann, *Erasme et les Débuts de la Réforme française* (Paris, 1934); H. Dörries, 'Calvin und LeFèvre', *Zeitschrift f. Kirchengeschichte* 44 (1925), 544–81; C. L. Salley, *The Ideals of the Devotio Moderna as reflected in*

the *Life and Writings of Jacques LeFèvre d'Etaples* (Dissertation, University of Michigan, 1953).

4. The date of Calvin's 'conversion' has been debated in scholarship. For a discussion, see Fritz Büsser, *Calvins Urteil über sich selbst* (Zürich, 1950), pp. 23–34, and, more exhaustively, Paul Sprenger, *Das Rätsel um die Bekehrung Calvins* (Neukirchen, 1960).

5. The translation used here is from Albert-Marie Schmidt, *John Calvin and the Calvinistic Tradition*, p. 29.

6. Simon Grynaeus (1493–1541), philologist, professor of New Testament at Basel, proponent of ecclesiastical independence from the city council.

7. Interpretive studies of the *Institutes* are found in John T. McNeill, *Books of Faith and Power* (New York, 1947) and Wilhelm Pauck, *The Heritage of the Reformation* (Glencoe, Ill., 1961). See also Benjamin B. Warfield, 'On the Literary History of Calvin's *Institutes*', *Calvin and Calvinism* (New York, 1931), pp. 373–478.

8. Calvin's view of the Church and church order are discussed by Ray C. Petry, 'Calvin's Conception of the *communio sanctorum*', *Church History*, 5 (1936), and J. S. Ramm, 'Church Discipline: A Comparative Study of Luther and Calvin', *Lutheran Church Quarterly*, 6 (1933).

9. The translation used here is from James H. Robinson, *Readings in European History*, I, 130–2.

10. For a study of Calvin's stay in Strassburg, see Paul Pannier, *Calvin à Strassbourg* (Paris, 1925).

11. Not much is known of Calvin's wife, Idelette de Bure, formerly the widow of an Anabaptist; see the older study of August Lang, 'Das häusliche Leban Johannes Calvins', *Reformation und Gegenwart* (Detmold, 1918), pp. 39–71.

12. The translation used here was made by Dr G. Aiken Taylor.

13. The translation used here is from James H. Robinson, *Readings in European History*, I, 134.

14. The translation used here is from James H. Robinson, *Readings in European History*, p. 130.

15. On Castellio, see Roland H. Bainton, *The Travail of Religious Liberty* (Philadelphia, 1951); *Castellioniana* (Leiden, 1951); H. R. Guggisberg, *Sebastian Castellio im Urteil seiner Nachwelt vom Späthumanismus bis zur Aufklärung* (Basel, 1956).

16. Hierosme Bolsec, died *c.* 1584, French Carmelite monk, turned Protestant, and was physician at Geneva. As a result of his attack on predestination he was expelled from Geneva and subsequently returned to the Catholic Church. See H. Fazy, *Procès de Bolsec* (Geneva, 1866).

Radical Reform Movements

DESPITE the widespread support for Luther in the early years of the Reformation the Protestant movement lacked homogeneity from the very beginning, which in turn prompted its disintegration no sooner than it had taken form. Not all of Luther's supporters were in his camp for the same reason and some, perhaps, did not belong there in the first place. German nationalism, economic grievances, and political power politics seem to have been for many as important a factor as the zeal to restore the Gospel.

But there were also true disciples, who were genuinely enthusiastic about the new evangelical proclamation. Their insistence that this proclamation entailed more extensive and radical consequences than Luther was willing to concede meant the emergence of a Protestant radicalism. These men became the 'deserting disciples', first in Wittenberg, then in Zürich, Nürnberg, Strassburg, and other Reformation centres. Finding the Reformers as little willing to be persuaded as they were themselves, they resolved to chart their own course. Their unanimous verdict was that the Reformers had not gone far enough in the reform of the Church, but had all too quickly compromised their insights in order not to disrupt the *status quo*. While all of the radicals agreed that the Reformation itself needed to be reformed, they disagreed about what constituted a restitution of genuine Christianity. Thus Protestant radicalism became a hopelessly heterogeneous phenomenon in which, none the less, three more or less distinct expressions can be discerned: Anabaptism, Spiritualism and Antitrinitarianism, each with its own peculiar characters and—to add to the confusion—common lines.

Wherever these radicals made bold to profess their faith they were met by severe and cruel persecution from the hands of governmental authorities to whom the theologians gave religious rationales. The story of the radical reformation is, therefore, above all one of suffering and martyrdom. But again, the blood of the martyrs proved to be the seed of the Church as men and women faced fire, sword and water steadfastly and

V

almost gladly—a contemporary observed that 'they went to the stakes as to a wedding'. The situation of the radicals was complicated by the fact that for the old and new Church, as well as for governmental authorities, theological deviates were not only heretics, but also revolutionaries who disturbed civil law and order. It mattered little that the radicals emphatically protested their innocence and disavowed all revolutionary tendencies. Most of them were true to their professions. But isolated instances of revolutionary zeal did occur which, for the authorities, were the proof of the pudding they had been waiting for. Since the codes of law everywhere made even theological matters a criminal offence—in the case of rebaptism punishable by death—the situation was, for the radicals, hopeless. Not until another century had passed and Europe was weary of religious controversy did the persecutions gradually cease. In the sixteenth century the radicals were outcasts—politically, socially and religiously, in Protestant no less than in Catholic lands. Since the radicals wanted to do no more and no less than what Luther had himself claimed, namely to hold a religious conviction until convinced otherwise by reason and Scripture, the persecution on the part of the Protestants is doubly regrettable. It shows, however, that the Reformation was far from proclaiming religious freedom and still believed in certain objective standards of faith which had to be adhered to or else communion was broken. It also indicated that Martin Luther, for one, was far from being a religious subjectivist—even though the appeal of the radicals to his position suggests that what for Luther was allegiance to the objective reality of the Scriptures could be seen by others as sheer subjectivism.

The earliest representative of such radicalism and by all odds also the most picturesque one, was Thomas Müntzer. Ever since the days of Luther and Melanchthon, this 'arch-devil of Allstedt', as these Reformers called him, has been a veritable bogy for respectable Protestants and consequently whoever wrote about him wrote against him. Only in recent decades has there been a more positive assessment. Theologians discovered that Müntzer had had some profound insights after all, and suggested that he was, next to Luther, the most creative spirit of the Reformation. Marxists recalled Müntzer's cursory statement that all things should be held in common and made him a sixteenth-century proletarian protagonist. The truth probably is that he was neither, though it is, perhaps, too early to tell. At any rate, he seems to have been better than his reputation.

Thomas Müntzer was probably born in 1488. Like Luther, he hailed from Saxony and, again like Luther, he was born into an economically respectable home. In 1506 he entered the University of Leipzig, later transferred to Frankfurt, and then to Mainz. At no place, however, did he undertake a regular course of study. He was the classic example of the brilliant but undisciplined student who is too restless to settle down to academic routine. This is not to say that he was not a serious student. Quite the contrary. He read much, perhaps too much, and soaked in insights and impressions without ever properly assimilating them. His thought, as well as his life, was restless and erratic.

After ordination to the priesthood, he fulfilled various ministerial responsibilities, about which not much is known. The Leipzig disputation of 1519 brought him under Luther's influence. At Luther's recommendation he went as minister to Zwickau, a small town in Eastern Saxony. The forthrightness of his preaching came into a city beset with religious and social problems. Serious tensions were the result and in April of 1521 Müntzer had to leave. He proceeded to Prague, the old Hussite centre, where he sought to rally popular support for his interpretation of the Christian faith. He was unsuccessful. For a year he disappeared from the limelight of history until, at Easter 1523, he settled as preacher of Allstedt, a small Saxon town. Here he had the opportunity to put theory into practice. He introduced a new form of worship and began a literary battle with Luther whom he denounced for his failure to preach the seriousness of the Gospel. He also strove to gather the truly elect in a covenant, or '*Bund*'. Several bouts with the Saxon authorities followed, occasioned by riotous developments in Allstedt, such as the burning down of a Catholic chapel. Müntzer was probably not directly responsible, but in August of 1524 he felt it best to leave Allstedt. Luther had in the meantime taken to the pen and had published his *Letter to the Rulers of Saxony Concerning the Rebellious Spirit*, in which he insisted that Satan himself had established a 'nest' in Allstedt. Müntzer proceeded to Mühlhausen, a nearby Saxon town, where he stayed for a short time, then travelled to South Germany, and possibly even to Switzerland. He was back in Saxony the following spring—at the time when the discontent of the peasants was about to break out into open insurrection. To what extent Müntzer was involved in the Peasants' War is uncertain. At no rate can he have played a significant role as instigator of the uprising—as was noted in an earlier chapter, the discontent among the peasants antedates the Reformation by many decades. But no doubt Müntzer identified himself with the peasants. But if (as we shall see) the peasants misunderstood Luther, then it must now be said that Müntzer misunderstood the peasants. It had increasingly become the *leitmotif*) of his theology that God's elect must assert their right against the godless. Müntzer found it easy to identify the peasants with the elect and the rulers with the godless: after all, he himself had experienced the rulers' hostility to his preaching. He joined the camp of the peasants and was present at the decisive Battle at Frankenhausen. The defeat of the peasants brought with it his catastrophe. He was apprehended after the battle, tortured, made to confess anything and everything, and eventually executed.

His thought, however, an explosive combination of medieval mysticism and Lutheran theology, lived on. Müntzer had participated in the theological controversy for less than two years. But during that time he had coined a number of suggestive slogans about Luther which caught the fancy of all those who had become dissatisfied with the Wittenberg programme of reform. Luther was Dr Liar, Sit-on-the-fence, and the Pope of Wittenberg. He had made, so Müntzer asserted, the Christian faith too easy, had proclaimed a honey-sweet Christ instead of a bitter one, and had said nothing about the commitment which one must make to become Christ's disciple.

Müntzer's biting attack and vivid epithets made the rounds. Thus, a 'brotherhood of the discontent' was in the making in the mid-twenties. The Reformers were accused of haphazardness because they retained infant baptism and of shallowness because they placed the locus of authority in the Bible without a proper guide to interpret it. Slowly this general and theologically vague discontent channelled itself into specific expressions. Of these, Anabaptism deserves, on account of chronology and importance, the first place.

ANABAPTISM

Anabaptism arose within the cradle of the Zwinglian Reformation in Zürich. Several young humanists and clerics who had been brought by Zwingli to a deepened understanding of the Christian faith became, late in 1523, impatient with the slowness of the reforming effort in Zürich. The October Disputation of 1523 brought the first indications of disagreement between Zwingli and some of his followers. Conrad Grebel, one of the radicals, insisted on that occasion that the preachers should be given practical instruction concerning the abolition of the mass. Zwingli replied that this was up to the City Council. Though this brief episode lacked dramatic exuberance, it indicated, none the less, a basic disagreement. The one wished to push forward; the other wanted to undertake ecclesiastical reform in consultation with the civil authorities.

Soon after this the radicals began to press for the establishment of a true Christian Church, completely reconstituted according to its apostolic pattern. The outward point of theological difference between Zwingli and the radicals became the problem of baptism, because here the divergent views of what constituted true Christianity and the true Church could find concrete expression. The radicals insisted that baptism should not be administered to infants who were passive and unaware of the significance of the act, but should be reserved for adults who voluntarily desired to receive it. Such deliberate commitment on the part of mature individuals would lay the foundation for a true Church. The autumn of 1524 saw various informal discussions between Zwingli and the radicals on the matter, but neither was able to persuade the other. In light of the growing restlessness and evident reluctance of parents to have their infants baptized, the Zürich city council called for a public disputation on the matter. It took place on 17th January 1525, and ended, as might well have been expected, with the vindication of Zwingli's position and the pronouncement that infant baptism was scriptural. The following day a city ordinance ordered the baptism of all unbaptized children. Three days later another ordinance prohibited all meetings of radical conventicles.

That evening, 21st January 1525, the radicals met. They had reached a crossroad; months of searching for the true Christian faith and extensive discussions with Zwingli and the other ministers lay behind them. Their own convictions were firm. But now both Church and State had taken a stand against them. The radicals faced the momentous decision of either defying these authorities or yielding to them. Their response was to administer, on this occasion, what they had theoretically advocated for some time—believer's baptism. This step was a signal expression of their unwillingness to compromise their convictions. Governmental suppression was now certain and indeed promptly set in. Though the situation of the Anabaptists was desperate, it was not altogether hopeless. There was still the possibility that they might find a more receptive atmosphere elsewhere. Such hope, and the impossibility of the situation in Zürich, precipitated a vigorous expansion of the Anabaptist message abroad. Within a few years a network of Anabaptist congregations was established in South Germany and Austria. But wherever the Anabaptist evangelists went, persecution set in almost simultaneously and forced the movement to go underground as soon as it had established itself. None the less, it appears that this persecution did not crush the vitality of the Anabaptist movement, even though most of the early leaders suffered martyrdom. If anything, it convinced the Anabaptists that theirs was the righteous cause which, so they felt, must in this world always suffer and be persecuted. The growing Anabaptist movement caused, in 1529, the German diet assembled at Speyer to address itself to the problem. It recalled that there was in the books an ancient decree forbidding rebaptism at the penalty of death, and reissued it. Henceforth the admission of Anabaptist convictions was sufficient to send a man to the stake or at least—in the case of benevolent authorities—to prison.

Only in Moravia did the Anabaptists find virtual toleration on the part of the local rulers. The news spread, and soon persecuted Anabaptists from everywhere migrated there to live their faith in peace and quiet. Under the energetic leadership of Jakob Hutter these Anabaptists created a new expression of Anabaptism which included the postulate of communal living among its tenets. Driven together by economic need, and inspired by the example of the apostolic Church, a group of Austrian Anabaptists on their way to Moravia put together all their possessions. This soon became general practice among Moravian Anabaptists, who were soon called Hutterites after their outstanding leader. They lived in communities of their own, called *Bruderhofs*, with their own shops, use of fields and woods, and schools; responsibilities and work were equally distributed among all. Theirs was a life of sharing. It produced a closely knit fellowship which incidentally survived the rigours of four hundred years and can still be found today in the Dakotas.

In Germany, meanwhile, Reformers and civil authorities received the proof for their contention that Anabaptism meant the disruption of law and order. In Münster the Anabaptists succeeded in accomplishing what elsewhere had proved to be impossible—they assumed control of the city. Münster, a town with a complicated administrative structure characterized by long-standing rivalry between the resident Catholic bishop and the city council, had officially become Lutheran in 1532. Soon a strong radical faction agitated for more extensive reforms. Its efforts were strengthened by the leading minister in the town, Bernhard Rothmann, who himself began to proclaim radical ideas. The radicals in Münster were more and more characterized by Anabaptist ideals—such as adult baptism—and though there remained to the end important differences between the Anabaptists at large and those in Münster, the similarities meant that the happenings at Münster were seen as the outgrowth of the Anabaptist spirit. In the summer of 1533 a disputation was held in Münster between Lutherans and Anabaptists. It became obvious that the latter did not yet have sufficient support to dominate the city. Rothmann was removed from his office and all unbaptized infants were ordered to be baptized. But the influx of Anabaptists to Münster continued, and Rothmann cared little about his official dismissal. He stayed on and supported the Anabaptist cause. In February 1534 the Anabaptists finally obtained control of the city when elections to the city council brought a majority for Anabaptists and Anabaptist sympathizers. The significance of the new orientation of Münster soon became evident. All who refused to be rebaptized were ordered to leave the city. Only the truly baptized believers remained— Münster had become the New Jerusalem.

But unlike its biblical paradigm, it was not destined to last. The Catholic bishop in whose diocese Münster was located was little willing to tolerate a town controlled by declared heretics, and undertook at once a siege. It was ineffective at first, but in the end a formidable amassment of military might was assembled with the help of the Emperor and the territorial rulers. The situation of the Anabaptists was hopeless.

The leadership in Münster during the first part of the Anabaptist rule was exercised by Jan Matthijs, a Dutchman, who had earlier played an important role in the expansion of Anabaptism in Holland. He proved to be a charismatic leader who rallied the people around him by pointing to the dream of the 'New Jerusalem' which was to be realized in Münster. The city council and the ministers, including Bernhard Rothmann, degenerated into powerless puppets. Matthijs' rule was of short duration. In April 1534, less than two months after the beginning of the Anabaptist rule in Münster, he was killed in battle.

Jan van Leyden, another Dutchman, still in his twenties, a tailor by trade, became the new 'prophet' and took Matthijs' place. Under the 'prophetic' leadership of Jan van Leyden radical changes were made in Münster in order to convert the city to its biblical image. All books except the Bible were burned; communism and polygamy were introduced.

In the autumn of 1534 Jan van Leyden proclaimed himself the King of the New Jerusalem. Though this added pageantry to biblical pretense, the continuing siege and the increasing famine made the situation more and more difficult. After a trying winter, Münster was taken by the besieging forces early in 1535. Jan van Leyden and the Anabaptist leaders who had not been killed in the fighting were tortured in a fashion common to savages, and eventually executed.

The Münster spectacle more than any other event served to cast dire suspicion upon all Anabaptists, since it now was thought to be evident that religious radicalism in the end would lead to immorality and civil rebellion. Everywhere persecution was intensified. But if the authorities thought they had learned a lesson, so did the Anabaptists. Though the events at Münster must not, despite certain parallels, be identified too intimately with Anabaptism proper, the movement at large felt the repercussions and underwent a process of inner renewal which emphasized simple piety and insisted that Münster had perverted the true Anabaptist genius.

The outstanding leader during subsequent development in North Germany and Holland was Menno Simons. Born in 1496 in Witmarsum, Holland, Menno was ordained without any religious conviction at the age of twenty-eight to the Catholic priesthood. He soon developed doubts concerning communion and baptism. The study of the Bible led him to the realization that the teaching of his Church was unscriptural in these two points. Thus inwardly alienated from his Church, Menno none the less continued outwardly as priest for several years. Then came the rise and fall of Anabaptism at Münster. For Menno this brought a conversion and the conviction that an open stand on his part could have avoided the tragic perversion of true Anabaptist principles there. In January 1536, Menno left his parish and went underground to join the Anabaptist movement. He spent the remainder of his life preaching and teaching, wandering from place to place in order to consolidate the theologically confounded Anabaptists. At the time of his death in 1561, Anabaptism was still beset by doctrinal divergencies and dissensions, but it had definitely repudiated the violence, force and chiliasm pursued at Münster. In its place Menno put the insistence on a simple Christian faith which expressed itself in a spotless life and doctrine.

Far from being a homogeneous phenomenon in the sixteenth century, Anabaptism everywhere meant a deliberate commitment on the part of the individual to be Christ's disciple. Thus Church and State were thought not to be identical—the true Church of Christ must be a persecuted minority, which faithfully walks the way of the Cross and follows the example of the Master. Though despised and persecuted, the Anabaptists of the sixteenth century deserve a prominent place in the annals of Christian history as untiring proponents of a Christianity which renounced compulsion and made the daily walk the test of faith.

▶   The first radical of widespread reputation was Thomas Müntzer.[1] A contemporary pamphlet summarized his life as follows:

After Dr Martin Luther had preached for several years and had taught the Gospel purely and clearly, the devil also sowed his seed and brought forth false and pernicious preachers through whom the Gospel was once more perverted and suppressed and much blood was shed. For Christ designated and described Satan as a murderer from the beginning who kills unto the end of the world.

Satan took possession of one whose name was Thomas Müntzer. He was well taught in the Holy Scriptures, but did not remain on their path. Satan fooled him and led him away from the Scriptures so that he no longer preached from the Gospel how men shall be saved. From a false understanding of the Holy Scriptures he deceitfully derived the false and seditious doctrine that all authority should be killed and all goods henceforth should be in common. Likewise there should be no ruler and no king.

This he vehemently preached to the masses, denouncing and scolding the rulers: How they suppressed, burdened, exploited and meanly treated the poor in order to retain their own unprofitable pomp and luxury. They lived sumptuously to the detriment of the poor, whereas Christian love demanded that no one should be above his brother—since everyone was free—and there should be community of goods.

To all these satanic doctrines he gave a good appearance. He insisted that he had revelations from heaven, that he taught and commanded nothing but what God had commanded him. One cannot fathom how much Satan must have taken possession of this man in order for him to glory in such heavenly revelations and so shamelessly and deceitfully to use God's name. Indeed, posterity will hardly believe that one man had the audacity to boast of things which were so altogether unfounded.

Such had happened in earlier times, however. Someone named 'Mani'[2] pretended to be the true Christ and the Son of God. He selected disciples and many people followed him. Satan led them into error and destroyed their bodies and souls.

The same has now happened again. Satan used such cunning that reason cannot understand it and inexperienced people cannot believe it.

There is a place in Thuringia, in the Harz near Saxony, called 'Allstedt', which belongs to the Elector of Saxony. To this place came Thomas Müntzer. Even though he boasted that he possessed the Holy Spirit, was unafraid, and had a divine command to preach in all the world, he none the less looked for a hole where he was under the safe protection of the pious ruler Duke Frederick, the Elector of Saxony, under whom the ministers preaching against old, unprofitable customs were safer than elsewhere.

After Müntzer had arrived in Allstedt he began to make himself a great name by denouncing both Pope and Luther. He asserted that both the papal and the Lutheran teaching were unprofitable. The Pope had kept the consciences bound with unreasonble burdens and ceremonies. Luther made them free from papal burdens, but left them in carnal freedom, and did not lead them on to God and the Spirit. Such babble amazed the people. They ran and wanted to hear the latest, just as Homer says that the crowd always considers the latest song the best one. . . .

Let us briefly relate what Thomas taught. True piety, he proclaimed, does not consist of the papal regulations which should be disregarded. One must come to genuine Christian piety: First one must desist from such public evils as adultery, murder, blasphemy, and the like. The body must be castigated and martyred with fasting and poor clothing. One should talk little, look sour, and not cut off one's beard. Such childish ways he called the 'mortification of the flesh' and the 'cross' of which the Gospels write.

Die Historie Thomae Müntzers : Otto H. Brandt,
Thomas Müntzer, pp. 38–39.

▶ **Müntzer's first theological pronouncement was the 'Prague Manifesto', which he published in the fall of 1521 in an attempt to rally popular support.**

I, Thomas Müntzer, of Stolberg, confess before all the Church and all the world, wherever this pronouncement may be found, that I can claim with Christ and all the elect who have known me from the days of my youth, that I have most industriously attempted, more so than other people I know, to have or receive a superior instruction in the holy and invincible Christian faith. Throughout my days—God knows I lie not—I could not learn from a monk or priest the right practice of the faith nor that fruitful trial which explains this faith in the spirit of the fear of God. . . . From no scholar did I learn the order of God, which is put into all creatures, with even the smallest word. . . . I heard from them mere Scripture which they stole from the Bible like murderers and thieves. Jeremiah, in his 23rd chapter, says that this is to steal the Word of God out of the mouth of one's neighbour—the Word which they themselves never heard from his mouth. They are sly preachers, I suppose, whom the devil ordained. . . .

Compassionately I took this unbearable and pernicious damage of Christendom to heart upon reading industriously the history of the Fathers. I found that after the death of the Apostles' disciples the immaculate and virgin Church became a harlot through spiritual adultery on account of the scholars who always want to sit on top. Hegesippus and after him Eusebius, in the fourth book and 22nd chapter, write about this.[3] I also do not find in any council a manifestation of the undeceivable Word of God. The councils have been children's pranks. This all has taken place because of the forbearing will of God so that the works of man should be manifest. Praise be to God that preachers and monkeys will not for ever make up the Christian Church! The elect friends of God's Word will learn to prophesy, as Paul teaches, so that they can truly experience in how friendly, indeed intimate, a way God talks with his elect. I am willing to sacrifice my life for the sake of God, that I might bring such doctrine to the light of day. God will do marvellous things with his elect, especially in this country. For here the new Church will arise. This people will be a reflection of the entire world. Thus I call upon every man to help so that God's Word can be defended and that I can visibly show you through the spirit of Elias those who have taught you to sacrifice to the idol Baal. If you will not do it, God will smite you through the Turk in the coming year. Truly, I know that what I say is true. I will suffer for it what Jeremiah had to suffer. Take it to heart, dear Bohemian Brethren. Not only I but also God demands an account from you, as the word of Peter teaches. I will give you an account of myself. If I do not know the art of which I so boldly boast, I will be a child of temporal and eternal death. I have no higher pawn. May God bless you. Given in Prague, in 1521, the day of All Saints.

Der Prager Anschlag: Otto H. Brandt, *Thomas Müntzer*, pp. 59–62.

▶   From 1523 to 1524 Müntzer was minister at Allstedt, where he ventured to put some of his radical ideas into practice. After the situation in the town had become tumultuous, Müntzer decided to leave—as the following letter indicates, in a hurry.

Regarding your request addressed to me I reply that the preacher, Thomas Müntzer, together with a goldsmith from Nordhausen, on Sunday after Sixtus during the night secretly crossed the city walls and departed without official farewell. The following day around noon he had a letter transmitted to the council in which he stated that it should not be suspicious, as he had business to attend to in the country. At the time, we thought that he would return. Two weeks later he wrote again and stated that he was now at Mühlhausen and wanted to take leave from Allstedt. (Both of these letters I transmitted yesterday to the Elector.) He also preached some sermons there. Whether the council has appointed him as a regular preacher, I have not as yet learned. As soon as I receive some word about it, I will convey it to you. Likewise I do not know if he uses his own order of the mass[4] in which the Epistle supposedly states that the rulers should be killed. While he was here, I never heard anything of this sort.

25th August 1524. Hans Zeys to Duke John of Saxony:
Otto H. Brandt, *Thomas Müntzer*, pp. 72–73.

▶ Müntzer had an abiding conviction that he was called to convert the world to his belief. Here is his fiery appeal to Count Ernst von Mansfeld of 12th May 1525, written when Müntzer had joined the camp of the rebellious peasants:

The authentic power and firm fear of God as well as the continuous ground of his righteous will be with you, Brother Ernst.

I, Thomas Müntzer, lately preacher at Allstedt, admonish you . . . that for the sake of the name of the living God you desist from your tyrannical raging and thereby no longer invoke God's wrath. You have begun to martyr the Christians. You have called the holy Christian faith a 'roguery'. You have undertaken to destroy the Christians. Tell me, you miserable, shabby bag of worms, who has made you a ruler of the people whom God has redeemed with his precious blood? You are called upon to prove whether you are a Christian. You ought to prove your faith, as I Peter 3 commands. You shall have safe conduct to testify to your faith. . . .

If you do not come to take care of this matter, I will proclaim to all the world that all brethren should confidently dare their blood, as against the Turks. You will be prosecuted and exterminated. Indeed, all will more eagerly earn indulgence with you than formerly they used to under the Pope. We do not know any other way to deal with you. You are not ashamed at all. God has hardened you like Pharaoh and the kings whom God wanted to destroy (Joshua 5 and 11). Alas to God, that the world did not recognize your raging tyranny any sooner! You have caused such evident, irreparable damage that God himself cannot have mercy on you. In short, through God's powerful authority you have been handed over to destruction. . . .

You should also know that we have a pertinent command: The eternal, living God has commanded that you be pushed from your chair with the power which is given us. You are unprofitable to Christendom. You are a pernicious sweeping-brush of the friends of God. God spoke of you and yours in Ezekiel 34 and 39, Daniel 7, as well as Micah 3. The prophet Obadiah says that your nest is to be torn out and destroyed.

We want to have your answer yet tonight or else we shall visit you in the name of the Lord of hosts. Act accordingly. We shall do immediately what God has ordered us. Do your best, also. I shall proceed on my way.

Written at Frankenhausen, Friday, after *Jubilate*, anno Domini 1525. Thomas Müntzer with the sword of Gideon.

12th May 1525. To Count Ernst of Mansfeld: Otto H. Brandt, *Thomas Müntzer*, pp. 77-78.

▶   Müntzer's somewhat enigmatic involvement in the Peasants'
War in 1525 overshadowed the last phase of his life. Here is a
last appeal of the peasants addressed to the rulers:

We confess Jesus Christ.

We are not here to harm anyone (John 2), but to maintain divine
justice. Thus we are not here to shed blood. If you are of the same mind,
we do not want to do anything to you. Let everyone preserve this.

15th May 1525. Otto H. Brandt, *Thomas Müntzer*, p. 79.

▶   The response of the rulers was brief and to the point:

To the brethren of Frankenhausen:

You have, through evil habit and the seductive teaching of your
perverter of the Gospel, proceeded in various ways against our Redeemer
Jesus Christ with murder, fire and other disrespect of God, especially
against the holy sacrament and in other blasphemy. As those whom God
has given the sword, we are here assembled to punish you as blasphemers
of God. Out of Christian love, and also because we feel that many a poor
soul has been seduced in evil manner, we have decided that, if you turn
over to us alive the false prophet, Thomas Müntzer, as well as his associates, and you submit yourselves to our grace and mercy, we will treat you
in such a way that you will find our grace as becomes this affair. We ask
for your speedy response.

15th May 1525. Otto H. Brandt, *Thomas Müntzer*, p. 79.

▶   The chronicler described the fate of the peasants and Thomas
Müntzer in the crucial battle at Frankenhausen:

Then they advanced towards the peasants and began to fire. The poor
people just stood there and sang, 'Now we pray the Holy Spirit', as if
they were insane. They neither resisted nor fled. Many comforted themselves in Thomas's great promise that God would send help from heaven,
since Thomas had said he would catch all bullets in his coat sleeves. . . .

After the battle they approached the village and occupied it. They
captured some three hundred men, who were beheaded. Thomas had
escaped into a house near the gate. He could have escaped in the meantime or hid himself better, had God not wanted him to be captured.
Nobody paid particular attention to him; nobody even looked for him.

A nobleman from Lüneburg had moved into the same house. By
accident his servant went up into the attic to see what kind of house they
were living in. He found a man lying on a bed as if he were sick. He asked
him who he was and if he was one of the rebels. Thomas had laid himself

into bed, as if he were weak, thinking that he could hide that way and escape. He answered the servant that he was a sick man and had fever and was very weak and had never taken part in the rebellion. The servant found a purse near the bed and took it, hoping to find some booty. He found letters, written by Count Albrecht of Mansfeld, which asked Thomas to desist from his wantonness. The servant inquired of him whence he had the letters and whether he were Thomas. Thomas was frightened and denied it vehemently, and did not want to be Thomas. Finally, when the servant began to threaten him, he confessed. Then he was arrested. . . .

He publicly confessed that he had done wrong. In the spring he admonished the princes that they should not be severe with the poor people. Then they would not encounter such danger again. He told them to read *Libros Regum*. After this talk he was beheaded. His head was put on a lance and placed in the field as a memorial.

Die Historie Thomae Müntzers: Otto H. Brandt, *Thomas Müntzer*, pp. 48–50.

▶ Shortly before his death Thomas Müntzer signed a confession and recantation.

The following articles were stated uncoerced and well thought-through by Thomas Müntzer, in the presence of the noble Lord Philipp, Count of Solms, etc., Master Gebhardt, Count and Lord of Mansfeld. . . . He asked that he be reminded of them in case he should forget, so that he could tell them with his own mouth to everyone just before his death.

First of all, he had opposed governmental authority and preached too lightly concerning it. Thus his listeners and he . . . had entered into wicked and wanton insurrection, rebellion and disobedience. He asked, for the sake of God, that they should not be offended thereby. He wanted especially to live obediently under the government ordained and ordered by God, and asked that they forgive his trespasses.

Secondly, he had also preached rebelliously and seductively some views, folly and errors concerning the blessed sacrament of the holy body of Christ much against the order of the universal Christian Church. He now would in peace and concord keep everything which this same Christian Church has always believed and still does believe. He would die as a true and reconciled member of this Church, asking it to witness such before God and the world, to pray to God for him and to forgive him in brotherly manner.

Finally, it would be his request that his recent letter be sent to those of Mühlhausen and that his wife and child might receive all his belongings.

17th May 1525. Otto H. Brandt, *Thomas Müntzer*, p. 84.

▶ Radical dissent found another concrete expression in the rise of Anabaptism[5] in Zürich. After increasing alienation between Zwingli and some of his followers concerning the nature of true Christianity and baptism, a theological disputation was convened to clarify the situation.

Thus a colloquy or disputation was called by the council for 17th January [1525], to be held in the City Hall before councillors and Zürich citizens as well as scholars. At that time . . . Mantz, Grebel, and also Reublin[6] were present to argue their case that children could not believe and did not understand the meaning of baptism. Baptism should be administered to believers to whom the Gospel had been preached, who understood it, and who therefore desired baptism, wanting to kill the old Adam and live a new life. Of this children knew nothing; therefore, baptism did not belong to them. They quoted passages from the Gospels and the Acts of the Apostles and showed that the Apostles did not baptize children, but only mature and understanding people. Thus should it be done today. Since there had been no proper baptism, infant baptism was not valid and everyone should be baptized again. Zwingli responded with the reasoning and argumentation which he subsequently published in a pamphlet dedicated to the people of St Gall entitled *Concerning Baptism, Rebaptism, and Infant Baptism*. The Anabaptists could neither refute his arguments nor maintain their own. . . . After the Disputation the Anabaptists were earnestly admonished by the council to desist from their position and to be quiet, since they could find no support in the Word of God. This, however, did not impress them. They said that they had to obey God rather than men. Restlessness and discord increased considerably. . . . Therefore, on 20th March a second disputation was held with them and their followers, of whom several had been arrested. In this second disputation they cited no more scriptural quotations than they had in the first. A lively discussion was held with them. Afterwards, the council talked earnestly with them and admonished them to retract their views, since such detrimental separation and division would not be tolerated any more. Several Anabaptists were kept in prison; others were banished from the region. This, however, resulted in nothing more than that they continued in their ways. . . . The Anabaptists also insisted that though a disputation had been held they had never received a real opportunity to present their case and that Zwingli would not let anyone talk freely. Restlessness and danger increased more and more. Therefore, the honourable city council of Zürich was prompted to call a colloquy which was to be especially free and open. Everyone was to say freely what could be supported with sacred Scripture. On the day of the disputation many Anabaptists from other places, such as St Gall, were present. The doctor from Waldshut, an Anabaptist [Hubmaier],[7] was expected, but did not come. Thus, Grebel and Mantz together with their associates represented the case. Against them stood Master Huldreich Zwingli, Master Leo Jud and Caspar Grossman. The propositions to be debated were the following: The children of Christians are no less the children of God than their parents, as was the case in the Old Testament. If they are the children of God, who will prevent them from receiving water baptism? Circumcision was to the men of old the same sign which baptism is to us. Inasmuch as circumcision was given to children, baptism shall likewise be given to children. Rebaptism finds no support, example or proof in the Word of God. Those who are rebaptized therefore crucify Christ anew— either because of stubbornness or innovation.

There were four chairmen of this disputation. . . . It began with prayer in the City Hall before councillors and citizens. . . . When the City Hall became too crowded barriers were put up in the nave of the Great Minster church as well as two tables and chairs. One table was reserved for the chairmen and the preachers, the other one for the Anabaptists. The latter were allowed to talk without restriction as long and as much as they wanted. The colloquy lasted throughout the entire day and two more days, November 6, 7 and 8. . . . A summary of the best arguments on both sides is briefly enumerated in Master Huldreich Zwingli's response to Dr Balthasar's [Hubmaier's] book. . . . After the colloquy, Grebel, Mantz and other Anabaptist patriarchs were cited before the council and admonished to desist from their views which had publicly been found to be false. Since these quarrelsome heads did not agree, they were kept in the tower. Soon, however, they were discharged and informed that if they continued their separatism they would be most severely punished.

Heinrich Bullinger, Reformationsgeschichte, I, 237–9.

▶   The result of the disputation was the formal affirmation of the practice of infant baptism on the part of the Zürich city council.

Erroneous opinion has arisen concerning baptism, that young children should not be baptized until they reach years of discretion and know the meaning of faith. Some have accordingly left their children unbaptized. Our Lords, the Mayors, Council and Great Council, called the Two

Hundred of Zürich, held a disputation concerning this matter to learn the view of the Holy Scripture. It was agreed that, contrary to such erroneous opinion, children should be baptized as soon as they are born. Therefore all those who have recently left their children unbaptized must have them baptized within eight days. Whoever does not want to do this must leave our town, jurisdiction and domain with his wife, children and property, or await further action against him. Everyone will know how to conduct himself.

18th January 1525. *Quellen zur Geschichte der Täufer*, Zürich, p. 35.

To the previous resolution concerning baptism, etc., is now added that it should be put into effect and that henceforth the special gatherings, arranged to deal with this matter, should be discontinued. Conrad Grebel and Mantz are to be informed that they should from now on desist from their disputation and opinion and accept the ruling of my lords. From now on no further disputations will be allowed. . . .

21st January 1525. *Quellen zur Geschichte der Täufer*, Zürich, p. 35.

▶   Another result was that the Zürich radicals, profoundly con-
     vinced of the rightness of their understanding, proceeded to
     perform baptism upon confession by faith. An Anabaptist
     Chronicle reported what happened.

But because God wished to have his own people, separated from all peoples, he willed for this purpose to bring in the right true morning star of his truth to shine in fullness in the final age of this world, especially in the German nation and lands, the same to strike home with his Word and to reveal the ground of divine truth. In order that his holy work might be made known and revealed before every man, there developed first in Switzerland an extraordinary awakening and preparation by God as follows:

It came to pass that Huldreich Zwingli and Conrad Grebel, one of the aristocracy, and Felix Mantz—all three much experienced and men learned in the German, Latin, Greek, and also the Hebrew languages— came together and began to talk through matters of belief among themselves and recognized that infant baptism is unnecessary and recognized further that it is, in fact, no baptism. Two, however, Conrad and Felix, recognized in the Lord and believed [further] that one must and should be correctly baptized according to the Christian ordinance and institution of the Lord, since Christ himself says that whoever *believes* and is baptized will be saved. Huldreich Zwingli, who shuddered before Christ's cross, shame and persecution, did not wish this and asserted that an uprising would break out. The other two, however, Conrad and Felix, declared that God's clear commandment and institution could not for that reason be allowed to lapse.

At this point it came to pass that a person from Chur came to them, namely, a cleric named George of the House of Jacob, commonly called 'Bluecoat' (*Blaurock*) because one time when they were having a discussion of matters of belief in a meeting this George Cajacob presented his view also. Then someone asked who it was who had just spoken. Thereupon someone answered: The person in the blue coat spoke. Thus thereafter he got the name of Blaurock. . . . This George came, moreover, with the unusual zeal which he had, a straightforward, simple parson. As such he was held by everyone. But in matters of faith and in divine zeal, which had been given him out of God's grace, he acted wonderfully and valiantly in the cause of truth. He first came to Zwingli and discussed matters of belief with him at length, but accomplished nothing. Then he was told that there were other men more zealous than Zwingli. These men he inquired for diligently and found them, namely, Conrad Grebel and Felix Mantz. With them he spoke and talked through matters of faith. They came to one mind in these things, and in the pure fear of God they recognized that a person must learn from the divine Word and preaching a true faith which manifests itself in love, and receive the true Christian baptism on the basis of the recognized and confessed faith, in the union with God of a good conscience, [prepared] henceforth to serve God in a holy Christian life with all godliness, also to be steadfast to the end in tribulation. And it came to pass that they were together until fear began to come over them, yea, they were pressed in their hearts. Thereupon, they began to bow their knees to the Most High God in heaven and called upon him as the knower of hearts, implored him to enable them to do his divine will and to manifest his mercy toward them. For flesh and blood and human forwardness did not drive them, since they well knew what they would have to bear and suffer on account of it. After the prayer, George Cajacob arose and asked Conrad to baptize him, for the sake of God, with the true Christian baptism upon his faith and knowledge. And when he knelt down with that request and desire, Conrad baptized him, since at that time there was no ordained deacon to perform such work. After that was done the others similarly desired George to baptize them, which he also did upon their request. Thus they together gave themselves to the name of the Lord in the high fear of God. Each confirmed the other in the service of the Gospel, and they began to teach and keep the faith. Therewith began the separation from the world and its evil works. *Die Älteste Chronik der Hutterischen Brüder*, pp. 45–47.

▶   The Anabaptist chronicler described the phenomenal spread of
     the Anabaptist movement:

Soon thereafter several others made their way to them, for example,
Balthasar Hubmaier of Friedberg, Ludwig Haetzer, and still others, men
well instructed in the German, Latin, Greek, and Hebrew languages, very
well versed in Scripture, some preachers and other persons, who were
soon to testify with their blood.

The above-mentioned Felix Mantz they drowned at Zürich because
of this true belief and true baptism, who thus witnessed steadfastly with
his body and life to this truth.

Afterward Wolfgang Ullmann, whom they burned with fire and put to
death in Waltzra, also in Switzerland, himself the eleventh, his brethren
and associates witnessing in a valorous and knightly manner with their
bodies and their lives unto death that their faith and baptism were
grounded in the divine truth. . . .

Thus did the movement spread through persecution and much tribulation. The Church increased daily, and the Lord's people grew in numbers.
This the enemy of the divine truth could not endure. He used Zwingli
as an instrument, who thereupon began to write diligently and to preach
from the pulpit that the baptism of believers and adults was not right and
should not be tolerated—contrary to his own confession which he had
previously written and taught, namely, that infant baptism cannot be
demonstrated or proved with a single clear word from God. But now,
since he wished rather to please men than God, he contended against the
true Christian baptism. He also stirred up the magistracy to act on imperial authorization and behead as Anabaptists those who had properly
given themselves to God, and with a good understanding had made covenant of a good conscience with God.

Finally it reached the point that over twenty men, widows, pregnant
wives and maidens were cast miserably into dark towers, sentenced never
again to see either sun or moon as long as they lived, to end their days on
bread and water, and thus in the dark towers to remain together, the living
and the dead, until none remained alive. . . .

Die Älteste Chronik der Hutterischen Brüder, pp. 47–49.

▶   The official response of the Zürich city council to the increasing
     spread of Anabaptism in Zürich territory was the severest one
     possible—rebaptism was made, on 7th March 1526, punishable
     by death.

Our Lords, the Mayors, Council and Great Council, called the Two
Hundred of Zürich, have for some time earnestly endeavoured to turn

the misguided and erring Anabaptists from their errors, etc. None the less, some of them, hardened against their oaths, vows and promises, have appeared disobedient to the detriment of public authority and government and the destruction of the common weal and true Christian institution. Several of them, both men, women and girls, were harshly punished and imprisoned by order of the Lords. It is therefore the earnest commandment, order and warning of these our Lords that no one in town, country and domain, whether man, woman or girl, shall henceforth baptize another. Whoever hereafter baptizes someone will be apprehended by our Lords and, according to this present decree, be drowned without mercy. It is hoped that everyone will know to avoid this lest he cause his own death. This pronouncement is to be proclaimed in the three parishes on Sunday. . . .

Quellen zur Geschichte der Täufer, Zürich, p. 180.

▶ An incidental, but in the long run quite important, by-product of the effort of the Zürich city council to suppress Anabaptism was the establishment of an official record of baptisms, marriages, etc. A mandate of the city council stated the reasons for the innovation.

Much trouble among Christian people everywhere has been caused by Anabaptists, so that some do not have their children baptized. Others claim that their children are baptized, whereas actually they are not. There are also some preachers and laymen who refuse to confirm marriage with public church attendance. Out of all this much confusion might arise among Christian people in future days. Therefore, the three people's priests desire that the Honourable Council permit them to inscribe in a list the names of the baptized children, as well as their parents and godparents, similarly those who formalize their marriage with public church attendance. Many reasons make this necessary. First of all, it seems good to know who is baptized and who is not, lest rebaptism become rampant overnight. One could always find in that book on which day of which year one was baptized as well as who presented him. Secondly, a marriage court seems advisable so that the age of sons and daughters can always be definitely known. For frequently fathers and mothers want to make the children younger than they actually are lest this cause problems concerning the actual date of the marriage. Thirdly, it seems advisable to record any publicly confirmed marriage so that it can be known who sits together as husband and wife, and who does not. The latter could be brought to a public announcement or to separation.

Emil Egli, *Aktensammlung zur Geschichte*, p. 466.

▶ The first victim of the stern persecution in Zürich was Felix
Mantz, a young humanist and early leader of the Zürich Anabaptist circle. For his involvement in Anabaptism he was
sentenced to drowning. The chronicler described his execution
on 5th January 1527.

When he was led from the Wellenberg to the fish market and . . . to
the boat, he praised God that he was to die for the sake of his truth, for
rebaptism was right and founded in the Word of God. Indeed, Christ had
prophesied that his own would have to suffer for the sake of truth. He
talked lengthily in this fashion, but was contradicted by the preacher who
accompanied him. When he was led out his mother and brother approached him and admonished him to remain steadfast. He was tied at the
little shed and was about to be pushed into the water by the executioner
when he sang with clear voice, '*In manus tuas, domine, commendo spiritum
meum*', or 'Lord, into thy hands I commend my spirit'. Then he was
pushed from the shed into the water and drowned. He was then taken to a
place and buried at St Jacob. Many people were upset by his courageous
death, though many were not concerned, since frequently those condemned in this fashion remain stubbornly in their false position. On the
same day on which Felix was thus sentenced, Jörg Blaurock was banished
from the city.

Heinrich Bullinger, *Reformationsgeschichte*, I, 382.

▶ Though there were among the early Anabaptists a number of
well-educated men, only one was a trained theologian—Balthasar Hubmaier, a doctor of theology and one-time professor at
the University of Ingolstadt. A vigorous opponent of infant
baptism, Hubmaier none the less attempted to advocate an
Anabaptist theology which had more in common with the major
Reformers than did most other Anabaptist thought. Like many
other Anabaptists, Hubmaier suffered martyrdom. The Anabaptist martyrology, the 'Martyrs' Mirror', has these words:

At the time of Zwingli there was also one Balthasar Hubmaier of
Friedberg, whom the papists called a doctor of the Holy Scriptures, a
learned and eloquent man. He was first a teacher and preacher at Ingolstadt, and subsequently came to Regensburg, where he preached mightily
against the Jews and their usury. Through the enlightenment of the Holy
Spirit, the abomination of popery was made manifest to him, in consequence of which he, according to the counsel of God, separated therefrom.
Subsequently he rejected, together with other errors, the self-invented
infant baptism, and taught with all his might the baptism of believers, as
commanded by Christ. But as the eyes of this dark world can not bear

the clear light of the holy Gospel, and since in this way their false faith and evil works are testified against, the above-mentioned Balthasar Hubmaier, together with many others, was hated and persecuted by the world. After many temptations, expulsions and imprisonments, he came to Nikolsburg, in Moravia. Afterwards they apprehended him and his wife, and brought them to Vienna, in Austria, where, after manifold trials and long imprisonment, he was burned to ashes, suffering it with great steadfastness, and his wife drowned; and thus both steadfastly confirmed with their death the faith which they had received from God.

Martyrs' Mirror, p. 465.

Brüderliche vereyni=
gung etzlicher kinder Gottes/
siben Artickel betreffend.

Item/Eyn sendtbrieff Michel sat=
lers/an eyn gemeyn Gottes/sampt kurtz=
em/doch warhafftigem anzeyg/wie
er seine leer zů Rottenburg am
Necker/mitt seinem blůt
bezeuget hat.

M. D. XXvij.

Title page of the Schleitheim Confession of 1527. The very simplicity (cf. p. 139) reflects rapid and secret printing.

▶ Early in 1527 a group of Anabaptists met at Schleitheim[8] in Switzerland and drew up what has come to be regarded as the most authoritative doctrinal document of early Anabaptism.[9]

Dear brethren and sisters, we who have been assembled in the Lord at Schleitheim on the Border, make known in points and articles to all who love God that as concerns us we are of one mind to abide in the Lord as God's obedient children, [his] sons and daughters, we who have been and shall be separated from the world in everything, [and] completely at peace. To God alone be praise and glory without the contradiction of any brethren. In this we have perceived the oneness of the Spirit of our Father and of our common Christ with us. For the Lord is the Lord of peace and not of quarrelling, as Paul points out. That you may understand in what articles this has been formulated you should observe and note [the following].

A very great offence has been introduced by certain false brethren among us, so that some have turned aside from the faith, in the way they intend to practise and observe the freedom of the Spirit and of Christ. But such have missed the truth and to their condemnation are given over to the lasciviousness and self-indulgence of the flesh. They think faith and love may do and permit everything, and nothing will harm them nor condemn them, since they are believers. . . .

But you are not that way. For they that are Christ's have crucified the flesh with its passions and lusts. You understand me well and [know] the brethren whom we mean. Separate yourselves from them, for they are perverted. Petition the Lord that they may have the knowledge which leads to repentance, and [pray] for us that we may have constancy to persevere in the way which we have espoused, for the honour of God and of Christ, his Son, Amen.

The articles which we discussed and on which we were of one mind are these: 1. Baptism; 2. The Ban [Excommunication]; 3. Breaking of Bread; 4. Separation from the Abomination; 5. Pastors in the Church; 6. The Sword; and 7. The Oath.

First. Observe concerning baptism: Baptism shall be given to all those who have learned repentance and amendment of life, and who believe truly that their sins are taken away by Christ, and to all those who walk in the resurrection of Jesus Christ, and wish to be buried with him in death, so that they may be resurrected with him, and to all those who with this significance request it [baptism] of us and demand it for themselves. . . .

Second. We are agreed as follows on the ban: The ban shall be employed with all those who have given themselves to the Lord, to walk in his commandments, and with all those who are baptized into the one body of Christ and who are called brethren or sisters, and yet who slip sometimes and fall into error and sin, being inadvertently overtaken. . . .

Third. In the breaking of bread we are of one mind and are agreed [as follows]: All those who wish to break one bread in remembrance of the broken body of Christ, and all who wish to drink of one drink as a remembrance of the shed blood of Christ, shall be united beforehand by baptism in one body of Christ which is the Church of God and whose head is Christ. . . .

Therefore it is and must be [thus]: Whoever has not been called by one God to one faith, to one baptism, to one Spirit, to one body, with all the children of God's Church, cannot be made [into] one bread with them, as indeed must be done if one is truly to break bread according to the command of Christ.

Fourth. We are agreed [as follows] on separation: A separation shall be made from the evil and from the wickedness which the devil planted in the world; in this manner, simply that we shall not have fellowship with them [the wicked] and not run with them in the multitude of their abominations. This is the way it is: Since all who do not walk in the obedience of faith, and have not united themselves with God so that they wish to do his will, are a great abomination before God, it is not possible for anything to grow or issue from them except abominable things. For truly all creatures are in but two classes, good and bad, believing and unbelieving, darkness and light, the world and those who [have come] out of the world, God's temple and idols, Christ and Belial; and none can have part with the other.

To us then the command of the Lord is clear when he calls upon us to be separate from the evil and thus he will be our God and we shall be his sons and daughters. . . .

Fifth. We are agreed as follows on pastors in the Church of God: The pastor in the Church of God shall, as Paul has prescribed, be one who out-and-out has a good report of those who are outside the faith. This office shall be to read, to admonish and teach, to warn, to discipline, to ban in the Church, to lead out in prayer for the advancement of all the brethren and sisters, to lift up the bread when it is to be broken, and in all things to see to the care of the body of Christ, in order that it may be built up and developed, and the mouth of the slanderer be stopped. . . .

Sixth. We are agreed as follows concerning the sword: The sword is ordained of God outside the perfection of Christ. It punishes and puts to death the wicked, and guards and protects the good. In the Law the sword was ordained for the punishment of the wicked and for their death, and the same [sword] is [now] ordained to be used by the worldly magistrates.

In the perfection of Christ, however, only the ban is used for a warning and for the excommunication of the one who has sinned, without putting the flesh to death—simply the warning and the command to sin no more. . . .

Seventh. We are agreed as follows concerning the oath: The oath is a confirmation among those who are quarrelling or making promises. In the Law it is commanded to be performed in God's name, but only in truth, not falsely. Christ, who teaches the perfection of the Law, prohibits all swearing to his [followers], whether true or false—neither by heaven, nor by the earth, nor by Jerusalem, nor by our head—and that for the reason which he shortly thereafter gives, for you are not able to make one hair white or black. So you see it is for this reason that all swearing is forbidden: we cannot fulfil that which we promise when we swear, for we cannot change [even] the very least thing on us. . . .

Dear brethren and sisters in the Lord: These are the articles of certain brethren who had heretofore been in error and who had failed to agree in the true understanding, so that many weaker consciences were perplexed, causing the name of God to be greatly slandered. Therefore there has been a great need for us to become of one mind in the Lord, which has come to pass. To God be praise and glory! . . .

Keep watch on all who do not walk according to the simplicity of the divine truth which is stated in this letter from [the decisions of] our meeting, so that everyone among us will be governed by the rule of the ban and henceforth the entry of false brethren and sisters among us may be prevented.

Eliminate from you that which is evil and the Lord will be your God and you will be his sons and daughters.

The Schleitheim Confession of Faith, pp. 247–53.

▶   The story of the vigorous expansion of the Anabaptist movement
     throughout Switzerland, Austria and Germany proved to be at
     once one of persecution and martyrdom.[10] Out of the numerous
     accounts of such Anabaptist martyrdom, three are printed
     below. The first deals with Michael Sattler, the outstanding
     South German Anabaptist,[11] the second and third with Dutch
     Anabaptists—Jan Claesz, Lucas Lamberts, and Elizabeth.

On the day of his departure from this world, the articles against him being many, Michael Sattler . . . requested that they might once more be read to him and that he might again be heard upon them. This the bailiff, as the attorney of his lord [the Emperor], opposed and would not consent to it. Michael Sattler then requested a ruling. After a consultation, the judges returned as their answer that, if his opponents would allow it, they, the judges, would consent. Thereupon the town clerk of Ensisheim, as the spokesman of the said attorney, spoke thus: 'Prudent, honourable and wise lords, he has boasted of the Holy Ghost. Now if his boast is true, it seems to me, it is unnecessary to grant him this; for, if he has the Holy Ghost, as he boasts, the same will tell him what has been done here.' To this Michael Sattler replied, 'You servants of God, I hope my request will not be denied, for the said articles are as yet unclear to me [because of their number].' The town clerk responded, 'Prudent, honourable and wise lords, though we are not bound to do this, yet in order to give satisfaction, we will grant him his request that it may not be thought that injustice is being done him in his heresy or that we desire to abridge him of his rights. Hence let the articles be read to him again.' . . .

Thereupon Michael Sattler requested permission to confer with his brethren and sisters, which was granted him. Having conferred with them for a little while, he began and undauntedly answered as follows: 'In regard to the articles relating to me and my brethren and sisters, hear this brief answer.

'First, that we have acted contrary to the imperial mandate, we do not admit. For the same says that the Lutheran doctrine and delusion is not to be adhered to, but only the Gospel and the Word of God. I appeal to the words of Christ.

'Secondly, that the real body of Christ the Lord is not present in the sacrament, we admit. . . .

'Thirdly, as to baptism we say infant baptism is of no avail to salvation. . . .

'Fourthly, we have not rejected the oil [of extreme unction]. For it is a creature of God, and what God has made is good and not to be refused, but that the Pope, bishops, monks and priests can make it better we do not believe; for the Pope never made anything good. . . .

'Fifthly, we have not insulted the mother of God and the saints. For the mother of Christ is to be blessed among all women because unto her was accorded the favour of giving birth to the Saviour of the whole world. But that she is a mediatrix and advocatess—of this the Scriptures know nothing, for she must with us await the judgment. . . . If they prove to us with the Holy Scriptures that we err and are in the wrong, we will gladly desist and recant and also willingly suffer the sentence and punishment for that of which we have been accused; but if no error is proven to us, I hope to God that you will be converted and receive instruction.'

Upon this speech the judges laughed and put their heads together, and the town clerk of Ensisheim said, 'Yes, you infamous, desperate rascal of a monk, should we dispute with you? The hangman will dispute with you, I assure you!'

Michael said, 'God's will be done.'

The town clerk said, 'It were well if you had never been born.'

Michael replied, 'God knows what is good.'

The town clerk: 'You archheretic, you have seduced pious people. If they would only now forsake their error and commit themselves to grace!'

Michael: 'Grace is with God alone.'

One of the prisoners also said, 'We must not depart from the truth.'

The town clerk: 'Yes, you desperate villain, you archheretic, I say, if there were no hangman here, I would hang you myself and be doing God a good service thereby.'

Michael: 'God will judge aright.' Thereupon the town clerk said a few words to him in Latin, what, we do not know. Michael Sattler answered him: 'Judge!'

The town clerk then admonished the judges and said, 'He will not cease from this chatter anyway. Therefore, my Lord Judge, you may proceed with the sentence. I call for a decision of the court.'

The judge asked Michael Sattler whether he, too, committed it to the court. He replied: 'Ministers of God, I am not sent to judge the Word of God. We are sent to testify and hence cannot consent to any adjudication, since we have no command from God concerning it. But we are not for that reason removed from being judged and we are ready to suffer and to await what God is planning to do with us. We will continue in our faith in Christ so long as we have breath in us, unless we be dissuaded from it by the Scriptures.'

The town clerk said, 'The hangman will instruct you; he will dispute with you, archheretic.'

Michael: 'I appeal to the Scriptures.'

Then the judges arose and went into another room, where they remained for an hour and a half and determined on the sentence. In the meantime some [of the soldiers] in the room treated Michael Sattler most unmercifully, heaping reproach upon him. One of them said, 'What have you in prospect for yourself and the others that you have so seduced them?' With this he also drew a sword which lay upon the table, saying, 'See, with this they will dispute with you.' But Michael did not answer upon a single word concerning himself, but willingly endured it all. One of the prisoners said, 'We must not cast pearls before swine.' . . .

The judges having returned to the room, the sentence was read. It was as follows: 'In the case of the attorney of his Imperial Majesty *versus* Michael Sattler, judgment is passed that Michael Sattler shall be delivered to the executioner, who shall lead him to the place of execution and cut out his tongue, then forge him fast to a wagon and thereon with red-hot tongs twice tear pieces from his body; and after he has been brought outside the gate, he shall be plied five times more in the same manner. . . .'

After this had been done in the manner prescribed, he was burned to ashes as a heretic. His fellow brethren were executed with the sword, and

TOMAS MVNCER PREDIGER ZV ALSTET IN DVRINGEN.

Thomas Müntzer. In the background his execution. (*Engraving by Christoph, V(an) S(ichem)*, Historische Beechrijvinge ende affbeelding . . ., *Amsterdam,* 1608)

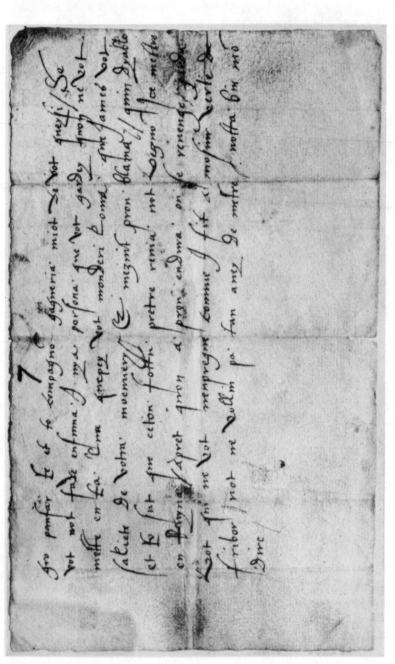

Jacques Gruet's anti-Calvin poster. (*Archives d'État, Geneva*)

the sisters drowned. His wife, also after being subjected to many entreaties, admonitions, and threats, under which she remained steadfast, was drowned a few days afterward.

Martyrs' Mirror, p. 465 (*BRN* II, 62–67; 645–50).

When Jan Claesz and Lucas Lamberts, an old man of eighty-seven years, called grandfather, came into court, they greeted each other with a kiss.

Jan Claesz said to the grandfather, 'My dear brother, how do you feel?'

The grandfather replied pleasantly with a glad countenance, 'Quite well, my dear brother.'

Then said Jan Claesz, 'Fear neither fire nor the sword. Oh, what a joyful feast will be prepared for us before the clock strikes twelve!'

Upon this they were separated.

The bailiff then said, 'You are rebaptized.'

Jan Claesz answered, 'I was baptized upon my faith, as all Christians ought to be, according to the Scriptures; read this.' Matt. 28.19.

They said to him again, 'You belong to the accursed Anabaptists, who originate strange sects, opinions, errors and contention among the people.' Acts 16.20; 17.6.

Jan Claesz: 'We are not such people; we desire nothing else than the true Word of God; if I am to suffer therefore, I demand the seven judges.'

He was then asked whether he did not confess that he was rebaptized four years ago or thereabouts.

Jan Claesz replied, 'Three years ago or thereabouts I was baptized as all Christians ought to be.'

The court said, 'You acknowledge it then?'

Jan Claesz: 'Yes.'

Court: 'Well, since you confess it, we have full power from the seven judges.' . . .

The four judges then went out to pronounce the sentence.

Lifting up his voice, Jan Claesz said, 'O merciful Father, thou knowest that we do not desire revenge' (Rom. 12.19), and he wrung his hands, saying, 'O merciful Father, grant them thy Spirit, that thou mayest not count this to them as wickedness.' Acts 7.60.

The four judges now returned into the court, and sat down to declare the sentence, saying, 'Jan Claesz, a native of Alkmaar, who has taught the people false doctrines, errors and new opinions—'

Upon this Jan Claesz answered, 'It is not so.'

The lords of the court then forbade Jan Claesz to speak, and good Jan Claesz observed silence, that he might hear his sentence. They then proceeded with their sentence, and said to the clerk, 'Read his crime.' He read that he had caused to be printed at Antwerp six hundred books, which he had concluded with Menno Simons, and scattered abroad in this country, containing strange opinions and sectarianism, and had kept school and held meetings, to introduce errors among the people (Acts 17.6), which is contrary to the decree of the Emperor, and our mother the holy Church, and which it is not proper for my lords of the court to tolerate, but to correct.

Here Jan Claesz reproved them as before, saying: 'They are not sectarianisms, but it is the Word of God.' Acts 24.14.

Then the lords of the court said: 'We sentence you to death, to be executed with the sword, the body to be placed on the wheel, and the head upon a stake; *we* do not sentence you, but the court does.'

As Jan Claesz went out of the court, he said, 'You citizens bear witness that we die for no other reason than for the true Word of God.' This occurred in the court. Having ascended the scaffold, Jan Claesz audibly addressed the people with these words: 'Hear, ye citizens of Amsterdam; be it known unto you, that I suffer not as a thief or murderer, or because we have sought the property or life of others. However, do not understand me as justifying or exalting myself; but I come with the prodigal son, and depend only on the pure Word of God.'

Upon this the executioner struck him on his breast. Jan Claesz turned around, and exclaimed with a loud voice:

'O Lord, forsake me not, now or in eternity. Lord, thou Son of David, receive my soul.'

Martyrs' Mirror, p. 471.

Elizabeth [Dirks] was apprehended on the 15th of January 1549. When those who had come to apprehend her entered the house in which she lived, they found a Latin Testament. Having secured Elizabeth, they said, 'We have got the right man; we have now the teacheress', adding: 'Where is your husband, Menno Simons, the teacher?'

They then brought her to the town-house. The following day two beadles took her between them to prison.

She was then arraigned before the council, and asked upon oath whether she had a husband.

Elizabeth answered, 'We ought not to swear, but our words should be yea, yea, and nay, nay; I have no husband.'

Lords: 'We say that you are a teacher, and that you seduce many. We have been told this, and we want to know who your friends are.'

Elizabeth: 'My God has commanded me to love my Lord and my God, and to honour my parents; hence I will not tell you who my parents are; for what I suffer for the name of Christ is a reproach to my friends.'

Lords: 'We will let you alone in regard to this, but we want to know whom you have taught.'

Elizabeth: 'Oh, no, my lords, let me in peace with this, but interrogate me concerning my faith, which I will gladly tell you.'

Lords: 'We shall make you so afraid that you will tell us.'

Elizabeth: 'I hope through the grace of God that he will keep my tongue, so that I shall not become a traitoress, and deliver my brother into death.'

Lords: 'What persons were present when you were baptized?'

Elizabeth: 'Christ said: Ask them that were present, or who heard it.' John 18.21.

Lords: 'Now we perceive that you are a teacher; for you compare yourself to Christ.'

Elizabeth: 'No, my lords, far be it from me; for I do not esteem myself above the offscourings which are swept out from the house of the Lord.'

Lords: 'What then do you hold concerning the house of God? Do you not regard our church as the house of God?'

Elizabeth: 'No, my lords, for it is written: "Ye are the temple of the living God; as God hath said, I will dwell in them, and walk in them."' II Cor. 6.16.

Lords: 'What do you hold concerning our mass?'

Elizabeth: 'My lords, of your mass I think nothing at all; but I highly esteem all that accords with the Word of God.' . . .

Lords: 'What are your views concerning infant baptism, seeing you have been rebaptized?'

Elizabeth: 'No, my lords, I have not been rebaptized. I have been baptized once upon my faith; for it is written that baptism belongs to believers.'

Lords: 'Are our children damned then, because they are baptized?'

Elizabeth: 'No, my lords, God forbid, that I should judge the children.'

Lords: 'Do you not seek your salvation in baptism?'

Elizabeth: 'No, my lords, all the water in the sea could not save me;

but salvation is in Christ (Acts 4.10), and he has commanded me to love God my Lord above all things, and my neighbour as myself.' . . .

The foregoing is the first confession.

Afterwards she was again brought before the council, and led into the torture chamber, Hans, the executioner, being present. The lords then said, 'We have thus long dealt with you in kindness; but if you will not confess, we will resort to severity with you.' The Procurator-General said, 'Master Hans, seize her.'

Master Hans answered, 'Oh, no, my lords, she will voluntarily confess.'

But as she would not voluntarily confess, he applied the thumbscrew to her thumbs and forefingers, so that the blood squirted out at the nails.

Elizabeth said, 'Oh! I cannot endure it any longer.'

The lords said, 'Confess, and we will relieve your pain.'

But she cried to the Lord her God: 'Help me, O Lord, thy poor handmaiden! For thou art a helper in time of need.'

The lords all exclaimed, 'Confess, and we will relieve your pain; for we told you to confess, and not to cry to God the Lord.'

But she steadfastly adhered to God her Lord, as related above; and the Lord took away her pain, so that she said to the lords, 'Ask me, and I shall answer you; for I no longer feel the least pain in my flesh, as I did before.'

Lords: 'Will you not yet confess?'

Elizabeth: 'No, my lords.'

They then applied the screws to her shins, one on each.

She said: 'O my lords, do not put me to shame; for never a man touched my bare body.'

The Procurator-General said, 'Miss Elizabeth, we shall not treat you dishonourably.'

She then fainted away. They said to one another: 'Perhaps she is dead.'

But waking up, she said, 'I live, and am not dead.'

They then took off all the screws, and plied her with entreaties.

Elizabeth: 'Why do you thus entreat me? This is the way to do with children.'

Thus they obtained not one word from her, detrimental to her brethren in the Lord, or to any other person.

Lords: 'Will you revoke all that you have previously confessed here?'

Elizabeth: 'No, my lords, but I will seal it with my death.'

Lords: 'We will try you no more; will you voluntarily tell us, who baptized you?'

Elizabeth: 'Oh, no, my lords; I have certainly told you that I will not confess this.'

Sentence was then passed upon Elizabeth, on the 27th of May [March], 1549; she was condemned to death.

Martyrs' Mirror, pp. 481-2.

▶ The governmental and legal efforts to suppress Anabaptism found many expressions. Here is a theological proposal for combating the movement in Flanders. The marginal comments of a jurist who had been asked to assess the document are found in parentheses.[12]

1. It should be made public at all those places where announcements usually are made that a woman who gives birth to a child must have the child baptized within twenty-four hours. If on account of some illness the child cannot live that long, it must be baptized immediately after birth, under penalty of . . .

2. The father must accompany the child to the baptism and must ask the pastor or chaplain to give his child the sacrament of baptism and thus accept it in the fellowship of the Christian Church.

3. If the child's father is absent at the time of its birth, he must go within twenty-four hours after his return to thank the pastor or chaplain for baptizing his child and accepting it in the fellowship of the Holy Roman Church, under penalty. . . .

4. After the purification and convalescence the child's mother must go to church, and as is customary stand outside until she is invited inside by the pastor or chaplain. The pastor will ask her first whether she accepts that her child has been baptized and accepted into the fellowship of the Holy Roman Church. If she agrees, she may enter the church; if not, she shall be forbidden to enter and the pastor will inform the officer, who will record the fact according to imperial command.

(To have to stand before the church is impractical and unusual; still the pastor could speak with her as the article says.)

5. No one may fail, when labour pangs begin, to send for two near neighbours, under penalty.

(Impractical; many nobles and wealthy persons would not want to call in their poor neighbours.)

6. If neighbours, friends or midwives know of some unbaptized child, they must report this within two days, under penalty.

(Unless waiting for the godparents.)

The next article deals with those who do not bear children and with travelling merchants.

7. Everyone over fourteen years old must receive the holy sacrament of the body and the blood of Christ at least once a year; this must take place between Palm Sunday and the last holiday after Easter . . .

8. To be able to see who is absent, it shall be ordained that in all cities and villages the neighbours shall take mass together, reckoning as a neighbourhood unit the part of the city between two bridges; villages shall be divided into four or eight parts, depending on their size.

(To these articles the mendicant monks will object, who now give communion without distinction, those who have dispensation; wherefore this could not be done without papal revocation of said privileges.)

9. If someone has travelled outside the city or village, he must, on the second or third day after his return, go to the pastor and receive the holy sacrament, thus uniting himself with all Christians in the unity of faith and the common peace. . . . He must also receive a certificate from the pastor or chaplain, after receiving the holy sacrament, to show, if necessary, to the police.

(This article is in conformity with the practice of the ancient Church, but would not be practical for application.)

10. Two of the nearest neighbours shall be obliged, after receiving the holy sacrament, to inform the pastor which of their nearest neighbours is absent; of whom the pastor or a policeman appointed for the purpose shall take note and keep watch, so that after his return he who was absent will not be found to be disobedient to these articles; if he is disobedient, the magistrate will be informed, and will constrain him to obey or else punish him according to imperial command.

11. No one shall contract marriage in secret; it shall take place publicly according to old ordinance and usage of the Holy Church. . . . Under penalty.

(Impracticable for those who have dispensations from their lords or bishops; contrary to custom. One cannot prove that all marriages have always been performed before the church door, though it is true that the practice of secret marriage covers many sects.)

If anyone, man or woman, unwilling to obey these orders, flees, the husband leaving his wife, or the wife leaving her husband, the remaining person shall notify the competent local officer. The remaining person shall with all due diligence ascertain where the fugitive has established residence, and inform the officer, who will inform his Royal Majesty's court, where a letter shall be written to all the lords of the land, instructing them to seize the fugitive, to ban him, or otherwise to punish such persons. (This one is not bad.) . . .

A. L. E. Verheyden, *Anabaptism in Flanders*, pp. 109-11. (Brussels Royal Archives, EA 1171/3).

▶ One illustration for spread of Anabaptism in the Low Countries is described indirectly in the following document.[13]

Philip, by the grace of God King of Castille, Leon, Aragon, England. . . . Be it known to everyone present and future, that we have received the humble supplication of Roelandt van Loo, son of Roelandt Vlesschouwere, seller of fish, burgher and resident of Ghent, certifying that Roelandt is an honest, peaceable man, descended from good honest parents, who taught and directed Roelandt to live according to the old order of the common and Catholic Church, which Roelandt has always tried to follow.

However, last summer there came to him one evening Victor Seysins, who also is a butcher, and asked Roelandt to go for a walk with him, to which Roelandt agreed, suspecting nothing.

Victor led Roelandt to the Burchstede, where he asked him to wait a moment on the street; Roelandt waited. Victor left, went into a side street, and shortly returned with a young man, absolutely unknown to Roelandt, who had never seen him before. This young man invited him to go along for a walk outside the gates early in the morning, saying, 'You will hear something there which will please you very much.'

For this reason Roelandt went, on the day fixed by the same person, and waited for a moment at the agreed place, where the said unknown person also arrived. Roelandt was led to a grain field, without knowing where he was going; the same person only said, 'Follow me.' When they reached the grain field, Roelandt saw sitting in it about ten or twelve people and three or four girls or women, who were all unknown to Roelandt, since he had never had any dealings with them before.

There Roelandt also heard another young man, unknown, speak for a long time, and he remembers among other things, 'that everyone should beware of evil and improve his life and that all drunkards and adulterers would not enter the kingdom of God'. Afterward one of the girls or women had black cherries in her lap, which were shared by all; then the group broke up and everyone went home.

A certain time after this meeting the same Victor Seysins again came to Roelandt and asked him again to go walking, which he did. Victor brought him past the Cuup Gate which stands in said city and into an alley, where Victor knocked on the door of a house with which Roelandt was not acquainted, which he had never seen. Opening the door, Victor entered, telling Roelandt to come along, which he did. Entering the house, he met three or four people, all of them unknown to him, as he had never seen them before, one of whom stated publicly 'that God is to be greatly praised and thanked, for all things were now revealed which had been hidden so long'. They had several talks and discussions, which Roelandt does not remember, because he did not understand. . . .

Roelandt did not desire to attend more such meetings nor listen to these people, therefore he avoided them for a long time and was on his guard. Several times people came to see him in the shop and on the street and asked why he no longer desired their society. He answered that he did not care for it and was busy with other things; finally the same fat man came and asked him the same questions, which Roelandt answered, saying he was too busy. The fat man asked him where he lived and whether he would consent to let four or five people meet in the evening in his home. Roelandt allowed this, without knowing who the people were whom they would bring to his house.

So the same man came to Roelandt's house, bringing eight or nine people along: Laureyns de Brauwere, Pieter de Cleerck, a miller, Willem Villeers, Gheert de Cortewaghencruudere, and some others not known to Roelandt. The same fat man preached from the Old and New Testaments without ever mentioning rebaptism; they left his house again. This was about three or four months ago and afterward Roelandt never met the same people again and never attended their meetings and he never had any evil feelings, even during those meetings and evil unseemly sermons, toward our Mother, the Holy Church, and he went to confession and received the sacraments and other things, as a child of the Holy Church should and must do, until Easter 1556, when he was in Holland on a business trip. He had also abstained for some time, because of those preachers who were attacking it, although he never agreed with their attacks.

A. L. E. Verheyden, *Anabaptism in Flanders*, pp. 114–16
(Ghent City Archives, 93 T, 417ff.).

▶ As the following court record from Bruges, in present-day Belgium, show, inquisitorial inquisitiveness knew no bounds when faced with the problem of apprehending Anabaptist suspects.[14]

Proceedings against Mennonites of Bruges arrested 24th and 29th June 1558.

Done at the Steen, 24th June. Present: The Burgomaster of the council, the Burgomaster of the guilds, the Governor, and Jan van Heede, council member.

Lievekin van der Veste, son of Jan Verveste, twelve years old, ribbon weaver, says that he was born at Ghent and lived there at the Techelrie for ten or eleven years; then he left for Holland with his father and mother, to Amsterdam for about a year; from there they came to Bruges and lived there for about two or three months.

Says he was christened in the St Jans Church at Ghent and that he went to church; always went to confession with his father and mother till about three or four years ago and not any more only because his father and mother will not allow it. Says that they came back from Holland because there was no work for his father; his father now works here for Franchois Dhondt. Says he hears his father and mother say, 'Things are better now than before.'

He saw his father and mother meet with several people, up to seven or eight, at his home, but does not know what they said, because they sent him out to play. His brothers and sisters are Hanskin, Betkin, Cyncken, Michielkin. The latter two live at Ghent, Cyncken with the man in the house "t mortaens hooft' across the street from the Franciscan Friars, together with her uncle, with whom she has lived ever since she was two, and Michielkin with Jacop Vroyelick, on the other side of the Jacobin Bridge. Cyncken is seven years old and Michielkin about eight. Besides these his father had three other children; Cornelis, who died when he was three, Neelken when she was two, and Zusannekin when she was one year old. None of them was baptized in the Church or in a basin at home or anywhere else, since, as Lievekin heard his father say, 'they know better now'. He has not been to church for four or five years, but he has prayed at every meal at home and sometimes reads the Lord's Prayer, but did not learn the Hail Mary because his mother told him that this was not good.

The two persons who were taken captive with him were his cousins, who live at Nieuport. One is a miller named Jacob, the other a cabinet-maker named Hanskin; he had heard them say at the table on the evening they were taken prisoner that they thanked God that they had found the truth and it grieved them that they had erred so long.

Betkin van der Veste, sister of Lievekin, thirteen years old, says that she was born at Ghent and lived there with Miss van der Catulle for about six months. Her father came from Holland to get her from there half a year ago, and she again lived with her father and his family at Amsterdam, until they came to Bruges. Previously she had lived at Antwerp with a Gheraewert Harinck to learn sewing and lived with him till the city officers came to look for him because he read the Bible, but they didn't find him, and she doesn't know whether he has been caught since then. Says it was about four or five years ago that she heard her father and mother say that they know better now, and that the baptism practised here is not right, but they understood now that there is another baptism; people should be baptized when they understand and change their lives, when they no longer lie and deceive.

She says further that it is about half a year since her father and mother were rebaptized. The baptism was performed off the Techelrie near the Oof Bridge, where Willem van Leuvene lived, who was the leader, and several persons were present, of whom some have been burned at Ghent, to wit, said Willem and Vincken his wife.

Says that she does not go to church and never went during the time she lived with her father and mother, which is about six months; at Amsterdam her father left her with a sick woman, whom she attended until about a month before they came to Bruges. At Ghent, living with Miss van der Catulle, she went to confession to Friar Pieter de Backere, a Jacobin monk, who punished her because she believed more what her father said than what Friar Pieter said. . . .

Hanskin van der Veste, brother of the above, fifteen years old, says that it is about five years that his father and mother knew of the new sect and that his friends therefore took him away from them and brought him to the home of Michiel de Draettreckere, who, however, also read the Bible, and then after about a year to the home of Jan de Meij, who is a shingler, whom he left about 13th June 1557. From then on he lived with his father at Amsterdam and Bruges; during which time he went neither to confession nor to church, because he had heard that that was not right, in such a way that he half-way believed it; but concerning baptism or rebaptism he knows nothing, except that a certain Willem van Leuvene used to come to the home of his father and mother, but they did not tell him what they did. . . .

His father and mother had had to leave Ghent because of the Scriptures and he understood that they were Anabaptists and that they were grieved by the fact that Hanskin did not join them and accept their teachings; furthermore that he heard them say that they baptized no one unless they desired it.

Vincken Verwee, wife of Jan Verveste, born at Deinse, says that she has lived at Ghent ever since she was eleven years old and about five years ago she accepted another faith, leaving the Roman Church, mass, and the other sacraments, because they are founded on human inventions and idolatries, giving as a reason: 'The vineyard which my father did not plant. . . .' Later she was rebaptized, about three years ago, in the city of Ghent at the home of a person she does not know, on Holstraet. He was Gillis van Haecke, she remembers, who was beheaded at Antwerp. She says she would not like to die as he died, for he gave up his faith. . . . Says she finds nothing of God in the Church and that she has not had her last child baptized. She also did not have her older and living children rebaptized because they had not asked for it and were not mature enough yet; should her youngest child die without baptism, she would not have it baptized before death. . . .

Her husband had been baptized together with her the same day and hour in the same house. She came in contact with this faith for the first time because her husband had to do with rhetoric and in this connection had to do with the Scriptures and she listened carefully and finally they joined this sect. . . . They call each other brethren and sisters.

This Vincken has been visited by the two sworn municipal midwives, because she had said she was ill; these declared under oath that they had not found her to be nearing childbirth. On 11th September, at about noon, she gave birth to a male child. The midwives said that the child had not yet begun to live; it was taken to a foster-mother the same day. 16th September the jailer reported that Vincken had a swollen head and a surgeon should be sent; the report was made to the council, which decided that the expenses should be charged to the inquisitor whose prisoner she was. Vincken died in the prison from the swelling which descended from her head and suffocated her 20th September. She was buried at night, with the authorization of the secretary in the inquisitor's absence, at St Jans in unconsecrated earth, because of her impenitence and obstinacy. . . .

Hans van den Broucke, unmarried, linen weaver, born at Ghent, says that about two years ago he was rebaptized in that city at the home of a shoemaker not far from the house of Lieven de Ooghe, out of obedience to the Scriptures, for he only knows about one baptism in the Scriptures and that is the one received by those who have come to the age of discretion; he received it at the age of twenty or twenty-one. He is not doubtful about it, for he is consoled by the Scriptures; furthermore he does not follow the Roman Church or the seven sacraments, which are not based on the Scriptures, but are human inventions.

He, Hans, lives at Oostende near the quai at the East Mill, with the miller, Jacob de Zwarte. He has discussed the Scriptures with him but does not remember telling him that he had been rebaptized; says he does not want to accuse or betray him; says that he has a father, living at Ghent at the place called 'up de mude', who is a carpenter, named Jan van den Broucke, with whom he discussed the Scriptures, but he did not want to believe him.

Decided by the council that if this Hans van den Broucke does not confess, he shall be strangled at the stake and burned to powder; if he confesses, he shall be executed with the sword. Decided 13th October 1558. Said Hans was executed by fire 15th October.

> A. L. E. Verheyden, *Anabaptism in Flanders*, pp. 116–19
> (Bruges City Archives, Bouc van den Sleene, 1558–9,
> fol. 89–95).

▶ One of the most dramatic early Anabaptists, responsible for the spread of the movement from South Germany to the North, was Melchior Hoffman.[15] Expecting the imminent return of Christ, Hoffman later on voluntarily entered the Strassburg prison to be found there in martyrdom when that glorious moment arrived. It never did, and Hoffman died in prison. Here are excerpts from the official Strassburg documents which describe his case.

4th May 1534: Melchior Hoffman desires to be put into the tower so that he will see neither sun nor moon until God will have mercy upon him and bring the matter to a conclusion. This present year is to be watched, for it is the year of which he has written for some time. He prophesies in a confusing fashion, says stupid things, etc.

> *Quellen zur Geschichte der Täufer*, Elsass II, 312.

9th September 1534: Melchior Hoffman said among other things that he was in the hands of my lords. But he counselled them not to shed his innocent blood. They should know that he was the prophet Elijah, who will precede the Last Judgment. God had sent him to us, but we did not want to know him. He is the last one. God would not send any more.

> *Quellen zur Geschichte der Täufer*, Elsass II, 386.

23rd November 1534: Melchior Hoffman desired to announce to the proper authorities that, first of all, this is the city which God had elected above all others to his glory. Secondly, that the rulers of this city would establish his perfect truth. . . . Concerning the first point he knew that all prophecies, old and new, concerning this city and its inhabitants would be revealed through his brethren in Holland, but kept from them here. He would like to reveal the prophecies to this city that they might be properly informed. For example, they had known before, through prophecies which said that a hundred would be expelled, that many of his followers would be banished. . . . Now the office of prophecy is also in this city, as Leonhard Jobst has indicated. Thus no harm should be done to him. He mentions Jonah, who preached on God's behalf to the city of Nineveh.

Quellen zur Geschichte der Täufer, Elsass II, 393.

15th April 1535: Melchior Hoffman reports to the city officials, as military authorities, that he volunteered in 1530 and 1534 to make statements concerning several prophecies. These he now wants to explain. First of all, he said that God had commanded that they should heed the Word of God. Secondly, the city should supply itself with food and all necessities, for it would suffer hunger and waste. It should also supply itself with arms. In the third year of his imprisonment, God will come.

Quellen zur Geschichte der Täufer, Elsass II, 444.

8th May 1539: Pfutzer and Gerfalck report that they had recently visited Melchior Hoffman when he was cleaned up. Both his face and legs were greatly swollen. He requests that my lords should let him out for a month until he feels better, then he will gladly go back.

Resolved: to let him out of the hole. He is to be carefully guarded, however.

Friedrich O. zur Linden, *Melchior Hofmann* (Haarlem, 1885), p. 470.

▶ Much disrepute was brought upon the Anabaptist movement by the development in the city of Münster,[16] where some Anabaptists, not altogether typical of the movement at large, undertook to realize a 'New Jerusalem'. After the Anabaptists had succeeded in obtaining control of the city, they sent out an appeal to those of like mind to come and join them.[17]

Dear friends, you are to know and recognize the work God has done among us so that everyone might arise to the New Jerusalem, the city of the saints, for God wants to punish the world. Let everyone watch lest he through carelessness fall under the judgment. Jan Bokelson, the prophet of Münster, has written us with all his helpers in Christ that no one can remain free under the dragon of this world, but will suffer bodily or spiritual death. Therefore let no one neglect to come unless he wishes to tempt God. There is turmoil in all the world and the prophet Jeremiah says in the 51st chapter: flee from Babylon that everyone may keep his soul, then your heart will not become discouraged on account of the call heard in the lands. I say nothing more, but command you in the name of the Lord to be obedient without delay and redeem the time. Let everyone heed and remember Lot's wife. Do not look after earthly goods, be it husband, wife or child, lest you be deceived. Let no one look after an unbelieving wife or husband, nor take them along, nor look after unbelieving children who are disobedient and are not under the rod, since they are of no profit to the congregation of the Lord. Here are available sufficient goods for the saints. Therefore do not take anything along, except money and clothes and food for travel. Whoever has a knife, lance or rifle should take it along. Whoever does not have such should buy himself such, for the Lord will redeem us through his mighty hand and through his servants, Moses and Aaron. Therefore be careful and watch for the evil one. Gather half a mile from Hasselt near the mountain cloister on 24th March around noon. Be careful in all things. Be not there before the appointed day nor later, for we will not wait for any. Let no one neglect to come. If anyone stays behind, I will be innocent of his blood. Emmanuel.

Harting, *De Munsterische Furie*, p. 78.

▶   **In Münster itself extensive changes were undertaken by the Anabaptists. Later on several nuns testified about their initial encounter with the new régime in the city.**

On the first Monday in Lent the agitators elected a new council, consisting of immigrants, shoemakers, tailors, furriers and other artisans. Already the previous Saturday several men—Bernt Knipperdoling, Kort Kruse and Klaus Snider—had come to our cloister. They inspected the cloister, but did not demand anything. On the contrary, they spoke some kind words. None the less, we were dismayed, since we could not know their intentions. The following Sunday, the first Sunday of Lent, the council informed us that we should tear down our garden house and the fence, or else it would be burned down. Some of the sisters had to leave the table—we were just eating—and go into the garden and tear them down. It was wet and cold outside and it rained and snowed heavily. . . . On Tuesday two new mayors were elected. They ordered us to leave and vacate our place or be baptized again. We delayed the decision. . . . The following day several Anabaptists came to our gate between eight and nine o'clock in the morning and asked that it be opened or else they would break in. When the gate was not immediately opened, they beat vehemently against it and caused us great dismay. Since they made such great noise, our priest, Master Egbert, opened the gate. They pushed their weapons, halberts, lances, and spears into the gate and thus entered forcibly. They entered our church, where they took the ornaments, first the three gilded silver chalices. The monstrance, which was also of gilded silver, had been hidden, in the hope that it might be kept. When the Anabaptists did not find it, they surrounded our priest in the church and threatened him with imprisonment and torture unless he would show it to them. They forced him and pressed him. In his fear he asked us to get it and give it to them; this we did. . . . They broke whatever they could not take along. Thus they broke the relics tablet. The priest had earlier taken the holy sacrament out of the monstrance and fed two of the sisters lest the intruders crush it with their feet as they have done elsewhere.

Chronik des Schwesterhauses Marienthal, pp. 430–2.
(Löffler, pp. 48–49.)

▶   In the spring of 1534 occurred the dramatic and unexpected death of the 'prophet' Jan Matthijs.

This same prophet, Jan Matthijs, and his wife were invited to a wedding of a fellow countryman. (Jan's wife incidentally became queen immediately after his death by marrying Jan van Leiden.) Jan Matthijs came to the house as guest together with his friends. They jovially sat at the table—whenever the Anabaptists came together they wanted to rejoice in the Lord according to the example of Paul and the prophets. They sat together, endeavouring to instruct one another. They wanted to be holy, but it was a foolish striving. Thus, they were jovially sitting at the table together with bride and groom. When the meat was about to be served, Jan Matthijs was overcome by the Anabaptist spirit. He sat quietly, clapped his hands, nodded with his head, and groaned greatly as if he were about to die. Those sitting nearby were silent and watched him. Finally Jan awoke and said with a sigh, 'Oh, dear Father, not as I will, but as thou wilt.' He stood up, shook hands all around, kissed everyone, and said, 'The peace of God be with you all.' Then he left with his wife. At that time the Anabaptists did not yet have several wives. The others sat down again and began to make merry. Finally, they also arose to leave, bid each other good night, and departed in peace.

The following day Jan Matthijs took ten or twenty men and left the town with them. When they reached the enemy they became involved in fighting. Together with his fellows, Jan Matthijs was killed. He was pierced with a spear. Afterwards the soldiers cut off his head, tore his body into a hundred pieces, which they threw around. They put the head on a stick and held it high in the air. Then the soldiers shouted to the Anabaptists in the city that they should come out and get their mayor. They did not know that Jan had been the highest prophet in the city.

Jan Matthijs had been from Holland. He was a tall man with a black beard. When he died the Dutchmen and Frisians in the city, as well as all Anabaptists, were greatly grieved, since they had lost their prophet. Afterwards the Anabaptists claimed that God had given a revelation to Matthijs during the wedding banquet that previous evening. No wonder, the Dutchmen, the Frisians, the preachers and the Anabaptists thought more highly of Jan Matthijs than of God.

Jan van Leyden. (*Woodcut by Erhard Schoen. Geisberg*, 1298)

Then Jan van Leiden became the highest prophet. He began to preach to the grey monks in the church yard: 'Dear brothers and sisters, you must not be dismayed that Jan Matthijs, our prophet, died. God will raise up someone else, who shall be higher and greater than Jan Matthijs was. It was God's will that he should die. His time had come. God has not done this without cause, but that you should not believe too much on Jan and not put him above God. God is more powerful than Jan Matthijs was. Whatever Jan did and prophesied he did through God, and not of himself. God can indeed raise up another prophet through whom he will reveal his will.' With such words Jan van Leiden calmed the people. Thus Jan van Leiden proclaimed that God was well pleased with the people who should be a holy people: 'All unrighteousness and all sin must be exterminated, for there is an example and you have entered into the apostolic Church and are holy. Holy is the Lord and you are his people.'

Meister Heinrich Gresbeck's Bericht, pp. 38–40.
(Löffler, pp. 74–75.)

▶ One of the radical innovations undertaken by the Anabaptists in Münster was the introduction of communism. Here is the chronicler's report:

The prophets, preachers and the entire council deliberated and felt that everything should be held in common. It was first ordered that everyone who had copper money should bring it to the City Hall, where he would receive a different currency. This was done. After the prophets and the preachers had reached an agreement with the council in this matter, it was announced in the sermons that all things should be held in common. Thus they said in the sermon: 'Dear brothers and sisters, inasmuch as we are one people, and are brothers and sisters one to another, it is God's will that we should bring our money, silver and gold together. Each one of us should have as much as any other. Therefore everyone is to bring his money to the chancellery near the City Hall. There the council will be present and receive the money.' Likewise preacher Stutenbernt said: 'A Christian should not have any money; everything which Christian brothers and sisters possess belongs to one as well as the other. You shall not lack anything, be it food, clothes, house, or goods. What you need, you shall receive, God will not suffer you to lack anything. One thing shall be held as much in common as the other. It belongs to all of us. It is mine as well as yours, and yours as well as mine.' Thus they persuaded the people so that some of them brought their money, silver and gold, indeed everything they owned. But there was much inequality in Münster, where one supposedly had as much as any other.

Some people in the city turned in all their money, silver and gold and did not keep anything. Others turned in part and kept part. Still others did not turn in anything.

Meister Heinrich Gresbeck's Bericht, pp. 32–33.
(Löffler, p. 67.)

▶ A new code, rampant with biblical allusions, formalized the changes in Münster.

The elders of the congregation of Christ in the holy city of Münster, called and ordained by the grace of the most high and almighty God, desire that the following duties and articles be faithfully and firmly observed by every Israelite and member of the house of God.

1. What the Holy Scriptures command or prohibit is to be kept by every Israelite at the pain of punishment.

2. Everybody is to be industrious in his vocation and fear God and his ordained government. Government authority does not carry the sword in vain, but it is the avenger of evildoers.

3. Every elder is to have a servant as assistant to carry out his orders.

4. Five elders are to supervise the day and night watches, personally inspecting them, lest the negligence of the watch lead the city into danger. . . .

6. Every day from seven to nine o'clock in the morning and from two to four o'clock in the afternoon, six elders are to sit on the market at the appointed place and settle all differences with their decisions.

7. What the elders in common deliberation in this new Israel have found to be good is to be proclaimed and announced by the prophet Jan van Leiden as faithful servant of the Most High and the holy government to the congregation of Christ and the entire congregation of Israel.

8. Lest among the sincere and unblemished Israelites open transgression against the Word of God be tolerated, and in order that the evildoer and transgressor, if apprehended at an obvious transgression, meet his just punishment, the swordbearer, Bernhard Knipperdoling, will punish him according to his deed. . . .

9. In order to keep the proper order concerning the administration of food, the food-masters are every day to prepare dishes of the kind as was hitherto customary for the brothers and sisters. These are to sit modestly and moderately at separate tables. They must not demand anything apart from what is served to them. . . .

10. Those having guard duty during the day are to eat only after the others have left, so that the necessary watches are not neglected. . . .

29. When a stranger who does not adhere to our religion, be it brother, countryman or relative, comes to this our holy city, he is to be referred to the swordbearer, Knipperdoling, so that he can talk with him. This is not to be done by anybody else.

30. A baptized Christian is not to converse with any arriving person or pagan stranger and is not to eat with him, lest there arise the suspicion of treacherous consultation. . . .

33. If, according to God's will, someone is killed by the enemy or departs otherwise in the Lord, nobody is to take his belongings, such as weapons, clothes, etc. They are to be brought to the swordbearer Knipper-

doling, who in turn will pass them on to the elders, who will then give them to the lawful heirs.

Ordnung des weltlichen Regiments. (Löffler, pp. 83–86.).

▶ After communism came—horror of horrors—the introduction of polygamy in the city. The chronicler who described the innovation knew that all had a very simple reason:

Thus Jan van Leiden—together with the bishop, the preachers and the twelve elders—proclaimed concerning the married estate that it was God's will that they should inhabit the earth. Everyone should take three or four wives, or as many as were desired. However, they should live with their wives in a divine manner. This pleased some men and not others. Husbands and wives objected that the marital estate was no longer to be kept.

Jan van Leiden was the first to take a second wife in addition to the one he had married in Münster. It was said that there was still another wife in Holland. Jan van Leiden continued to take more wives until he finally had fifteen. In similar fashion all the Dutchmen, Frisians and true Anabaptists had additional wives. Indeed, they compelled their first wives to go and obtain second wives for them. The devil laughed hard about this. Those who had old wives and wanted to take young ones had their way. . . . The Anabaptists in Münster, especially the leaders, such as Jan van Leiden and the twelve elders, were planning it well. They had done away with money, gold and silver, and had driven everyone from his property. They sat in the houses, held the property, and also wanted to have ten or twelve wives. I presume they called this the 'right baptism'.

Meister Heinrich Gresbeck's Bericht, pp. 60–61
(Löffler, pp. 112–13.)

▶ During the long siege of Münster several efforts were made by the besieging forces to learn about the conditions in the city. Hans Nagel, a nobleman and member of the besieging forces, found a rather unique way to do so. A 'newspaper' reported his spectacular feat.

In order to learn the secrets of Münster, he pretended that he had failed on the watch, which was against martial law and the articles of war. Supposedly to escape justice he had fled to Münster, where he showed them his armour, which had been marked with jags.

He was led before the king, questioned and finally thrown into the tower called the 'heathen tower' because of those who are taken into it. When he

The siege of Münster 1534–35.

volunteered, after three or four days, to accept their faith and be rebaptized, he was released and baptized. He was called to be a trabant or
servant, given a brown and black velvet jacket (which was the king's
colour) and a golden ring like the other courtiers.

He reported that the king rode about town on a fallow horse covered
with black-green velvet. He wore a golden crown on his head and held a
gilded rod in his hand. A gilded globe with two swords hung from his

(*Woodcut by Erhard Schoen. Geisberg, 1256–57*)

neck. In all respects he behaved like a king. He showed little confidence toward his subjects and through his secret and public informers he kept them from entering into secret arrangements. No one was allowed to meet secretly with others; indeed, all gatherings were prohibited. The king also had fourteen wives and had recently become father of a daughter.

Concerning food, he reported that there were not more than fifty cows in the city. These were spared, however, because of the milk, fat and calves. There were still some sixty horses. On Saturday, 3rd April, fifteen horses were killed to provide food. Virtually all the cats and dogs had been eaten and there were not more than three or four dogs left. There was no scarcity of bread, but he did not know if there was a size-able supply of wheat. Salt seemed to be available in sufficient quantity. Beer was also still brewed in the city. There were many who disliked the state of affairs in the city. They would gladly leave if they only had the opportunity.

Neue Zeitung. (Löffler, pp. 209–10.)

▶ **A captured prisoner also talked eagerly about conditions in the city.**

Yesterday, while I was inspecting the fortifications with a commanding officer, two 'brethren', a miller and the son of a riflemaker, were captured. Both stated that the common people in the city have nothing to eat but roots, sorrel, and the like. Even this is not sufficient. In the presence of the colonel and the rest of us, the miller insisted under oath that he had scraped the white off the walls, mixed it with water, and given it to his children to drink. He also said that others have done likewise and are still doing it. Both men stated that Münster certainly did not have more than two hundred men capable of bearing arms. All others were too weak and exhausted to be of any help. Men, women and children look pale like a bleached cloth; their bodies are bloated and they have huge stomachs and legs. . . . The king has elected twelve rulers whom he sent to twelve places in the city, particularly the gates. Each ruler was assigned several officers and soldiers. They are not to confer with each other without the know-ledge of the king. During the last few days the king executed four men who had talked against his rule and had planned to desert. Several prisoners reported that the king had said at that time that he would do the same with all worldly rulers, kings and emperors.

21st May 1535. Letter, Justinian von Holtzhausen, pp. 334–6.
(Löffler, p. 226.)

▶ **Yet another observer had this to say:**

The council in Münster decided to hire, if possible, some eight to ten thousand mercenaries who are to receive four gilders monthly and free plundering. They are to suppress all lords and rulers, ecclesiastical and temporal authorities. This recruitment is done in the North, in Friesland, Holland and Wesel.

The council also wanted to send for a nobleman who lives in the country. He was to receive 15,000 gilders and was to hire people secretly. Six men were sent from Münster. Jan van Geel, who was born in Geel near Utrecht, went to Strassburg. A merchant was sent to Friesland. They are to incite rebellion and insurrection in these towns and regions. A thousand books were sent from Münster to the surrounding towns and villages. Thereby the common people are to be incited to rebellion which in turn might relieve Münster. The book is entitled *Concerning Wrath*.

The food in Münster has almost all been eaten, with the exception of 300 cows and 44 horses. Twenty cows are needed to feed the people, as their number is very great. There are still some 1,300 men in the city and 6,000 women, not counting the children. Permission to leave has been given to everyone who desires to do so. Within two weeks over 200 persons left. . . . Twenty-five horses have already been eaten, cats are roasted on spears, and mice in pans.

I spoke with Bernhard Rothmann, who said, 'If God does not rescue us from our enemies, we know not what to do. Rye and barley are very scarce and will all be consumed within a month or two.' . . .

The king prophesied that the people would be delivered from their enemies before Easter. If this were not the case, they should take and burn him on the market square before all the people.

Statement, H. Graes. (Löffler, pp. 194–5.)

▶   At the height of the siege the oppressed Münster Anabaptists wrote to their opponents.

This time we do not want to keep quiet about our firm conviction. We are resolved to uphold the truth which by God's grace is with us undismayedly until death, unless we are instructed better. We will not willingly admit unproved guilt nor commit ourselves into your hands. If you are Christians, as you boast, you ought to treat us differently, in Christian fashion, which we frequently requested. You should give us a hearing regarding our presumed guilt, listen to our refutation and then pronounce a verdict. But this is what must take place. How else would the fourth beast, the fourth monarchy of earth (Daniel 7), which is the Roman Empire, trample on the saints of God, as is presently taking place? Now then, if we do not receive a proper hearing, but are smashed under the feet of the beast, let us according to God's pleasure be patient until the small stone smashes the feet of the image (Daniel 2) and the kingdom is turned over to his people, the saints of the Most High.

You write that we should not send any more men, women or children, or you would treat them according to your pleasure. You should know that we did not send you anybody and will not send you anybody. We permitted those to leave who desired to do so. You may do with them whatever you want to do. We do not refuse to receive anybody who comes to us in friendship. Likewise we do not refuse permission to anyone who wishes to leave the city. This we wanted you to know as our answer.

(Löffler, pp. 230–1.)

▶   The opponents were unimpressed and in due course captured the city. Jan van Leiden was among those who were captured alive. He was tortured and made the following confession.

Confession of Jan van Leiden, supposedly King of Münster, made on 25th July 1535, at Dülmen. . . .

Jan was born at Leiden and brought up there. His father's name was Bockel and was a magistrate at Soevenhaven near Leiden. His mother, Alit, was born near Horstmar in the Diocese of Münster. She lived with his father for seven years while his wife was still living. After the latter's death he married his mother. He went to school at Leiden and learned the tailor trade. From there he travelled to England, where he stayed for four years. Then he went to Flanders to work in his trade. Thereafter he returned to Leiden and took himself a wife who had at one time been married to a sailor. Since he engaged in trading, he went to Lisbon and then to Lübeck. He lost his property and returned home to go to Münster. His wife objected to this. . . . But he travelled against her will, since he had heard that in Münster the Word of God was preached in a most noble and exalted fashion. At that time he was not rebaptized. . . .

About All Saints of 1533, Jan Matthijs came to Leiden to the house of a tailor named Cornelis. Afterwards, Jan came to his house, instructed him in the Scriptures, and rebaptized him. Later on, Jan Matthijs and Melchior Rinck, or Hoffman, who is now imprisoned at Strassburg, differed in their views concerning baptism. Melchior asserted that the time for baptism had not yet come, since the persecution against them was so great. Jan replied that truth should not be compromised and that baptism should therefore be continued.

He and Gerrit were instructed by this Jan Matthijs to go to Münster with various messages and concerns. They arrived there the week after Epiphany in 1534 and first went to see Bernt Rothmann and the preachers. They delivered the messages from Jan Matthijs—namely, that they should no longer preach from church pulpits, but refrain from using churches altogether. Furthermore the wives should honour their husbands and call

them 'lord'. There were several other points which he has since forgotten.
From then on, the two of them taught and baptized in Münster.

Bekenntnis Johanns von Leiden, pp. 369–71. (Löffler, pp. 243–5.)

▶ The end, for Jan van Leiden and two other Anabaptist leaders
who had been captured, was execution.

The day after St Agnes was set as time of execution. The day before
the king was asked if he wanted to confess his sins to a priest. He replied
that he was not ashamed to converse and counsel with an understanding
man and asked for Johann von Syburg, the Bishop's chaplain. As he was
refused no request, the one whom he desired came at once. He could
reveal to the chaplain all the movements of his heart. When Johann von
Syburg afterwards returned to us he reported that this unfortunate man
showed extraordinary remorse. He had confessed openly that even if he
were executed ten times, he had deserved it. None the less, he could not
be brought to see his error regarding baptism and the human nature of
Christ. He had especially regretted, with great pain, that he had often
and wantonly rejected the faithful counsel of the illustrious Landgrave.
Now he realized that the Prince had rallied arms with the Bishop against
his madness and the city only after they had rejected the Landgrave's
admonitions. If the Landgrave were present, he would on his knees ask
for forgiveness. . . .

Knipperdoling, on the other hand, wanted no one to talk or counsel
with him. Earlier, under torture, he had boasted that he was not aware of
any shortcoming. He had only sought the glory of God and his salvation;
all other matters had been secondary. With similar boasting he declared
that the Lutherans were only evangelical in that they met from time to
time to sing a few Psalms. Since his baptism he, however, had shown his
Christian faith not through hymns, but through works. He had lived
according to the will of the Father and had not become guilty in anything.
Krechting exhibited the same stubbornness.

The following day they were brought, one after the other, before the
judge who read the indictment. The king was accused of the most serious
evils and crimes. Since they were known throughout Germany, no denial
was possible. He replied that he had failed against governmental authority,
but not against God. . . . However, he admitted rebaptism as well as insurrection and lese-majesty, for which he was sentenced to death. In the
same fashion the death sentence was pronounced over Knipperdoling and
Krechting, after they had been indicted of the same crimes and had been
unable to deny their deeds.

When the king was led as the first to the place of execution, he knelt and said, with folded hands, 'Father, into thy hands do I commend my spirit.' Then he was tied to a stake and tortured with fiery and glowing tongs and eventually killed, presumably under the applause and pleasure of the priests, whom Münster has always had in abundance. Their joy would have been full if the Lutherans had been given the same punishment. I will not mention the king's steadfastness in enduring torture. He did not even say one word to acknowledge his pain. After all, in earlier times even pagans showed such virtue; it is also certain that Satan gives power and steadfastness to those whom he entangles in his snares.

After the king had died, Knipperdoling was led to the same place. I do not know if he said anything as he was tied to the stake. Those who were not far from the place of execution insisted that he said, 'God be merciful unto me a sinner.' Otherwise there was continuous silence during his torture. Finally Krechting died through the same punishment. When the tongs were being used, we heard him say twice: 'Oh, Father, oh, Father.' There were many present for whom there could be nothing more pleasant than this sight. But we and some of the others who felt that everything which had happened here had taken place because of our sins were not so pleased.

After the deserved punishment had been administered to these criminal men, they were put into three iron cages so that they could be seen and recognized from afar. These cages were placed high on the steeple of St Lamberti's Church as a perpetual memorial and to warn and terrify the restless spirits lest they attempt something similar in the future. Such was the evil ending of this tragedy.

Corvinus Epistola (Löffler, pp. 267–8.)

▶   The catastrophe of Münster brought disrepute and confusion upon the Anabaptists of the North. Menno Simons,[18] of Holland, a former Catholic priest, emerged as leader of the movement, which, under his direction, returned to its earlier principles. Here Menno recalls his conversion and joining of the Anabaptist brotherhood.

It happened in the year 1524, the twenty-eighth of my life, that I assumed the duties of a priest in my paternal village called Pingjum. Two others of about my age also officiated in the same functions. The one was my pastor, fairly well educated. The other was below me. Both had read the Scriptures a little, but I had never touched them, for I feared if I should read them, I would be misled. Behold, such an ignorant preacher was I for nearly two years.

In the year following it occurred to me, as often as I handled the bread and wine in the mass, that they were not the flesh and blood of the Lord. I thought that the devil was suggesting this so that he might separate me from my faith. I confessed it often, sighed, and prayed; yet I could not come clear of the ideas.

MENNO   SIMONS. WT FRIESLANT.

Menno Simons. The Bible is open at I Cor. 3.11—Menno's motto. (*Engraving ,17th century, by C. von Sichem, Het Toonel der Hoofketteren*)

The two young men mentioned earlier and I spent our time emptily in playing [cards] together, drinking, and in diversions as, alas, is the fashion and usage of such useless people. And when we touched upon the Scriptures I could not speak a word with them without being scoffed at, for I did not know what I was driving at, so concealed was the Word of God from my eyes.

Finally, I got the idea to examine the New Testament diligently. I had not gone very far when I discovered that we were deceived, and my conscience, troubled on account of the aforementioned bread, was quickly relieved, even without any instructions. I was in so far helped by Luther, however, that human injunctions cannot bind unto eternal death. . . .

Afterwards it happened, before I had ever heard of the existence of brethren, that a God-fearing, pious hero named Sicke Snijder was beheaded at Leeuwarden for being rebaptized. It sounded very strange to me to hear of a second baptism. I examined the Scriptures diligently and pondered them earnestly, but could find no report of infant baptism.

After I had noticed this I discussed it with my pastor and after much talk he had to admit that there was no basis for infant baptism in Scripture. Still I dared not trust my own understanding, but consulted several ancient authors. They taught me that children are by baptism cleansed from their original sin. I compared this idea with the Scriptures and found that it did violence to the blood of Christ.

Afterwards I consulted Luther. For I sought for the basis of baptism. He taught me that children were to be baptized on account of their own faith. I perceived that this also was not in accordance with the Word of God.

Thirdly I consulted Bucer. He taught that infants are to be baptized so that they might be the more carefully nurtured in the way of the Lord. I perceived that this doctrine was also without foundation.

Fourthly I consulted Bullinger. He pointed to the covenant and to circumcision. This I found likewise to be incapable of Scriptural proof.

When I noticed from all these that writers varied so greatly among themselves, each following his own wisdom, then I realized that we were deceived in regard to infant baptism. . . .

Although I had now acquired considerable knowledge of the Scriptures, yet I wasted that knowledge through the lusts of my youth in an impure, sensual, unprofitable life, and sought nothing but gain, ease, favour of men, splendour, name and fame, as all generally do who sail that ship.

And so, my reader, I obtained a view of baptism and the Lord's Supper through the illumination of the Holy Ghost, through much reading and pondering of the Scriptures, and by the gracious favour and gift of God. . . .

Next in order the sect of Münster made its appearance, by whom many pious hearts in our quarter were deceived. My soul was much troubled, for I perceived that though they were zealous they erred in doctrine. I did what I could to oppose them by preaching and exhortations, as much as in me was. I conferred twice with one of their leaders, once in private, and once in public, but my admonitions did not help, because I myself still did that which I knew was not right.

The report spread that I could silence these persons beautifully.

Everybody defended himself by a reference to me, no matter who. I saw plainly that I was the stay and defence of the impenitent, who all leaned on me. This gave me no little qualm of conscience. I sighed and prayed: Lord, help me, lest I become responsible for other men's sins. My soul was troubled and I reflected upon the outcome, that if I should gain the whole world and live a thousand years, and at last have to endure the wrath of God, what would I have gained?

Afterwards the poor straying sheep who wandered as sheep without a proper shepherd, after many cruel edicts, garrottings and slaughters, assembled at a place near my place of residence called Oude Klooster. And, alas! through the ungodly doctrines of Münster, and in opposition to the Spirit, Word and example of Christ, they drew the sword to defend themselves, the sword which the Lord commanded Peter to put up in its sheath.

After this had transpired the blood of these people, although misled, fell so hot on my heart that I could not stand it, nor find rest in my soul. I reflected upon my unclean, carnal life, also the hypocritical doctrine and idolatry which I still practised daily in appearance of godliness, but without relish. I saw that these zealous children, although in error, willingly gave their lives and their estates for their doctrine and faith. And I was one of those who had disclosed to some of them the abominations of the papal system. But I myself continued in my comfortable life and acknowledged abominations simply in order that I might enjoy physical comfort and escape the cross of Christ.

Pondering these things my conscience tormented me so that I could no longer endure it. I thought to myself—I, miserable man, what am I doing? If I continue in this way, and do not live agreeably to the Word of the Lord, according to the knowledge of the truth which I have obtained; if I do not censure to the best of my little talent the hypocrisy, the impenitent, carnal life, the erroneous baptism, the Lord's Supper in the false service of God which the learned ones teach; if I through bodily fear do not lay bare the foundations of the truth, nor use all my powers to direct the wandering flock who would gladly do their duty if they knew it, to the true pastures of Christ—oh, how shall their shed blood, shed in the midst of transgressions rise against me at the judgment of the Almighty and pronounce sentence against my poor, miserable soul!

My heart trembled within me. I prayed to God with sighs and tears that he would give to me, a sorrowing sinner, the gift of his grace, create within me a clean heart, and graciously through the merits of the crimson blood of Christ forgive my unclean walk and frivolous easy life and bestow upon me wisdom, spirit, courage and a manly spirit so that I might preach his exalted and adorable name and holy Word in purity, and make known his truth to his glory.

I began in the name of the Lord to preach publicly from the pulpit the word of true repentance, to point the people to the narrow path, and in the power of the Scripture openly to reprove all sin and wickedness, all idolatry and false worship, and to present the true worship; also the true baptism and the Lord's Supper, according to the doctrine of Christ, to the extent that I had at that time received from God the grace.

I also faithfully warned everyone against the abominations of Münster, condemning king, polygamy, kingdom, sword, etc. After about nine months or so, the gracious Lord granted me his fatherly spirit, help and hand. Then I, without constraint, of a sudden, renounced all my worldly reputation, name and fame, my unchristian abominations, my masses, infant baptism, and my easy life, and I willingly submitted to distress and poverty under the heavy cross of Christ. In my weakness I feared God; I sought out the pious, and though they were few in number I found some who were zealous and maintained the truth. I dealt with the erring, and through the help and power of God with his Word, reclaimed them from the snares of damnation and gained them to Christ. The hardened and rebellious I left to the Lord.

And so you see, my reader, in this way the merciful Lord through the liberal goodness of his abounding grace took notice of me, a poor sinner, stirred in my heart at the outset, produced in me a new mind, humbled me in his fear, taught me to know myself in part, turned me from the way of death and graciously called me into the narrow pathway of life and the communion of his saints.

Menno Simons, *Reply to Gellius Faber: Complete Works*, pp. 668–72.

▶ In Moravia a group of Anabaptists, originally from Austria, developed a distinctive piety of their own, primarily characterized by a stress upon communal sharing.[19] The Anabaptist Chronicle reports on the beginning of the group, which after one of its early leaders, Jakob Hutter, was soon called Hutterite.

Thus some 200 persons, not counting children, gathered outside Nikolsburg. Several people mercifully came from town and wept with them. Others quarrelled with them. Then they proceeded to the vicinity of Tannewitz and Muschau. Here they found a deserted village, stayed for a day and a night, and counselled with one another on account of their present need. They appointed servants of temporal goods, namely Frantz Lutzinger of Leiben in Styria and Jacob Mändel, who had been an official for the Lord of Liechtenstein. Thomas Arbeiter and Urban Bader were appointed assistants. At this time these men spread a coat before the people and everybody laid down his possessions, voluntarily and un-coerced, so that the needy might be supported according to the teaching of the prophets and the apostles.

Die Älteste Chronik der Hutterischen Brüder, p. 87.

Picture of a Hutterite family and house. The two levels of dormers indi-cate the large attic dormitories in Hutterite houses. (*Woodcut from title page of C. Erhard, Historial Munich*, 1588)

▶   **In 1578 a visitor to one of the Hutterite communities described his impressions.**

On the 22nd of September the messenger from Znyam and I arrived around eleven o'clock at Wischnau and at once met Michael, the husband of my sister Catharine, who had died two years ago. I asked him if any-body from Württemberg or Knittlingen was among them. After some delay he answered very slowly: 'Yes, there were some.' He did not want to take me to them until he had recognized who I was. He took me to the tailor's room, where the Anabaptists eat their meals. He offered meat, wine and beer to the messenger and me and sent at once for my second sister, Margaretha, who lives, like my brother-in-law, here in Wischnau. While the messenger was eating she took us to her quarters. After tears of reunion had been shed, we spoke about various matters. My sister was greatly delighted about my coming and called for Christman, her husband. On our way to Stignitz my sister Margaretha and my brother-in-law Michael spoke of their affection and love to me. Often they had thought of me and wished for my presence. I replied that they had always been on my mind, indeed I had remembered them continuously before God in prayer. At this point Christman interjected that I was not to pray to God, as God does not hear the prayer of the godless, but considers it sin. I could not wish him anything good. When I scolded him as a proud hypocrite because of such a statement, he left us and walked behind us until my sister admonished him to be more friendly. Then he joined us again and asked me where I had been, what my experiences had been, etc.

Stignitz is a large village belonging to the Lord of Löben, who at one time had been supervisor in Moravia. It was reported to me at last Whitsuntide he and his wife attended the Anabaptist communion or breaking of bread. He is fond of them and does not burden them. At Stignitz I found my second sister, Sara, who is married to a vineyard worker. She herself looks after little children in the Anabaptist school. Each Anabaptist community has a school in which the children are placed to learn to pray and to read when they reach the age of two years. Until that time they stay with their mothers. The children do not study more than that. Girls only learn to pray and to read a little. Boys learn to write and read. When they grow up they learn a trade or some other work.

Once a day the children go into the fields or to the nearest woods, so that they are not always close together, but get some fresh air. Certain women do nothing else but watch for the children, wash them, care for them, and keep their beds and clothes clean. Two or three, according to their age, sleep together. Mornings and evenings they say their prayers that they may be brought up in the fear of God, that they may be given good rulers, that they may be kept in God's knowledge, that their brethren and sisters be kept from all harm. After this prayer, during which they kneel, they pray the Lord's Prayer.

My sister Sara did not want to marry her husband, but could not say anything against it. This is the way it is handled: On a certain Sunday, the elders call all marriageable young men and women together, place them opposite each other and give each girl the choice of two or three fellows. She has to take one of them. She is not compelled, but she is not to do anything against the elders. I met my step brother Sebastian at the brewery, but like Christman he did not offer me his hand. His first words were that I was a false prophet; therefore he would not give me his hand.

On the 23rd an elder who had diligently waited for me at the gate came to me. He asked Bastian if he were my brother. Afterwards he asked me whence I came, etc. Then he began to talk with me about the Christian churches, which boasted of their many Christians who were no Christians, since they did not do good works. A tree should be known by its fruit. There were many godless people in the world, much strife and quarrelling, and many sects. They, however, had left everything and followed Christ. Finally he began to speak about the community of goods, which he ventured to prove from I Cor. 10.24.

> *Quellen zur Geschichte der Wiedertäufer,*
> Württemberg, pp. 1105–7

Spiritualism and Antitrinitarianism

Spiritualism and Antitrinitarianism, the remaining two movements of the Radical Reformation, failed to assume a concrete sociological dimension in the first half-century of the Reformation. For the former this was impossible by definition, for the latter by circumstances. The ideals were propagated by individuals, mostly erudite intellectuals who preferred to go their own way, hoping to remain unmolested by ecclesiastical and political authorities.

The spiritualist saw the essence of religion not in externals, not even in doctrine, but in man's inward communion with God. Such an attitude detached him from the religious strife of the day. Since the value of externals was disregarded, the spiritualist found it possible to go through the routine of external observance of whatever tradition. It is difficult, therefore, to know exactly how widespread spiritualist ideals were in the early decades of the Reformation.

Perhaps the best illustration of sixteenth-century spiritualism is Sebastian Franck, who had started as a Catholic priest, had become a Lutheran preacher, and flirted with the Anabaptists—only, in the end, to renounce them all and insist that none was better than the other. Indeed, even Christianity is not better than the other religions, but all religions of all times and places have taught the same, namely an inward and spiritual religion for which outward forms are incidental.

Antitrinitarianism was also, at least during the early years of the Reformation, propagated by individuals and assumed ecclesiastical form only in the second half of the century. Persecution was too vehement earlier. The outstanding representative of antitrinitarian tendencies during the early years was a Spanish physician, geographer, Bible editor and lay theologian named Miguel Servetus, who enjoyed—if enjoyed be the appropriate word to use here—the singular distinction of having been burned by Catholics in effigy and by Protestants in reality. He must have been a fellow of sorts! Born in the Spanish town of Villanueva in 1509, Servetus had a deep passion concerning the restitution of what he considered true Christianity. Among the worst perversions of existing Christendom he numbered the traditional doctrine of the Trinity. At the age of twenty-two he wrote his first theological treatise, *Concerning the Errors of the Trinity*. The reaction of the theological world to this book which denounced the orthodox doctrine in no uncertain terms was, understandably enough, negative. But this did not thwart Servetus, for one year later he pronounced on the subject a second time with his *Two Dialogues Concerning the Trinity*. Though the preface contained a formal retraction of the earlier treatise—perhaps to convince the censors who, rather like students and book reviewers, do not read beyond the preface—the work itself was an emphatic restatement of the same negative position.

The controversy surrounding his two books must have convinced Servetus that the time was not quite ripe for his views. For almost a decade he vanishes from the historical scene until he appears again, in the early 1540s, as physician to the Catholic Archbishop of Vienne, near Lyons, in south-eastern France. Outwardly a faithful member of the Catholic Church, Servetus, now calling himself Villaneuve, was inwardly as convinced of his unorthodox views as ever. He had also retained his former passion to convince others. He singled out John Calvin, the Reformer of nearby Geneva, as the object of his 'evangelistic' endeavours, and commenced a vigorous but somewhat one-sided correspondence which ended abruptly when Calvin refused to be persuaded. Servetus was working, at the time, on a manuscript embodying not only his views on the Trinity, but on the reform of the Christian religion in general. He tried to bolster his case with Calvin by sending the Genevan reformer a few pages of his *Restitution of Christianity*. Calvin, however, did not even bother to return the pages.

Many years later, in 1553, the astonishing thing happened. Under the eyes of the Catholic Inquisition, Servetus's explosive manuscript was printed and appeared, of course, without the name of author or place and date of publication, on the book market. A few months later, alas, Servetus was arrested by the Inquisition. The leak, however, had occurred not at Vienne, but in Geneva: a Genevan resident, formerly of Vienne, had written letters to a cousin there, in which was charged, among other things, that the respectable physician Villaneuve was none other than the author of the abominable attack upon the Christian religion. The cousin in Vienne promptly informed the Inquisition. The difficulty lay in the fact that this could be nothing but a wild accusation, and so the cousin was instructed to write for evidence. This was provided, from Geneva, with the help of the manuscript pages still in Calvin's possession. Servetus was arrested, but denied everything, told a moving, yet fantastic, story, and used the first occasion to flee.

Four months later he appeared in—of all places—Geneva, and was promptly arrested. After almost two months' imprisonment and a lengthy trial in which the overtones of political power struggles in Geneva were not altogether absent, Miguel Servetus was burned at the stake outside Geneva. The day was 23rd October 1553. With the words 'Jesus, thou son of the eternal God, deliver me!' on his lips, Servetus died. As one of the bystanders observed, he could have saved his life by transposing the position of the adjective of his final sentence. So slight was the verbal distinction, and so profound the theological aberration!

▶ The first outstanding representative of antitrinitarian thought in the Reformation Era was the Spaniard Miguel Servetus.[20] His first book on what proved to be his lifelong theological concern was published in 1531. It bore the title 'Concerning the Errors of the Trinity'. Its opening section read as follows:[21]

BOOK I

Argument

Any discussion of the Trinity should start with the man. That Jesus, surnamed Christ, was not a *hypostasis* but a human being is taught both by the early Fathers and in the Scriptures, taken in their literal sense, and is indicated by the miracles that he wrought. He, and not the Word, is also the miraculously born Son of God in fleshly form, as the Scriptures teach—not a *hypostasis*, but an actual Son. He is God, sharing God's divinity in full, and the theory of a *communicatio idiomatum* is a confusing sophistical quibble. This does not imply two gods, but only a double use of the term God, as is clear from the Hebrew use of the term. Christ, being one with God the Father, equal in power, came down from heaven and assumed flesh as a man. In short, all the Scriptures speak of Christ as a man.

The doctrine of the Holy Spirit as a third separate being lands us in practical tritheism no better than atheism, even though the unity of God be insisted on. Careful interpretation of the usual proof-texts shows that they teach not a union of three beings in one, but a harmony between them. The Holy Spirit as a third person of the Godhead is unknown in Scripture. It is not a separate being, but an activity of God himself. The doctrine of the Trinity can be neither established by logic nor proved from Scripture, and is, in fact, inconceivable. There are many reasons against it. The Scriptures and the Fathers teach one God the Father, and Jesus Christ his Son, but scholastic philosophy has introduced terms which are not understood, and do not accord with Scripture. Jesus taught that he himself was the Son of God. Numerous heresies have sprung from this philosophy, and fruitless questions have arisen out of it. Worst of all, the doctrine of the Trinity incurs the ridicule of the Mohammedans and the Jews. It arose out of Greek philosophy rather than from the belief that Jesus Christ is the Son of God; and he will be with the church only if it keeps his teaching.

Two Treatises of Servetus on the Trinity, p. 3.

▸   One year later, in 1532, came Servetus's second attack upon the orthodox doctrine of the Trinity. It was entitled 'Dialogues on the Trinity' and had the following preface and opening section.[22]

Book I

Synopsis

1. Christians lack true knowledge of Christ, thinking him altogether different from man. 2. The Word foreshadowed Christ. 3. The invisible God, by speaking the word of creation, assumed a new role as a visible Creator, the Logos, or Elohim, manifested in the Person of Christ, who has taken the place of the Word that once was. 4. In seeing him we see the light of God reflected. 5. In creation God also became a Spirit, again foreshadowing Christ, in whom alone we can worship him. 6. The manifestation of God through angels also foreshadowed Christ. 7. The fullness of God and of all his properties dwells in Christ, who is of the same Substance with the Father. 8. Christ alone is the one in whom the Word became flesh. 9. In Christ the Substance of God also shared the Substance of flesh in the incarnation, making one being; thus he really came down from heaven. 10. Salvation comes only by faith that Christ is the Son of God, as is taught by Paul, Peter and Christ himself. 11. The schools teach two things in place of the one man Christ, the Son of God. 12. As Christians we are made like Christ in regeneration. 13. Just as in our old life we were like Adam.

To the Reader, Greeting

All that I have lately written, in seven books, against the received view as to the Trinity, honest reader, I now retract; not because it is untrue, but because it is incomplete, and written as though by a child for children. Yet I pray you to keep such of it as might help you to an understanding of what is to be said here. Moreover, that such a barbarous, confused and incorrect book appeared as my former one was, must be ascribed to my own lack of experience, and to the printer's carelessness. Nor would I have any Christian offended thereby, since God is wont sometimes to make his own wisdom known through

the foolish instruments of the world.
I beg you, therefore, to pay attention to the matter itself; for if
you give heed to this, my
halting words will not
stand in your way.
Fare you
well.

Dialogues on the Trinity
Book The First
Michael, Petrucius

Necessarily, according to the Scriptures, these three ought to agree, the Logos, Elohim, and Christ; as is proved by a mere comparison of the beginning of Genesis with the beginning of the Gospel of John.

Petrucius. I hear the man speaking whom I was looking for. Ho there! What are you saying to yourself here alone?

Michael. I am greatly tormented in mind when I see that the minds of Christians are so estranged from any knowledge of the Son of God.

Pet. I, too, have seen some carried away with their minds perfectly enraged against you because you are bent upon taking away from them a large part of their gods.

Mich. With what reasons, or by what Scriptures, do they censure me?

Pet. By none, so far as I have heard; but by shouting, and by appeals to the great councils. I have even seen some who fear that this may perhaps be to us a tradition like the Talmud and Alcoran, because it does not savour of the spirit of the Lord, and the Scripture in many ways suffers violence.

Mich. There are some whose blindness is so dense that if Christ were again to preach that he was the Son of God, they would crucify him

afresh. Just as they do not see that he is the head, so they do not acknowledge that they are the members. I should not expect ever to become a son
of God, unless I had a Nature in common with him who is the true Son,
upon whose sonship our own sonship depends, as members depend upon
the head. Yet they would have the Son be something altogether different,
although they can never prove it, nor does it contribute to the purpose
of our salvation.

Pet. You seem to assert some things that you cannot prove.

Mich. What things?

Pet. That the Word has ceased to be, or that it has become a mere
shadow.

Mich. I have never admitted that the Word has ceased to be. On the
contrary, I am ready to admit that the same Substance of the Word is in
the flesh today. As for my saying that there is now no such Word as there
once was, that will soon be explained. Moreover, I called it a shadow by
force of necessity, being unable otherwise to explain this mystery. Nor
am I willing to go so far as to say that the Word was a shadow which has
passed away and does not abide. On the contrary, this body now has the
same Substance that the Word once had. But Christ was there typified
and prefigured; for in the law were anticipated the mysteries and types of
things to come, which we can also call shadows. And in this very fact I
disclose the glory of Christ, since God is light, who typified Christ in
the very substance of light and of the Word. Nor does this fact detract
from the Word of God more than from God himself; even as I also do not
disparage the angels, even if I have said that a shadow of Christ pre-
existed in them. I wished with Paul to call whatever is seen in the law a
shadow, in order that the body, that is, the truth itself, may be Christ's.
And you came up opportunely with questions of this sort, for I was
meditating on this very thing when you saw me talking to myself.

The Two Treatises of Servetus on the Trinity, pp. 187–90.

▶ Almost ten years later, in 1541, Michael Servetus, now Michel de
Villeneuve, reappeared as a respectable physician in Lyons,
France. As Doctor of Medicine, Servetus discovered the pulmonary circulation of the blood—hiding his insight in an obscure
place of his 'magnum opus', the 'Restitution of Christianity'.
Commenting, in this work, on the distribution of the divine
spirit in the human body, he said the following:[23]

God breathed the divine spirit into Adam's nostrils together with a
breath of air, and thence it remains, Isaiah 2 and Psalm 103. God himself
maintains the breath of life for us by his spirit, giving breath to the

people who are upon the earth and spirit to those trading it, so that we live, move and exist in him, Isaiah 42 and Acts 17. Wind from the four winds and breath from the four breaths gathered by God revive corpses, Ezek. 37. From a breath of air God there introduces the divine spirit into men in whom the life of the inspired air was innate. Hence in Hebrew 'spirit' is represented in the same way as 'breath'. From the air God introduces the divine spirit, introducing the air with the spirit itself and the spark of the very deity which fills the air. . . .

I shall add here the divine philosophy which you will easily understand if you have been trained in anatomy. It is said that in us there is a triple spirit from the substance of three higher elements, natural, vital and animal. . . . But they are not three, but once again of the single spirit (*spiritus*). The vital spirit is that which is communicated through anastomoses from the arteries to the veins in which it is called the natural [spirit]. Therefore the first [i.e. natural spirit] is of the blood, and its seat is in the liver and in the veins of the body. The second is the vital spirit of which the seat is in the heart and in the arteries of the body. The third is the animal spirit, a ray of light, as it were, of which the seat is in the brain and the nerves of the body. In all these there resides the energy of the one spirit and of the light of God. The formation of man from the uterus teaches that the vital spirit is communicated from the heart to the liver. For an artery joined to a vein is transmitted through the umbilicus of the foetus, and in like manner afterward the artery and vein are always joined in us. The divine spirit of Adam was inspired from God into the heart before [it was communicated into] the liver, and from there was communicated to the liver. The divine spirit was truly drawn into the mouth and nostrils, but the inspiration extended to the heart. The heart is the first living thing, the source of heat in the middle of the body. From the liver it takes the liquid of life, a kind of material, and in return vivifies it, just as the liquid of water furnishes material for higher substances and by them, with the addition of light, is vivified so that [in turn] it may invigorate. The material of the divine spirit is from the blood of the liver by way of a remarkable elaboration of which you will now hear. Hence it is said that the divine spirit is in the blood, and the divine spirit is itself the blood, or the sanguineous spirit. It is not said that the divine spirit is principally in the walls of the heart, or in the body of the brain or of the liver, but in the blood, as is taught by God himself in Gen. 9, Lev. 7 and Deut. 12. . . .

The vital spirit has its origin in the left ventricle of the heart, and the lungs assist greatly in its generation. It is a rarefied spirit, elaborated by the force of heat, reddish-yellow (*flavo*) and of fiery potency, so that it is a kind of clear vapour from very pure blood, containing in itself the substance of water, air and fire. It is generated in the lungs from a mixture of inspired air with elaborated, subtle blood which the right ventricle of the heart communicates to the left. However, this communication is made not through the middle wall of the heart, as is commonly believed, but by a very ingenious arrangement the subtle blood is urged forward by a long course through the lungs; it is elaborated by the lungs, becomes reddish-yellow and is poured from the pulmonary artery into the pulmonary vein. Then in the pulmonary vein it is mixed with inspired air and through expiration it is cleansed of its sooty vapours. Thus finally the whole mixture, suitably prepared for the production of the vital spirit, is drawn onward from the left ventricle of the heart by diastole.

That the communication and elaboration are accomplished in this way through the lungs we are taught by the different conjunctions and the communication of the pulmonary artery with the pulmonary vein in the lungs. . . . Therefore that the blood is poured from the heart into the lungs at the very time of birth, and so copiously, is for another purpose. Likewise, not merely air, but air mixed with blood, is sent from the lungs to the heart through the pulmonary vein; therefore the mixture occurs in the lungs. That reddish-yellow colour is given to the spirituous blood by the lungs; it is not from the heart.

In the left ventricle of the heart there is no place large enough for so great and copious a mixture, nor for that elaboration imbuing the reddish-yellow colour. Finally, that middle wall, since it is lacking in vessels and mechanisms, is not suitable for that communication and elaboration, although something may possibly sweat through. By the same arrangement by which a transfusion of the blood from the portal vein to the vena cava occurs in the liver, so a transfusion of the spirit from the pulmonary artery to the pulmonary vein occurs in the lung. If anyone compares these things with those which Galen wrote in books VI and VII, *De usu partium*, he will thoroughly understand a truth which was unknown to Galen.

Charles Donald O'Malley, *Michael Servetus*, pp. 202–6.

▶ **Despite all odds Servetus succeeded in having his manuscript printed secretly. When copies of the 'Restitution' reached Geneva early the following year an ordinary correspondence between a Protestant citizen of Geneva and his Catholic cousin at Vienne took a rather dramatic turn. Here is the first of several important letters, written on 26th February 1553, by the Protestant in Geneva.**

I have no doubt that your attempt to recall me is actuated by friendship. Although I am not a learned man like you, I will do my best to answer your points. With the knowledge that God has given me I shall have something to say, for thanks be to God I am not so poorly grounded as not to know that Jesus Christ is the head of the Church . . . and that she consists only in the truth of God contained in Scripture. . . . To be brief, I am astounded that you reproach me with our lack of ecclesiastical discipline and order . . . whereas, thank God, I see vice better conquered here than in all your territories. And although we allow greater liberty in religion and doctrine, we do not suffer the name of God to be blasphemed. . . . I can give you an example which is greatly to your confusion. . . . You suffer a heretic, who well deserves to be burned wherever he may be. I have in mind a man who will be condemned by the papists as much as by us or ought to be. For though we differ in many things, yet we have this in common that in the one essence of God there are three persons and that the Father begat his Son, who is eternal Wisdom before all time, and that he has had his eternal power, which is the Holy Spirit. So then . . . a man says that the Trinity, which we hold, is a Cerberus and a monster of hell and he disgorges all possible villainies against the teaching of Scripture concerning the eternal generation of the Son of God. . . . And this man is in good repute among you, and is suffered as if he were not wrong. Where, I'd like to know, is the zeal which you pretend? Where is the police of this fine hierarchy of which you so boast? The man of whom I speak has been condemned by all the churches which you reprove, yet you suffer him and even let him print his books which are so full of blasphemies that I need say no more. He is a Portuguese Spaniard, named Michael Servetus. That is his real name, but he goes at present under the name of Villeneufve and practises medicine. He has resided for some time at Lyons. Now he is at Vienne, where his book has been printed by a certain Balthazar Arnoullet, and lest you think that I am talking without warrant I send you the first folio. You say that books which keep solely to the pure simplicity of Scripture poison the world, and if they get out, you cannot suffer them. Yet you hatch poisons that would destroy Scripture and even all that you hold of Christianity.

Roland H. Bainton, Hunted Heretic, pp. 151-3.

▶   The second letter from the Protestant in Geneva to his Catholic cousin in Lyons showed the development matters had taken. Dated 26th March 1553, it read as follows:

When I wrote the letter which you have communicated to those whom I charged with indifference, I did not suppose that the matter would go so far. I simply meant to call your attention to the fine zeal and devotion of those who call themselves the pillars of the Church, although they suffer such disorder in their midst, and persecute so severely the poor Christians, who wish to follow God in simplicity. . . . If they really wish to do anything, as you say, it does not seem to me that the matter is so very difficult, though I cannot for the moment give you what you want, namely the printed book. But I can give you something better to convict him, namely two dozen manuscript pieces of the man in question, in which his heresies are in part contained. If you show him the printed book he can deny it, which he cannot do in respect of his handwriting. The case then being absolutely proved, the men of whom you speak will have no excuse for further dissimulation or delay. All the rest is here right enough, the big book and the other writings of the same author, but I can tell you I had no little trouble to get from Calvin what I am sending. Not that he does not wish to repress such execrable blasphemies, but he thinks his duty is rather to convince heretics with doctrine than with other means, because he does not exercise the sword of justice. But I remonstrated with him and pointed out the embarrassing position in which I should be placed if he did not help me, so that in the end he gave me what you see. For the rest I hope by and by, when the case is further advanced, to get from him a whole ream of paper, which the scamp has had printed, but I think that for the present you have enough, so that there is no need for more to seize his person and bring him to trial.

Roland H. Bainton, Hunted Heretic, pp. 156–7.

▶ A third letter, going to the Catholic at Vienne on 31st March 1553, provided more incriminating material.

I hope that I shall have satisfied your requests in part at least by sending you the handwriting of the author. In the last letter which you have received you will find what he says about his name, which he disguised, for he excuses himself for having assumed the name Villeneuve, when he is really Servetus alias Reves, on the ground that he took the name from that of his native town. For the rest I will keep my promise, God willing, that if there is need I will furnish you with the manuscripts which he has printed, which are in his handwriting like the letters. I should have endeavoured already to secure them if they had been in this city, but they have been at Lausanne for two years. If Calvin had had them I think, for all they are worth, he would have sent them back to the author, but since he [Servetus] had addressed them to others as well, they have kept them.

When you have finished with the letters let me have them back.

Roland H. Bainton, Hunted Heretic, pp. 157–8.

▶ Supplied from Geneva with plenty of condemning material, the Inquisition at Vienne decided to cite 'Monsieur Villeneuve'.

On the fifth day of the month of April of the year 1553, we, Brother Matthieu Ory, Doctor of Theology, Penitentiary of the Holy Apostolic See, Inquisitor-General of the Faith in the kingdom of France and for all Gaul, and Louis Arzellier, Doctor of Laws, Vicar-General of the Most Reverend Monsignor Pierre Palmier, the Archbishop of Vienne, and Antoine de las Court, Lord of Tour de Buys, Doctor of Laws, Sheriff and Lieutenant-General for the district of Vienne, we went to the prisons of the palace at Vienne, and in the criminal chamber caused Michel de Villeneuve to be brought before us . . . and examined him.

Roland H. Bainton, *Hunted Heretic*, pp. 159–60.

▶ Servetus, obviously in trouble, responded with the following statement:

My Lords, I tell you the truth. When these letters were written at the time that I was in Germany about twenty-five years ago [they were written from Vienne], a book was printed in Germany by a certain Spaniard called Servetus. I do not know where he came from in Spain, nor where he lived in Germany, except that I have heard it was at Hagenau, where it is said his book was printed. This town is near Strassburg. Having read the book in Germany, when I was very young, about fifteen to seventeen, it seemed to me that he spoke as well or better than the others. However, leaving all that behind in Germany, I went to France without taking any books, merely with the intention of studying mathematics and medicine, as I have done since. But having heard that Calvin was a learned man, I wanted to write to him out of curiosity without knowing him otherwise, and in fact I did write, requesting that the correspondence should be confidential, and for brotherly correction, to see whether he could not convince me, or I him, for I could not accept his say so. . . . When he saw that my questions were those of Servetus he replied that I was Servetus. I answered that although I was not, for the purposes of discussion I was willing to assume the role of Servetus, for I did not care what he thought of me, but only that we should discuss our opinions. On those terms we wrote until the correspondence became heated, and I dropped it. For the last ten years there has been nothing between us and I affirm before God and you, sirs, that I never wished to dogmatize or assert anything contrary to the Church and the Christian religion.

Roland H. Bainton, *Hunted Heretic*, pp. 160–1.

▶   Servetus was subsequently arrested, but managed to escape. In
    August he made his way to Geneva, where he was promptly
    imprisoned. On 20th August 1553 Calvin informed Farel of the
    development.

We have now new business in hand with Servetus. He intended perhaps passing through this city; for it is not yet known with what design he
came. But after he had been recognized, I thought that he should be
detained. My friend Nicolas summoned him on a capital charge, offering
himself as security according to the *lex talionis*. On the following day he
adduced against him forty written charges. He at first sought to evade
them. Accordingly we were summoned. He impudently reviled me, just
as if he regarded me as obnoxious to him. I answered him as he deserved.
At length the Senate pronounced all the charges proven. Nicolas was
released from prison on the third day, having given up my brother as his
surety; on the fourth day he was set free. Of the man's effrontery I will
say nothing; but such was his madness that he did not hesitate to say that
devils possessed divinity; yea, that many gods were in individual devils,
inasmuch as deity had been substantially communicated to those, equally
with wood and stone. I hope that sentence of death will at least be passed
upon him; but I desire that the severity of the punishment may be
mitigated.

                          Calvin, *Letters* II, 417 (*CR* 42, No. 1772).

▶   Calvin, utterly convinced of the danger of Servetus's 'Restitution
    of Christianity', left nothing undone to extinguish the book. Here
    he wrote to ministerial colleagues in Frankfurt.

You have doubtless heard of the name of Servetus, a Spaniard, who
twenty years ago corrupted your Germany with a virulent publication,
filled with many pernicious errors. This worthless fellow, after being
driven out of Germany, and having concealed himself in France under a
fictitious name, lately patched up a larger volume, partly from his former
book, and partly from new figments which he had invented. This book
he printed secretly at Vienne, a town in the neighbourhood of Lyons.
Many copies of it had been conveyed to Frankfurt for the Easter fairs: the
printer's agent, however, a pious and worthy man, on being informed that
it contained nothing but a farrago of errors, suppressed whatever he had
of it. It would take long to relate with how many errors—yea, prodigious
blasphemies against God—the book abounds. Figure to yourselves a
rhapsody patched up from the impious ravings of all ages. There is no sort
of impiety which this monster has not raked up, as if from the infernal
regions. I had rather you should pass sentence on it from reading the book

itself. You will certainly find on almost every single page what will inspire you with horror. The author himself is held in prison by our magistrates, and he will be punished ere long, I hope; but it is your duty to see to it that this pestiferous poison does not spread farther. The messenger will inform you respecting the number and the repository of the books. The bookseller, if I mistake not, will permit them to be burnt.

Calvin, *Letters* II, 422 (*CR* 42, No. 1780).

▶   According to customary judicial procedure the following indict-
     ment was brought against Servetus on 14th August 1553, by a
     plaintiff, Nicholas de la Fontaine.[24]

Nicholas de la Fontaine asserts that he has instituted proceedings against Michael Servetus and on this account he has allowed himself to be held prisoner in criminal process.

1. I. In the first place that about twenty-four years ago the defendant commenced to annoy the churches of Germany with his errors and heresies, and was condemned and took to flight in order to escape the punishment prepared for him.

2. II. *Item*, that on or about this time he printed a wretched book, which has infected many people.

3. III. *Item*, that since that time he has not ceased by all means in his power to scatter his poison, as much by his construction of biblical text, as by certain annotations which he has made upon Ptolemy.

4. IV. *Item*, that since that time he has printed in secrecy another book containing endless blasphemies.

5. V. *Item*, that while detained in prison in the city of Vienne, when he saw that they were willing to pardon him on condition of his recanting, he found means to escape from prison.

VI. Said Nicholas demands that said Servetus be examined upon all these points.

VII. And since he is able to evade the questions by pretending that his blasphemies and heresies are nought else than good doctrine, said Nicholas proposes certain articles upon which he demands said heretic be examined.

6. VIII. To wit, whether he has not written and falsely taught and published that to believe that in a single essence of God there are three distinct persons, the Father, the Son, and the Holy Ghost, is to create four phantoms, which cannot and ought not to be imagined.

7. IX. *Item*, that to put such distinction into the essence of God is to cause God to be divided into three parts, and that is a three-headed

devil, like to Cerberus, whom the ancient poets have called the dog of hell, a monster, and things equally injurious.

8. X. *Item*, whether he has not maintained such blasphemies most injuriously, as much against the ancient doctors, such as St Ambrose, St Augustine, Chrysostom, Athanasius and the like as against all those who sought in our times to elevate Christianity, even to calling Melanchthon a man without faith, son of the devil, Belial and Satan.

9. XI. *Item*, whether he does not say that our Lord Jesus Christ is not the Son of God, except in so much as he was conceived of the Holy Ghost in the womb of the Virgin Mary.

10. XII. *Item*, that those who believe Jesus Christ to have been the word of God the Father, engendered through all eternity, have a scheme of redemption which is fanciful and of the nature of sorcery.

11. XIII. *Item*, that Jesus Christ is God, in so much as God has caused him to be such.

12. XIV. *Item*, that the flesh of Jesus Christ came from heaven and from the substance of God.

13. XV. *Item*, that divinity was imparted to Jesus Christ only when he was made man, and afterwards spiritually communicated to the apostles on the day of Pentecost. . . .

15. XVII. *Item*, whether he does not condemn those who seek in the essence of God his holy spirit, saying that all those who believe in the Trinity are atheists. . . .

21. XXIII. *Item*, that when St John says that the word was in God, it is the same as saying that the man Jesus Christ was there.

22. XXIV. *Item*, that the essence of the angels and of our soul is of the substance of God.

23. XXV. *Item*, that the substance of Jesus Christ is that which was in the skies, and that this is the same substance whence proceed the angels and our souls.

24. XXVI. *Item*, instead of conferring three persons in the essence of God, or three hypostases which have each his property, he says that God is a single entity, containing one hundred thousand essences, so that he is a portion of us, and that we are a portion of his spirit.

25. XXVII. *Item*, in consequence whereof not only the models of all creatures are in God, but also the material forms, so that our souls are of the substantial seed of the Word of God.

26. XXVIII. *Item*, that Jesus Christ is the Son of God because he has the elements of the substance of the Father, to wit: fire, air and water.

27. XXIX. *Item*, that the soul of man is mortal, and that the only thing which is immortal is an elementary breath, which is the substance

that Jesus Christ now possesses in heaven and which is also the elementary and divine and incorruptible substance of the Holy Ghost. . . .

29. XXXI. *Item*, that by the sin of Adam the soul of man as well as the body was made mortal.

30. XXXII. *Item*, that little children are sinless, and moreover are incapable of redemption until they come of age.

31. XXXIII. *Item*, that they do not commit mortal sin up to the age of twenty.

32. XXXIV. *Item*, that the baptism of little children is an invention of the devil, an infernal falsehood tending to the destruction of all Christianity. . . .

34. XXXVI. *Item*, that however much he confesses that the philosophers have erred in saying that the Word was God himself, he says that Jesus Christ, in so much as he is a man, was always in God and that from him is the divinity of the world.

35. XXXVII. *Item*, that the air is the Spirit of God and that God is called Spirit because he breathes life in all things by his spirit of air.

36. XXXVIII. *Item*, the soul of man in so much as it possesses many divine properties is full of an infinity of gods.

37. XXXIX. *Item*, that in the person of Calvin, minister of the Word of God in the Church of Geneva, he has defamed with printed book the doctrine which he preached, uttering all the injurious and blasphemous things which it is possible to invent.

38. XL. And because he knows well that his said book could not be tolerated even among papists, in so much as it destroyed all the foundations of Christianity, therefore he hid himself at the house of Guillaume Guerou, at that time proof corrector, as said Guerou has testified.

39. Said Nicholas demands that the said Servetus should be compelled to respond as to the fact of the articles here presented, without entering into dispute as to whether the doctrine is true or not, because that will appear later on.

CR 41, pp. 727–31.

▶   Early in September 1553 Calvin summarized in a letter the case
     against Servetus.

It was he whom that faithful minister of Christ, Master Bucer of holy memory, in other respects of a mild disposition, declared from the pulpit to be worthy of having his bowels pulled out, and torn to pieces. While he has not permitted any of his poison to go abroad since that time, he has lately, however, brought out a larger volume, printed secretly at Vienne, but patched up from the same errors. To be sure, as soon as the thing became known, he was cast into prison. He escaped from it some way or other, and wandered in Italy for nearly four months. He at length, in an evil hour, came to this place, when, at my instigation, one of the Syndics ordered him to be conducted to prison. For I do not disguise it, that I considered it my duty to put a check, so far as I could, upon this most obstinate and ungovernable man, that his contagion might not spread farther. . . . As respects this man, three things require to be considered. With what prodigious errors he has corrupted the whole of religion; yea, with what detestable mockeries he has endeavoured to destroy all piety; with what abominable ravings he has obscured Christianity, and razed to the very foundation all the principles of our religion. Secondly, how obstinately he has behaved; with what diabolical pride he has despised all advice; with what desperate stubbornness he has driven headlong in scattering his poison. Thirdly, with what proud scorn he at present avows and defends his abominations.

Calvin, *Letters* II, 428–9 (*CR* 42, No. 1793).

▶   **In September 1553 Servetus, after a month in prison, described his situation in a letter to the Geneva city council.**

I humbly beg that you cut short these long delays and deliver me from prosecution. You see that Calvin is at the end of his rope, not knowing what to say and for his pleasure wishes to make me rot here in prison. The lice eat me alive. My clothes are torn and I have nothing for a change, neither a jacket nor shirt, but a bad one. I have addressed to you another petition which was according to God and to impede it Calvin cites Justinian. He is in a bad way to quote against me what he does not himself credit, for he does not believe what Justinian has said about the Holy Church of bishops and priests and other matters of religion and knows well that the Church was already degenerated. It is a great shame, the more so that I have been caged here for five weeks and he has not urged against me a single passage.

My lords, I have also asked you to give me a procurator or advocate as you did to my opponent, who was not in the same straits as I, who am a stranger and ignorant of the customs of the country. You permitted it to him, but not to me, and you have liberated him from prison before knowing. I petition you that my case be referred to the Council of Two Hundred with my requests, and if I may appeal there I do so ready to assume all the cost, loss and interest of the law of an eye for an eye, both against the first accuser and against Calvin, who has taken up the case against himself. Done in your prisons of Geneva, 15th September 1553.

Roland H. Bainton, *Hunted Heretic*, p. 197.

▶ On 26th October 1553 sentence was passed against Michael Servetus.

The sentence pronounced against Michel Servet de Villeneufve of the Kingdom of Aragon in Spain who some twenty-three or twenty-four years ago printed a book at Hagenau in Germany against the Holy Trinity containing many great blasphemies to the scandal of the said churches of Germany, the which book he freely confesses to have printed in the teeth of the remonstrances made to him by the learned and evangelical doctors of Germany. In consequence he became a fugitive from Germany. Nevertheless he continued in his errors and, in order the more to spread the venom of his heresy, he printed secretly a book in Vienne of Dauphiny full of the said heresies and horrible, execrable blasphemies against the Holy Trinity, against the Son of God, against the baptism of infants and the foundations of the Christian religion. He confesses that in this book he called believers in the Trinity Trinitarians and atheists. He calls this Trinity a diabolical monster with three heads. He blasphemes detestably against the Son of God, saying that Jesus Christ is not the Son of God from eternity. He calls infant baptism an invention of the devil and sorcery. His execrable blasphemies are scandalous against the majesty of God, the Son of God and the Holy Spirit. This entails the murder and ruin of many souls. Moreover he wrote a letter to one of our ministers in which, along with other numerous blasphemies, he declared our holy evangelical religion to be without faith and without God and that in place of God we have a three-headed Cerberus. He confesses that because of this abominable book he was made a prisoner at Vienne and perfidiously escaped. He has been burned there in effigy together with five bales of his books. Nevertheless, having been in prison in our city, he persists maliciously in his detestable errors and calumniates true Christians and faithful followers of the immaculate Christian tradition.

Wherefore we Syndics, judges of criminal cases in this city, having witnessed the trial conducted before us at the instance of our Lieutenant against you 'Michel Servet de Villeneuve' of the Kingdom of Aragon in Spain, and having seen your voluntary and repeated confessions and your books, judge that you, Servetus, have for a long time promulgated false and thoroughly heretical doctrine, despising all remonstrances and corrections and that you have with malicious and perverse obstinacy sown and divulged even in printed books opinions against God the Father, the Son and the Holy Spirit, in a word against the fundamentals of the Christian religion, and that you have tried to make a schism and trouble the Church of God by which many souls may have been ruined and lost, a thing horrible, shocking, scandalous, and infectious. And you have had neither shame nor horror of setting yourself against the divine Majesty and the Holy Trinity, and so you have obstinately tried to infect the world with your stinking heretical poison. . . . For these and other reasons, desiring to purge the Church of God of such infection and cut off the rotten member, having taken counsel with our citizens and having invoked the name of God to give just judgment . . . having God and the Holy Scriptures before our eyes, speaking in the name of the Father, Son and Holy Spirit, we now in writing give final sentence and condemn you, Michael Servetus, to be bound and taken to Champel and there attached to a stake and burned with your book to ashes. And so you shall finish your days and give an example to others who would commit the like.

Roland H. Bainton, *Hunted Heretic*, pp. 207–9.

▶   The following day, 27th October 1553, Servetus died at the stake outside Geneva. Farel, who accompanied him on his walk, reflected as follows:

On the way to the stake, when some brethren urged him to confess freely his fault and repudiate his errors, he said that he suffered unjustly and prayed that God would forgive his accusers. I said to him at once, 'Do you justify yourself when you have sinned so fearfully? If you continue I will not go with you another step, but will leave you to the judgment of God. I intended to go along and ask everybody to pray for you, hoping that you would edify the people. I did not wish to leave you until you should draw the last breath.' Then he stopped and said nothing more of the sort. He asked forgiveness for his errors, ignorance and sins, but never made a full confession. He often prayed with us while we were exhorting, and asked the spectators several times to pray the Lord for him. But we could not get him openly to admit his errors and confess that Christ is the eternal Son of God.

Roland H. Bainton, *Hunted Heretic*, p. 211.

▶ Sebastian Castellio, whose book, 'Should Heretics be Persecuted?' (a skilful anthology of what eminent theologians had said about the persecution of heretics), was a vehement reaction against the condemnation and burning of Servetus, is an example of the spiritualists who considered inward piety to be of greater importance than outward adherence to doctrine.[25]

When I consider the life and teaching of Christ who, though innocent himself, yet always pardoned the guilty and told us to pardon until seventy times seven, I do not see how we can retain the name of Christian if we do not imitate his clemency and mercy. Even if we were innocent we ought to follow him. How much more when we are covered with so many sins? When I examine my own life I see so many and such great sins that I do not think I could even obtain pardon from my saviour if I were thus ready to condemn others. Let each one examine himself, sound and search his conscience, and weigh his thoughts, words and deeds. Then will he see himself as one who is not in a position to remove the mote from the eye of his brother before he has taken the beam from his own. In view of the many sins which are laid to us all, the best course would be for each to look to himself, to exercise care for the correction of his life and not for the condemnation of others. This licence of judgment which reigns everywhere today, and fills all with blood, constrains me to do my best to staunch the blood, especially that blood which is so wrongfully shed—I mean the blood of those who are called heretics, which name has become today so infamous, detestable and horrible that there is no quicker way to dispose of an enemy than to accuse him of heresy. The mere word stimulates such horror that when it is pronounced men shut their ears to the victim's defence, and furiously persecute not merely the man himself, but also those who dare to open their mouths on his behalf; by which rage it has come to pass that many have been destroyed before their cause was really understood. . . .

[Addressed to Christ:] O Creator and King of the world, dost thou see these things? Art thou become so changed, so cruel, so contrary to thyself? When thou wast on earth none was more mild, more clement, more patient of injury. As a sheep before the shearer thou wast dumb. When scourged, spat upon, mocked, crowned with thorns and crucified shamefully among thieves, thou didst pray for them who did thee this wrong. Art thou now so changed? I beg thee in the name of thy Father, dost thou now command that those who do not understand thy precepts as the mighty demand, be drowned in water, cut with lashes to the entrails, sprinkled with salt, dismembered by the sword, burned at the slow fire, and otherwise tortured in every manner and as long as possible?

Dost thou, O Christ, command and approve of these things? Are they thy vicars who make these sacrifices? Art thou present when they summon thee and dost thou eat human flesh? If thou, Christ, dost these things or if thou commandest that they be done, what hast thou left for the devil? Dost thou the very same things as Satan?

Sebastian Castellio, *Concerning Heretics*, pp. 125–6, 134–5.

▶   Sebastian Franck's 'Paradoxa' illustrates well the typical spiritualist understanding of the Christian faith.[25]

What does heresy do with Scripture but hit the unrhymed letter of Scripture here, or claim it there? Nobody watches for the pure interpretation and understanding of the irenic spirit. Rather everybody considers God and God's Word to be his Apollo, while it is only the manger of Christ, is only death, darkness, monstrance, arch, wall, lantern, testimony. keyhole, closed book. God's Word, however, is the holy Spirit, the light, the key, the sword, the life, the holy, the bread and Christ! The other are hardly the outer court of the holy. Thus nothing is more against the meaning of Scripture and nothing less against God's Word than Scripture understood according to the dead letter. Scripture is eternal allegory. One can hardly say which door to heresy is opened daily and which new sects arise. Also, what incomprehensible and incoherent results occur if Scripture is understood according to the dead letter. . . . To cut off one's hands, to pierce eyes, to eat the flesh of Christ and drink his blood, to be born again, to break the temple and rebuild it in three days. . . . You are Peter. Whoever believes will not die . . . to give one's robe for a sword, to hit as the prophet Jeremiah . . . not to wear shoes, to greet no one and speak to no one on the way, not to have gold and silver, to leave all things, to sell, to hate one's soul and life, to become fools and children, to walk naked and shamelessly through the streets . . . not to work like the birds and flowers in the field, to let the birds care. . . .

In the same fashion one would have to make a passible, changeable human being of God. In short, the Pharisees hit Christ to death with the letter, because he taught and lived against the letter, but not against the true meaning of Scripture, because he spoke and acted against the temple, the law and circumcision, broke the law, because, contrary to Scripture, he called the Cross and death a blessing, and spoke of fortune as a misfortune, much against the example of Lot and Abraham. In sum: Christ's whole Gospel, his life and testament, is a letter against the Old Testament, indeed it is its dissolution, so that they killed him with the letter of Scripture and still do it today. Oh, Christ's Gospel has an altogether different meaning and spiritual significance. It is alone recognized by the children of God and those who are truly spiritually minded. To all others it is eternally obscured, a parable, miraculous speech, a riddle and a closed book. . . .

We see how the Pharisees treated the letter. Yet we do not learn from such abuse nor understand Paul's simple statement that 'The letter kills.' Now, Scripture, letter, law and Old Testament are all one. Thus the statement really means that Scripture kills. Those who preach according to the meaning and sense of the letter are servants of Moses and of the letter and proclaim death. . . . The letter refers to the grammatical sense as does everything which the worldly wise through flesh and blood understand, tell and comprehend without spirit and grace. Scripture kills, for without the spirit it is never truly understood. The spirit makes that which is written alive and interprets it properly. The meaning of Christ and of the spirit is alone God's Word and makes alive when it livens, interprets and applies the letter in our heart. Otherwise it is of itself and by itself not only contradictory and disconcordant, but without such teacher, leader, guide, key, interpreter and this thesic thread it is also the bitter death, a closed book and a confused labyrinth. From the beginning until now have the Pharisees and scribes called the prophets, Christ and the apostles and all members of Christ liars and killed them. Thus the letter is, and always will be, the sword of the Antichrist and the place where he sits and fights against the saints. If the Antichrist has the letter, Christ has the meaning and the proper interpretation. . . .

Because the letter of Scripture is divided and disagrees with itself, it follows that the various sects do arise. One man touches the dead letter here, another man there. This man understands it as it sounds here, that man as it reads there. To be sure, all sects come from the devil and are a fruit of the flesh, are bound to time, place, person, law and elements. Only the free non-sectarian and impartial Christian faith is not tied to things, but stands freely in the spirit on God's Word and is apprehended by faith and not with eyes. Such a piety is neither tied to a sect, a time, a place, a law, a person, nor an element. And inasmuch as good and evil must remain together in one net and field until the end of the world, and Jerusalem is to be amidst the gentiles, I do not believe in a sectarian separation. Anyone can be pious all by himself, wherever he may be. He is not to run hither and yonder, seeking to establish a special sect, baptism, church or to look at a group of followers. . . .

This we can neither tell anybody nor write nor read it, but everyone will in himself experience it. Therefore one can neither say, read, nor write what is God, God's Word and truth. The holy Spirit does not allow itself to be regulated, nor suffers truth to be put into letters nor speak God's Word. It is all only picture and shadow what one can speak, rule, write or read, conceived as from afar.

Sebastian Franck, Paradoxa, pp. 5–8, 155.

BIBLIOGRAPHY

The best historiographical introduction is by George H. Williams, ed., *Spiritual and Anabaptist Writers* (London and Philadelphia, 1957), pp. 19–35. From the pen of the same writer comes the only recent monograph on the field, George H. Williams, *The Radical Reformation* (London and Philadelphia, 1962). A general introduction and thus broader than its title is Franklin H. Littell, *The Anabaptist View of the Church* (Boston, 1958). The four volumes of the *Mennonite Encyclopedia* (Scottdale, 1955–9) are indispensable. For Antitrinitarianism see Earl Morse Wilbur, *A History of Unitarianism, Socinianism and its Antecedents* (Cambridge, 1945). On Spiritualism, the older work of Rufus M. Jones, *Spiritual Reformers in the 16th and 17th Centuries* (London, 1914), is, despite various deficiencies, still the best.

The basic collection of primary materials is composed of the *Quellen zur Geschichte der Täufer*, of which eleven volumes have appeared so far. For Anabaptist martyrs, see Thielman Jan van Braght, *The Bloody Theatre or Martyrs' Mirror of the Defenceless Christians* (Scottdale, 1951). Reference must also be made to the *Corpus Schwenckfeldianorum*, 14 vols. (Leipzig, 1907–36), and *Bibliotheca Reformatoria Neerlandica* (abbrev. *BRN*) ('s-Gravenhage,1909). The *Mennonite Quarterly Review* published since 1927 contains source publications and scholarly contributions.

NOTES AND REFERENCES

1. There is no recent biography of Thomas Müntzer in English. The greatest interest in this radical reformer comes currently from Marxist historians, of whom M. M. Smirin, *Die Volksreformation des Thomas Müntzer und der grosse Bauernkrieg* (Berlin, 1952), has given the most competent treatment.

Traditionally oriented is Joachim Zimmermann, *Thomas Müntzer, ein deutsches Schicksal* (Berlin, 1925). There is a brief sketch of Müntzer's life in Karl Kupisch, *Feinde Luthers* (Berlin, 1951). Basic for Müntzer's relation to Luther is Carl Hinrichs, *Luther und Müntzer; ihre Auseinandersetzung über Obrigkeit und Widerstandsrecht* (Berlin, 1952), and the earlier essay by Karl Holl, 'Luther und die Schwärmer', *Gesammelte Aufsätze*, I (Tübingen, 1923). The collection of sources used is Otto H. Brandt, *Thomas Müntzer* (Jena, 1933). The *Historie Thomae Müntzer* was published anonymously in 1525 and ascribed for a long time to Melanchthon. Recent scholarship has absolved Melanchthon from responsibility for this strongly biased account. For an historiographical survey, see Max Steinmetz, 'Zur Entstehung der Müntzer-Legende', *Beiträge zum neuen Geschichtsbild* (Berlin, 1956).

2. Mani (216–*c*. 276), Persian religious leader, claimed to be the final divine revelation. See Henri-Charles Puech, *Le Manichéisme, la vie de son fondateur, sa doctrine* (Paris, 1949).

3. Hegesippus, a little known second-century Christian theologian who defended, against gnosticism, the purity of the apostolic teaching. Eusebius of Caesarea (died *c*. 339) is mostly known for his *Historia ecclesiastica*, a history of the Church up to 324.

4. Müntzer's three liturgical writings are reprinted in Emil Sehling, *Die evangelischen Kirchenordnungen des 16. Jahrhunderts*, Band I (Leipzig, 1902), pp. 472ff.

5. A recent popular treatment of Anabaptism is by John C. Wenger, *Even Unto Death* (Richmond, 1961). The rise of the movement in Zürich is recounted by Fritz Blanke, *Brothers in Christ* (Scottdale, 1961); Harold S. Bender, *Conrad Grebel, 1498–1526, Founder of the Swiss Brethren* (Goshen, 1950), tells in broader detail the same development in terms of the life of one of the leaders of Anabaptism in Zürich.

6. On Felix Mantz, Conrad Grebel, Wilhelm Reublin, Georg Blaurock and Michael Sattler, see the competent articles in the *Mennonite Encyclopedia*.

7. For Balthasar Hubmaier, see H. C. Vedder, *Balthasar Hubmaier, The Leader of Anabaptists* (New York, 1905) and the recent German work by Torsten Bergsten, *Balthasar Hubmeier, Seine Stellung zu Reformation und Täufertum* (Kassel, 1961).

8. On the Schleitheim Confession, see Robert Friedmann, 'The Schleitheim Confession (1527) and other Doctrinal Writings . . .', *Mennonite Quarterly Review* 16 (1942), 82–98. The translation used here is from Thieleman J. von Braght, *The Bloody Theatre or Martyrs' Mirror* (Scottdale, 1951).

9. The translation used here is from John C. Wenger, 'The Schleitheim Confession of Faith', *Mennonite Quarterly Review*, 19 (1945), 243ff.

10. A suggestive introduction to the *Martyrs' Mirror*, which collected the accounts of Anabaptist martyrs, is given by Orley Swartzendruber, 'The Piety and Theology of the Anabaptist Martyrs in van Braght's *Martyrs' Mirror*', *Mennonite Quarterly Review* 28 (1954), 5–26; 128–42.

11. The translation used here is from George H. Williams, ed., *Spiritual and Anabaptist Writers* (Philadelphia, 1957), pp. 138–44.

12. The translation used here is from A. L. E. Verheyden, *Anabaptism in Flanders* (Scottdale, 1961), pp. 109–12.

13. The translation used here is from A. L. E. Verheyden, *Anabaptism in Flanders*, pp. 114–16.

14. The translation used here is from A. L. E. Verheyden, *Anabaptism in Flanders*, pp. 116–19.

15. On Melchior Hofmann there is an unnecessarily complicated but competent study by Peter Kawerau, *Melchior Hofmann als religiöser Denker* (Haarlem, 1954).

16. On Münster Anabaptism, see the brief account by Hans Rothert, *Das Tausendjährige Reich der Wiedertäufer zu Münster, 1534–35* (Münster, 1948), the collection of sources by Klemens Löffler, *Die Wiedertäufer zu Münster 1534–35* (Jena, 1923), and the older, but thorough works by C. A. Cornelius, *Berichte der Augenzeugen über das Münsterische Wiedertäuferreich* (Münster, 1855), and *Geschichte des Münsterischen Aufruhrs . . .* (Leipzig, 1855). See also Fritz Blanke, 'Das Reich der Wiedertäufer zu Münster 1534–35', *Aus der Welt der Reformation* (Zürich, 1960), pp. 48–71; Robert Stupperich, *Das Münsterische Täufertum, Ergebnisse und Probleme der Forschung* (Münster, 1958).

17. D. Harting, *De Munsterische Furie* (Enkhuizen, 1850).

18. A balanced treatment of Menno's life and thought comes from H. W. Meihuizen, *Menno Simons* (Haarlem, 1962). Menno's writings are available in a definitive translation, *Menno Simons, The Complete Writings* (Scottdale, 1956). The translation used here is from this edition, pp. 668–72.

19. For a collection of essays on various aspects of the Hutterite Anabaptists, see Robert Friedmann, *Hutterite Studies* (Goshen, 1961).

20. The standard work on Servetus is Roland H. Bainton, *Hunted Heretic, The Life and Death of Servetus* (Boston, 1953). Servetus's two initial tracts on the Trinity were translated and edited by Earl Morse Wilbur, *The Two Treatises of Servetus on the Trinity* (Cambridge, 1932). Excerpts from Servetus's non-theological writings were translated by Charles D. O'Malley, *Michael Servetus, A Translation of his Geographical, Medical, and Astrological Writings . . .* (Philadelphia, 1953).

21. The translation used here is from Earl Morse Wilbur, ed., *The Two Treatises of Servetus on the Trinity* (Cambridge, 1932), pp. 3–5, 6f.

22. The translation used here is from Earl Morse Wilbur, ed., *The Two Treatises of Servetus on the Trinity* (Cambridge, 1932), pp. 187–90.

23. The translation used here is from Charles Donald O'Malley, *Michael Servetus* (Philadelphia, 1953), pp. 202–6.

24. The translation used here is from *Translations and Reprints from the Original Sources of European History*, vol. III, pp. 12–16. The Roman and Arabic numerals refer to the first and second draft of the indictment. The sources concerning Servetus's trial are available in R. Kingdon and J. F. Bergier, *Registres de la Compagnie des Pasteurs de Genève au Temps de Calvin*, II, 1553–1564: *Accusation et Procès de Michel Servet (1553)* (Geneva, 1962).

25. The translation used here is from Sebastien Chateillon, *Concerning Heretics: Whether They are to Be Persecuted . . .* [translated] by Roland H. Bainton (New York, 1935), pp. 125–6.

25. The quotation is from Sebastian Franck, *Paradoxa* (Jena, 1909). On Franck (1499–1542) see Rufus M. Jones, *Spiritual Reformers in the 16th and*

17th Centuries (London, 1914), pp. 46–63, and Eberhard Teufel, *Landräumig* (Neustadt, 1954). The *Paradoxa* were originally published in 1534.

Plate facing p. 241: *The sub-title reads, translated:* The entire apostolic Church is called to its threshold. The knowledge of God is restored, as is the faith in Christ, our justification, the regeneration of baptism and the eating of the Lord's Supper. Finally, the restitution of the heavenly kingdom for us means the end of the wicked Babylonian captivity and the destruction of the Antichrist and his host.

(Heb.) And at that time Michael shall rise
(Greek)   And war broke out in heaven

The Reformation in England and Scotland

THE Reformation in England began with the marital problems of King Henry VIII, that crowned head of England who, as Charles Dickens melodramatically observed, was 'a most intolerable ruffian and a blot of blood and grease on the history of England'. At other times such problems would have been a king's own business. In the religious turbulence of the early sixteenth century they led to England's break from Rome. To be sure, there were other factors in this break, perhaps in the long run even more important ones: the tradition of Wiclif, the influence of Luther and of Humanism. None the less, the course of ecclesiastical events during Henry's reign which transformed the Church in England into the Church of England is painfully— at least to the Protestant historian—untheological, it having been occasioned more by the amorous fancies of the King than by the pamphlets of the theologians.

Henry simply wanted to get rid of his wife and marry another one. But this was more easily said than done, for Henry's marital past was indeed a complex one. At the tender age of twelve (1503) Henry had been engaged to the Spanish princess Catherine of Aragon, who was almost six years his senior. This step had been prompted by political and financial considerations arising out of the untimely death of Henry's elder brother Arthur, to whom Catherine had been married for a little less than half a year. Catherine had come to England from Spain because an alliance between the two countries, cemented by royal matrimony, seemed an appropriate diplomatic manoeuvre. The death of Arthur did not change this consideration. As an alternative to sending the teenage Catherine back to her native Spain, it occurred to England's policy-makers that Prince Henry could well replace his deceased brother, particularly since the political situation which had originally prompted the proposed marital bond still existed.

An obstacle, however, lay in the fact that Christendom commonly rejected a marriage with a deceased brother's wife, a principle which was

VI

derived from a passage found in the book of Leviticus (20.21) which announced that it was an unclean thing to touch one's brother's wife. To be sure, a passage in Deuteronomy (25.5ff.) obligated a man to take his brother's wife into his tent, but somehow or other that passage never had played any significant part in Christian history. A papal dispensation was necessary to cover the marital impediment between Henry and Catherine. It was requested and duly received. And after old King Henry VII died, in the spring of 1509, Henry VIII succeeded him and shortly thereafter married his fiancée, Catherine. Though Henry shared the customary royal pastime of having mistresses—one of whom gave birth to a son— his marriage to Catherine was to all outward appearances happy enough. Indeed, Erasmus praised it as an example of chastity and love. Henry and Catherine, it seemed, were about 'to live happily ever after'.

Many years later, some time after 1525, Henry began to work toward an annulment of his marriage with Catherine. Frequently, the term 'divorce' is used in this connection. But this is inaccurate, for, among other things, Henry staunchly believed that divorce was impossible once a marriage had been properly consummated. None the less he insisted that his present marriage to Catherine was invalid because it rested upon a violation of the injunction of the book of Leviticus. Thus he approached the Pope, who had originally given the dispensation, to annul the 'marriage'—and the dispensation—and declare that the marriage had been actually null and void from the beginning.

It is not altogether clear what prompted Henry to take this step. Without doubt he was concerned about the absence of a male heir. Catherine had given birth to six children, but three of them had been stillborn, and only one girl, Mary, had survived infancy. A female heir was risky business for a not yet firmly established dynasty. For Henry, who was, in small measure, a devout and religiously sensitive person, this raised the question whether perhaps there was evident here divine disapproval of his 'marriage' and whether he might be living in sin. Finally, there was Anne Boleyn, a not unattractive lady-in-waiting at the royal court. Henry passionately desired her, but she was unwilling to be just another mistress and give herself to the King without the price of marriage.

Had Catherine been willing to go along with Henry's demands, no further trouble would have arisen. But she was stubborn, insisting on her rights in a duly contracted marriage, and declined to co-operate. Thereupon Henry turned to the Pope, recalling the many services he had rendered the Church (after all, his literary effort against Martin Luther had earned him the title *Fidei Defensor*), and asked for an annulment of his marriage with Catherine; simultaneously he requested a special papal dispensation to marry Anne, which was necessary because he had known, to use biblical terminology, her sister.

It so happened that Henry's request to the Pope came at a most inopportune moment. The soldiers of Charles V, Catherine's nephew, had occupied Rome in 1527 and had made Pope Clement VII virtually a prisoner of the Emperor. Clement could hardly afford to do anything which would enrage Charles. He stalled and the affair dragged on to interminable lengths. After some two years of such delay, Henry began to get impatient. He eagerly took up the suggestion of one of his advisers, Thomas Cranmer, that he present his case to the European universities to have them render their scholarly opinion, since the Pope obviously was not, under the present political circumstances, a free agent. Henry was enthusiastic. Much effort, financial and otherwise, was expended to assure a welcome outcome.

In January 1533, Henry secretly married Anne. In May an ecclesiastical court declared Henry's marriage to Catherine null and void, and in September the new Queen gave birth to a child. Contrary to the forecasts of the astrologers and physicians, it was a girl, Elizabeth. The Pope promptly countered the new development by excommunicating Henry. By that time King Henry had realized that the Pope could not be simply ignored, but that papal authority in England had to be removed. He discovered that the Pope was, after all, a foreign political power and that a fourteenth-century statute prohibited dealings with foreign powers. This meant, of course, that the entire English clergy were guilty. Henry said so and demanded the payment of exorbitant fines and the acknowledgment that none other than he was the head of the Church in England. The clergy put up surprisingly little struggle, doled out the money, and made the acknowledgment which the King wanted.

The same year Henry prohibited the English clergy from appealing to Rome. One year later the Act of Supremacy explicitly acknowledged the King as supreme head of the Church of England. Thus the break with Rome had become final. There were many who resented this course of events. It evoked opposition and accordingly brought persecution and martyrs, of whom Thomas More, the celebrated humanist and one-time Chancellor of the King, was the most prominent. The sole religious issue at stake was papal supremacy, for when Henry broke with Rome he did not mean to break with the old faith. The Statute of Six Articles of 1539 made this quite obvious, as it upheld such Catholic doctrine as transsubstantiation and the private mass. The only significant departure from traditional ecclesiastical custom was the official endorsement of an English translation of the Bible, which was to be placed into every church for everyone to read.

One must call attention to the fact that there were at this time in England other and wider issues of a genuinely religious character. On one side, the tradition of Wiclif was very strong in the country and many humanists longed for a reformation of the Church. On the other side, even Henry VIII himself had entered the theological arena with a staunch defence of the seven sacraments of the Catholic Church. His deed—if indeed it was his, for there were soon many who decided that the King could not have written this work—earned for him from the Pope the official title 'Defender of the Faith' and from Luther a rather fiery reply, in which he bluntly called Henry a liar.

If Henry continued to be religiously conservative, during the last years of his life his marital developments were all the more radical. Anne Boleyn was executed in 1536 on charges of adultery. Jane Seymour followed as wife number three. No wonder, that, when reflecting on the new marriage, one lady of nobility was prompted to express the hope that when the King was tired of Jane he would be able to find some occasion for getting rid of her, for, she said, wives will hardly be well contented if such customs become general. Fortunately, Jane died the following year in childbirth. Her place was quickly, though temporarily, taken by Anne of Cleves, who was thought to combine diplomatic ability with physical attraction; but the latter feature turned out to be largely the product of the idealizing brush of Holbein, the painter who was commissioned to draw her portrait. Henry took one look at Anne herself, called her the 'Mare of Flanders', and sent her back. Catherine Howard became the next queen, but experienced the same fate as her predecessor Anne Boleyn—only in her case the charges seem to have been more accurate. Catherine Parr, who completed the half-dozen, succeeded in the notable feat of surviving Henry.

The King's death came in 1547. He bequeathed the crown to his nine-year-old son, Edward, and the power of government to a group of advisers who were in sympathy with the Protestant Reformation. During the six years of Edward's reign official English theology shifted to a Protestant emphasis: in 1549 the Book of Common Prayer was introduced, that famous order of worship whose language has influenced English Christianity for the past 400 years. An *Act of Uniformity* not only prescribed the Prayer Book, but also prohibited all other forms of worship. Three years later a significant revision of the Book of Common Prayer made its Protestant orientation even more obvious. Though it emphatically stated that the first book had contained nothing but what was agreeable to the Word of God, the changes made were significant. Prayer for the dead and ritual vestments were abolished. The 'altar' became a 'table' and the famous *Black Rubric*, an appended note, explained that kneeling during communion did not mean the adoration of the sacrament. Also in 1552 an official confession of faith was drawn up— the Forty-two Articles of Faith, which, when revised into the Thirty-nine Articles under Queen Elizabeth, became a basic doctrinal pronouncement of the Church of England.

Edward VI died in 1553 and Mary, the daughter of Henry's first wife, Catherine, ascended the throne. A vigorous policy of re-Catholicization was instigated. Mary was deeply fond of her Church and of her husband. Since both were foreign, the one Roman, the other Spanish, she evoked much opposition, which eventually meant the failure of her plans. Though she was perhaps the only really pious English monarch of the sixteenth century, she has the name of 'Bloody Mary' in history primarily because she committed the blunder of making martyrs. Of these, Archbishop Cranmer was the most famous. He recanted his leadership in the Reformation and then recanted his recantation. Eventually he died at the stake. Later John Foxe collected fact and fiction concerning these martyrs in his *Book of Martyrs*, for centuries a veritable 'second Bible' in English homes, combining—even more than the Bible itself—excitement with devotion. Only in more recent times, when devotion has become a less popular pastime and excitement more easily obtainable elsewhere, has the popularity of Foxe decreased. If Foxe incited the English people to a horror of popery, he also gave Mary the bad name under which her memory has always laboured.

Queen Mary died in 1558. She was succeeded by her half-sister, Elizabeth, who upon hearing the news of Mary's death reportedly fell on her knees quoting Scripture: 'It is the Lord's doing, and it is marvellous in our eyes.' Soon every new gold coin carried the Queen's biblical, if presumptive, sentiments on the demise of her relative. Under Queen Elizabeth's guidance religious matters were brought to a settlement and England became the leading Protestant power in Europe. Elizabeth was probably little interested in religious matters for their own sake. Nevertheless, within a year after her ascension she had reintroduced the Uniformity Act and the ecclesiastical reforms of Edward. A new ruler had brought a new religion. The second Book of Common Prayer was reintroduced and became, once again, the basis for worship. Certain changes were made, of which the juxtaposition of key sections of both the 1549 and 1552 versions of the communion service was perhaps the most important one. Also, in the Litany the people no longer prayed to be delivered 'from the tyranny of the Bishop of Rome and his detestable enormities'. Four years later, in 1563, the Forty-two Articles were reworked into the Thirty-nine Articles. Relatively late in 1571 these Articles were officially recognized. By that time Elizabeth had been excommunicated by the Pope and Protestantism in England was firmly established.

North of the border, in Scotland, the expansion of Protestantism had been equally dramatic, but less turbulent. In this poor and very backward country, if anywhere, the Catholic Church was corrupt and exhibited little of the inner vitality necessary to stem the Protestant tide. Politics were intermingled with religion and the proponents of the Protestant cause were as eager to fight foreign and royal domination—these two were almost identical—as to uphold the Protestant Gospel.

The first influx of Protestant ideas is already discernible in the twenties. In 1546 George Wishart, a fiery evangelist of the Protestant Gospel, was arrested and burned at the stake at St Andrews. His last words had been a challenge to the bystanders to teach the bishops the Word of God. Shortly thereafter a commando of conspirators made its way into the Castle of St Andrews, the residence of hated Cardinal Beaton, and realized Wishart's challenge in a dramatically unique way: pierced by many swords, Beaton's body was thrown out of a window. John Knox, another fiery Protestant, joined the conspirators, called their deed 'a godly fact' and absolved them from any guilt. Knox paid for this, as did the others, with punishment to the galleys, which only intensified his hatred of the papal church—rowing chained to a galley for a year provides ample time for theological reflection. That Knox's galley bore the name of the Virgin certainly did not warm his sentiments for the Catholic Church. Eventually Knox found his way to the flourishing Protestant centre of Geneva, where he studied extensively and wrote his classic treatise *First Blast of the Trumpet Against the Monstrous Regiment of Women*—an unkind reference to the two Marys, mother and daughter, who held the reins of government in his native Scotland. Knox insisted that the people have a right to rebel against a godless government. A temporary return to Scotland inspired and intensified opposition. In 1557 several proponents of the Protestant cause concluded a covenant in which they pledged never to desist from combating 'satanic customs'.

The change of religious climate occasioned in England by Elizabeth's accession to the throne in 1558 had repercussions in Scotland. Exiles returned by the scores, anticipating a similar change in Scotland. Among those returning was John Knox, who at Perth in May 1559, preached a sermon which provoked iconoclasms and public disturbance. A short time later both Catholics and Protestants took up arms. No match for the well-equipped French soldiers of the Catholic queen, the Protestants appealed to Queen Elizabeth for help. Though little in sympathy with the kind of

Protestantism advocated by the 'thundering Scot', and indeed peeved on account of Knox's denunciation of women rulers, Elizabeth felt it wise politically to render some support. Knox's brand of Protestantism was the lesser evil compared with a French-dominated Scotland.

In July 1560 the conflict came to an end in the Treaty of Edinburgh, which simply provided for the future government of the land by a committee of Lords. These Lords promptly proceeded to reorganize not only government but also religion. A Protestant confession of faith was drawn up on behalf of the Scottish parliament and readily accepted—even by most of the clerical number. Papal jurisdiction in Scotland was outlawed and the celebration of the mass became an idolatry. Protestantism had achieved a major victory; indeed, the last one it achieved in Europe.

▶   **John Colet's[1] 'Convocation Sermon' of 1512 indicates, with its strong and deliberate appeal for reform, the humanist sensitivity to the state of the Church before the Reformation.**

You are come together today, fathers and right wise men, to enter council; in the which what you will do and what matters you will handle, yet we understand not. But we wish that once remembering your name and profession, you would mind the reformation of the Church's matter. For it was never more needed, and the state of the Church did never desire more your endeavours. For the spouse of Christ, the Church, whom you would should be without spot or wrinkle, is made foul and evil-favoured. . . .

To exhort you, reverend fathers, to the endeavour of reformation of the Church's estate, because that nothing has so disfigured the face of the Church as has the fashion of secular and worldly living in clerics and priests, I know not where more conveniently to take beginning of my tale than of the Apostle Paul in whose temple you are gathered together. For he, writing unto the Romans and under their name unto you, says: Be you not conformed to this world: but be you reformed in the newness of your understanding that you may prove what is the goodwill of God, well pleasing and perfect. . . .

In the which words the Apostle does two things: first, he does forbid that we be not conformable to the world and be made carnal. Furthermore, he does command that we be reformed in the spirit of God, whereby we are spiritual.

Intending to follow this order, I will speak first of conformation, then after of reformation.

'Be you not,' says he, 'conformable to this world.'

The Apostle calls the world, the ways and manner of secular living: the which chiefly does rest in four evils of this world, that is to say, in devilish pride, in carnal concupiscence, in worldly covetousness, in secular business. . . .

And, first, for to speak of pride of life: how much greediness and appetite of honour and dignity is nowadays in men of the Church? How run they, yea, almost out of breath, from one benefice to another; from the less to the more; from the lower to the higher. Who sees not this? Who seeing this, sorrows not? Moreover, these that are in the same dignities, the most part of them does go with so stately a countenance and with so high looks that they seem not to be put in the humble bishopric of Christ, but rather in the high lordship and power of the world; not knowing nor advertising what Christ, the master of all meekness, said unto his disciples whom he called to be bishops and priests. . . .

The second secular evil is carnal concupiscence. Has not this vice so grown and waxed in the Church as a flood of their lust so that there is nothing looked for more diligently in this most busy time of the most part of priests than that that does delight and please the senses? They give themselves to feasts and banqueting; they spend themselves in vain babbling; they give themselves to sports and plays; they apply themselves to hunting and hawking; they drown themselves in the delights of this world. . . .

Covetousness is the third secular evil: the which Saint John the apostle calls concupiscence of the eyes; Saint Paul calls it idolatry. This abominable pestilence has so entered in the mind almost of all priests, and so has blinded the eyes of the mind that we are blind to all things but only unto those which seem to bring unto us some gains. For what other thing seek we nowadays in the Church than fat benefices and high promotions? Yea, and in the same promotions, of what other thing do we pass upon than of our tithes and rents? That we care not how many, how chargeful, how great benefices we take, so that they be of great value. O covetousness! Saint Paul justly called it the root of all evil. Of it comes this heaping of benefices upon benefices. Of it, so great pensions assigned of so many benefices resigned. Of it, all the swing for tithes, for offering, for mortuaries, for dilapidations, by the right and title of the Church. For the which thing we strive no less than for our own life. . . .

The fourth secular evil that spots and makes ill-favoured the face of the Church is the continual secular occupation wherein priests and

bishops nowadays do busy themselves—the servants rather of men than
of God; the warriors rather of this world than of Christ.

The Sermon of Doctor Colet, made to the Convocation at Paul's,
pp. 293, 294–5, 296–7.

▶   The anticlerical sentiment in England during the early years of
         the Reformation is well illustrated by Simon Fish's famous 'A
         Supplication for the Beggars'[2] of 1529 which, addressed to the
         King, called attention to the abuses of the Church.

And this most pestilent mischief is come upon your said poor beads-
men by the reason that there is in the times of your noble predecessors
passed craftily crept into this your realm another sort (not of impotent
but) of strong puissant and counterfeit holy, and idle beggars and vagabonds which since the time of their first entry by all the craft and wiliness
of Satan are now increased under your sight not only into a great number,
but also into a kingdom. These are (not the herds, but the ravenous wolves
going in herds' clothing devouring the flock) the bishops, abbots, priors,
deacons, archdeacons, suffragans, priests, monks, canons, friars, pardoners and summoners. And who is able to number this idle ravenous
sort which (setting all labour aside) have begged so importunately that
they have gotten into their hands more than the third part of all your
realm? The goodliest lordships, manors, lands, and territories are theirs.
Besides this they have the tenth part of all the corn, meadow, pasture,
grass, wool, colts, calves, lambs, pigs, geese and chickens. Over and
besides the tenth part of every servant's wages the tenth part of the wool,
milk, honey, wax, cheese, and butter. Yea, and they look so narrowly
upon their profits that the poor wives must be accountable to them of
every tenth egg or else she gets not her rites at Easter, shall be taken as an
heretic; hereto have they their four offering days; what money pull they
in by probates of testaments, privy tithes, and by men's offerings to their
pilgrimages, and at their first masses? Every man and child that is buried
must pay somewhat for masses and dirges to be sung for him or else they
will accuse the dead's friends and executors of heresy; what money get
they by mortuaries, by hearing of confessions (and yet they will keep
thereof no counsel), by hallowing of churches, altars, super-altars, chapels,
and bells, by cursing of men and absolving them again for money? What
a multitude of money gather the pardoners in a year? How much money
get the summoners by extortion in a year, by citing the people to the
commissary's court and afterward releasing their appearance for money?
Finally, the infinite number of begging friars, what get they in a year?

Here if it please your grace to mark you shall see a thing far out of joint. There are within your realm of England 52,000 parish churches. And this standing, that there be but ten households in every parish, yet are there five hundred thousand and twenty thousand households. And if every of these households has every of the five orders of friars a penny a quarter for every order, that is for all the five orders five pence a quarter for every house. That is for all the five orders twenty pence a year of every house. *Summa :* five hundred thousand and twenty thousand quarters of angels. That is 260 thousand half-angels. *Summa :* 130 thousand angels. *Summa totalis :* 43 thousand pounds and £333 6s. 8d. sterling; whereof not four hundred years past they had not one penny. Oh, grievous and painful exactions thus yearly to be paid, from the which the people of your noble predecessors the kings of the ancient Britons ever stood free! And this will they have or else they will procure him that will not give it them to be taken as an heretic; what tyrant ever oppressed the people like this cruel and vengeable generation? What subjects shall be able to help their prince that be after this fashion yearly polled? What good Christian people can be able to succour us poor lepers, blind, sore and lame, that be thus yearly oppressed? Is it any marvel that your people so complain of poverty? . . .

And what do all these greedy sort of sturdy, idle, holy thieves with these yearly exactions that they take of the people? Truly nothing but exempt themselves from the obedience of your grace. Nothing but translate all rule, power, lordship, authority, obedience and dignity from your grace unto them. Nothing but that all your subjects should fall into disobedience and rebellion against your grace and be under them. . . . For the which matter your most noble realm wrongfully (alas for shame) has stood tributary (not unto any kind, temporal prince, but unto a cruel, devilish bloodsupper drunken in the blood of the saints and martyrs of Christ) ever since. Here were an holy sort of prelates that thus cruelly could punish such a righteous king, all his realm and succession, for doing right.

Here were a charitable sort of holy men that could thus interdict a whole realm, and pluck away the obedience of the people from their natural liege lord and king, for none other cause but for his righteousness. . . . Yea, and what do they more? Truly nothing but apply themselves by all the slights they may to have to do with every man's wife, every man's daughter, and every man's maid, that cuckoldry and bawdry should reign over all among your subjects, that no man should know his own child, that their bastards might inherit the possessions of every man to put the right begotten children clear beside their inheritance in subversion of all estates and godly order. These be they that by their abstaining from marriage do let the generation of the people whereby all the realm at length if it should be continued shall be made desert and unhabitable.

These be they that have made an hundred thousand idle whores in your realm which would have gotten their living honestly, in the sweat of their faces, had not their superfluous riches elected them to unclean lust and idleness. These be they that corrupt the whole generation of mankind in your realm, that catch the pox of one woman and bear them to another, that be burnt with one woman, and bear it to another, that catch the leprosy of one woman, and bear it to another, yea some one of them shall boast among his fellows that he has muddled with an hundred women. . . . What an infinite number of people might have been increased to have peopled the realm if these sort of folk had been married like other men? What breach of matrimony is there brought in by them? Such truly as was never since the world began among the whole multitude of the heathen.

Who is she that will set her hands to work to get three pennies a day and may have at least twenty pennies a day to sleep an hour with a friar, a monk or a priest? What is he that would labour for a groat a day and may have at least twelve pennies a day to be bawd to a priest, a monk or a friar? What a sort are there of them that marry priests' sovereign ladies but to cloak the priest's incontinency and that they may have a living of the priest themselves for their labour? How many thousands do such lubricity bring to beggary, theft and idleness which should have kept their good name and have set themselves to work had not been this excess treasure of the spirituality? What honest man dare take any man or woman in his service that has been at such a school with a spiritual man? Oh, the grievous shipwreck of the commonwealth, which in ancient time before the coming in of these ravenous wolves was so prosperous.

Simon Fish, *A Supplication for the Beggars*, pp. 3–5, 6, 7.

▶ **Thomas More, the celebrated humanist, wrote, also in 1529, his 'The Supplication of Souls'[3] as a vigorous rebuttal of Fish.**

Of all which cruel persons so procuring, not the minishment of your mercy towards us, but the utter spoil and robbery of our whole help and comfort that should come from you, the very worst and, thereby, the most deadly deviser of our pains and heaviness (God forgive him!) is that despiteous and despiteful person which of late, under pretext of pity, made and put forth among you a book that he named *The Supplication for the Beggars*. A book, indeed, nothing less intending than the pity that it pretendeth; nothing minding the weal of any man but, as we shall hereafter show you, much harm and mischief to all men; and among other great sorrow, discomfort and heaviness unto us, your even-Christians and nigh kin, your late neighbours and pleasant companions upon earth, and now poor prisoners here. . . .

And first, to begin where he beginneth, when he saith that the number of such beggars as he pretendeth to speak for—that is, as himself calleth them, 'the wretched, hideous monsters on whom', he saith, 'scarcely any eye dare look, the foul, unhappy sort of lepers and other sore people, needly, impotent, blind, lame and sick, living only of alms—have their number now so sore increased that all the alms of all the well-disposed people of the realm is not half enough to sustain them, but that for very constraint they die for hunger'. Unto all those words of his, were it not that though we well wist, ourself, [what] he said untrue, yet would we be loath so to lay as a lie to his charge anything whereof the untruth were not so plainly perceived, but that he might find some favourers which might say, he said true. Else would we, peradventure not let to tell him that for a beginning, in these few words, he had written two lies at once.

If we should tell you what number there was of poor sick folk in days passed long before your time, ye were at liberty not to believe us. Howbeit he cannot yet on the other side, for his part neither, bring you forth a bead-roll of their names. Wherefore we must for both our parts be fain to remit you to your own time, and yet not from your childhood (whereof many things men forget when they come to far greater age) but unto the days of your good remembrance. . . .

Now whereas he saith that 'the alms of all well-disposed people of this realm is not half enough to sustain them'—and the well-disposed people he calleth in this matter, all them that giveth them alms—and he speaketh not of one year or twain but of these many years now passed, for neither the number of the clergy nor their possessions nor the friars' alms, in which things he layeth the cause why the alms of good people is not half sufficient to keep and sustain the poor and sick beggars from famishing, any great thing increased in these ten or twelve or twenty years last passed; and therefore if that he said were true, then by all these ten years at the least, the alms of good people hath not been half able to sustain the poor and sick beggars from famishing. And surely if that were so that in four or five years in which was plenty of corn, the poor and sick beggars for lack of men's alms died so fast for hunger; though many should fall sick never so fast again, yet had they in the last two dear years died up of likelihood almost everyone. And whether this be true or not we purpose not to dispute; but to refer and report ourself to every man's eyes and ears, whether any man hear of so many dead or see so many the fewer.

Thomas More, The Supplication of Souls, pp. 226–7.

▶   **England was ruled, during the important years of the Reforma-
     tion, by Henry VIII.[4] He is described by contemporaries as
     follows:**

His Majesty is the handsomest potentate I ever set eyes on: above the
usual height, with an extremely fine calf to his leg; his complexion very
fair and bright, with auburn hair combed straight and short in the French
fashion, and a round face, so very beautiful that it would become a pretty
woman, his throat being rather long and thick.

Letters and Papers of the Reign of Henry VIII, IV, No. 395.

▶   **Henry VIII, and England, became involved in the religious con-
     troversy in Germany, when the King, in 1520, took to the pen to
     write a repudiation of Luther's treatise on the 'Babylonian
     Captivity of the Church' to assert the validity of the traditional
     seven sacraments.**

The King laid hold, on this occasion, to become the champion of the
Church, and wrote against Luther. His book, besides the title of 'Defender of the Faith', drew upon him all that flattery could invent to extol
it; yet Luther, not daunted by such an antagonist, answered it, and
treated him as much below the respect that was due to a king as his
flatterers had raised him above it. Tindal's translation of the New Testament, with notes, drew a severe condemnation from the clergy, there
being nothing in which they were more concerned than to keep the people
unacquainted with that book.

John Foxe, Book of Martyrs, p. 198.

▶   **Here are excerpts from Henry's dedicatory epistle to Pope Leo X,
     from the oration of John Clark on the occasion of presenting the
     book to the Pope, from the papal bull which bestowed the title
     'Defender of the Faith' upon Henry, and from the preface of the
     book itself:**

The Dedicatory Epistle

Most Holy Father: I most humbly commend myself to you, and
devoutly kiss your blessed feet. Whereas we believe that no duty is more
incumbent on a Catholic sovereign than to preserve and increase the
Christian faith and religion and the proofs thereof, and to transmit them

preserved thus inviolate to posterity, by his example in preventing them from being destroyed by any assailant of the faith or in any wise impaired, so when we learned that the pest of Martin Luther's heresy had appeared in Germany and was raging everywhere, without let or hindrance, to such an extent that many, infected with its poison, were falling away, especially those whose furious hatred rather than their zeal for Christian truth had prepared them to believe all its subtleties and lies, we were so deeply grieved at this heinous crime of the German nation (for whom we have no light regard), and for the sake of the Holy Apostolic See, that we bent all our thoughts and energies on uprooting in every possible way, this cockle, this heresy from the Lord's flock. When we perceived that this deadly venom had advanced so far and had seized upon the weak and ill-disposed minds of so many that it could not easily be overcome by a single effort, we deemed that nothing could be more efficient in destroying the contagion than to declare these errors worthy of condemnation, after they had been examined by a convocation of learned and scholarly men from all parts of our realm.

The Oration of John Clark

Most Holy Father:

What great troubles have been stirred up, by the pernicious opinions of Martin Luther; which of late years first sprung out of the lurking holes of the Hussite heresy, in the school of Wittenberg in Germany; from thence spreading themselves over most parts of the Christian world; how many unthinking souls they have deceived, and how many admirers and adherents they have met with; because these are all things very well known; and because, in this place, a medium is more requisite, than prolixity; I care not for relating. Truly, although many of Luther's works are most impiously by his libels, sperad abroad in the world: Yet none of them seems more execrable, more venomous, and more pernicious to mankind, than that, entitled, *The Babylonian Captivity of the Church*; in refuting which, many grave and learned men have diligently laboured.

My most serene and invincible Prince, Henry VIII, King of England, France and Ireland, and most affectionate son of your Holiness, and of the sacred Roman Church, hath written a book against this work of Luther's, which he has dedicated to Your Holiness; and hath commanded me to offer, and deliver the same; which I here present.

The Papal Bull

Considering that it is but just, that those, who undertake pious labours, in defence of the faith of Christ, should be extolled with all praise and honour; and being willing, not only to magnify with deserved praise, and approve with our authority, what your Majesty has with learning and eloquence writ against Luther; but also to honour your Majesty with such a title, as should give all Christians to understand, as well in our times, as in succeeding ages, how acceptable and welcome Your gift was to us, especially in this juncture of time: We, the true successor of St. Peter, (whom Christ, before his ascension, left as his vicar upon earth, and to whom he committed the care of his flock) presiding in this Holy See, from whence all dignity and titles have their source; have with our brethren maturely deliberated on these things; and with one consent unanimously decreed to bestow on your Majesty this title, viz. Defender of the Faith. And, as we have by this title honoured you; we likewise command all Christians, that they name your Majesty by this title; and that in their writings to your Majesty, immediately after the word KING, they add, DEFENDER OF THE FAITH.

The Preface of the Book

Although I do not rank myself amongst the most learned and eloquent; yet (shunning the stain of ingratitude, and moved by fidelity and piety;) I cannot but think myself obliged, (would to God my ability to do it, were equal to my good Will!) to defend my mother, the spouse of Christ: Which, though it be a subject more copiously handled by others; nevertheless I account it as much my own duty, as his who is the Church, and to oppose myself to the poisonous shafts of the enemy that fights against her: which this juncture of time, and the present state of things, require at my hand. For before, when none did assault, it was not necessary to resist; but now when the enemy, (and the most wicked enemy imaginable,) is risen up, who, by the instigation of the devil, under pretext of charity, and stimulated by anger and hatred, spews out the poison of vipers against the Church, and Catholic faith; it is necessary that every servant of Christ of what age, sex, or order soever, should rise against this common enemy of the Christian faith; that those, whose power avails not, yet may testify their good will by their cheerful endeavours.

Henry VIII, *Assertio Septem Sacramentorum*, 1521:
ed. Louis O'Donovan, New York, 1908, pp. 151, 156, 170, 186.

▶   **The Pope's reactions, upon reading Henry's treatise, are described in a letter sent from Rome.**

I suppose, if time and place and other business of no small importance had let him, he would never have ceased till he had read it over. . . .

And when his Holiness had read a great season, I assure your Grace he gave the book great commendation and said there was therein much wit and clerical conveyance and how that there were many great clerics that had written on the matter, but this book would seem to pass all others. His Holiness said that he would not have thought that such a book should have come from the King's Grace, who had been occupied necessarily with other facts, seeing that other men who had occupied themselves in studies all their lives cannot bring forth the like. I showed his Holiness that it should be for the King's Grace's great comfort that his Holiness liked his book so well.

Ellis, Original Letters, 3rd Series, I, 258–9.

▶   It did not take Martin Luther long to respond to Henry's treatise. His answer was published in 1522 and contained, alongside some vehement language, an incisive delineation of his own position.[5]

Our Lord Jesus Christ has smitten the whole realm of papal abomination with blindness and madness. For three years now, the mad giants have been struggling against Luther and they still do not grasp what my fight with them is all about. It seems, in vain have I published so many writings which testify openly that I seek to demonstrate that Scripture should count as the exclusive authority, as is right and fair; that human contrivances and doctrines should be given up as evil scandals or, at least, that once their poison is extracted (that is, the power to enforce them and to make them obligatory for the conscience), they should be regarded as a matter for free investigation just as any other calamity or plague in the world. Because they fail to understand this, they quote against me exclusively man-made laws, glosses on the writings of the fathers and from the history of old customs, in short: precisely what I reject and what I am contesting. . . . Thus, they study and teach until they turn grey—right to their grave—with endless labour and at great cost, the miserable men. They themselves cannot do anything else with their teaching; it is the only way they can dispute. And that is the reason why it happens that, if I always cry: 'Gospel! Gospel! Gospel!' they can only answer: 'Fathers! Fathers! Custom! Custom! Decretals! Decretals!' If then I answer that customs, fathers and decretals have often erred, that reform must be based upon sounder foundation because Christ cannot err, then they are silent like the fishes.

Antwort . . . auf König Heinrich: WA 10 II, 227f.

▶ **Thus involved in the theological controversy, Henry VIII responded once more to Luther—and showed amazing theological sensitivity—if he wrote it himself.[6]**

But as for me, I well know and acknowledge that I am unable of myself to come to the understanding thereof, and, therefore, calling for God's help, most humbly submit myself to the determination of Christ's Church and interpretations of the old holy Fathers whom his goodness plenteously enlightened with learning, illumined with grace, furnished with faith, garnished with good works, and, finally, with many miracles, declared their faith and living to like him. Where ye on the contrary side, setting all these old saints at nought and villainously blaspheming their memories, procuring the detraction of their honour, lest the reverence and estimation of their holy lives should stand in your light, admit no man's wit but your own (which only you admit in all things): and defending a manifest folly for wisdom, an open false heresy for a truth, you have nothing else to stand by, but only cry out that the Scripture is evident for your part, and all that ever took it otherwise were but fools—were they never so many, never so wise, never so well learned, never so holy.

And when ye have thus well and worshipfully quit yourself in words, then instigate and set out rude rebellious people under pretext of evangelical liberty to run out and fight for your faction.

If any man had so little wit to doubt which of these two ways were the better—yours now new begun, or the faith of the old Fathers—Our Saviour putteth us out of doubt when he saith: By their fruits ye shall know them. For of them no man doubteth but they were good men and of holy living, serving God in fasting, prayer and chastity, and all their writings full of charity; and of you, men doubt as little when they see that all your doing began of envy and presumption, proceedeth with rancour and malice, blown forth with pride and vain glory, and endeth in lechery.

And, therefore, cloak ye never so much your doctrine under the pretext of evangelical liberty: notwithstanding that I know how slender mine own learning is, yet it is not so slender that ye can make me believe that ye mean well when ye speak fast of the spirit and fall all to the flesh; when ye make as if ye would exhort all the world to live after the Gospel, and then exhort me from chastity, to which the Gospel effectually counselleth, and forsake yourself your vowed chastity, promised and dedicated to God, to the keeping and observance whereof all Holy Scripture bindeth you. . . .

Would God, Luther, that these words of yours were as true as I know them for contrary. For what charity build you upon faith, when ye teach that faith alone without good works sufficeth? For albeit that in your book, made against me, waxing for shame [and] half wary to hear thereof, ye laid to my charge that I did therein misreport you, yet did ye not only make none earthly answer to your own words which I laid to your charge, openly proving in you that detestable heresy, but also said the same again in the self book [*Contra Henricum Regem*] in which ye pretend yourself to have been wrongfully charged therewith before, saying that sacrilege it is and wickedness to have any will to please God by good works and not by only faith. Which words be as open as those ye wrote before in *Babylonica* where ye write this sentence:

> Thus thou seest (say ye) how rich is a Christian man, or he that is baptized, which though he would, cannot lose his salvation by any sins, be they never so great, but if he will not believe: for no sin can damn him but only lack of belief: for as for all other sins, if there stand still or come again faith and credence in God's promise that God made to His sacrament of baptism, they be supped up in a moment by the same faith.

These words of yours show so manifestly what ye mean that there neither needeth nor boteth any gloss. It can receive no colour but that contrary to Christ's words: The way is straight and narrow that leadeth to heaven. Ye, with your evangelical liberty, make a broad and easy way thither to win you favour of the people, teaching that it shall be enough to believe God's promise without any labour of good works, which is far from the mind of Saint Paul which teacheth us a 'faith that worketh by love' and also by faith.

The Answer of King Henry VIII . . . unto the letter of Martin Luther, pp. 408–9.

▶ Though his theological activity earned Henry the scorn and vehemence of Luther, it earned him the title 'Defender of the Faith' from the Pope.

I delivered the Pope's bull and his brief, brought in my charge opportune, and with the which the King was well contented: here at length showing unto me that it was very joyous to have these tidings from the Pope's holiness at such time as he had taken upon him the defence of Christ's Church with his pen, before the receipt of the said tidings; and that he will make an end of his book within these few weeks; and desiring your Grace to provide that within the same space all such as be appointed to examine Luther's books may be congregated together for his Highness's perceiving.

Ellis, *Original Letters*, II, No. 81.

▶ In the mid-twenties Henry began to have qualms about his marriage with Catherine, since it violated the biblical injunction. The chronicler writes:

He seemed to lay the greatest weight on the prohibition in the levitical law, of marrying the brother's wife, and being conversant in Thomas Aquinas's writings, he found, that he and the other schoolmen looked on those laws as moral, and for ever binding; and consequently the Pope's dispensation was of no force, since his authority went not so far as to dispense with the laws of God. All the bishops of England, Fisher of Rochester only excepted, declared under their hands and seals, that they judged the marriage unlawful. The ill consequence of wars that might follow upon a doubtful title to the crown were also much considered. It is not certain that Henry's affection for any other lady was the origin of these proceedings; but whatever be the determination of this point, it is certain that about this time he gave free scope to his affections towards Anne Boleyn.

John Foxe, *Book of Martyrs*, p. 199.

▶ The King himself gave his own version of the matter (which had soon become a public 'cause célèbre') in a speech to 'all his nobilitie, Iudges & counsailors with diuerse other persons' on 8th November 1528. Said Henry:

And although it has pleased Almighty God to send us a fair daughter of a noble woman and me begotten to our great comfort and joy, yet it has been told us by divers great clerks that neither she is our lawful daughter nor her mother our lawful wife, and that we live together abominably and detestably in open adultery, insomuch that when our ambassador was last in France and motion was made that the Duke of Orleans should marry our said daughter, one of the chief councillors to the French king said it were well done to know whether she be the King of England's lawful daughter or not, for well known it is that he begat her on his brother's wife which is directly against God's law and precept. Think you, my Lords, that these words touch not my body and soul, think you that these doings do not daily and hourly trouble my conscience and vex my spirits. Yes, we doubt not but and if it were your own cause every man would seek remedy when the peril of your soul and the loss of your inheritance is openly laid to you. For this only cause I protest before God and in the word of a prince I have asked counsel of the greatest clerks in Christendom, and for this cause I have sent for this legate as a man indifferent only to know the truth and to settle my conscience and for none other cause as God can judge. And as touching the Queen, if it be adjudged by the law of God that she is my lawful wife, there was never thing more pleasant nor more acceptable to me in my life both for the discharge and clearing of my conscience and also for the good qualities and conditions the which I know to be in her. For I assure you all, that beside her noble parentage of the which she is descended (as all you know) she is a woman of most gentleness, of most humility and buxomness, yea, and of all good qualities appertaining to nobility, she is without comparison, as I this twenty years almost have had the true experiment, so that if I were to marry again, if the marriage might be good, I would surely choose her above all other women. But if it be determined by judgment that our marriage was against God's law and clearly void, then I shall not only sorrow the departing from so good a lady and loving companion, but much more lament and bewail my unfortunate chance that I have so long lived in adultery to God's great displeasure.

Hall, *Chronicle*, pp. 754-5.

▶   Ann Boleyn[7] was described by an observer as follows:

Madam Ann is not one of the handsomest women in the world; she is of middling stature, swarthy complexion, long neck, wide mouth, bosom not much raised, and in fact has nothing but the English King's great appetite, and her eyes, which are black and beautiful, and take great effect on those who served the Queen when she was on the throne.

Venetian Calendar IV, p. 365.

▶   When the efforts to secure an annulment of the King's marriage to Catherine proved to be unsuccessful, Thomas Cranmer[8] made the intriguing suggestion to approach the universities of Christendom for their counsel in regard to the rightness of the King's marriage.

At this period, Dr Cranmer, a fellow of Jesus' College in Cambridge, meeting accidentally with Gardiner and Fox at Waltheim, and entering into discourse upon the royal marriage, suggested, that the King should engage the chief universities and divines of Europe, to examine the lawfulness of his marriage; and if they gave their resolutions against it, then it being certain that the Pope's dispensation could not derogate from the law of God, the marriage must be declared null. This novel and reasonable scheme they proposed to the King, who was much pleased with it.

John Foxe, *Book of Martyrs*, p. 202.

▶   **Among those consulted was Luther.**[9]

I like best the decision given by the University of Louvain and consider it preferable to all those others which are contrary to it. The King could follow its advice with a clear conscience and indeed must do so before God. That is to say, on no account can he separate himself from the Queen (his brother's wife) whom he has truly married; he may not, by means of such a divorce, taint the name of both the daughter and the mother with the shame of incest. I am not writing of the dispensation of the Roman Pope which permitted the marriage with the wife of his deceased brother. But this I will say: if we consider that the King may have sinned through his marriage with the wife of his late brother, then it would be a far greater and heavier sin to throw her off now that he has really taken her and to rend the bond of marriage in so cruel a manner. . . .

The King of England has sinned by taking the wife of his deceased brother, but it was only a sin under human and social law deriving from the Pope and the Emperor. If then the Pope and the Emperor granted a dispensation from their own law, then he has not sinned. For, if God approves of the Emperor's social laws, he also approves of an imperial law granted by the Emperor. . . .

Eventually it may well happen that the King, either by himself or in accordance with the advice of other doctors, will carry out the divorce; should that happen, you should still endeavour to persuade your friends that they should express their disapproval of the divorce. Even if the King is wholly misled by adversaries, still we should at least do all that is possible to protect the Queen, so that she may under no circumstances consent to the divorce, being willing to die rather than to burden her conscience with so great an evil before God. She should believe implicitly that she is the true and legitimate Queen of England, ordained and confirmed before God.

3rd September 1531. *WA, Br.* 6, 183f.

▶   **The deliberations at the University of Cambridge concerning the legitimacy of Henry's marriage to Catherine are described in the following letter.**

Upon Sunday at afternoon were assembled, after the manner of the University, all the Doctors, Bachelors of Divinity, and Masters of Art, being in number almost two hundred: In that Congregation we delivered your Grace's Letters, which were read openly by the Vice-Chancellor. And for answer to be made unto them, first the Vice-Chancellor calling apart the Doctors, asked their Advice and Opinion; whereunto they answered severally, as their Affections led them, *et res erat in multa confusione*. . . . Finally: The Vice-Chancellor, because the day was much spent in those altercations, commanding every man's mind to be known secretly, whether they would be content with such an Order as he had conceived for answer to be made by the University to your Grace's Letters; whereunto that night they would in no wise agree. And forasmuch as it was then dark night, the Vice-Chancellor continued the Congregation till the next day at one of the Clock; at which time the Vice-Chancellor proposed a Grace after the form herein inclosed; and it was first denied: When it was asked again, it was even on both Parties, to be denied or granted; and at the last, by labour of Friends to cause some to depart the House which were against it, it was obtained in such form as the Schedule herein enclosed purporteth; wherein be two Points which we would have left out; but considering by putting in of them, we allured many, and that indeed they shall not hurt the Determination for your Grace's part, we were finally content therewith. . . .

Your Highness may perceive by the Notes, that we be already sure of as many as be requisite, wanting only three; and we have good hope of four; of which four if we get two, and obtain of another to be absent, it is sufficient for our purpose.

Burnet, History of the Reformation, IV, 48–49.

▶ **John Foxe described the consultation of the universities in these words:**

The King now intending to proceed in the method proposed by Cranmer, sent to Oxford and Cambridge, to procure their conclusions. At Oxford, it was referred by the major part of the convocation to thirty-three doctors and bachelors of divinity, whom that faculty was to name: they were empowered to determine the question, and put the seal of the university to their conclusion. And they gave their opinions, that the marriage of the brother's wife was contrary both to the laws of God and nature. At Cambridge the convocation referred the question to twenty-nine; of which number, two thirds agreeing, they were empowered to put the seal of the university to their determination. These agreed in opinion with those of Oxford. The state of Venice would not declare themselves, but said they would be neutral, and it was not easy to persuade the divines of the republic to give their opinions, till a brief was obtained of the Pope, permitting all divines and canonists to deliver their opinions according to their consciences. The Pope abhorred this way of proceeding, though he could not decently oppose it: but he said, in great scorn, that no friar should set limits to his power. Crook was ordered to give no money, nor make promises to any, till they had freely delivered their opinion; which he is said to have faithfully observed.

He sent over to England a hundred several books, and papers, with many subscriptions; all condemning the king's marriage as unlawful in itself. At Paris, the Sorbonne made their determination with great solemnity; after mass, all the doctors took an oath to study the question, and to give their judgment according to their consciences; and after three weeks' study the greater part agreed on this: 'that the king's marriage was lawful, and that the Pope could not dispense with it'. At Orléans, Angiers and Toulouse, they determined to the same purpose.

John Foxe, Book of Martyrs, p. 203.

▶ **The King's intent followed its appointed course; on the first day of June 1533, Anne Boleyn was crowned queen.**

On Saturday, the last day of the month, also in the afternoon, she passed from the Tower to Westminster, with very great pomp, clad in silver tissue, with her hair over her shoulders, and a coronet on her head; being carried on a chair of cloth of gold, between two mules, which were also covered with silver damask, and under a canopy of cloth of silver, accompanied by the greater part of the nobility of this kingdom, with the utmost order and tranquillity, all the streets and the houses being crowded with persons of every condition, in number truly marvellous; and in many places there were triumphal arches, pageants and other decorations, as usually made on similar occasions.

Next morning, Whit-Sunday, she was conducted from the royal palace by the two archbishops of this kingdom, four of the chief bishops, and fourteen abbots, to the great church of Westminster, where she was most solemnly anointed and crowned by the Archbishop of Canterbury.

7th June 1533. Venetian Calendar IV, pp. 418–19.

▶ **After the curia had formally turned down the King's request, Henry in turn issued a proclamation forbidding his subjects to question the validity of his new marriage.**

Whereas the non-legitimate marriage between the King's Highness and the Lady Catherine Princess, relict-widow of Prince Arthur, has been legitimately dissolved by just ways and opinions, the divorce and separation having been made between his said Highness and the said Lady Catherine by the Right Reverend Father in God the Archbishop of Canterbury, Legate, Primate and Metropolitan of all England; and therefore the King's Majesty has espoused, and taken for his wife, according to the laws of the Church, the truly high and excellent Princess, the Lady Anne, now Queen of England, having had her solemnly crowned and anointed, as becoming the praise and glory and honour of the omnipotent God, the security of the succession and descent of the Crown, and to the great pleasure, comfort and satisfaction of all the subjects of this realm; all the which things have proceeded methodically, and took such good effect, by the common consent of the Lords Spiritual and Temporal, and of the Commons of this realm, by authority of the Parliament, as in like manner by the assent and determination of the whole clergy in its constant convocations held and celebrated in both the provinces of this kingdom.

It has been ordered, amongst other things, for the perfect and secure establishment of what is aforesaid, that no person or persons, whatever their state, grade, or condition, shall attempt to seek any sort of provision, or do or instigate any act or acts, or derogate from any of the said processes, sentences, and determinations as they stand and have been made, both concerning the said divorce, as also the solemnity of the legitimate marriage contracted and concluded been the King's Highness and the said Queen Anne. . . .

By reason whereof, and because the said divorce and separation is now made and finished, and the King's Highness is legitimately married, as afore heard, it is a thing therefore evident and manifest that the said Lady Catherine may not for the future have or use the name, style or title, or dignity of Queen of this realm, nor be in any guise reputed, taken or inscribed, by the name of Queen of this realm, but by the name, style, title and dignity of Princess Dowager, which name it is fitting she should have, because she was legitimately and perfectly married and conjoined with the said Prince Arthur; and all the officials, ministers, bailiffs, receivers, factors, servants, keepers of parks or forests of the said Princess Dowager, or any other person or persons, of whatever state, grade or condition, who, acting contrary to what is aforesaid, shall style, repute, acknowledge and address, or in any guise obey the said Lady Catherine in virtue of any sort of security, or shall write to her, addressing her by the name of 'Queen', or attempt to do or move any other act or acts, or any other thing or things to the impediment or derogation of such acts and processes as have been determined and completed, both by the celebration and confirmation of the said legitimate marriage, justly accomplished and concluded as aforeheard, will clearly and manifestly incur the said great pains and penalties comprised and specified.

5th July 1533. *Venetian Calendar* IV, pp. 430–1.

▶   Archbishop Cranmer reported to the ambassador to Germany on
     the divorce of Catherine.

It was thought convenient by the King and his learned Council that I
should repair unto Dunstable, which is within four miles unto Amptell,
where the said Lady Catherine keeps her house, and there to call her
before me, to hear the final sentence in this said matter. Notwithstanding
she would not at all obey thereunto, for when she was by Doctor Lee
cited to appear by a day, she utterly refused the same, saying that inasmuch as her cause was before the Pope she would have none other judge;
and therefore would not take me for her judge. Nevertheless the eighth
day of May, according to the said appointment, I came unto Dunstable,
my Lord of Lincoln being assistant unto me . . . and so there at our coming kept a court for the appearance of the said Lady Catherine, where
were examined certain witnesses which testified that she was lawfully
cited and called to appear, whom for fault of appearance was declared
contumax; proceeding in the said cause against her *in poenam contumaciam*
as the process of the law thereunto belongs; which continued fifteen days
after our coming thither. And the morrow after Ascension day I gave
final sentence therein, how that it was indispensable for the Pope to
license any such marriages.

                                    Ellis, *Original Letters*, First Series, II, 35–36.

▶   After Henry's marriage to Anne Boleyn the following reasons
     were officially drawn up as justification for his action:

Articles devised by the King's Council in justification of his marriage
with Anne Boleyn, and his proceedings in the divorce.

     1. The Archbishop of Canterbury's judgment against the first marriage
was founded on the decisions of the most famous universities in Christendom and of the whole English clergy. 2. Decisions of councils are against
removal of causes from the country in which they are initiated, and Parliament did not desire the inheritance of this realm to depend on 'the Bishop
of Rome, by some men called the Pope', who has detained the cause at
Rome, and 'would have made a commodiously and wealthy law lately,
both for us and him, by which good people, living within the limits of
true matrimony within this realm, shall not by malice or evil will be so
long detained and interrupted from their right as in times past, nor unjust
matrimony shall have his unlawful and incestuous demoure as by delays
to Rome it was wont to have'. Hence our Prince's long protracted cause
of matrimony has been ended here 'with brief success of issue already had
and other like to follow'. . . . 5. And any man, especially a prince, may

appeal from the Bishop of Rome to the Council. 6. After which appeal the Bishop of Rome ought to do nothing to the appellant's prejudice; so that, since the King's appeal, all his censures may be despised. 7. Excommunication ought not to be executed, except in cases of deadly sin, and then only on obstinate persons. 8. Bishops are bound first to admonish and reprove before excommunicating; which course has been followed by our good Archbishop of Canterbury since he came to his dignity, admonishing the King that he lived in unlawful matrimony. And how God is therewith pleased appears by many things, (1) issue being so soon had of this lawful matrimony; (2) so fair weather with plenty of corn and cattle; (3) peace and amity sought by foreign princes; (4) the purity of the air and freedom from pestilence for so long a time. 9. The Pope is undeserving of authority even by their own decree, 'for he is both baste, and came to his dignity by simony', and is guilty of heresy in refusing the King's appeal.

Letters and Papers VII, 1.

▶ A letter to Thomas Cranmer described the anti-papal argumentation of the time.

I have since the time of my licence given me by your Lordship to preach, made this year upon the point of threescore sermons, not failing in every one of them to speak effectually against the usurped power of the Bishop of Rome, and sometime, as the matter gave me occasion, against the abomination of him, his cardinals and his cloistered hypocrites, wherein I have taken this order:

First, I have shown them that Peter, by whom the Bishop of Rome challenges his primacy, never had such things given him by God.

Secondly, that the Scriptures whereby they would maintain the primacy of Peter were not spoken nor meant to Peter's person, but all bishops and priests and to the whole Church.

Thirdly, I lay the precedent of the Nicene Council naming four patriarchs, whereof the Bishop of Rome is last.

Fourthly, that *in primitiva ecclesia* the name and authority of bishop and priest were all but one thing unto the time that man's policy to avoid schism, devised the pre-eminence amongst priests by the name of a bishop.

Fifthly, I show that the bishops of Rome have always, for maintenance of their pomp and fruitless ceremonies, been cause of all the greatest schism that has been in Christ's Church.

Sixthly, I show that the special office of a bishop is to preach and teach which because the Bishop of Rome can nothing do here, nor in none other places, but only in Rome, I concluded that he can in no wise be bishop here or any other place, but only in Rome, and by consequence primate in no place but there, seeing that he challenges this primacy by his episcopal function only.

These things I declared, and proved by evident reason grounded upon Scripture, by authority of the ancient doctors, by the sayings of More and other papists themselves.

Ellis, *Original Letters*, 3rd Series, III, 3–5.

▶ The Reformation in England took place within the frame set by Henry's marital problems. It produced, however, notable theological documents and important legal pronouncements. The first of the latter came in May 1532 and has been called the 'Submission of the Clergy'.

We your most humble subjects, daily orators and bedesmen of your clergy of England, having our special trust and confidence in your most excellent wisdom, your princely goodness and fervent zeal to the promotion of God's honour and Christian religion, and also in your learning, far exceeding, in our judgment, the learning of all other kings and princes that we have read of, and doubting nothing but that the same shall still continue and daily increase in your majesty—

First, do offer and promise, *in verbo sacerdotii*, here unto your Highness, submitting ourselves most humbly to the same, that we will never from henceforth enact, put in ure, promulge or execute, any new canons or constitutions provincial, or any other new ordinance, provincial or synodal, in our Convocation or synod in time coming, which Convocation is, always has been, and must be, assembled only by your Highness's commandment of writ, unless your Highness by your royal assent shall license us to assemble our Convocation, and to make, promulge and execute such constitutions and ordinances as shall be made in the same; and thereto give your royal assent and authority.

Secondly, that whereas diverse of the constitutions, ordinances, and canons, provincial or synodal, which have been heretofore enacted, be thought to be not only much prejudicial to your prerogative royal, but also overmuch onerous to your Highness's subjects, your clergy aforesaid is contented, if it may stand so with your Highness's pleasure, that it be committed to the examination and judgment of your Grace, and of thirty-two persons. . . .

Gee and Hardy,[10] pp. 176–7.

▶ Using a century-old law, Henry VIII accused the clergy of recognizing foreign jurisdiction—the Roman pontiff. The clergy asked and received the King's pardon.

The King our sovereign lord, calling to his blessed and most gracious remembrance that his good and loving subjects the most reverend father in God the Archbishop of Canterbury and other bishops, suffragans, prelates and other spiritual persons of the province of the archbishopric of Canterbury of this his realm of England, and the ministers underwritten which have exercised, practised or executed in spiritual courts and other spiritual jurisdictions within the said province, have fallen and incurred into divers dangers of his laws by things done, perpetrated and committed contrary to the order of his laws, and specially contrary to the form of the statutes of provisors, provisions and praemunire; and his Highness, having always tender eye with mercy and pity and compassion towards his said spiritual subjects, minding of his high goodness and great benignity so always to impart the same unto them as justice being daily administered all rigour be excluded, and the great and benevolent minds of his said subjects largely and many times approved towards his Highness, and specially in their Convocation and Synod now presently being in the chapter house of the monastery of Westminster, by correspondence of gratitude to them to be requited: Of his mere motion, benignity and liberality, by authority of this his Parliament, hath given and granted his liberal and free pardon to his said good and loving spiritual subjects and the said ministers and to every of them, to be had, taken and enjoyed to and by them and every of them by virtue of this present act in manner and form ensuing, that is to wit: The King's Highness, of his said benignity and high liberality, in consideration that the said archbishop, bishops and clergy of the said province of Canterbury in their said Convocation now being have given and granted to him a subsidy of one hundred thousand pounds of lawful money current in this realm, to be levied and collected by the said clergy at their proper costs and charges and to be paid in certain form specified in their said grant thereof, is fully and resolutely contented and pleased that it be ordained, established and enacted by authority of this his said Parliament, That the most reverend father in God, William, Archbishop of Canterbury, metropolitan and primate of all England, and all other bishops and suffragans, prelates, abbots, priors, and their convents and every person of the same convents, and convents corporate . . . and all and every person and persons spiritual of the clergy of the said province of Canterbury in this present act of pardon hereafter not excepted or to the contrary not provided for, by whatsoever name or surname, name of dignity, pre-eminence or office they or any of them be or is named or called, the successors, heirs, executors and administrators of them and of every of them, shall be by authority of this present pardon acquitted, pardoned, released and discharged against his Highness, his heirs, successors and executors, and every of them, of all and all manner offences, contempts and trespasses committed or done against all and singular statute and statutes of provisors, provisions and praemunire.

Statutes of the Realm, III, 460–6.

▶ Another step in the direction of freeing the Church in England from its ties with Rome came early in 1532 with the Conditional Restraint of Annates. This act made it illegal to pay annates, that is one year's income from ecclesiastical benefices to the Pope.

Forasmuch as it is well perceived, by long-approved experience, that great and inestimable sums of money have been daily conveyed out of this realm, to the impoverishment of the same; and specially such sums of money as the Pope's Holiness, his predecessors, and the Court of Rome, by long time have heretofore taken of all and singular those spiritual persons which have been named, elected, presented or postulated to be archbishops or bishops within this realm of England, under the title of annates, otherwise called first-fruits: which annates, or first-fruits, heretofore have been taken of every archbishopric, or bishopric, within this realm, by restraint of the Pope's bulls, for confirmations, elections, admissions, postulations, provisions, collations, dispositions, institutions, installations, investitures, orders, holy benedictions, palls, or other things requisite and necessary to the attaining of those their promotions . . . by occasion whereof, not only the treasure of this realm has been greatly conveyed out of the same, but also it has happened many times, by occasion of death, unto such archbishops, and bishops, so newly promoted, within two or three years after his or their consecration, that his or their friends, by whom he or they have been holpen to advance and make payment of the said annates, or first-fruits, have been thereby utterly undone and impoverished:

And for because the said annates have risen, grown and increased, by an uncharitable custom, grounded upon no just or good title, and the payments thereof obtained by restraint of bulls, until the same annates, or first-fruits, have been paid, or surety made for the same; which declares the said payments to be exacted, and taken by constraint, against all equity and justice. . . .

And albeit that our said sovereign the King, and all his natural subjects, as well spiritual as temporal, be as obedient, devout, catholic and humble children of God and Holy Church, as any people be within any realm christened; yet the said exactions of annates, or first-fruits, be so intolerable and importable to this realm, that it is considered and declared, by the whole body of this realm now represented by all the estates of the same assembled in this present Parliament, that the king's highness before Almighty God is bound, as by the duty of a good Christian prince, for the conservation and preservation of the good estate and commonwealth of this his realm, to do all that in him is to obviate, repress and redress the said abuses and exactions of annates, or first-fruits. . . .

It is therefore ordained, established and enacted, by authority of this present Parliament, that the unlawful payments of annates, or first-fruits, and all manner contributions for the same, for any archbishopric or bishopric, or for any bulls hereafter to be obtained from the Court of Rome, to or for the aforesaid purpose and intent, shall from henceforth utterly cease, and no such hereafter to be paid for any archbishopric, or bishopric, within this realm, other or otherwise than hereafter in this present Act is declared.

Gee and Hardy, pp. 178–81.

▶ **Archbishop Cranmer wrote Henry VIII as follows concerning royal supremacy.**

Your Grace commanded all the prelates of your realm that they, with all acceleration and expedition, should do their diligence, every one in his diocese, fully to persuade your people of the Bishop of Rome's authority, that it was but a false and unjust usurpation, and that your Grace of very right and by God's law is the Supreme Head of this Church of England, next immediately unto God. I, to accomplish your Grace's commandment, incontinent upon my return from Winchester (knowing that all the country about Oxford and Knol, where my most abode was, were sufficiently instructed in those matters already) came up into this part of East Kent, only by perchance to persuade the people in the said two articles. And in my own church at Canterbury, because I was informed that that town in those two points was least persuaded of all my diocese, I preached there two sermons myself. . . . The scope and effect of both my sermons stood in three things. First, I declared that the Bishop of Rome was not God's Vicar in earth as he was taken, and, although it was so taught these three or four hundred years, yet it was done by the meanness of the Bishop of Rome, who compelled men by oaths so to teach, to the maintenance of his authority, contrary to God's word. . . . Second, because the See of Rome was called *Sancta sedes Romana*, and the Bishop was called *Sanctissimus Papa*, and many consciences peradventure could not be quiet to be separated from so holy a place and from God's most holy Vicar, I showed the people that this thing ought nothing to move them, for it was but a holiness in name; for indeed there was no such holiness at Rome. And thereupon I took occasion to declare the glory and pomp of Rome, the covetousness, the unchaste living, and the maintenance of all vices. Third, I spoke against the Bishop of Rome's laws, which he calls *divinas leges* and *sacros canones*, and makes them equal with God's laws. And here I declared that many of his laws were contrary to God's laws; and some of them which were good and laudable, yet they were not of such holiness as he would make them, that is, to be taken as God's laws; or, to have remission of sins by observance of them. And here I said that so many of his laws as were good, men ought not to condemn and despise them, and wilfully to break them: for those that be good your Grace had received as laws of your realm, until such time as others should be made. And therefore, as laws of your realm, they must be observed and not condemned. And here I spoke as well of the ceremonies of the Church, as of the aforesaid laws; that they ought neither to be rejected or despised, nor yet to be observed, with this opinion, that they of themselves make men holy, or that they remit sin. . . . And though it be good to observe them well for that intent they were first ordered, yet it is not good, but a contumely unto Christ, to observe them with this opinion, that they remit sin, or that the very bare observation of them in itself is an holiness before God; although they be remembrances of many holy things, or a disposition unto goodness. . . .

Though my two sermons were long, yet I have written briefly unto your Highness the sum of them both. And I was informed by sundry reports, that the people were glad that they heard so much as they did, until such time as the prior of the Black Friars at Canterbury preached a sermon, as it was thought and reported, clear contrary unto all the three things which I had preached before. For as touching the first part, where I had preached against the erroneous doctrine of the Bishop of Rome's power . . . the prior would not name the Bishop of Rome, but under colour spoke generally that the Church of Christ never erred. And as touching the second part, where I spoke of the vices of the Bishops of Rome and their See, the prior said that he would not slander the Bishops of Rome, and he said openly to me in a good audience, that he knew no vices by none of the Bishops of Rome; and he said also openly that I preached uncharitably, when I said that this many years I had daily prayed unto God that I might see the power of Rome destroyed, and that I thanked God and I had now seen it in this realm.

Ellis, *Original Letters*, Third Series, III, 23–28.

▶   The break with Rome became definite in February 1533, with the Restraint of Appeals, which placed supreme jurisdiction in all ecclesiastical appeals into the hands of the King.

In consideration whereof the King's Highness, his nobles, and commons, considering the great enormities, dangers, long delays and hurts, that as well to his highness, as to his said nobles, subjects, commons and residents of this his realm, in the said causes testamentary, causes of matrimony and divorces, tithes, oblations and obventions, do daily ensue, does therefore by his royal assent, and by the assent of the lords spiritual and temporal, and the Commons, in this present Parliament assembled, and by authority of the same, enact, establish and ordain, that all causes testamentary, causes of matrimony and divorces, rights of tithes, oblations and obventions . . . shall be from henceforth heard, examined, discussed, clearly, finally, and definitely adjudged and determined within the King's jurisdiction and authority, and not elsewhere, in such courts spiritual and temporal of the same, as the natures, conditions, and qualities of the causes and matters aforesaid in contention . . . shall require, without having any respect to any custom, use, or sufferance, in hindrance, let, or prejudice of the same, or to any other thing used or suffered to the contrary thereof by any other manner of person or persons in any manner of wise; any foreign inhibitions, appeals, sentences, summons, citations, suspensions, interdictions, excommunications, restraints, judgments, or any other process or impediments, of what natures, names, qualities, or conditions soever they be, from the see of Rome, or any other foreign courts or potentates of the world, or from and out of this realm, or any other the king's dominions, or marches of the same, to the see of Rome, or to any other foreign courts or potentates, to the let or impediment thereof in any wise notwithstanding. . . .

As also, that all the spiritual prelates, pastors, ministers, and curates within this realm, and the dominions of the same, shall and may use, minister, execute and do, or cause to be used, ministered, executed and done, all sacraments, sacramentals, divine services, and all other things within the said realm and dominions, unto all the subjects of the same, as catholic and Christian men ought to do; any former citations, processes, inhibitions, suspensions, interdictions, excommunications, or appeals, for or touching the causes aforesaid, from or to the see of Rome, or any other foreign prince or foreign courts, to the let or contrary thereof in any wise notwithstanding.

Gee and Hardy, pp. 189–91.

▶ **The 'First Act of Succession' of 1534, which stated that Anne Boleyn's offspring were to succeed to the English crown, summarized Henry's view of his first marriage.**

The marriage heretofore solemnized between your highness and the Lady Catherine, being before lawful wife to Prince Arthur, your elder brother, which by him was carnally known, as does duly appear by sufficient proof in a lawful process . . . shall be, by authority of this present Parliament, definitively, clearly and absolutely declared, deemed and adjudged to be against the laws of Almighty God, and also accepted, reputed and taken of no value nor effect, but utterly void and annulled . . . any licence, dispensation, or any other act or acts going afore, or ensuing the same, or to the contrary thereof, in any wise notwithstanding; and that every such licence, dispensation, act or acts, thing or things heretofore had, made, done, or to be done to the contrary thereof, shall be void and of none effect; and that the said Lady Catherine shall be from henceforth called and reputed only dowager to Prince Arthur, and not queen of this realm; and that the lawful matrimony had and solemnized between your Highness and your most dear and entirely beloved wife Queen Anne, shall be established, and taken for undoubtful true, sincere and perfect ever hereafter, according to the just judgment of the said Thomas, Archbishop of Canterbury, Metropolitan and Primate of all this realm, whose grounds of judgment have been confirmed, as well by the whole clergy of this realm in both the Convocations, and by both the universities thereof, as by the universities of Bologna, Padua, Paris, Orleans, Toulouse, Anjou, and divers others, and also by the private writings of many right excellent well-learned men. . . .

And furthermore, since many inconveniences have fallen, as well within this realm as in others, by reason of marrying within degrees of marriage prohibited by God's laws, that is to say, the son to marry the mother, or the stepmother, the brother the sister, the father his son's daughter, or his daughter's daughter, or the son to marry the daughter of his father procreate and born by his stepmother, or the son to marry his aunt, being his father's or mother's sister, or to marry his uncle's wife, or the father to marry his son's wife, or the brother to marry his brother's wife, or any man to marry his wife's daughter, or his wife's son's daughter, or his wife's daughter's daughter, or his wife's sister; which marriages, although they be plainly prohibited and detested by the laws of God, yet nevertheless at some times they have proceeded under colours of dispensations by man's power, which is but usurped, and of right ought not to be granted, admitted nor allowed; for no man, of what estate, degree, or condition soever he be, has power to dispense with God's laws. . . .

Be it therefore enacted by authority aforesaid, that no person or persons, subjects or residents of this realm, or in any your dominions, of what estate, degree or dignity soever they be, shall from henceforth marry within the said degrees afore rehearsed, what pretence soever shall be made to the contrary thereof. . . .

And also be it enacted by authority aforesaid that all the issue had and procreated, or hereafter to be had and procreated, between your Highness and your said most dear and entirely beloved wife Queen Anne, shall be your lawful children, and be inheritable, and inherit, according to the course of inheritance and laws of this realm, the imperial crown of the same, with all dignities, honours, pre-eminences, prerogatives, authorities and jurisdictions to the same annexed or belonging. . . .

Gee and Hardy, pp. 234–6, 237.

▶ In the spring of 1534 the ecclesiastical Convocations addressed themselves to the question of papal supremacy.

Convocation of Canterbury

On the last day of March, in the presence of the most reverend Ralph Pexsall, the clerk of the crown in the chancery of the lord the King, in the name of the said King, presented a royal writ for summoning Convocation and proroguing it to the fourth day of November following. And afterwards was exhibited a writing by William Saye, notary public, concerning the answer of the Lower House to the question, viz. 'Whether the Roman pontiff has any greater jurisdiction bestowed on him by God in the Holy Scriptures in this realm of England, than any other foreign bishop?' Noes 34, doubtful 1, ayes 4.

Convocation of York

We make known and declare to your royal highness, by the tenor of the presents, that when, according to the mandate of your royal majesty, the following conclusion was proposed in the presence of the prelates and clergy of the province of York, gathered together in the sacred synod of the province or Convocation of the prelates and clergy of the same province of York, held in the Chapter House of the metropolitan church of York, on the fifth day of May, in the present year of our Lord 1534, and continued from day to day: 'That the Bishop of Rome has not, in Scripture, any greater jurisdiction in the kingdom of England than any other foreign bishop.' And when further, on behalf of the presidents deputed by you in the same synod, the said prelates and clergy were asked and demanded to confirm and endorse that opinion by their consent, if they thought or judged it consonant to the truth and not repugnant to the Holy Scriptures; at length the said prelates and clergy of the province of York aforesaid, after careful discussion had in that behalf, and mature deliberation, unanimously and concordantly consented to the same.

Gee and Hardy, pp. 251–2.

► The 'Supremacy Act', of November 1534, declared the King to be the supreme head of the Church of England. The religious change in England was completed.

Albeit the King's Majesty justly and rightfully is and ought to be the supreme head of the Church of England, and so is recognized by the clergy of this realm in their Convocations, yet nevertheless for corroboration and confirmation thereof, and for increase of virtue in Christ's religion within this realm of England, and to repress and extirp all errors, heresies, and other enormities and abuses heretofore used in the same; be it enacted by authority of this present Parliament, that the King our sovereign lord, his heirs and successors, kings of this realm, shall be taken, accepted and reputed the only supreme head in earth of the Church of England, called *Anglicana Ecclesia*; and shall have and enjoy, annexed and united to the imperial crown of this realm, as well the title and style thereof, as all honours, dignities, pre-eminences, jurisdictions, privileges, authorities, immunities, profits and commodities to the said dignity of supreme head of the same Church belonging and appertaining; and that our said sovereign lord, his heirs and successors, kings of this realm, shall have full power and authority from time to time to visit, repress, redress, reform, order, correct, restrain, and amend all such errors, heresies, abuses, offences, contempts and enormities, whatsoever they be, which by any manner spiritual authority or jurisdiction ought or may lawfully be reformed, repressed, ordered, redressed, corrected, restrained, or amended, most to the pleasure of Almighty God, the increase of virtue in Christ's religion, and for the conservation of the peace, unity and tranquillity of this realm; any usage, custom, foreign law, foreign authority, prescription, or any other things to the contrary hereof notwithstanding.

Gee and Hardy, pp. 243–4.

▶ In 1535, Catharine of Aragon, Henry VIII's first wife, died. The 'Annals of the Emperor Charles V' contain for that year the following entry:[11]

Catharine, Queen of England, dies, a worthy but unfortunate woman. She wedded two brothers by virtue of a dispensation from Pope Julius. She was treated badly by her father-in-law, who in order to force her mother to marry him, gave her little or nothing to eat, and fared even worse with her second husband, who in order to marry his lady-in-waiting, put her away. She was very beautiful, so that King Henry VIII laboured hard to obtain her for his wife. She died happy in leaving such an excellent daughter as is Queen Mary, our Lady.

Annals of the Emperor Charles V, p. 100.

▶ An act of 1536 declared the authority of the 'Bishop of Rome' invalid in England.

Forasmuch as notwithstanding the good and wholesome laws, ordinances and statutes heretofore enacted, made and established . . . for the extirpation, abolition and extinguishment, out of this realm and other his Grace's dominions, seignories and countries, of the pretended power and usurped authority of the Bishop of Rome, by some called the Pope, used within the same or elsewhere concerning the same realm, dominions, seignories or countries, which did obfuscate and wrest God's holy word and testament a long season from the spiritual and true meaning thereof to his worldly and carnal affections, as pomp, glory, avarice, ambition and tyranny, covering and shadowing the same with his human and politic devices, traditions and inventions, set forth to promote and establish his only dominion, both upon the souls and also the bodies and goods of all Christian people, excluding Christ out of his kingdom and rule of man his soul as much as he may, and all other temporal kings and princes out of their dominions which they ought to have by God's law upon the bodies and goods of their subjects; whereby he did not only rob the King's Majesty, being only the supreme head of this his realm of England immediately under God, of his honour, right and pre-eminence due unto him by the law of God, but spoiled this his realm yearly of innumerable treasure, and with the loss of the same deceived the King's loving and obedient subjects, persuading to them, by his laws, bulls and other his deceivable means, such dreams, vanities and fantasies as by the same many of them were seduced and conveyed unto superstitious and erroneous opinions; so that the King's Majesty, the Lords spiritual and temporal, and the Commons in this realm, being overwearied and fatigated with the experience of the infinite abominations and mischiefs proceeding of his impostures and craftily colouring of his deceits, to the great damages of souls, bodies and goods, were forced of necessity for the public weal of this realm to exclude that foreign pretended power, jurisdiction and authority . . . and notwithstanding the said wholesome laws so made and heretofore established, yet it is come to the knowledge of the King's Highness and also to divers and many his loving, faithful and obedient subjects, how that divers seditious and contentious persons, being imps of the said Bishop of Rome and his see, and in heart members of his pretended monarchy, do in corners and elsewhere, as they dare, whisper, inculce, preach and persuade, and from time to time instill into the ears and heads of the poor, simple and unlettered people the advancement and continuance of the said bishop's feigned and pretended authority, pretending the same to have his ground and original of God's law, whereby the opinions of many be suspended, their judgments corrupted and deceived, and diversity in opinions augmented and increased, to the great displeasure of Almighty God, the high discontentation of our said most dread sovereign lord, and the interruption of the unity, love, charity, concord and agreement that ought to be in a Christian region and congregation. For avoiding whereof . . . Be it enacted, ordained and established by the King our sovereign lord and the Lords spiritual and temporal and the Commons in this present Parliament assembled, and by authority of the same, that if any person or persons, dwelling, demurring, inhabiting or resident within this realm . . . of what estate, dignity, preeminence, order, degree or condition soever he or they be . . . shall, by writing, ciphering, printing, preaching or teaching, deed or act, obstinately or maliciously hold or stand with to extol, set forth, maintain or defend the authority, jurisdiction or power of the Bishop of Rome or of his see, heretofore used, claimed or usurped within this realm or in any dominion or country being of, within or under the King's power or obeisance, or by any pretence obstinately or maliciously invent anything for the extolling, advancement, setting forth, maintenance or defence of the same or any part thereof, or by any pretence obstinately or maliciously attribute any manner of jurisdiction, authority or pre-eminence to the said see of Rome . . . that then every such person or persons so doing or offending, their aiders, assistants, comforters, abettors, procurers, maintainers, fautors, counsellors, concealers and every of them, being thereof lawfully convicted according to the laws of this realm, for every such default and offence shall incur and run into the dangers, penalties, pains and forfeitures ordained and provided by the statute of provision and praemunire made in the sixteenth year of the reign of the noble and valiant prince King Richard II against such as attempt, procure or make provision to the see of Rome or elsewhere for any thing or things to the derogation, or contrary to the prerogative royal or jurisdiction, of the Crown and dignity of this realm.

Statutes of the Realm, III, 663–6.

▶ **The sermons of Hugh Latimer, a leading churchman, spoke about the condition of the clergy as follows:[12]**

And now I would ask a strange question: who is the most diligentest bishop and prelate in all England that passeth all the rest in doing his office? I can tell, for I know him who it is; I know him well. But now I think I see you listening and hearkening that I should name him. There is one that passeth all the other, and is the most diligent prelate and preacher in all England. And will ye know who it is? I will tell you: it is the devil. He is the most diligent preacher of all other; he is never out of his diocese; he is never from his cure; ye shall never find him unoccupied; he is ever in his parish; he keepeth residence at all times; ye shall never find him out of the way, call for him when you will he is ever at home; the diligentest preacher in all the realm; he is ever at his plough; no lording nor loitering can hinder him; he is ever applying his business, ye shall never find him idle, I warrant you. And his office is to hinder religion, to maintain superstition, to set up idolatry, to teach all kind of popery. He is ready as he can be wished for to set forth his plough; to devise as many ways as can be to deface and obscure God's glory. . . . O that our prelates would be as diligent to sow the corn of good doctrine as Satan is to sow cockle and darnel. . . .

Hugh Latimer, *Sermons*, 70–71.

▶ **Theologically, the Reformation in England was conservative. This is shown by the 'Six Articles Act' of 1539, which affirmed, in six important questions, a Catholic position.**

Where the King's most excellent Majesty is, by God's law, supreme head immediately under him of this whole Church and congregation of England, intending the conservation of the same Church and congregation in a true, sincere and uniform doctrine of Christ's religion, calling also to his blessed and most gracious remembrance as well the great and quiet assurance, prosperous increase and other innumerable commodities, which have ever ensued, come and followed, of concord, agreement and unity in opinions, as also the manifold perils, dangers and inconveniences which have heretofore, in many places and regions, grown, sprung and arisen, of the diversities of minds and opinions, especially of matters of Christian religion, and therefore desiring that such a unity might and should be charitably established in all things touching and concerning the same . . . has therefore caused and commanded this his most High Court of Parliament, for sundry and many urgent causes and considerations, to be at this time summoned, and also a synod and Convocation of all the archbishops, bishops, and other learned men of the clergy of this his realm, to be in like manner assembled. . . .

First, that in the most blessed Sacrament of the altar, by the strength and efficacy of Christ's mighty word (it being spoken by the priest), is present really, under the form of bread and wine, the natural body and blood of our Saviour Jesus Christ, conceived of the Virgin Mary; and that after the consecration there remaineth no substance of bread or wine, nor any other substance, but the substance of Christ, God and man.

Secondly, that communion in both kinds is not necessary *ad salutem*, by the law of God, to all persons; and that it is to be believed, and not doubted of, but that in the flesh, under the form of bread, is the very blood; and with the blood, under the form of wine, is the very flesh, as well apart, as though they were both together.

Thirdly, that priests after the order of priesthood received, as afore, may not marry, by the law of God.

Fourthly, that vows of chastity or widowhood, by man or woman made to God advisedly, ought to be observed by the law of God; and that it exempts them from other liberties of Christian people, which without that they might enjoy.

Fifthly, that it is meet and necessary that private masses be continued and admitted in this the King's English Church and congregation, as whereby good Christian people, ordering themselves accordingly, do receive both godly and goodly consolations and benefits; and it is agreeable also to God's law.

Sixthly, that auricular confession is expedient and necessary to be retained and continued, used and frequented in the Church of God.

Gee and Hardy, pp. 303–6.

▶   **Among the changes, the approval of the reading of the Bible in English instead of Latin was, perhaps, the most significant.[14]**

When the King had allowed the Bible to be set forth to be read in all churches, immediately several poor men in the town of Chelmsford in Essex, where his father lived and he was born, bought the New Testa-

Henry VIII at the age of 49, in 1540, dressed for his wedding to Anne of Cleves. (*Painting after Hans Holbein, Galleria Nazionale, Rome*)

Catherine of Aragon (?), first wife of Henry VIII. (*Painting by Michael Sittow. Kunsthistorisches Museum, Vienna*)

Thomas Cranmer, Archbishop of Canterbury, with a copy of Paul's Epistles in his hands. (*Painting by Gerlach Flicke. National Portrait Gallery, London*)

Title page of Miles Coverdale's English Bible of 1535, which was officially licensed in 1537. (*British Museum*)

ment and on Sundays sat reading of it in the lower end of the church:
many would flock about them to hear their reading: and he among the
rest, being then but fifteen years old, came every Sunday to hear the glad
and sweet tidings of the Gospel. But his father observing it once angrily
fetched him away, and would have him say the Latin matins with him,
which grieved him much. And as he returned at other times to have the
Scripture read, his father still would fetch him away. This put him upon
the thoughts of learning to read English that so he might read the New
Testament himself; which, when he had by diligence effected, he and his
father's apprentice bought the New Testament, joining their stocks
together, and to conceal it laid it under the bedstraw, and read it at convenient times. One night his father being asleep, he and his mother
chanced to discourse concerning the crucifix, and kneeling down to it,
and knocking on the breast then used, and holding up the hands to it
when it came in by procession. This he told his mother was plain idolatry,
and against the commandment of God, when he saith, *Thou shalt not
make any graven image, nor bow down to it, nor worship it.* His mother,
enraged at him for this, said, 'Wilt thou not worship his cross, which was
about thee when thou wast christened, and must be laid on thee when
thou art dead?' In this heat the mother and son went to their beds. The
sum of the evening's conference she presently repeats to her husband,
which he impatient to learn, and boiling in fury against his son for denying worship to be due to the cross, arose up forthwith, and goes into his
son's chamber, and like a mad zealot, taking him by the hair of his head
with both his hands, pulled him out of the bed, and whipped him unmercifully. And when the young man bore his beating, as he related, with
a kind of joy, considering it was for Christ's sake, and shed not a tear, his
father seeing that was more enraged, and ran down and fetched a halter,
and put it about his neck, saying he would hang him. At length, with much
entreaty of the mother and brother, he left him almost dead.

Narrative of William Maldon, Harleian MS. 590, folio 77.

▶   The following proclamation of 1533 concerning the putting of
Bibles into every church shows also Henry's religious concern.

Whereby Injunctions heretofore set forth by the authority of the
King's Royal Majesty, Supreme Head of the Church of this his Realm
of England, it was ordained, and commanded, amongst other things, That
in all and singular Parish-Churches, there should be provided, by a certain
day now expired, at the costs of the Curates and Parishioners, Bibles containing the Old and New Testament in the English Tongue, to be fixed

and set up openly in every of the said Parish Churches; the which godly
Commandment and Injunction, was to the only intent that every of the
King's Majesties loving Subjects, minding to read therein, might, by
occasion thereof, not only consider and perceive the great and ineffable
Omnipotent Power, Promise, Justice, Mercy and Goodness of Almighty
God, but also to learn thereby to observe God's Commandments, and to
obey their Sovereign Lord, and High Powers, and to exercise Godly
Charity, and to use themselves according to their Vocations, in a pure
and sincere Christian Life, without murmur or grudging: By the which
Injunctions, the King's Royal Majesty intended that his loving Subjects
should have and use the commodities of the reading of the said Bibles,
for the purpose above rehearsed, humbly, meekly, reverently, and
obediently, and not that any of them should read the said Bibles with
high and loud Voices, in time of the Celebration of the Holy Mass, and
other Divine Services used in the Church; or that any his Lay-Subjects
reading the same, should presume to take upon them any common Disputation, Argument or Exposition of the Mysteries therein contained; but
that every such Layman should, humbly, meekly and reverently, read the
same for his own instruction, edification and amendment of his Life,
according to God's Holy Word therein mentioned. And notwithstanding
the King's said most godly and gracious Commandment and Injunction, in
form as is aforesaid, his Royal Majesty is informed, That divers and many
Towns and Parishes within this his Realm, have neglected their duties in
the accomplishment thereof; whereof his Highness marvelleth not a
little; and minding the execution of his said former most godly and
gracious Injunctions, doth straitly charge and command, That the
Curates and Parishioners of every Town and Parish within this his Realm
of England, not having already Bibles provided within their Parish
Churches, shall on this side the Feast of All-Saints next coming, buy and
provide Bibles of the largest and greatest Volume, and cause the same to
be set and fixed in every of the said Parish Churches, there to be used as is
aforesaid.

Burnet, History of the Reformation, IV, 138.

▶   **Of equal importance was Henry's dissolution of the monasteries.
    Here is the first of several Acts which spelled out the legal
    procedures.**[15]

Forasmuch as manifest sin, vicious, carnal and abominable living, is
daily used and committed amongst the little and small abbeys, priories
and other religious houses of monks, canons and nuns, where the congregation of such religious persons is under the number of twelve persons,

whereby the governors of such religious houses and their convent spoil, destroy, consume and utterly waste as well their churches, monasteries, priories, principal houses, farms, granges, lands, tenements and hereditaments, as the ornaments of their churches and their goods and chattels to the high displeasure of Almighty God, slander of good religion, and to the great infamy of the King's Highness and the realm if redress should not be had thereof. . . . In consideration whereof the King's most royal Majesty, being supreme head in earth under God of the Church of England, daily finding and devising the increase, advancement and exaltation of true doctrine and virtue in the said Church, to the only glory and honour of God and the total extirping and destruction of vice and sin, having knowledge that the premises be true, as well by the compts of his late visitations as by sundry credible informations, considering also that divers and great solemn monasteries of this realm wherein, thanks be to God, religion is right well kept and observed, be destitute of such full numbers of religious persons as they ought and may keep, hath thought good that a plain declaration should be made of the premises as well to the Lords spiritual and temporal as to other his loving subjects the Commons in this present Parliament assembled; whereupon the said Lords and Commons by a great deliberation finally be resolved that it is and shall be much more to the pleasure of Almighty God and for the honour of this his realm that the possessions of such spiritual religious houses, now being spent, spoiled and wasted for increase and maintenance of sin, should be used and converted to better uses, and the unthrifty religious persons so spending the same to be compelled to reform their lives; and thereupon most humbly desire the King's Highness that it may be enacted by authority of this present Parliament that his Majesty shall have and enjoy to him and to his heirs for ever all and singular monasteries, priories and other religious houses of monks, canons and nuns, of what kinds or diversities of habits, rules or orders so ever they be called or named, which have not in lands and tenements, rents, tithes, portions and other hereditaments above the clear yearly value of two hundred pounds; and in like manner shall have and enjoy all the sites and circuits of every such religious houses. . . .

Statutes of the Realm III, 575–6.

▶ Late in the sixteenth century a writer commented on what had taken place in regard to the monasteries.

They called the abbot and other officers of the house, and demanded all their keys, and took an inventory of all their goods both inside and outside; all the animals, horses, sheep, and cattle in pasture or grange places, the visitors caused to be brought into their presence, and when they had done so, turned the abbot with all his convent and household forth of the doors.

Which thing was not a little grief to the convent, and all the servants of the house departing one from another, and especially such as with their conscience could not break their profession; for it would have made a heart of flint to have melted and wept to have seen the breaking up of these houses and their sorrowful departing, and the sudden spoil that fell the same day of their departure from the house. And every person had everything good cheap, except the poor monks, friars, and nuns, that had no money to bestow on anything. . . .

Such persons as afterward bought their corn and hay, or such like, found all the doors either open, the locks and shackles plucked away, or the door itself taken away, went in and took what they found—filched it away. Some took the service books that lied in the church, and laid them upon their waine coppes to piece the same. Some took windows of the hayleith and hid them in their hay; and likewise they did of many other things. . . . It would have pitied any heart to see what tearing up of lead there was and plucking up of boards and throwing down of the spars; when the lead was torn off and cast down into the church and the tombs in the church all broken (for in most abbeys were divers noble men and women—yea, and in some abbeys, kings, whose tombs were regarded no more than the tombs of all other inferior persons; for to what end should they stand when the church over them was not spared for their cause!), and all things of Christ either spoiled, carped away, or defaced to the uttermost.

Ellis, Original Letters, Third Series, III, 33f.

▶   The dissolution of another monastery was described in a letter of 1539.

We came to Glastonbury on Friday last past, about ten of the clock in the forenoon; and for that the abbot was then at Sharpham, a place of his, a mile and somewhat more from the abbey, we, without any delay, went unto the same place, and there, after communication declaring unto him the effect of our coming, examined him in certain articles. And for that his answer was not then to our purpose, we advised him to call to his remembrance that which he had as then forgotten, and so declare the truth, and then came with him the same day to the abbey, and there anew proceeded that night to search his study for letters and books; and found in his study secretly laid, as well a written book of arguments against the divorce of the King's Majesty and the lady dowager, which we take to be a great matter, as also divers pardons, copies of bulls, and the counterfeit life of Thomas Becket[16] in print; but we could not find any letter that was material. And so we proceeded again to his examination concerning the articles we received from your lordship, in the answers whereof, as we take it, shall appear his cankered and traitorous heart and mind against the King's Majesty and his succession as by the same answers, signed with his hand . . . more plainly shall appear. And so with as fair words as we could, we have conveyed him from hence into the tower, being but a very weak man and sickly. And as yet we have neither discharged servant nor monk; but now the abbot being gone, we will, with as much celerity as we may, proceed to the dispatching of them. We have in money £300 and above. . . .

We have found a fair chalice of gold and divers other parcels of plate, which the abbot had hid secretly from all such commissioners as have been there in times past; and as yet he knows not that we have found the same. . . . It may please your lordship to advertise us of the King's pleasure by this bearer, to whom we shall deliver the custody and keeping of the house, with such stuff as we intend to leave there convenient to the King's use. We assure your lordship it is the goodliest house of that sort that we ever have seen. We would that your lordship did know it as we do; then we doubt not but your lordship would judge it a house meet for the King's Majesty and for no man else: which is to our great comfort; and we trust verily that there shall never come any double hood within that house again.

22nd September 1539. Thomas Wright, *Suppression of the Monasteries*,[17] pp. 255-6.

▶ **Of those who in the course of the Reformation in England lost their lives, Thomas More, the celebrated humanist, was surely the most prominent.[18]**

The sixth day of July was Sir Thomas More beheaded for the like treason before rehearsed, which, as you have heard, was for the denial of the King's supremacy. This man was learned, and was Lord Chancellor of England, and in that time a great persecutor of those who detested the supremacy of the Bishop of Rome, which he himself so highly favoured. He stood to it until he was brought to the scaffold on the Tower Hill, where on a block his head was stricken from his shoulders.

I cannot tell whether I should call him a foolish wise man or a wise foolish man, for undoubtedly he had a great wit besides his learning, but it was so mingled with taunting and mocking, that those who knew him best claimed that he thought nothing to be well spoken except he had included some mocking. When he came to the Tower one of the officers demanded his upper garment for his fee, referring to his gown. He answered he should have it and gave him his cap, saying that it was the uppermost garment that he had. Likewise, going to his death at the Tower gate, a poor woman besought him to declare that he had certain evidence of hers from his time in office (which after he was apprehended she could not come by), and that he would entreat she might have them again, or else she was undone. He answered, 'Good woman, be patient for a little while, for the King is so good unto me that within half an hour he will discharge me of all business, and help you himself.' When he went up the stair on the scaffold he asked one of the sheriff's officers to give him his helping hand, and said, 'When I come down again let me shift for myself as well as I can.'

As is custom, the hangman kneeled down to him asking him forgiveness of his death. He said to him, 'I forgive you, but I promise you that you shall never have honesty of the striking of my head, my neck is so short.' Even when he should lay down his head on the block he struck out his great grey beard, and said to the hangman: 'Please let me lay my beard over the block lest you should cut it.' Thus with a mock he ended his life.

Hall, *Chronicle*, p. 817.

> The so-called 'King's Book'—'A Necessary Doctrine and Erudition for any Christian Man'—of 1543 discussed theology in line with Henry's desires. Here are parts of the preface:

Like as in the time of darkness and ignorance, finding our people seduced and drawn from the truth by hypocrisy and superstition, we by the help of God and his word have travailed to purge and cleanse our realm from the apparent enormities of the same; wherein, by opening of God's truth, with setting forth and publishing of the scriptures, our labours (thanks be to God) have not been void and frustrate; so now, perceiving that in the time of knowledge the Devil (who ceaseth not in all times to vex the world) hath attempted to return again (as the parable in the gospel sheweth) into the house purged and cleansed, accompanied with seven worse spirits, and hypocrisy and superstition being excluded and put away, we find entered into some of our people's hearts an inclination to sinister understanding of scripture, presumption, arrogancy, carnal liberty, and contention; we be therefore constrained, for the reformation of them in time, and for avoiding of such diversity in opinions as by the said evil spirits might be engendered, to set forth, with the advice of our clergy, such a doctrine and declaration of the true knowledge of God and his word, with the principal articles of our religion, as whereby all men may uniformly be led and taught the true understanding of that which is necessary for every Christian man to know, for the ordering of himself in this life, agreeably to the will and pleasure of Almighty God. Which doctrine also the lords both spiritual and temporal, with the nether house of our parliament, have both seen and like very well. And for knowledge of the order of the matter in this book contained, forasmuch as we know not perfectly God but by faith, the declaration of faith occupieth in this treatise the first place; whereunto is next adjoined the declaration of the Articles of our Creed, containing what we should believe. And incontinently after them followeth the explication of the Seven Sacraments, wherein God ordinarily worketh, and whereby he participateth unto us his special gifts and graces in this life: which matters so digested and set forth with simplicity and plainness, as the capacities and understandings of the multitude of our people may easily receive and comprehend the same, there followeth conveniently the declaration of the Ten Commandments, being by God ordained the high way, wherein each man should walk in this life to finish fruitfully his journey here, and after to rest eternally in joy with him: which because we cannot do of ourselves, but have need always of the grace of God, as without whom we can neither continue in this life, we without his special grace do any thing to his pleasure, whereby to attain the life to come; we have, after declaration of the Commandments, expounded the seven petitions of our Paternoster, wherein be contained requests and suits for all things necessary to a Christian man in this present life; with declaration of the Ave Maria, as a prayer containing a joyful rehearsal, and magnifying of God in the work of the incarnation of Christ, which is the ground of our salvation, wherein the blessed virgin our lady, for the abundance of grace wherewith God endued her, is also with this remembrance honoured and worshipped. And forasmuch as the heads and senses of our people have been embusied, and in these days travailed with the understanding of free will, justification, good works, and praying for the souls departed; we have, by the advice of our clergy, for the purgation of erroneous doctrine, declared and set forth openly, plainly, and without ambiguity of speech, the mere and certain truth in them.

A Necessary Doctrine and Erudition for any Christian Man (London, 1543), Aii ff.
The King's Book (London, 1932), pp. 3 ff.

▶ Death came to Henry VIII in 1547. John Foxe, in assessing the King's stature, cannot avoid a cautious tone.

On the 27th of January 1547 his spirits sunk, and it was evident that he had not long to live. Sir Anthony Denny took the courage to tell him that death was approaching, and desired him to call on God for his mercy. He expressed in general his sorrow for his past sins, and his trust in the mercies of God in Christ Jesus. He ordered Cranmer to be sent for, but was speechless before he arrived; yet he gave a sign that he understood what he said to him, and soon after died, in the 56th year of his age, after he had reigned thirty-seven years and nine months. His death was concealed three days; and the parliament continued to sit till the 31st of January, when his decease was made public. It is probable the Seymours, uncles to the young king, concealed it so long, till they made a party for securing the government in their own hands.

The severities Henry used against many of his subjects, in matters of religion, made both sides write with great sharpness against him; his temper was imperious and cruel; he was sudden and violent in his passions, and hesitated at nothing by which he could gratify either his lust or his revenge. This was much provoked by the sentence of the Pope against him, by the virulent books Cardinal Pole and others published, by the rebellions that were raised in England by the popish clergy, and the apprehensions he was in of the Emperor's greatness, together with his knowledge of the fate of those princes, against whom the popes had thundered in former times; all which made him think it necessary to keep his people under the terror of a severe government.

John Foxe, *Book of Martyrs*, pp. 250–1.

▶ Under King Edward VI (1547–53) Protestantism was established in England. Giralamo Cardano, a physician from Milan, who visited the King in 1552, described him as follows:

All the graces were in him. He had many tongues when he was yet but a child; together with the English, his natural tongue, he had both Latin and French; nor was he ignorant, as I hear, of the Greek, Italian and Spanish, and perhaps some more. But for the English, French and Latin, he was exact in them and apt to learn everything. Nor was he ignorant of logic, of the principles of natural philosophy, nor of music. The sweetness of his temper was such as became a mortal, his gravity becoming the majesty of a king, and his disposition suitable to his high degree. In sum, that child was so bred, had such parts, was of such expectation, that he looked like a miracle of a man. These things are not spoken rhetorically and beyond truth, but are indeed short of it. . . . He was a marvellous boy.

Burnet, *History of the Reformation*, II, 3.

▶ Edward VI, despite his youth, showed an intriguing sensitivity for things religious, as the following excerpts show—the one a laconic entry in his autobiography, the other a lengthy statement about the function of religion in society.

A parliament was called, where an uniform order of prayer was instituted, before made by a number of bishops and learned men gathered together in Windsore. There was granted a subsidy, and there was a notable disputation of the sacrament in the parliament house. . . .

Prayers to God also must be made continually, of the people, and officers of the Church, to assist them with his grace. And those prayers must first, with good consideration, be set forth, and faults therein be amended. Next, being set forth, the people must continually be allured to hear them. For discipline, it were very good that it went forth, and that those that did notably offend in swearing, rioting, neglecting of God's word, or such like vices, were duly punished, so that those that should be the executors of this discipline, were men of tried honesty, wisdom, and judgment. But because those bishops who should execute, some for papistry, some for ignorance, some for age, some for their ill name, some for all these, are men unable to execute discipline; it is therefore a thing unmeet for these men: wherefore it were necessary, that those that were appointed to be bishops, or preachers, were honest in life, and learned in their doctrine; that by rewarding of such men, other might be allured to follow their good life.

As for the prayers, and the divine service, it were meet the faults were drawn out (as it was appointed) by learned men, and so the book to be established, and all men willed to come thereunto to hear the service.

Burnet, *The History of the Reformation*, V, 7, 96.

▶ Here are instructions issued by a visitation committee established in order to enforce the new Protestant practices of Edward's rule.

Injunctions given by the king's majesty's visitors, to all and every the clergy and laity, now resident within the deanery of Duncastre.

Item. You shall not hereafter, in the pulpit or elsewhere, on the

Sunday, or any other day, give knowledge to your parishioners, when or what day in the week any of the abrogate holy-days were solemnized or kept in the church, but omit the same with silence as other working-days, for the utter abolishing of the remembrance thereof.

Item. You shall teach your parishioners, that fasting in the Lent, and other days, is a mere positive, that is to say, man's law; and by the magistrates, upon considerations, may be altered, changed, and dispensed with: and that therefore all persons having just cause of sickness, or other necessity, or being licensed thereto, may temperately eat all kinds of meat, without scruple or grudge of conscience.

Item. You shall every day, that an high mass is said or sung at the high altar, before the same mass, read openly in your churches the English suffrages, for the preservation and safeguard of the king's majesty's people, and prosperous success of his affairs.

Item. You shall every Sunday, at the time of your going about the church with holy-water, into three or four places, where most audience and assembly of people is, for the declaration of the ceremonies, say, distinctly and plainly, that your parishioners may well hear and perceive the same, these words,

Remember Christ's blood-shedding, by the which most holy sprinkling, of all your sins you have free pardon.

Burnet, *The History of the Reformation*, V, 185.

▶ **During the rule of her brother, Mary resented the religious changes undertaken. Here Duke Somerset, who guided the affairs of England during the first few years of Edward's rule, explained the changes to her:**

And where your grace writeth also, That there was a godly order and quietness left by the king our late master, your grace's father, in this realm at the time of his death; and that the spirituality and the temporality of the whole realm, did not only, without compulsion, fully assent to his doings and proceedings, especially in matters of religion, but also in all kind of talk, whereof, as your grace wrote, ye can partly be witness yourself; at which your grace's sayings I do something marvel: for if it may please you to call to your remembrance what great labours, travails, and pains, his grace had, before he could reform some of those stiff-necked Romanists or papists: yea, and did not they cause his subjects to rise and rebel against him, and constrained him to take the sword in his hand, not without danger to his person and realm? Alas, why should your grace so shortly forget that great outrage done by those generations of vipers unto his noble person only for God's cause? Did not some of the same ill kind also, I mean that Romanist sect, as well within his own realm as without, conspire oftentimes his death, which was manifestly and oftentimes proved, to the confusion of some of their privy assisters. Then was it not that all the spirituality, nor yet the temporalty, did so fully assent to his godly orders as your grace writeth of? Did not his grace also depart from this life before he had fully finished such godly orders as he minded to have established to all his people, if death had not prevented him? Is it not most true, that no kind of religion was perfected at his death, but left all uncertain, most like to have brought us into parties and divisions, if God had not only helped us? And doth your grace think it convenient it should so remain? God forbid. What regret and sorrow our late master had, the time he saw he must depart, for that he knew the religion was not established as he purposed to have done, I and others can be witness and testify.

Burnet, *The History of the Reformation*, V, 169f.

> The state of the Church in England is well illustrated by the following answers of ministers to questions concerning the Apostles' Creed [A], the Ten Commandments [C], and the Lord's Prayer [LP].

John Henburie, minister, says the Commandments are ten, Ex. 20, and repeated them from memory. Can also repeat the Articles of the Faith and prove them by authority of Scriptures. Can repeat Lord's Prayer and knows it was delivered by Christ to his apostles and is written in Matt. 6. *Communicants* about 360.

. . . Humphrey Wilkins, vicar, has not come to examination owing to his great infirmity. John Jones, minister. C *s* [satisfactory]. A: Can repeat them but not prove them directly from Scripture. LP *s. C* about 400. . . .

. . . John Hanley, minister. C: Says they are ten, in Ex. 20, but cannot repeat them from memory as there contained. A: Recited them, but did not prove them from Scripture. LP *s. C* about 140.

. . . Ralph Tilley, rector, has not been examined, because he resides in another benefice. Thos. Astill, minister. C: Says they are ten, and written in the New Testament, but knows not where, nor can repeat them well. A: Repeated them, but cannot prove them from Scriptures. LP: Can repeat it, but knows not by whom it was delivered or where written. C about 53.

. . . Mr Horowde patron. Ric. Davias, rector. C: Says they are ten, in Ex. 20, but cannot repeat them as there contained. A: Can repeat them but not confirm them by Scriptures. LP: Recited it, but knows not by whom it was delivered or where written. *C* about 20.

. . . Geo. Roo, minister. *C s.* A: Can repeat but not prove them by Scriptures. LP: Repeated it, but knows not by whom it was delivered or where written. *C* about 700.

. . . John Lawrence, rector. *C s.* A: Can repeat but not prove them from Scriptures. LP: Can repeat it, but knows not by whom it was delivered or where written. *C* about 30.

> Articles about which all ministers were examined concerning the commandments delivered by Moses from God (in Exodus 20), the articles of faith, and the Christian prayer.[13]

▶ **With Queen Mary's[19] succession to the English throne a Catholic reaction set in. Here a Venetian ambassador described the Queen and her people.**

Queen Mary, the daughter of Henry VIII and his queen Catherine, daughter of Ferdinand the Catholic, King of Aragon, is a princess of great worth. In her youth she was rendered unhappy by the event of her mother's divorce; by the ignominy and threats to which she was exposed after the change of religion in England, she being unwilling to unbend to the new one; and by the dangers to which she was exposed by the Duke of Northumberland, and the riots among the people when she ascended the throne.

She is of short stature, well made, thin and delicate, and moderately pretty; her eyes are so lively that she inspires reverence and respect, and even fear, wherever she turns them; nevertheless she is very shortsighted. Her voice is deep, almost like that of a man. She understands five languages—English, Latin, French, Spanish, and Italian, in which last, however, she does not venture to converse. She is also much skilled in ladies' work, such as producing all sorts of embroidery with the needle. She has a knowledge of music, chiefly on the lute, on which she plays exceedingly well. As to the qualities of her mind, it may be said of her that she is rash, disdainful and parsimonious rather than liberal. She is endowed with great humility and patience, but withal high-spirited, courageous and resolute, having during the whole course of her adversity not been guilty of the least approach to meanness of deportment; she is, moreover, devout and staunch in the defence of her religion. . . .

Religion, although thriving in this country, is, I apprehend, in some degree the offspring of dissimulation. The Queen is far from being lukewarm; she has already founded ten monasteries, and is about to found more. Generally speaking, your Serene Highness may rest assured that with the English the example and authority of the sovereign is everything, and religion is only so far valued as it inculcates the duty due from the subject to the prince. They live as he lives, they believe as he believes, and they obey his commands, not from any inward moral impulse, but because they fear to incur his displeasure; and they would be full as zealous followers of the Mohammedan or Jewish religions did the king profess either of them, or command his subjects to do so. In short, they will accommodate themselves to any religious persuasion, but most readily to one that promises to minister to licentiousness and profit.

Ellis, Original Letters, Second Series, II, 236ff.

▶ A few weeks after Queen Mary's succession to the English throne in July 1553 she issued the following proclamation. England became Catholic again.

The Queen's Highness well remembering what great inconvenience and dangers have grown to this her Highness's realm in times past through the diversity of opinions in questions of religion, and hearing also that now of late, since the beginning of her most gracious reign, the same contentions be again much renewed, through certain false and untrue reports and rumours spread by some light and evil-disposed persons, has thought good to do to understand to all her Highness's most loving and obedient subjects her most gracious pleasure in manner and form following.

First, her Majesty being presently by the only goodness of God settled in her just possession of the imperial crown of this realm, and other dominions thereunto belonging, cannot now hide that religion, which God and the world know she has ever professed from her infancy hitherto; which as her Majesty is minded to observe and maintain for herself by God's grace during her time, so doth her Highness much desire, and would be glad, the same were of all her subjects quietly and charitably embraced.

And yet she doth signify unto all her Majesty's loving subjects, that of her most gracious disposition and clemency, her Highness minds not to compel any her said subjects thereunto, unto such time as further order, by common assent, may be taken therein; forbidding nevertheless all her subjects of all degrees, at their perils, to move seditions or stir unquietness in her people, by interrupting the laws of this realm after their brains and fancies . . . and therefore wills and straitly charges and commands all her said good loving subjects to live together in quiet sort and

Christian charity, leaving those new-found devilish terms of papist or heretic and such like, and applying their whole care, study and travail to live in the fear of God, exercising their conversations in such charitable and godly doing, as their lives may indeed express that great hunger and thirst of God's glory and holy word, which by rash talk and words many have pretended; and in so doing as they shall best please God and live without dangers of the laws, and maintain the tranquillity of the realm, whereof her Highness shall be most glad, so if any man shall rashly presume to make any assemblies of people, or at any public assemblies or otherwise shall go about to stir the people to disorder or disquiet, she minds, according to her duty, to see the same most severely reformed and punished, according to her Highness's laws.

And furthermore, forasmuch also as it is well known that seditions and false rumours have been nourished and maintained in this realm by the subtlety and malice of some evil-disposed persons, which take upon them, without sufficient authority, to preach and interpret the word of God after their own brain in churches and other places, both public and private, and also by playing of interludes, and printing of false fond books and ballads, rhymes, and other lewd treatises in the English tongue, concerning doctrine in matters now in question and controversy touching the high points and mysteries of Christian religion, which books, ballads, rhymes and treatises are chiefly by the printers and stationers set out to sale to her Grace's subjects, of an evil zeal for lucre, and covetous of vile gain; her Highness therefore straitly charges and commands all and every of her said subjects, of whatsoever state, condition or degree they be, that none of them presume from henceforth to preach, or by way of reading in churches or other public or private places, except in the schools of the University, to interpret or teach any Scriptures or any manner points of doctrine concerning religion; neither also to print any book, matter, ballad, rhyme, interlude, process or treatise, nor to play any interlude, except they have her Grace's special licence in writing for the same, upon pain to incur her Highness's indignation and displeasure.

Gee and Hardy, pp. 373–5.

▶   **In 1554 the Venetian Ambassador to Queen Mary sent home a lengthy report on English affairs. Here is the section of the report dealing with the religious changes in England.**

On the accession of Queen Mary, immediately on arriving in London, she had the mass performed, and the first Parliament restored all the ancient ceremonies and the doctrine of the sacrament, and everything else, in accordance with the custom of the Roman Church, so that in this brief period such progress has been made that the mass and divine service are performed in all the churches, and attended by a good number of persons. Though the majority of the population is perhaps dissatisfied, yet may it be hoped that the Almighty will support her Majesty's good intentions. Nothing remains for adjustment with the Roman Church, save the obedience to the Church, which the Parliament has not hitherto confirmed, but will doubtless give its assent, provided the church property already distributed by the crown, remain in the hands of its present possessors, as having been given, sold, and exchanged, for so long a while, it can scarcely be supposed that the present possessors would restore it; and indeed it would be almost impossible by reason of the endless law-suits which would ensue; nor is it the Queen's intention to renounce the church property, of which she lately sold some, of considerable value, although she is quite bent on the union. . . . She had always been inclined to live according to the religion in which she was born, and that thus did she desire to continue, so that she did not believe she had incurred any ecclesiastical censure, having never consented to the things which took place against the religion, but that nevertheless to put her mind more at ease she moreover wished for absolution from the Pope, not only for herself but also for the whole kingdom; though as everything was still so unsettled that the publication of her demand might seriously injure the affairs of the kingdom, and perhaps endanger her life, she charged him to communicate this her wish solely to him (Soranzo). . . . proceeding subsequently straight to Rome, there to kiss the Pope's feet in her Majesty's name, and to make this request, as he did; but at Rome the secret was not kept as it ought to have been, and the Pope conceded the absolution to her Majesty and all those who were heartily disposed to resume their obedience to the Roman church.

Calendar of State Papers: Venice V, 556f.

▶   Queen Mary's two devotions—to her religion and to her husband
   —found an intriguing expression in this letter to her husband:

Wherefore, my Lord, as humbly as is possible for me, your most loyal and obedient wife (which I confess that I ought to be and indeed am more than all other wives, having such a husband as you . . .), I beseech you that both you and I pray to God and put our firm trust in him that we may live and meet again and that the same God who has the conduct of the hearts of kings in his hand will doubtless enlighten us so that the outcome will be to his glory and your contentment. Please forgive me assurance of

God's grace. But, though I have never deserved it, I have truly experienced it beyond the expectation of the world and I continue in that same hope in him which always has been mine.

John Strype, *Ecclesiastical Memorials* VII, 269f.

▶   **Mary energetically undertook to stamp out heresy in England. Here is her order for the execution of Bishop John Hooper.**

Whereas John Hooper, who of late was called Bishop of Rochester and Gloucester, by due order of the laws ecclesiastic, condemned and judged for a most obstinate, false, detestable heretic, and committed to our secular power, to be burned according to the wholesome and good laws of our realm in that case provided; forasmuch as in those cities, and the diocese thereof, he has in times past preached and taught most pestilent heresies and doctrine to our subjects there, we have therefore given order that the said Hooper who yet persisteth obstinate, and hath refused mercy when it was graciously offered, shall be put to execution in the said city of Gloucester, for the example and terror of such as he has there seduced and mistaught, and because he hath done most harm there. . . . And forasmuch also as the said Hooper is, as heretics be, a vainglorious person, and delighteth in his tongue, and, having liberty, may use his said tongue to persuade such as he hath seduced, to persist in the miserable opinion that he hath sown among them, our pleasure is therefore, and we require you to take order, that the said Hooper be neither, at the time of his execution, nor in going to the place thereof, suffered to speak at large, but thither to be led quietly and in silence, for eschewing of further infection and such inconvenience as may otherwise ensue in this part. Wherefore fail not, as ye tender our pleasure.

Goldsmid, *Collection of Documents*, II, 16.

▶   **The most prominent of Mary's victims was Archbishop Cranmer. His execution was described by an eyewitness.**

I think there was none that pitied not his case and bewailed his fortune, and feared not his own chance, to see so noble a prelate, so grave a counsellor, of so long-continued honour, after so many dignities, in his old years to be deprived of his estate, adjudged to die and in so painful a death to end his life. I have no delight to increase it. . . . But to come to the matter: on Saturday last, being the 21st of March was his day appointed to die. And because the morning was rainy, the sermon appointed by Mr Dr Cole to be made at the stake was made in St Mary's church.

When he had ended his sermon, he desired all the people to pray for him, Mr Cranmer kneeling down with them and praying for himself. I think there was never such a number so earnestly praying together. For they that hated him before now loved him for his conversion and hope of continuance. They that loved him before could not suddenly hate him, having hope of his confession again of his fall. So love and hope increased on every side. . . .

When praying was done, he [Cranmer] stood up, and having leave to speak said, 'Good people, I have intended to desire you to pray for me, which, because Mr Dr hath desired and you have already done, I thank you most heartily for it. And now will I pray for myself, as I could best devise for mine own comfort, and say the prayer, word for word, as I have here written it.' And he read it standing, and after kneeled down and said the Lord's Prayer, and all the people on their knees devoutly praying with him. . . . Then rising he said. . . .

'And now I come to the great thing that troubleth my conscience more than any other thing that ever I said or did in my life; and that is, the setting abroad of writings contrary to the truth. Which here now I renounce and refuse as things written with my hand, contrary to the truth which I have in my heart, and writ for fear of death and to save my life, if it might be: and that is all such bills which I have written or signed with mine own hand since my degradation, wherein I have written many things untrue. And forasmuch as my hand offended in writing contrary to my heart, therefore my hand shall first be punished. For if I may come to the fire, it shall be first burned. And as for the Pope, I refuse him as Christ's enemy and Antichrist, with all his false doctrine.'

And here being admonished of his recantation and dissembling, he said, 'Alas, my Lord, I have been a man that all my life loved plainness and never dissembled till now against the truth, which I am most sorry for.' He added hereunto, that for the Sacrament, he believed as he had taught in his book against the Bishop of Winchester. And here he was suffered to speak no more. . . .

Coming to the stake with a cheerful countenance and willing mind, he put off his garments with haste, and stood upright in his shirt. And a Bachelor of Divinity, named Elye, of Brasenose College, laboured to convert him to his former recantation, with the two Spanish friars. But when the friars saw his constancy, they said in Latin one to another, 'Let us go from him; we ought not to be nigh him, for the devil is with him.' But the Bachelor of Divinity was more earnest with him. Unto whom he answered, that as concerning his recantation he repented it right sore, because he knew it to be against the truth, with other words more. Whereupon the Lord Williams cried, 'Make short, make short.' Then the Bishop took certain of his friends by the hand. But the Bachelor of Divinity refused to take him by the hand, and blamed all others that did so, and said he was sorry that ever he came in his company. And yet again he required him to agree to his former recantation. And the Bishop answered (showing his hand), 'This is the hand that wrote it, and therefore shall it suffer first punishment.'

Fire being now put to him, he stretched out his right hand and thrust it into the flame, and held it there a good space, before the fire came to any part of his body, where his hand was seen of every man sensibly burning, crying with a loud voice, 'This hand hath offended.' As soon as the fire was got up, he was very soon dead, never stirring or crying all the while.

His patience in the torment, his courage in dying, if it had been taken either for the glory of God, the wealth of his country, or the testimony of truth, as it was for a pernicious error and subversion of true religion, I could worthily have commended the example and matched it with the fame of any father of ancient time; but seeing that not the death, but the cause and quarrel thereof, commendeth the sufferer, I cannot but much dispraise his obstinate stubbornness and sturdiness in dying, and specially in so evil a cause.

Harleian MS. 422.[20]

▶   Queen Elizabeth[21] brought a religious settlement to England which was distinctly Protestant in character. A contemporary describes the Queen.

She was a lady upon whom nature had bestowed and well placed many of her fairest favours: of stature mean, slender, straight and amiably composed; of such state in her carriage as every motion of her seemed to bear majesty; her hair was inclined to pale yellow, her forehead large and fair, a seeming seat for princely grace; her eyes lively and sweet, but shortsighted; her nose somewhat rising in the midst; the whole compass of her countenance somewhat long, but yet of admirable beauty, not so much in that which is termed the flower of youth, as in a most delightful composition of majesty and modesty in equal mixture.

The Annals of Queen Elizabeth, by Sir John Hayward.[22]

▶   The nature of the religious policy pursued by Queen Elizabeth is well illustrated by the following 'Injunctions' of 1559.

The Queen's most royal Majesty, by the advice of her most honourable council, intending the advancement of the true honour of Almighty God, the suppression of superstition throughout all her Highness's realms and dominions, and to plant true religion to the extirpation of all hypocrisy, enormities and abuses (as to her duty appertaineth), doth minister unto her loving subjects these godly Injunctions hereafter following. . . .

I. The first is, that all deans, archdeacons, parsons, vicars and all other ecclesiastical persons shall faithfully keep and observe, and as far as in them may lie, shall cause to be observed and kept of other, all and singular laws and statutes made [for the] restoring to the crown, the ancient jurisdiction over the state ecclesiastical, and abolishing of all foreign power, repugnant to the same. . . .

III. Item, that they, the persons above rehearsed, shall [preach] in their churches, and every other cure they have, one sermon every [month] of the year at the least, wherein they shall purely and sincerely declare the word of God, and in the same exhort their hearers to the works of faith, [as] mercy and charity especially prescribed and commanded in Scripture; and that [the] works devised by man's fantasies, besides Scripture (as wandering [of] pilgrimages, [setting up of candles], praying upon beads, or such like superstition), have not only no promise of reward in Scripture for doing them, but contrariwise great threatenings and maledictions of God. . . .

V. Item, that every holy-day through the year, when they have no sermon, they shall immediately after the Gospel openly and plainly recite to their parishioners in the pulpit the pater noster, the creed, and the ten commandments, in English, to the intent that the people may learn the same by heart; exhorting all parents and house holders to teach their children and servants the same, as they are bound by the law of God and conscience to do. . . .

XXI. Also, forasmuch as variance and contention is a thing that most displeases God, and is most contrary to the blessed communion of the Body and Blood of our Saviour Christ, curates shall in no wise admit to the receiving thereof any of their cure and flock, [which be openly known to live in sin notorious without repentance, or] who hath maliciously and openly contended with his neighbour, unless the same do first charitably and openly reconcile himself again, remitting all rancour and malice, whatsoever controversy hath been between them. . . .

XXIII. Also, that they shall take away, utterly extinct, and destroy all shrines, coverings of shrines, all tables, candlesticks, trindals, and rolls of wax pictures, paintings, and all other monuments of feigned miracles, pilgrimages, idolatry and superstition, so that there remain no memory of the same in walls, glass windows, or elsewhere within their churches and houses; [preserving nevertheless, or repairing both the walls and glass windows;] . . .

XXXIV. Item, that no innholders or alehouse-keepers shall use to sell meat or drink in the time of common prayer, preaching, reading of the Homilies or Scriptures.

XXXV. Item, that no persons keep in their houses any abused images, tables, pictures, paintings, and other monuments of feigned miracles, pilgrimages, idolatry and superstition.

XXXVI. Item, that no man shall willingly let or disturb the preacher in time of his sermon, or let or discourage any curate or minister to sing or say the divine service now set forth; nor mock or jest at the ministers of such service. . . .

LIII. Item, that all ministers and readers of public prayers, chapters, and homilies shall be charged to read leisurely, plainly and distinctly; and also such as are but mean readers shall peruse over before, once or twice, the chapters and homilies, to the intent they may read to the better understanding of the people, and the more encouragement to godliness. . . .

Item, where also it was in the time of King Edward VI used to have the sacramental bread of common fine bread, it is ordered for the more reverence to be given to these holy mysteries, being the sacraments of the Body and Blood of our Saviour Jesus Christ, that the same sacramental bread be made and formed plain, without any figure thereupon, of the same fineness and fashion round, though somewhat bigger in compass and thickness, as the usual bread and water, heretofore named singing cakes, which served for the use of the private mass.

Gee and Hardy, pp. 417-40.

▶   The martyrdom of George Wishart constitutes the first significant incident in the history of the Scottish Reformation. John Knox described it as follows:

Upon the last of February, was sent to the prison, where the servant of God lay, the Dean of the town, by the commandment of the Cardinal and his wicked council, and they summoned the said Master George that he should, upon the morn following, appear before the Judge then and there to give account of his seditious and heretical doctrine. . . .

They caused Master George to ascend into the pulpit, there to hear his Accusation and Articles. For right against him stood up one of the fed flock, a monster, John Lauder, laden full of cursings, written in paper, of the which he took out a roll both long and also full of cursings, threatenings, maledictions, and words of devilish spite and malice, saying to the innocent Master George so many cruel and abominable words, and hit him so spitefully with the Pope's thunder, that the ignorant people dreaded lest the earth then would have swallowed him up quick. Notwithstanding, he stood still with great patience hearing their sayings, not once moving or changing his countenance. When that this fed sow had read throughout all his lying menacings, his face running down with sweat, and frothing at the mouth like a bear, he spat at Master George's face, saying, 'What answerest thou to these sayings, thou runagate, traitor, thief, which we have duly proved by sufficient witness against thee?' Master George hearing this, sat down upon his knees in the pulpit, making his prayer to God. When he had ended his prayer, sweetly and Christianly he answered to them all in this manner: . . .

'First and chiefly, since the time I came into this realm, I taught nothing but the Ten Commandments of God, the Twelve Articles of the Faith, and the Prayer of the Lord, in the mother tongue. Moreover, in Dundee, I taught the Epistle of Saint Paul to the Romans; and I shall show your discretions faithfully what fashion and manner I used when I taught, without any human dread, so that your discretions give me your ears benevolent and attent.'

Suddenly, then, with an high voice, cried the Accuser, the fed sow, 'Thou heretic, runagate, traitor and thief, it was not lawful for thee to preach. Thou hast taken the power at thine own hand, without any authority of the Church. We forethink that thou hast been a preacher so long.' Then said all the whole congregation of the Prelates, with their complices, these words, 'If we give him licence to preach, he is so crafty, and in Holy Scriptures so exercised, that he will persuade the people to his opinion, and raise them against us.' . . .

And shortly for to declare, these were the Articles following, with his Answers, as far as they would give him leave to speak; for when he intended to mitigate their lesings, and show the manner of his doctrine, by and by they stopped his mouth with another Article. . . .

THE SECOND ARTICLE

Thou false Heretic did say that a priest standing at the altar saying Mass was like a fox wagging his tail in July.

THE ANSWER

My Lords, I said not so. These were my sayings: The moving of the body outward, without the inward moving of the heart, is nothing else but the playing of an ape, and not the true serving of God; for God is a secret searcher of men's hearts: Therefore, who will truly adorn and honour God, he must in spirit and verity honour him.

Then the Accusator stopped his mouth with another Article.

THE THIRD ARTICLE

Thou false Heretic preachest against the Sacraments, saying, That there are not seven Sacraments.

THE ANSWER

My Lords, if it be your pleasure, I taught never of the number of the Sacraments, whether they were seven, or an eleven. So many as are instituted by Christ, and are shown to us by the Evangel, I profess openly. Except it be the word of God, I dare affirm nothing. . . .

THE THIRTEENTH ARTICLE

Thou false Heretic hast preached plainly, saying, That there is no Purgatory; and that it is a feigned thing, any man, after this life, to be punished in Purgatory.

THE ANSWER

My Lords, as I have oftentimes said heretofore, without express witness and testimony of Scripture I dare affirm nothing. I have oft and divers times read over the Bible, and yet such a term found I never, nor yet any place of Scripture applicable thereunto. Therefore, I was ashamed ever to teach of that thing, which I could not find in Scripture. . . .

When the fire was made ready, and the gallows, at the West part of the Castle, near to the Priory, my Lord Cardinal, dreading that Master George should have been taken away by his friends, therefore he commanded to bend all the ordnance of the Castle right against the place of execution, and commanded all his gunners to be ready, and stand beside their guns, unto such time as he were burned. All this being done, they bound Master George's hands behind his back and led him forth with their soldiers, from the Castle, to the place of their cruel and wicked execution. . . .

When that he came to the fire, he sat down upon his knees, and rose again; . . . and said these words: 'I beseech you, Christian brethren and sisters, that ye be not offended at the word of God for the affliction and torments which ye see already prepared for me. But I exhort you, that ye love the word of God, your salvation, and suffer patiently, and with a comfortable heart, for the word's sake, which is your undoubted salvation and everlasting comfort. Moreover, I pray you, show my brethren and sisters, which have heard me oft before, that they cease not nor leave off to learn the word of God, which I taught unto them, after the grace given unto me, for no persecutions nor troubles in this world, which lasteth not. And show unto them that my doctrine was no wives' fables, after the constitutions made by men; and if I had taught men's doctrine, I had greater thanks by men.' . . . And last of all, he said to the people on this manner, 'I beseech you, brethren and sisters, to exhort your Prelates to the learning of the word of God, that they at the last may be ashamed to do evil, and learn to do good; and if they will not convert themselves from their wicked error, there shall hastily come upon them the wrath of God, which they shall not eschew.'

Many faithful words said he in the meantime, taking no heed or care of the cruel torments which were then prepared for him. Then, last of all, the hangman, that was his tormentor, sat down upon his knees and said, 'Sir, I pray you, forgive me, for I am not guilty of your death.' To whom he answered, 'Come hither to me.' When he was come to him he kissed his cheek and said, 'Lo! Here is a token that I forgive thee. My heart, do thine office.' And then, by and by, he was put upon the gibbet, and hanged, and there burnt to powder.

John Knox, History of the Reformation, II,
233, 234, 235, 236, 237, 241, 244, 245.

▶ The story of the Scottish Reformation is inextricably linked with the name of John Knox. A contemporary described the 'thundering Scot' with the following words:

In bodily stature he was rather below the normal height. His limbs were straight and well proportioned; his shoulders broad; his fingers somewhat long. His head was of medium size, with black hair; his appearance swarthy, yet not unpleasant. His countenance, which was grave and stern, though not harsh, bore a natural dignity and air of authority; in anger his very frown became imperious. Under a rather narrow forehead his eyebrows rose in a dense ridge; his cheeks were ruddy and somewhat full, so that it seemed as though his eyes receded into hollows. The eyes themselves were dark-blue, keen and animated. His face was somewhat long, with a long nose, a full mouth, and large lips of which the upper one was slightly the thicker. His beard was black, flecked with grey, thick, and falling down a hand and a half long.

Sir Peter Young to Theodore Beza, 13th November 1579:
Hume Brown, John Knox (Edinburgh, 1895), II, 322–4.

John Knox. See p. 359. (*Theodor Beza*, Icones, 1580)

▶   Here John Knox describes, in his 'History of the Reformation in Scotland', his own call to preach the Gospel.

Said John Rough, preacher, directed his words to the said John Knox, saying, 'Brother, ye shall not be offended, albeit that I speak unto you that which I have in charge, even from all those that are here present, which is this: In the name of God, and of his Son Jesus Christ, and in the name of these that presently call you by my mouth, I charge you, that ye refuse not this holy vocation, but that as ye tender the glory of God, the increase of Christ his kingdom, the edification of your brethren, and the comfort of me, whom ye understand well enough to be oppressed by the multitude of labours, that ye take upon you the public office and charge of preaching, even as ye look to avoid God's heavy displeasure, and desire that he shall multiply his graces with you.' And in the end he said to those that were present, 'Was not this your charge to me? And do ye not approve this vocation?' They answered, 'It was; and we approve it.' Whereat the said John, abashed, burst forth in most abundant tears, and withdrew himself to his chamber. His countenance and behaviour, from that day till the day that he was compelled to present himself to the public place of preaching, did sufficiently declare the grief and trouble of his heart; for no man saw any sign of mirth of him, neither yet had he pleasure to accompany any man, many days together.

John Knox, *History of the Reformation*, I, 83.

▶   **The assassination of the hated Cardinal Beaton marked the dramatic prelude to the Reformation in Scotland.**

But early upon the Saturday, in the morning, the 29th of May, were they in sundry companies in the Abbey kirk-yard, not far distant from the Castle. First, the yetts being open, and the drawbridge let down, for receiving of lime and stones, and other things necessary for building (for Babylon was almost finished)—first, we say, essayed William Kirkcaldy of Grange, younger, and with him six persons, and getting entrance, held purpose with the porter, 'If my Lord was walking?' who answered, 'No.' (And so it was indeed; for he had been busy at his accounts with Mistress Marion Ogilvy that night, who was espied to depart from him by the privy postern that morning; and therefore quietness, after the rules of physic, and a morning sleep was requisite for my Lord.) While the said William and the porter talked, and his servants made them to look the work and the workmen, approached Norman Leslie with his company; and because they were in no great number, they easily got entrance. . . . The porter, fearing, would have drawn the brig; but the said John, being entered thereon, stayed, and leapt in. And while the porter made him for defence, his head was broken, the keys taken from him, and he cast in the fosse; and so the place was seized. The shout arises: the workmen, to the number of more than a hundred, ran off the walls, and were without hurt put forth at the wicket yett. The first thing that ever was done, William Kirkcaldy took the guard of the privy postern, fearing that the fox should have escaped. Then go the rest to the gentlemen's chambers . . . The Cardinal, awakened with the shouts, asked from his window, What meant that noise? It was answered, That Norman Leslie had taken his Castle. Which understood, he ran to the postern; but perceiving the passage to be kept without, he returned quickly to his chamber, took his two-handed sword, and gart his chamber child cast kists, and other impediments to the door. In this meantime came John Leslie unto it, and bids open. The Cardinal asking, 'Who calls?' he answers, 'My name is Leslie.' He re-demands, 'Is that Norman?' The other says, 'Nay; my name is John.' 'I will have Norman,' says the Cardinal, 'for he is my friend.' 'Content yourself with such as are here; for other shall ye get none.' There were with the said John, James Melville, a man familiarly acquainted with Master George Wishart, and Peter Carmichael, a stout gentleman. In this meantime, while they force at the door, the Cardinal hides a box of gold under coals that were laid in a secret corner. At length he asked, 'Will ye save my life?' The said John answered, 'It may be that we will.' 'Nay,' says the Cardinal, 'swear unto me by God's wounds, and I will open unto you.' Then answered the said John. 'It that was said, is unsaid'; and so cried, 'Fire, fire' (for the door was very stark); and so was brought a chimney full of burning coals. Which perceived, the Cardinal or his chamber child (it is uncertain), opened the door, and the Cardinal sat down in a chair and cried, 'I am a priest; I am a priest: ye will not slay me.' The said John Leslie (according to his former vows) struck him first, once or twice, and so did the said Peter. But James Melville (a man of nature most gentle and most modest) perceiving them both in choler, withdrew them, and said, 'This work and judgment of God (although it be secret) ought to be done with greater gravity'; and presenting unto him the point of the sword, said, 'Repent thee of thy former wicked life, but especially of the shedding of the blood of that notable instrument of God, Master George Wishart, which albeit the flame of fire consumed before men, yet cries it a vengeance upon thee, and we from God are sent to revenge it: For here, before my God, I protest, that neither the hetterent of thy person, the love of thy riches, nor the fear of any trouble thou could have done to me in particular, moved, nor moves me to strike thee; but only because thou hast been, and remains an obstinate enemy against Christ Jesus and his holy Evangel.' And so he struck him twice or thrice through with a stog sword; and so he fell, never word heard out of his mouth, but 'I am a priest, I am a priest: fye, fye: all is gone.'

John Knox, *History of the Reformation*, I, 76–78.

▶   **Of great importance for John Knox was his early travel to Geneva.**

The said John [Knox] was first appointed preacher to Berwick, then to Newcastle; last he was called to London, and to the south parts of England, where he remained to the death of King Edward the Sixth. When he left England, then he passed to Geneva, and there remained at his private study till that he was called by the English congregation, that then was assembled at Frankfurt to be preacher to them. Which vocation he obeyed (albeit unwillingly) at the commandment of that notable servant of God, John Calvin. At Frankfurt he remained, till that some of the learned (whose names we suppress), more given to unprofitable ceremonies than to sincerity of religion, began to quarrel with the said John; and because they despaired to prevail before the Magistrate there, for the establishing of their corruptions, they accused him of treason committed against the Emperor, and against their Sovereign Queen Mary, that, in his *Admonition to England*, he called the one little inferior to Nero, and the other more cruel than Jezebel. The Magistrate perceiving their malice, and fearing that the said John should fall in the hands of his accusators, by one means or by other, gave advertisement secretly to him to depart their city; for they could not save him if he were required by the Emperor, or by the Queen of England in the Emperor's name; and so the said John returned to Geneva, from thence to Dieppe, and thereafter to Scotland.

John Knox, *History of the Reformation*, I, 110–11.

▶ From the very beginning Knox was uncompromising in his conviction.

At the first coming of the said John Knox, he perceiving divers who had a zeal to godliness make small scruple to go to the Mass, or to communicate with the abused sacraments in the papistical manner, began as well in privy conference as in doctrine to show the impiety of the Mass, and how dangerous a thing it was to communicate in any sort with idolatry. Wherewith the conscience of some being effrayed, the matter began to be agitated from man to man, and so was the said John called to supper by the Laird of Dun, for that same purpose. . . . The question was proponed, and it was answered by the said John, 'That no-wise it was lawful to a Christian to present himself to that idol.'

John Knox, *History of the Reformation*, I, 120.

▶ Early in 1556, John Knox, at that time residing in Geneva, received an urgent plea to return to Scotland.

Dearly beloved in the Lord, the faithful that are of your acquaintance in these parts (thanks be unto God) are steadfast in the belief whereinto ye left them, and have a godly thirst and desire, day by day, of your presence again; which, if the Spirit of God will so move and permit time unto you, we will heartily desire you, in the name of the Lord, that ye will return again in these parts, where ye shall find all faithful that ye left behind you, not only glad to hear your doctrine, but will be ready to jeopard lives and goods in the forward setting of the glory of God, as he will permit time. And albeit the Magistrates in this country be as yet but in the state ye left them, yet, at the making hereof, we have no experience of any more cruelty to be used nor was before; but rather we have belief that God will augment his flock, because we see daily the Friars, enemies to Christ's Evangel, in less estimation both with the Queen's Grace and the rest of the Nobility of our realm. This in few words is the mind of the faithful, being present, and others absent. The rest of our minds this faithful bearer will show you at length. Thus, fare ye well in the Lord.

These letters were delivered to the said John in Geneva. . . . Which received, and advised upon, he took consultation as well with his own Church as with that notable servant of God, John Calvin, and with other godly ministers who, all with one consent, said, 'That he could not refuse that vocation, unless he would declare himself rebellious unto his God, and unmerciful to his country.' And so he returned answer, with promises to visit them with reasonable expedition, and so soon as he might put order to that dear flock that was committed to his charge. And so, in the end of the next September after, he departed from Geneva, and came to Dieppe.

John Knox, *History of the Reformation*, I, 132–3.

▶   **On his way back to Scotland, John Knox took time out to write to the men he was going to serve.**

I would your Wisdoms should consider that our God remaineth one, and is immutable; and that the Church of Christ Jesus hath the same promise of protection and defence that Israel had of multiplication; and further, that no less cause have ye to enter in your former enterprise, than Moses had to go to the presence of Pharaoh; for your subjects, yea, your brethren are oppressed, their bodies and souls held in bondage: and God speaketh to your consciences (unless ye be dead with the blind world) that you ought to hazard your own lives (be it against kings or emperors) for their deliverance.

John Knox, *History of the Reformation*, I, 135.

▶   **As a result of this letter, some of the Scottish Protestants banded together, in December 1557, to subscribe to the following covenant:**

We, perceiving how Sathan in his members, the Antichrists of our time, cruelly doth rage, seeking to downthring and to destroy the Evangel of Christ, and his Congregation, ought, according to our bounded duty, to strive in our Master's cause, even unto the death, being certain of the victory in him: The which our duty being well considered, we do promise that we (by his grace) shall with all diligence continually apply our whole power, substance, and our very lives, to maintain, set forward, and establish the most blessed word of God and his Congregation; and shall labour at our possibility to have faithful Ministers purely and truly to minister Christ's Evangel and Sacraments to his people. We shall maintain them, nourish them, and defend them, the whole Congregation of Christ, and every member thereof, at our whole powers and waring of our lives, against Sathan, and all wicked power that does intend tyranny or trouble against the foresaid Congregation. Unto the which holy word and Congregation we do join us, and also does forsake and renounce the congregation of Sathan, with all the superstitions, abomination and idolatry thereof: And moreover, shall declare ourselves manifestly enemies thereto, by this our faithful promise before God, testified to his Congregation, by our subscriptions at these presents—at Edinburgh, the third day of December, the year of God 1557.

John Knox, History of the Reformation, I, 136–7.

▶   **Later John Knox arrived back in Scotland.**

In the meantime that the Preachers were summoned, to wit, the second of May 1559, arrived John Knox from France, who lodging two nights only in Edinburgh, hearing the day appointed to his brethren, repaired to Dundee, where he earnestly required them, 'That he might be permitted to assist his brethren, and to give confession of his faith with them': which granted unto him [he] departed unto Saint Johnston with them; where he began to exhort, according to the grace of God granted unto him. The Queen, perceiving that the preachers did not compear, began to utter her malice; and notwithstanding any request made in the contrary, gave commandment to put them to the horn, inhibiting all men under pain of their rebellion to assist, comfort, receive, or maintain them in any sort.

John Knox, History of the Reformation, I, 161.

▶   **Within a month of his return Knox addressed himself to the Scottish Lords:**

The present troubles, Honourable Lords, ought to move the hearts, not only of the true servants of God, but also of all such as bear any favour to their country, and natural countrymen, to descend within themselves and deeply to consider what shall be the end of this pretended tyranny. The rage of Sathan seeketh the destruction of all those that within this realm profess Christ Jesus; and they that inflame the Queen's Grace, and you the Nobles against us, regard not who prevail, provided that they may abuse the world, and live at their pleasure, as heretofore they have done. Yea, I fear that some seek nothing more than the effusion of Scottish blood, to the end that their possessions may be more patent to others.

But, because that is not the principal which I have to speak, omitting the same to be considered by the wisdom of those to whom the care of the commonwealth appertaineth—

1st. I most humbly require of you, my Lords, in my name, to say to the Queen's Grace Regent, that we, whom she in her blind rage doth persecute, are God's servants, faithful and obedient subjects to the authority of this realm; that that religion, which she pretendeth to maintain by fire and sword, is not the true religion of Christ Jesus, but is express contrary to the same; a superstition devised by the brain of man; which I offer myself to prove against all that within Scotland will maintain the contrary, liberty of tongue being granted unto me, and God's written word being admitted for judge.

2nd. I further require your Honours, in my name, to say unto her Grace, that as of before I have written, so now I say, that this her enterprise shall not prosperously succeed in the end, albeit for a time she trouble the saints of God; for she fighteth not against man only, but against the eternal God and his invincible verity. And therefore, the end shall be her confusion, unless betimes she repent and desist.

These things I require of you, in the name of the eternal God, as from my mouth, to say unto her Grace; adding that I have been and am, a more assured friend to her Grace than they that, either flattering her are servants to her corrupt appetites, or else inflame her against us, who seek nothing but God's glory to be advanced, vice to be suppressed and verity to be maintained in this poor realm.

John Knox, *History of the Reformation*, I, 173–4.

▶   **In May of 1559 another covenant was made by those who were uncompromising in their Protestant conviction.**

At Perth, the last day of May, the year of God 1559, the Congregations of Fife, Perth, Dundee, Angus, Mearns and Montrose, being convened in the town of Perth, in the name of Jesus Christ, for forthsetting of his glory, understanding nothing more necessary for the same than to keep a constant amity, unity and fellowship together, according as they are commanded by God, are confederate, and become bound and obliged in the presence of God, to concur and assist together in doing all things required of God in his Scripture, that may be to his glory; and at their whole power to destroy, and away put, all things that do dishonour to his name, so that God may be truly and purely worshipped. And in case that any trouble be intended against the said Congregations, or any part, or member thereof, the whole Congregation shall concur, assist and convene together, to the defence of the same Congregation, or person troubled, and shall not spare labours, goods, substance, bodies and lives, in maintaining the liberty of the whole Congregation, and every member thereof, against whatsoever power that shall intend the said trouble, for cause of religion, or any other cause dependent thereupon, or lay to their charge under pretence thereof, although it happen to be coloured with any other outward cause.

John Knox, *History of the Reformation*, I, 178.

▶ On 27th April 1560, a group of Scottish noblemen pledged themselver at Leith to work for the reformation of the Church.

We, whose names are underwritten, have promised and oblist ourselves faithfully, in the presence of our God, and by these presents promise, that we altogether in general, and every one of us in special, by himself, with our bodies, goods, friends, and all that we may do, shall set forward the Reformation of Religion, according to God's word; and procure, by all means possible, that the truth of God's word may have free passage within this realm, with due administration of the sacraments, and all things depending upon the said word.

John Knox, *History of the Reformation*, I, 314.

▶ The victory of the Reformation in Scotland came in 1560 with the approval of a Protestant Confession of Faith by the Scottish Parliament. Here is the request of its Protestant members for a religious change.

First, Seeing that God of his great mercy by the light of his word, has manifested to no small number of this realm, that the doctrine of the Roman Kirk, received by the said Clergy, and maintained through their tyranny by fire and sword, contained in the self many pestiferous errors, which cannot but bring damnation to the souls of such as therewith shall be infected; such as are the doctrine of Transubstantiation; of the Adoration of Christ his body under the form of bread, as they term it; of the merits of Works, and Justification that they allege comes thereby; together with the doctrine of the Papistical Indulgences, Purgatory, Pilgrimage, and Praying to Saints departed; which all either repugn to the plain Scriptures, or else have no ground of the doctrine of our Master Jesus Christ, his Prophets, nor Apostles. We humbly therefore crave of your Honours, that such doctrine and idolatry as by God's word are condemned, so may they be abolished by Act of this present Parliament, and punishment appointed for the transgressors.

Secondly, Seeing that the Sacraments of Jesus Christ are most shamefully abused and profaned by that Roman harlot and her sworn vassals; and also because that the true discipline of the ancient Kirk is utterly now amongst that sect extinguished: for who within the realm are more corrupt of life and manners than are they that are called the Clergy, living in whoredom, adultery, deflowering virgins, corrupting matrons, and doing all abomination, without fear of punishment; We humbly therefore desire your Honours to find remedy against the one and the other.

Thirdly, Because that Man of Sin often most falsely claims to himself the titles of 'The Vicar of Christ; the Successor of Peter; the Head of the Kirk; that he cannot err; that all power is granted unto him', etc., by the which usurped authority, he takes upon him the distribution and possession of the whole patrimony of the Kirk, whereby the true ministers of the word of God long time have been altogether neglected, the godly learning despised, the schools not provided, and the poor not only defrauded of their portion, but also tyrannously oppressed; We likewise hereof desire remedy.

John Knox, History of the Reformation, I, 336–7.

▶   John Knox described the acceptance of the Confession in Parliament as follows:

Our Confession was publicly read, first in audience of the Lords of Articles, and after in audience of the whole Parliament; where were present, not only such as professed Christ Jesus, but also a great number of the adversaries of our religion, such as the forenamed Bishops, and some others of the Temporal Estate, who were commanded in God's name to object, if they could, any thing against that doctrine. Some of our Ministers were present, standing upon their feet, ready to have answered, in case any would have defended the Papistry, and impugned our affirmatives: but while that no objection was made, there was a day appointed to voting in that and other heads. Our Confession was read, every article by itself, over again, as they were written in order, and the votes of every man were required accordingly. Of the Temporal Estate, only voted in the contrary the Earl of Atholl, the Lords Somerville and Borthwick; and yet for their dissenting they produced no better reason, but, 'We will believe as our fathers believed.' The Bishops (papistical, we mean) spake nothing. The rest of the whole three Estates by their public votes affirmed the doctrine; and many, the rather, because that the Bishops would nor durst say nothing in the contrary; for this was the vote of the Earl Marischal—'It is long since I have had some favour unto the truth, and since that I have had a suspicion of the Papistical religion; but, I praise

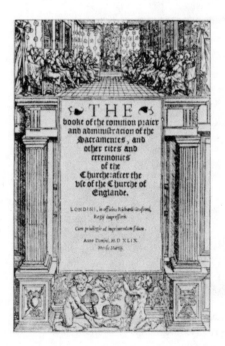

Title page of the so-called *Great Bible*, issued by order of Henry VIII in 1539. The top shows the King presenting copies to Archbishop Thomas Cranmer, on his right, and Thomas Cromwell, Lord Privy Seal, on his left (*British Museum*)

Title page of the first Book of Common Prayer, which was officially sanctioned in 1549 by the first Act of Uniformity. (*British Museum*)

The martyrdom of Bishops Latimer and Ridley in 1556, as seen in a woodcut in John Foxe's *Actes and Monuments* of 1563. (*British Museum*)

Luther's hymn 'A Mighty Fortress' as it appeared for the first time in a hymnal published at Wittenberg. (*Lutherhalle, Wittenberg*)

my God, this day has fully resolved me in the one and the other. For seeing that my Lords Bishops who, for their learning can, and for the zeal that they should bear to the verity would, as I suppose, gainsay anything that directly repugns to the verity of God; seeing, I say, my Lords Bishops here present speak nothing in the contrary of the doctrine proponed, I cannot but hold it to be the very truth of God, and the contrary to be deceivable doctrine. And therefore, so far as in me lieth, I approve the one and damn the other: And do further ask of God that not only I, but also my posterity, may enjoy the comfort of the doctrine that this day our ears have heard.'

John Knox, *History of the Reformation*, I, 338–9.

BIBLIOGRAPHY

A host of Government publications makes available extensive sources pertaining to the rules of Henry VIII, Edward IV, Mary, and Elizabeth. The following are to be noted: *Letters and Papers, Foreign and Domestic, of the Reign of Henry VIII* (London, 1856ff.), 20 vols. (London, 1862–1910); *Calendar of State Papers* [papers preserved in Rome, 1 vol.; in Spain, 15 vols.; in Venice, 22 vols.; in Ireland, 10 vols.; foreign papers of Edward VI, 1 vol.; of Mary Tudor, 1 vol.; of Elizabeth I, 19 vols.].

A concise collection of sources is by Henry Gee and William J. Hardy, *Documents Illustrative of English Church History* (London, 1896). There is also Henry Ellis, *Original Letters Illustrative of English History*, three series (London, 1825–1846). Among the outstanding sixteenth-century chroniclers of events was John Foxe, whose *Actes and Monuments* (London, 1563) is better known as *Book of Martyrs*. An edition of Foxe was published at London in 1870; a recent and positive assessment of Foxe comes from J. F. Mozley, *John Foxe and His Book of Martyrs* (London, 1940), who stresses the accuracy of Foxe. Also to be noted is John G. Nichols, ed., *Narrative of the Days of the Reformation* (Westminster, 1859). Then there is John Knox, *History of the Reformation in Scotland* (Glasgow (?), 1586/87). The older volume of R. Keith, *The History of the Affairs of Church and State of Scotland*, 3 vols. (Edinburgh, 1884ff.), is useful for its inclusion of many documents. See also Edmund Goldsmid, *Collection of Documents Illustrative of the Reigns of the Tudor and Stuart Sovereigns* (Edinburgh, 1886); C. R. N. Routh, *They Saw It Happen. An Anthology of Eye-Witness Accounts of Events in British History 1485–1688* (Oxford, 1957). Economic documents were published by R. H. Tawney and E. Powers, *Tudor Economic Documents*, 3 vols. (London, 1951). There is an excellent bibliographical introduction, Conyers Read, *Bibliography of British History, Tudor Period*, 2nd ed. (Oxford, 1959).

See also G. R. Elton, *The Tudor Constitution* (Cambridge, 1960) for a valuable collection of documents; G. R. Elton, *England Under the Tudors* (London, 1956).

The most comprehensive treatment of the English Reformation is by Philip Hughes, *The Reformation in England*, 3 vols. (London, 1950–4). Brief, but characteristically incisive are T. M. Parker, *The English Reformation* (Oxford,

1950) and E. Gordon Rupp, *Studies in the Making of the English Protestant Tradition Mainly in the Reign of Henry VIII* (Cambridge, 1947). See also E. Cardwell, *Documentary Annals of the Reformed Church of England, 1546–1716* (Oxford, 1839), and G. Burnet, *The History of the Reformation of the Church of England*, ed. N. Pocock (Oxford, 1865).

On Scotland, see Gordon Donaldson, *The Scottish Reformation* (Cambridge, 1960), a work limiting its scope to the development and operation of ecclesiastical institutions; on John Knox, Geddes McGregor, *The Thundering Scot: A Portrait of John Knox* (Philadelphia, 1952), and Elizabeth Whitley, *Plain Mr Knox* (London, 1960). See also M. B. MacGregor, *The Sources and Literature of Scottish Church History* (Glasgow, 1934), and Ian B. Cowan, *Blast and Counterblast. Contemporary Writings on the Scottish Reformation* (Edinburgh, 1960).

NOTES AND REFERENCES

1. John Colet (1467?–1519), English humanist and theologian, 1504 Dean of St Paul's in London. See J. H. Lupton, *A Life of John Colet, D.D.* (Hamden, Conn., 1961), a work first published in 1887 from which our selection is taken. A more recent study is E. W. Hunt, *Dean Colet and his Theology* (London, 1956).

2. On Simon Fish, 'of Gray's Inn, Gentleman', see the introduction to the edition used here: *Simon Fish, A Supplication for the Beggars* (London, 1878).

3. The edition used here is found in *The Thought and Culture of the English Renaissance: An Anthology of Tudor Prose 1481–1555*, ed. Elizabeth M. Nugent (Cambridge, 1956).

4. An older biography, with many documents, is by J. S. Brewer, *The Reign of Henry VIII*, 2 vols. (London, 1884). See also A. F. Pollard, *Henry VIII* (London, 1905).

A recent study of Henry VIII and his role in the Reformation (which is adequate on the humanist reformers, but not on Luther) is H. M. Smith, *Henry VIII and the Reformation* (London and New York, 1948). Henry's divorce is discussed by Hans Thieme, *Die Ehescheidung Heinrichs VIII. und die europäischen Universitäten* (Karlsruhe, 1957). The Catholic documents pertaining to Henry's divorce were published by St Ehses, *Römische Dokumente zur Geschichte der Ehescheidung Heinrichs VIII von England. 1527–34* (Paderborn, 1893). See also the telling, though at times gossipy, sources in J. A. Froude, *The Divorce of Catherine of Aragon, as told by the Imperial Ambassador* (London, 1891).

5. The translation used here is from Erwin Doernberg, *Henry VIII and Luther. An Account of Their Personal Relations* (London and Stanford, 1961), pp. 27–28.

6. The edition used here is found in *The Thought and Culture of the English Renaissance. An Anthology of Tudor Prose 1481–1555*, ed. Elizabeth M. Nugent (Cambridge, 1956).

7. On Anne Boleyn, see Philip W. Sergeant, *The Life of Anne Boleyn* (New York, 1924).

8. Thomas Cranmer (1489–1556), fellow of Jesus College at Cambridge, from 1533 Archbishop of Canterbury, suffered martyrdom under Mary Tudor.

See Francis E. Hutchinson, *Cranmer and the English Reformation* (New York, 1951); Theodore Maynard, *The Life of Thomas Cranmer* (Chicago, 1956); G. W. Bromiley, *Thomas Cranmer Theologian* (New York, 1956) and Jasper Ridley, *Thomas Cranmer* (Oxford, 1962).

9. The translation used here is from Erwin Doernberg, *op. cit.*, pp. 86-90.

10. This, and all other quotations from Henry Gee and William J. Hardy, *Documents Illustrative of English Church History* (London, 1896), are used with permission of Macmillan & Co.

11. *Annals of the Emperor Charles V*, by Francisco Lopez de Gomara (Oxford, 1912).

12. Hugh Latimer, *Sermons* (Cambridge, 1844).

13. 'Bishop Hooper's Visitation of Gloucester', *English Historical Review*, 19 (1904), 101ff.

14. As found in John Strype, *Memorials of the Most Reverend Father in God, Thomas Cranmer* (Oxford, 1840), I, 91. See also M. D. Knowles, *The Religious Orders in England*, vol. 3 (Cambridge, 1959).

15. There are two major studies on the dissolution of the monasteries, F. A. Gasquet, *Henry VIII and the English Monasteries* (London, 1895), and G. Baskerville, *English Monks and the Suppression of the Monasteries* (London, 1940). The study by J. A. Youings, 'The Terms of the Disposal of the Devon Monastic Lands', *English Historical Review* 69 (1954), rejects the customary view of a waste of the property by the Crown.

16. Thomas Becket (1118-70), aggressive and ambitious cleric and statesman under King Henry II, became Chancellor in 1154, Archbishop of Canterbury in 1163. Subsequently opposed the King, spent six years in exile and was, upon his return to England, murdered in the cathedral of Canterbury. Canonized in 1173. See David Knowles, *Archbishop Thomas Becket, A Character Study* (London, 1952).

17. Thomas Wright, *Three Chapters of Letters Relating to the Suppression of Monasteries* (London, 1843).

18. E. Hall, *Chronicle: or The Union of the Two Noble and Illustre Families of Lancaster and York* (London, 1809). See also James H. Robinson, *Readings in European History*, I, 143-4.

19. On Mary Tudor, see H. F. M. Prescott, *Mary Tudor* (London, 1952). A broader study, which ably relates to the Elizabethan religious scene, is C. H. Garret, *The Marian Exiles. A Study in the Origins of Elizabethan Puritanism* (Cambridge, 1938).

20. As quoted in John Strype, *Memorials of the Most Reverend*, etc., II, 384ff.

21. On Elizabeth, see J. E. Neale, *Queen Elizabeth* (London, 1934); A. L. Rowse, *The England of Elizabeth I: The Structure of Society* (London, 1950); E. T. Davies, *Episcopacy and the Royal Supremacy in the Church of England in the XVIth Century* (Oxford, 1950). On the Parliamentary background of the Elizabethan Settlement see J. E. Neale, *Elizabeth I and Her Parliaments* (London, 1953). For the settlement see Carl S. Meyer, *Elizabeth I and the Religious Settlement of 1559* (St Louis, 1960).

22. As quoted in *They Saw It Happen*, pp. 63-65. Used with permission of Blackwell and Mott.

The Political and Organizational Consolidation of the Reformation in Germany

AFTER his abdication Emperor Charles V is reported to have observed that the greatest blunder of his rule was to have honoured the pledge of safe-conduct for Martin Luther's appearance before the Diet at Worms. Such insight of hindsight is intriguing, though somewhat questionable, as it simplifies greatly the course of Reformation events after May 1521. In a sense, the removal of Luther's overpowering personality might possibly have thwarted the aggressive expansion of reformatory ideas. On the other hand, the observer must note that from 1521 onward the efforts at religious reform become more and more part of political and diplomatic manoeuvres which made the contributions of the theologians seem altogether dispensable.

Indeed, following the Diet of Worms there was widespread belief that Martin Luther was dead—he was so removed from the scene. Only a few people knew that Luther had been taken, at the instigation of Elector Frederick, to the Wartburg, a castle in Saxon territory. Here he was to spend ten eventful months. Sporting a new beard and a new name, Luther lived in secret seclusion, greatly beset by uncertainty regarding his own future and his prophetic vocation. At Worms the full impact of his stand against what seemed to be 1,500 years of Christian history had become obvious to him. This weighed heavily upon him. His prolific creativeness during his stay on the Wartburg is therefore all the more noteworthy. A host of letters, tracts and sermons, some of which belong to his most beautiful works, issued from his pen. They are overshadowed, however, by his work on a German translation of the New Testament for which he used Erasmus's recently published Greek text as a basis. When this translation appeared in 1522 as the *September Bible* it was a sensation. There had been other German translations before, but in power of expression and beauty of style Luther's surpassed them all. There were countless editions and reprints which gave the common people the chance to read and decide for themselves.

Wittenberg, during Luther's stay on the Wartburg, was a pilotless

ship. Tragically enough, the leader of the Reformation was removed at precisely the time when theological theory demanded to be translated into ecclesiastical practice. The implications of Luther's various pronouncements had been, beyond doubt, far-reaching enough—the postulate of the priesthood of all believers, the repudiation of several sacraments and of the mass, all had definite bearing on ecclesiastical practice. A thousand practical questions arose and demanded answers.

None of Luther's colleagues at Wittenberg was prepared and equipped to assume the role of leadership. There was young Philipp Melanchthon: born in 1497, he enrolled at the University of Heidelberg at the age of twelve and wrote a Greek grammar at the age of twenty-one. He joined the Wittenberg faculty in 1518, delivering an ambitious but profound inaugural address *On the Reform of Academic Studies*. He taught Greek to Luther and published the first systematic exposition of the new theology— the *Loci Communes*. Though a brilliant mind, Melanchthon was too young and too academic to fill Luther's place. It was Andreas Carlstadt who exuberantly carried the programme of reform forward and emerged as leader. In December 1521, Carlstadt announced his engagement to a young girl as well as his intention to observe communion in simple fashion under both kinds after Christmas. He performed the ceremony in ordinary street clothes and let the people themselves hold the cup. Not everybody at Wittenberg favoured such drastic changes and early in 1522 the tensions in the city mounted. Wittenberg became a hotbed for would-be reformers; iconoclasms occurred and in the end it appeared that only Luther himself could restore direction.

Luther, well informed of these developments, returned in March and began at once to preach a series of sermons in which he delineated his principles for the reform of the Church. The radicals, so he asserted, had become unduly impatient in their concern for reform. They had done the right things at the wrong time. Inward change had first to take place and would then, at the proper time, result in external change. To change externals before the inner man had been changed was a gross error. The subsequent course of the Wittenberg reformation followed Luther's programmatic pronouncement. It was conservative and some of the reforms were long in coming. This is not to say that there were no external reforms. In 1523 Luther published a hymn book to provide for more extensive congregational participation in worship. In the same year he wrote a German 'church order' so that the congregation could understand the meaning of the service. Three years later there followed another. Gradually, a new Church, stripped of what was considered Catholic abuse, was emerging.

Luther himself was not unwilling to face the practical consequences of his theology; in June 1525 he married. His bride, Catherine von Bora, was a former nun whom he had attempted, albeit unsuccessfully, to marry to someone else. Though Luther's marriage gave his enemies an opportunity to revile him as a heretical monk who had married an apostate nun—Erasmus scoffed that what had begun as tragedy was now ending as comedy—it marked one of Luther's greatest contributions to Protestant Christendom: the Protestant parish.

Luther had married at a time of pronounced social and political unrest. The peasants, long discontent with their diminishing role in society, had proceeded to outright insurrection in 1524-5. The connection between the Peasants' Rebellion and the religious revolution was more than accidental. Though the grievances of the peasants antedate the outbreak of the Reformation, there can be little doubt that the slogans of the Reformation provided for many peasants convenient theological support for their social and economic programme. The famous *Twelve Articles* of the peasants clothed the demand for free use of woods, water and pasture and the refusal to accept new taxes and obligations in the language of the Reformation and the Bible. After all, it had been asserted that all Christians were priests, able to decide matters of the Christian faith. Did it not follow, then, that Christians could also order their political affairs according to their own understanding? Could they not simply apply the Bible, as they understood it, to social and economic problems? Early in 1525 the first instances of violence occurred among the discontented peasants. Monasteries were burned, castles destroyed, clergy and nobility tortured and defamed. But force resulted only in counterforce. The rulers were little willing to tolerate insurrection and resorted to arms. The unorganized bands of peasants were no match for the rulers' well-trained armies. Without serious effort the various uprisings were crushed and the peasants ruthlessly punished.

Luther was intimately involved in all this. For one, the Protestant tenor of the peasants' demands implicated him and he was prevailed upon to speak on the issue. His *Admonition to Peace Concerning the Twelve Articles* of April 1525 marked an even more direct involvement. The peasants were addressed as 'my dear brethren' and vehement words were reserved for the lords. At the same time Luther vigorously denounced the confusion of the Gospel and human demands in the articles of the peasants. The Christian must suffer injustice rather than use the Gospel for worldly demands. Luther's peaceful admonitions had no results—at least not those Luther had hoped for. The peasants were too concerned about their grievances, and furthermore read in Luther's treatise only what they wanted to read: namely, the harsh words against the lords. When the peasants became openly violent, Luther took to the pen again and wrote his tract *Against the Murderous and Plundering Hordes of the Peasants.* It was a restatement of his earlier position, but now couched in more vehement words against the peasants, who had, after all, disregarded his admonition. And so Luther exhorted the rulers to stab, slay, and kill the peasants wherever they were to be found.

This, of course, the rulers were already doing. Afterwards the common man remembered Luther's words and felt that he had been betrayed. Disappointed, he began to seek his religious pastures elsewhere. Though the Lutheran Reformation continued to achieve new gains in the years to come and continued to be an aggressive movement, the wave of popular enthusiasm began to disappear. But if the common people drifted away from Luther, he in turn drifted away from them. The Reformer lost his confidence in the common people and went forth to build the new Church with the help of the territorial rulers.

The subsequent history of the Reformation is characterized therefore by an increasing political involvement of the cause and course of religious reform. This is not to say that there were no theological or ecclesiastical issues in the years after 1521. But it is evident that the consolidation of Protestantism was as much the result of political manoeuvring as it was of theological controversy.

The year following the Diet of Worms had brought, on account of Emperor Charles's immediate preoccupation with a war against France, as well as the intensive popular enthusiasm for Luther, no determined enforcement of the Edict of Worms. When Charles victoriously concluded the first armed conflict against France it became possible for him to devote his attention to the burning German religious question. He announced a diet to be held at Speyer in 1526 to settle the problem. When the diet convened, however, foreign considerations preoccupied the Emperor once more. Harsh peace terms had prompted France to enter into an alliance with the Pope and with several states, thereby constituting a severe threat against Charles. With the determined Emperor absent, the middle course favoured by most of the territorial rulers in matters of ecclesiastical disagreement won the day. Until the time of a general council the territories were to deal with the edict issued at the Diet of Worms as they thought justifiable before God and the Emperor.

The territorial rulers with Lutheran inclinations felt this pronouncement was the justification for going ahead with what they deemed to be urgently needed reform. The ecclesiastical differences between the various territories were thereby formalized; the religious division of Germany began to be an established fact.

Three years later, in 1529, a diet, again meeting at Speyer, tackled the religious problem anew. This time the majority demanded the implementation of the Edict of Worms. The Lutheran territories protested. The pronouncement of 1526 could not, they asserted, be revoked by simple majority, since it had then been passed unanimously. It was incidentally this protest which gave a name to Luther's supporters— Protestants. The majority of the diet none the less agreed on the implementation of the Edict of Worms.

Emperor Charles had been absent from the diet, once again preoccupied with a war against France. No sooner had it been victoriously concluded than he summoned a diet for the following year to meet at Augsburg to 'consider everyone's opinion'.

Apart from settling the religious differences at the diet, Charles also hoped to receive financial aid from the territories for a war against the Turks, who stood outside Vienna, threatening to overrun central Europe. The Emperor's problem was that he was equally eager to crush the Turks and the Protestants, but that he needed the support of the latter against the former. The Lutheran territories wisely demanded that the religious differences should be discussed first. For this purpose, they submitted a confession of faith, the so-called *Augsburg Confession*. Written by Melanchthon, it was conciliatory in tone and more concerned about showing the agreement of the Lutherans' Protestantism with the early tradition of the Church than about accentuating the differences with Catholicism. The Emperor called for a Catholic repudiation, the *Confutation*. After it had been presented to the diet early in August, Charles declared that the Lutheran confession had been refuted. Understandably, the Protestants did not concur. They drew up a response, the *Apology*, but as far as the Emperor was concerned, the matter was closed. He gave the Protestants until the following April to return to the 'faith of the Pope, the Emperor, all the princes, and the whole Christian world'.

April came and went. Charles was unable to enforce his decree, for in the meantime the Lutheran territories had formed the League of Schmalkald and had thereby become a political power in the Empire. In 1532 the Turks renewed their attack upon Vienna, and the Emperor, in need of support from the German territories, agreed to the Peace of Nürnberg, which postponed a final decision in the disputed religious matters until a general council. Peace and concord should prevail until then. Afterwards Charles departed from Germany for almost a decade, soon to become involved in another armed conflict with France. Protestantism achieved remarkable gains during that decade, particularly in northern Germany. Everywhere an inner consolidation of the new Lutheran churches took place.

None the less the Lutheran territories suffered an incisive setback, foreshadowing worse things to come. In 1540 the political bulwark of Protestantism, Landgrave Philipp of Hesse, became involved in a public scandal in which the theological bulwark of Protestantism, Martin Luther, was more than an innocent bystander. The *cause célèbre* was Philipp's bigamy and the fact that Luther had counselled him into it. Philipp, like other crowned heads, was dynastically married to a woman he did not love, which did not prevent him, however, from having ten children by her. The woman he loved made marriage the prerequisite of other considerations. Divorce seemed out of the question, but not, surprisingly enough, bigamy. Martin Luther, approached in the matter, discovered that in the Old Testament polygamy evidently had been practised without divine disapproval and counselled Philipp into a second, albeit secret, marriage. Before long the secret was out—one might suggest that too many women were in on it! Luther counselled 'a good, strong lie for the good of the Christian Church' in order to clear the air, but Philipp now decided that lying was sin. He was furthermore concerned about losing the good grace of the Emperor. After all, he had broken the accepted moral and criminal code, for which the Emperor could hold him responsible. Charles assured him of his benevolence and Philipp agreed, in turn, to prevent the inclusion of European powers in the League of Schmalkald.

This episode weakened Protestantism morally and politically. Charles, on the other hand, found by the middle of the decade the political situation to be more convenient than ever. After another armed conflict—it was the fourth—France agreed in 1544 to offer support for crushing both the Turks and the Protestants. Charles concluded a truce with the former to deal with the latter. Since he was now determined to solve the Protestant problem at all costs, war became inevitable. It broke out in the summer of 1546, shortly after Luther's death.

Luther had not exactly grown old gracefully. The years after 1525 had seen him increasingly removed from the heart of the course of the Reformation in Germany. He busied himself with his professorial duties at Wittenberg, answered practical questions on the organizational consolidation of the Lutheran churches, had bouts with his kidney stones, and issued innumerable pamphlets from his pen which, towards the end of his life, became more vehement and bitter. One must not psychologize too much at this point, but there can be no question that the awareness of having been primarily responsible for the schism of the Church lay heavily upon him. Death came to him in February 1546 at his birthplace, where he had returned on an errand of Christian love to mediate in a long-standing family feud between the counts of Mansfeld. When war broke out between the Emperor and the League of Schmalkald, the latter was inadequately prepared and could offer no resistance. Wittenberg was occupied, Duke John Frederick of Saxony and Landgrave Philipp of Hesse were taken prisoner. The peace concluded in 1547 meant political catastrophe for German Protestantism. Charles was at the height of his power in Germany. But then it became evident that by crushing the Protestant princes he wanted to destroy not only Protestantism, but also the princes; not only Catholicism was to be firmly established in Germany, but also Emperor Charles himself. In both, he failed. For one, the religious question could hardly be settled without the Pope and certainly not against him. Pope Paul III had convened, late in 1545, a council at Trent. The attitude prevailing there was to refine the Catholic position rather than to conciliate the Protestants, as was Charles's intention. Furthermore, when Charles's political intentions could be clearly discerned, he quickly lost the support of some of the territorial rulers. The formal outcome of the war and the Emperor's efforts was the *Augsburg Interim* of 1548, which was to be a first step toward the re-Catholicization of Protestant territories. The details of this *Interim* were Catholic—though the communion cup was temporarily granted to the Protestants and married priests were permitted to remain married. However, the document remained a mere scrap of paper. This fact was indicative of the depth and the extent of Protestant sentiment at that time. Popular Protestant reaction was extensive, vigorous, and irrepressible.

Without the necessary ecclesiastical and political support, and endangered by a Turkish threat (indeed a somewhat stereotyped aspect of Reformation history), Charles agreed in 1552 to the *Peace of Passau*. It provided for a temporary truce in religious matters until the next diet. Three years later this diet convened at Augsburg. It promulgated the *Peace of Augsburg* and sealed thereby the religious division of Germany into two factions. The territorial rulers were given the right to determine the religious orientation of their territories, though only Catholicism and Lutheranism were legitimate options. It was the individual territorial ruler, therefore, who occupied the crucial role in the subsequent ecclesiastical developments in Germany and it was the individual territory in which these developments took place.

The *Peace of Augsburg* concluded the Reformation era in Germany. Its various provisions entailed many unresolved tensions. None the less, it provided a settlement of religious affairs in Germany without the bloodshed and civil strife which occurred elsewhere in Europe.

► Luther's sudden disappearance following the Diet of Worms caused, among his many enthusiastic supporters, alarm and dismay. The tenseness of the situation, when nobody knew what had happened, is well described by a report sent to the Pope from Germany by the Papal Nuncio Aleander.[1]

Last Sunday the news arrived here that Martin had been arrested, and it was widely rumoured that we were the instigators of this deed. We found ourselves in greatest danger, for the supporters of Luther incited the people by pointing out how Luther was a man filled with the Holy Spirit and how we had broken the safe-conduct. For more than one reason we were forced to conclude that the Elector of Saxony was involved in this. The Emperor, all the territorial rulers, and virtually the entire court agreed with our view so emphatically that the Elector had to make a statement before the Diet that he knew nothing about this matter and could swear any oath. He seemed to be considerably dismayed. However, one can trust neither his glance, which is always directed down to the ground, nor his words—especially not when it comes to the Lutheran question. This rumour persisted for two days, and one messenger after another reported in identical fashion that Luther had dismissed the herald a four days' journey from here properly signing the release from his safe-conduct. This is a fact. Then he continued on to the town of Eisenach, which is situated about an eight to ten days' journey from here. There he preached on the Day of the Discovery of the Cross contrary to the explicit order of the Emperor. Leaving the doctors behind, he proceeded alone in a carriage with his monastic brother and his uncle, who wanted to be close to him. He intended to visit a friend living nearby. Thus he was apprehended along the way, but his company released.

Such was my news of Sunday. The informants claimed that they themselves had been in Eisenach and had heard Luther's uncle bemoan the happening. They were unanimous in their statements regarding place and time, regarding the five armed men who apprehended him and all the other described circumstances. And now some blame us to be the instigators of this attack, others point to the Archbishop of Mainz. Would to God that the latter had been so decisive! . . .

But many believe that it was a secret undertaking of the Elector of Saxony, who wanted to get him into safety before the expiration of the safe-conduct. He likewise wanted to have an excuse that others apprehended him, no matter whether he himself would retain or release him in the future. Later on someone reported to the Emperor—as I learned from his confessor—that he knew Martin's present location. A Frankonian

knight, Hektor Behem, who several months ago had been involved in a
quarrel with the Elector, had apprehended Luther out of spite and was
retaining him now. If it only were so! After all, Luther had broken his
safe-conduct already by his preaching! None the less the entire court was
furious against us and threatened that, if such had really happened, the
people would strangle first us and then all the priests in Germany.

Luther at the Wartburg as 'Junker
Jörg' with beard and dagger. (*Woodcut
by Sebald Beham. Geisberg*, 302)

But the greatest misfortune was yet to come. All of a sudden the news
arrived yesterday that Luther had been found dead in a silver mine,
pierced with a sword. This caused a tremendous uproar here, directed
especially against me. At the court even outside the Emperor's quarters
many influential persons approached me and gave me warning that I
would not be safe even in the arms of the Emperor. Later more persons
visited me in my lodging to inform me about the numerous pacts and
conspiracies concluded to murder me. Signor Carraciolo received similar
word. I will refrain from mentioning all the pranks which were played on
us. All this notwithstanding, we have continued to fulfil, individually and

collectively, our responsibilities. We will not let ourselves be hindered even by death, which is threatening a thousand times. The Lord's will be done! It is his cause we defend.

Depeschen des Nuntius Aleander, pp. 192–5; 196–7.

▶ When the painter Albrecht Dürer heard of Luther's mysterious disappearance he recorded his reaction in his diary.[2]

On Friday before Whitsunday, 1521, the news reached me at Antwerp that Martin Luther had been treacherously taken prisoner. He had been given a herald of Emperor Charles for safe-conduct. But no sooner had the herald taken him to an unfriendly place near Eisenach than he announced that he could go no further and rode away. Soon ten horsemen appeared who treacherously took away the pious man, who was inspired by the Holy Spirit, a disciple of Christ and of the Christian faith. I do not know if he is still living or if they have murdered him. He suffered for the sake of Christian truth and because he rebuked the unchristian papacy . . . which strives to deprive us of the work of our blood and sweat which is then shamefully consumed by idlers. The poor and sick people must die of starvation. . . .

Oh, God in heaven, have mercy upon us! Oh, Lord Jesus Christ, pray for thy people, deliver us in thy appointed time, keep us in the true Christian faith. . . . If we lose this man—who has written more clearly than anyone else in 140 years, to whom thou hast given a true evangelical spirit—we pray thee, our heavenly Father, to give thy Holy Spirit to another who will gather thy holy Christian Church so that we may all be found in pure Christian manner. . . . Anyone reading Dr Martin Luther's books will see how his teaching so clearly proclaims the holy Gospel. They are, therefore, to be greatly honoured and not to be burned—unless his opponents, who always drive against truth, be also thrown into the fire with their opinions, which want to make gods out of men. Afterwards Luther's books should be printed anew. Oh God, if Luther is dead, who is going to proclaim the holy Gospel so clearly to us? Oh God, what could he have written in ten or twenty years? Oh, pious Christians, help me eagerly bewail this God-inspired man and pray that God may send us another.

Ernst Heidrich, *Albrecht Dürers schriftlicher Nachlass*, pp. 95–96.

▶ From the Wartburg, Luther actively participated in the ongoing course of events. This is well illustrated by a vehement letter he wrote to the Archbishop of Mainz, Albert of Hohenzollern.

You doubtlessly remember vividly and well that I wrote you twice in

Latin. The first letter came at the beginning of the deceitful indulgence which was propagated under your name. In it I faithfully warned you and, out of Christian love, set myself against those licentious, enticing, and greedy preachers and their heretical and idolatrous books. . . .

Anti-catholic cartoon showing a cardinal or a fool according to which head is uppermost. (*Woodcut by an unknown master. Staatliche Graphische Sammlung, Munich*)

Such faithful admonition brought me only derision and ingratitude instead of gratitude. When I wrote a second time, humbly asking to be instructed, I received a harsh, improper, unepiscopal and unchristian answer, and the matter of my instruction was passed on to higher authorities. In spite of the fact that these two letters did not help any, I am not giving up and am now sending you, according to the Gospel (Matt. 18.17) a third warning, this time in German. Perhaps such a superfluous and unnecessary warning and supplication will help—even though it is not my responsibility.

You have again put up at Halle that idol which robs the poor simple Christians of their money and souls. Thereby you have freely and publicly

Anti-catholic cartoon depicting the covetousness of the monks. By folding the top part the two lower versions become visible—on the left the wolf devouring the lamb, on the right devouring the widow's house. (*Stadt- und Universitäts-bibliothek, Bern*)

proven that Tetzel's unseemly and shameful deeds were not his alone, but also those of the Bishop of Mainz, who, though I spared him then, now wants to assume some responsibility himself. Perhaps you think that I am no longer to be reckoned with and you want to be safe from me and have this monk taken care of by imperial authority. This may be, but you should know that I will do what Christian teaching demands of me, notwithstanding the gates of hell, much less the popes, cardinals, the bishops and the ignorant. I will not stand it and will not remain silent when the Bishop of Mainz pretends that he need not instruct the poor people who wish to be instructed, or who pretends that it is improper to do so. At the same time he does well know what is going on and boldly continues activities which bring him financial gain. I will not be fooled in this. One must speak of such matters and listen.

I therefore humbly beseech you to leave the poor people undeceived and unrobbed and to show yourself as bishop and not as wolf. . . .

Remember the beginning! What a frightful fire has the little despised spark become, from which all the world thought itself so secure. Everyone thought that this single poor beggar was far too weak for the Pope and had dared the impossible. Despite this God has pronounced his judgment. . . .

This God is still living. Let no one doubt this. And he knows how to withstand a Cardinal of Mainz, even if four emperors would support him. . . .

You must not think that Luther is dead. Freely and gladly he trusts in the God who humbled the Pope. He will begin a little game with the Cardinal of Mainz for which not many are prepared. Rally together, dear bishops. You may continue to be worldly rulers, but you will not silence or deaden this spirit. Should this become an amusement for you for which you are not prepared, this will be my warning to you.

Therefore I announce to you definitely with this letter: If the idol is not taken down, I shall be necessarily, urgently and inescapably forced on account of divine teaching and Christian salvation to attack you publicly as I did the Pope in order to protest against your activity. The Bishop of Mainz will be made responsible for all of Tetzel's earlier abominations. All the world will be shown the difference between a bishop and a wolf. . . .

Secondly I beg you to restrain yourself and to leave in peace those priests who, in order to avoid unchastity, have entered the marital estate or who are about to do so. Do not deprive them of what God has given them. You have no ground, source or authority to do such a thing, and arbitrary wickedness does not become a bishop.

What does it help you bishops to use force boldly, only to embitter hearts against you, and yet you are unable to present the ground and rightness of your action. What do you think, anyhow? Have you become giants and Nimrods of Babel? Do you not know, you poor people, that wickedness and tyranny, when no longer supported by the appearance of right, cannot claim the prayer of the congregation and cannot exist long? You are foolishly falling into your own misfortune, which will come to you sooner than you expect.

You may be assured: If this matter is not taken care of, a great clamour will arise from the Gospel. People will say that it would become the bishops first to cast the beam out of their own eyes, and that it would be better if the bishops would first put away their mistresses before they separate pious wives from their husbands. I pray that you make it possible, for your own sake, that I remain silent.

1st December 1521. *WA, Br.* 2, 406–7.

▶ Luther's stay at the Wartburg brought, above all, the German translation of the New Testament. This was a contribution whose historical significance has been both literary and theological.[3] The translation included a general introduction to the New Testament as well as comments on the various books. Part of the introduction is printed below. When a translation of the entire Bible appeared in 1541, important sections of the original introduction (which are here put in brackets) were omitted.

[It would be right and proper for this book to go forth without any prefaces or extraneous names attached and simply have its own say under its own name. However, many unfounded interpretations and prefaces have scattered the thought of Christians to a point where no one any longer knows what is Gospel or law, New Testament or Old. Necessity demands, therefore, that there should be a notice or preface, by which the ordinary man can be rescued from his former delusions, set on the right track, and taught what he is to look for in this book, so that he may not seek laws and commandments where he ought to be seeking the Gospel and promises of God. . . .]

'Gospel' is a Greek word and means in Greek a good message, good tidings, good news, a good report, which one sings and tells with gladness. For example, when David overcame the great Goliath, there came among the Jewish people the good report and encouraging news that their terrible enemy had been struck down and that they had been rescued and given joy and peace; and they sang and danced and were glad for it [I Sam. 18.6].

Thus this Gospel of God or New Testament is a good story and report, sounded forth into all the world by the apostles, telling of a true David who strove with sin, death and the devil, and overcame them, and thereby rescued all those who were captive in sin, afflicted with death and overpowered by the devil. Without any merit of their own he made them righteous, gave them life and saved them, so that they were given peace and brought back to God. For this they sing, and thank and praise God, and are glad for ever, if only they believe firmly and remain steadfast in faith. . . .

[Which are the true and noblest books of the New Testament?]

[From all this you can now judge all the books and decide among them which are the best. John's Gospel and St Paul's epistles, especially that to the Romans, and St Peter's first epistle are the true kernel and marrow of all the books. They ought properly to be the foremost books, and it would be advisable for every Christian to read them first and most, and by daily reading to make them as much his own as his daily bread. For in them you do not find many works and miracles of Christ described, but you do find depicted in masterly fashion how faith in Christ overcomes sin, death and hell, and gives life, righteousness and salvation. This is the real nature of the Gospel, as you have heard. . . .

John's Gospel is the one, fine, true and chief Gospel, and is far, far to be preferred over the other three and placed high above them. So, too, the epistles of St Paul and St Peter far surpass the other three Gospels, Matthew, Mark and Luke.

In a word, St John's Gospel and his first epistle, St Paul's epistles, especially Romans, Galatians and Ephesians, and St Peter's first epistle are the books that show you Christ and teach you all that is necessary and salvatory for you to know, even if you were never to see or hear any other book or doctrine. Therefore St James's epistle is really an epistle of straw, compared to these others, for it has nothing of the nature of the Gospel about it. But more of this in the other prefaces.]

Luther's Works 35, 357–62 (*WA, DB* 6, 2–11).

> ▶ **The widespread praise for Luther's translation was countered by severe criticism on the part of opponents. Here Luther's Catholic foe Cochläus comments:[4]**

Who can sufficiently point out what welcome opportunity and tinder for division, distress and apostasy Luther's translation of the New Testament has been? For in it this disgraceful fellow has deliberately perverted, omitted from and added to the ancient authentic text of the Church. He

The seven-headed beast, the papacy. On the cross
with the crown of thorns, the sponge, the whip, but
not Christ, only the sign 'for money a sack full of
indulgence'. Below, the inscription: 'the kingdom of
Satan'. An allusion to the Book of Revelation.
(*Unknown master. Geisberg*, 1575)

has forced different meanings and added many annoying glosses in the
margin. He omitted no piece of villainy, particularly in the prefaces, in
order to draw the reader to his side. No wonder then that some Germans
mentioned and listed over a thousand errors and changes in this translation. Hieronymus Emser accordingly published a special pamphlet in
which he not only—more industriously than anyone else—collected all
the erroneous glosses, perversions and falsifications in Luther's translation, but also made available at the same time as acceptable medicine
against Luther's poison a version of his own which agrees with the
accepted and established Latin text of the Church. This was to the special
comfort of Catholics who with the help of this pamphlet could see and
understand Luther's dangerous errors and counter the evangelical
glorying and boasting of the eloquent Lutheran fools.

Septiceps Lutherus, ybiq3 sibi, suis
scriptis, cõtrari⁹, in Visitationẽ Saxonicã, p D.D.Ioã.Cocleũ, ẽditus

Luther as a seven-headed, self-contradicting
monster. The allusion is, once again, to the Book of
Revelation, only now used by a Catholic. (*Woodcut
from the title-page of Johannes Cochlaeus,* Lutherus
Septiceps, *Leipzig,* 1529. *Lutherhalle, Wittenberg*)

But before Emser's work saw the light of day Luther's New Testament
had been so propagated and widely spread by the book printers that even
tailors and shoemakers, indeed women and other simple idiots, who had
accepted this new Lutheran gospel—though they could read only a little
German—read it eagerly as if it were a fountain of all truth. Some carried
it in their bosoms and learned it by heart. Thus they claimed within a
few months such skill and experience that without timidity they debated
not only with Catholic laymen, but also with priests and monks, indeed
with masters and doctors of Sacred Scripture concerning faith and the
Gospel. What is more, there were some despicable women who published

German books and propositions proudly rejecting the supposed ignorance of men, thereby engaging in debate not only with laymen and other private persons, but also with licentiates, doctors and entire universities. This is illustrated by Argula von Staufen, a lady of nobility. These Lutheran women, lacking all female modesty, arrogantly usurped the office of preaching and judging in the church, something expressly condemned by Paul. They did not lack Lutheran supporters who claimed that Paul had prohibited the preaching of women only if no capable men for teaching and instruction were present. Were this not the case or were men too inept, women should assume this responsibility. In this vein Luther had been teaching for some time that wives of Christians were priests and indeed that everyone who had received baptism had been consecrated as popes, bishops and priests. . . .

Since the fickle common people always tend to push the new to extremes rather than to retain traditional customs, it happened that the Lutheran crowd studied the translated Scriptures in an external fashion more industriously than the Catholics. Among the latter the laymen made this a responsibility of priests and monks. Thus Lutheran laymen were likely, in meetings and conversations, to quote without hesitation more Scripture than Catholic monks and priests.

Johann Cochläus, *Historia Lutheri*, pp. 120–3.

✓ ▶ The year 1525 brought, at several places in Germany, uprisings of the peasants.[5] The programmatic statement of the goals of the peasants was pronounced in the 'Twelve Articles' of March 1525. Here the influence of Luther's message upon the long-standing economic grievances of the peasants is clearly evident.

To the Christian Reader Peace and the Grace of God through Christ.

There are many Antichrists who on account of the assembling of the peasants, cast scorn upon the Gospel, and say: Is this the fruit of the new teaching, that no one obeys but all everywhere rise in revolt, and band together to reform, extinguish, indeed kill the temporal and spiritual authorities? The following articles will answer these godless and blaspheming fault-finders. They will first of all remove the reproach from the Word of God and secondly give a Christian excuse for the disobedience or even the revolt of the entire peasantry. . . . Therefore, Christian reader, read the following articles with care, and then judge. Here follow the Articles:

The First Article.—First, it is our humble petition and desire, indeed our will and resolution, that in the future we shall have power and authority so that the entire community should choose and appoint a minister, and that we should have the right to depose him should he conduct himself improperly. The minister thus chosen should teach us the holy Gospel pure and simple, without any human addition, doctrine or ordinance. For to teach us continually the true faith will lead us to pray God that through his grace his faith may increase within us and be confirmed in us. For if his grace is not within us, we always remain flesh and blood, which avails nothing; since the Scripture clearly teaches that only through true faith can we come to God. Only through his mercy can we become holy. . . .

The Second Article.—Since the right tithe is established in the Old Testament and fulfilled in the New, we are ready and willing to pay the fair tithe of grain. None the less it should be done properly. The Word of God plainly provides that it should be given to God and passed on to his own. If it is to be given to a minister, we will in the future collect the tithe through our church elders, appointed by the congregation and distribute from it, to the sufficient livelihood of the minister and his family elected by the entire congregation, according to the judgment of the whole congregation. The remainder shall be given to the poor of the place, as the circumstances and the general opinion demand. . . .

The Third Article.—It has been the custom hitherto for men to hold us as their own property, which is pitiable enough considering that Christ has redeemed and purchased us without exception, by the shedding of his precious blood, the lowly as well as the great. Accordingly, it is consistent with Scripture that we should be free and we wish to be so. Not that we want to be absolutely free and under no authority. God does not teach us that we should lead a disorderly life according to the lusts of the flesh, but that we should live by the commandments, love the Lord our God and our neighbour. . . .

The Fourth Article.—In the fourth place it has been the custom heretofore that no poor man was allowed to catch venison or wild fowl, or fish in flowing water, which seems to us quite unseemly and unbrotherly, as well as selfish and not according to the Word of God. . . . Accordingly, it is our desire if a man holds possession of waters that he should prove from satisfactory documents that his right has been wittingly acquired by purchase. We do not wish to take it from him by force, but his rights should be exercised in a Christian and brotherly fashion. . . .

The Fifth Article.—In the fifth place we are aggrieved in the matter of wood-cutting, for our noble folk have appropriated all the woods to themselves alone. . . . It should be free to every member of the community to help himself to such firewood as he needs in his home. Also, if a man requires wood for carpenter's purposes he should have it free, but with the approval of a person appointed by the community for that purpose. . . .

The Sixth Article.—Our sixth complaint is in regard to the excessive services demanded of us, which increase from day to day. We ask that this matter be properly looked into, so that we shall not continue to be oppressed in this way, and that some gracious consideration be given us, since our forefathers served only according to the Word of God.

The Seventh Article.—Seventh, we will not hereafter allow ourselves to be farther oppressed by our lords. What the lords possess is to be held according to the agreement between the lord and the peasant. . . .

The Eighth Article.—In the eighth place, we are greatly burdened by holdings which cannot support the rent exacted from them. The peasants suffer loss in this way and are ruined. We ask that the lords may appoint persons of honour to inspect these holdings and fix a rent in accordance with justice, so that the peasant shall not work for nothing, since the labourer is worthy of his hire.

The Ninth Article.—In the ninth place, we are burdened with the great evil in the constant making of new laws. We are not judged according to the offence, but sometimes with great ill will, and sometimes much too leniently. In our opinion we should be judged according to the old written law, so that the case shall be decided according to its merits, and not with favours.

The Tenth Article.—In the tenth place we are aggrieved that certain individuals have appropriated meadows and fields which at one time belonged to the community. These we will take again into our own hands unless they were rightfully purchased.

The Eleventh Article.—In the eleventh place we will entirely abolish the custom called *Todfall* [heriot], and will no longer endure it, nor allow widows and orphans to be thus shamefully robbed against God's will. . . .

Conclusion.—In the twelfth place it is our conclusion and final resolution, that if any one or more of these articles should not be in agreement with the Word of God, which we do not think, we will willingly recede from such article when it is proved to be against the Word of God by a clear explanation of the Scripture. . . . For this we shall pray God, since he can grant all this and he alone. The peace of Christ abide with us all.

*Die zwölf Artikel der Bauern 1525. Kaiser, Reich und
Reformation 1517 bis 1525*, pp. 50–59.

✓ ▸   A contemporary chronicler reports on the Peasants' Revolt in
Rothenburg in South Germany.[5a]

. . . Through certain citizens here in Rothenburg who adhere to the
heresy of Luther and Carlstadt, it has come about that bad, false teaching
has greatly got the upper hand, owing also to the dissimulation and concessions of some of the town authorities. Dr Andreas Carlstadt has appeared in person, preached here, and asked to be received as a citizen.

On 21st March, a Tuesday, thirty or forty peasants got together in a
mob in Rothenburg, bought a kettledrum, and marched about the town,
a part going to Pretheim and a part toward Orenbach. They got together
again on Thursday and on Friday, as many as four hundred. . . .

March 24. This evening between five and six o'clock someone knocked
off the head of Christ's image on a crucifix and struck off the arms. . . .

March 26. Chrischainz, the baker, knocked the missal out of the priest's
hand in the chapel of Our Lady and drove away the priest from mass.
Today the peasants let themselves be seen in the field outside the Gal-
genthor.

The following Monday, while the priest was performing service in the
parish church and chanting '*Adjuva nos, deus salutaris noster*', Ernfried
Kumpf addressed him rudely, saying that if he wished to save himself he
would better leave the altar. Kumpf then knocked the missal on to the
floor and drove the scholars out of the choir. . . .

On Good Friday all services were suspended in the churches of
Rothenburg, for there was neither chanting nor preaching, except that
Dr Johann Teuschel preached against emperor, kings, princes and lords,
ecclesiastical and lay, with foul abuse and slander, on the ground that they
were hindering God's Word.

On Easter Day there was neither singing nor preaching. Monday, Dr
Andreas Carlstadt again attacked the holy sacrament with abusive words.
In the night some millers attacked the church at Cobenzell and threw the
pictures and images into the Tauber.

April 18. The reforms of the committee are proclaimed. The younger
priests may, and should, marry, and may enjoy their benefices for three
years. The old priests shall have theirs for life. There is a struggle between Kueplein and his followers, on the one hand, who want to destroy
a picture of the Virgin, and the pious old Christians, on the other, who
wish to protect it. Some knives are drawn.

April 19. The peasants take three casks of wine from the priest at
Scheckenpach and drink it up. . . .

On the same day [20th April], Thursday after Easter, the women run up and down Hafengasse with forks and sticks, declaring that they will plunder all the priests' houses, but are prevented. . . .

In Rothenburg the citizens are summoned to decide whether, like the neighbouring towns of Heilbronn, Dinkelsbühl, and Wimpfen, they will aid the peasants. The majority decide to send them guns and pikes, powder and lead.

May 12. The clergy forced to take arms like the rest. All monks are compelled to lay aside their cowls and the nuns their veils.

May 15. The bell summoned the community. In spite of the protests of the old Christians, they are forced to obey the majority, and Rothenburg that day fell away from the empire and joined the peasants. In the meantime a gallows was erected in the market place as a warning, according to their ideas of brotherhood. . . .

May 15. The peasants attack the castle of Würzburg and scale the walls, but are all killed. The peasants attempt to get possession of Rothenburg by conspiracy, but are ejected without bloodshed. . . .

On Friday after Corpus Christi, mass was once more chanted in Rothenburg, as formerly.

June 17. Vespers, compline and matins are once more sung. . . .

June 30. The citizens of Rothenburg are summoned to the market place by a herald and surrounded by pikemen. They are accused of deserting the empire and joining the peasants, and are threatened with the vengeance they deserve.

The names of a number of citizens are read off, and they are beheaded on the spot. Their bodies are left on the market place all day.

Quellen zur Geschichte des Bauernkrieges aus
Rothenburg ob der Tauber, pp. 593ff.

▶ **During the turmoil of the Peasants' War, Luther married.[6] The following letter announced his marriage to his friends:**

What an outcry I have caused with my little pamphlet against the peasants! Everything God has done the world through me is forgotten. Now lords, priests and peasants are all against me and threaten me with death.

Well, since they are so frantic and foolish, I will prepare myself to be found, when my end comes, in the state which God has created. I will do my best so that nothing of my earlier popish life remains. This should make my enemies even more frantic and foolish before the final farewell. I sense that God will finally grant me his grace.

Thus I have now, according to the desire of my dear father, entered

Catherine von Bora. (*Woodcut by Hans
Brosamer. Geisberg,* 424)

the marital estate. I have done so quickly lest bad tongues would stop it.
Tuesday a week, which is Tuesday after St John the Baptist, I am planning to have a small and joyful housewarming party. I did not want to
hide this before you, my good friends and masters, and pray that we may
have your blessing.

Since these are difficult and dangerous times I did not want to ask you
to be present. If, however, you would find it possible to come, together
with my dear father and mother, it would be a special pleasure for me.
Whatever good friends you bring along will be welcome. I am only asking
you to let me know through this messenger.

15th June 1525. *WA, Br.* 3, 531.

> Though the course of the Reformation was, after 1521, decided
> largely in the councils of statesmen, Luther remained an im-
> portant and colourful figure. The satirical, but friendly, 'Luci-
> fer's Letter to Luther' is illustrative of the popular support for
> the Wittenberg Reformer.

We, Lucifer, Master and Owner of eternal darkness, powerful ruler

Martin Luther (*Woodcut by Hans Brosamer.*
Geisberg, 423)

and lord of the entire world, of all property, and all treasures and riches found therein, etc.: Disgrace and wrath to you, Martin Luther. Our dear and faithful servants, Laurentius Campeggio[7] and Matthias Lang, of Salzburg, legates of our governor in Rome and cardinals have humbly communicated to us together with others of our officials recently assembled at Regensburg through messengers that you have continuously set yourself without any reason to work to their disadvantage and against us with vehement pamphlets and sermons, which has led to the deprivation of our annual income. They report that your attitude and intentions are daily enlarged and getting stronger, indeed having as goal the doing away of these our servants and officials, extinguishing them altogether. Furthermore, we find upon consultation of our registries and soul books that for the seven years you have turned away from us many souls through your writing, teaching and preaching. You directed them, instead, to Christ, who also at one time harmed our realm considerably. This does not seem altogether proper in light of your obligation and vow which you fulfilled for us earlier as a monk, but in which you have now become faithless. To

Luther (*b*) leads the faithful Christians out of Egyptian darkness (*a*). They worship the crucified Saviour (*c*), while the Pope (*d*), three of Luther's Catholic opponents, (*g*, *f*, *h*) and the indulgence salesmen (*e*) stand in the background. (*Woodcut by monogram H. Geisberg*, 927)

show the hostility of your wicked will and obstinate mind against us and our servants and in order to be even more pernicious and detrimental against our realm, you use the Bible and the books of the Gospels, which according to our order have not been used much for several hundred years. Indeed, we and our appointed counsellors, meeting at several places and lately, in particular at Köstnitz, prohibited their preaching and debating. Accordingly we had two criminals and transgressors of this command, namely John Huss and Jerome of Prague, who also wanted to oppose us, gruesomely punished and burned. Furthermore you cause monks and nuns who had honoured us to no small measure with the sin which we invoked upon the people and the cities of Sodom and Gomorrah to leave their monasteries and to take wives and husbands. For us, as well as priests and monks, our faithful servants, you diminish and do away with auricular confession, preventing thereby their easy accomplishment of adultery, fornication and rape, which was all caused by this. People are thus no longer instructed in our path. And you are not only in these said articles against us and our servants, but you also use industriously all sorts of other evil tricks and cunning by which we and our servants are daily belittled, reviled and ridiculed. Inasmuch as friendly requests and the offer of great gifts and wealth are rejected by you and not well esteemed, as we have sufficiently learned, and furthermore you will not let your hard head be softened by friendly or serious admonition, not heeding our support, power and authority from both bishops and worldly rulers, we and our counsellors have decided, after a thorough consideration of the shame and damage caused by you, to persecute both you and all your followers and supporters. Thus we announce to you and yours through this open letter our ill will, enmity, feud and denunciation. This we proclaim on behalf of ourselves, our Pope, cardinals, bishops and all our servants and officials under our authority, in our service, or otherwise belonging to us. We wish to proceed cruelly against you and yours with fire, beheading, drowning, and the taking of you and your children's body and goods in whatever way we can. . . .

In witness whereof we have affixed our hellish seal at the end of this letter. Given in our city of eternal damnation on the last day of September 1524.

Absag oder Fehdschrift Lucifers an Luther, 1524, pp. 364-7.

✓ ▸   A visitor to Wittenberg reflected on his meeting with Luther.[8]

I found several young men there, highly trained in Hebrew, Greek and Latin. Of these, Philipp Melanchthon is held to be the first of all in his thorough knowledge of the Scriptures and of doctrine. This young man of twenty-six years certainly showed during my three days' stay greatest erudition and a most amiable personality. Through his mediation I informed Luther about the reason for my journey as follows: It is thought that he who did not see the Pope in Rome or Luther in Wittenberg did not see anything at all. Therefore I desired to see him and to speak with him. Lest there be any distrust I assured him that I had no further desire than to greet him and say good-bye. For not every person has access to him. He welcomed me, however, without difficulties. Together with Melanchthon I visited him toward the end of the evening meal to which he had invited some of the brothers of his order who were clad in robes of white colour, but cut according to the rule. Thus they were known as brothers, though their hair did not distinguish them from peasants. Luther stood up, self-consciously gave me his hand, and asked me to sit down. We sat down and for almost four hours talked until late at night about many things. I found him to be a man of discernment, knowledge and eloquence. Apart from words of contempt and arrogance, as well as acid comments concerning the Pope, the Emperor and several other rulers, he did not say, however, anything of significance. . . . Luther conveys the same impression in his countenance as in his books. His eyes are penetrating and almost sparkle in a sinister fashion as one can observe it at times among mentally ill. The King of Denmark has similar eyes and I believe that they were both born under the same constellation of stars. His manner of speech is vehement, abounding in insinuations and ridicule. His apparel hardly distinguishes him from a courtier. When he leaves the house in which he lives—it was formerly the cloister—he wears, it is said, the robe of his order. Sitting together with him we did not merely talk but also drank beer and wine in a good mood, as is custom there. In every respect he seems to be 'a good fellow', as they say in German. The integrity of his life, which is frequently praised among us here, does not distinguish him from the rest of us. Easily one can recognize his arrogance and presumptuousness. Slander, calumny and ridicule seem to be part of him. His books point this out clearly. It is said that he is well read and that he writes much. At present he is translating the Books of Moses from Hebrew into Latin, whereby he uses mostly the help of Melanchthon. Among all the learned men in Germany this young man pleases me most of all. With Luther he does not agree in everything.

Franz Hipler, Nikolaus Kopernikus und Martin Luther, pp. 54–56.

▶   According to a Venetian ambassador, the German Emperor Charles took the following view of the religious situation:

Two remedies only present themselves to him: either he must go to Germany, and punish the heretics with severity, or a general council must be convoked. As it is impossible for him to go soon to Germany, he begs the Pope to decide what he ought to do. Promises his holiness, as a good son of the Church, to stake his person and his states to suppress a sect which is evidently dangerous to all religious authority. As the Germans have asked the legate, Cardinal Campeggio, to propose to the Pope a general council to be held in Germany, it would be well if his holiness would anticipate the conventicle at Speyer by the convocation of a general council at Trent. The Germans consider Trent as a German city, although it is, properly speaking, Italian. Although the council ought to be convoked at Trent early next spring, it can afterwards be prorogued and transferred to another city in Italy, Rome, for example, or wherever the Pope likes. Promises to obey the orders of the Holy Father. . . .

18th July 1524. Calendar of State Papers: Spanish II, No. 662.

▶ Among the unending questions which the Reformation raised, none was, in the long run, more important than that of the organizational structure of the new Protestant churches. Church Orders were drawn up everywhere.[9] The excerpt below from Braunschweig indicates to what extent such changes affected public life.

First, of the Poor-Chests. In all large parishes there shall openly stand a Common Chest for the indigent, the poor and others in need. To it shall come all free-will offerings which men shall put therein throughout the year, as each is disposed; item, all bequests and benefactions; item, the customary offerings on St Auctor's day . . .; item, what men have hitherto vainly offered for the dead; item, what they have also offered when a bride comes to church . . .; item, if anyone wishes to have the bells rung at a death . . . the money for the ringing (save what is due to the sexton) shall be put into the Poor-Chest; item, whatever pious Christian people can devise for the help of these chests shall belong thereto; item, the Deacons of the Poor shall . . . go round on holydays before and after the sermon in church with bags whereon shall be a little bell so that they need not ask but that the people shall hear that they are there . . . and preachers shall in their sermons recommend such service of the poor as Divine Service. . . . For these chests there shall be chosen three deacons by the council and by the members of the congregation in the district.

The deacons shall keep an account of their receipts and expenditure, and a list of the names and houses of those who from week to week are in need of assistance, so that their reckoning may be the simpler and clearer. . . . Every Sunday, or other appointed day in the week, the deacons shall meet together in each parish to distribute to the poor according to need, and to consider what is necessary for each sick or poor man. And when there is no money there, or too little, the preacher shall warn the people to come to the assistance of the Common Chest. . . .

These deacons or treasurers shall pay the stipends to the preachers of their churches every quarter, as also to the sacristans and the organists. They shall also provide and maintain a dwelling near the church for their preachers, and, where they are willing and able to do so, for their schoolmaster who is appointed in their church to sing with the children, in case he wishes to marry and to keep house. . . . They shall also keep the churches in repair and provide what is needful therein. These four persons shall have authority from the congregation in company with the council to appoint a preacher, as is above set down, one of the four being a member of the council.

Emil Sehling, *Die evangelischen Kirchenordnungen des XVI Jahrhunderts*, VI. Band, 1. Hälfte (Tübingen, 1955), pp. 450–4.

√ ▶ The 1529 diet at Speyer[10] withdrew the concession to the Lutheran territories made at the diet at Speyer in 1526. Here are excerpts[11] from the Emperor's pronouncement which refers to the resolutions of the (Catholic) majority and the (Lutheran) minority. The protest of the minority gave the new movement its lasting name—Protestants.

Whereas in the Recess of the Diet of Speyer, made in 1526, it was said that 'the Electors, Princes and Estates of the Empire, and the ambassadors of the same unanimously agreed and resolved, while waiting for the Council, with our subjects, in matters which the edict published by his Majesty at the diet held at Worms may concern, each one so to live, govern and carry himself as he hopes and trusts to answer it to God and his Majesty, etc.'; and whereas, from the same article, as hitherto understood, expounded and explained at their pleasure by several of the Estates of the Holy Empire, marvellous great trouble and misunderstanding has arisen against our holy Christian faith, as also against the magistrates through the disobedience of their subjects, and much other disadvantage, your Majesty conceives no small astonishment thereat; and to the end that, for the future, the said article may be no further taken and expounded at every man's pleasure, and that the consequences, which hitherto have proved so disastrous to our holy faith, may be averted, your Majesty hereby repeals, revokes and annuls the above-mentioned article contained in the aforesaid Recess, now as then, and then as now, all out of your own Imperial absolute power. . . .

Whereas, moreover, said article has been by many used and expounded under a complete misapprehension, to excuse many new doctrines and sects; therefore, to stop such and to avert further falling away . . . the Electors, Princes and other Estates have resolved that those who have hitherto adhered to Imperial Edict should continue to abide by the same till the coming Council, and hold their subjects thereto.

That the other Estates, with whom the other doctrine originated and with whom, to some degree, it cannot be abandoned without considerable tumult, trouble and danger, shall nevertheless prevent all further innovation till the coming Council, so far as is humanly possible.

That, in particular, such doctrines and sects as deny the most worthy sacrament of our Lord Jesus Christ's body and blood shall in no wise be tolerated by the Empire, nor be henceforth allowed . . . to be preached in public; nor shall the celebration of the holy mass be done away; nor shall anyone, in places where the new doctrine has got the upper hand, be forbidden to celebrate or to hear mass, nor be hindered or forced therefrom.   *Deutsche Reichstagsakten* VII, 667.

Landgrave Philipp of Hesse, the leading
Protestant territorial ruler and chief
spokesman at Speyer in 1529 and in Augsburg in 1530. (*Woodcut by Hans Brosamer.*
Geisberg, 414)

▶ A diet at Augsburg, in 1530, was to deal definitively with the
religious question. The Lutheran territories presented the famous 'Augsburg Confession' at Augsburg, which underscored the
agreement of the new Lutheran faith with the early Fathers.
None the less, conciliation did not take place. Here are the
Emperor's words with which he announced the diet.

We have resolved to undertake a general diet and assembly, and . . .
to hold the same in our Imperial City of Augsburg; by which time we
hope that we shall have settled affairs in Italy so as to be present in
person on that day, as we have finally resolved to do. This day, then, we
hereby announce to you, our well-beloved, commanding you by the
authority of our Roman Empire and by the duty wherewith you are bound
to us and to the Empire, straitly bidding and willing you to appear that
day in person at Augsburg, and together with us and other our Electors,
Princes and Estates of the Holy Empire, whom we have summoned in

like manner, to assist in undertaking, debating, resolving and concluding how weighty provision may be made for the removal of the grievous burden and invasion into Christendom of the aforesaid Turks, with good deliverance, defences and steady help according to need, in addition to the measures formerly taken in that behalf; and, further, how, in the matter of errors and divisions concerning the holy faith and the Christian religion we may and should deal and resolve, and so bring it about, in better and sounder fashion, that divisions may be allayed, antipathies set aside, all past errors left to the judgment of our Saviour, and every care taken to give a charitable hearing to every man's opinions, thoughts and notions, to understand them, to weigh them, to bring and reconcile men to a unity in Christian truth, and to dispose of everything that has not been rightly explained or treated of on the one side or the other. . . .

> Förstemann, *Urkundenbuch zu der Geschichte des Reichstages in Augsburg 1530*, I, 1.

▶ **The situation at Augsburg during the time of the diet was described by a Venetian observer as follows:**[12]

This city is divided into three factions, viz. the papists who still have here their churches, images, masses, canonical hours, and bells, though they are in very small number as compared with the other inhabitants. . . .

The second faction is that of the Lutherans, who are numerous, and complain greatly of the dismissal by the Government of some of their preachers, because they did not agree with certain other preachers of the faction of Zwingli in the matter of the eucharist; but the Government acted thus for the public peace.

The third faction, which is that of Zwingli, is the greatest, and it comprises beyond comparison many more of the citizens, so that yesterday they celebrated the communion *more Zwinglij*, and side with him in all things as you know, and all the Evangelical preachers are unanimously in his favour. . . .

On holidays, the aforesaid preachers preach '*la scriptura sacra*' in five places, some of them expounding Matthew, some Paul . . . before the sermon, there being present a very great concourse of people evincing much devotion; and they go without much ringing of bells, which merely strike the hours. All the people sing the Psalms of David, most melodiously, causing great spiritual joy and consolation to the hearers; so that after the sermon, they always sing a psalm; and then the preacher exhorts them to give alms, which are most abundant, in such wise that the need of such as are unable to help themselves is provided for. He also exhorts them to pray for all sorts and conditions of men, as likewise for the propagation of the Gospel. They live very frugally, with regard both to apparel, household furniture, and daily food; and they administer exemplary justice.

They also give daily lectures in Hebrew, Greek and Latin; and attend more than ever was the practice formerly to the education of youth, both as concerns literature and sound Christian morality.

Calendar of State Papers: Venetian IV, 511.

▶ In 1545 an Italian broadside reported the alleged death of Luther. When the Wittenberg Reformer, who was still very much alive, received a copy, he added some comments and published it. Here is both the broadside and Luther's comments.

God has given a terrible and incredible sign in the ignominious death of Martin Luther, who is damned in body and soul. This is clearly put forth in a chapter from the letter of the ambassador of the Most Christian King, to the honour and praise of Jesus Christ and to the strengthening and comfort of the pious.

Copy of the Chapter

When Martin Luther was ill, he desired the holy sacrament of the body of our Lord Jesus Christ. Upon having received it, he died. When he saw that his illness was very serious and death was near, he asked that his body should be placed on an altar and worshipped as a god. But divine goodness and providence wanted to end such error and silence it for ever; it revealed therefore such miraculous signs as were greatly necessary to make the common people renounce such great error, destruction and corruption as has been caused by said Luther in this world. No sooner had his corpse been laid in the grave than a terrible roar and noise were heard, as if devil and hell had collapsed. All those present were greatly terrified, frightened and afraid. When they looked up into heaven they saw distinctly the most sacred host of our Lord Jesus Christ, which this unworthy man had been permitted to receive. All those present also saw the most sacred host suspended in the air. Thus they showed great reverence and veneration toward the most sacred host. Accordingly, the roar and hellish rumbling were not heard any more that day.

But the following night everybody heard an even greater roaring at the place where Luther's corpse had been buried. The people awakened and were greatly afraid and dismayed. When daylight came, they went to Luther's grave, opened it. They saw clearly that there was neither body nor flesh nor bones nor clothes, but a sulphurous odour which sickened all those who stood around.

Many returned to a life in the holy Christian faith, to the honour, praise and glory of Jesus Christ and the strengthening of his holy Christian Church which is a pillar of truth.

And I, Martin Luther, confess and witness with this statement that I received this furious story of my death on 21st March. I read it gladly and joyfully indeed, except for the fact that such blasphemy is attributed to divine majesty. Otherwise, I do not really care about it that the devil and his followers, Pope and papists, are so hostile to me. May God convert them from the evil! If my prayer for their venial sin is in vain, may God let them fill their cup by the writing of such booklets for their joy and comfort. May they go to hell; they have deserved it. They wanted it.

> Martin Luther, *Ein wälsche Lügenschrift von Doctoris Martini Luthers Tod*, 1545 (*WA* 54, 192–4).

▶ In fact, death came to Luther on 18th February 1546, at Eisleben, where he had travelled to conciliate the feuding counts of Mansfeld. His death occasioned a flood of descriptive accounts which all purported to describe the Reformer's last hours.[13] Here is the most authentic account:

Dr Luther also considered at the dinner-table of his last evening the question whether we would be able to recognize each other in that blessed future eternal gathering and congregation. When we eagerly approached him for a comment, he said, 'What about Adam? He had never seen Eve. He lay there and slept. Upon waking up he did not say, "Where from do you come? Who are you?" Rather he said, "This is flesh of my flesh and bone of my bone." Whence did he know that this woman was not made of stone? He was full of the Holy Spirit and true recognition of God. We through Christ will be renewed to such knowledge and insight in that life so that we shall know father, mother, and each other from face to face better than Adam and Eve.'

Not long after these words he arose and went into his room, together with his two young sons, Martin and Paul. Celius followed him. As was his custom he sat at the window of his room to pray. Then Celius came down again and Johann Aurifaber went to be with him. The doctor said, 'I am feeling sick in my chest as before.' Then Johann said, 'When I was teacher of the young lords I saw how the countess gave them unicorn when they had pain in the chest or elsewhere. If you want me to I can get some.' To this the doctor responded affirmatively. Before going to the countess Johann hurried downstairs and called Dr Jonas and Celius who had been there not longer than the time of two Lord's Prayers. They quickly came upstairs. . . .

About nine o'clock he lay down on his couch and said, 'If I could sleep for half an hour, I would feel much better.' He slept gently and naturally for about an hour and a half until ten o'clock, during which time Dr Jonas and Celius, together with his servant, Ambrosius, and two of his sons, Martin and Paul, stayed with him.

When he woke up at exactly ten o'clock he said, 'I see you are still here. Do you not want to retire?' We answered, 'No, we wish to wake and wait on you.' He then got up from his couch and went to the bedroom adjacent to the parlour, where all the windows had been closed. Though he did not complain, he said when he crossed the threshold into the bedroom, 'I am going to bed, God willing. *In manus tuas commendo spiritum meum, redemisti me, Domine Deus veritatis.*'

His bed had been prepared with warm bedding and pillows. When he retired, he lay down, shook our hands and bid us good night: 'Dr Jonas, and Celius and all others, pray for our Lord God and for his Gospel that it may prosper, for the Council of Trent and the abominable Pope are quite angry against him.' . . .

He slept well, breathing naturally, until the clock struck one o'clock. He woke up, called for his servant Ambrosius and asked him to heat the room. Since the room had been kept warm throughout the night, Dr Jonas asked him upon Ambrosius's return if he felt weak again. He said, 'O dear God, I feel so badly. O dear Dr Jonas, I think I shall remain here at Eisleben where I was born and baptized.' Thereupon Dr Jonas and Ambrosius, the servant, answered, 'O reverend father, God our heavenly Father will help you through Christ whom you have preached.' Then he walked without help or support from the room to the parlour, saying at the threshold the same words he had spoken when he retired: '*In manus tuas commendo spiritum meum, redemisti me, Domine Deus veritatis.*' Once or twice he walked back and forth in the parlour, then lay down on the couch and complained about a pain in his chest, but none in his heart. He asked to be rubbed with warm cloths as he was used to at Wittenberg, and pillows and bedding were warmed for him. He commented that it felt good to be kept warm. Before this and before the doctor lay down at the couch Celius came from his room and afterwards Johann Aurifaber.

At that time the innkeeper Johann Albrecht, the city clerk and his wife were hurriedly wakened, together with the two physicians of the town, who came within fifteen minutes, since they lived nearby. First the innkeeper came with his wife, then Simon Wild, a physician, and D. Ludwig, another medical man. They were soon joined by Count Albert with his wife, who brought several herbs and refreshments and continuously sought to make him comfortable. All during this time the doctor

Martin Luther in the last year of his life. (*Woodcut by Lucas Cranach the Younger. Geisberg, 672*)

said, 'Dear God, I have much pain. I am passing on. I shall stay at Eisleben.' Dr Jonas and Celius comforted him and said, 'Reverend father, call upon your Lord Jesus Christ, our High Priest and only Mediator! You have sweated well. God will be gracious and it will get better.' He answered, 'Indeed, I had the cold sweat of death. I shall give up my spirit, for my sickness increases!' Then he said, 'My heavenly Father, God and Father of our Lord Jesus Christ! I thank thee, thou God of all comfort, that thou hast revealed to me thy dear son, Jesus Christ, whom I believed, preached and confessed, loved and praised, who is denounced, persecuted and blasphemed by the evil Pope and all the godless. I pray, my dear Lord Jesus Christ, and commend my soul to thee. O heavenly Father, though I must leave this body and depart this life, I know indeed that I will eternally be with you and no one will pluck me out of thy hands.' And he said in Latin, 'For God so loved the world that he gave his only begotten Son, that whosoever believeth in him should not perish, but have everlasting life.' He also spoke the words of the sixty-eighth Psalm, 'Our God is a God of salvation; and to God, the Lord, belongs escape from death.' . . .

Then he said three times in rapid succession, 'Father, into thy hands I commend my spirit. Thou hast redeemed me, O God of Truth.' After he had thus commended his spirit into the hands of God, the heavenly Father, he became quiet. He was shaken, rubbed, cooled and shouted at; but his eyes remained closed and there was no answer. The wife of Count Albert and the doctors applied strong aromatic solutions to his pulse, which his physicians had sent him and which he was accustomed to using.

When he was so quiet, Dr Jonas and Celius spoke to him: 'Reverend father, will you die firmly in Christ and the teaching which you have preached?' And he answered with a clear voice, 'Yes.' Then he turned to his right side and began to sleep for almost fifteen minutes so that there was thought of improvement. The physicians and we felt that such sleep could not be trusted and frequently took the light and looked into his face. . . .

Soon thereafter Dr Luther became pale in his face and his feet and nose became cold. He took a deep, yet gentle breath, and then gave up his spirit in quietness and great patience, moving neither finger nor leg. No one could observe (this we testify before God with our conscience) any restlessness, gloating of his body, or pain of death. He departed peacefully and gently in the Lord as Simeon proclaims. Thus the words of John in the eighth chapter were fulfilled: 'Truly, I say unto you, he who keeps my word shall nevermore see death. . . .'

After the body had been put into the church, Dr Jonas preached a sermon pointing out, first, the person and gifts of Dr Martin, secondly, resurrection and eternal life, thirdly, an admonition to the opponents that death would have power against the realm of Satan. Such he preached according to I Thessalonians 4.

Vom Christlichen abschied aus diesem tödlichen leben,
1546 (*WA* 56, 488–93).

▶ Not all the accounts of Luther's death were friendly in character. From hostile sources came the following:[14]

During supper on Wednesday evening he was in a good mood and caused all to laugh by his fables and jokes. Around eight o'clock he began to complain about not feeling well, as the written report states. After midnight two physicians were suddenly called to him, of whom the one was a doctor and the other one a master, who when they arrived found no more pulse. None the less they immediately wrote a prescription to give him an enema.

Thus the pharmacist was wakened at three o'clock and was ordered to prepare an enema and bring it to Luther. When he came in by order of the physicians, prepared the enema and warmed it, he believed that Luther was still alive. But when the body had been turned in order to give him the enema, the pharmacist realized that he was already dead and said to the physicians, 'He is dead, why do we need an enema?' Present were Count Albert and some scholars. The physicians answered, 'What about it? Use the enema. Perhaps there is some life in him, and he will come back.' . . .

The two physicians quarrelled with each other concerning the cause of death. The doctor said it was a stroke, for it was clear that the face on the entire right side had turned black. The master, however, who felt that such a holy man was not to die by God's hand of a stroke, said that death had been caused by suffocation. After this had taken place, the other counts came. Jonas, who was sitting near the head of the deceased, moaned and wrung his hands. When he was asked whether Luther had complained about pain the previous evening—for the following day, namely Thursday, February 18th, had already begun—he replied, 'But no, yesterday he was as joyful as he ever had been. Oh, Lord God, Lord God, etc.' In the meantime, the counts brought precious smelling water to rub the body of the deceased.

> Johann Cochläus, *Ex compendio actorum Martini Lutheri,*
> *caput ultimum et ex epistola quadam Mansfeldensi*
> *historica narratio* . . . (Mainz, 1548).

▶   **Philipp Melanchthon, Luther's colleague, made the following announcement to his students at Wittenberg when the news of Luther's death arrived:**

Dear Students:

You know that we have undertaken a grammatical exposition of the Epistle to the Romans in which is contained the true doctrine concerning the Son of God whom God has revealed to us in this time with singular benevolence through our reverend father and our beloved teacher, Dr Martin Luther.

Today said news has arrived here, increasing my pain so much that I do not know whether I can continue this lecture. On the advice of the other Lords, I will tell you the following, that you know how the matter truly took place, so that you do not believe the spreading false rumour and do not yourself spread fables. On Wednesday, February 17th, shortly before supper the doctor began to suffer from his constant illness, namely the pressure of liquid to the stomach opening, from which he had suffered occasionally in earlier times. Afterwards pain began again. While he was suffering he desired to be taken to the adjacent room, where he lay for almost two hours while the pain increased. Since Dr Jonas slept in the same room, Dr Martin called him and awakened him with the order to stand up and see to it that the educator of his children, Ambrosius, should heat the room. But when he was gone in came the Count Albert of Mansfeld and his wife, and many others whose names, on account of the hurry, are not mentioned in this letter. When, shortly before four o'clock on the following day, February 18th, he sensed that the end of his life had come, he commended himself to God with the following prayer. . . .

After he had uttered this prayer several times, he was called by God to eternal rest and joy in which he will delight in the fellowship with the Father, Son, Holy Spirit and all prophets and apostles.

Alas, now has died the charioteer and chariot of Israel who guided the Church in this last age of the world. It was not through human wisdom that the teaching of the remission of sins and the faith of the Son of God was perceived; but it was disclosed by God through this man whom we saw to have been aroused by God. Let us cherish therefore his memory and the doctrine which he delivered. May we be modest and consider the immense calamities and great changes which will follow this death.

CR 6, 58–59.

▶   After the Reformer's death, the following sentences were found
        on a slip of paper, containing, evidently, his last writing:

No one can understand Virgil's Bucolics and Georgics unless he was, for five years, a shepherd or farmer. No one understands Cicero's letters, I imagine, unless he occupied an eminent public office for twenty years. No one can understand the sacred Scriptures sufficiently unless he guided the churches together with the Prophets for a hundred years. Thus there is something exceedingly wonderful about, first, John the Baptist, second, Christ, third, the Apostles. Do not manipulate this divine Aeneas, but worship its footsteps. We are beggars, this is true.

Enders, 17, 60 (*WA, TR* 5, 5677).

Two kinds of preaching: left, the Protestant, based on the Bible;
The man behind the pillar calls attention to both.

► **In Wittenberg, Philipp Melanchthon delivered the funeral
sermon:**

Some well-meaning men have complained that Luther was rougher
than he should have been. This I will not deny, recalling that Erasmus
often said, 'On account of the great evil in this most depraved time, God
gave a rough physician'. . . . I will also not deny that Luther was occasionally quite vehement. But no one is altogether without mistakes in light of
our natural weakness. . . . Such was Luther, as we knew him. . . . What
else shall I say about Luther's noble character? Frequently I was present
when with tears he spoke his prayers for the Church. Almost every
day he devoted some time to the reciting of the Psalms, which he in-

right, the Catholic without the Scripture but with the Rosary.
(*Woodcut by Georg Pencz. Geisberg*, 997)

cluded, with lament and tears, in his intercession. . . . Contrary to the
opinion of many, he neither neglected the common good nor failed to
heed the will of others. He was competent in governmental affairs and
clearly discerned the mind and the intentions of those with whom he
came into contact. Despite this penetrating mind, Luther read industriously old and new theological writings and historical narratives whose
teachings he applied with unique competence to the present.

Well do we bewail that such a man has been taken from us. For we
must be compared to orphans who have been deprived of a caring and
faithful father. . . . Let us seek to understand that he was salutary, too,
of God and let us earnestly heed his teachings. Likewise, let us imitate

his virtues as much as is possible in our mediocrity: his fear of God, his faithfulness and industriousness in his vocation, his purity in fulfilment of spiritual responsibilities, the immaculateness of the walk of his life, the insight and care with which he avoided rebellious counsel, and finally his eagerness to learn.

CR 11, 726–34.

▶   **The Peace of Augsburg, of September 1555, formalized the religious schism in Germany by the recognition of Lutheranism (but not Calvinism) as a legitimate territorial religion. The Peace thus concluded, in an external manner, the Reformation in Germany.**[15]

In order to bring peace into the holy Empire of the German Nation between the Roman Imperial Majesty and the Electors, Princes and Estates: let neither his Imperial Majesty nor the Electors, Princes, etc., do any violence or harm to any estate of the Empire on account of the Augsburg Confession, but let them enjoy their religious belief, liturgy and ceremonies as well as their estates and other rights and privileges in peace; and complete religious peace shall be obtained only by Christian means of amity, or under threat of the punishment of the imperial ban.

Likewise the Estates espousing the Augsburg Confession shall let all the Estates and Princes who cling to the old religion live in absolute peace and in the enjoyment of all their estates, rights and privileges. . . .

And since it has proved to be matter of great dispute what was to happen with the bishoprics, priories and other ecclesiastical benefices of such Catholic priests as would in course of time abandon the old religion, we have in virtue of the powers of Roman Emperors ordained as follows: Where an archbishop, bishop or prelate or any other priest of our old religion shall abandon the same, his archbishopric, bishopric, prelacy and other benefices, together with all their income and revenues which he has so far possessed, shall be abandoned by him without any further objection or delay. The chapters and such as are entitled to it by common law or the custom of the place shall elect a person espousing the old religion, who may enter on the possession and enjoyment of all the rights and incomes of the place without any further hindrance and without prejudging any ultimate amicable settlement of religion.

Some of the abbeys, monasteries and other ecclesiastical estates having been confiscated and turned into churches, schools and charitable institutions, it is herewith ordained that such estates as their original owners had not possessed at the time of the treaty of Passau shall be comprised in the present treaty of peace. . . .

No Estate shall try to persuade the subjects of other Estates to abandon their religion nor protect them against their own magistrates. Such as had from ancient times the rights of patronage are not included in the present article.

In case our subjects, whether belonging to the old religion or to the Augsburg Confession, should intend leaving their homes, with their wives and children, in order to settle in another place, they shall neither be hindered in the sale of their estates after due payment of the local taxes nor injured in their honour.

Quellen zur neueren Geschichte, pp. 44–47.

BIBLIOGRAPHY

There are no monographs covering the entire development, though all the general histories of the Reformation contain discussions.

NOTES AND REFERENCES

1. Aleander played an important diplomatic role in the early years of the Reformation as papal representative in Germany. His reports to Rome are invaluable documents. See Theodor Brieger, *Aleander und Luther, 1521. Die vollständigen Aleanderdepeschen vom Wormser Reichstag* (Gotha, 1884). A German translation was published by Paul Kalkoff (Halle, 1897).

2. For an English translation of Dürer's diary passage and a brief discussion of the disputed problem of Dürer's Protestantism see *The Writings of Albrecht Dürer*, translated and edited by William M. Conway (New York, 1958), pp. 154–61.

3. For studies of Luther's work as translator see M. Reu, *Luther's German Bible* (Columbus, Ohio, 1934); Heinrich Bornkamm, 'Luther's Translation of the New Testament', *Luther's World of Thought* (St Louis, 1958), pp. 273–83. See also Roland H. Bainton, *Here I Stand* (New York, 1950), pp. 326–35. Werner Schwarz, 'Examples of Luther's Biblical Translation', *Journal of Theological Studies* 6 (1955), 199–209; Werner Schwarz, *Principles and Problems of Biblical Translation* (Cambridge, 1955).

Luther addressed himself to the problem of translating in his *Sendbrief vom Dolmetschen. 1530 (WA* 30, 2, 627–46), translated as *On Translating: An Open Letter*, in *Works of Martin Luther* (Philadelphia, 1931), pp. 10–28.

4. Johann Cochläus (1479–1552), chaplain at various German courts, was Luther's foremost literary opponent, though he was at first quite friendly toward the Wittenberg reformer. His biography of Luther, *Commentarius de actis et scriptis M. Lutheri*, of 1549, has been until recently the basic source for all Catholic studies of Luther. See Adolf Herte, *Das katholische Lutherbild im*

Banne der Lutherkommentare des Cochläus, 3 vols. (Münster, 1943). The work of Emser cited is *Das naw testament nach lawt der Christlichen kirchen bewerten text, corrigirt und widerumb zurecht gebracht* (Dresden, 1527).

5. There is no recent and competent account of the German peasants' war in English. Of the older works, that of J. S. Schapiro, *Social Reform and the Reformation* (New York, 1909) is the most useful. The authoritative work comes from the pen of Günther Franz, *Der deutsche Bauernkrieg* (Darmstadt, 1956). Authorship and background of the Twelve Articles is discussed by Günther Franz, 'Die Entstehung der "Zwölf Artikel" der deutschen Bauernschaft', *Archiv für Reformationsgeschichte* 36 (1939), 193–213. A collection of eyewitness accounts of the peasants' war is found in Otto H. Brandt, *Der grosse Bauernkrieg. Zeitgenössische Berichte, Aussagen und Aktenstücke* (Jena, 1926). For parts of our translation Kidd, *Documents,* pp. 174 ff., was consulted.

5a. The translation used here is from Robinson, *Readings in European History,* II, 101 ff.

6. On Catherine von Bora, Luther's wife, see Ernst Kroker, *Katharine von Bora, Martin Luthers Frau* (Berlin, 1956); Ingetraut Ludolphy, 'Katherine von Bora, die Gehilfin Martin Luthers', *Luther* (1961), 69–84; and the popular C. L. Deutler, *Katherine Luther of the Wittenberg Parsonage* (Philadelphia, 1924).

7. Lorenzo Campeggio (1474–1539) was professor of law at the University of Bologna, and entering, after the death of his wife, the ecclesiastical estate, became cardinal in 1517. In 1522 he proposed far-reaching proposals for the reform of the Church. In 1528 he was in England attempting to mediate in King Henry's effort for the annulment of his marriage with Catherine. See E. V. Cardinal, *Cardinal Lorenzo Campeggio* (Boston, 1935). Matthias Lang (1468–1540), diplomat in the service of the German Emperor, cardinal in 1511, Archbishop of Salzburg in 1519, was an opponent of Luther, causing thereby unrest in Salzburg in 1523.

The document printed is found in *Flugschriften aus den ersten Jahren der Reformation,* hrsg. O. Clemen, Band 3, Heft 7 (Leipzig, 1909).

8. Franz Hipler, *Nikolaus Kopernikus und Martin Luther, nach ermländischen Archivalien* (Königsberg, 1868).

9. The authoritative edition of Protestant Church Orders in Germany is by Emil Sehling, *Die evangelischen Kirchenordnungen des XVI. Jahrhunderts* (Leipzig, 1902ff.).

The translation used here is from Kidd, *Documents,* pp. 241–2.

The sources for the Diet at Speyer, 1529, are found in *Deutsche Reichstagsakten,* VII. Band (Gotha, 1937). See also Johannes Kühn, *Die Geschichte des Speyrer Reichstages 1529* (Leipzig, 1929).

10. The sources for the diet have not yet been published. The standard monograph is that of Hans von Schubert, *Der Reichstag von Augsburg im Zusammenhang der Reformationsgeschichte* (Leipzig, 1930). An important transcript of the proceedings at Augsburg was made by Valentin von Tetleben and has been published by Herbert Grundmann, *Protokoll des Augsburger Reichstages 1530* (Gütersloh, 1958). For an English translation of the Augsburg Confession see Theodore Tappert, *The Book of Concord* (Philadelphia, 1959). See

also Williard D. Allbeck, *Studies in the Lutheran Confessions* (Philadelphia, 1952).

11. The translation used here is from Kidd, *Documents*, p. 258.

12. C. E. Förstemann, *Urkundenbuch z. Geschichte des Reichstages von Augsburg 1530*, Band I (Halle, 1833).

13. The various accounts of Luther's death are discussed in *WA* 54, 478ff. An unfriendly study of the various accounts is by J. A. Kleis, *Luthers 'heiliges' Leben und 'heiliger' Tod* (Mainz, 1896). Luther's death fell into a time of tense diplomatic relations between the League of Schmalkald and the Emperor.

14. J. A. Kleis, *Luthers 'heiliges' Leben und 'heiliger' Tod* (Mainz, 1896), pp. 209ff.

15. The translation used here is from B. J. Kidd, *Documents*, pp. 363–4. For an authoritative text see *Quellen zur neueren Geschichte*, herausg. vom hist. Seminar der Universität Bern, Heft 7 (Bern, 1946).

Catholic
Response and Renewal

NY history of the Reformation of the sixteenth century must also speak of the response of the Catholic Church to the religious upheaval occasioned by the Protestant Reformers. Two facts deserve particular mention here. One is that it was the spectacular and blatantly negative response of the Roman Church to Luther's initial pronouncements which made a public figure out of the Wittenberg professor. The other is that none the less the Church did not fully realize the significance of the threat it was facing. Pope Leo spoke of Luther as a drunken German monk and seemed to assume that this monkish squabble would soon disappear. Thus, both a comprehensive response to the Protestant challenge and an energetic renewal of the deplorable state of the Church were long in coming.

The dual efforts of the Catholic Church to respond to Protestantism and to renew itself are not easy to keep separate since they often merged with one another. None the less, the differentiation is necessary, if for no other reason than to point out that Catholic efforts at renewal must not be seen exclusively as a result of the Protestant Reformation. This is pointedly illustrated by the existence of various reform efforts, particularly in Italy and Spain, even before the outbreak of the indulgence controversy. From 1512 to 1517 the Fifth Lateran Council met at Rome and alleviated—on paper—some of the glaring ecclesiastical abuses. Humanists everywhere called for reform of the Church and churchmen, in some measure, shared this concern. Sooner or later the Church would have revitalized and 'reformed' itself—as it had often done in the past.

As matters stood, however, the strength of the Protestant Reformation was related to the weakness of its opponent. At the root of the problem lay the inability of the defenders of the old Church to undertake a common course of action. Too many cooks often spoil the broth—and they did so here. For too many years the most prominent Catholics—the popes and the German Emperor Charles V—were disagreeing and feuding with each other. To be sure, they all wanted to be good Catholics, but the

VIII

popes were too Italian and the Emperor was too Spanish to agree on how to deal with Luther and his followers. Had these two forces been able to work together in the early years of the Reformation, the Lutheran 'heresy' might have been suppressed or at least the course of the Reformation altered. When they finally did get together in the middle of the century—after Charles V had abdicated in favour of Philip II—it was too late. The schism of the Church was a fact and the differences between the old and the new Church were firmly established. By that time, however, both Catholic response and renewal had gained momentum. Though the religious schism persisted and the one Christian Church under the headship of the Roman pontiff remained but a dream, the remainder of the century proved to be in a real sense the time of a revitalized, indeed aggressive Catholic Church.

Several expressions of the Catholic response and renewal, as they emerged in the early decades of the Reformation, should be properly noted. The most glaring abuses were quickly discontinued. Of far greater importance, however, was the fact that true spirituality and devotion, which despite all the gross perversion had never left the Church, now became more distinct and prominent—possibly even apart from the direct stimulus of the Protestant Reformation. A new mysticism, exemplified by St Teresa of Jesus or her follower, St John of the Cross, emphasized personal religion and thereby channelled strength into the Church. A wave of new theological learning was evident throughout the Catholic Church, particularly in Spain, which was indeed geographically the centre of the revitalization.

More formal and more formidable was the renewal of the Inquisition as an instrument for the apprehension of heretics. In some parts of the medieval Church, such as Spain, it had had a long and somewhat infamous history. Now it became a church-wide institution. The Inquisition received complete control over the Church, over both its most prominent and its most lowly members. A blanket endorsement of all Inquisitorial action was issued by the Pope, who reserved for himself only the right of pardon. Particularly in Italy and Spain the Inquisition succeeded with the help of civil authorities in eradicating completely all traces of Protestant heresy. *Autos-da-Fé*, acts of faith, became the notorious public spectacles where the accused and convicted heretic—the mere reading of the Psalms was sufficient for both accusation and conviction—was burned at the stake.

Hand in hand with the Inquisition went a minute supervision of all printed matter. Ever since the invention of printing in the preceding century there had been local and fragmentary lists of books which the faithful were not to read. The veritable flood of Protestant writings created all the more urgency in this regard. At mid-century the first list of prohibited books began to appear. In 1559 Pope Paul IV issued a general *Index Librorum Prohibitorum*—a list of prohibited books. This so-called Index of Trent has become a basic Catholic institution. Since then numerous names have been added and a few taken off. Even today Catholic books contain the explicit *nihil obstat* (nothing conflicts) and *imprimatur* (it may be printed) as ecclesiastical guides that they are not on the official *Index*. In the sixteenth century the *Index* proved to be a powerful weapon which made, in Catholic countries, the dissemination of heretical ideas virtually impossible. Among the vast number of books prohibited were all translations of the New Testament into the vernacular, not specifically authorized by the Church. Not even scholars or high church officials were allowed to read the prohibited books unless they obtained special permission from the Pope.

The incarnation of the Catholic Reformation, as well as the Counter Reformation, was a Spanish nobleman named Inigo de Onez y de Loyola. Almost to the day of the Edict of Worms in May 1521, Inigo, then thirty years of age, was seriously wounded in a battle of the first war between Spain and France. A cannon ball had struck him between his legs. Recovery was painful and tedious, indeed nothing but prolonged torture. Though the healing process eventually was satisfactory, one leg turned out to be shorter than the other. One thing was certain: Ignatius's military career was over.

This was a shocking realization for Ignatius and surely at first as painful as his operations. After all, he had been a military man through and through—a typical roughneck, involved with women, duelling and drinking, and the law. But his lengthy hospital stay had been a sobering experience. With ample time at his disposal he was able to read extensively. He always had loved to read—stories of valiant knights and fair maidens. Now the only books he could lay his hands on were a life of Christ and lives of the saints. But what started with embarrassment ended with profound conviction. The longer Ignatius read, the more he found himself strangely attracted to these men of God and their acts of devotion. Increasingly, he asked himself the question whether perhaps despite his physical limitation he could not do as they had done.

And so he decided. He vowed to go barefoot to Jerusalem eating only herbs. To prepare himself properly he undertook a pilgrimage to the shrine of Mary in the monastery of Montserrat. For three days he made a general confession and dedicated his military armour, now no longer usable, to the Virgin.

Then he was on his way to the Holy Land, there to fight the infidel. An outbreak of plague prevented his voyage and forced him to wait on the Spanish coast for almost a year. This time of waiting became for Ignatius immensely important and has been compared to Luther's monastic experience. The German monk had despaired of ascetic regimentation as a way to a gracious God. Not so Ignatius. The most important document from his pen, the *Spiritual Exercises*, which he began to write at this time, reflects his religious genius. For in this profound handbook of spiritual living one can clearly discern the Ignatius who had been a soldier, who was a mystic, and who might have been a monk. The four weeks' spiritual pilgrimage described in the *Exercises* take place like a military manoeuvre—everything, even visions and tears, are subjected to a methodical pattern. And so is the minute self-examination of thought, word and deed which leaves nothing uncovered. As a soldier, Ignatius knew the value of discipline. Though one would suspect that such a routine breeds spiritual poverty, there are, undoubtedly, few books in Christian history whose significance for those who not only read, but practised it, was greater.

In February 1523, Ignatius set out for the Holy Land, luckily enough finding a vessel which took him *gratis*. In light of his poverty, this was an important consideration. When he reached the Holy Land he found the propagation of the Gospel among the infidels not as easy as he had envisioned. After all, they were the rulers of the land and even the few Franciscan monks who somewhat symbolically kept the holy places felt it best to advise Ignatius to return to Europe. Early the following year Ignatius was back in Spain, convinced above everything else of the need for further schooling. For the next eleven years he studied, first in Spain, then at Paris. His dynamic personality gathered a small group of six followers, who did the *Spiritual Exercises* and were committed to 'helping souls'.

In 1534 came a memorable occasion for the small group. On the feast of the Assumption of that year Ignatius and his six companions met at dawn in a small church in Paris. After the only priest among them had celebrated mass, the group made a vow not only to live in poverty and chastity, but also to go to the Holy Land and work there for the conversion of the infidels. If this should prove to be impossible—an echo of Ignatius's own unhappy experience back in 1523—they would proceed to Rome and offer their services to the Pope 'to be sent anywhere the supreme pontiff wished'. Three years passed before Ignatius and his companions—their number had meanwhile increased to nine—were in Venice ready to embark for the Holy Land. But war between Spain and the Turks made a voyage impossible. The group proceeded to Rome instead, where it eagerly undertook religious works of all sorts, especially among the outcasts of society. Asked who they were, they responded, 'The company of Jesus'—and this name stuck, though many felt it to be sacrilegious. Their religious fervour and zeal evoked suspicion of Lutheran heresy, until a thorough investigation by the Inquisition affirmed their orthodoxy. Support came also from highest places: Pope Paul III was willing at this crucial time to utilize the services of all who pledged themselves to fight heresy. 'This is the finger of God,' Paul is said to have exclaimed when he saw the plans for the formalization of the new order. In 1540 the papal bull, *Regimini militantis ecclesiae*, recognized the Company of Jesus or *Societas Jesu* as a new order. Its end was to propagate the faith. Its means were new and unusual. A long 'apprenticeship' was to make sure that only the most capable minds became members of the order. The strictly military organization of the order meant administrative efficiency. The members of the order were freed from all the customary monastic obligations—such as the canonical hours—to concentrate all efforts along the lines suggested by the order.

The order spread—an indication that many were eager to serve the Church. At first its number was restricted to sixty, but this limitation was soon removed. By the time of Ignatius's death in 1556 over a thousand Jesuits were actively and aggressively at work all over the world. In Asia, India and Japan worked Francis Xavier, effecting mass conversions unceasingly until his early death. In Germany the efforts of Peter Canisius were responsible for the re-Catholicization of the south.

The Jesuits were the feared and formidable storm-troops of the Counter Reformation. Though their major influence came in the late sixteenth and throughout the seventeenth century, after the period customarily described as the Reformation, their significance even at mid-century was great. The zeal and conviction of the Jesuits were so appropriate to the problem the Catholic Church was facing that something would have been 'missing' in the Counter Reformation had there been no Jesuit order.

Catholic reaction and renewal found its formal and definitive expression in the Council of Trent which met, intermittently, for almost two decades (1545–63). The idea of a council correcting abuses within the Church when the papacy was seemingly unable to do so had gained momentum in the early sixteenth century. Widespread hope prevailed that a council was the appropriate way for bringing about the reform of the Church. At first even Luther thought so, for he formally appealed to a council as early as 1518. The following year, however, he admitted at Leipzig that even a council could err and was, therefore, no inerrant source of faith. None the less Luther asserted, in 1520, in his *Open Letter to the Christian Nobility* the need for a council. Three years later the Diet of Nürnberg went on record that the existing religious disorder could be remedied only by a free Christian council.

If despite such sentiments some twenty-five years passed before a council convened at Trent, in northern Italy, the delay must be attributed in large measure to the reluctance of the papacy. The popes were fearful that a council might mean the resurgence of the conciliar idea. It is said that whenever a council was mentioned in Rome all saleable church offices decreased in value. But not all the blame must be laid at papal doorsteps. After all, Pope Paul III had in 1536 summoned a council to meet the following year. The fact that it took almost a decade for the council to gather was due to the machinations of Charles V. The trouble with Charles was that he thought himself a faithful son of the Catholic Church, while constantly thwarting her efforts. Not only did he have his own ideas on how the German religious conflict should be settled; his perennial conflict with France was another major obstacle. Thus the council was postposed time and time again. Finally, the council convened at Trent in December 1545, but less than three dozen delegates were present—a meagre representation for what was supposed to be a gathering of the universal Church. It was rather—this is not meant disrespectfully—a denominational synod, firmly controlled by the Pope. Since most of the delegates were from Italy and voting was to take place according to heads rather than nations, as had been the case at earlier councils, a papal majority was assured on all questions from the very beginning. None the less, the initial accomplishments of the council were spectacular: a number of important doctrinal pronouncements defined the position of the Roman Catholic Church in regard to some of the contested doctrines. The Protestant positions were repudiated in each instance.

Understandably enough, the Protestants showed little inclination to attend the council. In the meantime Charles had engaged in armed conflict with the Lutheran League of Schmalkald. Early in 1547 his victory appeared imminent. This, together with the death of his archrival Francis at the same time, made Charles's position as strong as it ever had been and raised the prospect of having the council dominated by him, particularly since Trent was situated in Charles's territory. When an epidemic threatened to break out, it provided the welcome justification for transferring the council to Bologna, which was in papal territory. Charles thereupon announced that all deliberations and decisions made there were null and void. A rump council continued at Bologna; in 1549 it adjourned. Two years later it convened again. This time some Protestant representatives were present, brought there by Charles's pressure. Since he was the powerful figure of this session, the French Church refused to attend. Again there was, therefore, no universal representation. After one year the council adjourned anew—supposedly for two years, which grew into ten. From 1562 to 1563 the council held its third and final session. Serious inner-Catholic tensions about the duties of a bishop to reside in his diocese and the primacy of the Pope prolonged the proceedings. In January 1564, Pope Pius IV confirmed the decrees and canons of the council.

One can hardly overestimate the significance of the Council of Trent inasmuch as it marks the official Roman Catholic repudiation of the Protestant Reformation. By the time of the council, coming as late as it did, the tensions between the two religious factions were too pronounced and too firmly established to afford any real possibility of conciliation. The course of deliberations tended to confirm this fact. The council affirmed the ties of the Church with its rich Catholic heritage, rather than venture into a possibly dangerous concord with Protestantism. The Council of Trent is a milestone in the history of the Catholic Church.

▶   The Catholic Church entered the Reformation with the Fifth Lateran Council which met at Rome from 1512 to 1517. The Council addressed itself to many abuses in the Church and prescribed relief—though not, interestingly enough, concerning that abuse which a few months after the adjournment of the Council was to receive widespread attention, namely, indulgences. Here are excerpts from the decrees of the Council.[1]

That clerics especially may live chastely and continently as required by the sacred canons, we decree that those who do the contrary be severely punished. If anyone, cleric or layman, be convicted of the crime on account of which the anger of God came upon the children of unbelief, let him be punished in accordance with the sacred canon or the civil law respectively. *Concubinarii*, whether clerical or lay, shall be punished in accordance with the same canons. Toleration by superiors, contrary custom or any other subterfuge cannot be accepted as justifiable excuses; these must be corrected and those who tolerate them punished in accordance with the law.

For the peace and benefit of the cities and of all localities subject to the Roman Church, we hereby renew the *Constitutiones Aegidii olim episcopi Sabinensis* (1356) and prescribe their strict observance.

That that nefarious pest known as simony be for ever banished from

the Roman curia and from all Christendom, we hereby renew the constitutions published by our predecessors against it, decreeing their strict
observance and the imposition of the penalties prescribed therein on
delinquents.

Supernae dispositionis arbitrio (Schroeder, pp. 496–7).

With the approval of the holy council we decree and ordain that no
clerics, whether seculars or members of any of the mendicant orders or
any other order to which the office of preaching pertains by right, custom,
privilege, or otherwise, be admitted to exercise that office unless they
have first been carefully examined by their respective superiors and found
competent and fit as regards moral integrity, age, knowledge, upright-
ness, prudence and exemplariness of life. . . .

We command all who are engaged in this work and who will be so
engaged in the future that they preach and explain the truth of the Gospel
and the Holy Scriptures in accordance with the teaching, interpretation
and exposition of the doctors of the Church, whom the Church or long
usage has approved and the reading of whom she has thus far accepted
and in the future will accept, without adding thereto anything that is
contrary to or in any way at variance with their teaching. . . .

Supernae majestatis praesidio (Schroeder, p. 505).

▶   Erasmus of Rotterdam, the celebrated humanist, illustrates well
    the nobler spirituality within Catholicism at the eve of the
    Reformation. Thus he wrote in the preface to his Greek New
    Testament:

I do not at all share the opinion of those who do not want laymen to
read the Sacred Scriptures in the vernacular, as though Christ had taught
something enigmatic to be scarcely understood by a few theologians.
They seem to think that the Christian religion is best protected by
ignorance. I wish all women would read the Gospels and the letters of
Paul. I wish they would be translated into all the languages. I wish the
peasants would sing them behind the plough, the weaver at his loom, the
pilgrim on his way.

Novum Instrumentum (Basel, 1516), Paraclesis.

▶   Erasmus's critique of the abuses and perversions of the Church
    led many to connect him with Luther. But Erasmus, who hated
    open conflict, was quick to defend himself against such insinua-
    tions. Thus he wrote, in November 1519, to Archbishop Albert of
    Mainz:

Luther is a perfect stranger to me, and I have never had time to read his books beyond merely glancing over a few pages. If he has written well, no praise is due to me; if not, it would be unjust to hold me responsible. . . . Luther had written to me in a very Christian tone, as I thought; and I replied, advising him incidentally not to write anything against the Roman pontiff, nor to encourage a proud and intolerant spirit, but to preach the Gospel out of a pure heart . . . I am neither Luther's accusor, nor advocate, nor judge; his heart I would not presume to judge—for that is always a matter of extreme difficulty—still less would I condemn.

> 1st November 1519. *Opus Epistolarum Des.*
> *Erasmi* IV, 100–1.

▶   **A similar letter was addressed in September 1520 to Pope Leo X.**

I do not know Luther, nor have I ever read his books, except perhaps ten or twelve pages, and those only superficially. From what I saw, he seemed to be well qualified to expound the Scriptures in the manner of the Fathers—in an age more excessively given to mere subtleties than to important questions. Accordingly, I have favoured his good, but not his bad qualities, or rather I have favoured Christ's glory in him.

I was among the first to see that there was danger that this matter might end in uproar and no one has ever hated uproar more than I. Indeed, I even approached the printer Johann Froeben not to publish his books any more. I wrote frequently and industriously to my friends to admonish this man to observe Christian meekness in his writings and always serve the peace of the Church. And when he himself wrote me two years ago, I lovingly admonished him what I wished him to avoid. Oh, if he would have followed my advice! This letter, I hear, has even been shown to your Holiness, I presume in order to evoke hatred against me, even though it ought rather to conciliate your Holiness's favour towards me.

> 13th September 1520. *Opus Epistolarum Des.*
> *Erasmi* IV, 345.

▶   **Since Erasmus had so vigorously attacked the abuses in the Church before Luther, it was a surprise that neither he nor indeed many of the humanists subsequently joined the Protestant movement. In a letter to the Reformer Martin Bucer, Erasmus strove to explain his attitude.[2]**

You assemble a number of conjectures as to why I have not joined your Church. But you must know that the first and most important of all the reasons which withheld me from associating myself with it was my conscience: if my conscience could have been persuaded that this movement proceeded from God, I should have been now long since a soldier in your camp. The second reason is that I see many in your group who are strangers to all evangelical soundness. I make no mention of rumours and suspicions; I speak of things learned from experience, nay, learned to my own injury—things experienced not merely from the mob but from men who appear to be of some worth, not to mention the leading men. It is not for me to judge of what I know not; the world is wide. I know some as excellent men before they became devotees of your faith, what they are now like I do not know: at all events I have learned that several of them have become worse and none better, so far as human judgment can discern.

The third thing which deterred me is the intense discord between the leaders of the movement. Not to mention the Prophets and the Anabaptists, what embittered pamphlets Zwingli, Luther and Osiander[3] write against each other! I have never approved the ferocity of the leaders, but it is provoked by the actions of certain persons; when they ought to have made the Gospel acceptable by holy and forbearing conduct, if you really had what you boast of. Not to speak of the others, of what use was it for Luther to indulge in buffoonery in that fashion against the King of England, when he had undertaken a task so arduous with the general approval? . . . I seem to see a cruel and bloody century ahead, if the provoked section gets its breath again, which it is certainly now doing. You will say there is no crowd without an admixture of wicked men. Certainly it was the duty of the principal men to exercise special care in matters of conduct, and not be even on speaking terms with liars, perjurers, drunkards and fornicators. As it is I hear, and almost see, that things are far otherwise. If the husband had found his wife more amenable, the teacher his pupil more obedient, the magistrate the citizen more tractable, the employer his workman more trustworthy, the buyer the seller less deceitful, it would have been great recommendation for the Gospels. As things are, the behaviour of certain persons has had the effect of cooling the zeal of those who at first, owing to their love of piety and abhorrence of Pharisaism, looked with favour on this movement; and the princes, seeing a disorderly host springing up in its wake made up of vagabonds, fugitives, bankrupts, naked, wretched and for the most part even wicked men, are cursing, even those who in the beginning had been hopeful.

It is not without deep sorrow that I speak of all this. . . . Certain rascals say that my writings are to blame for the fact that the scholastic theologians and monks are in several places becoming less esteemed than they would like, that ceremonies are neglected, and that the supremacy of the Roman pontiff is disregarded; when it is quite clear from what source this evil has sprung. They are stretching too tight the rope which is now breaking. They almost set the Pope's authority above Christ's, they measured all piety by ceremonies, and tightened the hold of the confession to an enormous extent, while the monks lorded it without fear of punishment, by now meditating open tyranny. As a result 'the stretched string snapped', as the proverb has it; it could not be otherwise. But I sorely fear that the same will happen one day to the princes, if they too continue to stretch their rope too tightly. . . . And they [the leaders of the movement] should not have heedlessly wrecked anything without having something better ready to put in its place. As it is, those who have abandoned the Hours do not pray at all. Many who have put off pharisaical clothing are worse in other matters than they were before. Those who disdain the episcopal regulations do not even obey the commandments of God. Those who disregard the careful choice of foods indulge in greed and gluttony. It is a long-drawn-out tragedy, which every day we partly hear ourselves and partly learn of from others. I never approved of the abolition of the mass, even though I have always disliked those mean and money-grabbing mass-priests. There were other things also which could have been altered without causing riots. As things are, certain persons are not satisfied with any of the accepted practices; as if a new world could be built of a sudden. There will always be things which the pious must endure. If anyone thinks that mass ought to be abolished because many misuse it, then the sermon should be abolished also, which is almost the only custom accepted by your party. I feel the same about the invocation of the saints and about images.

11th November 1527. *Opus Epistolarum Des.*
Erasmi VII, 231–2.

▶ The following letters of the humanist and jurist Ulrich Zasius[4] typically represented the position of those whose early enthusiasm for Luther was juxtaposed with continued allegiance to the Church.

There is much I should like to discuss with you concerning Martin Luther, if a short letter could accomplish matters. In Luther there is much one can praise and defend. But again other aspects seem a bit offensive. He rightly calls all our good works a gift of God and attributes nothing but evil to our own will. This he supports with many authorities. The book of Psalms bears it out almost in every line. Chrysostom in several places in his commentary on Matthew; Gregory quite openly in his sermons, and also others whom I brought together to support the cause of this upright man in this regard—if the Lord permits. Concerning

HVLDRICHVS ZASIVS
Iurisconsultus.

Iam Sophia Zasius,quam Iuris doctor in arte
Sum bonus: hoc passim fama susurrat anus.
M. D. XXXV.   D iiij

Ulrich Zasius. (*Woodcut in Porträtsammlung,*
Universitätsbibliothek, Basel)

indulgences I have my thoughts, but do not want to express them. I have
no desire to get involved in trouble. This is an old complaint, yet unde-
cided, according to the commentary on ecclesiastical law. A conciliar
decision is necessary, personal views make little difference. Luther has
tried repeatedly with more boldness than success to cut the Gordian
knot. There are many, however, who believe that his writings are altogether true. Imagine! What Luther wrote concerning penitence and
faith, I also regard as salutary. For our entire life is a call to cast off vice
and grow in virtue. We must be ready in the struggle against the enemy,
must humble ourselves at the Cross, tame our body, and thus daily improve: such is the true task of a Christian. He who flees from it, flees

from salvation. He who fights it, destroys himself. This task consists of nothing else but penitence. Who would deny that faith is the main aspect in the sacraments? I will leave this to the theologians, since it is not my profession to discuss these matters. They must be truth-loving theologians, however.

In these points I agree with Luther and admire him. As my simple, untheological profession allows it, I am prepared to defend him. But there are in Luther's teaching some blemishes which I dislike. His assertion, for example, that we sin even when performing a good work is a misplaced proposition unless it is understood rightly. His assertion can be accepted if we consider the man who does a good work not in terms of the particular deed, but in terms of his character which, even in case of a righteous man, is imperfect and at fault in many things. Thus far I understand Luther. I agree with his opinion, for it takes away pride, increases humility, excites love and reverence for God, and is founded on the sacred Scripture. . . . He thinks it proved that the Pope is not universal bishop by divine right. I cannot say emphatically enough how much this displeases me. To begin with, it violates the decrees of Pope Leo and other popes. Of course, Luther disparages them and almost spits on them as if they were altogether irrelevant and does so without law and reason.

13th November 1519. *Zwinglis Sämtliche Werke* VII, 218ff.

In 1522 Pope Adrian VI issued, in an instruction to the papal legate Chieregati, a profound confession of the shortcoming of the Church. The paper was presented by Chieregati to the German Diet in January 1523.

If anyone should strongly assert that Luther was condemned by the Apostolic See unheard and undefended and that he should be completely heard and not be condemned before he has been convicted, reply as follows: What concerns faith is to be believed on account of divine authority and is not to be questioned. . . . And surely we acknowledge that he should not be refused a defense in regard to questions of fact—if he has really said, preached, or written such and such, or not. But concerning the divine Law and the sacraments we are called upon to stand with the authority of the saints and the Church. You may add that almost everything in which Luther departs from the consensus is already condemned by various councils. What general councils and the universal Church have approved as matters of faith must not be called into question. Otherwise an injustice is done to the assembly of the Church, if a true decision is revoked in doubt. How could there ever be certainty among men, how could there be an end to disputations and contention, if a presumptuous and perverted man is given freedom and license to depart from that which is confirmed not by a single man or a few, but by the consensus of the centuries and by the wisest men and the Catholic Church which God never permits to err in matters concerning faith. . . .

You may say that we freely confess that God permits this persecution of his Church to be brought about on account of the sins of men and, most of all, of the priests and the prelates of the Church. . . . We know that in this Holy See there has been for several years great abomination, abuse in spiritual matters, excess in mandates; indeed, everything has been changed into perversion. It is not astonishing that the sickness penetrated from the head to the members, from the highest pontiffs to the lower prelates. We all, prelates and ecclesiastics, have each one fallen in his ways and, for a long time, there was none, not even one, who did good. Wherefore it is necessary that we all give the glory to God and humble our minds before him and that each one of us may behold the cause of his fall. Let each one judge himself rather than to be judged by God with the rod of his wrath. Concerning ourselves you may promise that we will do everything so that first this See, from whom this evil powerfully progressed, will be reformed, so that, even as corruption came from there into all lower parts, likewise from there healing and reform may emanate. To accomplish this we consider ourselves the more definitely obligated, since we see how eagerly the entire world desires reform. As we have told you, we never sought this pontificate, but desired, as much as was within us, rather to live a private life serving God through a holy solitude. . . . No one should be astonished, if we will not correct all error and abuse at once. The disease is too long established and not simple, but varied and complex.

In hoc libello Pontificii oratoris continetur . . . Deutsche Reichstagstaken, Jüngere Reihe (Gotha, 1910), III, 396ff.

▶ Ignatius of Loyola, founder of the Jesuit Order, is surely the most famous representative of sixteenth-century Catholicism. Here are descriptions of him by an associate and a contemporary:[5]

Inigo de Loyola, whom divine Providence deigned to choose as the first of this company, was a native of Guipuzcoa province, belonging to one of its noblest families. . . . His education was more conformed to the spirit of the world than to that of God, inasmuch as from his boyhood, instead of proceeding to learn something more than reading and writing, he commenced to follow the Court as a page.

. . . He was valiant and loyal, spirited and enterprising. . . . Although attached to his faith, his life was not in keeping with his beliefs, and his mind was far from spiritual things; he did not avoid sin, being particularly without restraint in gaming, affairs with women, duelling, and armed affrays. . . . Once he composed a poem in honour of St Peter. . . . In affliction and trials he never blasphemed against God. . . .

Chronicle of Father Polanco (Fontes Narrativi, I, 153–4).

Not very tall, white skinned, with a high colour in his cheeks, he was genial looking if somewhat serious. He had very beautiful red hair, but was going bald on the temples and forehead. . . .

A little bit of a Spaniard, slightly lame, with joyful, lively eyes.

He was of medium height; perhaps it would be more correct to describe him as on the small side and short-legged, though all his brothers had been tall, well-built men. His face was that of one bearing authority and responsibility. His forehead was broad and smooth, though bearing the traces of wrinkles; his eyes were sunken and their eyelids shrunken and wrinkled because of the tears he so often shed. He had medium-sized ears, and his nose was high and curved; his colour was inclined to be high; in his later years his baldness gave him a venerable aspect. His expression was joyfully grave and gravely joyful, so that his serenity rejoiced those who beheld him while his gravity calmed them. He limped a little on one leg, but was not deformed; and he walked in so careful a manner that it was hardly noticeable. His two feet were all calloused, severely so, having gone for such a long time barefoot and walked so many journeys.

He allowed his beard to grow fairly long; later in life, when he went to live in Rome, he trimmed it shorter; his portraits show how he kept it.

In contrast to his lack in inches he was inclined to bulkiness of chest and torso. He must have possessed a wonderful constitution and enjoyed great health and strength when young, for the fact remains that in his mature years, though weakened by fasting and suffering from chronic stomach and liver ailments, he nevertheless put on weight easily. . . . His face was not long, as some painters have portrayed him, but short and round; his chin was the shape of a shield.

Monumenta Ignatiana, I, 243; II, 83–87, 490.

▶   An injury in battle proved to be the turning-point of Ignatius's
     life. He himself reflected as follows:[6]

Up to his twenty-sixth year he was a man given over to the vanities of
the world, and took a special delight in the exercise of arms, with a great
and vain desire of winning glory. He was in a fortress which the French
were attacking, and although the others were of the opinion that they
should surrender on terms of having their lives spared, as they clearly
saw there was no possibility of a defence, he gave so many reasons to the
governor that he persuaded him to carry on the defence against the judgment of the officers, who found some strength in his spirit and courage.
. . . After the assault had been going on for some time, a cannon ball
struck him in the leg, crushing its bones, and because it passed between
his legs it also seriously wounded the other.

With his fall, the others in the fortress surrendered to the French, who
took possession, and treated the wounded men with great kindliness and
courtesy. . . . Here he found himself in a very serious condition. The
doctors and surgeons whom he had called from all parts were of the
opinion that the leg should be operated on again and the bones reset,
either because they had been poorly set in the first place, or because the
jogging of the journey had displaced them so that they would not heal.
Again he went through this butchery, in which as in all the others that
he had suffered he uttered no word, nor gave any sign of pain other than
clenching his fists.

His condition grew worse. Besides being unable to eat he showed other
symptoms which are usually a sign of approaching death. The feast of
St John drew near, and as the doctors had very little hope of his recovery
they advised him to make his confession. He received the last sacraments
on the eve of the feast of Sts Peter and Paul, and the doctors told him that
if he showed no improvement by midnight, he could consider himself as
good as dead. The patient had some devotion to St Peter, and so our
Lord wished that his improvement should begin that very midnight.
So rapid was his recovery that within a few days he was thought to be out
of danger of death.

When the bones knit, one below the knee remained astride another,
which caused a shortening of the leg. The bones so raised caused a protuberance that was not pleasant to the sight. The sick man was not able
to put up with this, because he had made up his mind to seek his fortune
in the world. He thought the protuberance was going to be unsightly and
asked the surgeons whether it could not be cut away. They told him that
it could be cut away, but that the pain would be greater than all he had

already suffered, because it was now healed and it would take some time to cut it off. He determined, nevertheless, to undergo this martyrdom to gratify his own inclinations. . . .

Many ointments were applied and devices employed for keeping the leg continually stretched which caused him many days of martyrdom. . . . In everything else he was quite well, but he was not able to stand upon that leg, and so had to remain in bed. He had been much given to reading worldly books of fiction and knight errantry, and feeling well enough to read he asked for some of these books to help while away the time. In that house, however, they could find none of those he was accustomed to read, and so they gave him a life of Christ and a book of the lives of the saints in Spanish.

By the frequent reading of these books he conceived some affection for what he found there narrated. Pausing in his reading, he gave himself up to thinking over what he had read. At other times he dwelt on the things of the world which formerly had occupied his thoughts. Of the many vain things that presented themselves to him, one took such possession of his heart that without realizing it he could spend two, three, or even four hours on end thinking of it, fancying what he would have to do in the service of a certain lady, of the means he would take to reach the country where she was living, of the verses, the promises he would make her, the deeds of gallantry he would do in her service. He was so enamoured with all this that he did not see how impossible it would all be, because the lady was of no ordinary rank; neither countess, nor duchess, but of a nobility much higher than any of these.

Nevertheless, our Lord came to his assistance, for he saw to it that these thoughts were succeeded by others which sprang from the things he was reading. In reading[7] the life of our Lord and the lives of the saints, he paused to think and reason with himself, 'Suppose that I should do what St Francis did, what St Dominic did?'

St Ignatius' Own Story, pp. 7–9.

> ▶ Ignatius's decision to dedicate himself to the service of God was
>   followed by a general confession.

He continued his way to Montserrat, thinking as usual of the great deeds he was going to do for the love of God. As his mind was filled with the adventures of Amadis of Gaul and such books, thoughts corresponding to these adventures came to his mind. He determined, therefore, on a

Martin Luther. The lines were to enable easy copying. It is interesting to observe the similarity with the portrait on page 48— as well as the change in Luther's appearance as shown on pages 395, 406. (*Woodcut by Lucas Cranach the Elder, 1528. Staatl. Kunstsammlungen, Weimar*)

Erasmus of Rotterdam. (*Louvre, Paris*)

Ignatius of Loyola.
(*Posthumous painting based on a death mask by Sánches Coello*)

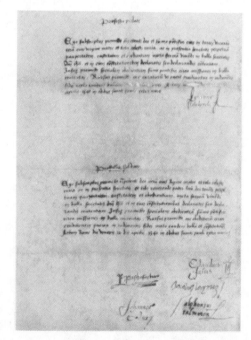

The vow signed by Ignatius and his companions in Paris in 1534.

watch of arms throughout a whole night, without ever sitting or lying down, but standing a while and then kneeling before the altar of our Lady of Montserrat, where he had made up his mind to leave his fine attire and to clothe himself with the armour of Christ. Leaving, then, his place, he continued, as was his wont, thinking about his resolutions, and when he arrived at Montserrat, after praying for a while and making an engagement with his confessor, he made a general confession in writing which lasted three days. He arranged with the confessor to have the mule taken away, and his sword and dagger hung in the church at the altar of our Lady. This man was the first to whom he had made known his purpose, because up to then he had not revealed it to any confessor.

St Ignatius' Own Story, p. 15.

▶ **Many years later someone recalled having met Ignatius on that occasion.**

We were walking along on the homeward journey, all together, and chatting a little, when, just as we neared the little chapel of the Apostles, a poor beggar dressed all in sacking such as pilgrims wear came out towards us. He was not very tall; his skin was white and his hair red; he was good-looking, if somewhat serious, and kept his eyes fixed on the ground. . . . He walked very wearily and with a limp in the right foot. . . . He asked my mother if she knew of any hospital nearby where he could find lodging. She noted that he looked a good and honourable person whose glance moved one to devotion and piety; she also noticed that he was beginning to go bald. She told him that the nearest hospital was three leagues away in Manresa, from which town she had come and towards which she was now returning; she added that, if he wished to accompany or follow our group, she would endeavour to secure accommodation for him. Thanking her in Christian and honourable words, he decided to follow us, we all going slowly because of his lameness, so that he could come along in our company.

M. Purcell, *The First Jesuit*, p. 83.
(*MI, Scripta*, II, 395.)

▶ **An epidemic delayed Ignatius's journey to the Holy Land.**

At Manresa also, where he remained almost a year, after he began to feel God's consolations and saw the fruit produced in the souls with whom he dealt, he gave up those outward extremes he formerly adopted, and trimmed his nails and hair. One day, in this town, when he was hearing mass in the church of the monastery already mentioned, during the elevation he saw with the inner eyes of the soul something like white rays that came from above. Although he cannot explain this after so long a time, yet what he clearly saw with his understanding was how Jesus Christ our Lord is present in that most holy sacrament.

St Ignatius' Own Story, p. 23.

▶   After a short stay in the Holy Land, Ignatius returned to his native Spain, then went to France, in order to obtain further schooling. Everywhere his personality attracted like-minded followers.

By this time he had finished the course in philosophy, and studied theology for several years and gathered about him a number of companions. . . .

By this time they had come to some decision as to what they were going to do. Their plan was to go to Venice and from there to Jerusalem, where they were to spend the rest of their lives for the good of souls. If they were refused permission to remain in Jerusalem they would return to Rome, offer themselves to the Vicar of Christ, asking him to make use of them wherever he thought it would be more to God's glory and the good of souls. They proposed to wait a year in Venice before sailing, and if during that year there was no chance of taking passage for the East, they would be released from their vow to go to Jerusalem and could go to the Pope. . . .

This was the year 1535, and according to their agreement the companions were to leave Paris in 1537, on the feast of the Conversion of St Paul [25th January]. But because of the war, they were forced to anticipate that date, and left in November of 1536. But just as he was about to leave, the pilgrim heard that an accusation had been lodged against him with the Inquisitor, and a process begun. Knowing this, and seeing that he had not been summoned, he went in person to the Inquisitor and told him what he had learned, that he was about to leave for Spain, and that he had associates. For this reason he asked him to pass sentence. The Inquisitor said that it was true there had been an accusation, but that he did not see that there was anything of importance in it. He only wanted to see what he had written in the *Exercises*. When he saw them, he praised them highly, and asked the pilgrim to leave him a copy. This he did. Nevertheless, the pilgrim insisted that his case be brought to trial and that sentence be passed. But, as the Inquisitor seemed unwilling to do this, the pilgrim brought a public notary and witnesses to the Inquisitor's house and received formal testimony of the whole affair.

St Ignatius' Own Story, pp. 58–59.

▶   **By 1537, Ignatius and his companions arrived in Venice to fulfil**
     their vow. Again a delay became necessary.

During those days in Venice he spent some time giving the *Exercises* and in other spiritual associations. . . .

In Venice also another persecution was begun against the pilgrim. There were many who said that his likeness had been burned in Spain and in Paris. Matters came to such a pass that a trial was held and sentence rendered in favour of the pilgrim.

The nine companions arrived in Venice in the beginning of 1537. There they separated to serve the sick in the different hospitals. After two or three months they all went to Rome to get the Pope's blessing before setting out on their journey to Jerusalem. The pilgrim did not go with them, because of Doctor Ortiz and the Theatine Cardinal, who had just been created. The companions returned from Rome with drafts for two or three *scudi* which they were given as alms to help them on their way to Jerusalem. They did not wish to receive the money, except in cheques, and since they did not go to Jerusalem later, they returned the cheques to those who had given them.

The companions returned to Venice just as they had left it, that is, on foot and begging, but divided into three parties, which were always made up of different nationalities. Those who were not priests were ordained in Venice, and received faculties from the Nuncio, who was in Venice at the time, and who was later called Cardinal Verallo. They were ordained under the title of poverty, all taking the vows of poverty and chastity. . . .

As the year went by and they found no passage to Jerusalem, they decided to go to Rome. . . .

They went to Rome in three or four groups, the pilgrim with Faber and Laynez,[8] and in this journey he received many special favours from God.

He had made up his mind after taking orders to wait a year before saying mass, preparing himself and praying our Lady to place him with her Son. One day, a few miles before they reached Rome, while he was praying in a church, he felt such a change in his soul, and saw so clearly that God the Father placed him with Christ his Son, that he would not dare to doubt that the Father had placed him with his Son.

St Ignatius' Own Story, pp. 64–66.

/ ▶   **The group devoted itself to charitable works in Rome.**[9]

No eminent person seemed worried over the situation. No one took the trouble to visit the hospitals, indeed no one bothered to inquire into the calamitous misery or gave any show of compassion. . . . To remedy, inasmuch as in them lay, such great necessity, the companions begged and collected money and bread in all quarters; they made some herb stews and searched for the poor in the streets and piazzas and fetched them to the house; there, having washed their feet, they fed them, doctored their ills and sores, and taught them some catechism. . . . Sometimes they put the sick in their own beds, they themselves sleeping on the floors; and they begged hay and fuel and food from their friends, carrying such alms home on their backs through the city. At times as many as two or three hundred were crowded into their house, all being fed and comforted. The companions also visited almost two thousand people shivering in the wretched houses of Rome's poorest streets, helping them with the money which had been given as alms to the company by friends.

Chronicle of Cornelio di Fine (Tacchi-Venturi, *Storia della Compagnia di Gesù in Italia* II, I, p. 163).

/ ▶   **The following incident, involving Francis Xavier, describes the willingness of the 'pilgrims' to serve their fellows.**[10]

In the hospital of the Incurabili there was a leper or a man very like a leper, as he was covered all over with foul suppurating sores. As my friend one day was passing by, this unfortunate man cried out to him, 'Ho, there! Pray, rub my back', which he at once turned to do until suddenly overcome by sensations of horror and nausea, fearing that he might catch the loathsome disease himself. But desiring rather to crush his rebellious feelings than to avoid the contagion, he scraped some of the pus together with his fingers and swallowed it. Next morning, he told me with a smile how he had dreamt in the night that the leprosy of the afflicted man remained stuck in his throat and that he could not get rid of it by coughing or other means, short of being very sick. In fact, however, it happened with him as our Lord said, 'If they drink any deadly thing it shall in no wise hurt them'.

Fontes Narrativi I, 110.

► **Ignatius and his companions ran into opposition.**[11] ✓

Inigo of Loyola, a wolf going about Rome in the guise of a shepherd; a jailbird, a fellow who had cheated the Inquisition at Alcala,[12] Paris and Venice. Loyola and his *Exercises* raised a storm in Paris, which was still remembered in university circles there. . . . And all this can be borne out by a man of incorruptible faith who, attracted at first by Inigo of Loyola, has—in common with other Spaniards—now left him, renouncing him and his works with horror.

Fontes Narrativi I, 201.

► **But the opposition was soon overcome. On 27th September 1540** ✓
the Bull 'Regimini Ecclesiae Militantes' established canonically
the Society of Jesus.[13]

We have recently learned that our beloved sons Ignatius de Loyola, Peter Faber, James Laynez, Claude le Jay, Pasquier Brouet, Francis Xavier, Alfonzo Salmeron, Simon Rodriguez, John Lodure, and Nicholas de Bobadilla, priests, masters of arts, and graduates of the University of of Paris, and students of some years' standing in theology coming from several parts of the world, inspired, as they piously believe, by the Holy Spirit, united themselves some time ago to dedicate their lives corporately to the perpetual service of our Lord Jesus Christ and ourselves and our successors. For many years they have laboured laudably in the vineyard of the Lord by publicly preaching the Word of God according to a stated permission, by privately admonishing the faithful to a good and blessed life, by stimulating them to pious meditation, by ministering to the sick, by instructing the young and ignorant in the essential doctrines of the Christian faith, indeed by fulfilling all commandments of love for the consolation of souls in whatever lands they visited. Thereupon they gathered in this beautiful city and remained within its confines in order to complete the union of their society in Christ. In accordance with the principles which they have learned by experience will further their ends, they have drawn up a rule of life in conformity with evangelical precepts and the canonical sanctions of the Fathers. Their rule is the following:

Whoever desires to fight for God under the banner of the Cross in our society—which we want to be characterized by the name of Jesus—and who wishes to serve the Roman pontiff, his vicar on earth, shall, after a solemn vow of perpetual chastity, remind himself that he is a member of a society founded for the special purpose of providing spiritual consolation for the furtherance of souls in Christian living and doctrine, the propagation of faith by public preaching, and the ministry of the Word of God, spiritual exercises and deeds of mercy, and above all the instruction of the ignorant in the Christian religion and by hearing the confession of Christian believers. He shall take care that he constantly keep God and the purpose of this society, which is virtually a way to God, always before his eyes. . . . Only the superiors have a right to give orders. All members should know that the entire society and its individual members are fighting for God in faithful obedience to our most holy lord, the Pope, and to the other Roman bishops who succeed him. And although the Gospel teaches, as we know and confess, that all Christian believers are subject to the Roman pontiff as their head and as vicar of Christ, yet we have considered it appropriate that . . . we should pledge ourselves to a special vow, in addition to the general obligation, that we are pledged to fulfil whatever the present Roman pontiff, or any future one, may decree concerning the welfare of souls and the propagation of the faith. We are to fulfil furthermore within our ability any task assigned to us without excuse or pretence. Even if he should send us to the Turks or any other infidels, even those living in the region called India, or to the heretics, schismatics or believers of whatever kind.

Therefore those who wish to become members of our society shall reflect long and deeply before they take this burden upon their shoulders, . . . whether the Holy Spirit promises them sufficient grace that they can hope, with his help, to fulfil their difficult vocation. If they have, under God's inspiration, enrolled in this army of Jesus Christ, then they must have their loins girded day and night and be prepared for the fulfilment of such a mighty task.

Nor shall there be amongst us any ambition or rivalry whatsoever for missions and provinces. . . . Subordination shall, indeed, both for the sake of the wide activities of the order and also for the assiduous practice —never sufficiently to be commended—of humility, be bound always to obey the commander in every matter pertaining to the organization of the society, and shall recognize Christ as present in him, and shall do him reverence as far as is seemly. . . .

Whereas, moreover, we have found that the happier, purer and more edifying life is that removed as far as possible from all contagion of avarice and patterned as much as possible after evangelical poverty, and whereas we know that our Lord Jesus Christ will furnish the necessities of food and clothing to his servants who seek only the kingdom of God, therefore each and every member shall vow perpetual poverty, declaring that neither individually nor even in common for the support or use of the society will he acquire any civil right over any permanent property, rents or incomes whatever, but that he will be content with the use only of such articles as shall be given him to meet his necessities. They may, however, maintain in universities a college or colleges with means or possessions to be applied to the needs and exigencies of the students; all control or supervision of any sort over the said colleges and students being vested in the commander and the society. . . .

The foregoing is what, by the permission of our lord Paul and the apostolic see, we have been allowed to set forth as a general ideal for our profession. We have taken this step at this time in order that by this brief document we might inform the persons who are inquiring now about our way of life, and also posterity—if, by God's will, there shall be those to follow us in the path upon which (attended though it be by many grave difficulties) we have entered. We have further judged it expedient to prescribe that no one shall be received into this society until he has been long and thoroughly tried; but when he has proved himself wise in Christ as well as in doctrine, and exalted in the purity of the Christian life, then at length he shall be admitted into the army of Jesus Christ. May he deign to prosper our feeble undertaking to the glory of God the Father, to whom alone be ever praise and honour throughout the ages. Amen.

Whereas nothing may be discovered in the foregoing which is not pious or devout, in order that these associates who have made their humble application to us may be the better forwarded in their religious plan of life for feeling themselves included in the grace of the apostolic see and finding their projects meeting our approval, we do, through apostolic authority, approve, confirm, bless and fortify with a bulwark of ever-lasting power the whole and every part of the aforesaid organization, and we take these associates under the protection of ourselves and this holy apostolic see. . . . We will also that persons who desire to profess the rules of life of this society be admitted into it and counted with the said society up to the number of sixty and no more. To no man whatsoever be it permitted to infringe or violate this statement of our approbation, benediction and justification. If any one shall presume to attempt it, let him be assured that he incurs the wrath of Almighty God and of the blessed Peter and Paul, his apostles.

Bulla Romanorum VI, 303ff.

▶ On 30th June 1556, Ignatius died. What took place was duly recorded.[14]

We deferred his burial until Saturday after vespers. The concourse of the pious and their devotion was great, though he remained in the room where he died. Some kissed his hands; others, his feet; they touched his body with their rosaries. . . . We did all we could to keep off those who wanted to take away bits of his biretta or clothes. . . . They took his shoe-laces, his nightcap, and other belongings of his, though we gave nothing and, when we found what they were doing, did not allow the like to continue. Some artists made likenesses of him, which he had never permitted during his lifetime, though often asked.

Monumenta Ignatiana I, 764f.

► Ignatius's piety can perhaps be best discerned from his 'Spiritual Journal', an intimate record of his spirtual life which he kept for several weeks in the spring of 1544 and, again, of 1545.[15]

The Name of Jesus

Friday [8th February].—After notable devotion and tears at prayer, beginning with preparation for mass, and during it with deep devotion and tears also, holding my tongue when I could, with the decision for perfect poverty.

Soon after mass, with devotion and not without tears, going through the elections for an hour and a half or more and making an offering of what seemed to be better supported by reason, and by a stronger inclination of will, that is, to have no revenue, wishing to present this to the Father through the mediation and prayers of the Mother and the Son, I prayed first to her to help me with her Son and the Father, and then prayed to the Son to help me with his Father in company with the Mother, I felt within me an impulse to go and betake myself to the Father, and in doing so my hair stood on end with a most remarkable warmth in my whole body. Following on this, tears and the deepest devotion (V).[16]

Reading this later, and thinking it was good to have written it out, a fresh devotion came upon me, not without water in my eyes, (V) and later, recalling these graces I had received, a fresh devotion. . . . Our Lady in the Temple. Simeon.

Friday [15th February].—At the first prayer, when naming the Eternal Father, etc., a sensible interior sweetness came and lasted, not without a movement to tears, and later with deep devotion, which became much deeper at the end, without, however, revealing any mediators or persons.

Later, on going out to say mass, when beginning the prayer, I saw a likeness of our Lady, and realized how serious had been my fault of the other day, not without some interior movement and tears, thinking that the Blessed Virgin felt ashamed at asking for me so often after my many failings, so much so that our Lady hid herself from me, and I found no devotion either in her or from on high. After this, as I did not find our Lady, I sought comfort on high, and there came upon me a great movement of tears and sobbing with a certain assurance that the Heavenly Father was showing himself favourable and kindly, so much so that he gave a sign that it would be pleasing to him to be asked through our Lady, whom I could not see.

While preparing the altar, and after vesting, and during the mass, very intense interior movements, and many and intense tears and sobbing, with frequent loss of speech, and also after the end of mass, and for long periods during the mass, preparing and afterwards, the clear view of our Lady, very propitious before the Father, to such an extent, that in the prayers to the Father, to the Son, and at the consecration, I could not help feeling and seeing her, as though she were a part, or the doorway, of all the grace I felt in my soul. At the consecration she showed that her flesh was in that of her Son, with such great light that I cannot write about it. I had no doubt of the first oblation already made. . . .

St Mark
Friday [25th April].—Tears at mass and before it.

Holy Spirit
Saturday [26th April].—No tears.

Day
Sunday [27th April].—Tears during mass and before it.

Trinity
Monday [28th April].—Tears at mass and before it.
Tuesday [29th April].—With tears.
Wednesday [30th April].—With tears.
Thursday [1st May].—With tears.
Friday [2nd May].—No tears.
Saturday [3rd May].—Tears.
Sunday [4th May].—With tears.
Monday [5th May]. ⎫
Tuesday [6th May]. ⎬ Tears, I think.
Wednesday [7th May]. ⎫
Thursday [8th May]. ⎬ No tears, I think.
Friday [9th May]. ⎭
Saturday [10th May].—Many tears at mass.
Sunday [11th May].—Tears before mass and during it an abundance of them, and continuing, together with the interior *loquela* during the mass. It seems to me that it was given miraculously, as I had asked for it

that same day, because in the whole week, I sometimes found the external *loquela*, and sometimes I did not, and the interior less, although last Saturday I was a little more purified.

The Spiritual Journal of St Ignatius Loyola,
pp. 2, 7, 8, 43.

▶	Ignatius pursued an extensive correspondence, which reveals his varied interests.[17] The following excerpt shows his concern for the proper education of youth.

. . . I have been reflecting on how young minds are by nature disposed to receive and retain early impressions, whether they be good or harmful. And these first impressions, together with the good or bad example and instructions they receive, have a very important influence on their later lives. In the light of this truth I realize that the books which are read, especially in courses of literature, such as Terence, Virgil, and others, while they contain many things that are profitable for the learned and far from useless in the practical aspects of life, also contain many things that are profane, immodest, and harmful even when they are no more than alluded to. Scripture tells us that 'the imagination and thought of man's heart are prone to evil from his youth'. This will be truer still if such things are placed before young boys in books which they study, hear explained, and keep ever ready at hand.

22nd June 1549. *Letters of St Ignatius of Loyola,*
p. 189 (*MI* II, No. 743).

▶	The most celebrated of Ignatius's letters dealt with obedience.

. . . We may allow ourselves to be surpassed by other religious orders in fasts, watchings, and other austerities, which each one following its institute holily observes. But in the purity and perfection of obedience together with the true resignation of our wills and the abnegation of our judgment, I am very desirous, my dear brothers, that they who serve God in this society should be conspicuous, so that by this virtue its true sons may be recognized as men who regard not the person whom they obey, but in him Christ our Lord, for whose sake they obey. For the superior is to be obeyed not because he is prudent, or good, or qualified by any other gift of God, but because he holds the place and the authority of God, as Eternal Truth has said, 'He that heareth you, heareth me; and he that despiseth you, despiseth me.' Nor on the contrary, should he lack prudence, is he to be the less obeyed in that in which he is superior, since he represents him who is infallible wisdom, and who will supply what is wanting in his minister; nor, should he lack goodness or other desirable qualities, since Christ our Lord, having said, 'The scribes and the Pharisees have sitten on the chair of Moses,' adds, 'All things, therefore, whatsoever they shall say to you, observe and do; but according to their works do ye not.'

Therefore I should wish that all of you would train yourselves to recognize Christ our Lord in any superior, and with all devotion reverence and obey his Divine Majesty in him. . . . You can judge, when a religious is taken not only as superior, but expressly in the place of Christ our Lord, to serve as director and guide in the divine service, what rank he ought to hold in the mind of the inferior, and whether he ought to be looked upon as man or rather as the vicar of Christ our Lord.

I also desire that this be firmly fixed in your minds, that the first degree of obedience is very low, which consists in the execution of what is commanded, and that it does not deserve the name of obedience, since it does not attain to the worth of this virtue unless it rises to the second degree, which is to make the superior's will one's own in such a way that there is not merely the effectual execution of the command, but an interior conformity, whether to wish or not wish a thing done. . . .

Now, because this disposition of will in man is of so great worth, so also is the offering of it, when by obedience it is offered to his Creator and Lord. How great a deception it is, and how dangerous for those who think it lawful to withdraw from the will of their superior, I do not say only in those things pertaining to flesh and blood, but even in those which of their nature are spiritual and holy, such as fasts, prayers, and other pious works! . . . The activity of Martha was holy, and holy the contemplation of Magdalene, and holy the penitence and tears with which she bathed the feet of Christ our Lord. But all this was to be done in Bethania, which is interpreted to mean the house of obedience. It would seem, therefore, that Christ our Lord would give us to understand, as St Bernard remarks, 'that neither the activity of good works, nor the leisure of contemplation, nor the tears of the penitent would have pleased him out of Bethania.'

Therefore, my dear brothers, try to make the surrender of your wills entire. Offer freely to God through his ministers the liberty he has bestowed on you. Do not think it a slight advantage of your free will the ability of restoring it wholly in obedience to him who gave it to you. In this you do not lose it, but rather perfect it in conforming your will wholly with the most certain rule of all rectitude, which is the divine will, the interpreter of which is the superior who governs you in place of God.

For this reason you must never try to draw the will of the superior (which you should consider the will of God) to your own will. This would not be making the divine will the rule of your own, but your own the rule of the divine, and so perverting the order of his wisdom. It is a great delusion in those whose understanding has been darkened by self-love to think that there is any obedience in the subject who tries to draw the superior to what he wishes. . . .

Would to God that this obedience of the understanding were as much understood and practised as it is necessary to anyone living in religion and acceptable to God our Lord. I say necessary, for, just as in the celestial bodies, if the lower is to receive movement and influence from the higher it must be subject and subordinate, the one body being ordered and adjusted to the other; so, when one rational creature is moved by another, as takes place in obedience, the one that is moved must be subject and subordinated to the one by whom he is moved, if he is to receive influence and virtue from him. Now, this subjection and subordination cannot be had unless the understanding and the will of the inferior is in conformity with the superior.

Now, if we regard the end of obedience, as our will so our understanding may be mistaken as to what is good for us. And therefore we think it expedient to conform our will with that of the superior to keep it from going astray, so the understanding ought to be conformed with his to keep it from straying likewise. 'Lean not upon thy own prudence,' says Scripture. Thus, they who are wise judge it to be true prudence not to rely on their own judgment even in other affairs of life, and especially when personal interests are at stake, in which men as a rule, because of their lack of self-control, are not good judges. This being so, we ought to follow the judgment of another (even when he is not our superior) rather than our own in matters concerning ourselves. How much more, then, the judgment of the superior whom we have taken as a guide to stand in the place of God and to interpret the divine will for us? And it is certain that this guidance is all the more necessary in men and matters spiritual, as the danger in the spiritual life is great when one advances rapidly in it without the bridle of discretion. . . .

On the other hand, without this obedience of the judgment, it is impossible for the obedience of will and execution to be what they should. For the appetitive powers of the soul naturally follow the apprehensive, and in the long run the will cannot without violence obey against one's judgment. When it does obey for some time, misled by the common apprehension that it must obey when commanded amiss, it cannot do so for any length of time. And so perseverance fails, or at least the perfection of obedience, which consists in obeying with love and cheerfulness. But when one acts in opposition to one's judgment, one cannot obey lovingly and cheerfully as long as such repugnance exists. . . . That renowned simplicity of blind obedience fails, when we call into question the justice of the command, or even condemn the superior because he bids us do something that is not pleasing. Humility fails, for although on the one hand we submit, on the other we prefer ourselves to the superior. Fortitude in difficult tasks fails, and in a word all the perfections of this virtue.

On the contrary, when one obeys without submitting one's judgment, there arise dissatisfaction, pain, reluctance, slackness, murmurings, excuses, and other imperfections and obstacles of no small moment, which strip obedience of its value and merit. . . .

Indeed, if we look to the peace and quiet of mind of him who obeys, it is certain that he will never find it who has within himself the cause of his disquiet and unrest, that is, a judgment of his own opposed to what obedience lays upon him. . . .

I seem to hear some of you say, most dear brothers, that you see the importance of this virtue, but that you would like to see how you can attain to its perfection. To this I answer with Pope St Leo, 'Nothing is difficult unto the humble, and nothing hard unto the meek.' Be humble and meek, therefore, and God our Lord will bestow his grace, which will enable you to maintain sweetly and lovingly the offering that you have made to him.

In addition to these means, I will place before you three especially which will give you great assistance in attaining this perfection of obedience.

The first is that, as I said at the beginning, you do not behold in the person of your superior a man subject to errors and miseries, but rather him whom you obey in man, Christ, the highest wisdom, immeasurable goodness and infinite charity, who, you know, cannot be deceived and does not wish to deceive you. And because you are certain that you have set upon your own shoulders this yoke of obedience for the love of God, submitting yourself to the will of the superior in order to be more conformable to the divine will, be assured that his most faithful charity will ever direct you by the means which you yourselves have chosen. Therefore, do not look upon the voice of the superior, as far as he commands you, otherwise than as the voice of Christ. . . . Thus, if you do not look upon man with the eyes of the body, but upon God with those of the soul, you will find no difficulty in conforming your will and judgment with the rule of action which you yourselves have chosen.

The second means is that you be quick to look for reasons to defend what the superior commands, or to what he is inclined, rather than to dis-approve of it. A help towards this will be to love whatever obedience shall enjoin. From this will come a cheerful obedience without any trouble. . . .

The third means to subject the understanding, which is even easier and surer and in use among the holy fathers, is to presuppose and believe, very much as we are accustomed to do in matters of faith, that what the superior enjoins is the command of God our Lord and his will. Then to proceed blindly, without inquiry of any kind, to the carrying out of the command, with a kind of passion to obey. So we are to think Abraham did when commanded to sacrifice his son Isaac. Likewise in the New Testa-ment, some of those holy fathers to whom Cassian refers, such as the Abbot John, who did not question whether what he was commanded was profitable or not, as when with such great labour he watered a dry stick throughout a year. Or whether it was possible or not, when he tried so earnestly at the command of his superior to move a rock which a large number of men would not have been able to move. . . .

It is by this means that Divine Providence gently disposes all things, bringing to their appointed ends the lowest by the middlemost, and the middlemost by the highest. Even in the angels there is the subordination of one hierarchy to another, and in the heavens and all the bodies that are moved, the lowest by the highest, and the highest in their turn, unto the Supreme Mover of all.

> 26th March 1553. *Letters of St Ignatius of Loyola,*
> pp. 288–95 (*MI* IV, No. 3304).

✓ ▶   Ignatius's constant concern was the check of Protestantism. Here he suggests appropriate methods for this enterprise:

Seeing the progress which the heretics have made in a short time, spread-ing the poison of their evil teaching throughout so many countries and peoples, and making use of the verse of the Apostle to describe their progress, 'And their speech spreadeth like a canker', it would seem that our society, having been accepted by Divine Providence among the efficacious means to repair such great damage, should be solicitous to prepare the proper steps, such as are quickly applied and can be widely adopted, thus exerting itself to the utmost of its powers to preserve what is still sound and to restore what has fallen sick of the plague of heresy, especially in the northern nations.

The heretics have made their false theology popular and presented it in a way that is within the capacity of the common people. They preach it to the people and teach it in the schools, and scatter booklets which can be bought and understood by many, and make their influence felt by means of their writings when they cannot do so by their preaching. Their success is largely due to the negligence of those who should have shown some interest; and the bad example and the ignorance of Catholics, especially the clergy, have made such ravages in the vineyard of the Lord. Hence it would seem that our Society should make use of the following means to put a stop and apply a remedy to the evils which have come upon the Church through these heretics.

In the first place, the sound theology which is taught in the universities and seeks its foundation in philosophy, and therefore requires a long time to acquire is adapted only to good and alert minds; and because the weaker ones can be confused and, if they lack foundations, collapse, it would be good to make a summary of theology to deal with topics that are important but not controversial, with great brevity. There could be more detail in matters controversial, but it should be accommodated to the present needs of the people. It should solidly prove dogmas with good arguments from Scripture, tradition, the councils, and the doctors, and refute the contrary teaching. It would not require much time to teach such a theology, since it would not go very deeply into other matters. In this way theologians could be produced in a short time who could take care of the preaching and teaching in many places. The abler students could be given higher courses which include greater detail. Those who do not succeed in these higher courses should be removed from them and put in this shorter course of theology.

The principal conclusion of this theology, in the form of a short catechism, could be taught to children, as the Christian doctrine is now taught, and likewise to the common people who are not too infected or too capable of subtleties. This could also be done with the younger students in the lower classes, where they could learn it by heart. . . .

Another excellent means for helping the Church in this trial would be to multiply the colleges and schools of the society in many lands, especially where a good attendance could be expected. There might possibly be need of a dispensation to accept colleges with a smaller number of students than our Institute demands, or else that classes be accepted without undertaking perpetual charge of a college, if there is among ours, or elsewhere, someone to teach the said theology to the students and preach sound doctrine to the people, which with the administration of the sacraments will promote their spiritual welfare.

Not only in the places where we have a residence, but even in the neighbourhood, the better among our students could be sent to teach the Christian doctrine on Sundays and feast days. Even the extern students, should there be suitable material among them, could be sent by the rector for the same service. Thus, besides the correct doctrine, they would be giving the example of a good life, and by removing every appearance of greed they will be able to refute the strongest argument of the heretics— a bad life, namely, and the ignorance of the Catholic clergy.

The heretics write a large number of booklets and pamphlets, by means of which they aim at taking away all authority from the Catholics, and especially from the society, and set up their false dogmas. It would seem expedient, therefore, that ours here also write answers in pamphlet form, short and well written, so that they can be produced without delay and bought by many. In this way the harm that is being done by the pamphlets of the heretics can be remedied and sound teaching spread. These works should be modest, but lively; they should point out the evil that is abroad and uncover the evil machinations and deceits of the adversaries. A large number of these pamphlets could be gathered into one volume. Care should be taken, however, that this be done by learned men well grounded in theology, who will adapt it to the capacity of the multitude.

With these measures it would seem that we could bring great relief to the Church, and in many places quickly apply a remedy to the beginnings of the evil before the poison has gone so deep that it will be very difficult to remove it from the heart. But we should use the same diligence in healing that the heretics are using in infecting the people. We will have the advantage over them in that we possess a solidly founded, and therefore an enduring, doctrine. . . .

13th August 1554. *Letters of St Ignatius of Loyola,*
pp. 345-7 (*MI* XII, No. 27).

▶   The Jesuit order soon engaged actively in missionary activity outside Europe. Ignatius here makes suggestions for the work in Ethiopia.

Some suggestions which may help to bring the kingdom of Prester John into union with the Catholic faith and Church.

Since, humanly speaking, the principal factor in this undertaking will be found primarily in Prester John, King of Ethiopia, secondarily in the people, a few suggestions will be offered which may be of help in winning over Prester John. They will be followed by others which may help in dealing with the people and Prester John conjointly.

For the King
Besides the bulls which the Pope addresses to him, the letters which are

written him from here will afford some help in winning over the heart of Prester John. They recall to mind the submission which his father David sent to the Holy See, and contain certain recommendations of those who are sent and accredited to him. They also make other friendly advances. But the principal and final help, after that of God our Lord, for winning the heart of Prester John must come from the King. Not merely letters from his Highness, but, if he will agree to it, a special ambassador will be required, who on the part of the King will call on Prester John and present the patriarch, the coadjutor bishops, and the other priests, and explain the order that will be followed, so that it will be no longer necessary to take patriarchs from Moorish lands or from schismatic Christians. . . .

It might be good to see whether his Highness thinks that some presents should be sent, especially of things that are held in esteem in Ethiopia; and in offering them he could indicate that a true union of friendship will exist among Christian princes when they all hold the one religion. When this is recognized, he could send him every kind of official he desired, and God will give him the grace to overcome the Moors, so far as this will be for God's greater service.

Some letters from the King to individuals will also be of help, especially to those who are closer to Prester John and with whom he consults and whom he holds in esteem, notably the Portuguese. Other letters, if the King agrees, could be brought unaddressed, the proper addresses being supplied in Ethiopia. But whether by letter or otherwise an effort should be made to make such men friendly. . . .

The patriarch and those with him should try to be on familiar terms with Prester John and gain his goodwill by every honourable means. Should he be receptive and the opportunity present itself, give him to understand that there is no hope of salvation outside the Roman Catholic Church, and whatever she determines about faith or morals must be believed if one is to be saved. If you succeed in convincing Prester John of this general truth, you have already gained many particular points which depend on this fundamental truth and which can little by little be deduced from it.

If you can win over men of influence who have great weight with Prester John, or, on the other hand, if you can get him to make the *Exercises* and give him a taste for prayer and meditation and spiritual things, this will be the most efficacious means of all to get them to think less of and even to abandon the extreme views which they entertain concerning material things.

Remember that they have a prophecy to the effect that in these times a king from this part of the West (apparently they have no other in mind than the King of Portugal) is destined to destroy the Moors. This is an additional reason for a closer friendship with him, and this in turn will be recommended by a closer uniformity.

> 20th (?) February 1555. *Letters of St Ignatius of Loyola*,
> pp. 382–3 (*MI* VIII, No. 2).

▶   **An associate of Ignatius instructs the members of the Society to learn the language of the country where they are living.**

It seems to be required for the benefit and edification of the peoples among whom our society is living and for the increase of union and charity and kindliness among ours, that in places where we have a college or a house all who do not know the language which is in common use should learn it and as a rule speak it. If each one spoke his mother tongue, there would be much confusion and lack of union, seeing that we are of different nations.

For this reason our father has given orders that in all places where the society exists, all of ours should speak the language of that country. In Spain, Spanish; in France, French; in Germany, German; in Italy, Italian; and so on. He has given orders that here in Rome all should speak Italian, so that every day there are lessons in Italian grammar to help those learn it who are unable to use it. No one is allowed to speak to another except in Italian, unless it be to make clear the meaning of some words and thus be better understood. Once a week in the refectory, either at dinner or supper, there is an Italian sermon in addition to the *toni* which are ordinarily held. Care is taken that some of those who are skilled in Italian help the others, so that they can compose their sermons with greater ease. A good penance is given to those who fail in their observation of this regulation.

Likewise our father has given orders that this same rule be written out and kept everywhere in the society as carefully as possible, due consideration being had for differences of places and persons. For this reason we are writing to your reverence to see that the regulation is kept. Let us know when you receive this.

May Jesus Christ be with us all.

> 1st January 1556. *Letters of St Ignatius of Loyola*,
> pp. 412–13 (*MI* X, No. 6068).

▶   The propagation of the Catholic faith was the goal of the Jesuit
     order—in Europe as well as in the regions beyond. In August
     1539, King John of Portugal inquired, from his ambassador in
     Rome, about the willingness of Ignatius and his companions to
     do missionary work in India. An official stimulus was thus given
     the Jesuit efforts.[18]

I was recently informed by Mestre Diogo de Gouvea that certain
clerics of good attainment and virtuous life had departed from Paris,
after vowing themselves to the service of God, and that, living solely
on the alms of the faithful, they went about preaching and doing a great
deal of good. One of them wrote to the same Diogo at Paris on 23rd
November last, saying that, if it should please the Holy Father, to whom
they have vowed their services, they would go to India. I enclose you a
copy of the letter . . . and commission you with all earnestness to inquire
into the lives of those men, their learning, their habits, their aims, letting
me know the result, so that I may be sure whether their purpose is to
increase and profit the faith by their prayers and example. As the sanction
of the Holy Father is necessary in the case, you will petition him in my
name to have the goodness to issue the order required. . . .

                                          August 1539 (*MI* I, 738).

▶   The Jesuit missionary efforts are inextricably connected with
     the name of Francis Xavier, who preached in India, Japan and
     China. The following document describes the perils of a voyage
     across the seas, such as Francis undertook, at a time when ships
     were ships, and men were men.[19]

The perils and hardships suffered on this expedition are very extensive and terrifying. The first hardship is lack of accommodation. True,
the ships are large and powerful, but so packed with passengers, mer-
chandise and provisions that there is little room left for anyone to move
about, and the ordinary people aboard, for whose comfort there is no
arrangement whatever, must stand all day on deck in the blazing sun and
sleep there somehow all night in the cold. On the other hand, the berths
put at the disposal of noble or wealthy persons are so low, so narrow, so
confined, that it is all a man can do to fit himself into them. The second
hardship has to do with food and drink. Though his Highness the King
provides daily rations of biscuit, meat, fish, water and wine sufficient to
keep the passengers alive, the meat and fish are so salty, and the provision
of utensils to collect the rations so inadequate, that the suffering on this
account, especially among the soldiers, beggars description. The third
hardship among the general run of the voyagers is due to their being poor

and happy-go-lucky. They set out with insufficient clothing, the little they bring soon rots on their backs, and they suffer dreadfully in lower latitudes, both from the cold and from the stench of their rags. The fourth hardship is caused by the calms off the Guinea Coast, which may last for forty, fifty or sixty days. During that time the passengers almost sweat their souls out and suffer torments from the heat beyond the power of my pen to set forth. The fifth hardship, and the worst of any, is the lack of water. During much of the voyage, the water doled out in the daily ration is so foul and malodorous that it is impossible to bear the stench of it, and the passengers have to put a piece of cloth before their mouths to filter off the corruption. This liquid is distributed only once a day, and many fail to get their portion through having no jugs in which to collect it. Others drink their entire ration at one gulp, the result being that large numbers die of thirst. The sixth hardship results from disease of every description among the passengers, who suffer a thousand miseries before dying or recovering. The King appoints a surgeon to each ship, but he and his remedies soon cease to be of any use.

Alexandro Valignano, *Biography of St Francis*:
James Brodrick, *St Francis Xavier*, pp. 98–99.

▶   The surgeon of the ship on which Francis had made the voyage
      across the seas gave in later years the following testimony:[20]

I came out from Portugal on the same ship as Father Francis, and often watched him at his charitable occupations and while he taught Christian doctrine. He used to beg alms from other passengers for the poor and sick persons. He took personal charge of such as were ailing or prostrated by illness. From this work of mercy, and from his hearing of confessions, he allowed himself never a moment's respite, but cheerfully accomplished it all. Everybody held him for a saint, and that was my own fixed opinion. At Mozambique, the Father gave himself so completely to the service of those who were taken from the five ships already ill, and to those who fell ill afterwards during the winter spent on the island, that only forty or forty-one of the sufferers died. Everybody regarded this as a marvellous thing, indeed as a real miracle due under God to the devotedness and goodness of the Father. He fell sick himself in consequence of his crushing labours, and I took him to my lodging to care for him. So bad did he become that I had to bleed him nine times, and for three whole days he was out of his senses. I noticed that while in delirium he raved unintelligibly about other things, but in speaking of the things of God was perfectly lucid and coherent.

Monumenta Xaveriana II, 187–8.

▶ **On another occasion Francis himself had this to say:**[21]

The natives esteem themselves to be Christians and are very proud of it. They can neither read nor write, possess no books or other sources of information, and are extremely ignorant. But they have churches, crosses, and ritual lamps, and in each village there is a *caciz*, who corresponds to a priest among us. Though, like the rest, unable to read or write, these functionaries know a great number of prayers by heart, and officiate in the churches four times a day, at midnight, in the morning, and at the hours of Vespers and of Compline. Having no bells, they summon the people to services with wooden clappers, such as we use during Lent. They do not understand the meaning of the prayers which they recite, because they are in a language not their own. I think it is Chaldean. On my two visits to the island I wrote down three or four of those prayers. The people are devotees of the Apostle St Thomas and claim to be descendants of the Christians he converted in that part of the world. While reciting the prayers, the priests exclaim Alleluia! Alleluia! every now and then, pronouncing the word as we do. They do not baptize nor even know what baptism is. When I was on the island I baptized a large number of children, to the great satisfaction of their fathers and mothers. With much kindness and goodwill, they tried to make me accept such presents as their poverty afforded, and I was touched by the way they pressed me to take a quantity of their dates. They begged me very earnestly to stay with them, promising that if I did they would all, old as well as young, come to be baptized.

20th September 1542. Schurhammer, *Epistolae S. Francisci Xaverii* I, 123–5.

▶ **Francis explained his missionary methods in India:**[22]

I give out the First Commandment, which they repeat, and then we say all together, *Jesus Christ, Son of God, grant us grace to love thee above all things.* When we have asked for this grace we recite the Pater Noster together, and then cry with one accord, *Holy Mary, Mother of Jesus Christ, obtain for us grace from the Son to enable us to keep the First Commandment.* Next we say an Ave Maria, and proceed in the same manner through each of the remaining nine Commandments. And just as we said twelve Paters and Aves in honour of the twelve articles of the Creed, so we say ten Paters and Aves in honour of the Ten Commandments, asking God to give us grace to keep them well. . . . I require all of them to say the Confiteor, especially those about to be baptized, and then we have the Creed. I question the candidates individually about each article to see whether they believe it firmly. If they reply that they do, I go on to explain to them the law of Christ which must be observed in order to save one's soul, and then I baptize them. . . .

As I go my rounds visiting the Christian villages, I pass many pagodas. One of those places contained more than two hundred *bragmanes*. They came out to see me, and among many other matters discussed between us I put to them the following question, 'What do the gods and idols whom you adore command you to do in order to attain salvation?' There was much dispute among them as to who should answer me. It fell to one of the oldest, an octogenarian, who asked me to tell him first the demands made of his followers by the God of the Christians. Perceiving his malice, I refused to say anything until he had dealt with my question, and thus he was forced to exhibit his ignorance. He answered that the gods had two commandments for all men desiring to attain to their heaven, the first being not to kill cows but to adore in them the gods themselves, and the second, to give alms to the *bragmanes* who served the pagodas. On hearing this I was overcome with sadness that the devil should so lord it over our neighbour as to draw to himself the adoration due to God alone. So I jumped up and, bidding the *bragmanes* to remain seated, I gave out to them at the top of my voice the Creed and the Commandments in their own tongue, pausing a little after each Commandment. Then, also in their language, I delivered an exhortation on the subject of Heaven and Hell, and told them who go to the one place and who to the other. After the sermon, the *bragmanes* all rose and embraced me warmly, saying that the God of the Christians was indeed the true God, since his Commandments are so conformable to all right reason.

15th January 1544. Schurhammer, Epistolae S. Francisci
Xaverii I, 162–4, 171–2.

▶   Here Francis reports on some of his conversions:[23]

. . . As for news of these parts, I must tell you how in a kingdom out here which I traversed God moved many persons to become Christians. It was so that in a single month I baptized more than ten thousand men, women and children. My method, on arriving in a heathen village, was to assemble the men and boys apart, and to begin by teaching them to make the Sign of the Cross three times as a confession of faith in Father, Son and Holy Ghost, three persons in one only God. I then recited in a loud voice the General Confession, the Creed, the Commandments, the Pater Noster, the Ave Maria, and the Salve Regina. Two years ago I copied out those prayers and formulae in the Tamil language which is spoken here, and know them by heart. I put on a surplice for the occasion. All, little and big, then repeated the prayers after me, and that done I gave them an instruction on the articles of faith and the Commandments, in Tamil. Next, I required them one and all to ask pardon from God for the sins of their past lives, and that publicly and loudly, in the presence of heathens who did not desire to become Christians. This was done for the confusion of bad men and the consolation of the good. . . . When they had finished, I asked them severally, young and old, whether they believed sincerely each article of the Creed, to which they replied that they did. I then went again through the Creed article by article, asking after each if they believed it, and they answered me, with their arms folded on their breasts in the form of a cross, 'I do believe.' Thereupon I baptized each one, and handed him his new Christian name written on a slip of paper. . . . I went thus from village to village making Christians, and in each place I left a written copy of the doctrine and prayers in their language, with instructions that they were to be taught daily, each morning and evening.

27th January 1545. Schurhammer, *Epistolae S. Francisci Xaverii* I, 273–4.

▶   Here is another description of Francis's missionary methods.[24]

He went up and down the streets and squares with a bell in his hand, crying to the children and others to come to the instructions. The novelty of the proceeding, never seen before in Goa, brought a large crowd around him which he then led to the church. He began by singing the lessons which he had rhymed and then made the children sing them so that they might become the better fixed in their memories. Afterwards he explained each point in the simplest way, using only such words as his young audience could readily understand. By this method, which has since been adopted everywhere in the Indies, he so deeply engrained the truths and precepts of the faith in the hearts of the people that men and women, children and old folk, took to singing the Ten Commandments while they walked the streets, as did the fisherman in his boat and the labourer in the fields, for their own entertainment and recreation.

Monumenta Xaveriana II, 842, 843–4.

▶   When Francis reached, on his eastward journey, the Indonesian islands, he reported the following to his European brethren.[25]

There are islands whose folk eat the bodies of enemies killed in their tribal wars. When one of them dies from sickness his hands and heels are eaten, and considered a great delicacy. Such barbarians are they on some islands that a man, wishing to hold a great feast, will ask his neighbour for the loan of his father, if he is very old, to serve him up as a dish, at the same time promising to give his own father when ripe for the purpose and the neighbour is desirous of having a banquet.

> 10th May 1546. Schurhammer, *Epistolae S. Francisci
> Xaverii* I, 331.

▶ While in the Far East, the most picturesque of the miracles attributed to Francis is supposed to have happened. A chronicler wrote:[26]

Voyaging one day from Amboina to another island, Xavier in his boat was assaulted by furious headwinds. He took from his breast his crucifix, which was about a finger in length, and from the side of the boat dropped it into the sea by its cord. But the cord slipped from his hands and the waves swallowed up the crucifix. He was greatly distressed by the loss and made no secret of his grief. The following day, twenty-four tempestuous hours after the disaster to his crucifix, he reached the Island of Veranula [old Portuguese name for Ceram]. Accompanied by a man named Fausto Rodriguez, born at Viana de Alvito [Portugal], he had walked about five hundred paces along the shore towards the village of Tamalo when both he and Rodriguez saw a crab come out of the sea with the crucifix held upright in its claws or pincers. The new standard-bearer of Christ crawled towards the Saint and stood before him with the divine banner hoisted. Xavier went on his knees, and the crab waited until he had taken the crucifix, whereupon it immediately returned to the sea. The Saint kissed his recovered treasure a thousand times and pressed it to his heart. He remained on his knees in prayer for half an hour, as did his companion also, both giving God their profoundest thanks for so illustrious a miracle.

> *Oriente Conquistado a Jesu Christo pelos Padres da
> Companhia de Jesus* I, 370–1.

▶ Off the coast of China, Francis died on 3rd December 1552, aged forty-six.[27]

Next morning he returned to the island where I had remained, carrying under his arm a pair of cloth breeches which he had been given on the ship as a protection against the great cold, and also a handful of almonds as a remedy for his infirmity. He arrived in so dread a fever that a Portuguese merchant [Diogo Vaz] compassionately carried him to his hut as his guest and begged him to allow himself to be bled, as he was more seriously ill than he imagined. The Father replied that he was not used to being bled, but in that matter as in everything else pertaining to his illness, his friend was to do with him as he thought best. He was bled forthwith and fainted for a brief time under the knife, because, as you know well, dear Brother, he was of the coleric-sanguine temperament. It was a Wednesday, and there followed on the blood-letting so great a nausea that he was unable to swallow anything. Next day, he underwent the operation again, and again fainted. He asked to be purged when he came to, but the fever went on increasing, causing him the most grievous anguish. But he bore it all most patiently, without the slightest murmur or any appeal for relief. His mind began to wander at this time, and in his delirium his words, incoherent though they were, showed him to be thinking of his brethren in the Society of Jesus. . . . With eyes raised to Heaven and a very joyful countenance, he held long and loud colloquies with our Lord in the various languages which he knew. I heard him repeat several times the words: *Jesu, fili David miserere mei; tu autem meorum peccatorum miserere.* So he remained until Monday, November 28, which was the eighth day of his illness. On that day he lost the power of speech altogether and continued silent for three days, until midday on Thursday. During that time he recognized nobody and ate nothing. At noon on Thursday he regained his senses, but spoke only to call upon the Blessed Trinity, Father, Son and Holy Ghost, always one of his tenderest devotions. I heard him again repeat the words: *Jesus, Son of David, have mercy on me,* and he exclaimed again and again: *O Virgin Mother of God, remember me!* He continued to have these and similar words on his lips until the night of Friday passed on towards the dawn of Saturday, when I could see that he was dying and put a lighted candle in his hand. Then, with the name of Jesus on his lips he rendered his soul to his Creator and Lord with great repose and quietude.

Vida del Bienaventurado Padre Francisco Xavier:
Monumenta Xaveriana II, 894–6.

▶ On 22nd May 1542, Pope Paul III called for a general council to ✓ meet at Trent. His bull 'Initio Nostri' read, in part, as follows:[28]

Even though there must be, according to our faith, 'one flock and one shepherd of the flock of our Lord' [John 10.16] for the strengthening of the pure Christian community and the hope of heavenly things, the unity of Christendom has been torn apart by division, controversy and heresy. We sincerely wished for a Christendom safe from the arms and wiles of infidels, but our errors and our guilt (or rather: the wrath of God coming on account of our sins) have caused great damage: Rhodes was lost, Hungary aggressively assailed, war on land and sea planned against Italy, Austria and Illyria. Our godless and merciless enemy, the Turk, never sleeps and considers the hatred and disagreement among us as an opportune moment to carry out his plans.

In the midst of this vehement storm of heresy, discord and war, we are called to guide responsibly the ship of Peter. We put little trust in our own strength, but cast all our cares on the Lord to sustain us [Psalm 54.23] and equip our hearts with firmness and our spirits with insight and wisdom.

We reflected that our truly enlightened and holy predecessors often convened, in times of great danger of Christendom, general councils and assemblies of bishops as the best and most appropriate means of salvation. Therefore we also considered the possibility of such a council.

We sought the views of rulers whose assent seemed particularly valuable and useful. We found that they did not want to absent themselves from such a holy undertaking. Therefore we summoned an ecumenical council and general assembly of all bishops and other concerned fathers to meet at Mantua on 23rd May 1537, the third year of our pontificate. Our letters and documents will bear this out. We hoped that the Lord, had we there assembled, would be in our midst, according to his promise, and would dispel graciously and mercifully all storms of the time and remove all danger by the breath of his mouth.

But the enemy of man always pursues his good works. Contrary to our hope and expectation we were refused the town of Mantua unless we agreed to conditions which were altogether against the precepts of our predecessors, current practice, and the dignity and freedom of the Holy See, indeed the universal church. This we pointed out in another letter.

Thus we had to seek a new site and select another city. Since we were unsuccessful in our immediate efforts, we were forced to postpone the solemn assembly until 1st November.

In the meantime our eternal and cruel enemy, the Turk, attacked Italy with a large navy. He occupied, destroyed and plundered several towns on the Apullian coast and took men away as captives. Fear and danger abounded. We had to fortify our shores and aid our neighbours. None the less, we constantly deliberated with Christian rulers, asking them for their views concerning an appropriate site for the gathering. Since they answered in indefinite and contradictory fashion, we selected with the best intentions and, as we thought, after extensive consideration, Vicenza, a prominent town suggested to us by Venice, whose courage, reputation and power guaranteed safe travel and freedom and safety.

Time had advanced too rapidly, however, to allow the announcement of the selection of the new town. November 1st was near and winter, which would make any announcement impossible, stood outside. We were therefore forced to postpone the church council again to the first of May of the following year. This having been firmly decided, we proceeded with preparations to have, by God's help, a sacred and good council. We felt that it would be profitable both for the council and entire Christendom if the Christian princes would find themselves in peaceful concord. Thus we asked our beloved sons in Christ, the Roman Emperor Charles, and the Most Christian King Francis, to meet with us for consultation.

With letters, nuncios and legates from the ranks of our reverend brethren we asked unceasingly that after all the enmity and discord they should unite themselves to firm alliance and true friendship and thereby aid Christendom in its shaky state. After all, God had especially given them power, so we asserted, to save Christendom. If they did not act and show concern in their policies for the common good of Christendom, God would demand a strict account of them. Finally the rulers heeded our admonition and proceeded to Nizza where we also, despite our advanced age, travelled, in order to restore peace, with God's help.

When the time of the council approached we sent three virtuous and reputable legates from the ranks of our cardinals to Vicenza. They were to open the council, receive the arriving prelates, and undertake whatever appeared necessary until we, upon return from the peace talks, could ourselves direct everything. . . .

Though no permanent peace was concluded at Nizza between the two rulers, on account of our sins, a ten-year truce was agreed upon. We hoped that one of its results would be that the council could convene unhindered and that a lasting peace could thereupon be brought about by the council by its authority. We admonished the rulers to attend the council themselves, to bring along their prelates, and call the absent ones. They did neither and excused themselves with the necessity to return to their realms and the complete exhaustion of their prelates, who had to recover from their travel and financial obligations. They asked postponement of the council. We refused, but then received word from our legates at Vicenza that even after the day appointed for the council hardly a foreign prelate had arrived at the city. Learning this news, we realized that the council could not possibly be held at this time.

We therefore conceded to the rulers and postponed the opening of the council to the next feast of the Resurrection of our Lord. . . . Motivated by hope for peace and constrained by the will of powerful rulers, we decided to suspend the general council, in order to avoid the often fruitlessly used word 'postponement', especially since we realized that no further prelates had come to Vicenza for Easter. . . .

In the meantime the situation of Christendom worsened from day to day. The Hungarians called the Turks for help after the death of their king while King Ferdinand was arming against them. The Belgians had been incited to desert the Emperor. To suppress the insurrection the Emperor marched, in agreement with the most Christian King—an indication of mutual benevolence—through France to Belgium. From there he proceeded to Germany, where he deliberated with rulers and towns in order to achieve concord. When the hopes for peace disappeared and it seemed that conversations were only leading to more pronounced differences, we felt led to return to the earlier proposal of a general council. Our cardinal legate proposed this for some time to the Emperor, last at the Diet of Regensburg, where our beloved son, Caspar Contarini, Cardinal of St Praxedis, represented us with profound learning and pure motives. As we had feared, the diet demanded the acknowledgment from us that several articles, deviating from ecclesiastical teaching should be tolerated until they had been examined and decided by a general council. Neither the truth of Christ and the Catholic Church nor the dignity of the Apostolic See allowed such a concession. We decided, therefore, emphatically to propose a council to be held as early as possible. Indeed, we never had any other intent than to convene a general assembly of the Church. We hoped that this would give peace to the Christian people and unity to the Church of Christ. However, we wanted to achieve this only in agreement with the Christian rulers. Waiting for their approval, watching for the hidden time, the 'time of thy grace, O Lord' [Psalm 68.14], we were led to the decision that any time is pleasing to God as long as sacred matters are discussed which pertain to the salvation of Christian believers. For with pain we had to observe that the situation of Christendom worsened daily: Hungary was suppressed by the Turks, Germany was in danger, all the world was in fear and sorrow. Thus we decided not to wait for the consent of the rulers, but to trust only in the will of God Almighty and the salvation of Christendom.

Since Vicenza is no longer possible as site of the council, and since we—selecting another place—considered not only the salvation of Christendom, but the difficulties of Germany, and learned that Trent was preferred by the Germans to some other possibilities, we gave in to their demands, even though the deliberations might have been undertaken more suitably in Italy.

Thus we decided that the general council is to convene on 1st November at Trent. We consider this location appropriate, since German bishops and prelates can easily repair there, as can Spanish and French bishops, as well as others, without too much difficulty. We have decided on the date in light of the fact that the time appears sufficient to announce this decision to all Christian peoples and allows enough travel time to the prelates. We did not give the customary year's time for the change of place, as is commanded in earlier pronouncements, since we did not want to delay our aid to oppressed and unfortunate Christendom. We recognize the present difficulties and have no far-reaching hopes. It is written: 'Commit thy ways unto the Lord and trust in him. He will bring it to pass' [Psalm 36.5]. Thus we are resolved to trust more in God's grace and mercy than to mistrust our weakness. In a good work, God's grace accomplished often what human planning cannot do.

Thus we decide, proclaim, summon, order and rule, trusting the authority of God Almighty, Father, Son and Holy Spirit, as well as the Apostles Peter and Paul, an authority with which we are entrusted here on earth, with the counsel and approval of our reverend brethren, the cardinals of the holy Catholic Church, that on 1st November 1542, in the city of Trent, which is a convenient, free, easily reached place, a general, holy council is to begin, continue, and, with God's help, to his honour and glory and the salvation of all Christendom, be concluded and perfected.

Concilium Tridentinum IV, 226–31.

▶ **Cardinal Reginald Pole of England delivered a deeply sensitive and searching address to the council on 7th January 1546.**

As the matters to be dealt with in this sacred Congress for God's glory and the Church's good increased, we who bore the office of Presidents and Legates of the Apostolic See thought it our bounden duty often to use words of exhortation or of warning. Nor must we change our way in this second session, which, we hope, has been given as a happy beginning to the council.

All the more willingly shall we fulfil this duty because when we exhort you to do what befits so great a gathering or on the contrary warn you, we are exhorting or warning ourselves, who are in the same bark with you, and are exposed with you to the same dangers and the same storms. We bestir ourselves, I say, to watch lest, on the one hand, we run on the rocks which certainly are all too many in these matters, or on the other hand by our sloth we are storm-beaten and wrecked by the very flood of affairs; but rather steadied by faith and hope we may steer our course where the harbour of safety may most clearly show itself to the glory of God in Jesus Christ.

Therefore, that we may begin as we should, let all be warned in this beginning: each of us should above all things keep before his eyes the things that are expected of this holy council. Each one will easily see therein what is the duty resting upon him. To put it briefly, these duties are what are contained in the bull summoning the council, viz. the uprooting of heresies, the reformation of ecclesiastical discipline and of morals, and lastly the external peace of the whole Church. These are the things we must see to, or rather for which we must untiringly pray in order that by God's mercy they may be done. This again, at the outset of the council and before all else, must be made an admonition to each and all of us who have here foregathered—and especially to us who are presiding in this sacred office—lest at any time we should think the many ills now oppressing the flock of Christ could be withstood either by any one of us who have come here or by the whole council, even if all the pastors of the whole earth were met. If, indeed, we think the thing can be accomplished by us, or by any other than by Christ himself, whom God the Father has made the sole Saviour and Shepherd and to whom he has given all power, we shall err in the very foundation of all our actions, and we shall provoke still further the divine wrath.

To the former evils which have come upon us because we left the well of living waters, we shall have added the greater sin of wishing to heal these ills by our own power or prudence, so that justly it may be said of us what the prophet in the name of God spoke in accusation of the chosen people: 'This people hath wrought two evils. They have left me, the well of living water, and they have dug to themselves cisterns that cannot hold water' [Jer. 2.13]. These cisterns are all the counsels which spring from our prudence without the breathing of the divine spirit. They cannot hold the people in godliness and obedience as cisterns hold water. But the more we toil to pen the waters by these devices the more rapidly and flood-like shall they flow from us and leave us. This may we learn from our experience in many places and in these latter years. And this may warn us that there is one only way left for curing these ills. First we must acknowledge that all our remedies are useless, and indeed are more powerful to strengthen than to destroy these evils. Secondly, we who have the office of Fathers must act in everything by faith and hope and place our trust in the power of Christ, whom God the Father calls his right hand, and in the wisdom of Christ, who is the wisdom of the Father, whose ministers in all things we acknowledge ourselves to be. . . .

What, then, shall we do that we now be sufficient ministers of Christ in renewing the Church? The selfsame thing that Christ, the shepherd of our souls, did when he came to found and form his Church. The selfsame, indeed, Fathers, must be done by us that the very wisdom of the Father did when he came to lead many children into glory; this indeed ought again to be our purpose. For when he found all burdened by sins, he took upon himself all the sins of all—in the sight of God he made himself for all the one culprit and offender. He bore all the penalty due to us as if he had committed all the misdeeds and sins we had committed. Yet he was wholly untainted by any sin, since 'He had done no sin nor was guile ever found on his lips' [I Peter 2.22].

Therefore what in his great love of God the Father and his mercifulness towards our race Christ did, justice itself now enacts of us that we should do. Before the tribunal of God's mercy we, the shepherds, should make ourselves responsible for all the evils now burdening the flock of Christ. The sins of all we should take upon ourselves, not in generosity but in justice; because the truth is that of these evils we are in great part the cause and therefore we should implore the divine mercy through Jesus Christ.

If any should think that in calling ourselves, who are the shepherds, a cause of the evils burdening the Church, we are using undue bitterness and exaggeration of speech, rather than the truth, facts themselves which cannot lie will bear us witness. Let us therefore scan for a moment the evils burdening the Church and, at the same time, our own sins.

Yet who can count these sins? Like the other evils, they outnumber the sands of the seashore and raise their voice to the very heavens. We must therefore narrow this so great a mass of evils within the limits set by this council itself, which is called to cure the greatest of them, viz. the three we have named above: (1) heresy, (2) the decline in ecclesiastical morals, and (3) internal and external war.

Since the Church has been beset for many years by these woes, let us now look and think what is their source—and if we gave them birth or increase. Consider, then, the birth of these heresies, which in these days are everywhere rife. We may indeed wish to deny that we have given them birth, because we ourselves have not uttered any heresy. Nevertheless, wrong opinions about faith, like brambles and thorns, have sprung up in the God's-garth entrusted to us. Hence, even if, as is their wont, these poisonous weeds have spread of themselves, nevertheless if we have not tilled our field as we ought—if we have not sowed—if we took no pains at once to root up the springing weeds—we are no less to be reckoned their cause than if we ourselves had sowed them; and all the more since all these have their beginning and increase in the tiller's sloth. Here, therefore, the tillers of God's-garth should examine themselves, should question their conscience what pains they have taken in tilling and sowing. Whoever will do this, especially in these days when so few have a care to till God's-garth, will, we think, have no doubt that the guilt of these heresies spreading in the Church is upon him. But we have said enough by way of warning about what comes under the first heading.

Let us come to the second, which embraces the breaking-down of right living and what is called 'abuses'. Herein no good is served by a long inquiry as to who are the causes of these evils, seeing that we cannot even name any other causes but ourselves!

Therefore let us approach the third, which embraces in itself the hindrances to the Church's peace, such as wars domestic or external. These, indeed, have already disturbed and still disturb the Church's peace. We will say of them that if these wars are (and God shows by most sure signs that they are) his scourges to chasten us because we cannot deny that we are guilty under the two former heads—even of these wars we cannot deny that we ourselves are the chief cause. We are of opinion that God sends these scourges to punish our sinning and to turn our gaze towards these very sins by which we greatly offend his Majesty.

Here, if anyone would estimate in what ways the Church has been troubled by war, let him deliberate within himself what are those things especially in which the Church suffers most because of wars. Nor does it matter whose wars they are—whether the intestine wars of our own princes, or the external wars of the Turks, which in past years have wrought such havoc on us, or of those who have given up obedience to their shepherds and indeed have driven them from their sees. In a word, all that is to be said of every kind of war, whether men have taken up arms against us, have driven the shepherds from their churches, have thrown the orders into confusion, have set laymen in the place of bishops, have robbed church property, have hindered the preaching of God's Word, we may sum up in this: if they are willing to read the Book of the Abuses of Shepherds, the greater number of those who claim this name will find it stated in the clearest terms that there is none of these things which has not been done by themselves. It will be found that our ambition, our avarice, our cupidity have wrought all these evils on the people of God; and that, on account of this, shepherds are being driven from their churches, and the churches starved of the Word of God, and the property of the Church, which is the property of the poor, stolen, and the priesthood given to the unworthy and to those who differ from lay-folk

Title page of volume II of the Spanish edition of Ludolph of Saxony's *Vita Christi* (Alcala, 1502), undoubtedly the edition read by Ignatius during his convalescence (*Fogg Art Museum, Harvard University*)

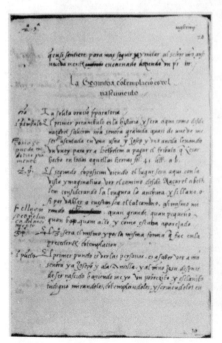

Page from the original of the *Spiritual Exercises*, giving the meditation on the birth of Christ.

A session of the Council of Trent. (*Painting by Titian, Louvre, Paris*)

only in dress (if even in that!). Which of these things can we deny having done during these latter years? If, then, the Turks and the heretics do the same to us, what else are we witnessing than our crimes and at the same time the just judgment of God—a judgment, indeed, fully of mercy? If he punished us as we deserved, we should have been long since as Sodom and Gomorrha.

In all these afflictions of ours we see God's judgment—but would that we did see his judgment; it would be the first step towards avoiding all God's judgments and scourges and of entering into grace and true glory. This has been our motive for somewhat sharply and lengthily recalling these things. Unless indeed these things are well known and seen to, it is useless to call upon the Holy Spirit, who is wont to make his first step in men's souls when men condemn themselves so that they may afterwards condemn the world of sin. Therefore unless this Spirit first condemns us before ourselves we cannot profess that he has yet come to us; nor will he come if we refuse to hear about our own sinfulness. . . .

This council, as having the character of consulters and judges, will both consult about whatever has to do with the Church's well-being and will judge both of things and of persons; for we sit as judging the twelve tribes of Israel, in which are comprised the whole people of God. Hence it is now the time for warning ourselves against what is wont to weaken in us the power of consulting or judging. These are the passions of the soul. They are also called 'perturbations' because they disturb and swerve the right and true judgment and feeling about things. These passions especially are to be shunned which, as the pagan wisely warns us, should be cast aside in counsel-taking, when he says, 'Every man that would consult about things doubtful should be free from anger, hatred, friendship.' For all classes of men are prone to this; and those especially who serve princes. They have strong affection, they easily speak for love or for hate, according as they think their princes are affected, from whom they await reward. . . .

It clearly appears what is to be done by us who have forgathered here to save the Church from the great evils that overwhelm it. We must confess our own sins and those of the princes and the people. This we are now fitly doing in a spirit of sorrow. But we should do it even more fully in word, if these princes were present to join with us in confessing and weeping. For as the prophets say, the sins of priests, princes and people are intertwined into such a rope of sin that hardly can we search into the sin of one class without laying bare the sins of another class.

'Cardinal Pole's *Eirenikon*', *Dublin Review*, 198 (1936), 150–8.

▶ The most formidable manifestation of the determination of the
Catholic Church to suppress the Protestant 'heresy' was the
Inquisition. This following report, submitted in 1566 by an agent
of the Inquisition, indicates some of the means utilized by the
Catholic Church to extirpate heresy.

By order of Don Francis d'Alua I associated in Montpellier, a French
town, with several Lutherans who have close contacts with Spain in
order to learn if they ship books to Spain or know of heretics there. In
order to gather this information conveniently and without gaining undue
attention, I pretended to be a heretic myself and indicated my intention
to take some books, such as the works of John Calvin and Theodore Beza,
to Spain. Since I was afraid of the Inquisition, I did not dare to purchase
any there. If they, as believers, desired to help me in this regard, I would
take books pertaining to their religion along. These I would send to
several ladies and other friends who had eagerly requested them. A
bookseller and a merchant volunteered to bring the books secretly to
Barcelona to the home of one of their friends who were, as they said, of
their faith.

A thousand deceptions were necessary to gather this information.
Eventually Don Francis gave me permission to buy several books and the
merchant took them. In order to save expenses he will send them around
the middle of Lent to the house of one of their friends. He gave me a
letter which introduces me. Don Francis presumably informed you already
of further details. He allowed me to proceed to Barcelona to uncover this
deception. I learned the names of all his friends from him, for he told me
that they were of his religion. I am staying here and expect the books in
order to further the transaction for the service of God and your Majesty.

Hernando de Ayala, Simancas arch. gen. S. 39, Leg. 641
(E. Schäfer, *Beiträge zur Geschichte*, pp. 71–72).

▶ In 1559 the Inquisition of Toledo reported a manifestation of
heresy and the measures undertaken to apprehend it.[29]

Even without special order I shall never fail to submit a report whenever developments warrant it. Such is now the case. Last Saturday, the
fourteenth of this month, five pamphlets were found in five chapels of
our church here. I am herewith transmitting one of these pamphlets to
you. There was no trace of the culprit. All were in the same handwriting
and had the same content. It rained very heavily that night and more than
thirty additional pamphlets were found at many doors, virtually throughout the entire town. They were all written by the same hand and again

identical in content. Despite great efforts no trace has been found thus
far. We are carefully and secretly applying ourselves to this task. The
following has been done: All teachers were called in, one after the other,
and were asked under oath if they knew the handwriting. They were
given the first three lines, without the title, to have the pupils identify
the writing without knowing the reason for the inquiry. All inns and hos-
tels in Toledo have been reached to learn who has stayed there during the
past two months, from whence they came and what papers they had in
their possession. This search was also undertaken in the hospitals. All
writers were sought out and messengers were sent into outlying villages
to learn if perchance someone lives there and writes. Notaries were called
to identify the handwriting. These and other methods are used, according
to the situation in all secrecy, for it seems that it is the intent of these
manifestoes to cause public commotion. No trace has been found, however. In light of the content of the pamphlets it appears that an apostate
monk is the author.

Don Diego Ramirez, Simancas arch. gen. S. 39, Leg. 911
(E. Schäfer, *Beiträge zur Geschichte*, p. 107).

▶   'Autos-da-fé', 'acts of faith', were, particularly in Spain, the
public spectacles in which those indicted by the Inquisition for
heresy were condemned.

Jesus

Report on Another Solemn *Auto* which took place at Sevilla, 24th
September 1559, and on the Order Observed.

On the square of San Francisco two large platforms were erected—
one for the Inquisitors and the cathedral chapter, the supreme tribunal
and the monks of San Francisco. The other platform was for the penitents,
the clergy and monks of other orders. An altar was erected here for the
degradation of the Licentiate Juan Gonzalez. On one side of the square
another large platform was erected for the town chapter; alongside the
platform of the Inquisitors a platform for the duchess of Bejar, other
marquises, and eminent gentlemen. Many noble ladies were found here.
Alongside the platform for the penitents was another platform for other
earls and lords and noble ladies. All around the square were numerous
scaffolds upon which stood a great throng of people. It was said that some
people who came to see the *auto* had arrived three days early. The crowd
of people was so huge that it was impossible to find lodging in the city.
. . . Between two and three hundred men, equipped with lances,

well-dressed and decorated, were selected to accompany the penitents. They were a pleasure to behold. They marched orderly with drums and flags to the Castle, where they received the penitents with whom they then walked to the square. About four o'clock in the morning fifty priests arrived with the cross of St Ann and went to the Castle, where forty monks of all orders had gathered. Together they accompanied the penitents . . . eighty penitents with habit and candles, twenty-one persons condemned to fire with a statue of Francisco de Cafra (who had escaped). Then came the magistrates with their marshal, then the Cathedral Chapter with the sextons in front. Finally came the Inquisitors with their banner. . . .

Don Juan Ponce de Leon was turned over to them so that his confession could be heard and he brought back to the Catholic faith. He was a damned Lutheran who, despite two years in prison, had not given up his Lutheran errors. The rector heard his confession and led him back to the faith. Don Juan swore that he would die as a true Christian. He had been involved in great error and heresy: for example, that there was no purgatory, that the Inquisitors were antichristian, that one should not believe or obey the Pope. Also that one should not accept any papal bulls or heed the Pope's word in any matter; that it was not necessary to make confession to monks or priests, but only to God, everyone in his heart. Also the most holy sacrament should not be adored.

On one occasion he had stood in the yard of the cathedral when the most holy sacrament was carried by. He had quickly hidden behind a pillar and counselled the people he met to do the same. He persuaded them not to adore the sacrament. He was the first to receive Lutheran books from Germany. He confessed that, upon receiving a letter from Germany, he had asked the messenger about the books. The messenger told him that they were hidden in a field because bringing them to town would have meant danger of discovery. Don Juan Ponce de Leon told him that he would go to get the books. He went with a mule, put the books into baskets, and brought them to his house. The next morning he already began to distribute the books to trustworthy people. The messenger received twenty ducats for his expenses. Later Don Juan and others met on a fast day. They talked about this damned and devilish sect and then killed several pigeons and ate them. Several days later they agreed that it would be profitable to have a room at some place to be used for reading and instruction in this damned sect. Don Juan offered to buy a house and install some sort of mosque to proclaim that damned heresy. Don Juan appointed a certain person, a cleric, as teacher, whose name was not mentioned in the sentence.

On certain days he went to the site of execution and said, raising his hands to the sky, 'May it please the Lord that I might soon be burned to dust for the defence of our holy faith, for I want to be redeemed this way and hope that my wife and children will here suffer with me for the defence of our faith.' This he did many times. At one of their meetings he said, 'I wish to God that I had an income of 20,000 ducats and could use them to spread our faith all over Spain so that people might be enlightened to become Christians and know their faith.'

He pretended that he went to confession. When he wanted to take communion he sent his servants away with orders so that they were of the opinion, upon their return, that he had received communion in the meantime. . . . This Don Juan was sentenced to die at the stake. . . . But our Lord, in his immeasurable goodness, caused him to see his error, and led him back to the holy Catholic faith. He died with many tears of remorse over his sins. Indeed, still at the stake he endeavoured to persuade the others to desist from their errors and to convert themselves to the holy Catholic faith and to the Roman Church.

Madrid, bibl. nac., Cod. R. 29, fol. 310–15
(E. Schäfer, *Beiträge zur Geschichte* pp. 271–3).

▶ The suppression of Protestantism by government authorities is illustrated by the following mandate of Emperor Charles V, issued in 1550.[30]

No one, whatsoever his rank or condition, shall print, transcribe, copy, or knowingly have by him, receive, carry, keep, conceal, have in his possession, sell, buy, give, distribute, scatter, or let fall in churches, or on the street, or in other places, any books or writings composed by Martin Luther, Johann Oecolampadius, Huldreich Zwingli, Martin Bucer, John Calvin, or other heretics or promoters of their sects, or of other bad and false sects condemned by the holy Church. . . .

No one shall represent, or cause to be represented, sell, or offer for sale, have, keep, or possess, any scandalous figures, pictures, or images of the Virgin Mary, or of the saints canonized by the Church, or of the clergy. Nor shall anyone break, destroy, or pull down the images or pictures made in their honour.

No one shall, in his house or elsewhere, hold, or suffer to be held, any secret conventicles or improper assemblies, nor attend such, in which said heretics and seducers sow and privily inculcate their errors, rebaptizing and conspiring against the holy Church and the Government.

Catholic cartoon showing the ship of the Church sailing safely past the dangers of various heresies to the heavenly kingdom. Both Pope and Emperor are on the ship which is retarded by the chains of the devil, the flesh and the world. The 'rocks' of various heresies—Arius, Sabel-

lius, Huss, Pelagius, etc.—obstruct the voyage, but the wind of proper
philosophy propels the ship forward.

(*Woodcut title-page, Conrad Wimpina,* Sectarum Errorum . . .,
Frankfurt, 1528)

Moreover we forbid everyone, laymen and others, to discuss or argue about the holy scriptures, whether in secret or in public, especially touching important and doubtful matters; or to read aloud or teach to others the holy scriptures, unless they be theologians versed in theology and approved by some well-known university. . . .

In case anyone is discovered to have violated any of the provisions herein stated the punishment shall be fitting for seditious persons who are a peril to our realm and the common good. They shall be executed, the men by the sword, the women by being buried alive, if they show no disposition to maintain or defend their errors. Should they, however, persist in their opinions, errors and heresies, they shall be burned alive, and in every case their goods shall be confiscated and declared forfeit to us. . . .

Apologie de Guillaume de Nassau, Prince d'Orange, etc.,
ed. Lacroix, Brussels, 1858, pp. 275ff.

▶   Among the means utilized by the Catholic Church to combat
     Protestant thought was the close supervision of all printed
     material, which eventually led to the 'Index of Prohibited Books'.
     Here are two early specimens from England:[31]

A proclamation for resisting and withstanding of most damnable heresies sown within this realm by the disciples of Luther and other heretics (1530):

Books prohibited

A disputation between the father and the son.

A book of the old god and new.

Godly prayers.

The Christian state of matrimony.

The burying of the mass.

The sum of the scripture.

Matins and evening songs, VII psalms and other heavenly psalms, with the commination, in English.

An exposition upon the VIIth chapter of the first espistle to the Corinthians.

The chapters of Moses, called Genesis.

The chapters of Moses, called Deuteronomy.

The matrimony of Tindall.

David's psalter, in English.

The practice of prelate.

Hortulus animae, in English.
A B C against the clergy.
The examination of William Thorpe, etc.

Wilkins, III, 739.

Memorandum of a proclamation made at Paul's Cross on the first Sunday in Advent, 1531, against the buying, selling or reading of the following books:
The disputation between the father and the son.
The supplication of beggars.
The revelation of Antichrist.
Liber qui de veteri et novicio Deo inscribitur.
Precaciones.
Economica christiana.
The burying of the mass, in English rhyme.
An exposition into the VII chapter to the Corinthians.
The matrimony of Tyndal.
A B C against the clergy.
Ortulus animae, in English.
A book against Saint Thomas of Canterbury.
A book made by Friar Reye against the seven sacraments.
An answer of Tyndal to Sir Thomas More's dialogue, in English.
A disputation of purgatory, made by John Frythe.
The first book of Moses, called Genesis.
A prologue in the second book of Moses, called Exodus.
A prologue in the third book of Moses, called Leviticus.
A prologue in the fourth book of Moses, called Numeri.
A prologue in the fifth books of Moses, called Deuteronomy.
The practice of prelates.
The New Testament in English, with an introduction to the epistle to the Romans.
The parable of the wicked Mammon.
The obedience of a Christian man.
The book of Thorpe or of John Oldecastell.
The sum of Scripture.
The primer in English.
The psalter in English.
A dialogue between the gentleman and the plowman.
Jonas in English.

Calendar of State Papers V, 18.

▶ The Index of Pope Pius IV of 1559, the so-called Index of Trent, made the position of the Church regarding erroneous books official. Here are some excerpts:

First of all it must be observed that each letter of the alphabet in this Index has three sections. In the first are not books, but writers of books who have been suspected to be heretics or to give indication of heresy. Such a catalogue was needed so that everyone might see whose writings— already published or to be published—are prohibited. . . . In the second section not authors are listed, but books which are rejected on account of unsound or suspect doctrine or on account of the offence against the morals of the faithful, even if their authors have never withdrawn from the Church. The third and final section lists books which have been published anonymously and which contain such doctrine as the Roman Church and the Catholic faith must repudiate and reject. . . . Not all anonymous books are condemned, however, since we have often known of learned and devout men from whose watchfulness the Christian community has profited greatly, though they themselves wished to evade vain glory and published their best books without their name. Included are only those books which either contain clearly false or dubious doctrine or are detrimental to morals. . . .

Rule I

All books which were condemned prior to 1515 by popes or ecumenical councils, and are not listed in this Index, are to stand condemned in the original fashion.

Rule II

Books of arch-heretics—those who after 1515 have invented or incited heresy or who have been or still are heads and leaders of heretics, such as Luther, Zwingli, Calvin, Hubmaier, Schwenckfeld, and the like—whatever their name, title or argumentation—are prohibited without exception. As far as other heretics are concerned, only those books are condemned without exception which deal *ex professo* with religion. Others will be permitted after Catholic theologians have examined and approved them by the order of bishops and inquisitors. Likewise, Catholic books written by those who subsequently fell into heresy or by those who after their lapse returned into the bosom of the Church can be permitted after approval by a theological faculty or the inquisition.

Rule III

Translations of older works, including church fathers, made by condemned authors, are permitted if they contain nothing against sound doctrine. However, translations of books of the Old Testament may be allowed by the judgment of bishops for the use of learned and pious men only. These translations are to elucidate the Vulgate so that Sacred Scripture can be understood, but they are not to be considered as a sacred text. Translations of the New Testament made by authors of the first sections in this Index are not to be used at all, since too little usefulness and too much danger attends such reading.

Rule IV

Since experience teaches that, if the reading of the Holy Bible in the vernacular is permitted generally without discrimination, more damage than advantage will result because of the boldness of men, the judgment of bishops and inquisitors is to serve as guide in this regard. Bishops and inquisitors may, in accord with the counsel of the local priest and confessor, allow Catholic translations of the Bible to be read by those of whom they realize that such reading will not lead to the detriment but to the increase of faith and piety. The permission is to be given in writing. Whoever reads or has such a translation in his possession without this permission cannot be absolved from his sins until he has turned in these Bibles. . . .

Rule VI

Books in the vernacular dealing with the controversies between Catholics and the heretics of our time are not to be generally permitted, but are to be handled in the same way as Bible translations. . . .

Rule VII

Books which contain, relate or teach licentious and immoral matters *ex professo* are prohibited without exception, since not only faith but also morals must be considered and they can be easily corrupted by the reading of such books. Whoever possesses such books is to be severely punished by the bishops. Ancient books, written by classical authors, are permitted because of the elegance and beauty of their language. They are not to be used for the instruction of youth, however. . . .

Rule X

If a book is to be published in Rome it is to be examined, first of all, by a vicar of the Pope and the Master of the Sacred Palace or a person designated by the Pope. In the case of books to be published at other places the bishop, or a censor appointed by him, and the inquisitor are to examine the book and affix their signature with their own hand at once and without charge. . . . The approval of the book must be in writing and must appear in authentic form in the front of the book.

Die Indices Librorum Prohibitorum des sechzehnten Jahrhunderts (Tübingen, 1886), pp. 246f.

▶ Catholic renewal in the sixteenth century found a profound expression in the life and thought of several Spanish mystics, of whom St Teresa of Avila (1515–82) came to be the most important. Already in her youth, so her later autobiographical reflections reveal, she dreamed of martyrdom and works for God.[32]

I had one brother almost of my own age. It was he whom I most loved, though I had a great affection for them all, as had they for me. We used to read the lives of saints together; and, when I read of the martyrdoms suffered by saintly women for God's sake, I used to think they had purchased the fruition of God very cheaply; and I had a keen desire to die as they had done, not out of any love for God of which I was conscious, but in order to attain as quickly as possible to the fruition of the great blessings which, as I read, were laid up in heaven. I used to discuss with this brother of mine how we could become martyrs.

We agreed to go off to the country of the Moors, begging our bread for the love of God, so that they might behead us there; and, even at so tender an age, I believe the Lord had given us sufficient courage for this, if we could have found a way to do it; but our greatest hindrance seemed to be that we had a father and a mother. It used to cause us great astonishment when we were told that both pain and glory would last forever. We would spend long periods talking about this and we liked to repeat again and again, 'For ever—ever—ever!' Through our frequent repetition of these words, it pleased the Lord that in my earliest years I should receive a lasting impression of the way of truth.

Life, Peers I, 11.

▶ Already as a youth Teresa thought about a religious vocation.

I began to fear that, if I had died of my illness, I should have gone to hell; and though, even then, I could not incline my will to being a nun, I saw that this was the best and safest state, and so, little by little, I determined to force myself to embrace it.

Life, Peers I, 18–19.

▶ Teresa's mystic experience was characterized by the gift of tears which took place when the soul contemplated God's goodness and greatness.

If to this there be added a little love, the soul is comforted, the heart melts, and tears begin to flow: sometimes we seem to produce these tears by force; at other times the Lord seems to be drawing them from us and we cannot resist him. For the trifling pains we have taken his Majesty appears to be requiting us with the great gift of the comfort which comes to a soul from seeing that it is weeping for so great a Lord; and I do not wonder at this, for it has ample reason to be comforted. For here it finds encouragement, and here it finds joy.

Life, Peers I, 58.

▶ **Teresa reflects on the presence of the Holy Spirit within her soul:**

So I began to meditate on the place in hell which I deserved for my sins, and I gave great praises to God, for so changed was my life that I seemed not to recognize my own soul. While I was meditating in this way a strong impulse seized me without my realizing why. It seemed as if my soul were about to leave the body, because it could no longer contain itself and was incapable of waiting for so great a blessing. The impulse was so exceedingly strong that it made me quite helpless. It was different, I think, from those which I had experienced on other occasions, and I did not know what was the matter with my soul, or what it wanted, so changed was it. I had to seek some physical support, for so completely did my natural strength fail me that I could not even remain seated.

While in this condition I saw a dove over my head, very different from those we see on earth, for it had not feathers like theirs, but its wings were made of little shells which emitted a great brilliance. It was larger than a dove; I seemed to hear the rustling of its wings. It must have been fluttering like this for the space of an Ave Maria. But my soul was in such a state that, as it became lost to itself, it also lost sight of the dove.

Life, Peers I, 270–1.

▶ **Teresa's vision of hell was no less vivid than her vision of the Holy Spirit.**

The entrance, I thought, resembled a very long, narrow passage, like a furnace, very low, dark, and closely confined; the ground seemed to be full of water which looked like filthy, evil-smelling mud, and in it were many wicked-looking reptiles. At the end there was a hollow place scooped out of a wall, like a cupboard, and it was here that I found myself in close confinement. . . . I felt a fire within my soul the nature of which I am utterly incapable of describing. My bodily sufferings were so intolerable that, though in my life I have endured the severest sufferings of this kind—the worst it is possible to endure, the doctors say, such as the shrinking of the nerves during my paralysis and many and divers more, some of them, as I have said, caused by the devil—none of them is of the smallest account by comparison with what I felt then, to say nothing of the knowledge that they would be endless and never-ceasing. And even these are nothing by comparison with the agony of my soul, an oppression, a suffocation and an affliction so deeply felt, and accompanied by such hopeless and distressing misery, that I cannot too forcibly describe it. . . . In that pestilential spot, where I was quite powerless to hope for comfort, it was impossible to sit or lie, for there was no room to do so. I had been put in this place, which looked like a hole in the wall, and those very walls, so terrible to the sight, bore down upon me and completely stifled me. There was no light and everything was in the blackest darkness. I do not understand how this can be, but, although there was no light, it was possible to see everything the sight of which can cause affliction. At that time it was not the Lord's will that I should see more of hell itself, but I have since seen another vision of frightful things, which are the punishment of certain vices. . . . I was terrified by all this, and, though it happened nearly six years ago, I still am as I write: even as I sit here, fear seems to be depriving my body of its natural warmth. I never recall any time when I have been suffering trials or pains and when everything that we can suffer on earth has seemed to me of the slightest importance by comparison with this; so, in a way, I think we complain without reason. I repeat, then, that this vision was one of the most signal favours which the Lord has bestowed upon me: it has been of the greatest benefit to me, both in taking from me all fear of the tribulations and disappointments of this life and also in strengthening me to suffer them and to give thanks to the Lord.

Life, Peers I, 215-17.

▶   A contemporary describes Teresa's last days and death on 4th October 1582.

The holy Mother was so weak and in such pain that she fainted. It made us all dreadfully sorry to see her like that, and we had nothing to give her but a few figs, which had to last her the night, for in the whole village we could not find so much as an egg. I was in anguish at seeing her in such straights and being unable to help her in any way, but she comforted me and told me not to be grieved—the figs were extremely good and there were many poor people who would have less. This she said to comfort me, but as I was aware of her great patience and of what she was enduring and what joy it gave her to suffer, I guessed that she was in greater straits than her remark suggested; and so, on the next day, we went on to another village to try to get her some relief. Here we got some cabbage, cooked with a great deal of onion, and she took some of this, although it was very bad for her complaint. On the same day we reached

Alba, but our Mother was now so ill that she was unable to talk to the nuns. She said she felt so broken in health that she thought she had not a sound bone in her body. She went on with her work from that day, which was the eve of Saint Matthew, down to Michaelmas Day, when she went to communion. But on her return she came straight back and lay down on her bed, and had a haemorrhage, which, it is understood, was the cause of her death.

Two days before she died she asked to be given the Most Holy Sacrament, for she knew now that she was dying. On seeing that they were bringing it to her she sat up in bed in such a spirited way that it looked as if she were going to get up, so they had to restrain her. Then she said, with great joy, 'My Lord, it is time to set out; may the journey be a propitious one and may thy will be done.' . . . On Saint Francis' Day, at nine o'clock in the evening, our Lord took her to be with him and left us all in such sorrow and grief that, if I had to describe it here, there would be a great deal to say. I heard a few things which the holy Mother said before she expired, but so wonderful are they that I shall not set them down here: my superiors can relate them if they think it well to do so.

Life, Peers III, 360–2.

GENERAL BIBLIOGRAPHY

The best work in English is, despite its lack of imagination, B. J. Kidd, *The Counter-Reformation 1550–1600* (London, 1933). Competent Catholic treatments are F. Mourret, *A History of the Catholic Church*, vol. 5 (St Louis, 1930), and P. Janelle, *The Catholic Reformation* (Milwaukee, 1949). All the general works on the Reformation cited in Chapter One do include, of course, a discussion of what goes variously under the nomenclature Catholic Reformation or Counter-Reformation. Recent scholarship is discussed by George H. Tavard, 'The Catholic Reform in the 16th Century', *Church History*, 26 (1957).

For the Jesuits the monumental *Monumenta Historica Societas Jesu* in eighty volumes is indispensable. The section dealing with Ignatius is entitled *Monumenta Ignatiana (MI)* and contains Iganatius's almost 7,000 letters and his autobiography (Series I, 12 vols.), the *Spiritual Exercises* (Series II, 1 vol.), the *Constitutions of the Society of Jesus* (Series III, 3 vols.), and writings about Ignatius (Series IV, 2 vols.). There are also two volumes *Fontes Narrativi* (Series V). The outstanding treatment of Jesuit history is Pietro Tacchi-Venturi, *Storia della Compagnia di Gesù in Italia*, 2 vols. (Rome, 1950–1). In English there is the account of Heinrich Böhmer, *The Jesuits* (Philadelphia, 1928), James Brodrick, *The Origins of the Jesuits* (London and New York, 1940), and James Brodrick, *The Progress of the Jesuits* (London and New York, 1947).

A convenient historical table is the *Synopsis historiae Societas Jesu* (Louvain, 1950). Of biographies of Ignatius the following are to be noted: The first was written within thirteen years of Ignatius's death by Pedro Ribadeneira, *Vida del P. Ignacio de Loyola* (Madrid, 1594), translated into English as *The Life of B. Father Ignatius of Loyola* (Paris [?], 1616). Among recent biographical attempts there is Paul Dudon, *St Ignatius of Loyola* (Milwaukee, 1949); Mary Purcell, *The First Jesuit* (Westminster, 1957); the superbly illustrated *St Ignatius of Loyola, A Pictorial Biography* (Chicago, 1956).

The most recent edition of Ignatius's autobiography is *St Ignatius' Own Story as told to Luis Gonzalez de Camara, With a Sampling of His Letters*, translated by William J. Young (Chicago, 1956). A selection of Ignatius's letters is edited by William J. Young, *Letters of St Ignatius of Loyola* (Chicago, 1959).

On Francis Xavier, see James Brodrick, *Saint Francis Xavier* (1506–1552) (New York, 1952). Xavier's letters and writings were first published in two volumes of *Monumenta Xaveriana* in the *Monumenta Historica Societas Jesu* in 1899 and 1912, and were re-published by G. Schurhammer and J. Wicki, *Epistolae S. Francisci Xaverii aliaque ejus scripta*, 2 vols. (Rome, 1944–5).

The definitive six-volume (of which two have appeared) biography will be from the pen of G. Schurhammer, *Franz Xavier, Sein Leben und seine Zeit* (Freiburg i. Br., 1955ff.).

The sources of the Council of Trent are published in *Concilium Tridentinum, Diariorum, Actorum, Epistularum, Tractatuum nova collectio*. The two first histories of the Council came from the pen of Paolo Sarpi, who used the pseudonym of Pietro Soave, *Historia del Concilio Tridentino, Nella quale si scoprono tutti gl'artificii* . . . (London, 1619) (an English translation appeared under the title *The History of the Council of Trent* [London, 1620]), and Sforza Pallavicino, *Istoria del Concilio di Trento*, 2 vols. (Rome, 1656–7). These, and other historiographical aspects are ably considered by Hubert Jedin, *Das Konzil von Trient. Ein Überblick über die Erforschung seiner Geschichte* (Rome, 1948). A symposium of important essays on the Council is in G. Schreiber, ed., *Das Weltkonzil von Trient. Sein Werden und Wirken*, 2 vols. (Freiburg i. Br., 1951).

The definitive history will be the work of Hubert Jedin, *Geschichte des Konzils von Trient*, vol. I, *Der Kampf um das Konzil*; vol. II, *Die erste Trienter Tagungsperiode 1545–7* (Freiburg i. Br., 1951–7); the first two volumes have been translated into English under the title *A History of the Council of Trent* (London, 1957ff.).

Reginald Pole (1500–58), an Erasmian humanist, 1556 Archbishop of Canterbury, was one of the three papal legates who represented the Pope at the first assembly of the Council of Trent and presided over the sessions. A recent biography of Pole is by W. Schenk, *Reginald Pole* (New York, 1950). There is also the older work by M. Haile, *Life of Reginald Pole* (Edinburgh, 1910).

On the Inquisition, see G. G. Coulton, *Inquisition and Liberty* (New York, 1938). The classic treatment, despite certain weaknesses, is H. C. Lea, *History of the Inquisition in Spain*, 4 vols. (New York, 1922).

On the Index of Prohibited Books, see G. H. Putnam, *Censorship of the Church of Rome*, 2 vols. (New York and London, 1906–7) and F. S. Betten, *The Roman Index of Forbidden Books* (Chicago, 1935).

On St Teresa of Avila and Spanish mysticism, see Bruno de Jesus Marie, *Three Mystics: El Greco, St John of the Cross, St Teresa of Avila* (New York, 1949); M. Lepee, *Sainte Therese d'Avila, le realisme chrétien* (Paris, 1947). For the doctrinal pronouncement of the Council of Trent, see H. J. Schroeder, *The Canons and Decrees of the Council of Trent* (St Louis and London, 1941).

There is no modern critical edition of Erasmus's works. See therefore the old *Desiderii Erasmi opera omnia*, 10 vols. (Leiden, 1703–6). Erasmus's correspondence was ably edited by P. S. Allen, ed., *Opus Epistolarum Desid. Erasmi Roterodami*, 11 vols. (Oxford, 1893–1947).

The best introduction to Erasmus is by Johan Huizinga, *Erasmus and the Age of the Reformation* (New York, 1957). There is also P. S. Allen, *Erasmus, Lectures and Wayfaring Sketches* (Oxford, 1934), M. Mann Phillips, *Erasmus and the Northern Renaissance* (New York, 1950). Controversial is Siro A. Nulli, *Erasmo e il Rinascimento* (Turin, 1955).

NOTES AND REFERENCES

1. The translation used here is from H. J. Schroeder, *Disciplinary Decrees of the General Councils* (St Louis, 1937).

2. The translation used here is from Johan Huizinga, *Erasmus and the Age of the Reformation* (New York, 1957), pp. 231–2. In 1520 Erasmus drew up greatly interesting *axiomata* about the Lutheran affair; they are available in *Erasmi opuscula*, ed. W. K. Ferguson (The Hague, 1933), p. 329.

3. Andreas Osiander (1498–1552) was a Lutheran theologian, reformer of Nürnberg, in his later years a major protagonist in a theological controversy concerning the meaning of justification.

4. Zasius (1461–1536), humanist and jurist, was professor at Freiburg.

5. The translation used here is from Mary Purcell, *The First Jesuit* (Dublin, 1956; Westminster, 1957), pp. 3, 17, 201–2.

6. The translation used here is from *St Ignatius' Own Story* (Chicago, 1957).

7. The two books which Ignatius read were *The Life of Christ*, by Ludolph of Saxony (d. 1377), which was translated into Spanish in 1502 and 1503, and *Flos Sanctorum*, by James de Voraigne (d. 1298).

8. Pietro Faber (1506–46), canonized in 1872, was the first priest of the Jesuit Order. Diego Laynez (1512–65) was the second general of the Jesuit Order, represented towards the final sessions of the Council of Trent, Mary's immaculate conception and papal primacy.

9. The translation used here is from Mary Purcell, *The First Jesuit* (Westminster, 1957), p. 275.

10. The translation used here is from James Brodrick, *Saint Francis Xavier* (New York, 1952), pp. 56–57.

11. The translation used here is from Mary Purcell, *The First Jesuit* (Westminster, 1957), p. 272.

12. Heinrich Boehmer, *Ignatius von Loyola* (Stuttgart, 1941) prints in convenient form the records of the various inquisitorial proceedings against Ignatius in Spain.

13. For parts of the present translation the version of James H. Robinson, *Readings in European History*, pp. 163–4, was consulted.

14. The translation used here is from Mary Purcell, *The First Jesuit*, pp. 351–2.

15. The translation used here is from *The Spiritual Journal of St Ignatius Loyola* (Woodstock, 1958), pp. 2, 7, 8, 43.

16. V indicates that Ignatius wished to record a vision for that day.

17. The translation used here is from *Letters of St Ignatius of Loyola* (Chicago, 1959).

18. The translation used here is from James Brodrick, *Saint Francis Xavier* (New York-London, 1952), p. 75.

19. Brodrick, pp. 98–99.

20. Brodrick, pp. 103–4.

21. Brodrick, pp. 110–11.

22. Brodrick, p. 142.

23. Brodrick, pp. 207–8.

24. Brodrick, p. 120.

25. Brodrick, p. 257.

26. Brodrick, pp. 262–3.

27. Brodrick, pp. 525–6.

28. The translation used here is from 'Cardinal Pole's *Eirenikon*', *The Dublin Review*, 198 (1936).

29. The source used here and subsequently is Ernst Schäfer, *Beiträge zur Geschichte des spanischen Protestantismus im 16. Jahrhundert*, 2. Band (Gütersloh, 1902).

30. The translation used here is from James H. Robinson, *Readings in European History*, p. 173.

31. The source used here is David Wilkins, *Councils and Ecclesiastical Documents relating to Great Britain and Ireland* (Oxford, 1869).

32. From *The Complete Works of Saint Teresa, translated and edited by E. Allison Peers from the critical edition of P. Silverio de Santa Teresa, C. D.*, published in three volumes by Sheed & Ward, Inc., New York. Used by permission.

Bibliographical Addendum

Bibliographical Addendum

R. H. Bainton and E. W. Gritsch, eds., *Bibliography of the Continental Reformation. Materials Available in English* (Hamden, Conn., 1972).

G. R. Elton, *Reformation Europe 1517–1559* (New York, 1963).

R. L. DeMolen, ed., *The Meaning of Renaissance and Reformation* (Boston, 1974).

R. Forster and J. Green, eds., *Preconditions of Revolutions in Early Modern Europe* (Baltimore, 1970).

R. Wohlfeil, ed., *Reformation oder fruhburgerliche Revolution?* (Munchen, 1972).

L. W. Spitz, *The Religious Renaissance of the German Humanists* (Cambridge, 1963).

Ch. Trinkaus and H. Oberman, eds., *The Pursuit of Holiness in Late Medieval and Renaissance Religion* (Leiden, 1974).

B. Moeller, "Piety in Germany Around 1500," in S. Ozment, ed., *The Reformation in Medieval Perspective* (Chicago, 1971).

H. G. Koenigsberger, "The Unity of the Church and the Reformation," *Journal of Interdisciplinary History 1* (1970/71), 407-17.

J. Wicks, *Man Yearning for Grace: Luther's Early Spiritual Teaching* (Washington, 1956).

R. Walton, *Zwingli's Theocracy* (Toronto, 1967).

B. Moeller, *Imperial Cities and the Reformation* (Philadelphia, 1972).

P. Blickle, *Die Revolution von 1525* (Munchen, 1975).

B. Moeller, *Bauernkriegsstudien* (Gutersloh, 1975).

W. Elliger, *Aussenseiter der Reformation: Thomas Muntzer, Ein Knecht Gottes* (Gottingen, 1975).

S. Ozment, *Mysticism and Dissent, Religious Ideology and Social Protest in the Sixteenth Century* (New Haven, 1973).

J. Stayer, *Anabaptists and the Sword* (Lawrence, Kansas, 1972).

G. H. Williams, *The Radical Reformation* (Philadelphia, 1962).

C. P. Clasen, *Anabaptism: A Social History* (Ithaca, 1972).

J. J. Scarisbrick, *Henry VIII* (London, 1968).

L. B. Smith, *Henry VIII: The Mask of Royalty* (New York, 1972).

G. R. Elton, *Policy and Police* (New York, 1972).

G. R. Elton, *Studies in Tudor and Stuart Politics and Government. Papers and Reviews 1946–1972* (London, 1974).

J. Youings, *The Dissolution of the Monasteries* (London, 1971).

K. R. Davis, *Anabaptism and Asceticism: A Study in Intellectual Origins* (Scottdale, 1974).

D. Kempff, *A Bibliography of Calviniana 1959–1974* (Studies in Medieval and Reformation Thought 15) (Leiden, 1975).

T. H. L. Parker, *John Calvin: A Biography* (London, 1975).

L. J. Richard, *The Spirituality of John Calvin* (Atlanta, 1974).

T. H. L. Parker, *John Calvin: A Biography* (London, 1975).

H. O. Evenett, *The Spirit of the Counter Reformation* (Notre Dame, 1970).

Index

Index

Twin Brooks Series

Barclay, William
Educational Ideals in the Ancient
World

Bass, Clarence B.
Backgrounds to Dispensationalism

Battenhouse, Roy W. (ed.)
A Companion to the Study of
St. Augustine

Bavinck, Herman
The Doctrine of God
Our Reasonable Faith
The Philosophy of Revelation

Beardslee, John W., III (ed. & tr.)
Reformed Dogmatics

Beckwith, Isbon T.
The Apocalypse of John

Beecher, Willis Judson
The Prophets and the Promise

Berkhof, Hendrikus
Christ the Meaning of History

Berkhof, Louis
The History of Christian Doctrines
Introduction to Systematic Theology

Bright, John
The Authority of the Old Testament

Bushnell, Horace
Christian Nurture

Carnell, Edward John
A Philosophy of the Christian
Religion

Clark, Gordon H.
A Christian View of Men and Things
Thales to Dewey

Dargan, Edwin C.
A History of Preaching

Davies, J. G.
The Early Christian Church

Davis, John D.
Genesis and Semitic Tradition

Deissmann, Adolf
Light from the Ancient East

De Ridder, Richard R.
Discipling the Nations

Dodd, C. H.
The Apostolic Preaching and Its
Developments

Eck, John
Enchiridion of Commonplaces

Edersheim, Alfred
The History of the Jewish Nation
Prophecy and History

Ellis, E. Earle
Paul's Use of the Old Testament

Eusebius
The Proof of the Gospel

Farrar, Frederic W.
History of Interpretation

Frend, W. H. C.
Martyrdom and Persecution in the
Early Church

Gasper, Louis
The Fundamentalist Movement

Gerstner, John H.
Reasons for Faith
The Theology of the Major Sects

Goppelt, Leonhard
Apostolic and Post-Apostolic Times

Green, William Henry
General Introduction to the Old
Testament
The Higher Criticism of the
Pentateuch
The Unity of the Book of
Genesis

Henry, Carl F. H.
Aspects of Christian Social Ethics
Christian Personal Ethics

Henry, Carl F. H. (ed.)
Basic Christian Doctrines
Fundamentals of the Faith
Revelation and the Bible

Heppe, Heinrich
Reformed Dogmatics

Hillerbrand, Hans J.
The Reformation
The World of the Reformation

Hort, Fenton John Anthony
Judaistic Christianity

Jerome
Commentary on Daniel

Kevan, Ernest F.
The Grace of Law

Klotsche, E. H.
The History of Christian Doctrine

Kuiper, R. B.
God-Centered Evangelism

Kurtz, J. H.
Sacrificial Worship of the Old
Testament

Kuyper, Abraham
Principles of Sacred Theology

Law, Robert
The Tests of Life

Lecerf, Auguste
An Introduction to Reformed
Dogmatics

Lightfoot, J. B.
The Apostolic Fathers

Longenecker, Richard N.
The Christology of Early Jewish
Christianity
Paul, Apostle of Liberty

Machen, J. Gresham
The Virgin Birth of Christ

Manson, T. W.
The Servant-Messiah

Mayor, Joseph B.
The Epistle of James
The Epistles of Jude and II Peter

McDonald, H. D.
Theories of Revelation

Meeter, H. Henry
The Basic Ideas of Calvinism

Niesel, Wilhelm
The Theology of Calvin

Orr, James
Revelation and Inspiration

Rackham, Richard Belward
The Acts of the Apostles

Ramm, Bernard
The Evangelical Heritage
Varieties of Christian Apologetics

Raven, John Howard
The History of the Religion of Israel

Sandeen, Ernest R.
The Roots of Fundamentalism

Seeberg, Reinhold
Textbook of the History of
Doctrines

Sherwin-White, A. N.
Roman Society and Roman Law in
the New Testament

Smith, David
The Days of His Flesh

Smith, James
The Voyage and Shipwreck of St.
Paul

Steinmetz, David C.
Reformers in the Wings

Stonehouse, Ned B.
Origins of the Synoptic Gospels
The Witness of the Synoptic Gospels
to Christ

Sweet, William Warren
The Story of Religion in America

Theron, Daniel J.
Evidence of Tradition

Trench, Richard Chenevix
Notes on the Miracles of Our Lord
Notes on the Parables of Our
Lord
Studies in the Gospels

Trueblood, David Elton
General Philosophy
Philosophy of Religion

Turretin, Francis
The Atonement of Christ

Van Til, Henry
The Calvinistic Concept of Culture

Vos, Geerhardus
The Pauline Eschatology

Westcott, B. F.
A General Survey of the History of
the Canon of the New Testament

Wilson, Robert Dick
Studies in the Book of Daniel

Young, Warren C.
A Christian Approach to Philosophy

BAKER BOOK HOUSE   BOX 6287   GRAND RAPIDS, MI 49506